15916

W9-AUF-251

Making a Difference

HARCOURT BRACE SOCIAL STUDIES

HARCOURT BRACE & COMPANY

Orlando Atlanta Austin Boston San Francisco Chicago Dallas

New York Toronto London

 Visit The Learning Site at http://www.hbschool.com

Acknowledgments

For permission to reprint copyrighted material, grateful acknowledgment is made to the following sources:

August House, Inc.: "The Red and Blue Coat" from *Wisdom Tales from Around the World* by Heather Forest. Text copyright 1996 by Heather Forest. "An Old Man and a Boy" from *East African Folktales from the Voice of Mukamba* by Dr. Vincent Muli Wa Kituku. Text © 1997 by Vincent Muli Wa Kituku.

BridgeWater Books, an imprint of Troll Communications L.L.C.: "Talking to the Clay" from *Four Ancestors* by Joseph Bruchac. Text copyright © 1996 by Joseph Bruchac.

The Lois Lenski Covey Foundation, Inc.: "Like Me" from *The Life I Live* by Lois Lenski. Text copyright © 1965 by Lois Lenski.

Doubleday, a division of Bantam Doubleday Dell Publishing Group, Inc.: From "Demeter and Persephone" in *What Your Second-Grader Needs to Know* by E. D. Hirsch. Text copyright © 1991 by Core Knowledge, Inc.

Harcourt Brace & Company: "Home, Sweet Home" from *The Music Book* by Eunice Boardman and Barbara Andress. Text copyright © 1984 by Holt, Rinehart and Winston, Inc.

HarperCollins Publishers: "The Quarrel" from *Eleanor Farjeon's Poems for Children* by Eleanor Farjeon. Text copyright 1933, renewed 1961 by Eleanor Farjeon. Originally published in *Over the Garden Wall* by Eleanor Farjeon. "Old Log House" from *A World to Know* by James S. Tippett. Text copyright 1933 by Harper & Row, renewed 1961 by Martha Tippett. "Trucks" from *I Go A-Traveling* by James S. Tippett. Text copyright 1929 by Harper & Row, Publishers, Inc.; text copyright © 1957 by James S. Tippett.

Henry Holt & Company, Inc.: "At the Store" from *Is Somewhere Always Far Away?* by Leland B. Jacobs. Copyright © 1993 by Allan D. Jacobs.

Alfred A. Knopf, Inc.: "Puget Sound" by Harold W. Felton from *Legends of Paul Bunyan*, compiled and edited by Harold W. Felton. Text copyright 1947 by Alfred A. Knopf, Inc., renewed © 1975 by Harold W. Felton.

Little, Brown and Company: "You and I" from *My Song Is Beautiful* by Mary Ann Hoberman. Text copyright © 1994 by Mary Ann Hoberman. "Four Generations" from *Fathers, Mothers, Sisters, Brothers* by Mary Ann Hoberman. Text copyright © 1991 by Mary Ann Hoberman.

Marian Reiner: From *Earth Songs* by Myra Cohn Livingston. Text copyright © 1986 by Myra Cohn Livingston. Published by Holiday House.

Elizabeth M. Roach: "Fourth of July" from *Around and About* by Marchette Chute. Text copyright 1957 by E. P. Dutton; text copyright renewed 1984 by Marchette Chute.

Printed in the United States of America

ISBN 0-15-312105-X

3 4 5 6 7 8 9 10 032 01 00 99

Contents

Making a Difference

Tabbed Section

Harcourt Brace Social Studies
Components

For content updates and new ideas for teaching *Harcourt Brace Social Studies,* see the Harcourt Brace home page on the Internet. You can find it at http://www.hbschool.com

	K	1	2	3	4	5	6
Student Support Materials							
Pupil Editions*		•	•	•	•	•	•
Literature Anthology Big Books*	•						
Unit Big Books*		•	•				
Activity Books*	•	•	•	•	•	•	•
Social Studies Libraries*	•	•	•	•	•	•	•
Teacher Support Materials							
Teacher's Editions*	•	•	•	•	•	•	•
Activity Book, Teacher's Editions*				•	•	•	•
Assessment Programs*		•	•	•	•	•	•
Write-On Charts*	•	•	•	•			
Vocabulary Picture Cards*		•	•				
Take-Home Review Books		•	•				
Big Book Libraries		•	•				
Daily Geography	•			•	•	•	•
Overhead Transparencies*		•	•	•	•	•	•
Unit Posters*	•	•	•	•	•	•	•
Desk Maps		•	•	•	•	•	•
Text on Tape Audiocassettes*	•	•	•	•	•	•	•
Music Audiocassettes	•			•	•	•	•
The Map Book				•	•	•	•
Atlases	•	•	•	•	•	•	•
Game Time!		•	•	•	•	•	•
Reading Support and Test Preparation		•	•	•	•	•	•
Language Books—Cambodian, Cantonese, Hmong, Vietnamese	•	•	•	•	•	•	•
Reading Rainbow Videotape Series	•	•	•	•			
Video Experiences: Social Studies				•	•	•	•
Making Social Studies Relevant Videos					•	•	•
Technology							
The Amazing Writing Machine and Resource Packages		•	•	•	•	•	•
Graph Links*		•	•	•	•	•	•
Looking Ahead: Earning, Spending, Saving						•	•
Imagination Express*	•	•	•	•	•	•	
Destination Neighborhood	•	•	•	•			
Destination Castle							•
Destination Ocean			•		•		•
Destination Rain Forest				•			•
Destination Time Trip		•	•	•	•	•	
Destination Pyramids							•
TimeLiner*					•	•	•
TimeLiner Data Disks						•	•
Decisions, Decisions						•	•
Revolutionary Wars						•	
Immigration						•	
Colonization						•	
Building a Nation						•	
Feudalism							•
Ancient Empires							•
Choices, Choices	•	•	•	•			
Taking Responsibility	•	•	•				
On the Playground	•	•	•				
Kids and the Environment	•	•	•	•			
Geography Search						•	•
National Inspirer					•	•	
MapSkills					•	•	•
Neighborhood MapMachine	•	•	•	•			
Trudy's Time and Place House	•	•	•				

*Available in Spanish

Making a Difference

HARCOURT BRACE SOCIAL STUDIES

Series Authors

Dr. Richard G. Boehm

Claudia Hoone

Dr. Thomas M. McGowan

Dr. Mabel C. McKinney-Browning

Dr. Ofelia B. Miramontes

Dr. Priscilla H. Porter

Series Consultants

Dr. Alma Flor Ada

Dr. Phillip Bacon

Dr. W. Dorsey Hammond

Dr. Asa Grant Hilliard, III

HARCOURT BRACE & COMPANY

Orlando Atlanta Austin Boston San Francisco Chicago Dallas
New York Toronto London

 Visit The Learning Site at http://www.hbschool.com

Series Authors

Dr. Richard G. Boehm
Professor and Jesse H. Jones Distinguished
Chair in Geographic Education
Department of Geography and Planning
Southwest Texas State University
San Marcos, Texas

Claudia Hoone
Teacher
Ralph Waldo Emerson School #58
Indianapolis, Indiana

Dr. Thomas M. McGowan
Associate Professor
Division of Curriculum and Instruction
Arizona State University
Tempe, Arizona

Dr. Mabel C. McKinney-Browning
Director
Division for Public Education
American Bar Association
Chicago, Illinois

Dr. Ofelia B. Miramontes
Associate Professor of Education and
Associate Vice Chancellor for Diversity
University of Colorado
Boulder, Colorado

Dr. Priscilla H. Porter
Co-Director
Center for History–Social Science
Education
School of Education
California State University,
Dominguez Hills
Carson, California

Series Consultants

Dr. Alma Flor Ada
Professor
School of Education
University of San Francisco
San Francisco, California

Dr. Phillip Bacon
Professor Emeritus of Geography and
Anthropology
University of Houston
Houston, Texas

Dr. W. Dorsey Hammond
Professor of Education
Oakland University
Rochester, Michigan

Dr. Asa Grant Hilliard, III
Fuller E. Callaway Professor of Urban
Education
Georgia State University
Atlanta, Georgia

Media, Literature, and Language Specialists

Dr. Joseph A. Braun, Jr.
Professor of Elementary Social Studies
Department of Curriculum and Instruction
Illinois State University
Normal, Illinois

Meredith McGowan
Youth Services Librarian
Tempe Public Library
Tempe, Arizona

Rebecca Valbuena
Language Development Specialist
Stanton Elementary School
Glendora, California

Grade-Level Consultants

Barbara Abbott
Adams Elementary School
San Diego, California

Janice Bell
Hammel Street Elementary School
Los Angeles, California

Carol Hamilton Cobb
Gateway School
Metropolitan Nashville Public Schools
Madison, Tennessee

Janet J. Eubank
Language Arts Curriculum Specialist
Wichita Public Schools
Wichita, Kansas

Billie M. Kapp
Teacher (Retired)
Coventry Grammar School
Coventry, Connecticut

Carol Siefkin
Garfield Elementary School
Carmichael, California

Grade-Level Reviewers

Esther Booth-Cross
School-Wide Coordinator
Bond Elementary School
Chicago, Illinois

Kristen Caplin
Murwood Elementary School
Walnut Creek, California

Nodjie Conner
Old Richmond Elementary School
Tobaccoville, North Carolina

Bob Davis
Office of Social Studies
Newark Public Schools
Newark, New Jersey

Maryfran Goetz
Notre Dame de Sion
Kansas City, Missouri

Patricia Guillory
Director, Social Studies
Fulton County Administrative Center
Atlanta, Georgia

Sharon Hamid
Williams Elementary School
San Jose, California

Nancy Kelly
Pinedale Elementary School
Pinedale, California

Mickey McConnell
Central Heights Elementary School
Blountsville, Tennessee

Gwen Mitsui
Solomon Elementary School
Wahiawa, Hawaii

Ronald R. Paul
Curriculum Director, Retired
Mehlville School District
St. Louis, Missouri

Ida Rebecca Ross
Woolmarket Elementary School
Biloxi, Mississippi

Marie Singh
Harden School
Salinas, California

Else Sinsigalli
Erikson Elementary School
San Jose, California

J. Mark Stewart
Social Studies Supervisor
Columbus Public Schools
Columbus, Ohio

Sheree Thomas
Cottage Elementary School
Sacramento, California

Renarta Tompkins
Morrow Elementary School
Morrow, Georgia

Contents

UNIT 1

We Belong to Many Groups 8

UNIT 5

Being a Good Citizen 182

vii

F.Y.I.

Literature and Primary Sources

Skills

Features

Biography

Brainstorm

Making Social Studies Real

Maps

Charts, Graphs, Diagrams, Tables, and Time Lines

Atlas

Geo Georgie invites you to visit new places this year. The maps in this book will help you to know where you are. When you see Geo Georgie, stop and learn how to use the maps.

Come back to this Atlas often as you travel through your book. It will help you see where you are!

Atlas • A1

Atlas

The World

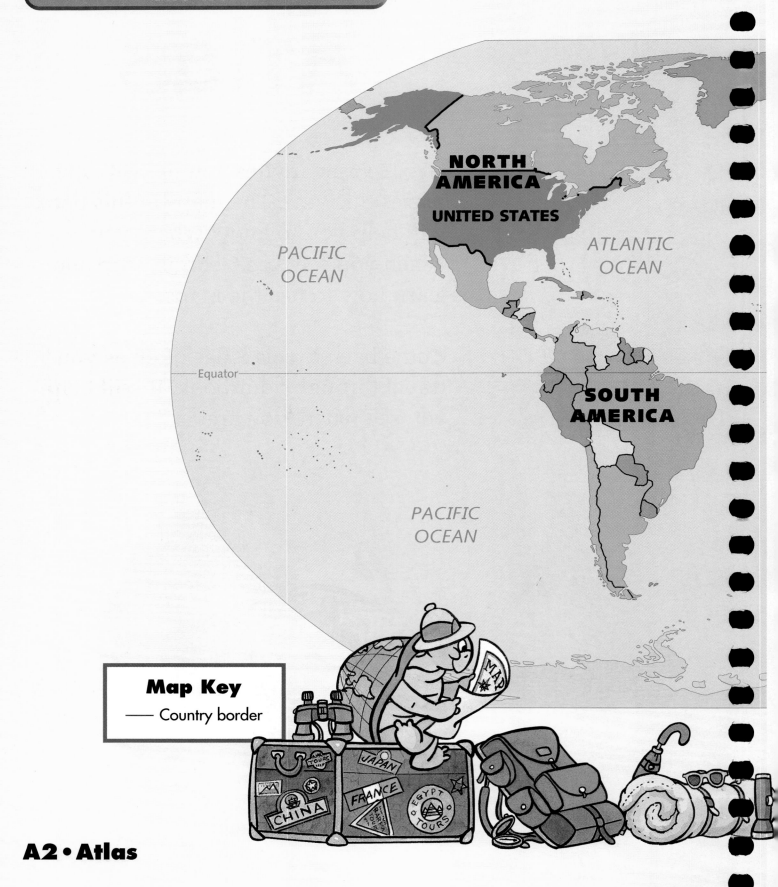

NORTH
AMERICA

UNITED STATES

PACIFIC
OCEAN

ATLANTIC
OCEAN

Equator

SOUTH
AMERICA

PACIFIC
OCEAN

Map Key

— Country border

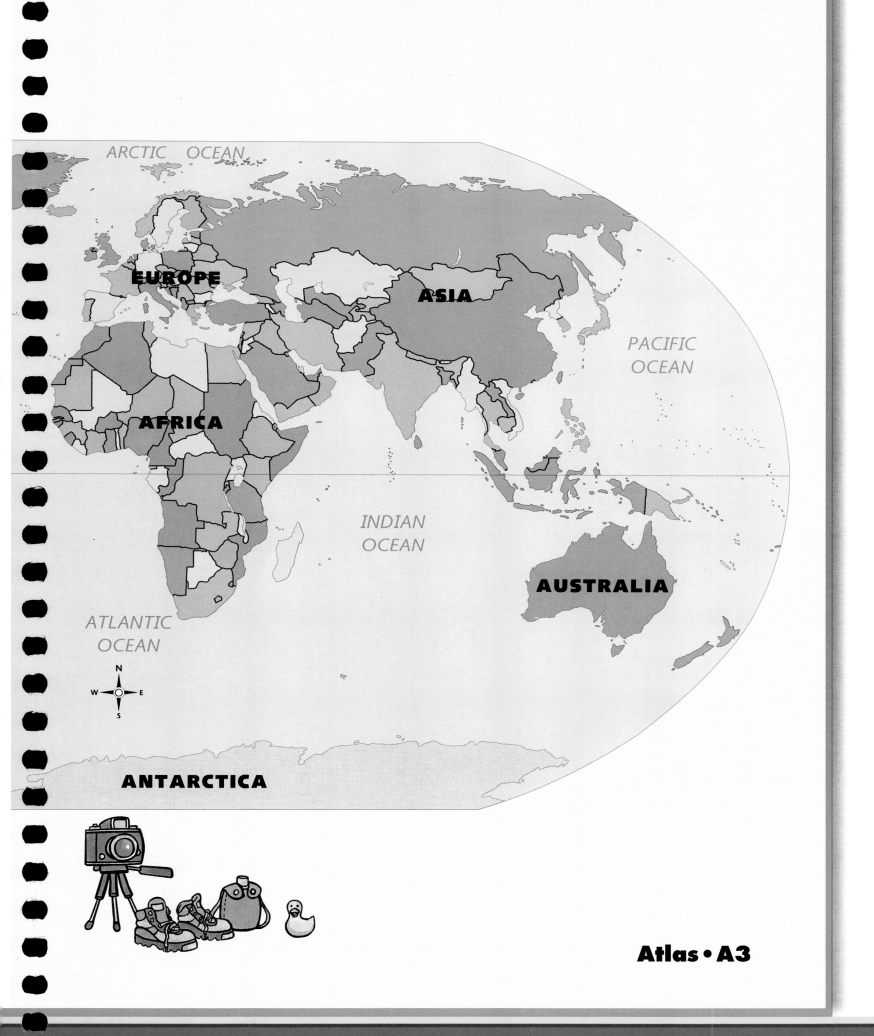

ARCTIC OCEAN

EUROPE

ASIA

PACIFIC
OCEAN

AFRICA

INDIAN
OCEAN

AUSTRALIA

ATLANTIC
OCEAN

N
W E
S

ANTARCTICA

Atlas

The United States

CANADA

RUSSIA

ARCTIC OCEAN

Alaska (AK)

CANADA

Bering Sea

Juneau

PACIFIC OCEAN

Washington (WA)
★ Olympia

★ Salem

Montana (MT)
Helena ★

Oregon (OR)

Boise ★
Idaho (ID)

Wyoming (WY)

Cheye...

PACIFIC OCEAN

Great Salt Lake
★ Salt Lake City

Sacramento ★

Carson City ★

Nevada (NV)

Utah (UT)

Der...

Colorado (CO)

California (CA)

Santa Fe ★

Arizona (AZ)

New Mexico (NM)

★ Phoenix

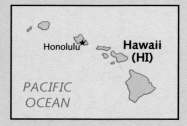

Honolulu ★
Hawaii (HI)

PACIFIC OCEAN

MEXICO

N
W ○ E
S

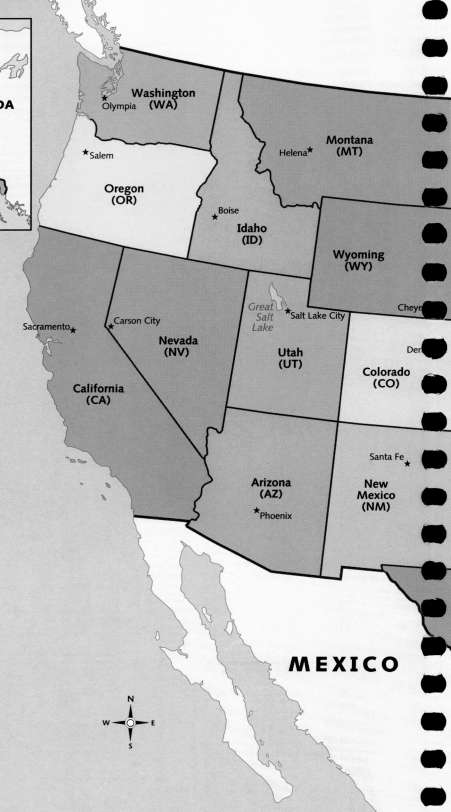

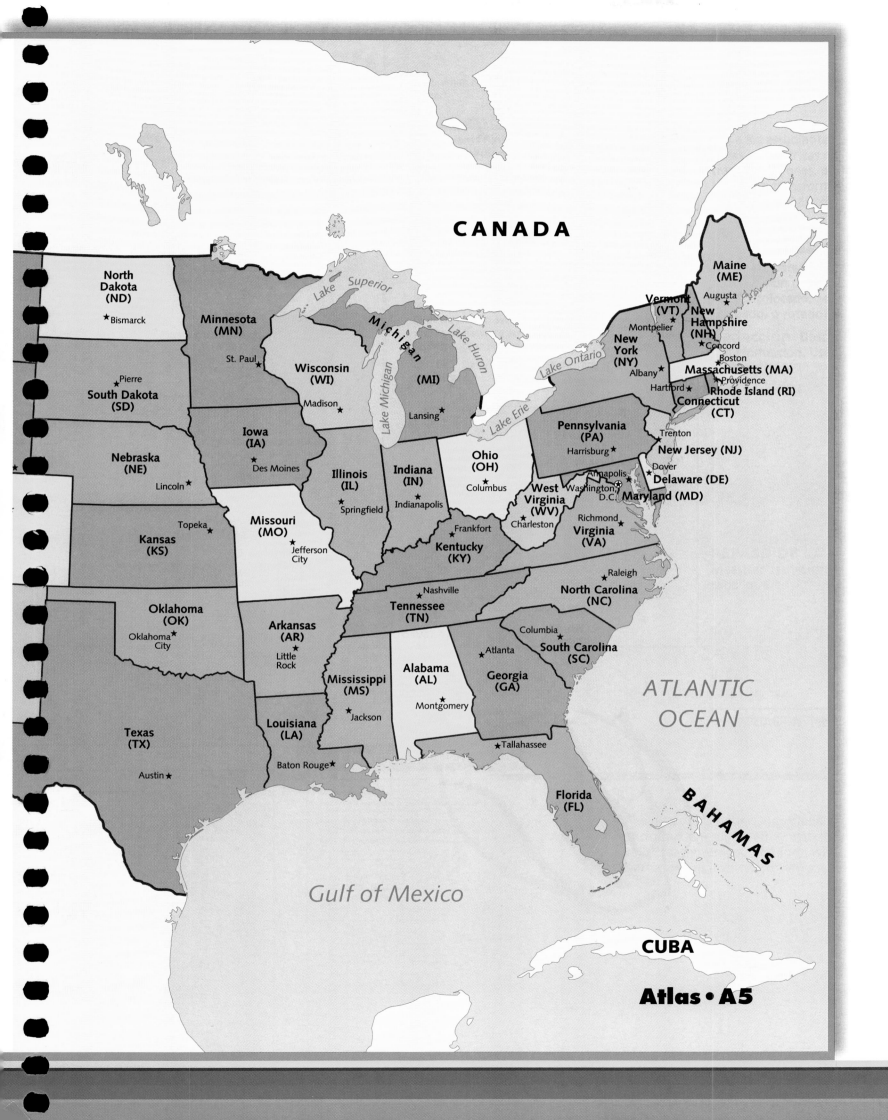

CANADA

North Dakota (ND)
★Bismarck

Minnesota (MN)
St. Paul★

South Dakota (SD)
★Pierre

Nebraska (NE)
Lincoln★

Kansas (KS)
Topeka★

Oklahoma (OK)
Oklahoma City★

Texas (TX)
Austin★

Wisconsin (WI)
Madison★

Iowa (IA)
Des Moines★

Missouri (MO)
Jefferson City★

Arkansas (AR)
Little Rock★

Louisiana (LA)
Baton Rouge★

Lake Superior

Michigan (MI)
Lansing★

Lake Michigan

Lake Huron

Illinois (IL)
Springfield★

Indiana (IN)
Indianapolis★

Lake Erie

Lake Ontario

Ohio (OH)
Columbus★

Kentucky (KY)
Frankfort★

Tennessee (TN)
Nashville★

Mississippi (MS)
Jackson★

Alabama (AL)
Montgomery★

Georgia (GA)
Atlanta★

Florida (FL)

West Virginia (WV)
Charleston★

Virginia (VA)
Richmond★

North Carolina (NC)
Raleigh★

South Carolina (SC)
Columbia★

Pennsylvania (PA)
Harrisburg★

New York (NY)
Albany★

Vermont (VT)
Montpelier★

New Hampshire (NH)
Concord★

Maine (ME)
Augusta★

Massachusetts (MA)
Providence★
Boston★

Rhode Island (RI)

Connecticut (CT)
Hartford★

Trenton
New Jersey (NJ)

Dover
Delaware (DE)

Annapolis
Washington, D.C.
Maryland (MD)

ATLANTIC OCEAN

BAHAMAS

Gulf of Mexico

CUBA

Atlas • A5

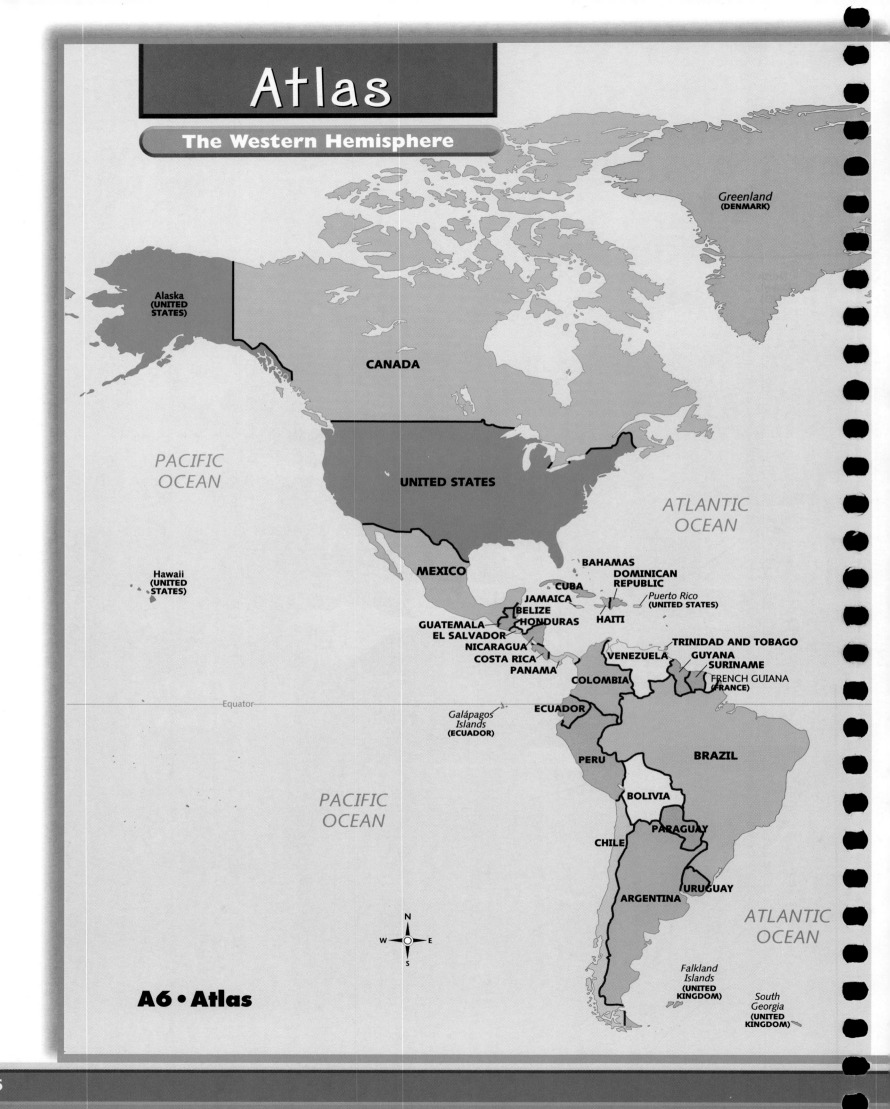

Atlas

The Western Hemisphere

PACIFIC OCEAN

Greenland (DENMARK)

Alaska (UNITED STATES)

CANADA

UNITED STATES

ATLANTIC OCEAN

Hawaii (UNITED STATES)

MEXICO

BAHAMAS

CUBA

DOMINICAN REPUBLIC

JAMAICA

Puerto Rico (UNITED STATES)

BELIZE

HONDURAS

HAITI

GUATEMALA

EL SALVADOR

NICARAGUA

TRINIDAD AND TOBAGO

COSTA RICA

VENEZUELA

GUYANA

PANAMA

SURINAME

COLOMBIA

FRENCH GUIANA (FRANCE)

Equator

ECUADOR

Galápagos Islands (ECUADOR)

PERU

BRAZIL

PACIFIC OCEAN

BOLIVIA

PARAGUAY

CHILE

URUGUAY

ARGENTINA

ATLANTIC OCEAN

N
W—E
S

Falkland Islands (UNITED KINGDOM)

South Georgia (UNITED KINGDOM)

A6 • Atlas

Atlas

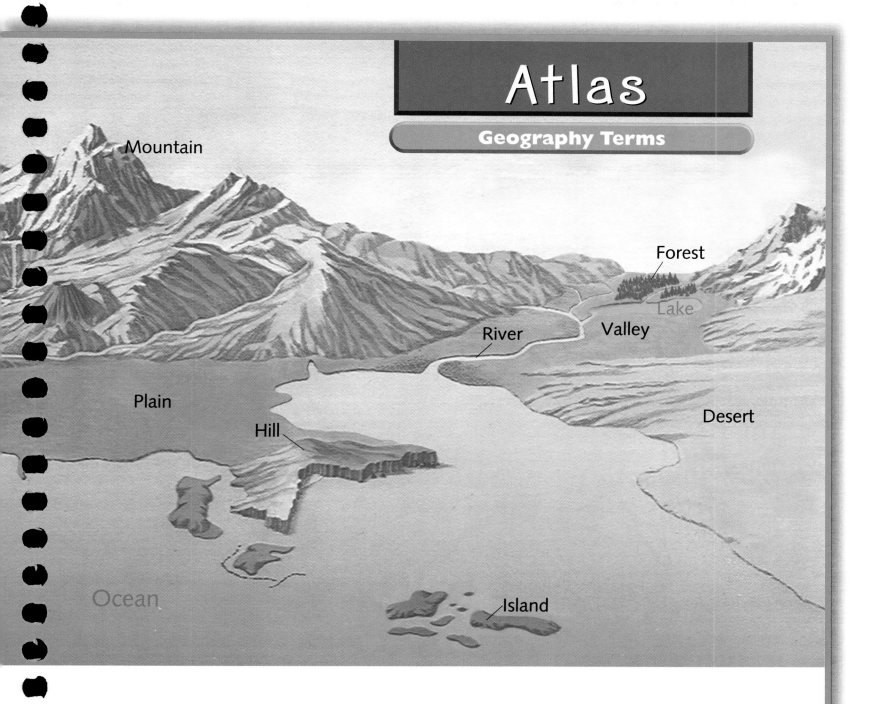

Mountain
Forest
Lake
River
Valley
Plain
Desert
Hill
Ocean
Island

desert dry land with few plants

forest large area of land where many trees grow

hill land that rises above the land around it

island land that has water on all sides

lake body of water with land on all sides

mountain highest kind of land

ocean body of salt water that covers a large area

plain flat land

river large stream of water that flows across the land

valley low land between hills or mountains

Atlas • A7

UNIT 1

WE BELONG TO MANY GROUPS

The major objectives in this unit are organized around the following themes:

UNIT THEMES

► **INTERACTION WITHIN DIFFERENT ENVIRONMENTS**

► **CONFLICT & COOPERATION**

► **COMMONALITY & DIVERSITY**

Preview Unit Content

Unit 1 tells the story of a child interacting with his or her immediate environment. Children will focus on the groups to which they belong and the groups and resources in the community that help them meet their basic needs. Through a study of group interaction, children will explore means of cooperation to avoid conflict, identify the usefulness of rules and order, and demonstrate the importance of sharing opinions. Children will look at how communities everywhere have common characteristics, despite physical and cultural differences.

You may wish to begin the unit with the Unit 1 Picture Summary Poster and activities. The illustration that appears on the poster also appears on pages 36–37 in the Pupil Book to help children summarize the unit.

UNIT POSTER

Use the UNIT 1 PICTURE SUMMARY POSTER to preview the unit.

Planning Chart

TEACHER'S EDITION	THEMES • Strands	VOCABULARY	MEET INDIVIDUAL NEEDS	RESOURCES INCLUDING ► TECHNOLOGY
UNIT INTRODUCTION **Introduce the Unit** Preview Set the Scene with Literature **"Sing a Song of People"** by Lois Lenski Use the Literature Big Book pp. 8–13A			Auditory Learners, p.11 English Language Learners, p. 13	**Pupil Book/Unit Big Book, pp. 8–13** **Write-On Chart 30** Picture Summary Poster Home Letter Text on Tape Audio Asian Translations Vocabulary Cards *One Afternoon*
LESSON 1 **Learning Together at School** pp. 14A–17A	**INTERACTION WITHIN DIFFERENT ENVIRONMENTS** • Culture	group leader rule	Visual Learners, p. 14A Auditory Learners, p. 15 English Language Learners, p. 16 Extend and Enrich, p. 17 Reteach the Main Idea, p. 17	**Pupil Book/Unit Big Book, pp. 14–17** **Write-On Chart 25** Clings Activity Book, p. 1
LESSON 2 **Living at Home and in the Neighborhood** pp. 18A–21A	**INTERACTION WITHIN DIFFERENT ENVIRONMENTS** • Culture • Civics and Government • Economics	neighborhood needs community	Kinesthetic Learners, p. 18 Visual Learners, p. 18 English Language Learners, p. 19 Extend and Enrich, p. 20 Reteach the Main Idea, p. 21	**Pupil Book/Unit Big Book, pp. 18–21** **Write-On Charts 1, 29** Activity Book, p. 2 Music Audio, "People in Your Neighborhood" ► **GRAPH LINKS** ► **IMAGINATION EXPRESS: DESTINATION NEIGHBORHOOD**
SKILL **Learn from a Picture and a Map** pp. 22A–23A	**BASIC STUDY SKILLS** • Map and Globe Skills	map	Tactile Learners, pp. 22A, 22 Visual Learners, p. 22A Extend and Enrich, p. 22 Reteach the Skill, p. 23	**Pupil Book/Unit Big Book, pp. 22–23** Activity Book, p. 3 Transparencies 1, 19
LESSON 3 **In and Around the City** pp. 24A–27A	**INTERACTION WITHIN DIFFERENT ENVIRONMENTS** • Civics and Government • Economics	city law goods services	Auditory Learners, p. 24A Extend and Enrich, p. 26 Reteach the Main Idea, p. 26	**Pupil Book/Unit Big Book, pp. 24–27** **Write-On Charts 2, 29** Activity Book, p. 4 Vocabulary Cards Music Audio, "Let's Take a Trip" Video, Reading Rainbow, *Ox-Cart Man* ► **THE AMAZING WRITING MACHINE**

21 DAYS

TIME MANAGEMENT

DAY 1	DAY 2	DAY 3	DAY 4	DAY 5	DAY 6	DAY 7	DAY 8	DAY 9	DAY 10	DAY 11	DAY 12
Unit Introduction		Lesson 1			Lesson 2			Skill	Lesson 3		

TEACHER'S EDITION	THEMES • Strands	VOCABULARY	MEET INDIVIDUAL NEEDS	RESOURCES INCLUDING ▶ TECHNOLOGY
SKILL **Read a Map** pp. 28A–29B	**BASIC STUDY SKILLS** • **Map and Globe Skills**	map key symbol compass rose direction	Kinesthetic Learners, p. 28 Extend and Enrich, p. 28 Reteach the Skill, p. 29	**Pupil Book/Unit Big Book, pp. 28–29** Activity Book, p. 5 Transparencies 2, 19 ▶ TRUDY'S TIME AND PLACE HOUSE ▶ NEIGHBORHOOD MAPMACHINE
BRAINSTORM **A Park Is for Everyone** pp. 30–31A	**BUILDING CITIZENSHIP** • **Critical Thinking Skills** • **Participation Skills**			**Pupil Book/Unit Big Book, pp. 30–31** **Write-On Chart 3** ▶ CHOICES, CHOICES: KIDS AND THE ENVIRONMENT
LESSON 4 **Our Country of Many People** pp. 32A–33B	**COMMONALITY & DIVERSITY** • **Civics and Government**	citizen country	Auditory Learners, p. 32A Extend and Enrich, p. 33 Reteach the Main Idea, p. 33	**Pupil Book/Unit Big Book, pp. 32–33** **Write-On Chart 4** Activity Book, p. 6 Vocabulary Cards Desk Maps Music Audio, "People in Your Neighborhood" ▶ THE AMAZING WRITING MACHINE
MAKING SOCIAL STUDIES REAL **The Big Help** pp. 34–35	**BUILDING CITIZENSHIP** • **Participation Skills**			**Pupil Book/Unit Big Book, pp. 34–35** ▶ INTERNET
UNIT WRAP-UP Picture Summary Unit 1 Review Cooperative Learning Workshop pp. 36–41B			English Language Learners, p. 37	**Pupil Book/Unit Big Book, pp. 36–41** Picture Summary Poster Vocabulary Cards Assessment Program, Standard, pp. 15–17 Performance, p. 18 Take-Home Review Book Game Time! ▶ THE AMAZING WRITING MACHINE

DAY 13	DAY 14	DAY 15	DAY 16	DAY 17	DAY 18	DAY 19	DAY 20	DAY 21
Skill		Brainstorm	Lesson 4		Making Social Studies Real	Unit Wrap-up		Unit Test

Multimedia Resource Center

Books

Easy

Allard, Harry. *Miss Nelson Is Missing!* Illus. by James Marshall. Houghton Mifflin, 1985. The kids in Room 207 take advantage of their teacher's good nature until she disappears and they are faced with a vile substitute.

Craft, Ruth. *The Day of the Rainbow.* Illus. by Niki Daly. Puffin, 1991. On a hot day, three cranky people have a chance to help each other find lost items.

Finchler, Judy. *Miss Malarkey Doesn't Live in Room 10.* Illus. by Kevin O'Malley. Walker, 1995. A first-grade boy is shocked, then pleased, when he discovers that his teacher has a life away from school.

Mennen, Ingrid, and Niki Daly. *Somewhere in Africa.* Illus. by Nicolaas Maritz. Dutton, 1992. Vibrant illustrations enhance this story of a young boy's life in an African city. The book is useful in dispelling stereotypes regarding Africa.

Polacco, Patricia. *Mrs. Katz and Tush.* Little Rooster, 1992. With the help of a tailless kitten, Mrs. Katz and her young friend, Larnel, find out that their separate family histories have a lot in common.

Soentpiet, Chris K. *Around Town.* Lothrop, Lee & Shepard, 1994. This book celebrates city life.

Average

Best, Cari. *Taxi! Taxi!* Illus. by Dale Gottlieb. Little, Brown, 1994. Tina spends each Sunday with her father, a taxi driver.

Derby, Sally. *My Steps.* Illus. by Adjoa J. Burrowes. Lee & Low, 1996. A young African American girl describes her favorite playground —the front steps of her home on which she and her friends play.

Gibbons, Gail. *Marge's Diner.* HarperCollins, 1989. Marge, the diner's owner, takes readers through her busy day ordering supplies, preparing for mealtime rushes, and interacting with customers.

Hall, Donald. *Ox-Cart Man.* Illus. by Barbara Cooney. Viking, 1979. The book describes the day-to-day life of an early nineteenth-century New England family throughout the changing seasons.

Jakobsen, Kathy. *My New York.* Little, Brown, 1993. This book depicts a young girl's tour of New York City.

Lord, John Vernon. *The Giant Jam Sandwich.* Houghton Mifflin, 1987. A tall tale shows how people in a community work together to solve a problem when millions of wasps invade their town.

Low, William. *Chinatown.* Henry Holt, 1997. A boy and his grandmother wind their way through the streets of Chinatown, enjoying all the sights and smells of the Chinese New Year's Day.

Lundgren, Mary Beth. *We Sing the City.* Illus. by Donna Perrone. Clarion, 1997. An ethnically diverse group of children describe the wonderful diversity of their city .

Moss, Marissa. *Mel's Diner.* BridgeWater, 1994. Mabel enjoys helping her father and mother run their diner, a friendly and comfortable place where she loves to spend time.

Spinelli, Eileen. *If You Want to Find Golden.* Illus. by Stacey Schuett. Albert Whitman, 1993. A trip through the city streets brings contact with many colors, from an orange construction sign to gray pigeons.

Torres, Lela. *Subway Sparrow.* Farrar, Straus and Giroux, 1993. People of different ages, genders, and cultures work together when a sparrow trapped in their subway car needs help.

Challenging

Anno, Mitsumasa, and Raymond Briggs. *All in a Day.* Philomel, 1988. Brief text and illustrations by ten internationally known artists chronicle a day in the lives of children in eight different countries, showing the similarities and differences.

Dorros, Arthur. *Abuela.* Illus. by Elisa Kleven. Dutton, 1991. A young girl imagines taking a flight over New York City with her *abuela*, or grandmother. Also, *Isla*, 1995.

Henderson, Kathy. *A Year in the City.* Illus. by Paul Howard. Candlewick, 1996. A month-by-month description in pictures and words of what goes on in a city during the year.

Rosa-Casanova, Sylvia. *Mama Provi and the Pot of Rice.* Illus. by Robert Roth. Atheneum, 1997. Mama Provi takes chicken and rice to her sick granddaughter Lucy, who lives upstairs.

Tamar, Erika. *The Garden of Happiness.* Illus. by Barbara Lambase. Harcourt Brace, 1996. Marisol and her neighbors turn a vacant New York City lot into a lush community garden.

Williams, Suzanne. *Emily at School.* Illus. by Abby Carter. Hyperion, 1996. Emily learns some of the good and bad things about being in second grade.

LIBRARY

Use the **GRADE 2 SOCIAL STUDIES LIBRARY** for additional resources.

Audiocassettes

Family Folk Festival. Scholastic. Traditional sing-along favorites and new songs feature Pete Seeger, Maria Muldaur, and others. Lyrics included. Toll free: 1-800-724-6527

People in Our Neighborhood: Community Helpers and Workers. By Ron Hiller. Kimbo Educational Records. Rock-to-rap songs about various jobs, from traditional community workers to jobs in computers and fiber optics. Available on Cassette or CD. Toll free: 1-800-631-2187

Computer Software

Floppy Disk

TimeLiner—A Day in the Life of . . . Tom Snyder Productions, Inc. Available for Mac 3.5 or Windows 3.5. Network versions: Appleshare or Novell-based. Children can look at a day, a week, a year, or many years in the lives of people in various careers and from different cultures. Requires TimeLiner 4.0 software. Toll free: 1-800-342-0236

CD-ROM

Arthur's Teacher Trouble. Educational Resources. Mac/IBM. When Arthur starts third grade, he discovers that he has the most undesirable teacher in the school: the one who assigns tons of homework. Children learn how giving someone the benefit of the doubt can pay off. Toll free: 1-800-624-2926.

Sim Town. Electronic Arts Direct. Windows 3.1/Mac/DOS.Children are able to design, create, and control a growing town. Toll free: 1-800-336-2947

Street Atlas USA. DeLorme. Mac/Windows. Children get a detailed view of the country. The package includes every street in the United States. Toll free: 1-800-227-1656

Video

Film or VHS Cassettes

I'm No Fool with Safety at School. Disney Educational Productions. Jiminy Cricket and a live-action Pinocchio pay an educational visit to an elementary school and playground. They provide important tips on using equipment properly, following directions, and cooperating with others to avoid problems. 13 minutes. Toll free: 1-800-295-5010

Rules to the Rescue. Alfred Higgins Productions, Inc. Rules can mean the difference between order and chaos, between safety and danger. The audience is shown the advantages of following rules, as well as the natural consequences of not following them. 16 minutes.
6350 Laurel Canyon Blvd. North Hollywood, CA 91606

A Trip to the Firehouse. SVF & Churchill Media. Join Jackie the Dalmatian, who narrates a visit to the firehouse. Children can watch firefighters respond to a fire call. 16 minutes. Toll free: 1-800-829-1900

Art to Zoo, Teaching with the Power of Objects. Quarterly teaching guide on science, social studies, and art. Current and selected back issues are available online, or write for free subscription.

Office of Elementary and Secondary Education
Arts & Industries Building
Room 1163, MRC 402
Smithsonian Institution
Washington, DC 20560
Internet: http://educate.si.edu/lessons/art-to-zoo/azindex.html

National SAFE KIDS Campaign
Checklist of top ten steps parents and caregivers can take to ensure the safety of children. Send SASE. Free.
National SAFE KIDS Campaign
1301 Pennsylvania Avenue, NW
Suite 1000
Washington, DC 20004-1707
(202) 662-0600
Fax: (202) 393-2072

Smithsonian Resource Guide for Teachers.
An 84-page listing of more than 450 free or low-cost educational materials available from Smithsonian Institution, Kennedy Center, National Gallery of Art, and Reading Is Fundamental. $5 per copy.
Office of Elementary and Secondary Education
Arts & Industries Building
Room 1163, MRC 402
Smithsonian Institution
Washington, DC 20560

Welcoming Diversity - Classroom Connections. Newsletter shares ideas for using children's books to teach about cultural diversity and environmental issues. Contains news, book lists, tips, and classroom activities. Free.
Tilbury House Publishers
132 Water St.
Gardiner, ME 04345
(207) 582-1899

Note that information, while correct at time of publication, is subject to change.

Linking Social Studies

READING CENTER

All-American Stories

Materials: books with American characters from a variety of backgrounds (Mama, Do You Love Me?; Annie and the Old One; Time of Wonder); 3" squares of lined writing paper glued onto larger squares of red, white, and blue construction paper; pencils

Invite children to read one or more of the stories and to notice similarities and differences between the lives of the characters and their own lives. Have children record similarities on red squares and differences on blue squares. Ask each child to write his or her name on a white square and the name of one of the book characters on another white square. At the end of the unit, invite children to arrange the squares to make an All-American Quilt.

We both have brothers and sisters.

My grandmother tells me stories, too.

She lives in the snow and I live where it is warm.

Her family raises sheep and my mom works in the city.

MULTICULTURAL CENTER

Aerial View of a Spanish Town

Materials: blocks or small boxes, adding machine tape, art materials for making miniatures

Explain to children that many Spanish towns are built around a square area called a plaza. Point out that the people gather there to visit with neighbors, to shop, to celebrate national holidays, and to discuss local issues. Invite children to arrange blocks as buildings around a square area and to use adding machine tape as streets. Encourage children to place miniature people, fountains, trees, gardens, musicians, and vendors in the plaza. Have children draw an aerial view of the town.

LANGUAGE ARTS CENTER

Write a Narrative

Materials: puppets, pictures of safety signs, pencils, paper, crayons, construction paper for covers, stapler

Invite pairs of children to use puppets to act out a story about taking a walk and obeying safety signs. After the puppet show, have the partners retell the story by writing a narrative. Have children illustrate the story, make a cover, and bind the pages to make a book. Make children's stories available in the center or classroom library for others to enjoy.

Across the Curriculum

ART CENTER

Sign Art

Materials: visuals showing examples of business and store signs, art materials, posterboard

Have children find and discuss a variety of styles of signs and billboards. You may wish to explain how some people use logos or icons to distinguish their businesses. Invite children to invent names for a new store or business. Then have them create signs for their businesses. Advise children to sketch drafts of their signs, think about which art materials they would like to use, and then transfer their designs to posterboard and complete the signs.

MATH CENTER

Give Speeding Tickets

Materials: toy cars; notecards; calculators; spinner with the numbers 20, 30, 40, 50, 60, 70

Fold notecards tent-style and make speed limit signs of 20 mph, 35 mph, 45 mph, and 55 mph. Post a schedule of fines based on the difference between a driver's speed and the speed limit. Invite partners to take turns placing a toy car next to one of the speed limit signs and then spinning the spinner to find out the speed the driver is going. If the driver is speeding, the other partner uses the calculator to determine the difference between the driver's speed and the speed limit and writes a ticket for the amount shown on the schedule of fines.

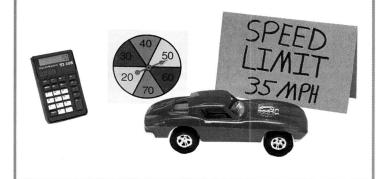

HOW TO INTEGRATE YOUR DAY
Use these topics to help you integrate social studies into your daily planning.

READING THEMES	INTEGRATED LANGUAGE ARTS	MATHEMATICS	SCIENCE	ART
Self and Others	Write a Narrative, p. 8G	Give Speeding Tickets, p. 8H	Plants and Animals, p. 20	Sign Art, p. 8H
	Integrated Spelling, p. 16	Data and Graphing, p. 19		About the Artist, p. 12
Families	Poetry, p. 18A	Numbers, p. 28A		Illustration, p. 9
	Journal, pp. 8, 24A, 32A, 35			Angle and Perspective, p. 22
Neighborhoods	Descriptive Writing, p. 32A			Create a Poster, p. 35
Communicating with Others		**HEALTH AND PHYSICAL EDUCATION**	**MUSIC**	**WORLD LANGUAGES**
Near and Far		Team Games, p. 28	Music for a Purpose, p. 25	Spanish, p. 14A
			Dance, p. 32	Spanish, German, Italian, p. 32
Explorations/ Problem Solving				

BULLETIN BOARD

Create a bulletin board titled *Good Citizens Are Winners*. Have children fold a sheet of drawing paper vertically. Then invite children to draw on the left-hand side of the sheet a harmful or careless behavior and, on the right, an opposite and appropriate behavior. Provide small blue ribbons and have children attach one to the drawing that shows what a good citizen would do. Display children's work around a large blue ribbon.

Assessment Options

The assessment program allows all learners many opportunities to show what they know and can do. It also provides ongoing information about each child's understanding of social studies.

FORMAL ASSESSMENT

▶ *Unit Review*
(**Pupil Book,** pp. 38–41)

▶ *Unit Assessment*
(**Assessment Program:**
Standard Test, pp. 15–17
Performance Task, p. 18)

STUDENT SELF-EVALUATION

▶ *Individual End-of-Project Checklist*
(**Assessment Program,** p. 6)

▶ *Group End-of-Project Checklist*
(**Assessment Program,** p. 7) for use after cooperative learning activities

▶ *Individual End-of-Unit Checklist*
(**Assessment Program,** p. 8)

INFORMAL ASSESSMENT

▶ *What Do You Know? Questions*
(**Pupil Book,** at end of lessons)

▶ *Think and Do*
(**Pupil Book,** at end of skill lessons)

▶ *Picture Summary*
(**Pupil Book,** pp. 36–37)

▶ *Check Understanding*
(**Teacher's Edition,** in Close, at end of lessons)

▶ *Think Critically*
(**Teacher's Edition,** in Close, at end of lessons)

▶ *Social Studies Skills Checklist*
(**Assessment Program,** pp. 4–5)

PERFORMANCE ASSESSMENT

▶ *Show What You Know*
(**Teacher's Edition,** in Close, at end of lessons)

▶ *Cooperative Learning Workshop*
(**Teacher's Edition,** pp. 41A–41B)

▶ *Performance Task: Who Are We?*
(**Assessment Program,** p. 18)

▶ *Scoring the Performance Task*
Use the *Scoring Rubric for Individual Projects*
(**Assessment Program,** p. 9)

▶ *Scoring Rubric for Group Projects*
(**Assessment Program,** p. 10)

▶ *Scoring Rubric for Presentations*
(**Assessment Program,** p. 11)

PORTFOLIO ASSESSMENT

Student-selected items may include:

▶ *Using the Activity Book,* map
(**Activity Book,** p. 3)

▶ *Link to Language Arts,* journal
(**Teacher's Edition,** p. 24A)

▶ *Extend and Enrich,* research
(**Teacher's Edition,** p. 26)

Teacher-selected items may include:

▶ *My Best Work*
(**Assessment Program,** p. 12)

▶ *Portfolio Summary*
(**Assessment Program,** p. 13)

▶ *Portfolio Family Response*
(**Assessment Program,** p. 14)

Assessment Options

STANDARD TEST

Name _____ Date _____

Unit 1 Test

Vocabulary

Circle the word that goes best with each picture. 5 points each

1. (community) / country

2. (law) / leader

3. symbol / (services)

4. neighborhood / (group)

5. (goods) / services

6. (map) / city

Name _____

Main Ideas 5 points each

Circle four workers who provide goods or services that people in communities need.

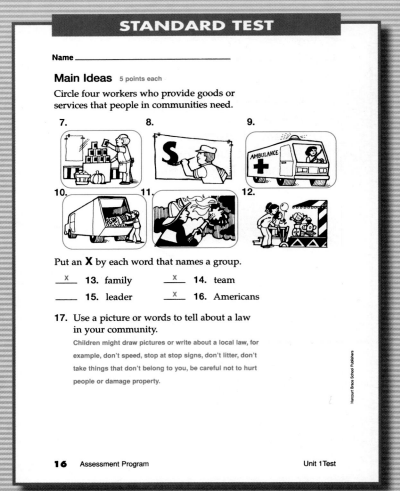

7. 8. 9.

10. 11. 12.

Put an **X** by each word that names a group.

| X | 13. family | X | 14. team |
| ___ | 15. leader | X | 16. Americans |

17. Use a picture or words to tell about a law in your community.

Children might draw pictures or write about a local law, for example, don't speed, stop at stop signs, don't litter, don't take things that don't belong to you, be careful not to hurt people or damage property.

Objectives

▶ Describe the classroom and school environment. (p. 14A)

▶ Identify roles within groups at school. (p. 14A)

▶ Explore appropriate classroom behavior. (p. 14A)

▶ Recognize and respect the authority of school workers. (p. 14A)

▶ Describe family roles and shared responsibilities. (p. 18A)

▶ Recognize a neighborhood as a place where families live and work to meet their needs. (p. 18A)

▶ Identify people and places in the neighborhood on which families depend. (p. 18A)

▶ Distinguish between eye-level and aerial views of identical sites. (p. 22A)

▶ Recognize that maps are drawn from an aerial view. (p. 22A)

▶ Define *city*. (p. 24A)

▶ Explain the need for people to follow rules and obey laws. (p. 24A)

▶ Describe the goods and services people get in a city. (p. 24A)

▶ Identify a map by its title. (p. 28A)

▶ Use symbols in a map key to identify places on a map. (p. 28A)

▶ Use cardinal directions to describe locations on a map. (p. 28A)

▶ Define themselves as citizens of the United States. (p. 32A)

▶ Identify the diversity of the American people. (p. 32A)

▶ Recognize that Americans have talents and skills that contribute to the country's common good. (p. 32A)

STANDARD TEST

Name _____

Skills 5 points each

Tania's family is going to the Canfield Fair. The map shows where they will find things at the fair.

Map of the Canfield Fair

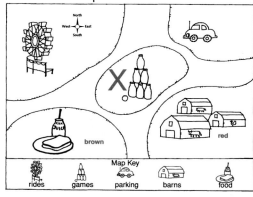

Use the map and map key to answer the questions.

18. Where should Tania's family go to play games? Put an **X** on this place.

19. After riding the Ferris wheel, what direction would they go for lunch? south

20. Where should they go to see farm animals? Color this place red.

Unit 1 Test   Assessment Program **17**

PERFORMANCE TASK

Name _____ Date _____

Performance Task

Who Are We?

Abdul is visiting the United States. He wants to know more about Americans. Draw a picture to show Abdul that Americans can be different from each other in many ways. Put yourself in the picture, too. Then tell how Americans are the same.

☆ **How Americans Are Different**

> Drawings might show people of different sizes, people with different features and coloring, people with different styles of hair and clothing, people doing different jobs, people engaging in different customs.

☆ **How Americans Are the Same**

Sample responses: They follow the same laws, they choose their

government leaders, they make many choices by voting, they live

in a free country.

18 Assessment Program   Unit 1 Test

Rubrics

SCORING RUBRICS The scoring rubrics for evaluating individual projects, group projects, and children's presentations may be found in the *Assessment Program*, pages 9–11.

CRITERIA The criteria listed below may be used when looking for evidence of the children's understanding of social studies content and ability to think critically.

▶ *Performance Task: Who Are We?* [**Assessment Program,** p. 18]

▶ *Scoring the Performance Task—* Use the *Scoring Rubric for Individual Projects* [**Assessment Program,** p. 9], and look for evidence of the child's ability to:

↵ Recognize that he or she is an American.

↵ Use art to show that Americans are different in many ways (size, dress, features, etc.).

↵ Describe how he or she is like other Americans (e.g., same government and laws).

REMINDER

You may wish to preview the performance assessment activity in the COOPERATIVE LEARNING WORKSHOP on Teacher's Edition pages 41A–41B. Children may complete this activity during the course of the unit.

*I*NTRODUCE THE *U*NIT

Link Prior Learning

Ask children to list the different groups of which they are members. Provide examples of groups such as school, class, family, Scouts, and teams. Suggest children share their lists with the rest of the class.

KWL Chart

Create a three-column chart on chart paper. Label the first column *What We Know*, the second column *What We Want to Know*, and the third column *What We Learned*. Invite children to tell what they know about communities. Record all suggestions in the first column. Then ask children what they would like to find out about communities. Record their responses in the second column. After completing this unit, return to the KWL chart to help children list what they learned about communities. Record children's findings in the third column and discuss whether their questions were answered.

What We Know	What We Want to Know	What We Learned
People live in a community. You can buy things in a community.	Are there different kinds of communities?	

Preview Vocabulary

The vocabulary words listed on page 8 represent the key concepts for this unit. Suggest that children use the words to predict what the main ideas of the unit will be. Ideas for teaching the vocabulary are provided on pages 10 and 11.

UNIT 1
We Belong to Many Groups

Vocabulary

group
community
map
law
goods
services

8

ACTIVITY CHOICES

Home Involvement

Invite children to discuss with family members the different groups to which they belong. Suggest children make a list of the different groups. Children may wish to share their lists with the rest of the class.

Link to Language Arts

JOURNAL Invite children to keep a daily record of the things they learn about communities. This information can be used at the end of the unit to complete the KWL chart.

HOME LETTER

Use UNIT 1 HOME LETTER. See Teacher's Edition pages HL1–2.

WRITE-ON CHARTS

Use WRITE-ON CHART 30 to create the KWL chart.

9

PUPIL BOOK **OR** UNIT BIG BOOK

Personal Response

Direct children's attention to the opening photograph. Help them to notice that the children are wearing pinnies of two different colors. Have them speculate about the activity of the two groups in the photo. *teams preparing to compete in a game or sport*

Q. **Why do you think people belong to groups?** *to have fun, to do good things, to share interests*

Tell children that in this unit they will learn that people belong to many kinds of groups. Help children understand that these groups not only help the community, they also help people meet their basic needs.

> ## **❝ PRIMARY SOURCE ❞**
>
> In his fourth inaugural address, President Franklin D. Roosevelt said, "We have learned to be citizens of the world, members of the human community." Tell children that they will discover groups of all sizes and interests.

Options for Reading

Read Aloud Read each lesson aloud as children follow along in their books. Strategies for guiding children through working with text and visuals are provided with each lesson.

Read Together Have pairs or small groups of children read the lesson by taking turns reading each page or paragraph aloud. Encourage children to use the new vocabulary words as they discuss what they read. Remind them that a reading group is one more example of a group to which they belong.

Read Alone Strong readers may wish to read the lessons independently before you read or discuss each lesson with the class.

Link to Art

ILLUSTRATION Invite children to draw a picture of a group to which they belong. Ask them to show people in the group working or playing together. Have children discuss their roles in the group. Display children's pictures on a bulletin board titled *We Belong to Many Groups.*

AUDIO

Use the UNIT 1 TEXT ON TAPE AUDIOCASSETTE for a reading of this unit.

ASIAN TRANSLATIONS

For students who speak Cambodian, Cantonese, Hmong, or Vietnamese, use the ASIAN TRANSLATIONS for Unit 1. The Harcourt Brace program is also available in a SPANISH EDITION.

PREVIEW THE UNIT

THINK ABOUT WORDS

Help children become familiar with the picture glossary in the back of their books. Tell children that both the pictures and the words will help them understand what each vocabulary word means. Ask children to tell what they think the word *group* means. Then have them find *group* in the glossary and read the definition provided. Invite a volunteer to read the context sentence aloud to reinforce the meaning. Repeat the process several times until children are familiar with the picture glossary.

group

A number of people doing an activity together.

community

A place where people live and the people who live there.

map

A drawing that shows where places are.

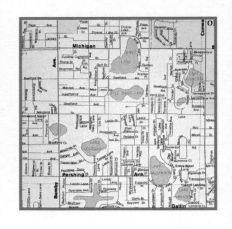

10

Meet Individual Needs

ENGLISH LANGUAGE LEARNERS
Invite children whose first language is not English to begin a vocabulary notebook of new words for each unit. Children might write the word in English and ask a family member to write it in their native language. They could then copy the definition or illustrate the word. Suggest that they add information about the word meanings as they work through the lessons.

Link to Language Arts

JOURNAL Invite children to begin their own picture glossary in a journal. Have them write new or unfamiliar words and their definitions and then draw a picture to represent each entry. Remind children to add to their journals as they study each unit.

law

A rule that everyone must follow.

goods

Things that people make or grow.

services

Jobs people do that help others.

11

WORK WITH WORDS

Invite children to turn to pages 10–11 in their Pupil Book. Then direct their attention to the words and their definitions on the pages. Explain that the words at the beginning of each unit are some of the main ideas that they will explore as they study the unit. Invite volunteers to read each word and its definition aloud. (Note: For additional vocabulary, see the Planning Chart on pages 8C–8D in this Teacher's Edition.) Use the words and the questions that follow to stimulate a general discussion of the new vocabulary.

Q. **How many reading groups do we have in our class? Where have you seen maps? What rules do we follow in our classroom? What kinds of things do people make or grow? What are some jobs that help others?**

VOCABULARY BLACKLINES

You may wish to reproduce individual copies of the vocabulary words for this unit. They are found in the back of your Teacher's Edition.

VOCABULARY CARDS

Display the picture side of the VOCABULARY PICTURE CARDS for Unit 1 on the chalk ledge. Then play "I Spy," giving clues from the lesson, for example: *I spy a picture that shows a rule everyone must follow. Which picture card am I? What word am I? (law)*

Meet Individual Needs

AUDITORY LEARNERS Use the tune to "Mary Wore Her Red Dress" to help children become familiar with the vocabulary words. Sing the lyrics below, and have children identify the word.

Can you read the [first] word,
[First] word, [first] word?
Can you read the [first] word
On this page?

SET THE SCENE WITH LITERATURE

PREVIEW

Invite the class to examine the picture on pages 12–13. Then read aloud the title of the poem. Ask children what they think the poem will be about. Lead children in a discussion about the different people they see each day.

Q. **What are some ways that other people are different from you?**
Responses may include that some people are shorter or taller, some people walk slower while others walk faster, some people like dogs and others like cats. All sorts of things make us different.

Set the Scene with Literature

Sing a Song of People

by Lois Lenski
illustrated by Cathy Diefendorf

Sing a song of people
Walking fast or slow;
People in the city,
Up and down they go.

People on the sidewalk,
People on the bus;
People passing, passing,
In back and front of us.
People on the subway
Underneath the ground;
People riding taxis
Round and round and round.

12

ACTIVITY CHOICES

Background

ABOUT THE POET Lois Lenski (1893–1974) was a Newberry award-winning author of hundreds of books and poems for young children. She began her career as an artist, illustrating some of her own early works. Lois Lenski grew up in Ohio, studied art in New York City, lived on a farm in Connecticut, and spent her last years on the Gulf Coast of Florida. Her stories and poems share the lives of people from diverse parts of our country.

Link to Art

ABOUT THE ARTIST Ever since she was a little girl, Cathy Diefendorf has loved to paint and draw. She is inspired by everyday life in nature and by children. This piece is typical of Cathy's approach. Most of the elements are generated from photographs of the cityscape in Albany, New York, where she lives. Cathy also gets family members and friends to model for her bright, colorful illustrations. Invite children to use photographs to paint community scenes in bright colors.

People with their hats on,
Going in the doors;
People with umbrellas
When it rains and pours.
People in tall buildings
And in stores below;
Riding elevators
Up and down they go.

People walking singly,
People in a crowd;
People saying nothing,
People talking loud.
People laughing, smiling,
Grumpy people too;
People who just hurry
And never look at you!

Sing a song of people
Who like to come and go;
Sing of city people
You see but never know!

13

READ & RESPOND

Ask children to take turns reading aloud the poem on pages 12–13. Encourage them to notice the different ways people act in a city.

Q. **How do you think people act in a small town? How is it different from the way people do things in a city?** People in a small town might drive in a car to work while people in a city might ride a bus, take a taxi, or ride the subway. People in a small town know most of the people who live there, and they speak to neighbors as they take a walk. People in a city might know only a few people, and they do not speak to most of the people on the street.

Meet Individual Needs

ENGLISH LANGUAGE LEARNERS
Use the illustration on the page to help children who have difficulty pronouncing or understanding some of the words and phrases such as *taxis*, *sidewalk*, *hurry*, *walking singly*, *buildings*, and *crowd*. For example, say the word *taxi* and ask children to put their fingers on a taxi shown on the page and pronounce the word.

Link Literature

Invite children to begin the unit by reading *Around Town* by Chris K. Soentpiet. (Lothrop, Lee & Shepard, 1994) The book celebrates the uniqueness and beauty of city life and describes many opportunities that can be found there. Ask children to share a time they visited a city and to describe what they saw.

AUDIO

You may wish to play the UNIT 1 TEXT ON TAPE AUDIOCASSETTE for "Sing a Song of People" and have children tell about the people they find familiar.

LITERATURE
BIG
BOOK

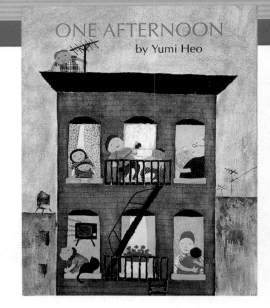

ONE AFTERNOON
by Yumi Heo

Invite children to read *One Afternoon* by Yumi Heo. The distinctively detailed art and simple story make a fine introduction to the concepts taught in Unit 1. The story follows a boy on an afternoon shopping trip with his mother. Readers are introduced to the people and resources in the community that help the boy and his family meet their basic needs.

About the Author/Illustrator

Yumi Heo has illustrated several children's books, including *The Lonely Lioness and the Ostrich Chicks: A Masai Tale* by Verna Aardema and *The Rabbit's Escape* and *The Rabbit's Judgment* by Suzanne Crowder. *One Afternoon* was her first book as both author and illustrator.

Yumi Heo grew up in Korea. Her mother gave her her first box of crayons when she was five and encouraged her to draw throughout her childhood. She now lives near New York City with her husband, Steve.

Reading the Story

Read and discuss the literature to address the following objectives:

1. Recognize a community as a place where people live and work to meet their needs.
2. Identify people and places that families depend on in a community.
3. Describe the goods and services people get in a community.
4. Recognize that communities everywhere have common characteristics.

Social Studies Connection

Invite children to compare the community in the story with their own neighborhoods.

Q. **What places does Minho visit with his mother?** laundromat, beauty salon, ice cream store, pet store, shoe repair store, supermarket

How is your neighborhood like Minho's neighborhood? How is it different?

Provide children with art supplies, and ask them to draw a place they have visited in their community. If necessary, suggest that they reread the story to get ideas. Ask children to include the sights and sounds they remember from the experience.

1

LEARNING TOGETHER AT SCHOOL

OBJECTIVES

1. Describe the classroom and school environment.
2. Identify roles within groups at school.
3. Explore appropriate classroom behavior.
4. Recognize and respect the authority of school workers.

VOCABULARY

group (p. 14)
leader (p. 16)
rule (p. 16)

RESOURCES

Pupil Book/Unit Big Book, pp. 14–17
Write-On Chart 25
Clings
Pattern P1
Activity Book, p. 1

ACTIVITY CHOICES

Meet Individual Needs

VISUAL LEARNERS Display your classroom calendar, and invite children to compare and contrast it with the calendar on page 15 by noting the year, month, and special holidays and events on both. Display the calendar on Write-On Chart 25, and invite children to help record their class schedule for the week. You may wish children to use the Day and Month Clings.

Link to World Languages

SPANISH On the board, write the days of the week in both Spanish and English. Invite children to say the Spanish words after you, or ask a child who is fluent in Spanish to teach the words to the class. Ask children to note how the English and Spanish words are alike and how they are different. Ask children who speak other languages to teach the class the days of the week in their languages.

lunes (LOO•nes)	Monday
martes (MAHR•tes)	Tuesday
miércoles (MIER•koh•les)	Wednesday
jueves (HWEH•ves)	Thursday
viernes (VIER•nes)	Friday
sábado (SAH•bah•doh)	Saturday
domingo (doh•MEEN•goh)	Sunday

1. ACCESS

Invite children to preview the lesson by looking at the pictures and identifying where the children are. Then focus attention on the calendar on page 15. Review with children that a calendar is a way of showing the months, weeks, and days of a year. Encourage children to tell how they use a calendar in their own classroom. Emphasize that a calendar can help them keep track of important events and things they have to do.

Q. **Look again at the calendar and the pictures. What event do you think the children are getting ready for?** Accept reasonable responses, such as an Open House or a program.

Why do you think so? The children seem to be working together to make or do something special.

Focus on the Main Idea

In this lesson children will explore working together for the success of the group. They will identify different roles within a group, explore appropriate classroom behavior, and learn why it is important to respect the authority of school workers. Tell children they will discover how to work together successfully in groups in their own classroom as they read about children in another classroom who are getting ready for a special event.

2. BUILD

Key Content Summary

When working in groups, people often have different roles or jobs. One member may be the leader, who guides the rest of the group. He or she directs and assists other group members. Some group members may work alone, but all work to contribute to a common goal.

How to Read Social Studies

Invite children to review pages 14–17 and locate the labels *lesson number, title, story, picture, new word, main idea, detail,* and *question* as you read them aloud. Explain that knowing what these terms mean and how to recognize and use them will help children become better readers in social studies. Focus attention on the lesson title, and have a volunteer read it aloud.

Q. **How can the title help you?** It tells you what the lesson is about.

Ask for a volunteer to identify the new word and read aloud the sentence in which it appears. Explain that throughout the book all important words will be in yellow.

Q. **What can you do when you read a new word and do not know the meaning?** You can look it up in a dictionary or in the glossary at the end of the book; you can keep a notebook of new words and their definitions and practice using them.

LESSON

Learning Together at School

2. title

3. story

1. lesson number

Visitors are coming to our classroom. We want to show what we can do. First, our teacher, Mrs. Warren, helps us make a plan. For some jobs we will work alone. For other jobs we will work together in a **group**.

4. new word

5. picture

14

ACTIVITY CHOICES

Reading Support

IDENTIFY THE MAIN IDEA Ask children to reread the main idea labeled on page 16. Review the jobs and assignments of the children in the lesson. Use the chart to help children identify which jobs are done alone and which are done in a group.

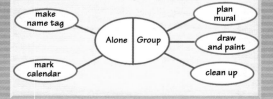

make name tag — Alone / Group — plan mural
mark calendar — draw and paint
clean up

Link Literature

Expand your discussion of appropriate classroom behavior and respect for school workers by sharing *Miss Nelson Is Missing!* by Harry Allard. (Houghton Mifflin, 1985) In the story, schoolchildren take advantage of their teacher's good nature until she disappears and is replaced by a mean substitute teacher. Ask children to point out some rules that are being broken in Miss Nelson's classroom.

We all make name cards for our desks. We get help from our art teacher.

Judy works on a calendar to show the activities of our busy class. She has marked our Open House on September 30.

September

Sunday	Monday	Tuesday	Wednesday	Thursday	Friday	Saturday
			1	2	3	4
5	6	7 Spelling	8	9	10	11
12	13 Book Report	14	15	16	17	18
19	20	21	22	23	24	25
26	27	28	29	30		

15

Meet Individual Needs

AUDITORY LEARNERS Provide clues about tools that enable children to learn and express themselves in school. For example: *I have keys, but they do not unlock doors. I have a screen, but it is not like the kind on windows. What am I?* (a computer) Challenge children to guess what those tools are. Then invite children to create their own riddles.

Background

SCHOOLS AND EDUCATION
During the early 1800s leaders like Thomas Jefferson recognized that the United States would have a better future if its citizens were educated. Leaders wanted each state to set up a school system that was free, had mandatory attendance, was supported by taxes, and was not run by religious groups. Certain religious groups maintained their own schools in the 1800s and some still do today.

Next, ask for a volunteer to describe the photograph labeled *picture*. Explain that pictures and photographs, as well as maps, charts, and diagrams, are important parts of their social studies book.

Q. **What should you do when you see a picture?** You should look for details and think about how the picture goes with the lesson.

Continue by asking for a volunteer to read aloud the sentences labeled *story*. Explain that the sentences form a paragraph and that each paragraph gives important information about things we need to learn.

Then focus children's attention on the labels *main idea* and *detail* on page 16. Explain that the main idea sentence tells what the paragraph is about and that detail sentences give information about the main idea. Tell them that recognizing main ideas and details will help them read social studies.

Vocabulary

Define *group* as a number of people who have something in common. Ask children to identify the groups they see on pages 14–17.

Q. **Why do you think some of the children are working in groups while others are working alone?** Small jobs can be done by one person, but other jobs may be too difficult for just one person; some people like to work in groups, and others like to work alone.

Culture

Organizations and Institutions Remind children that they all belong to a large group—their class. Then ask children to identify the goal of the class in the lesson. Guide children to understand that though some are working alone and some are working in groups, the classmates are all working together toward the same goal.

Q. **Why do you think Mrs. Warren is helping the children to plan the Open House?** so everyone knows what must be done and who must complete each job

Continue by explaining that the art teacher is also helping. Ask children to identify workers in their own school and to review what their roles are.

Vocabulary

Define *leader* as someone who takes responsibility for a group's getting a job done. Have children identify the leader of the group planning to make the mural. Point out that the other group members each have an important job to do. Explain that by working together, group members will reach their group's goal (to make a mural) and at the same time contribute to the class's goal (to get ready for an Open House). Emphasize that when people work in groups, they have to follow certain rules. Explain that a *rule* is a statement that tells us what to do or what not to do.

Q. **Why do you think it is necessary for most groups to have rules?** Rules help people to get the job done by telling what is expected and helping to keep order and prevent wasted time.

Culture

Thought and Expression Discuss how the teachers and children in the photos are expressing their thoughts and ideas by listening to and speaking with one another, by writing and reading, and by drawing. Next, point out materials, tools, and resources that the children are using, such as the calendar, board and chalk, notebook, books, and art supplies. List the materials on the board and invite children to add to the list.

Q. **What are some of the ways you learn together in our classroom?** in cooperative groups, with partners, as a class, in small groups

How do you think the tools that schoolchildren use have changed since your great-grandparents were children? Now we have tools such as computers, televisions, VCRs, and calculators, and we have electricity and batteries to run them.

3. CLOSE

Ask children to summarize the lesson by telling about groups they are part of at school, their roles within the groups, and the behavior expected of group members. Suggest that they also tell about school workers, how the workers help the children, and how the workers usually act toward children.

---

6. main idea

My group is making a mural to hang on the wall. We want to show what we learn in school.

7. detail

Everyone in my group has a special job to do. Juan is the leader. A **leader** makes sure the group follows the rules. **Rules** help us listen, share, and work together fairly.

Biography

There are many ways to learn. Helen Keller could not see, hear, or speak until a teacher came to help her. Anne Sullivan made the letters of the alphabet in Helen's hand. Helen felt Anne's throat and learned to speak. Helen Keller wrote books and taught the world that all people can learn.

16

Juan is the leader.

ACTIVITY CHOICES

Link to Reading

FIND MAIN IDEA AND DETAILS Invite children to read *It Takes a Village, Our Home Is the Sea, Stellaluna,* and *There's a Dragon in My Sleeping Bag.* Ask them to identify the main ideas and important details.

Link to Language Arts

INTEGRATED SPELLING Invite children to begin a notebook to record new words with synonyms and a sentence using each word.

Meet Individual Needs

ENGLISH LANGUAGE LEARNERS Have fluent English speakers work with children who are learning English to review the red tabs in this lesson. English learners should recognize that they can use the title and pictures to understand the focus of each lesson. They may also need to spend more time with the highlighted words.

Sandy and I make a list of the scenes we want to show on our mural. Then the rest of our group helps draw and paint the mural. Finally, we all clean the room and enjoy our work.

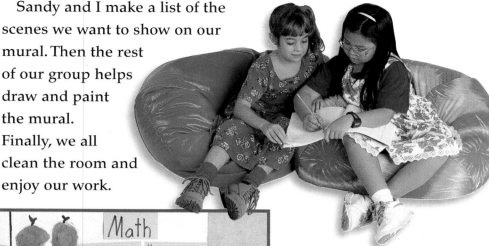

8. question

What Do You Know?

1. What does the leader of a group do?

2. How do you learn together in your classroom?

1. A leader makes sure the group follows the rules.

2. Children's responses might focus on the importance of cooperation.

17

PUPIL BOOK **OR** UNIT BIG BOOK

Extend and Enrich

MAKE RULES Propose situations in which rules are needed, and ask children to suggest which rules are appropriate. For example: *A soccer sign-up is being held in the school gym. Many people push one another toward the table where coaches are taking applications. The soccer coaches help whoever yells the loudest.* Possible rules include *line up as you come in; take numbers as you come in.* Have children discuss the consequences of ignoring rules.

Reteach the Main Idea

DRAW A GROUP Ask children to draw a picture of a group to which they belong, such as their family or class. Ask them to tell what the people in their group have in common. Invite them to tell who the *leader* of the group is and what he or she does. Then ask them to talk about the jobs of the other people in the group.

Check Understanding

The child can
___ describe the classroom and school environment.
___ identify roles within groups at school.
___ explore appropriate classroom behavior.
___ recognize and respect the authority of school workers.

Think Critically

Q. **How does following rules help you learn at school?** The rules help keep group members focused on the group's purpose; when everyone is working toward the same goal, the goal can be reached more quickly.

Show What You Know

Performance Assessment Invite children to contribute to a class mural showing things they do in the classroom and around the school. After they are finished, call attention to the things that made the project a success, such as sharing ideas and taking turns.

What to Look For Look for evidence that the child understands how to work in groups successfully and what behavior is appropriate in the classroom.

Using the Activity Book Distribute copies of Activity Book page 1. Ask children to read the story. Then invite them to underline the main idea, circle one detail, and answer the questions about the story.

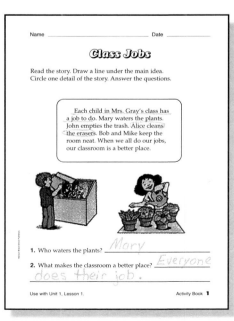

Activity Book page 1

HANDS-ON OPTION

Our Group Guide

Objective: Identify roles within groups at school.

Materials: heavy drawing paper, crayons, markers

Have children create and publish a class Group Guide. One child can create a list of all the activity groups, clubs, or special classes in which members of the class participate. Another child can organize cooperative groups of children, and each cooperative group will work together to create pages in the guide for one of the activity groups. One child can draw pictures of the activity, and another can write captions to tell about the activity. A third can list the activity group's members, leaders, and rules. Another child can design a cover for the guide, and yet another can collect and bind the pages. Place the guide in the library center for children to review. **(TACTILE/VISUAL)**

Class Rules

Objective: Explore appropriate classroom behavior.

Materials: one index card for each pair or small group, chart paper

Help children generate a list of classroom rules to guide behavior at school as you write the list on chart paper. Organize children into pairs or small groups. Invite each group to choose a rule from the chart and write it on an index card. Then ask groups to plan a role-play to show what happens when children do not follow the rule and what happens when children do follow the rule. Set aside time for children to act out the scenes for the class or other small groups. **(AUDITORY/KINESTHETIC)**

School Worker Interview

Objective: Recognize and respect the authority of school workers.

Materials: poster paper, crayons or markers, audiocassette recorder (optional)

Ask children to brainstorm a list of school workers in your building. Invite children to work in small groups to select a worker to interview about his or her job. Encourage them to work together to make a list of questions to ask. Children can share with the class the information they get from the interviews. Some children may make and display posters about the workers and the work they do. Others may write scripts and present their findings in a television news show format. **(AUDITORY/KINESTHETIC)**

School Puzzle

Objective: Describe the classroom and school environment.

Materials: Pattern P1, crayons or markers, heavy paper or light cardboard, scissors, glue, envelopes

Invite each child to draw and color a picture of some part of the school—the classroom, the playground, the cafeteria, the library—onto the Puzzle Pattern. Then ask children to glue their pictures onto a sheet of heavy paper or light cardboard. The children should then cut out the pieces of the puzzle. Ask children to place their puzzle pieces in an envelope and exchange with another child. Invite them to take turns putting together each other's puzzles and guessing what part of their school the picture illustrates. **(TACTILE/VISUAL)**

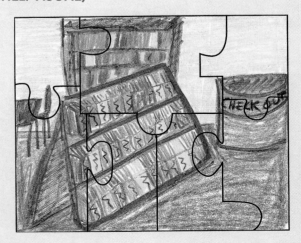

2
LIVING AT HOME AND IN THE NEIGHBORHOOD

OBJECTIVES

1. Describe family roles and shared responsibilities.
2. Recognize a neighborhood as a place where families live and work to meet their needs.
3. Identify people and places in the neighborhood on which families depend.

VOCABULARY

neighborhood (p. 18)
needs (p. 18)
community (p. 21)

RESOURCES

Pupil Book/Unit Big Book, pp. 18–21
Write-On Charts 1, 29
Vocabulary Blacklines
Activity Book, p. 2
Music Audio, "People in Your Neighborhood"
Graph Links
Imagination Express: Destination Neighborhood

ACTIVITY CHOICES

Link to Language Arts

POETRY Read the following verse to the children from *Is Somewhere Always Far Away?* by Leland B. Jacobs.

At the Store
A lady cat once kept a store.
Her store was just for kittens.
Now, what do you think the kittens bought?
Calico for mittens,
Bright ribbons for around their necks,
And catnip sweets for chewing,
And little cans of fish for lunch,
And books to study mewing.

Ask children to brainstorm a list of all the things they have used today that were probably bought at a store for people.

Home Involvement

Suggest that children talk with family members about whom in the neighborhood their family depends on and what the family gets from those people. Give children an opportunity to share what they learned.

WRITE-ON CHARTS

Use WRITE-ON CHART 29 to list things children do during the day and the people who enable them to do those things.

1. ACCESS

Ask children to brainstorm a list of everything they have done so far today, such as wake up, wash, get dressed, eat breakfast, and walk or ride to school. List their responses on the board. Then ask children to think about the people who enabled them to do these things, such as those who made or sold the bed, bedding, soap, toothpaste, and clothing, and those who grew the food, sold it, and prepared it. Talk about what it would be like if children and their families had to grow their own food, make their own clothing, and build and drive a school bus. Point out that they depend upon many people in their everyday lives.

Focus on the Main Idea

In this lesson children will be introduced to the idea of division of labor. They will see that they are part of different groups, such as the family, school, and neighborhood, and that these groups help them meet their needs. They will learn about ways families fulfill their needs and depend on their neighbors. Point out that the girl in the lesson is building a model of her community. Tell children that in this lesson they will build a similar model of a community.

2. BUILD

Key Content Summary

Most families live in neighborhoods. Many neighborhoods together make up a community. Communities are places where people work together to do things that one family or one neighborhood could not do by itself.

Culture

Organizations and Institutions Discuss how families are one type of group whose members depend on one another. Invite children to tell about jobs they do at home, such as making their beds and putting away their clothes. Discuss the importance of family members sharing responsibility.

Q. **Why is it important for everyone to help with jobs at home?** Things get done quickly and there is time for other activities.

Vocabulary

Discuss that a *neighborhood* is the area surrounding many people's homes. Ask children to look at the buildings pictured in the lesson and describe the places they see. Have them point out the buildings that resemble the ones in their neighborhoods and those that do not.

Q. **What other kinds of places might be in a neighborhood?** Children might name banks, drugstores, and police stations.

LESSON

2 Living at Home and in the Neighborhood

You are part of other groups, such as your family and your neighborhood. A **neighborhood** is a place where people live. Lisa is making a model of her neighborhood. Read what she says about her home and neighbors.

My family works together to meet our **needs**. We need food and clothing and a safe place to live.

18

ACTIVITY CHOICES

Reading Support

LOOK FOR WORD PARTS Write the lesson title on the chalkboard. Point to the word *Neighborhood*. Ask children if they can identify the two parts of this large word. Draw boxes around the word *Neighbor* and the word part *hood*. Then have children identify the whole word.

Meet Individual Needs

KINESTHETIC LEARNERS Invite children to take turns acting out different jobs family members do to help at home.

VISUAL LEARNERS Display pictures of different kinds of neighborhoods. Invite children to point out such features as houses, parks, stores, and schools. Point out people and ask children what those people are doing. Ask children to note features that are alike and different from those of their own neighborhoods.

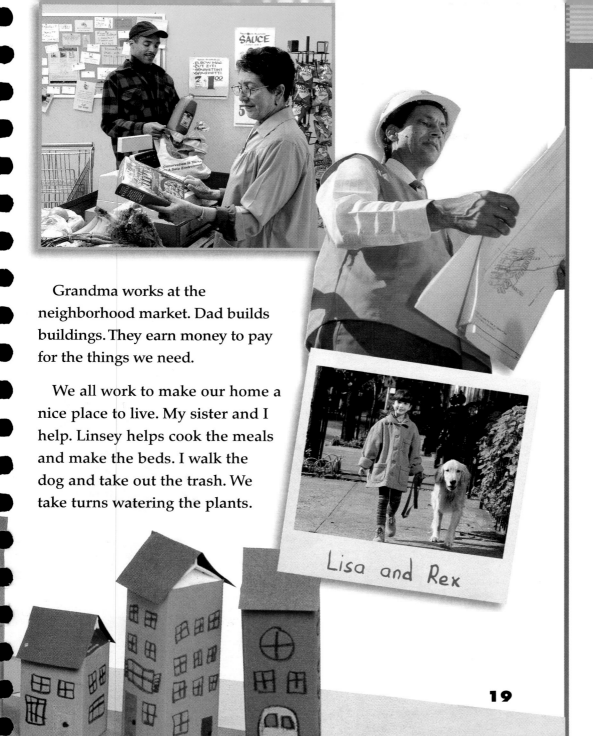

Grandma works at the neighborhood market. Dad builds buildings. They earn money to pay for the things we need.

We all work to make our home a nice place to live. My sister and I help. Linsey helps cook the meals and make the beds. I walk the dog and take out the trash. We take turns watering the plants.

Lisa and Rex

Explain that many places in a neighborhood supply the needs of the people who live there. Define *needs* as things people must have to stay healthy and safe. Ask children to name some things their families need—such as food, clothing, and shelter—and to tell how they get them.

Civics and Government

Civic Values Discuss Neighborhood Watch, Neighborhood Associations, or any other civic groups whose members meet to share ideas on the quality of life in a neighborhood.

Q. **Who is responsible for taking care of neighborhoods?** Children's responses may focus on emergency services and maintenance facilities. Direct them to the understanding that those who live there should also be concerned about taking care of the neighborhood and each other.

19

PUPIL BOOK OR UNIT BIG BOOK

Link to Mathematics

DATA AND GRAPHING Invite children to take a survey to find out what jobs are most often done by children in the class to help their families. Help them tally the jobs by stacking interlocking cubes. Then invite children to compare the stacks to discover the results of the survey.

Community Involvement

Invite neighborhood businesspeople to visit the class or arrange for the class to visit their places of work. Ask the businesspeople to talk about their work and how it helps the neighborhood.

Meet Individual Needs

ENGLISH LANGUAGE LEARNERS Provide pictures showing people in different neighborhoods. Point to each of the pictures, and model sentences such as these: *The woman needs the shoe store to buy shoes for her family. The family needs the mail carrier to deliver its mail.* Invite children to name a person or place that their family needs and to tell why.

TECHNOLOGY

Use GRAPH LINKS to complete this activity.

Economics

Productivity and Economic Growth
Direct attention to the photos on pages 20–21. Invite children to identify each business and tell whether similar ones exist in their neighborhoods. Review businesses in their neighborhoods that are not shown.

Q. **Why do neighborhoods have businesses like those in the pictures?** People depend on others for the things they need.

Help children make connections between the people in the neighborhood who work at different jobs. Point out, for example, that the grocer needs to have clothes cleaned, to be safe from fires, and to buy gasoline. Discuss how others need the grocer. Emphasize that this division of labor helps people because they do not have to provide everything for themselves.

Vocabulary

Develop the meaning of *community* as a group of neighborhoods and a feeling of connectedness. Note that a community's size can vary.

Q. **How would you describe your community?** Children's answers may include a river, a bridge or highway, ethnic makeup, town or city limits, or a sports team.

3. CLOSE

VOCABULARY BLACKLINES

Distribute the word cards for *neighborhood* and *needs*. Ask children to write a definition on the back of each card. Have them write a description of their neighborhood on the neighborhood card and to list three of their needs on the needs card.

Check Understanding

The child can

____ describe family roles and shared responsibilities.

____ recognize a neighborhood as a place where families live and work to meet their needs.

____ identify people and places in the neighborhood on which families depend.

People in our neighborhood help each other, too. Our neighbor Ms. Lee gives me piano lessons. I feed her cat when she visits her daughter.

Our next-door neighbor is a firefighter. He helps save lives and homes in our neighborhood. Other people work as police officers to help keep our neighborhood safe.

20

ACTIVITY CHOICES

Extend and Enrich

INTERVIEW NEIGHBORS Invite children to interview good neighbors about why they like their neighborhood and what it offers them. Ask the children to report their findings.

WRITE-ON CHARTS

Meeting Needs Now and Long Ago
Use WRITE-ON CHART 1 to extend and enrich this lesson. See Teacher's Edition page W2.

Link to Science

PLANTS AND ANIMALS If possible, have children observe ants in a colony or share the book *Ant Cities,* by Arthur Dorros. Have children observe how the ants all seem to have jobs and how they work together. Invite children to compare their observations with their family situations.

Many places in the neighborhood help us meet our needs. We have a food store and a gas station. Sometimes we eat at the restaurant.

My neighborhood is part of a community. A **community** is a place where people live, work, play, and help each other.

What Do You Know?

1. What needs do families have? food, clothing, and a safe place to live

2. How is your neighborhood like Lisa's neighborhood?

21

Reteach the Main Idea

MAKE SENTENCE STRIPS Ask children to make sentence strips showing how a family meets its needs and how a neighborhood meets its needs. Then mix the sentence strips. Ask children to select one, read it, and tell whether it describes how a family meets needs or how a neighborhood meets needs.

TECHNOLOGY

HARCOURT BRACE

Use IMAGINATION EXPRESS:™ DESTINATION NEIGHBORHOOD to complete the Reteach activity.

Think Critically

Q. **Some families live in places where they have few or no neighbors. How might they meet their needs?** They might grow their own food, travel long distances to buy supplies, learn to do without some things, and have some items delivered to them.

Show What You Know

Performance Assessment Have children use various-sized milk cartons and cereal boxes to make a tabletop version of their own neighborhood. They can add toy or clay figures of people and vehicles and then role-play situations in which neighbors interact.

What to Look For In evaluating the models and children's role-plays, look for evidence of the child's understanding that neighborhoods are places where families live and work to meet their needs.

Using the Activity Book Distribute copies of Activity Book page 2. Invite children to draw a picture of something they do to help at home and to draw a picture of someone in their neighborhood who helps them.

Activity Book page 2

HANDS-ON OPTION

"People in Your Neighborhood"

Objective: Identify people and places in the neighborhood on which families depend.

Materials: Music Audio, "People in Your Neighborhood"

Play the audiocassette "People in Your Neighborhood" for children. Lead them in singing along with the tape. As the children sing, encourage them to pantomime the idea they are singing about. After each verse, encourage them to tell why families need the people in the song. Invite children to create original verses to tell about other people they depend on. (AUDITORY/KINESTHETIC)

Family Mural

Objective: Describe family roles and shared responsibilities.

Materials: mural paper, crayons or markers

Make an outline on mural paper of a house or an apartment building. Divide the building into four parts and label them *Food, Clothing, Shelter,* and *Help.* Have children think about ways family members help one another fulfill each need. Invite children to draw pictures to illustrate these ways, and then add those drawings to the mural. Ask children to write a sentence in the appropriate box to describe the family member and how he or she helps. (TACTILE/VISUAL)

Neighborhood Diorama

Objective: Recognize a neighborhood as a place where families live and work to meet their needs.

Materials: shoe boxes, craft materials, glue, scissors, crayons or markers

Organize children into cooperative groups to brainstorm ways neighbors take care of and improve their neighborhoods, such as through Neighborhood Watch programs, through cleanup campaigns, and by planning for parks and playgrounds. Then invite each group to choose one of these to illustrate in a diorama. One child can paint the inside of a shoe box to create the background; pairs of children can work together to add details to the neighborhood, such as people, buildings, and trees. Have children write a caption telling how families are working together in the neighborhood to meet their needs. (TACTILE/VISUAL)

Semantic Maps

Objective: Identify people and places in the neighborhood on which families depend.

Materials: mural or heavy drawing paper, index cards, crayons or markers, magazines, scissors, glue

Ask children to create semantic maps with four categories in which children will name places in their neighborhood where people *Live, Work, Shop,* and *Play.* Have children draw pictures, cut out magazine pictures, and write sentences or names of places on index cards and paste them around the categories. Begin a discussion about how and why the people in the neighborhood depend on each place. (TACTILE/VISUAL)

LEARN FROM A PICTURE AND A MAP

OBJECTIVES

1. Distinguish between eye-level and aerial views of identical sites.
2. Recognize that maps are drawn from an aerial view.

VOCABULARY

map (p. 23)

RESOURCES

Pupil Book/Unit Big Book, pp. 22–23

Activity Book, p. 3

Transparencies 1, 19

ACTIVITY CHOICES

Meet Individual Needs

TACTILE LEARNERS Arrange several items—such as a book, a book bag, a box of crayons, and a toy car—on a desk or table. Invite children to sit so they are viewing the items at eye level. Have them talk about what they see. Then arrange the same items similarly on the floor. Ask children to stand so they are viewing the items from above and to talk about what they see. Have the children compare the two views by putting their fingers on the part they can see of each object.

VISUAL LEARNERS Suggest children look with family members through newspapers and magazines to find photos that show places shown at eye level and places shown from above. Ask them to bring the photos to class and share them with others.

TRANSPARENCY

Use TRANSPARENCY 1.

1. ACCESS

Walk children around the school playground, stopping several times to have them describe the playground and any equipment or other structures on it. Ask them where one object is in relation to objects around it. Then invite them to imagine that they are flying over their playground in an airplane. The airplane is close enough to the ground for children to clearly see the playground equipment. Ask them to discuss what they see. Elicit from children that from the sky, they would probably see only the tops of things.

Q. **Which view of the playground tells you more about what it is like? Why?** Children may say that the view from the airplane shows more because you can see the whole playground in one glance. The playground equipment can't get in the way of your seeing the whole playground.

2. BUILD

Visual Analysis

Compare Maps and Photographs Ask children to look at the photo on page 22 and the map on page 23. Ask them to tell how the picture and the map are alike and how they are different. Invite volunteers to point out specific places in both the photo and the map. Have others tell whether the photo was taken at eye level or from above. Tell children that an *aerial view* is a photo taken from the sky.

Vocabulary

Remind children that a *map* is a special kind of picture that shows what a place looks like from above. Both photos and maps show what places look like, but maps usually use shapes and colors to represent real objects. Unlike photos, which show everything, maps only show some information.

Q. **How is a map different from a photograph?** It does not show all the details; it just shows some things. It uses shapes and colors to stand for real things; a photo shows real things.

Learn from a Picture and a Map

We can learn about a neighborhood by looking at a picture.

 Look at this picture. Tell what you see.
buildings, streets

 Think about how the picture was taken. Do you think you can see more from the air or the ground?
from the air

22

ACTIVITY CHOICES

Meet Individual Needs

TACTILE LEARNERS Have children arrange various objects—like books and pencils—on the tops of their desks. Suggest that each child look down at his or her desktop and draw an aerial view of the arrangement on one half of a sheet of paper and a map of the same arrangement on the other half. Remind them that the drawing should show the actual objects but that the map should show symbols.

Link to Art

ANGLE AND PERSPECTIVE Invite groups of children to work together to create simple 3-D scenes on tabletops. When they have finished, ask children to draw eye-level views and aerial views of their scenes. Have them compare the two. Then ask them to cut the aerial views apart into six to eight squares and to scramble them. Invite other groups to rearrange them correctly.

Extend and Enrich

MAKE A CLASSROOM MAP Take a photo of your classroom while standing on a ladder so the view will be as close to an aerial view as possible. Discuss with children what the photo shows. Then help them make a map of the portion of the classroom shown in the photo. Have children choose shapes for objects, such as desks and windows, and have them place the shapes appropriately on the map. When it is complete, have children compare the map to the photo.

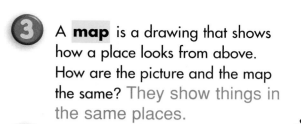

3 A **map** is a drawing that shows how a place looks from above. How are the picture and the map the same? They show things in the same places.

4 What things do you see in the picture that are not on the map? trees, cars, sidewalks, building details

Think and Do

Make a list of the places you see in the picture and on the map.

23

Reteach the Skill

BUILD A BLOCK CITY Provide blocks and invite pairs of children to build a block city. Then take photos of their city to show eye-level and aerial views. Display the pictures and ask children to pair the eye-level view of each city with the aerial view. Have them identify which view is which and tell how they know.

TRANSPARENCY

Use TRANSPARENCY 19 to prepare an aerial view of your school and the surrounding neighborhood.

3. CLOSE

Think and Do

Children's lists should include the places that are common to both the photo and the map, such as homes, apartment buildings, streets, and a school. Have children discuss why certain places in the photo were included on the map.

Review the skill with children by asking the following questions:

Q. What can you tell about a photo taken from above as compared with one taken at eye level? The one taken from above will usually show more; it shows the tops of things instead of the sides, fronts, or backs.

If you are making a map, would you use a photo that shows a place from above or at eye level? Why? From above; it would show a more complete view of the area.

Using the Activity Book Distribute copies of Activity Book page 3. Have children draw a map to match the aerial view.

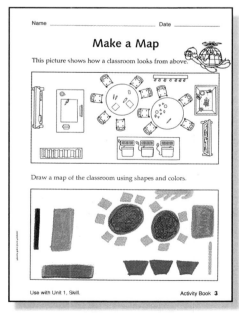

Activity Book page 3

HANDS-ON OPTION

Treasure Map

Objectives: Distinguish between eye-level and aerial views of identical sites. Recognize that maps are drawn from an aerial view.

Materials: construction paper, crayons or markers, four or five bags of marbles

Organize children into four or five groups and give each group a small bag of marbles. Provide time for each group to select a location to hide the bag of marbles, either on the playground or in the classroom. Then have members of each group work together to make a treasure map that shows where the marbles are hidden. A few children from each group can be responsible for listing important landmarks that should be included on the map. Other children can then use the lists to draw the maps. Have each group discuss whether its map should show things at eye level or from above.

Invite children to be creative with their maps, and tell them to use an X to mark the spot where the "treasure" is hidden. Groups can then exchange maps and take turns locating each bag of marbles. Ask children what would happen if they tried to draw all their maps at eye level. **(KINESTHETIC/TACTILE/VISUAL)**

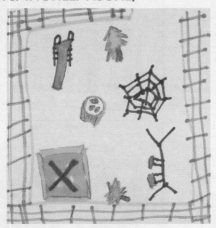

Maps All Around You

Objective: Recognize that maps are drawn from an aerial view.

Materials: fire escape maps for your classroom

Take children on a walking tour of the school. Ask volunteers to point out different kinds of maps and tell how they think they are used. Then have children study the fire escape map for your classroom. Discuss the route the class would take in case of a fire. Provide each child with a copy of the fire escape map and hold a practice fire drill. Have children follow the directions on the map to leave the building. If your school does not use fire escape maps, your class might enjoy creating some and displaying them in the hallways. **(AUDITORY/KINESTHETIC/VISUAL)**

Garden Map

Objective: Recognize that maps are drawn from an aerial view.

Materials: drawing paper, colored pencils, books showing photos of flowers and vegetable plants

Invite children to plan a class garden. Display books with photos of different flowers and vegetable plants, and help children list things they would like to grow. Then have children use the list to make maps that show where each kind of seed will be planted in the garden. Remind them that a map showing an aerial view of the garden might make it easier to see each row. When children have completed their garden maps, display them on a wall or bulletin board. If possible, children might like to use one of the maps to actually plant a class garden. **(KINESTHETIC/TACTILE/VISUAL)**

3

IN AND AROUND THE CITY

OBJECTIVES

1. Define *city*.
2. Explain the need for people to follow rules and obey laws.
3. Describe the goods and services people get in a city.

VOCABULARY

city (p. 24)   goods (p. 26)
law (p. 25)   services (p. 27)

RESOURCES

Pupil Book/Unit Big Book, pp. 24–27

Write-On Charts 2, 29

Pattern P2

Activity Book, p. 4

Vocabulary Blacklines

Vocabulary Picture Cards

Music Audio, "Let's Take a Trip"

Video, Reading Rainbow, Ox-Cart Man

The Amazing Writing Machine

ACTIVITY CHOICES

Meet Individual Needs

AUDITORY LEARNERS   Encourage children to think about the sounds they hear and the kinds of things they see where they live. Make a class list to compare and contrast those sounds and sights with those of the cities they will read about.

Link to Language Arts

JOURNAL   Invite children to begin a personal social studies journal. Note that they may write in it whatever they choose and that you will also make suggestions from time to time. They should be reassured that sharing their journal activities is voluntary.

Ask children to imagine they just moved from a town to a city. Suggest they write a letter to a friend, telling at least one good thing and one bad thing about living in the city.

TECHNOLOGY

Use THE AMAZING WRITING MACHINE™ to complete this activity.

1. ACCESS

Share with children poems about cities and city sounds, such as "City Street" by Lois Lenski.

Q. **What are some things you might see and hear on a city street?** tall buildings, traffic, many people, noisy vehicles, people speaking many languages, people wearing many types of clothing

Focus on the Main Idea

In this lesson children will learn what a city is and recognize ways it is similar to and different from other kinds of communities. They will also recognize the need for people to obey laws. They will distinguish between goods and services and describe some goods and services available in a city. Tell children that in this lesson they will read what a boy wrote in his journal about his visit to a city.

2. BUILD

Key Content Summary

Cities are vast communities made up of a multitude of neighborhoods and a large variety of stores, schools, and services. Many different groups of people live and work in a city. Although the groups of people are diverse, they must work together to meet the needs of the community as a whole.

Visual Analysis

Learn from Pictures Explain that Jesse, the boy in the story, keeps a journal to help him remember what he sees. Invite children to look at the photos on pages 24–27 while you read the text aloud. Have them compare and contrast what they view in these city pictures with what they see in their community.

Vocabulary

Have children use the pictures and text to define *city* as a large community with many neighborhoods. Invite children to identify a skyscraper and a small shop in the photos.

Q. **Why do you think there are skyscrapers in big cities?** More people can live and work using less land.

LESSON 3

In and Around the City

Today Jesse went into the city with his mom. A **city** is a very large community with many neighborhoods. Read Jesse's journal to find out what he learned.

Morning

Time to go to the city. I fasten my safety belt.

Many cars, trucks, and buses are on the expressway. I wonder where they are all going.

24

ACTIVITY CHOICES

Reading Support

USE CONTEXT CLUES Have children pause when they finish reading page 24 to check for understanding. Ask them if they have ever seen the word *city.* Remind them of clues that can help a reader know the meaning of a new word:
• the other words in the sentence
• the pictures on the page

Background

ABOUT THE PICTURES The city pictured in the lesson is Boston, Massachusetts. Boston is the largest city in New England and is located on Boston Bay.

AUDIO

Use the UNIT 1 MUSIC AUDIOCASSETTE to hear the song "Let's Take a Trip."

VIDEO

Use READING RAINBOW,™ OX-CART MAN to explore how people met their needs long ago.

I can't believe that so many people work in the city! Some work in small shops and stores. Others work in giant skyscrapers.

Traffic is moving very slowly. I see a police officer. Police officers make sure that people follow laws. Laws are rules for a community. I'm glad the officer is here.

25

Civics and Government

Rights and Responsibilities   Review the term *rule* from Lesson 1. Define a *law* as a rule that everyone must obey. Tell children that communities have laws to enable people to live and work together in ways that are healthy, safe, and fair.

Q. **What kinds of laws do police officers enforce?** traffic, safety, protection of property, crowd control

66 PRIMARY SOURCE 99

Invite a local law enforcement agent to your class to discuss the laws in the community that most directly affect children and their families and where these laws can be found. You may wish to have children prepare interview questions prior to the visit.

Vocabulary

Define *goods* as products that people make or grow. Tell children you can touch and see goods; they have size and weight. Then define *services* as activities that help people. Point out that a carpenter or plumber sells services and that a grocer or a furniture maker sells goods.

Multicultural Link

Point out that the character of a city usually reflects the heritages of its citizens. Talk about examples such as ethnic food stores and restaurants, people speaking different languages, and people performing various holiday customs. Have children cite examples from their own community.

Link to Music

MUSIC FOR A PURPOSE   Invite children to play a game of Here We Go Through the City Streets, sung to the tune of "Here We Go Round the Mulberry Bush." Have children create verses and sing about different activities they could do in the city, such as "This is the way we go up in the elevator," ". . . look down from the skyscraper," ". . . rush to work." Encourage children to pantomime actions as they sing.

WRITE-ON CHARTS

The Laws We Live By
Use WRITE-ON CHART 2 to extend and enrich this lesson. See Teacher's Edition page W5.

Economics

Productivity and Economic Growth
Have children review the photos and text on pages 26–27. Help them differentiate between goods and services by having them create two-column charts labeled *Goods* and *Services*. Have children list suggestions from the book in the appropriate columns and then add others that are generated in the discussion.

Q. **Which are more important to a community, goods or services?**
They are equally important. People must have goods and services to live happy, healthy, and successful lives.

VOCABULARY BLACKLINES

Organize children into small groups, and give each group the word cards for the vocabulary developed in this lesson. Have children take turns selecting one card at a time and using it in a sentence. Continue the activity until each child has had a turn and all the cards have been used.

3. CLOSE

Invite children to make business cards to represent different types of jobs people have in a city, or use cards that were made in the Hands-On activity. Collect, shuffle, and redistribute the cards, one card to each

Traffic is slow because big trucks are taking goods to stores and shops. Goods are things people make or grow to sell.

It's time to shop! There are so many places to buy clothes, toys, books, and other things for our home. Mom and I even buy fresh flowers.

26

ACTIVITY CHOICES

Extend and Enrich

RESEARCH A CITY Have children choose one of these cities: Chicago, Los Angeles, Dallas, San Francisco, Philadelphia, Kansas City, Atlanta, Phoenix, Portland. Ask them to look in an encyclopedia and write about something they would like to see if they visited that city.

Reteach the Main Idea

ANALYZE PICTURES Provide magazines, newspapers, and travel brochures for children to find pictures of cities. Invite them to tell about what they see in the pictures by pointing out the buildings, people, vehicles, and so on, and by comparing and contrasting these with those in their own communities.

WRITE-ON CHARTS

Use WRITE-ON CHART 29 to list goods and services.

VOCABULARY CARDS

Have children look at the VOCABULARY PICTURE CARDS for the lesson to help them use the words correctly in sentences.

Afternoon

After lunch, Mom and I visit the Computer Museum. The guide tells us about a big computer map. A guide gives a service. Services are jobs that people do for others. I learned a lot from our guide.

Mom and I meet Aunt Leanne for dinner. We talk about the fun we had in the busy city. I can't wait until my next visit!

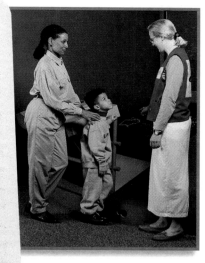

1. Answers might include guide, bus driver, waitress, police officer, window washer.

What Do You Know?

1. Name a service job someone might do in a city.

2. What would you enjoy doing in a city?

27

Community Involvement

Distribute promotional materials from a large city's Chamber of Commerce. Point out the different types of activities that you can enjoy in a city. Also, point out that the larger the city, the more choices of entertainment you have.

Link Literature

Share *My New York* by Kathy Jakobsen. (Little, Brown, 1993) This book depicts a young girl's tour of New York City. Before children read the book, suggest they look for and list places where they might buy different goods or where a service is being provided. Also, suggest they list examples of where a law is being followed.

---

child. Ask children who provide a service to stand in one part of the room and children who provide goods to stand in another part of the room.

Check Understanding

The child can
—— define *city*.
—— explain the need for people to follow rules and obey laws.
—— describe the goods and services people get in a city.

Think Critically

Q. **What might it be like in your community if there were no laws?** People might not get along. People might not be safe.

Show What You Know

 Performance Assessment Invite children to use their journals to record things that happen in their community on a given day.

What to Look For In evaluating children's journals, look for evidence that children recognize the community as a place where people live, work, and play. They may refer to laws, goods, and services.

Using the Activity Book Distribute copies of Activity Book page 4. Invite children to imagine they are on a trip to the city. Ask them to write journal entries to reflect what is happening in the pictures.

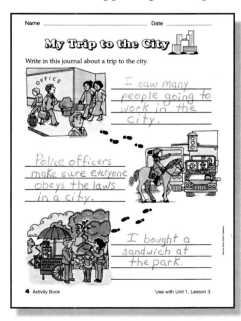

Activity Book page 4

HANDS-ON OPTION

City Skyline

Objective: Define *city*.

Materials: construction paper, magazines, glue, scissors, pencils, crayons, string

Invite children to draw outlines of buildings they might see in a city. Have children use a variety of shapes. Then invite children to draw or cut out pictures of the types of businesses and fun places in a city and to paste the pictures onto the appropriate building shapes. String all the pictures together to form a city skyline, and display it in the hall or in the classroom. **(KINESTHETIC/TACTILE)**

You Are Our Business

Objective: Describe the goods and services people get in a city.

Materials: variety of store and office props, such as empty food containers, toy stethoscope, play money, boxes; markers; scissors; construction paper; and hand-held calculators

Organize children into cooperative groups. Ask them to work together to set up pretend stores and offices and to role-play situations that involve selling goods or providing services. Ask children in each group to discuss and choose roles they might assume, such as customer, cashier, stock clerk, citizen, librarian, and doctor. Suggest children make business cards to exchange with one another. If necessary, provide real business cards for children to model. **(KINESTHETIC/TACTILE)**

Living Together Peacefully

Objective: Explain the need for people to follow rules and obey laws.

Materials: notebooks, pencils, instant camera (optional), drawing paper, crayons

Take children on a walk through the school's neighborhood to look for evidence of laws in their community, such as traffic lights, speed-limit signs, someone wearing a bike helmet, or someone putting litter into a trash can. Ask children to use a notebook or a camera to record what they see. After the walk, discuss the laws and the consequences of disobeying them. **(KINESTHETIC/VISUAL)**

Goods and Services Wheel

Objective: Describe the goods and services people get in a city.

Materials: Pattern P2, brads, markers, cardboard, glue

Have the children form small groups, and provide each with a Wheel Pattern and materials. Ask them to put together a Goods and Services Wheel. Children should brainstorm and choose eight businesses that provide goods and services to write and illustrate on the wheel. Help them glue the wheels to sturdy backings and to affix the arrows with brads. Have children take turns moving the arrow to different businesses. Ask them to name the types of goods and services provided by each business in turn.
(AUDITORY/TACTILE)

READ A MAP

OBJECTIVES
1. Identify a map by its title.
2. Use symbols in a map key to identify places on a map.
3. Use cardinal directions to describe locations on a map.

VOCABULARY
map key (p. 28)
symbol (p. 28)
compass rose (p. 28)
direction (p. 28)

RESOURCES
Pupil Book/Unit Big Book, pp. 28–29
Activity Book, p. 5
Transparencies 2, 19
Trudy's Time and Place House
Neighborhood MapMachine

ACTIVITY CHOICES

Link to Mathematics

NUMBERS Provide children with connecting cubes. Make flash cards showing the symbols for *greater than, less than,* and *equal to.* Divide cubes into equal and unequal groups. Invite children to pick the symbol that expresses the correct relationship between two groups. Explain that >, <, and = are symbols that describe how two numbers relate to each other.

Multicultural Link

Use pictures to introduce children to Chinese, Japanese, or Korean characters, explaining that the characters are symbols and part of an alphabet. Point out that, unlike the English alphabet, where each letter stands for a sound, these alphabets have characters that stand for either a word or an idea.

TECHNOLOGY

Use TRUDY'S TIME AND PLACE HOUSE and NEIGHBORHOOD MAPMACHINE™ to reinforce finding directions.

1. ACCESS

Ask children to recall what they know about maps. Review the idea that a map is a drawing that shows what a real place looks like from above.

Q. **How do maps help us?** They show us where things are, and they help us find our way.

Review relative location terms by inviting children to play a game. Have one child use directional terms to describe the location of a person or object in the room while other children try to find the person or object. For example, a child might describe the location of a globe by saying, "This object is in the back of the room, on top of the shelf." Encourage children to use location terms such as *right, left, above, below, far away,* and *near.*

Critical Thinking

Explain to children that a *symbol* is a drawing that stands for something else. Then write the words *sunshine* and *rain* on the board. Provide children with drawing paper, and invite them to draw a picture to represent each word. Explain that their drawings are *symbols* for the words on the board.

Q. **Why do people use symbols instead of words?** They can be read by everyone; they fit in smaller spaces, as on a map.

2. BUILD

Vocabulary

Tell children that in this lesson they will discover how mapmakers use symbols to show things on a map. Explain that a *map key* tells what each symbol represents.

🌐 Geography

Location Have children look at the map and share the text on page 28. Ask children to identify the title of the map.

Have children locate the map key and answer the questions. Point out that some symbols look like what they stand for and that others do not.

Q. If you were designing this map, what might you use as a symbol for a park? Why? a bench or a flower, because these are associated with parks

Explain that a *compass rose* is a symbol on maps and globes that shows *directions*—north, south, east, and west.

Ask children to brainstorm a list of other things they might see on a map of a city, such as a railroad, tunnel, or bridge. Then have them suggest symbols they might use to represent each thing you listed. Invite children to practice using the compass rose to describe where they might put their new symbols on the map of Boston.

Map and Globe Skills

Read a Map

How do you think Jesse and his mom know where to go in the city? Perhaps they read a map. Maps help you find places. A **map key** shows you how to read a map.

1 What is the title of this map? Boston

2 **Symbols** are pictures that stand for things on a map. What symbols are shown in this map key? Children should list the ten symbols.

3 Find the symbol for the Computer Museum. On what street is the museum located? Sleeper Street.

4 Find the compass rose on the map. A **compass rose** gives the directions on a map. The four main **directions** are north, south, east, and west.

5 In which direction would you walk to get from the Pedestrian Mall to Boston Common? west

Map Key

🏛 **City Hall**

💻 **Computer Museum**

🐟 **New England Aquarium**

👪 **Pedestrian Mall**

🚌 **Peter Pan Bus Terminal**

🍴 **Pier 1 Restaurant**

🏛 **Quincy Market**

🌳 **Park**

▭ **Street**

28

ACTIVITY CHOICES

Link to Physical Education

TEAM GAMES Use masking tape on the floor of the gym to create a map of the school's neighborhood. Outline streets, and tape on symbols to stand for places. Make a map key on a chart. Then challenge children to play a game of Simon Says, using directions that involve reading symbols. Say, for example, "Simon says hop west to the basketball courts."

Meet Individual Needs

KINESTHETIC LEARNERS Help children make a large mural map, or use Transparency 19 to show the school and the surrounding neighborhood. Take the class on a walk around the neighborhood, noting street names and landmarks. In the classroom, outline streets on the mural paper or on the transparency. Ask children to compile a list of places they want to show on the map and to decide on symbols. Help them create a map key to explain the symbols.

Extend and Enrich

MAKE A FLOOR PLAN Ask children to make a large floor plan of their school using symbols to show where different rooms are located. Have them title the map and create a map key.

TRANSPARENCY

Use TRANSPARENCY 2 to locate the map title, map key, and compass rose.

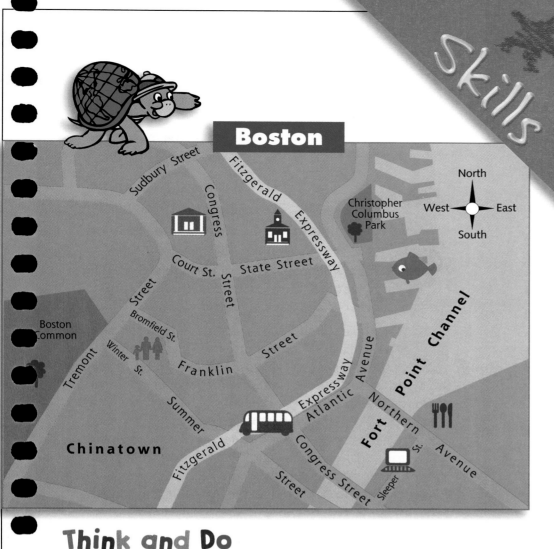

Boston

Sudbury Street · **Congress** · **Fitzgerald Expressway** · **Christopher Columbus Park** · **Court St.** · **State Street** · **Street** · **Bromfield St.** · **Boston Common** · **Winter St.** · **Tremont** · **Summer** · **Franklin** · **Street** · **Chinatown** · **Fitzgerald** · **Congress Street** · **Sleeper St.** · **Expressway** · **Atlantic Avenue** · **Congress Street** · **Fort Point Channel** · **Northern Avenue**

North · West · East · South

Think and Do

- Find City Hall. What streets would you take to get from City Hall to Christopher Columbus Park?

- In which direction would you go?

- What would you pass along the way?

29

Reteach the Skill

MAKE MAP SYMBOLS Discuss objects that can be used to stand for various buildings and structures children might see in a neighborhood. Invite children to place these objects on a tabletop and draw a map using symbols to represent each object. Remind them to include a map key, compass rose, and title.

Home Involvement

Ask children to look through newspapers and magazines at home for maps—local maps or maps of places around the world. Suggest they talk with family members about the maps, their titles, and the symbols on them.

3. CLOSE

Think and Do

Children should trace a path from City Hall south on Congress Street to State Street and then east to Christopher Columbus Park on Atlantic Avenue. Along the way, children should locate City Hall, Quincy Market, the expressway, Fort Point Channel, Christopher Columbus Park, Congress Street, State Street, and Atlantic Avenue.

Review the skill with children by asking:

Q. **If Jesse and his mom took a bus into Boston, where would they stop first?** Peter Pan Bus Terminal

What direction would they go to get to the Computer Museum? east

Jesse and his mom are leaving the museum. They are supposed to meet Jesse's aunt at the Pier 1 Restaurant. What street should they take? Sleeper Street

Using the Activity Book Distribute copies of Activity Book page 5. Have children draw symbols in the map key and design their own maps. Then have them write a map title. When they are finished, suggest that partners use their questions to ask each other how to get from one place to another, naming the things they would pass along the way.

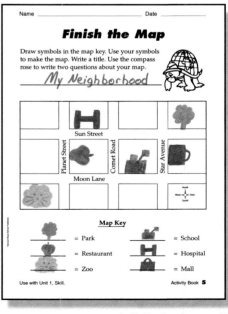

Activity Book page 5

HANDS-ON OPTION

Create a Map

Objectives: Identify a map by its title. Use symbols in a map key to identify places on a map.

Materials: Teacher's Edition page 29B, colored pencils, assorted objects of different sizes and shapes

Provide each child with a copy of the map on page 29B. Invite children to create a map of a new community. They should use a different symbol for each item listed in the map key. Point out that they can place more than one feature on their maps, but they must trace the same symbol each time they repeat something. Remind children to draw the symbols in the map key and to name their community. **(TACTILE/VISUAL)**

Make a Map from a Picture

Objectives: Identify a map by its title. Use symbols in a map key to identify places on a map. Use cardinal directions to describe locations on a map.

Materials: books and magazines showing aerial views of different locations, drawing paper, crayons, markers, colored pencils

Invite children to find aerial photographs of towns, neighborhoods, zoos, amusement parks, and so on. Challenge them to use the photographs to draw maps of the same areas. Have children create map keys that list their symbols. Tell them to add compass roses to their maps and title them. Ask children to write questions about their maps using the four cardinal directions. Then have them exchange with partners and answer each other's questions. **(KINESTHETIC/TACTILE/VISUAL)**

A Weather Map

Objectives: Identify a map by its title. Use symbols in a map key to identify places on a map.

Materials: wall map, national newspaper showing a five-day weather forecast, construction paper, crayons, markers, scissors, double-sided tape

COOPERATIVE LEARNING Invite children to be weather reporters for an imaginary TV news station. Organize the class into cooperative groups. Ask one group to read the weather section in a national newspaper and write down the five-day forecast. If possible, children may enjoy searching the Internet for national weather information. Ask another group to create a variety of weather symbols showing clouds, sunshine, rain, wind, snow, and so on. Some of the children can draw the weather symbols on construction paper. Other children can color the symbols, cut them out, and put double-sided tape on the backs. Ask a volunteer to make a map key by drawing the different weather symbols on a sheet of drawing paper and writing what each one means. Attach the map key to the bottom of a United States wall map.

Suggest that children watch a weather forecast on television at home, or, if possible, tape one and allow them to watch it in class. Then have groups work together, using the forecast information, the weather symbols, and the wall map, to create their own weather maps for the coming week. Invite a volunteer to be the "weather reporter" each day, explaining what the different symbols represent as they report the weather. **(AUDITORY/KINESTHETIC/TACTILE/VISUAL)**

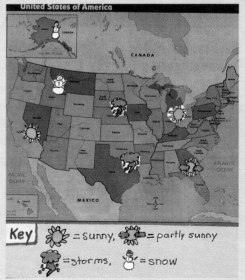

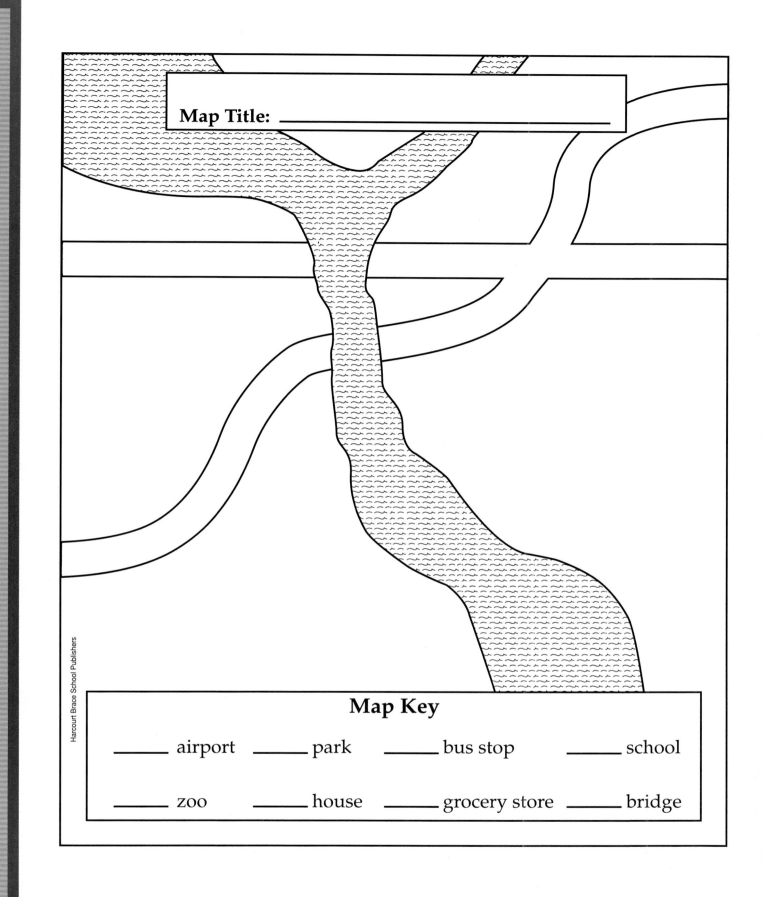

Map Title: _____

Map Key

_____ airport _____ park _____ bus stop _____ school

_____ zoo _____ house _____ grocery store _____ bridge

Harcourt Brace School Publishers

DEFINE THE PROBLEM

Ask children to look at the picture and tell where they think the people are going and why. Help children recognize that people of all ages with many different needs are entering the park to enjoy such activities as skating, walking, bicycling, and jogging.

Q. **Suppose you were planning a park. What kinds of things should you think about as you plan?** things to have in the park, the needs of the people who will be using the park, and all possible problems

What kinds of problems do you think there could be? how to make and keep the park safe and fun for everyone and how to protect park property

USE PROBLEM-SOLVING SKILLS

Organize children into small groups, and review cooperative-group strategies. Suggest each group select a leader and a recorder for the activity. Then challenge each group to plan a park for everyone to enjoy. Have children read the suggestions and use the questions on page 30 as a guide. Have children list the features they would like to have in their parks, such as places to sit, things to climb, and a track or trail to ride on. They should

---

Solving Problems

A Park Is for Everyone

How could you make the park a safe place for everyone to enjoy? Work with some friends. Think of ways to use the park.

● What special needs does each person have?
● What problems need to be solved?

Show Your Ideas

Choose a way to show your ideas to the class.

● Make a model of the park.
● Write a story.
● Draw a picture.

30

ACTIVITY CHOICES

Link to Reading

READ TO SET THE SCENE Read aloud a book about rain, such as *Rain* by Peter Spier, *Lost in the Storm* by Carol Carrick, or *Bringing the Rain to Kapiti Plain* by Verna Aardema. Then ask children to pretend that water covers the whole world. Have children use the problem-solving steps to decide what kind of house they would live in. Invite them to draw pictures to show what they think would be the best kind of house.

Background

PROBLEM SOLVING The purpose of the Brainstorm is to help children realize that solving problems successfully depends on careful thinking. Problem solving is a skill. Review with children the following steps to solving problems.

Steps to Solving Problems
1. Name the problem.
2. Think of some solutions.
3. Compare the solutions and pick the best one.
4. Plan how to carry out the solution.
5. Solve the problem and evaluate the solution.

consider the needs of all people—including the young, the old, and the physically challenged—and think of solutions to potential problems.

Q. **What rules and regulations might you have in your park?**
Do not litter; do not speed; do not bike or skate on the foot path; all dogs must be kept on a leash.

SHOW SOLUTIONS

Provide children with art supplies, drawing paper, craft sticks, small boxes, and modeling clay. Invite them to make a model or a drawing of their park or to write a story telling how it would be a place for everyone in the community to enjoy. Review the steps for solving a problem.

1. Define the problem.
2. Record possible solutions.
3. Discuss the advantages and disadvantages of each solution.
4. Agree on the best solution.
5. Solve the problem.

PUPIL BOOK OR UNIT BIG BOOK

Role-Play

Invite children to role-play how they would solve the following problems.

- You are a new student, and you do not have any friends in this school.
- You do not understand something that has been taught, and you are too embarrassed to raise your hand to say so.
- You are often the last person picked for a team, and your feelings are hurt.
- You forgot to do your homework. Now what do you do?

WRITE-ON CHARTS

Signs of Safety

Use WRITE-ON CHART 3 to extend and enrich this lesson. See Teacher's Edition page W8.

TECHNOLOGY

Use CHOICES, CHOICES:™ KIDS AND THE ENVIRONMENT for making responsible choices about the environment.

A Red and Blue Coat

Solving problems usually involves considering different points of view. Children can consider different perspectives when they read stories with conflict. Fables and folktales from around the world offer opportunities for such discussions. Share the following folktale from the Congo in Central Africa. You may wish to stop before reading the end of the story to have children consider who is at fault.

There once were two childhood friends who were determined to remain close companions always. When they were grown, they each married and built their houses facing one another. Just a small path formed a border between their farms.

One day a trickster from the village decided to test their friendship. He dressed himself in a two-color coat that was divided down the middle, red on the right side and blue on the left side. Wearing this coat, the man walked along the narrow path between the two houses. The two friends were each working opposite each other in their fields. The trickster made enough noise as he traveled between them to cause each friend to look up from his side of the path at the same moment and notice him.

At the end of the day, one friend said to the other, "Wasn't that a beautiful red coat that man was wearing today?"

"No," replied the other. "It was blue."

"I saw that man clearly as he walked between us!" said the first. "His coat was red."

"You are wrong!" the second man said. "I saw it too. It was blue."

"I know what I saw!" insisted the first man. "The coat was red."

"You don't know anything," replied the second angrily. "It was blue!"

"So," shouted the first, "you think I am stupid? I know what I saw. It was red!"

"Blue!" the other man said.

"Red!" "Blue!" "Red!" "Blue!"

They began to beat each other and roll around on the ground.

Just then the trickster returned and faced the two men, who were punching and kicking each other and shouting, "Our friendship is over!"

The trickster walked directly in front of them, displaying his coat. He laughed loudly at their silly fight. The two friends saw that his two-color coat was divided down the middle, blue on the left and red on the right.

The two friends stopped fighting and screamed at the man in the two-colored coat, "We have lived side by side all our lives like brothers! It is all *your* fault that we are fighting! You started a war between us."

"Don't blame me for the battle," replied the trickster. "I did not *make* you fight. *Both* of you are wrong. And *both* of you are right. Yes, what each one said was true! You are fighting because you only looked at my coat from your *own* point of view."

4

OUR COUNTRY OF MANY PEOPLE

OBJECTIVES

1. Define themselves as citizens of the United States.
2. Identify the diversity of the American people.
3. Recognize that Americans have talents and skills that contribute to the country's common good.

VOCABULARY

citizen (p. 32)
country (p. 32)

RESOURCES

Pupil Book/Unit Big Book, pp. 32–33
Write-On Chart 4
Activity Book, p. 6
Desk Maps
Music Audio, "People in Your Neighborhood"
The Amazing Writing Machine

ACTIVITY CHOICES

Meet Individual Needs

AUDITORY LEARNERS Seat children in a circle. Ask them to look at one another and to think about who they are and all the ways they are special. Then invite each child in turn to tell about a special talent, skill, or interest that he or she has. Afterward ask children to suggest why their differences are important and how they may use them as members of a family, a class, and the community.

Link to Language Arts

JOURNAL Invite each child to jot down what he or she thinks it means to be an American or to live in the United States. At the end of the lesson, ask children to look at what they wrote and make additions or changes.

DESCRIPTIVE WRITING Have children think about jobs they might like to have someday or hobbies they would like to try. Then invite children to write descriptive paragraphs about their choices.

1. ACCESS

Remind children of the song they sang in Lesson 2, "People in Your Neighborhood." Ask children to think about *all* the different people in their own neighborhoods who help to make it a good place to live—family members, friends, neighbors, shopkeepers, dance teacher, soccer coach, as well as the letter carriers and firefighters they sang about in the song. Emphasize that everyone is important to the neighborhood in some way. Then remind children that they are also Americans, even though they come from different places and backgrounds.

Focus on the Main Idea

In this lesson most children will identify themselves as Americans, or citizens of the United States. They will recognize that although they and their fellow citizens may come from different places and cultural backgrounds, they are alike in many ways. Tell children that in this lesson they will look at a collage that shows some of the people who help to make the United States a great place to live.

TECHNOLOGY

Use THE AMAZING WRITING MACHINE™ RESOURCE PACKAGE to complete this activity.

2. BUILD

Key Content Summary

Americans come from many places and backgrounds, and they display a variety of skills, talents, interests, and abilities. Yet Americans share a common bond and the responsibility to follow the country's laws and to work together to help make our country a great place to live.

Vocabulary

Remind children that they live in the country called the United States of America. Define *country* as a separate land where the people have their own leaders and their own laws. Explain that *citizens* are people who belong to communities—a town, city, state, or country.

Have children use a globe or their Desk Maps to expand their location from a town or city to their state, country, and the world.

Civics and Government

Rights and Responsibilities of Citizens
Use the photos and text to discuss how Americans contribute to their country. Have children identify and describe the activities of the people in the photos.

Q. **Why do you think people work?**
to support their families; because their jobs are interesting; to contribute to the community

Emphasize that our backgrounds, interests, skills, abilities, and talents play an important role in what we decide to do as individual citizens.

3. CLOSE

Invite children to summarize the lesson by telling how they would answer a person from another country who asks what it means to be an American. Ask them to use the words *citizen* and *country* and to tell about the responsibilities to be good Americans.

LESSON 4
Our Country of Many People

Our class made a collage of American citizens. **Citizens** are a group of people who belong to a community. We are citizens of our **country**, too. The United States of America has more than 250 million citizens.

Americans are different in many ways. We live in different places, eat different foods, and work at different jobs. But Americans are also alike in special ways. We follow our country's laws. We cooperate, or work together, to make our country a great place to live.

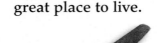

32

ACTIVITY CHOICES

Reading Support

USE CONTEXT CLUES Complete the word map with children to help them understand the meaning of the word *country*.

What is it?
• a place

country

What is it like?
• It has its own land.
• It has laws.
• It has holidays.

What are some examples?
• United States
• Canada
• Mexico

Link to World Languages

SPANISH, GERMAN, ITALIAN
Help children list foreign words that have become part of the English language, such as *canyon* and *patio* from Spanish; *kindergarten* from German; and *costume* and *laundry* from Italian.

Link to Music

DANCE Point out the dancer who is *clogging*. If possible, have someone demonstrate clogging and other folk dances to children.

What Do You Know?

1. **What is the name of our country?** the United States of America

2. **How can you be a good member of this large group of Americans?** Answers should reflect an understanding of the need to cooperate, obey laws, and respect people's differences. **33**

PUPIL BOOK OR UNIT BIG BOOK

Extend and Enrich

RESEARCH A JOB Children can research what talents and skills are required to become a musician, a logger, a driver, a teacher, or any of the other jobs shown on the collage.

Reteach the Main Idea

ANALYZE A PHOTO Invite pairs of children to choose a photograph from the collage and discuss how the citizen is working to make the country a great place to live.

Multicultural Link

Discuss that many different ethnic groups bring with them their customs, traditions, language, and beliefs. Use a world map to point out the origins of different ethnic groups.

WRITE-ON CHARTS

Children of the World

Use WRITE-ON CHART 4 to extend and enrich this lesson. See Teacher's Edition page W11.

Check Understanding

The child can
— define himself or herself as a citizen of the United States.
— identify the diversity of the American people.
— recognize that Americans have talents and skills that contribute to the country's common good.

Think Critically

Q. **What do you see in your community that tells you Americans come from many different backgrounds?** People speak different languages, eat different foods, wear many different styles of clothes, practice different religions, and celebrate different holidays.

Show What You Know

 Performance Assessment Have children look for pictures they can use to create a bulletin-board collage of American citizens in action.

What to Look For The collage should illustrate people of various ages, genders, and ethnicities working at different jobs.

Using the Activity Book Distribute copies of Activity Book page 6. Tell children to study the pictures and use them to make lists under the heading *Good Citizens Do . . .* or *Good Citizens Do Not . . .*

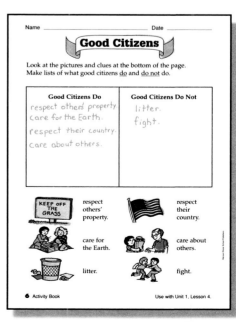

Activity Book page 6

HANDS-ON OPTION

The "Hands-On Option" is an alternative way to address all objectives for this lesson or to enrich the content found in the Pupil Book/Unit Big Book.

I Am an American!

Objectives: Define themselves as citizens of the United States. Identify the diversity of the American people. Recognize that Americans have talents and skills that contribute to the country's common good.

Materials: large sheets of drawing paper, crayons or markers, pencils

Invite children to choose partners to create individual profiles of each other. Have children take turns using a black crayon or marker to make a side-view outline on paper of each other's heads. Then have children identify their partners by making a list of their qualities, skills, accomplishments, and backgrounds. Have children begin by writing *American Citizen* at the top of the list. Display the completed profiles on a bulletin board display entitled *Who Am I?* Afterward, encourage children to discuss the diversity of America's citizens. **(TACTILE/VISUAL)**

The People of America

Objectives: Identify the diversity of the American people. Recognize that Americans have talents and skills that contribute to the country's common good.

Materials: audiocassette player; blank cassette; Music Audio, "People in Your Neighborhood"

Play "People in Your Neighborhood" for children, and invite them to sing along. Then rename the song "The People of America," and invite children to make up new words to tell about some of the people who contribute their talents and skills to our country. Invite children to perform the song with the new words. **(AUDITORY/KINESTHETIC)**

The Alphabet Game

Objectives: Identify the diversity of the American people. Recognize that Americans have talents and skills that contribute to the country's common good.

Materials: children's reference books about the 50 states, writing paper or premade forms, markers

 Invite children to form groups to play the alphabet game. Assign several letters of the alphabet to each group, omitting letters such as X and Z. Write the following on the board as a model:

_____ (letter)

My name is _____.

I eat _____.

I play a(n) _____.

I like _____.

I want to be a(n) _____.

Ask groups to fill in the blanks with words beginning with the assigned letter. For example, for the letter *A* children might list *Albert, avocados, accordion, airplanes,* and *astronomer.* For each letter they are assigned, have the group record and complete the sentences on the board. Invite the groups to read their sentences aloud. Then compile the pages into a class book. **(TACTILE/VISUAL)**

The Peacock's Gift

ADAPTED FROM AESOP'S FABLE

"Our Country of Many People" focuses on the diversity of Americans. As you read the following story adapted from Aesop's fable, have children think about ways that Americans depend on each other.

One day lion and lioness, the rulers of the animal world, called to the birds to find out if they were doing their jobs.

First came the eagle, spreading broad wings. "My job is to fly," said the eagle. "My great wings carry me across the sky, so I can watch over all on the earth."

Next spoke the nightingale sweetly, "My job is to sing the world to sleep at night."

Then the parrot chattered, "My job is to speak. People laugh when they hear me repeat the words they teach me."

Last came the peacock, looking embarrassed and ashamed. "And what is your job?" asked the lion and the lioness.

"I have no job," said the peacock. "I can neither fly, nor sing, nor speak. What good am I?"

Immediately the other birds disagreed. Eagle answered, "It is your beauty that makes me strong. I see the colors of earth and sky in your tail and am inspired to fly."

So, too, the nightingale chimed, "Your rainbow tail makes me so happy that I must sing."

Even the parrot mimicked the thought, "You are a pretty bird, pretty bird, pretty bird!"

And so the lion and lioness helped the birds to see that all of their special gifts—the strength of an eagle, the song of the nightingale, the speech of the parrot, and the splendor of the now proud peacock—gave them important jobs to do.

MAKING
SOCIAL
STUDIES
REAL

READ AND RESPOND

Read aloud pages 34–35 and discuss *The Big Help*. Explain that *The Big Help* is a program created by Nickelodeon to show children how they can make the world a better place by volunteering. Tell children that Megan Halbrook lives in Woodinville, Washington. Invite volunteers to find Woodinville on a map. Then discuss how Megan found a way to volunteer in her own community.

Q. **What did Megan do?** She worked five hours helping an elderly man named Ray; she did chores for a man who needed help. **What are some ways to volunteer in your community?** Responses may include picking up trash, recycling, painting over graffiti, collecting food and clothing for people in need, visiting a nursing home, planting trees and flowers, and helping at an animal shelter.

Lead children in a discussion about why community service is important. Children should understand that it is the responsibility of people living in a community to help one another.

Q. **Why is it important to help people who cannot help themselves?** Responses may include that we should treat people the way we would like to be treated.

❝ PRIMARY SOURCE ❞

If possible, have children use the Internet to find more information about *The Big Help*. The address is **http://www.nick.com**. If children wish, they can print out a "Certificate of Thanks" just for visiting *The Big Help*.

The Big Help

Megan Halbrook loves to help people. At school she looks for ways to help classmates. At home she helps her mom and dad with many jobs. Now Megan has some new ideas about helping others. She wrote about the ideas in a story for a contest at school. This is how Megan began.

"One day, when I was watching television, I saw something called The Big Help. I sat wondering what The Big Help was. Then they explained it. The Big Help was about kids doing community service. Community service is helping other people or helping the world."

Woodinville, Washington

34

ACTIVITY CHOICES

Background

THE BIG HELP *The Big Help* is Nickelodeon's ongoing grassroots campaign to connect children to their communities through volunteering. Since its creation in 1994, over 18 million children have pledged 175 million volunteer hours in communities across the country. As an added benefit, the children build self-esteem as they engage in positive and constructive activities.

Each year Nickelodeon hosts an eight-hour *Big Help-a-thon* to give children an opportunity to commit some of their time to volunteering. *The Big Help* has also joined forces with more than twenty partner organizations across the country to facilitate volunteer projects for children on a local level.

To send for *The Big Help* classroom kit, write to P.O. Box 929, New York, NY 10108.

Megan saw children helping their community in different ways. They picked up trash, painted over graffiti, and helped people. Megan liked the last idea best. She pledged, or promised, to work five hours helping someone.

Megan's dad told her about a Day of Caring she could join in his workplace. On that day, Megan's father took her to the house of a seventy-five year old man named Ray. Ray could no longer keep up with his chores. Megan cleaned out drawers, vacuumed floors, and washed dishes. Megan said that helping Ray made her feel "very, very good inside."

  What Can You Do?

 Find out how you and your classmates can help your community.

Talk with your family about things you can do to help others.

Visit the Internet at
http://www.hbschool.com
for additional resources.

35

Culture

Shared Humanity and Unique Identity
Invite children to discuss how people in the community decide what services they can volunteer. Discuss how the age of the volunteer, his or her special talents, the number of people who will help, and the needs of the community might affect the choice.

Q. **What kinds of helpful activities can people do alone?** They can help older people or plant flowers and trees. **What activities are better done by a group?** Responses might include raising money to help people in need and cleaning up neighborhoods.

Critical Thinking

Help children understand the definition of a volunteer. Explain that when people volunteer, they do not get paid for their time or the work that they do.

Q. **Why do you think volunteers are willing to work without pay?** It makes them feel good to help others; they enjoy making their communities and the world a better place to live.

PUPIL BOOK OR UNIT BIG BOOK

Link to Language Arts

JOURNAL Suggest that children research organizations in their communities for which they might volunteer. Invite them to record some of the ways they would like to help make their community a better place to live. Allow children to share their findings and their ideas with the class.

Link to Art

CREATE A POSTER Invite children to work together in small groups to create posters about volunteering. Suggest that each group show a different way to volunteer. Children may want to review the lists of local volunteer organizations they recorded in their journals. Display the finished posters in the hallway or in the front entrance of the school.

Community Involvement

Invite spokespersons from a variety of local volunteer organizations to speak to the class about ways children can help their communities. You may want to organize an event at which the children can volunteer as a class.

PICTURE SUMMARY

TAKE A LOOK

Remind children that the picture summary is a way to visually represent the main ideas or events in a story. Explain that this summary reviews some of the main ideas in Unit 1. Help children realize that they are looking at a picture of people living, working, and playing in a community and of the different groups to which they belong.

Visual Analysis

Learn from Pictures Organize children into small groups. Invite them to examine the picture summary and to react to its images. Ask children to describe the various scenes and to compare and contrast each scene to people, places, and activities in their own communities.

VOCABULARY BLACKLINES

Distribute the individual word cards for this unit and have children use the words as they discuss the picture summary.

UNIT
1
Review

Picture Summary

Look at the pictures. They will help you remember what you learned.

Talk About the Main Ideas

1. People belong to many groups.

2. Children in school learn together in groups.

3. Families help each other in neighborhoods.

4. Cities are busy places where people live, work, and play.

5. Communities have laws for order and safety.

6. Our country is home to many different Americans.

Write a List Many people help you meet your needs. Make a list of some of these people. Tell how they help you.

36

UNIT POSTER

Use the UNIT 1 PICTURE SUMMARY POSTER to summarize the unit.

VOCABULARY CARDS

Have children use the VOCABULARY CARDS for this unit to review key concepts.

Picture Summary Key

All panels represent the groups to which people belong. In addition, the numbered panels correspond directly to the main ideas on page 36.

Help children expand from the smaller groups to community and country.

SUMMARIZE MAIN IDEAS

Ask children to read the summary statements on page 36 and to relate each one to a specific scene in the picture summary. Lead a class discussion about each scene, and challenge children to offer supporting details for each main idea illustrated. Review children's predictions on the KWL chart at the beginning of the unit, on Teacher's Edition page 8.

Help children focus on the groups to which they belong and the people in their communities who help them meet their needs.

Sharing the Activity

Provide time for children to complete the Write a List activity on page 36. Invite children to share their lists within small groups or with the whole class. Have them discuss how the people on their lists relate to the main ideas illustrated in the picture summary.

PUPIL BOOK OR UNIT BIG BOOK

Meet Individual Needs

ENGLISH LANGUAGE LEARNERS Write the following sentences on the chalkboard. Invite children to copy each sentence and write *yes* if the sentence is true or *no* if it is not true.

1. People belong to only one group.
2. Children in school learn together in groups.
3. People in a neighborhood never help each other.
4. Cities are very quiet places where only a few people live.
5. Laws bring order and safety.
6. Our country is home to many different people.

TECHNOLOGY

Use the AMAZING WRITING MACHINE™ RESOURCE PACKAGE to summarize the unit.

USE VOCABULARY

1 community
2 map
3 law
4 services
5 group
6 goods

CHECK UNDERSTANDING

1 Children might name family, class, church, Scouts, team, choir, community, country, and other groups.
2 Children might say that people in a community depend on firefighters, teachers, farmers, trash collectors, police officers, grocers, and other workers who provide services or goods.
3 Children might respond that laws keep people safe. Traffic laws help people avoid accidents.
4 As Americans, we may have different jobs, eat different foods, and live in different places. But we all live in a free country and follow the same laws.

THINK CRITICALLY

1 Without laws, people would not know what they should and should not do. People and property might not be safe.
2 It is important to respect people's differences so everyone can get along and be happy.

UNIT
1
Review

Use Vocabulary

Which word goes with each meaning?

law
community
services
goods
group
map

1 a place where people live, work, and play
2 a drawing that shows where places are
3 a rule that everyone must follow
4 jobs that people do for others
5 a number of people doing something together
6 things that people make or grow to sell

Check Understanding

1 Name two groups to which you belong.
2 What people in the community help families meet their needs?
3 How do laws help people in a community?
4 In what ways are American citizens different from one another? How are they the same?

Think Critically

1 What might happen if there were no laws in a city?
2 Why should we respect people's differences?

38

Apply Skills

Read a Map

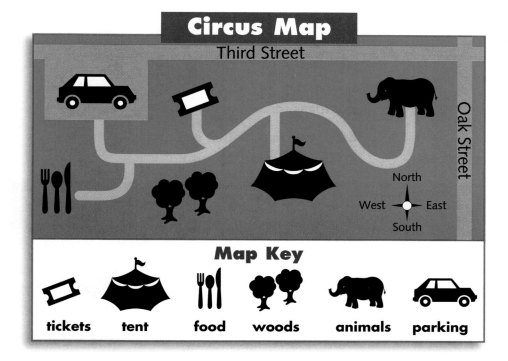

Circus Map

Third Street

Oak Street

North
West — East
South

Map Key

tickets   tent   food   woods   animals   parking

1 Does the map show the circus from the ground or from the air?

2 What symbol stands for a circus tent?

3 What is between the food place and the animals?

4 On which street is the parking lot?

5 What is east of the parking lot?

39

APPLY SKILLS
Read a Map and Map Key
1 from the air
2 the tent symbol
3 the tent, the woods, the tickets
4 Third Street
5 tickets

APPLY SKILLS

Do It Yourself

Children should list some or all of the following places: school, parking lot, playground, basketball court, field, road, house, driveway, woods.

Remind children that they are making a map from an aerial view. Children's maps should reveal an understanding of the use of symbols. Children should also remember to delete nonessential details from their maps. You may wish to pair children to practice telling directions with places on their maps.

Apply Skills

Do It Yourself

Look at the picture. Make a list of the places you see.

Draw a map to show the places in the picture.

Make a map key for your map. Be sure to add a compass rose.

Share your map with a classmate.

40

··········Unit Activity··········

Make a "World on a String" Mobile

Make a mobile of people and the groups they belong to.

⭐ Cut out shapes of your state and country.

⭐ Find and cut out pictures of all different kinds of people.

⭐ Glue your cutouts to pieces of yarn and tie them to a hanger.

⭐ Hang your mobile in the classroom.

Visit the Internet at http://www.hbschool.com for additional resources.

Read More About It

The Giant Jam Sandwich by John Vernon Lord. Houghton Mifflin. A tall tale shows how people in a community work together to solve a problem.

Marge's Diner by Gail Gibbons. HarperCollins. Interesting people come into Marge's diner.

Mrs. Katz and Tush by Patricia Polacco. Dell. A young boy helps a neighbor and learns that all people share the same feelings.

41

PUPIL BOOK OR UNIT BIG BOOK

UNIT ACTIVITY

Make a "World on a String" Mobile

Materials: plastic clothes hanger, posterboard, index cards, magazines, scissors, glue, hole punch, markers, yarn outline maps of the United States and your state for children to cut up

In their discussions and through the mobiles they create, children should exhibit an understanding that our country is made up of people who are alike in some ways and different in others. Children should recognize the shapes of the United States and their state.

READ MORE ABOUT IT

Additional books are listed in the Resource Center on page 8E of this Teacher's Edition.

TAKE-HOME BOOK
Use the TAKE-HOME REVIEW BOOK for UNIT 1.

ASSESSMENT
Use UNIT 1 TEST Standard, pp. 15–17. Performance, p. 18.

GAME TIME!
Use GAME TIME! to reinforce content.

COOPERATIVE LEARNING WORKSHOP

GET THE NEWS HERE!

Provide local newspapers for children to examine. Help them identify the different types of stories, features, and ads. Children might also enjoy reading *The Furry News: How to Make a Newspaper* by Loreen Leedy (Holiday House, 1993). Then invite children to contribute to a community newspaper. Explain that their newspaper will tell others about the people and places in their community. Provide drawing paper and lined paper of the same size. Organize children into small groups, and assign the following tasks, helping children complete any necessary research.

Materials: local newspaper, paper, pencils, crayons or markers, stapler

Task 1: Interview a community worker, such as the mayor, the school principal, a police officer, a county nurse, or a firefighter. Write a story about how this person helps the community. Draw pictures to show the worker's tools.

Task 2: Write about places in your community, such as museums, parks, or lakes, that are fun to visit. Draw pictures to show the places.

Task 3: Take a poll in your school. Ask children and teachers who they think are the most important leaders in your community and why they think as they do. Make a chart and write a story about the results of your poll.

Task 4: Make advertisements for your favorite stores. Write sentences and draw pictures to tell readers why they should shop at these stores.

What to Look For In their discussions and through the newspaper they create, children should exhibit an understanding of the people and places that make up a community. They should be able to

▶ explain why rules and laws are necessary.

▶ tell how people in their neighborhood help one another.

▶ describe ways to make their community a better place in which to live.

▶ use appropriate vocabulary.

Task 5: Interview your teacher. Ask, "What do you like best about your job?" Write a story and draw pictures that tell about your teacher doing his or her job.

After children have completed their work, have them choose a name for their paper. Then ask a small group of volunteers to create a masthead for the paper that includes the name of the paper and date of publication. Compile children's drawings, writings, and the masthead into a newspaper by stapling the pages together. Invite each group to share its contributions with the class.

REMIND CHILDREN TO:

• Share their ideas.
• Cooperate with others to plan their work.
• Plan and take responsibility for their tasks.
• Show their work.
• Discuss their own and the group's performance.

WHERE WE LIVE

The major objectives in this unit are organized around the following themes:

UNIT THEMES

▶ **INTERACTION WITHIN DIFFERENT ENVIRONMENTS**

▶ **COMMONALITY & DIVERSITY**

Preview Unit Content

Unit 2 tells the story of people interacting with their physical environment. Children will explore different landscapes and the ways in which people have adapted to and changed their surroundings. In addition, children will consider how people interact with their location in a cultural sense—through recreation, art, and architecture. By looking at the ways food is produced, transported, and marketed, children will develop an appreciation of the many people who work to supply their needs. Finally, children will focus on how the management and use of available resources affect the people of an area.

You may wish to begin the unit with the Unit 2 Picture Summary Poster and activities. The illustration that appears on the poster also appears on pages 92–93 in the Pupil Book to help children summarize the unit.

UNIT POSTER

Use the UNIT 2 PICTURE SUMMARY POSTER to preview the unit.

Planning Chart

This program is also available in a **SPANISH EDITION.**

TEACHER'S EDITION	THEMES • Strands	VOCABULARY	MEET INDIVIDUAL NEEDS	RESOURCES INCLUDING ▶ TECHNOLOGY
UNIT INTRODUCTION **Introduce the Unit** Preview Set the Scene with Literature **"Always Wondering"** by Aileen Fisher Use the Literature Big Book pp. 42–47A			English Language Learners, pp. 45, 47 Tactile Learners, p. 45	**Pupil Book/Unit Big Book, pp. 42–47** **Write-On Chart 27** Picture Summary Poster Home Letter Text on Tape Audio Asian Translations Vocabulary Cards *Bread Is for Eating*
LESSON 1 **Looking Around Communities** pp. 48A–53A	**COMMONALITY & DIVERSITY** • **Geography**	geography plain city desert suburb ocean landform island mountain river valley lake	Kinesthetic Learners, p. 48A Visual Learners, p. 48A English Language Learners, p. 48 Visual and Tactile Learners, p. 50 Extend and Enrich, p. 53 Reteach the Main Idea, p. 53	**Pupil Book/Unit Big Book, pp. 48–53** **Write-On Charts 5, 6** Activity Book, p. 7 Vocabulary Cards Music Audio, "The Bear Went Over the Mountain" ▶ **THE AMAZING WRITING MACHINE**
SKILL **Find Land and Water on a Map** pp. 54A–55A	**BASIC STUDY SKILLS** • **Map and Globe Skills**		Visual Learners, p. 54 Extend and Enrich, p. 55 Reteach the Skill, p. 55	**Pupil Book/Unit Big Book, pp. 54–55** Activity Book, p. 9 Transparencies 3, 20, 21, 22
LESSON 2 **Life in Different Places** pp. 56A–59A	**COMMONALITY & DIVERSITY** • **Geography** • **Culture** • **Economics**		Advanced Learners, p. 56A Extend and Enrich, p. 58 Reteach the Main Idea, p. 58	**Pupil Book/Unit Big Book, pp. 56–59** **Write-On Charts 5, 30, 35** Clings Activity Book, p. 10 Vocabulary Cards Desk Maps Video, Reading Rainbow, *My Little Island*
SKILL **Use a Globe** pp. 60A–61A	**BASIC STUDY SKILLS** • **Map and Globe Skills**	globe continent equator	English Language Learners, p. 60A Kinesthetic Learners, p. 60 Auditory Learners, p. 60 Extend and Enrich, p. 61 Reteach the Skill, p. 61	**Pupil Book/Unit Big Book, pp. 60–61** **Write-On Chart 34** Clings Activity Book, p. 11 Transparencies 4, 23
LESSON 3 **Using the Land** pp. 62A–65A	**INTERACTION WITHIN DIFFERENT ENVIRONMENTS** • **Geography** • **History** • **Economics**	crop	Visual Learners, p. 62A English Language Learners, p. 62 Tactile Learners, p. 63 Extend and Enrich, p. 64 Reteach the Main Idea, p. 64	**Pupil Book/Unit Big Book, pp. 62–65** **Write-On Charts 26, 29** Clings Activity Book, p. 12 Music Audio, "Garden Song"

24 DAYS

TIME MANAGEMENT

DAY 1	DAY 2	DAY 3	DAY 4	DAY 5	DAY 6	DAY 7	DAY 8	DAY 9	DAY 10	DAY 11	DAY 12
Unit Introduction		Lesson 1			Skill	Lesson 2		Skill	Lesson 3		Lesson 4

	TEACHER'S EDITION	THEMES • Strands	VOCABULARY	MEET INDIVIDUAL NEEDS	RESOURCES INCLUDING ► TECHNOLOGY
LESSON 4	**Where Does Our Food Come From?** pp. 66A–69A	**INTERACTION WITHIN DIFFERENT ENVIRONMENTS** • **Geography** • **Economics**	flow chart	English Language Learners, p. 66 Extend and Enrich, p. 69 Reteach the Main Idea, p. 69	**Pupil Book/Unit Big Book, pp. 66–69** Activity Book, p. 13
LESSON 5	Learn Geography through Literature **How to Make an Apple Pie and see the world** by Marjorie Priceman pp. 70A–81A	**COMMONALITY & DIVERSITY** • **Geography** • **Culture** • **Economics** • **History**	resource	English Language Learners, pp. 73, 76 Advanced Learners, p. 80 Extend and Enrich, p. 81 Reteach the Main Idea, p. 81	**Pupil Book/Unit Big Book, pp. 70–81** **Write-On Charts 7, 29, 30** Activity Book, p. 14 Text on Tape Audio Desk Maps ► **THE AMAZING WRITING MACHINE**
SKILL	**Read a Table** pp. 82A–83B	**BASIC STUDY SKILLS** • **Chart and Graph Skills**	table	English Language Learners, p. 82A Visual Learners, p. 82 Extend and Enrich, p. 83 Reteach the Skill, p. 83	**Pupil Book/Unit Big Book, pp. 82–83** **Write-On Chart 7** Activity Book, p. 15 Transparencies 5, 20, 21
BRAINSTORM	**What Would Happen If . . .** pp. 84–85A	**BUILDING CITIZENSHIP** • **Critical Thinking Skills** • **Participation Skills**		Advanced Learners, p. 85 Visual Learners, p. 85	**Pupil Book/Unit Big Book, pp. 84–85**
LESSON 6	**Caring for the Earth** pp. 86A–89B	**INTERACTION WITHIN DIFFERENT ENVIRONMENTS** • **Geography** • **History** • **Civics and Government** • **Economics**	conservation	Extend and Enrich, p. 88 Reteach the Main Idea, p. 88	**Pupil Book/Unit Big Book, pp. 86–89** **Write-On Charts 8, 33** Activity Book, p. 16 ► **THE AMAZING WRITING MACHINE** ► **IMAGINATION EXPRESS: DESTINATION RAIN FOREST**
MAKING SOCIAL STUDIES REAL	**Tree Musketeers** pp. 90–91	**BUILDING CITIZENSHIP** • **Participation Skills**	pollution		**Pupil Book/Unit Big Book, pp. 90–91**
UNIT WRAP-UP	Picture Summary Unit 2 Review Cooperative Learning Workshop pp. 92–97B			English Language Learners, p. 93	**Pupil Book/Unit Big Book, pp. 92–97** Picture Summary Poster Vocabulary Cards Assessment Program, Standard, pp. 19–21 Performance, p. 22 Take-Home Review Book Game Time! ► **THE AMAZING WRITING MACHINE**

DAY 13	DAY 14	DAY 15	DAY 16	DAY 17	DAY 18	DAY 19	DAY 20	DAY 21	DAY 22	DAY 23	DAY 24
	Lesson 5			Skill	Brainstorm	Lesson 6		Making Social Studies Real	Unit Wrap-Up		Unit Test

Multimedia Resource Center

Books

Easy

Badt, Karin Luisa. *Let's Go.* Childrens Press, 1995. Transportation around the world is compared in this book.

Carlstrom, Nancy White. *Wild Wild Sunflower Child Anna.* Aladdin Books, 1991. This narrative poem is about a girl who has fun exploring nature.

Clark, Emma Chichester. *Across the Blue Mountains.* Harcourt Brace, 1993. Miss Bilberry can't help but wonder what life would be like on the other side of the mountains.

MacLachlan, Patricia. *All the Places to Love.* Illus. by Mike Wimmer. Harper-Collins, 1994. Filled with wonderful words and beautiful paintings, this book pays homage to the American farm.

Shannon, George. *Climbing Kansas Mountains.* Illus. by Thomas B. Allen. Bradbury, 1993. Father and son share some special moments as they spend the afternoon climbing a Kansas mountain.

Williams, Vera B. Illus. by Vera B. Williams and Jennifer Williams. *Stringbean's Trip to the Shining Sea.* Scholastic, 1990. Stringbean describes his trip west in a series of postcards.

Average

Accorsi, William. *Rachel Carson.* Holiday House, 1993. This book is the true story of a woman who worked to make the Earth a healthful place to live.

Aliki. *Milk: From Cow to Carton.* HarperCollins, 1992. This book describes how a cow produces milk, how the milk is processed in a dairy, and how various other dairy products are made from milk.

Cooney, Barbara. *Miss Rumphius.* Puffin, 1994. Miss Rumphius's dreams come true after she enjoys the sea, visits faraway places, and finally helps make her community a more beautiful place.

dePaola, Tomie. *The Legend of the Indian Paintbrush.* G.P. Putnam's Sons, 1988. Little Gopher becomes an artist for his people and is able to bring the colors of the sunset down to the Earth.

Kellogg, Steven. *Johnny Appleseed.* Morrow, 1988. The story of John Chapman tells about his love of nature, his kindness to animals, and his physical fortitude.

Laan, Nancy Van. *Round and Round Again.* Illus. by Nadine Bernard Westcott. Hyperion, 1994. Mama recycles everything until the house is complete, with walls covered with candy wrappers and shingles that used to be flapjack flappers. Later the whole town turns out to see her handmade rocket ship.

Mora, Pat. *The Desert Is My Mother/El desierto es mi madre.* Arte Público Press, 1994. In this poem a girl describes how the desert is like a mother because it provides for her needs.

Robbins, Ken. *Make Me a Peanut Butter Sandwich and a glass of milk.* Scholastic, 1992. How to make each part of a peanut butter sandwich is shown from field to store to table.

Wittstock, Laura Waterman. *Ininatig's Gift of Sugar: Traditional Native Sugarmaking.* Photos by Dale Kakkak. Lerner, 1993. Each spring, Porky, an Indian from Minnesota, teaches people about the sugar-making process and about his heritage.

Ziefert, Harriet. *A New Coat for Anna.* Illus. by Anita Lobel. Knopf, 1986. Even though there is no money, Anna's mother finds a way to make Anna a badly needed winter coat.

Challenging

Coats, Laura Jane. *The Almond Orchard.* Macmillan, 1991. The narrator watches an almond orchard grow and change with the seasons.

Diller, Harriett. *Grandaddy's Highway.* Illus. by Henri Sorensen. Boyds Mills Press, 1993. Maggie imagines heading west on Route 30 with her grandfather all the way to the Pacific.

Dorros, Arthur. *Radio Man—Don Radio: A Story in English and Spanish.* HarperCollins, 1993. Told in both Spanish and English, this story describes the life of a migrant worker as seen through the eyes of a young boy.

Hall, Donald. *The Milkman's Boy.* Illus. by Greg Shed. Walker, 1997. The Graves family delivered milk from their dairy in the years before trucks and shopping centers replaced them.

McDonald, Megan. *My House Has Stars.* Illus. by Peter Catalanotto. Orchard, 1996. Young people describe the different kinds of homes they live in around the world.

Patent, Dorothy Hinshaw. *Wheat: The Golden Harvest.* Photos by William Muñoz. Dodd, Mead, 1987. Text and photos describe how different varieties of wheat are planted, harvested, and processed into foods.

Thompson, Colin. *The Tower to the Sun.* Knopf, 1996. The richest man in the world decides to build a tower so that his grandson can experience the sun.

Turner, Ann. *Apple Valley Year.* Illus. by Sandi Wickersham Resnick. Macmillan, 1993. The Clark family keeps busy through all four seasons.

LIBRARY

Use the Grade 2 SOCIAL STUDIES LIBRARY for additional resources.

Audiocassettes

The Cactus Cafe. The Smithsonian Institution. Introduces children to the cactus ecology of the Sonoran Desert. (202) 357-2425

Smilin' Island of Song. Cedella Marley-Booker, Taj Mahal & Friends. This is a collection of songs from the Caribbean Islands. Music for Little People. Toll free: 1-800-346-4445

Computer Software

CD-ROM

Big Job. Follett Library Resources. Mac/DOS. Users participate in a variety of jobs, including farming, construction, and fire rescue. Toll free: 1-800-435-6170

5-a-Day Adventures America. Follett Library Resources. Mac/DOS. Users join Bobby Banana and his friends in the town of 5-a-Day, where they encourage children to eat five servings of fruits and vegetables a day. Cookbook included. Toll free: 1-800-435-6170

Our Earth. National Geographic Educational Services. Mac/Windows. Children can use their map skills and understandings as they explore the physical geography of the Earth. Toll free: 1-800-368-2728

Video

Film or VHS Cassettes

The Carrot Highway. Whisper Production Company. Tells the story of the carrot, with some animation to teach viewers about food and farming. Toll free: 1-800-631-6263

A Day on the Farm. Kiddie-O Video. Affable Annie gives a tour of a Maryland farm. She also visits a home vegetable garden and a neighborhood supermarket to explain the products and processes of farming. Toll free: 1-800-307-0477

Short Walk to Everywhere. NASA Johnson Space Center, 1988. Children can tour an environmental awareness camp for grades K–3. 18 minutes. (281) 483-2975

FREE & INEXPENSIVE MATERIALS

Beautify Your School! Free catalog offers wide variety of plants for your schoolyard. If you join the National Arbor Day Foundation, you will receive ten free Colorado blue spruce seedlings. Membership fee is $10.

> National Arbor Day Foundation
> 100 Arbor Avenue
> Nebraska City, NE 68410

A Better World Starts at Home. Informational poster discusses environmental problems and how to combat them.

> Office of Environmental Awareness
> S. Dillon Ripley Center
> Room 3123, MRC 705
> Smithsonian Institution
> Washington, DC 20560

Keep America Beautiful. Send for one or all of these environmentally friendly brochures: *Tips for Preventing Litter, Take Care of America,* and *Community Cleanup.* Send request and legal-sized SASE. Free.

> Keep America Beautiful
> 1010 Washington Boulevard
> Stamford, CT 06901
> Internet: www.kab.org

Kids for Saving Earth. Packet contains colorful Earth sticker and information on how to join *Kids for Saving Earth Worldwide* (KSE) and on how to start your own club to help save the Earth. Send legal-size SASE (55-cent stamp). Free.

> KSE Worldwide
> P.O. Box 421118
> Plymouth, MN 55442
> (612) 559-1234
> Internet: kseww@aol.com

Natural Resources Kits. Program includes teacher's guide, student activity pages, and posters. Request one or more of the titles *Everyday Uses of Minerals, A Study of the Earth,* or *Everything We Have and Everything We Use Comes from Our Natural Resources.* Free.

> Mineral Information Institute
> 475 17th St., Suite 510
> Denver, CO 80202

Wildlife and Conservation. Posters and pamphlets on wildlife and conservation. Free.

> West Virginia U.S. Fish and Wildlife Service
> National Conservation Training Center
> Division of Training and Education Materials Production
> Publications Unit
> Rt. 1, Box 166
> Shepherdstown, WV 25443
> (304) 876-7203
> Fax: (304) 876-7689

Woodsy Owl. Woodsy Owl educational and promotional materials. Free.

> USDA Forest Service
> Northeast Interagency Fire Cache
> 402 11th St., SE
> Grand Rapids, MN 55744
> Attention: Woodsey Owl Order
> (218) 327-4578

Note that information, while correct at time of publication, is subject to change.

TECHNOLOGY

HARCOURT BRACE

Visit the Internet at **http://www.hbschool.com** for additional resources.

Linking Social Studies

MATH CENTER

Venn Diagram

Materials: Write-On Chart 28, dry-erase markers

Use Write-On Chart 28 to model the following activity. Label one circle *Mountains* and one *Island*. Also provide a list with the following words: *snow, swimming, hiking, boats, sand, fishing.* Ask children to decide whether each item or activity belongs in the circle labeled *Mountains* or *Island* or in both. Invite them to draw intersecting circles and a picture in the appropriate place to show where each item belongs. The intersecting section of the circles is where they would draw pictures of things that could belong in either region. Invite children to think of other pictures to draw in the circles.

ART CENTER

Soap Carving

Materials: bars of soap, craft sticks or plastic knives, toothpicks, craft paper, tempera paints, paintbrushes

Many people of the Appalachian region enjoy the craft of woodcarving as a hobby. If possible, display a collection of small decorative objects made from wood. Ask children to discuss how sculptures can show us things about the Earth. Provide the materials, and invite children to carve a bar of soap into an object such as a bird, canoe, or musical instrument. Once children have made the outline of the shape, have them use toothpicks to carve details. Children may use paint to add color to their soap carvings. Encourage children to share their carvings with the class.

LANGUAGE ARTS CENTER

Write a Narrative

Materials: watercolors, small paintbrushes, drawing paper

Invite children to think about outdoor places, such as a park, lake, or farm, that they have visited or would like to visit. Ask children to use watercolors to paint a picture of themselves on the trip. Children can write a few sentences about the visit and tell why it is important to take care of the Earth. Tape children's writings to the watercolor pictures and display them.

This is me at the seashore. I like to swim and fish. It is important to keep the water clean.

Across the Curriculum

MULTICULTURAL CENTER

Harvest Dolls

Materials: corn husks, pipe cleaners, circle stickers

Share the Iroquois legend of the corn doll. They believed that a corn goddess lived underground and moved up the stalk as the corn grew. They feared that when the corn was harvested, the goddess would have no place to live. To keep her in the community, they gathered cornstalks, wove them into dolls, and returned them to the soil the following spring. Invite children to make their own harvest dolls by twisting a pipe cleaner around the middle of a corn husk, bending the ends of the pipe cleaner into arms. Then ask children to flatten the top of the husk to make a face. Have them stick on eyes and fray the top to look like hair. Children can fray the bottom to make a skirt.

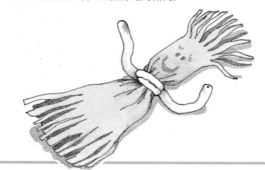

SCIENCE CENTER

Desert Home

Materials: colored clay, toothpicks, sand, box lids or trays

Fill trays with sand to resemble a desert. Set out brown, tan, green, and orange clay and toothpicks. Invite children to mold cacti, sagebrush, and other plants for their desert community. Have children complete the scene by making clay animals that might be found in this dry environment. Pairs of children may work together to make animals that live inside the cacti and in homes under the sand. Invite learners to explore ways that animals protect themselves from the heat.

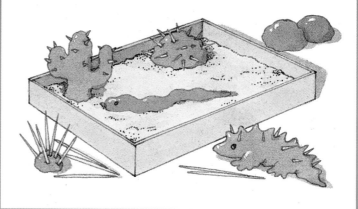

HOW TO INTEGRATE YOUR DAY
Use these topics to help you integrate social studies into your daily planning.

READING THEMES	INTEGRATED LANGUAGE ARTS	MATHEMATICS	SCIENCE	ART
Homes and Shelters	Write a Narrative, p. 42G	Venn Diagram, p. 42G	Desert Home, p. 42H	Soap Carving, p. 42G
	Write a Description, p. 50	Measurement, p. 79	Models and Scale, pp. 52, 60	About the Artist, p. 46
Near and Far	Journal, p. 76	Data, p. 82A	Air, Weather, Climate, p. 57	Sculpture, p. 60A
	Write to Explain, p. 70A	Addition and Subtraction, p. 87	Observation, pp. 79, 84	Illustration, p. 85
Water Ways	Write Letters, pp. 66A, 86A		Interdependence of Life, p. 86	Graphic Art, p. 86
Earth				

	HEALTH AND PHYSICAL EDUCATION	MUSIC	WORLD LANGUAGES
Ecology	Nutrition, p. 63	Vocal, p. 62A	Other Languages, p. 77
Nature	Community Health, p. 91	Melody, p. 68	

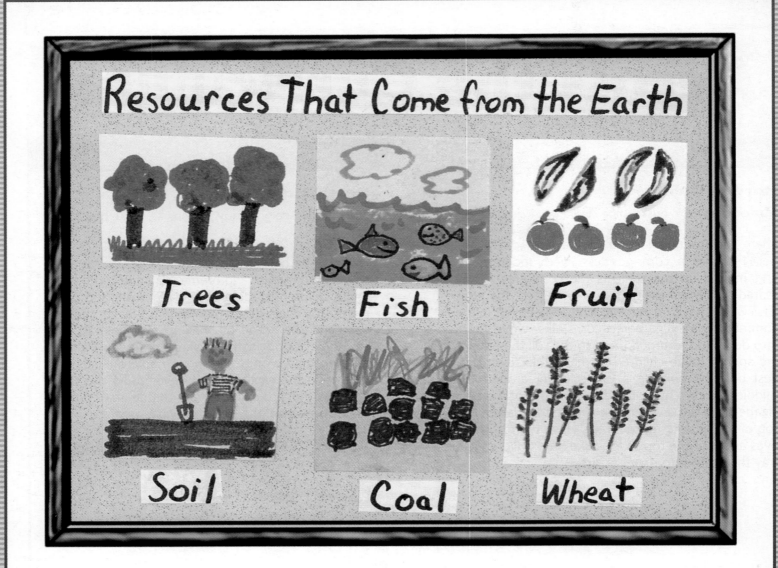

BULLETIN BOARD

Introduce the concept of natural resources with a bulletin board titled *Resources That Come from the Earth*. Tell children that natural resources are things from nature that help us live or satisfy our needs. Ask children to draw pictures or to cut out from magazines pictures of things we get from the Earth. Help children label each picture and place it on the bulletin board.

Assessment Options

The assessment program allows all learners many opportunities to show what they know and can do. It also provides ongoing information about each child's understanding of social studies.

FORMAL ASSESSMENT

▶ *Unit Review*
(**Pupil Book**, pp. 94–97)
▶ *Unit Assessment*
(**Assessment Program:**
Standard Test, pp. 19–21
Performance Task, p. 22)

STUDENT SELF-EVALUATION

▶ *Individual End-of-Project Checklist*
(**Assessment Program**, p. 6)
▶ *Group End-of-Project Checklist*
(**Assessment Program**, p. 7) for use after cooperative learning activities
▶ *Individual End-of-Unit Checklist*
(**Assessment Program**, p. 8)

INFORMAL ASSESSMENT

▶ *What Do You Know? Questions*
(**Pupil Book**, at end of lessons)
▶ *Think and Do*
(**Pupil Book**, at end of skill lessons)
▶ *Picture Summary*
(**Pupil Book**, pp. 92–93)

▶ *Check Understanding*
(**Teacher's Edition**, in Close, at end of lessons)
▶ *Think Critically*
(**Teacher's Edition**, in Close, at end of lessons)

▶ *Social Studies Skills Checklist*
(**Assessment Program**, pp. 4–5)

PERFORMANCE ASSESSMENT

▶ *Show What You Know*
(**Teacher's Edition**, in Close, at end of lessons)
▶ *Cooperative Learning Workshop*
(**Teacher's Edition**, pp. 97A–97B)
▶ *Performance Task: Splish! Splash!*
(**Assessment Program**, p. 22)
▶ Scoring the Performance Task
Use the *Scoring Rubric for Individual Projects*
(**Assessment Program**, p. 9)
▶ *Scoring Rubric for Group Projects*
(**Assessment Program**, p. 10)
▶ *Scoring Rubric for Presentations*
(**Assessment Program**, p. 11)

PORTFOLIO ASSESSMENT

Student-selected items may include:
▶ *Link to Language Arts,* description
(**Teacher's Edition**, p. 50)
▶ *Home Involvement,* graphic
(**Teacher's Edition**, p. 54A)
▶ *Extend and Enrich,* report
(**Teacher's Edition**, p. 88)

Teacher-selected items may include:
▶ *My Best Work*
(**Assessment Program**, p. 12)
▶ *Portfolio Summary*
(**Assessment Program**, p. 13)
▶ *Portfolio Family Response*
(**Assessment Program**, p. 14)

Assessment Options

STANDARD TEST

Name _____ Date _____

Unit 2 Test

Vocabulary

Draw a line under the meaning of the word. 5 points each

1. globe
   - <u>a model of the Earth</u>
   - a photograph of the Earth

2. continent
   - a large community
   - <u>one of the largest bodies of land on the Earth</u>

3. geography
   - <u>the study of the Earth and its people</u>
   - the study of the laws of our country

4. landform
   - <u>a kind of land, such as mountains</u>
   - a kind of crop, such as wheat

5. resource
   - something built to honor someone
   - <u>something people use that comes from the Earth</u>

6. conservation
   - leaving litter in a forest or park
   - <u>working to save or protect things</u>

Unit 2 Test   Assessment Program **19**

STANDARD TEST

Name _____

Main Ideas 5 points each

Circle the best answer to each question.

7. What is a crowded place that has busy streets, tall buildings, and many things to do?
   (a city)   a suburb

8. Where do many city workers live?
   on farms   (in suburbs)

Finish the table.

Kinds of Land and Water on the Earth	
Land	**Water**
mountain	ocean
9. Sample responses: hill, valley, plain, island, desert	10. Sample responses: lake, river
11. _____	12. _____

13. Tell one way in which people change the land.

   Sample responses: People build homes and other buildings; they plow fields and plant crops; they dump trash; they make roads, playgrounds, and parks.

14. List the people who help bring food to your table.

   Answers should include people who grow, make, move, and sell food.

15. Draw two important resources and name them.

   Drawings should show things people use that come from the Earth, such as water, oil, food from plants, trees or wood products.

20   Assessment Program   Unit 2 Test

Objectives

- Distinguish between city, suburban, and small-town or farm settings. (p. 48A)
- Identify various landforms and bodies of water. (p. 48A)
- Compare physical features of the land. (p. 48A)
- Use colors and symbols to read a physical map. (p. 54A)
- Distinguish land and water on a map. (p. 54A)
- Identify examples of how people live in different locations. (p. 56A)
- Identify how land and climate affect people's work and the recreation they enjoy. (p. 56A)

- Compare a map and a globe. (p. 60A)
- Identify and locate the oceans and continents on a globe. (p. 60A)
- Find the equator and poles on a globe. (p. 60A)
- Describe how people depend on the land. (p. 62A)
- Identify ways people adapt to and change their environments to meet their needs. (p. 62A)
- Recognize how seasonal changes can affect the land and land use. (p. 62A)
- Recognize the many people who work to supply our daily needs. (p. 66A)
- Explain the steps in a flow chart that follows a food's production from farm to market. (p. 66A)

- Describe the jobs of workers involved in food processing. (p. 66A)
- Define *resource*. (p. 70A)
- Identify various natural resources. (p. 70A)
- Explain how people depend on resources. (p. 70A)
- Identify the parts of a table. (p. 82A)
- Draw logical conclusions about resources and goods from a table. (p. 82A)
- Identify precious resources. (p. 86A)
- Define *conservation*. (p. 86A)
- Draw logical conclusions about the importance of protecting our land and resources. (p. 86A)

STANDARD TEST

Name _____

Skills 5 points each

Use the globe to answer the questions.

16. Is Australia closer to the North Pole or the South Pole? South Pole

17. Which ocean is between North America and Europe? Atlantic Ocean

18. What is one continent that the equator passes through? Africa, South America, Asia

Large Rivers	
River	Continent
Amazon	South America
Hwang	Asia
Mississippi	North America
Nile	Africa
Rhine	Europe

Use the table to answer the questions.

19. What is the Nile? a river

20. Where is the Amazon? in South America

Unit 2 Test   Assessment Program   **21**

PERFORMANCE TASK

Name _____ Date _____

Performance Task

Splish! Splash!

You see people wasting water every day. Make three drawings to help people see why water is important to them. Then complete the sentences.

> Drawings might show people using water for drinking; for washing themselves or other things; for watering plants; and for activities, such as swimming, fishing, and sailing.

⭐ Water is important to people because Sample responses: They need it for drinking, washing things, and swimming; they can't live without it.

⭐ One way to help save this resource is to Sample responses: Turn off the water while you are brushing your teeth; take a shower instead of a bath; never use more water than you need; get a dripping faucet fixed.

22   Assessment Program   Unit 2 Test

Rubrics

SCORING RUBRICS The scoring rubrics for evaluating individual projects, group projects, and children's presentations may be found in the *Assessment Program*, pages 9–11.

CRITERIA The criteria listed below may be used when looking for evidence of the children's understanding of social studies content and ability to think critically.

▶ *Performance Task: Splish! Splash!* [**Assessment Program**, p. 22]

▶ *Scoring the Performance Task*—Use the *Scoring Rubric for Individual Projects* [**Assessment Program**, p. 9], and look for evidence of the child's ability to:

- ↙ Recognize that people depend on water.
- ↙ Identify how people can save water.
- ↙ Communicate ideas clearly through art and writing.

REMINDER

You may wish to preview the performance assessment activity in the COOPERATIVE LEARNING WORKSHOP on Teacher's Edition pages 97A–97B. Children may complete the activity during the course of the unit.

INTRODUCE THE UNIT

Link Prior Learning

Invite small groups to take turns performing an impromptu radio commercial about their community. Each child in the group could discuss a different aspect of the community, such as the weather, the news, or interesting things to do and see.

Anticipation Guide

Find out what children know by having them categorize the following statements as true or false. Then discuss what they are interested in learning more about.

1. _____ You can drive your car to an island.
2. _____ Suburbs can be different sizes.
3. _____ Farmers change the land.
4. _____ We can get everything we need in our own community.
5. _____ Resources for the future depend on me.

Preview Vocabulary

The vocabulary words listed on page 42 represent the key concepts for this unit. Suggest that children use the words to predict what the main ideas of the unit will be. Ideas for teaching the vocabulary are provided on pages 44 and 45.

UNIT 2
Where We Live

Vocabulary

geography
landform
continent
globe
resource
conservation

42

ACTIVITY CHOICES

Community Involvement

Contact your local chamber of commerce or tourist information bureau and invite a guest speaker to share information about your area with the class. Ask the person to bring brochures and posters to display. You may wish to have your class prepare a set of questions for the guest to preview.

Background

THE LARGE PICTURE   San Francisco is one of the largest cities on the Pacific Coast. It lies on the tip of a peninsula between the Pacific Ocean and San Francisco Bay. It is connected to Marin County in the north by the Golden Gate Bridge and to Oakland in the east by the San Francisco-Oakland Bay Bridge (pictured) across Yerba Buena Island. Distinctive buildings mark its skyline, including the Transamerica Pyramid. Neighborhoods grew up on and around its famous hills—Nob Hill, Telegraph Hill, Russian Hill, Portrero Hill, and Twin Peaks.

HOME LETTER

Use UNIT 2 HOME LETTER. See Teacher's Edition pages HL3–4.

43

PUPIL BOOK **OR** UNIT BIG BOOK

Personal Response

Direct children's attention to the opening photograph. Discuss the different places where people can live. Then invite children to describe their physical surroundings.

Q. **How would you describe the land where you live? Is it flat or hilly? Is it rocky or sandy? Are you close to water? If you are, is it a lot or a little?**

Tell children that in this unit they will learn how land and water affect the way people live.

> ### 66 PRIMARY SOURCE 99
>
> John Wesley Powell, a Civil War veteran, explored the Grand Canyon in the 1800s. He saw "a painted desert—not a desert plain, but a desert of rocks cut by deep gorges . . . rocks of bright colors, golden, vermilion, purple and azure hues . . . a vision of glory!" (from *Land of Living Rock* by C. Gregory Crampton)
> Have children talk about ways to describe the beautiful landforms of our country.

It is important for children to begin to realize that where people live affects the way they live. People both adapt to and change their environment to meet their needs. Help children recognize these adaptations and changes as they work through each lesson. Point out, for example, how environment affects what people wear, what jobs they have, what they do for fun, and what types of transportation they most often use.

Options for Reading

Read Aloud Read each lesson aloud as children follow along in their books. Strategies for guiding children through working with text and visuals are provided with each lesson.

Read Together Have pairs or small groups of children read the lesson by taking turns reading each page or paragraph aloud. Encourage children to use the new vocabulary words as they discuss what they read.

Read Alone Strong readers may wish to read the lessons independently before you read or discuss each lesson with the class.

PREVIEW THE UNIT

THINK ABOUT WORDS

Reproduce the following word web:

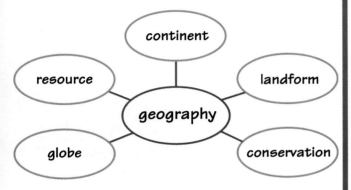

Write the word *geography* in the middle of a word web. Have children suggest words that they think have something to do with geography. Help them understand that geography is the study of the Earth and how people live on it.

Unit 2 Preview

geography
The study of the Earth and its people.

landform
A kind of land.

continent
One of the largest bodies of land on the Earth.

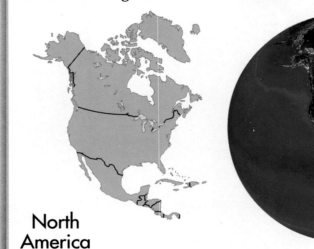

North America

44

ACTIVITY CHOICES

WRITE-ON CHARTS
Use WRITE-ON CHART 27 to preview vocabulary.

Home Involvement
Invite children to ask older family members about their experiences on or near different kinds of landforms. Have children suggest questions they could ask, such as *Have you ever been to the mountains?* or *What oceans have you seen?*

globe

A model of the Earth.

resource

Something people use that comes from the Earth.

conservation

Working to save resources or make them last longer.

SAVE THE BEACH

45

Work with Words

Invite children to turn to pages 44–45 in their Pupil Book. Then direct their attention to the words and their definitions on the pages. Explain that these words tell the main ideas of Unit 2. Invite volunteers to read aloud each word and its definition. Add the words on pages 44–45 to the web if they have not been suggested. (Note: For additional vocabulary, see the Planning Chart on pages 42C–42D in the Teacher's Edition.) Then use the questions that follow to stimulate a general discussion of the new vocabulary.

Q. **What does the picture of the landform show? Why would a globe be a good model for the Earth? Which is a resource: a plant or a pencil? What continent does the picture show?**

VOCABULARY BLACKLINES

You may wish to reproduce individual copies of the vocabulary words for this unit. They are found in the back of your Teacher's Edition.

Meet Individual Needs

ENGLISH LANGUAGE LEARNERS
By providing travel brochures that show varied places, you can help children make the connection between the word *landform* and the concept of different kinds of land.

TACTILE LEARNERS Give children an opportunity to examine a classroom globe. Invite them to read the words on the globe and to look for names of places that they have heard or read about.

VOCABULARY CARDS

Place the VOCABULARY PICTURE CARDS for *geography, landform, continent, globe, resource,* and *conservation* on the chalk ledge. Invite children to approach the ledge, a pair at a time. Have one child choose a card and interview his or her partner, asking two questions that use the vocabulary word. Then have partners switch roles and repeat, with a different word. For example, a child can ask, On what continent do you live? or What countries can you find on the globe?

SET THE SCENE WITH LITERATURE

PREVIEW

Have the class look at pages 46–47. Discuss what land and water is shown in the picture. Invite children to share experiences they may have had driving or hiking around the country. Then read aloud the title of the poem. Ask children to tell what they think the poet is wondering.

Q. **What kind of land can you see in the picture?** flat land and mountains

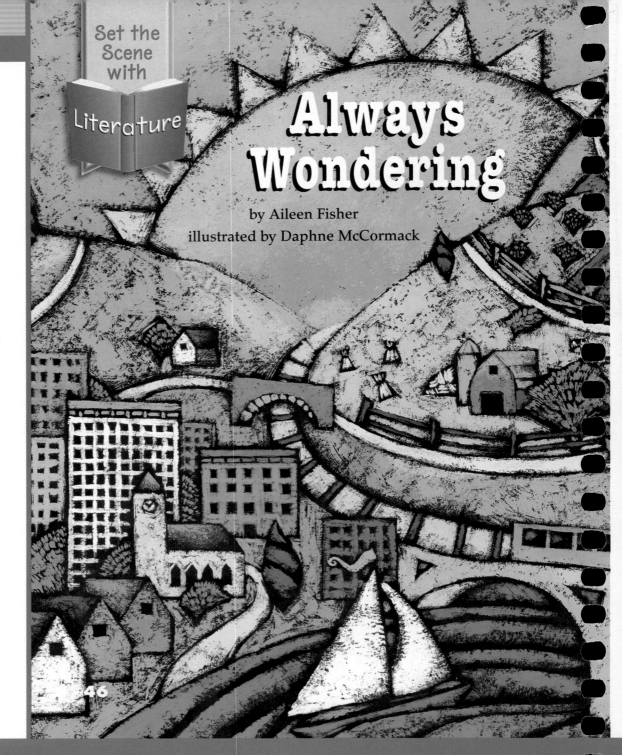

Set the Scene with **Literature**

Always Wondering

by Aileen Fisher

illustrated by Daphne McCormack

46

ACTIVITY CHOICES

Background

ABOUT THE POET Aileen Fisher was born in Iron River, Michigan, in 1906. She is the author of numerous plays, poems, and stories. She says, "My first and chief love in writing is writing children's verse." Growing up on a farm and later living on a ranch in Colorado, Fisher became an outstanding nature poet. In 1978, she received the National Council of Teachers of English Award for Excellence in Poetry for Children for the body of her work.

Link to Art

ABOUT THE ARTIST Daphne McCormack's use of texture and bright colors gives her work a sense of fun and play. First, she paints rough watercolor paper a solid black, using India ink. Then she uses a kind of water-based paint called gouache, which is slightly chalky upon drying. She applies the paint lightly over the paper to give a rough, loose effect. The bright colors contrast with the black, and the edges and linework are thick and somewhat "clumsy." Invite children to paint landscapes in this style.

Roads run by
and paths run by
and tracks
where trains go thundering

Past green and brown
of field and town
and over-ing and under-ing.

Brooks run by
and creeks run by
and rivers
big and blundering,

And where they end,
around what bend,
I'm always, always wondering.

47

READ & RESPOND

Ask children to follow along as a volunteer reads aloud the poem "Always Wondering." Lead children in a discussion about the kinds of land the person in the poem can see. Point out that people live on different kinds of land.

Q. **How is the land in the picture like the land where you live? How is it different?** Children should compare their physical surroundings to the land shown in the photograph.

Meet Individual Needs

ENGLISH LANGUAGE LEARNERS
Children whose first language is not English may be confused by the words *over-ing* and *under-ing*. Help children understand that these are not real words, that the poet made them up to describe how roads, paths, and railroad tracks seem to go over and under the land, the fields, the water, and so on. Point out that the poet probably also created *under-ing* to rhyme with *thundering, blundering,* and *wondering*.

AUDIO

You may wish to play the TEXT ON TAPE AUDIOCASSETTE for "Always Wondering" as children study the picture.

Link Literature

Children might enjoy beginning the unit with *The Desert Is My Mother/El desierto es mi madre* by Pat Mora. (Arte Publico Press, 1994) In this narrative poem a girl describes how the desert is like a mother because it provides for her needs. She enjoys the warmth, rest, food, and beauty that the land has to offer. Have children name things that their environment provides for them.

Use the
LITERATURE
BIG
BOOK

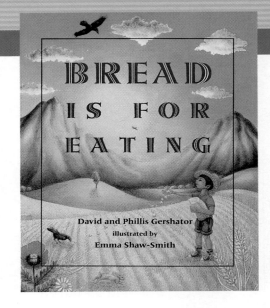

BREAD IS FOR EATING

David and Phillis Gershator
illustrated by
Emma Shaw-Smith

Invite children to begin the unit by reading *Bread Is for Eating* by David and Phillis Gershator. The rhythmic, bilingual text and warm illustrations explain the process by which bread is produced, from seed to supermarket. Children learn how people depend on the land and other resources to meet their basic needs. They are also reminded of the importance of not wasting valuable resources.

About the Authors and the Illustrator

Phillis and David Gershator live on St. Thomas in the United States Virgin Islands. Phillis is a former librarian and the author of several picture books, including *The Iroko Man* and *Rata-pata-scata-fata*. Her husband, David, is a songwriter, translator, and poet.

Emma Shaw-Smith was born and raised in Ireland but now lives in Memphis, Tennessee. Her fascination with different cultures led her to illustrate books about Jamaica, Egypt, and China. *Bread Is for Eating* is her first children's picture book.

Reading the Story

Read and discuss the literature to address the following objectives:

1. Describe how people depend on land, water, and sunshine.
2. Identify the people involved in making bread.
3. Recognize that people all around the world eat bread.
4. Discuss the importance of not wasting food.

Social Studies Connection

Lead children in a discussion of what they know about bread and how it is made.

Q. **How do farmers help make bread?** Farmers plant the wheat seeds and grow and harvest the wheat that people use to make flour for bread.

What different kinds of bread can you name? Responses may include sliced white bread, whole-wheat bread, pita bread, tortillas, rolls, biscuits, and bagels.

List on the board or on chart paper some of the events from the story.

▶ The sun and the rain help the wheat seeds grow.
▶ The farmer harvests the wheat.
▶ The baker makes bread from the flour.
▶ People around the world eat bread.

Invite children to draw a picture to show one of the workers who help in bringing us bread.

1

LOOKING AROUND COMMUNITIES

OBJECTIVES

1. Distinguish between city, suburban, and small-town or farm settings.
2. Recognize human-made features of the land.
3. Identify various landforms and bodies of water.
4. Compare physical features of the land.

VOCABULARY

geography (p. 48)
city (p. 48)   desert (p. 51)
suburb (p. 49)   ocean (p. 52)
landform (p. 50)   island (p. 52)
mountain (p. 50)
valley (p. 50)   river (p. 53)
plain (p. 51)   lake (p. 53)

RESOURCES

Pupil Book/Unit Big Book, pp. 48–53

Write-On Charts 5, 6

Vocabulary Blacklines

Vocabulary Cards

Activity Book, p. 7

Music Audio, "The Bear Went Over the Mountain"

The Amazing Writing Machine

ACTIVITY CHOICES

Meet Individual Needs

KINESTHETIC LEARNERS Organize the class into two teams. Invite one team at a time to pantomime activities people might do in various types of land or water areas. If children need help thinking of an area, you might suggest city, farm, desert, mountain, ocean, river, or plain.

VISUAL LEARNERS Display magazine pictures of various geographic features. Ask children what they think they would find if they visited those places. Have children draw pictures of people doing activities appropriate to their physical surroundings.

1. ACCESS

Invite children to describe their community and the land around it. Children may wish to look out of classroom windows for ideas. They should consider size and shape in commenting on the physical or human-made features they see.

Focus on the Main Idea

In this lesson children will learn the names for communities of various sizes. They will also observe and learn the names of the landforms and bodies of water that separate and surround communities. Tell children that in this lesson they will be using photographs as windows to places around the Earth that they cannot see from their classroom.

2. BUILD

Key Content Summary

The Earth has a variety of features. Some are human-made. These include cities, farms, towns, and suburbs. Others are physical features, such as mountains, islands, deserts, oceans, lakes, plains, and rivers. Both human-made and physical features affect how people live in different places.

Geography

Human-Environment Interactions
Invite children to compare the photos on pages 48–49. Discuss which kind of area would have the most animals and which would have the most people. Then ask children to discuss the various kinds of communities shown in the photographs. Look again at the city in the opening photograph of the unit.

Q. **What are some reasons people might choose to live in a city?**
more jobs, near family, things to do, schools

What are some reasons people might choose to live on a farm?
quieter, near family, like animals, cleaner air, like farm work

Vocabulary

Define *suburb* as a town or area of homes near a city. Explain that many people who live in suburbs work and shop in the city.

LESSON 1

Looking Around Communities

The study of the Earth and its people is called **geography**. This photo album shows that people live in communities of different sizes.

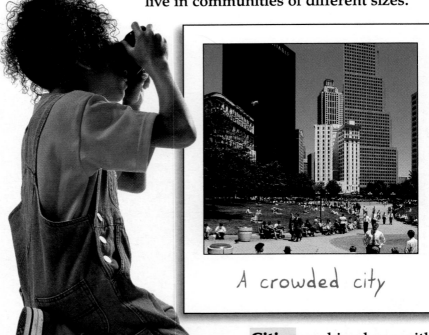

A crowded city

Cities are big places with many people and lots of things to do. People live and work in tall buildings and travel on busy streets.

48

ACTIVITY CHOICES

Reading Support

USE CONTEXT CLUES As you read the lesson with children, pause at the name of each landform or body of water to check for understanding. Ask children if they have ever seen each key word. Remind them of clues that can help a reader know the meanings of new words:
• the other words in the sentence
• the pictures on the page

Meet Individual Needs

ENGLISH LANGUAGE LEARNERS
Ask children to write *city*, *suburb*, *town*, and *farm* on a sheet of paper in their vocabulary notebooks. Then have them write short, simple words they can use to help them remember the meaning of each word.

A suburb near a city

A **suburb** is a community near a city. It has quieter neighborhoods and less traffic than the city. Many people go to the city each day to work.

A small town

People also live in small towns or on farms. Neighbors in these places know each other. They help one another and have fun together.

49

Q. **Why do you think people might move to a suburb?** more space and less traffic than a city

What kind of community do you live in? How do you know? Ask for a show of hands to determine in which setting children would prefer to live. Have children give their reasons for their choices.

Geography

Place Have children study a political map of your state or a population map, if you have one. Help them identify areas where large cities are located. Ask them to find areas where there are no towns, few towns, or small towns. Explain that cities and the places around them are called urban areas, while places with small towns, farms, and countryside are called rural areas. Make sure children connect the suburb with an urban area. Review the pictures on pages 48–49, having children identify them as either urban or rural.

Q. **Why do you think the city shown in the beginning of this unit grew into an urban area?** Responses might include because it is located near water and easy to get to; because it is a pretty place to live; because there are lots of jobs for people to do there.

PUPIL BOOK OR UNIT BIG BOOK

Home Involvement

Suggest that children discuss with their families the place where they live. Have they ever lived in other places? How did their family come to settle in the area? How much do jobs or recreation have to do with why they enjoy where they live? Invite interested children to share some family history with their classmates.

Link Literature

Invite children to read *Wild Wild Sunflower Child Anna* by Nancy White Carlstrom (Aladdin, 1991). This poem is about a girl who has fun exploring nature. She twirls through a field, climbs a tree, makes a daisy chain, and at the end, falls asleep. Then ask volunteers to read parts of the poem while others pantomime the actions of Anna. Invite children to pantomime other things Anna might do while exploring nature.

Geography

Place Explain that a landform is any land feature on the Earth's surface. Invite children to compare the photos on pages 50–51. Emphasize the landforms mountain, valley, and plain. Note that a desert is a kind of land vegetation rather than a landform. Point out that deserts are not always sandy and that many kinds of desert plants may grow there.

Q. **How are these places different from one another?** Responses may include that plains and deserts are usually flat, mountains are high, and valleys are low.

Vocabulary

Ask children to explain the difference between a mountain and a hill (hills are smaller with rounded tops). Define a mountain range as a line or row of mountains and a mountain peak as the pointed top of a mountain. Remind children of the fields in the poem "Always Wondering." Tell them that another name for flat land with few trees is a *plain*.

Communities have different kinds of land near them. The land may be flat or hilly. The shapes of the land are called **landforms**.

Mountains are the highest kind of land. High places are colder than low places. The air at the tops of tall mountains is so cold that the snow never melts.

Tall, rocky mountains

Between mountains or hills are lower lands called **valleys**. People may live in the valleys.

A valley between mountains

50

ACTIVITY CHOICES

Meet Individual Needs

VISUAL AND TACTILE LEARNERS Ask children to collect picture postcards and newspaper and magazine photos that show the landforms and bodies of water found in their state. Use the pictures to make a bulletin-board collage. Have children discuss activities associated with each natural feature and tell how these places benefit their state.

Link to Language Arts

WRITE A DESCRIPTION Ask children to write a description of the land found in a place they have visited or would like to visit. Challenge them to use the lesson vocabulary in their descriptions.

TECHNOLOGY

Use **THE AMAZING WRITING MACHINE™ RESOURCE PACKAGE** to complete this activity.

A flat plain

Large, flat parts of the Earth are called **plains**. The land in most plains is good for farming and for raising animals.

Dry desert land

Deserts are dry lands that get little rain. They are often hot in the daytime and cool at night.

51

PUPIL BOOK **OR** UNIT BIG BOOK

WRITE-ON CHARTS

Home, Sweet Home

Use WRITE-ON CHART 5 to extend and enrich this lesson. See Teacher's Edition page W14.

VOCABULARY CARDS

Have partners use the lesson VOCABULARY PICTURE CARDS to challenge each other to identify landforms and bodies of water.

Auditory Learning

Learn from a Poem Read the following verses from *Earth Songs*, a book of poems by Myra Cohn Livingston.

> *Patched together*
> *With land and sea,*
> *I am earth,*
> *Great earth.*
> *Come with me!*

Uplands clamber over me, climbing
skyward. Hummocks, hillocks, small knolls
roll in circles, slope and tumble down.
Round hills rise to bluffs. My highlands
    change—
Range over me! Look! My shapes grow
    strange.

Mountains rise above me, their slopes white,
bright with fresh snow, tall peaks glistering.
Blistering brown domes bend over,
    hunched,
bunched together. Some, chained in deep
    folds,
molded in waves, sleep, wrinkled and old.

Lowlands slide down me. Dip and hollow
follow the path to dell and ravine,
careen to broad valley, rocky gorge,
forge giant fissures. My canyons deep
sleep in stone walls, black, silent and steep.

Deserts sleep on me, restless, shifting,
drifting mounds of sand whipped by dry
    wind.
Skinned and barren, these dun, arid dunes
strewn with scorched tumbleweed, slumber,
    cursed,
submersed in mirage and endless thirst.

Review the descriptive words in the poem, helping children see the images conveyed by the poet. Invite volunteers to use their own words to describe the landforms listed in their books. You may wish to construct a class poem similar to the one above.

VOCABULARY BLACKLINES

Distribute the individual word cards for the lesson found in the back of your Teacher's Edition. Ask children to write the meaning of the word on the back of each card.

Vocabulary

Review the definitions of *ocean, river, lake,* and *island,* and invite children to compare the photos on pages 52–53. Point out that people choose to live near bodies of water for different reasons—sometimes for a way to make a living and sometimes for recreation.

Q. **Why do you think people might choose to live near a large body of water?** They might want to fish, operate a restaurant or store for tourists, swim or surf or do other water sports, or transport goods to other places over the water.

Geography

Place Point out that there are many bodies of water on Earth. Display a globe and guide children to discover that there is more water on Earth than land. Ask volunteers to point out bodies of water on the globe and identify them as rivers, lakes, or oceans.

Q. **How are oceans, rivers, and lakes different from one another?** Oceans are very large and contain salt water; rivers flow across land and have fresh water; lakes have land all around them, and most have fresh water.

3. CLOSE

Ask children to summarize the lesson by describing the Earth's human-made and physical features. Challenge them to use the terms *suburb, landform, desert, island, lake, mountain, ocean, plain, valley,* and *river* in their descriptions.

Check Understanding

The child can
____ distinguish between city, suburban, and small-town or farm settings.
____ recognize human-made features of the land.
____ identify various landforms and bodies of water.
____ compare physical features of the land.

Communities may also be near different kinds of bodies of water. Water may be salty or fresh, flowing or still.

Oceans are the largest bodies of water. Their salty waves fall on beaches all over the world.

Ocean waves

There are islands in some bodies of water. An **island** is a landform with water all around it.

An island in the ocean

52

ACTIVITY CHOICES

Background

ISLANDS Many islands are the tops of volcanoes that have been built up from the ocean floor by repeated eruptions. The Hawaiian Islands are habitable islands formed by volcanoes that are still active.

Link to Science

MODELS AND SCALE Discuss with children the landforms and bodies of water found in the community where they live. Then provide them with modeling clay and blue construction paper, and invite them to build a model of their community. Remind them to include all landforms and bodies of water.

A flowing river

Rivers have fresh water, not salt water. Rivers start as small streams. They flow down mountains and across the land to the oceans. Rivers can flow through towns and cities.

Sailboats on a lake

Lakes are bodies of still water with land all around them. Most have fresh water. Lakes can be many different sizes.

What Do You Know?

1. **What is a suburb?** a community near a city
2. **What pictures would be in a photo album of your community?**

53

PUPIL BOOK OR UNIT BIG BOOK

Extend and Enrich

LOOK AT A MAP Display a physical map of the United States. Ask volunteers to point out the part of the country where they live. Discuss the communities, land, and water in this area.

Reteach the Main Idea

DRAW LAND OR WATER Talk with children about the characteristics of one landform or body of water. Then have them draw a picture to show the place discussed.

WRITE-ON CHARTS

A World of Water
Use WRITE-ON CHART 6 to extend and enrich this lesson. See Teacher's Edition page W18.

Think Critically

Q. **Why are communities often located near bodies of water?** to have water for people, plants, animals, and businesses; for transportation of goods and people

Show What You Know

Performance Assessment Have children use "Looking Around Communities" as a model for making a photo album of communities, landforms, and bodies of water found in your area of the country. If a camera is not available, ask children to choose a variety of scenes to draw for the album.

What to Look For In evaluating the album, look for evidence of the child's understanding of human-made and physical features of the Earth.

Using the Activity Book Invite pairs of children to choose one of the scenes on Activity Book page 7. Have them color and cut out either the desert or the mountain scene and fold the paper on the dotted lines. Have children paste their scenes onto heavy paper or posterboard. Invite them to draw on the paper to add to the scene. They might also color and cut out trees and other plants, rocks, or bodies of water to paste onto the posterboard to create a three-dimensional diorama. Display the dioramas in the classroom.

Activity Book page 7

LESSON 1 • 53

HANDS-ON OPTION

The "Hands-On Option" is an alternative way to address all objectives for this lesson or to enrich the content found in the Pupil Book/Unit Big Book.

"The Bear Went Over the Mountain"

Objective: Identify various landforms and bodies of water.

Materials: Music Audio, "The Bear Went Over the Mountain"

Lead children in singing "The Bear Went Over the Mountain." Invite children to make up additional verses with names of other land and water features, such as "The bear swam down the river" or "The bear walked in the desert." Ask children to pantomime the actions as they sing. After each verse, invite volunteers to name some things the bear might see in that environment. **(AUDITORY/KINESTHETIC)**

Travel Postcards

Objectives: Compare physical features of the land. Recognize human-made features of the land.

Materials: heavy drawing paper, sample postcards, crayons, markers, scissors, paste, magazines

Display sample postcards and explain that people often send these cards to tell friends and family about their trips. Invite children to imagine they are visiting one of the areas from the lesson. Have each child create a postcard to send home, including a brief message to tell what they are seeing and doing. Ask children to draw a picture or paste a magazine picture on the front of their cards. Then have them write their messages on the back. Suggest that children address their cards to family members or classmates. **(TACTILE/VISUAL)**

Travel Guides

Objectives: Distinguish between city, suburban, and small-town or farm settings. Compare physical features of the land.

Materials: magazines, travel books and brochures, maps, scissors, paste, paper

 Organize children into cooperative groups to develop a travel plan for one of the areas pictured on pages 48–53. One child can cut out or draw pictures of clothing suitable for the trip. Another child can find or draw methods of transportation, and a third can list things they want to see on their trip.

Remaining members of each group can make a travel booklet. Remind them to provide information about their area, what to bring, what to do for fun, what to see, and so on. Provide resources, including travel books and brochures, for children to use. Ask groups to present their travel plans and guides to the class.

Place the travel booklets in a center for children to use in dramatic play activities. **(TACTILE/VISUAL)**

FIND LAND AND WATER ON A MAP

OBJECTIVES

1. Use colors and symbols to read a physical map.
2. Distinguish land and water on a map.

RESOURCES

Pupil Book/Unit Big Book, pp. 54–55
Activity Book, p. 9
Transparencies 3, 20, 21, 22

ACTIVITY CHOICES

Home Involvement

Ask children to use books and maps with family members to learn more about their community and state. Have them draw and label the landforms and bodies of water in the area. Invite children to share their drawings and to use them to describe what they discovered about the land and water in their community.

TRANSPARENCY

Use TRANSPARENCY 3.

 1. ACCESS

Display a large physical map, and ask children how they can tell the difference between land and water on a map. Elicit from children that water is usually colored blue on maps.

Vocabulary

Review the definitions for *map key* and *symbol* from Unit 1. Remind children that a map key tells what the symbols on a map represent. Point out the map key on page 55, and ask what is different about this key. Help children realize that this type of map key uses colors as well as symbols to represent land and water on the map.

Q. **What colors are used in the map key? What colors are used to show land areas? What color shows bodies of water?**
Brown, green, and orange show land areas; blue shows water.

2. BUILD

Visual Analysis

Learn from Maps As children look at the map key, invite volunteers to tell what each color and symbol represents. Help children recognize that the map key shows various landforms, bodies of water, and desert regions in the United States.

Explain that a map shows the separation between land areas in a general way. Some people who live in an area shown as plains may be able to see mountains rising a few miles away.

Q. How can you find mountains on a map? Look at the key and use the symbol and color to find them.

Geography

Place Focus attention on the map key symbols. Help children notice that the first three items are land features—they have different colors and symbols. The last two items are bodies of water. They have the same color, blue, but different symbols.

Q. Into what large bodies of water do the rivers flow? into the gulfs and oceans

Location Ask children to look at the symbol and color for mountains. Work with them to identify all the mountain areas shown on the map. Repeat the procedure for each of the landforms and bodies of water.

Q. How do you think mapmakers choose the colors and symbols for each feature? They try to make the colors and symbols look like the colors and shapes of the real features.

Map and Globe Skills

Find Land and Water on a Map

Maps often use colors and symbols to show different kinds of land and bodies of water.

1 Look at the map key. What color is used to show deserts? orange

2 Use the map key to find the symbol for mountains. Which side of the country has more mountains? Which ocean is it near? west side; Pacific Ocean

3 Find some lakes and rivers on the map. Which body of water flows between the United States and Mexico? Which bodies of water are between Canada and the United States? a river; lakes

PACIFIC OCEAN

54

ACTIVITY CHOICES

Meet Individual Needs

VISUAL LEARNERS Display a classroom map of the United States. Invite small groups to identify by name the mountains, deserts, and major bodies of water that are shown but not labeled on the pupil page. Children might identify the Appalachian and Rocky mountains, the Sierra Nevada, and the Coast Ranges; the Sonoran, Painted, Mojave, and Chihuahuan deserts; the Rio Grande and the Mississippi, Ohio, Missouri, Colorado, and Columbia rivers; the Great Lakes; and the Gulf of Mexico.

TRANSPARENCY

Use TRANSPARENCIES 20, 21, and 22 to label landforms and bodies of water.

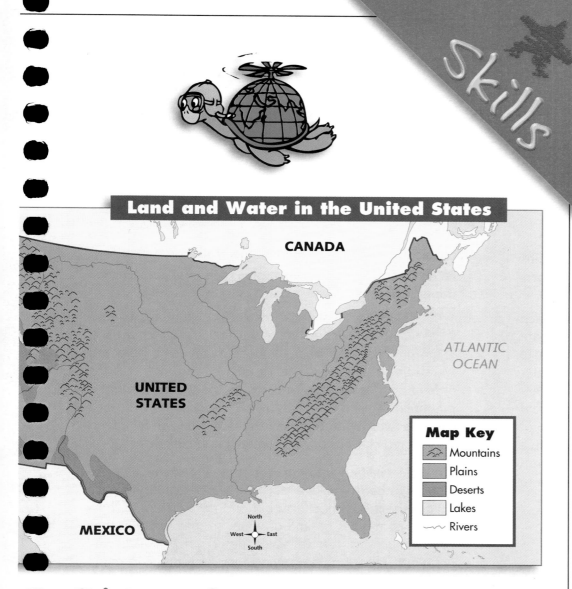

Land and Water in the United States

CANADA

ATLANTIC OCEAN

UNITED STATES

MEXICO

Map Key
- Mountains
- Plains
- Deserts
- Lakes
- Rivers

North
West — East
South

Think and Do

Where are our country's longest rivers?
How do you think they help the land?

55

Extend and Enrich

DRAW A MAP Invite children to draw a map of an imaginary country. Ask them to include a map key that uses colors and symbols to represent land and water. Have them exchange their maps with partners, who will describe the countries by using the map keys.

Reteach the Skill

FIND LAND AND WATER Display a wall map that uses color to distinguish land and water. Have children examine the map and map key. Then call on volunteers to place a brown square on an area of the map that represents land. Invite another child to place a blue square on an area that represents water. Repeat the task until each child has had a turn.

3. CLOSE

Think and Do

Children should note the three major rivers that flow through the plains on their maps. Help them identify the rivers as the Missouri, Mississippi, and Ohio rivers. Children should recognize that these rivers provide water to large areas of land, which may be used for farming and ranching.

Review the skill with children by asking the following questions:

Q. **How can you show features such as land and water on a map?** by using colors and symbols **What kinds of symbols and colors are used in a map key?** Answers should reflect an understanding of the map key on page 55.

Using the Activity Book Distribute copies of Activity Book page 9. Have children use crayons to color the map key first and then the map on the page. Check that children have shown the landforms and bodies of water in different colors.

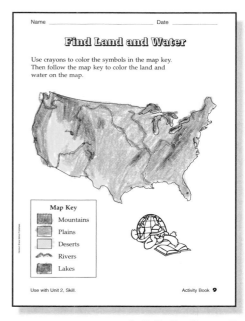

Activity Book page 9

HANDS-ON OPTION

HANDS-ON OPTION

Map Collage

Objective: Distinguish land and water on a map.

Materials: map, in color, showing several bodies of water; blue yarn; blue construction paper; scissors; glue

Distribute a black-and-white copy of the map to each child. If possible, use a local map. Ask children to locate water areas on the map. Then invite them to cut and paste the blue yarn and construction paper to cover the water areas. Display the color version of the map. Suggest children check their work by looking at this map. Remind them to use the map key to help them locate the bodies of water. Children may also wish to compare their map with a classmate. After the glue dries, suggest that children run their hands over the map to feel the texture as well as to look at the colors. **(VISUAL/TACTILE)**

Surveying the Terrain

Objective: Use colors and symbols to read a physical map.

Materials: state physical maps, clay, tools for working with clay such as blunt pencils and craft sticks, paint, paintbrushes

Invite children to create a three-dimensional map of a state with mountains, plains, lakes, and rivers. Suggest that they examine several state maps and select one they want to make. After the clay dries, have them use paint to show the different kinds of land and water as they are shown on the map. Display the models for other classes to enjoy. **(VISUAL/ TACTILE)**

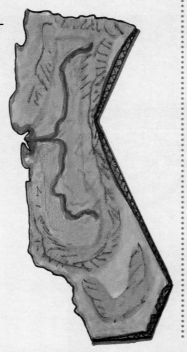

Interpreting Map Symbols

Objectives: Use colors and symbols to read a physical map. Distinguish land and water on a map.

Materials: magazines, glue, scissors, construction paper, crayons

 Display a physical map. Ask volunteers to take turns selecting one of the land and water symbols and telling what someone might see if he or she were to visit that area. Then ask children to name all the different types of land and water they have learned—mountains, plains, deserts, rivers, oceans, forests, and lakes—as you write them on the board. Have volunteers use colored chalk to draw a symbol beside each one.

Organize children into small groups and invite them to work together to make a land and water scrapbook. Each child in the group should cut out or draw a picture to show one or more types of land or water so that together they cover mountains, forests, plains, deserts, rivers, lakes, and oceans. If children are drawing their pictures, you might suggest that they include a few of the animals that might be found in that area. Then have them glue their pictures on separate sheets of construction paper. Children should draw an appropriate map symbol and write the name of the kind of land or water under each picture. Help children staple their pages together to make a book with a blank sheet for the front cover. Then tell them to decide on a title and design the cover for their book. **(TACTILE/VISUAL)**

2
LIFE IN DIFFERENT PLACES

OBJECTIVES

1. Identify examples of how people live in different locations.
2. Identify how land and climate affect people's work and the recreation they enjoy.
3. Recognize the multicultural diversity of the Western Hemisphere.

RESOURCES

Pupil Book/Unit Big Book, pp. 56–59
Write-On Charts 5, 30, 35
Clings
Pattern P3
Vocabulary Cards
Vocabulary Blacklines
Activity Book, p. 10
Desk Maps
Video, Reading Rainbow, *My Little Island*

ACTIVITY CHOICES

Meet Individual Needs

ADVANCED LEARNERS Invite children to discuss what they do for fun. Focus attention on the kinds of activities that depend on the geography of the area in which they live. Help children make a class chart of activities. When the chart is complete, reread the list and ask children to identify activities they do that may not be possible in other kinds of environments, such as swimming in the ocean or mountain skiing.

Role-Play

Organize children into groups of three or four, and have them choose one child to be a visitor from a different part of the country. The visitor's role is to ask questions of the rest of the group about what life is like in the area. The rest of the group plays the part of local people who want to introduce the newcomer to their home area. Allow time for groups to share their presentations with the whole class.

1. ACCESS

Remind children that they have learned how land and climate affect the kinds of homes people build. Invite children to preview this lesson by looking at the pictures. Lead them to discover that they are going to read letters from three children who live in different places. Ask them what they would write in a letter about where they live and what kinds of pictures they would want to send to a new pen pal.

Focus on the Main Idea

Tell children that in this lesson they will read three letters from pen pals who live in different places. They will see some of the ways these children spend their leisure time and how they and their families live, work, and celebrate. These things all tell something about the places they live in.

VIDEO

Use READING RAINBOW,™ MY LITTLE ISLAND to explore life on a Caribbean Island.

2. BUILD

Key Content Summary

Three pen pals share descriptions of everyday life in New York, Grenada, and New Mexico. Their letters provide insights into life in regions of our hemisphere that have diverse geographical features.

Critical Thinking

Direct attention to pages 56–59. Have children examine the pictures and then read the letters written by the children.

Q. What do the photos tell you about the person who wrote each letter? Each child lives in a different geographical area.

Geography

Location Display a large map showing the Western Hemisphere. Help children locate New York, New Mexico, and Grenada. Explain that life in these places is different because of their location in the world.

Q. How is life the same in these areas? How is it different? Children should mention the similarities and differences in the weather and in the types of activities described.

LESSON

2 Life in Different Places

Three pen pals share what life is like in a mountain community, an island community, and a desert community. Read their letters.

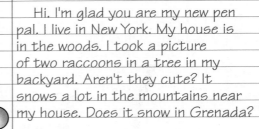

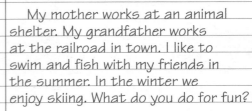

Dear Felicia,

Hi. I'm glad you are my new pen pal. I live in New York. My house is in the woods. I took a picture of two raccoons in a tree in my backyard. Aren't they cute? It snows a lot in the mountains near my house. Does it snow in Grenada?

My mother works at an animal shelter. My grandfather works at the railroad in town. I like to swim and fish with my friends in the summer. In the winter we enjoy skiing. What do you do for fun?

Your pal,
Jared

56

ACTIVITY CHOICES

Reading Support

PREVIEW AND PREDICT Ask children what a pen pal is and what pen pals might write about. Make a web of children's ideas. Then read the story aloud, and ask children to add to the idea web.

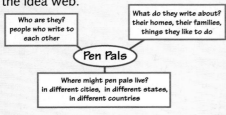

Background

GRENADA Grenada is a small independent island nation in the Windward Islands of the Caribbean Sea. The land is mainly mountainous, and the climate is moist and hot. The people are mainly of African descent. English is their official language. Most of the people work in the agriculture or service industries.

WRITE-ON CHARTS

Use WRITE-ON CHART 35 and Star Clings to locate New York, New Mexico, and Grenada.

Dear Jared,

I live on a small island. I like to fish, too. My family has a fishing farm. On Saturdays I help my father and my uncle on our boat.

Last week we had a big carnival in our town. Almost everybody came. Do you like my costume? My sister painted my face for the parade.

I took a picture of some of my friends at school. It is warm here all the time. I've never even seen snow! What does it feel like? Please write soon.

Your friend,

Felicia

P.S. April is my other pen pal. She is writing you a letter, too.

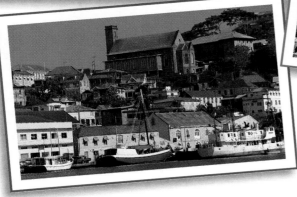

57

Link to Science

AIR, WEATHER, CLIMATE Suggest children look at weather maps in newspapers for several days and record the temperatures from different areas in the Western Hemisphere on their Desk Maps.

VOCABULARY CARDS

Use VOCABULARY PICTURE CARDS to reinforce the meanings of *island, lake, landform, mountain, ocean, plain, desert, river, suburb,* and *valley.*

Culture

Shared Humanity and Unique Identity Have children compare the carnival in Grenada and the Pueblo Feast Day in New Mexico and discuss what they think people might do at these celebrations.

Q. **What kinds of celebrations might Jared have where he lives?** Answers might include traditions associated with Christmas, Thanksgiving, Columbus Day, or other holidays.

Economics

Productivity and Economic Growth Discuss the various types of jobs mentioned in the letters and shown in the pictures, such as fish farm owner, railroad worker, artist, farmers' market worker, and animal shelter worker. Ask how these occupations help the community. Invite children to think of other jobs that could be done in the various areas.

Q. **Which of these jobs could be done only in a certain area?** Answers will vary but should include types of jobs that could be done only at the beach, in the mountains, or in the desert.

Which job would you like to have? Why? Children may choose a job that sounds exciting to them or one that is similar to one of their family members' jobs.

VOCABULARY BLACKLINES

Invite partners to select three or four of the vocabulary words from Lesson 1. Challenge them to use the words to make up and illustrate a story about life in one of the areas they have read about in the letters.

3. CLOSE

Ask children to summarize their learning by choosing New York, Grenada, or New Mexico and telling how its geography and environment affect the way people there live and play.

Check Understanding

The child can
—— identify examples of how people live in different locations.
—— identify how land and climate affect people's work and the recreation they enjoy.
—— recognize the multicultural diversity of the Western Hemisphere.

Think Critically

Q. **How does weather affect the way people live and work?** Weather makes certain jobs and types of recreation possible in some places—for example, fishing in Grenada and skiing in New York. Weather also makes certain jobs and types of recreation impossible or difficult in other places—for example, snow skiing or fishing in the deserts of New Mexico.

How is having pen pals a good way to learn about other places? Getting to know other people helps you find out interesting things about the way they live.

Dear Jared,

I live with my grandparents in the Cochiti Pueblo in New Mexico. We live in an adobe house. It is very dry here.

Our class went on a field trip. We saw a place where people lived a long time ago. Their houses were built into the side of the mountain.

58

ACTIVITY CHOICES

Multicultural Link

To the Cochiti people of New Mexico, making pottery and storytelling are important traditions. Many potters make storyteller figures (like the Cochiti Pueblo storyteller pictured on page 59) to celebrate these traditions. The figures usually represent a grandparent, and the smaller figures are the children who hear the ancient stories that pass on the traditions of the people.

Extend and Enrich

MAKE TRAVEL GUIDES Provide a collection of travel magazines. Invite children to find pictures showing geographic features similar to those of one of the three places in the lesson. Suggest that children who choose the same geographic area work together to create travel guides by pasting the pictures they find onto posterboard. Then have them prepare an oral presentation about the area.

Reteach the Main Idea

DESCRIBE THE LAND Call on children to give details about the land features of New York, Grenada, and New Mexico. As each place is described, invite them to ask one another questions about the weather, recreational activities, and the work people do; for example, *Can you go to the beach in New York? Could I build a snow figure in Grenada?*

My grandparents make beautiful pottery. They sell it to people who come to see Cochiti Pueblo. I am learning to make pots and dolls out of clay.

Pueblo Feast Day is a special day. Everyone wears a costume. We all dance and sing. Maybe you and Felicia can come to a Feast Day. That would be fun! Please write.

Your pen pal,

April

What Do YOU Know?

1. How is the weather different for Jared and Felicia?
2. What would you write in a letter about where you live?

1. Jared's home has snow in winter; Felicia's does not. **59**

PUPIL BOOK OR UNIT BIG BOOK

Background

PEN PALS Contact one of the following organizations for information on how your class or interested children can become pen pals. (Pen pal services may require a small fee.)
Worldwide Friendship International
3749 Brice Run Road, Suite A
Randallstown, MD 21133
International Friendship League, Inc.
22 Batterymarch Street
Boston, MA 02109
American Sharing Program
3255 Gateway #57
Springfield, OR 97477

International Pen Friends
P.O. Box 1491
Fitchburg, MA 04120
Dear Pen Pal
P.O. Box 4054
Santa Barbara, CA 93101
Caravan House
132 E. 65th Street
New York, NY 10021
Childlife Magazine
c/o Pen Pals
P.O. Box 567B
Indianapolis, IN 46206

Performance Assessment Have children write their own letters to pen pals. Suggest that they choose an area of the world in which they are interested. Remind them to write about the land features, the weather, and the activities that people enjoy doing where they live and to ask questions about the area in which they are interested.

What to Look For Children's letters to pen pals should identify the land features, weather, and recreational activities of the area in which you live.

Using the Activity Book Distribute copies of Activity Book page 10. Invite children to list items they might need for a summer vacation in Florida and then items they might need for a winter vacation in Colorado. Suggest that children look at a map to determine what they think the weather would be like in each place. Point out that some items could be taken to both places.

Activity Book page 10

HANDS-ON OPTION

Getting the Picture

Objective: Identify examples of how people live in different locations.

Materials: Write-On Chart 30, paper, markers

Label the columns on the three-column chart *Mountains, Island,* and *Desert.* Ask children to name a job that people might do in a mountain area, on an island, and in a desert. As each is suggested, record the job in the appropriate column(s). Repeat, naming recreational activities. Then ask children to choose one area. Invite them to draw a picture showing how people in that area live and write a few sentences describing what it is like to live there. Display pictures from similar environments together. **(TACTILE/VISUAL)**

Friendship Letters

Objective: Identify how land and climate affect people's work and the recreation they enjoy.

Materials: Write-On Chart 5, paper, pencils, box

Invite children to examine the various photos of shelters that are shown on Write-On Chart 5. Ask children to imagine that they live in one of those homes. Tell them to write a letter to a pen pal in the classroom. Their letter should describe the land on which they live, the kinds of work their family members do, and the things the adults and children where they live do for enjoyment. Collect the letters, put them in a box, and mix them up. Have each child choose one letter from the box and read it aloud. Ask the child to make a guess about the type of home the pen pal is writing from. The writer of the letter must say whether the guess is correct. **(AUDITORY/TACTILE)**

Create a Cultural Filmstrip

Objective: Recognize the multicultural diversity of the Western Hemisphere.

Materials: Pattern P3, books about several countries

 COOPERATIVE LEARNING Help children recall the many differences between the cultures of the three children who wrote the letters in the lesson. Then suggest that children might like to research a country or a culture that is different from their own.

Organize children into cooperative groups. Provide books about several areas in the Western Hemisphere. Assign each group to research aspects of one of the countries or cultures. As children investigate, suggest each group member choose one or more of the following questions to answer.

1. What kinds of homes or shelters do the people have?
2. What kinds of celebrations do the people have? What do they do at these celebrations?
3. What kinds of music do they play?
4. What foods do the people eat?
5. What is the land like where these people live?
6. What is the weather like? What kinds of clothes do the people wear?

Then invite children to use the Filmstrip Pattern to present the information they found. Children should draw pictures on the frames to illustrate their discoveries and also write a script to go along with the pictures. Children may wish to record their script or read it aloud as other children view the filmstrip. **(VISUAL/TACTILE)**

USE A GLOBE

OBJECTIVES

1. Define *continent, globe,* and *equator.*
2. Compare a map and a globe.
3. Identify and locate the oceans and continents on a globe.
4. Find the equator and poles on a globe.

VOCABULARY

continent (p. 60)
globe (p. 60)
equator (p. 61)

RESOURCES

Pupil Book/Unit Big Book, pp. 60–61
Write-On Chart 34
Clings
Activity Book, p. 11
Transparencies 4, 23

ACTIVITY CHOICES

Link to Art

SCULPTURE Children can use balloons and papier-mâché to make their own globes. Have them dip strips of newspaper into wallpaper or wheat paste and wrap the strips around a balloon, overlapping the strips and applying several layers. When strips are dry, have children paint their globes blue for water. When the blue paint has dried, children can use other colors to paint the continents over the blue. Save the globes for labeling later in the lesson.

Meet Individual Needs

ENGLISH LANGUAGE LEARNERS
Ask children to write the word *globe* and then its equivalent in their first language. Help them compare a map (flat) to a globe (round). Have them find and name aloud the parts of the globe—continent, equator, pole—as they are discussed.

TRANSPARENCY

Use TRANSPARENCIES 4 and 23 to locate New York, Grenada, New Mexico, and children's home state.

1. ACCESS

Begin by having children find New York, Grenada, New Mexico, and their home state on a map. Review how to distinguish between land and water on the map. Show pictures of the Earth taken from space, and invite children to describe what they see. Point out the shapes of various land formations and water bodies. Guide children to notice that the Earth is not flat.

Vocabulary

Display a globe. Explain to children that a *globe* is a round model of the Earth that shows land, water, and other features. Call on volunteers to locate areas of land on the globe. Explain that the land on Earth is divided into seven large areas called *continents.* Assist children in locating and naming the seven continents.

Q. **On what continent do you live? How do you know?** North America; the United States is on that continent

Remind children that the northernmost and southernmost points on the Earth are called poles. Invite children to trace with their fingers a circle around the middle of the globe, halfway between the North Pole and South Pole. Explain that this make-believe circle is called the *equator.*

2. BUILD

Geography

Location After children read pages 60 and 61, organize them into pairs. Invite one pair to use the globe, another to use a wall map of the world, and the rest to use the world maps in their books. Name the continents, oceans, poles, and equator, one at a time, for the groups to locate on the maps and the globe. Rotate pairs so that all children have a chance to find places on the globe and wall map. Ask children whether they find it easier to use a map or a globe, and have them explain their answer.

Regions Display a globe, and tell children that they are going to label the continents. Ask volunteers to name one of the seven continents and label it with a self-stick note. Then have children remove the labels as they name each continent. Repeat the procedures for the oceans, the poles, and the equator.

Q. Which cover more of the Earth's surface—the oceans or the continents? the oceans

Explain that islands close to continents are considered to be part of those continents. Point out examples such as Australia and New Zealand, Asia and Japan, and Europe and Great Britain.

Map and Globe Skills

Use a Globe

The places you just read about are in North America. North America is a large land area called a **continent**. You can see continents and oceans on a globe. A **globe** is a model of the Earth.

Look at the picture of the globe. How does a globe look like the Earth? How is a globe different from a map? The globe and the Earth are the same shape. Maps are flat, and land shapes may look different from those on a globe.

60

ACTIVITY CHOICES

Meet Individual Needs

KINESTHETIC LEARNERS Play a game using a world map and a globe. Ask one child to give a clue about a continent, an ocean, a pole, or the equator. For example: *Where is an ocean that begins with A?* Others try to identify this place, first on the map and then on the globe.

Meet Individual Needs

AUDITORY LEARNERS Write the names of the continents and oceans on separate slips of paper, making enough so that every child will have one. Establish two label centers: continents and oceans. Have children go to the appropriate area and prove he or she is in the right group by saying, for example, *I have Asia. Asia is a continent.*

Link to Science

MODELS AND SCALE Help children find Grenada and New York on a map and a globe. Do the same with the equator and North Pole. Explain that Grenada is warm year-round because it is close to the equator. Then have children compare the distances from New York to the equator and to the North Pole. Help them understand why New York is cold in the winter.

2 Now look below at the drawings of a globe. How many continents do you see? Name them. seven: North America, South America, Antarctica, Africa, Europe, Asia, Australia

3 How many oceans do you see? Name them. four: Pacific, Atlantic, Indian, Arctic

Skills

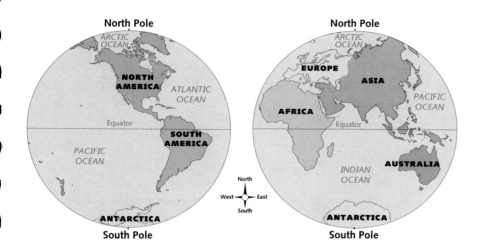

4 Find the North Pole and South Pole on each drawing. Then put your finger on the line drawn halfway between the two poles. This is the **equator**. It is a make-believe line that divides the Earth in half.

Think and Do

Find the equator on a globe. Which three continents does the equator cross?

61

PUPIL BOOK OR UNIT BIG BOOK

Extend and Enrich

MATCH CONTINENTS Provide cardboard models so that children can trace and cut out the continents. Children can take turns selecting a shape, matching it to the land mass on the globe, and naming it. Ask questions about other features that have been taught, such as the oceans, the poles, and the equator.

Reteach the Skill

LABEL GLOBES Have children draw and label the equator on their papier-mâché globes. Ask them to label the seven continents, the four oceans, and the poles.

WRITE-ON CHARTS

Use WRITE-ON CHART 34 and Geometric Symbol Clings to identify the continents, oceans, poles, and equator.

---

3. CLOSE

Think and Do

Children's responses should show that the equator passes through South America, Africa, and Asia. They may need a reminder that the islands of Indonesia are part of the continent of Asia.

Review the skill with children by asking the following questions:

Q. **What is the difference between a map and a globe? How are they alike?** A map is flat, but a globe is shaped like a ball. Each shows where places are on the Earth.

What are the seven continents? Asia, Europe, Africa, Australia, Antarctica, North America, and South America

What are the four oceans? Pacific, Atlantic, Indian, Arctic

Using the Activity Book Distribute copies of Activity Book page 11. Have children identify the continents, poles, oceans, and equator on the drawing of the globe by writing the appropriate letter in each circle.

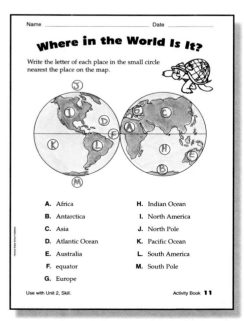

Activity Book page 11

HANDS-ON OPTION

Make a Map

Objectives: Compare a map and a globe. Identify and locate the oceans and continents on a globe.

Materials: tracing paper, pencils, tape, large globe, posterboard, glue, markers

COOPERATIVE LEARNING Organize the class into small groups. Have each group member trace one of the continents from the globe onto tracing paper as other children hold the globe steady. Challenge children to identify each continent as it is traced. Have group members cut out their continents and arrange them on a sheet of posterboard to create a flat map. Children may rearrange them until they are satisfied with their placement. Then have them tape their pages to the posterboard and retrace the continents with colored markers. You may wish to hang their maps on the walls of the room or in the hall.

(VISUAL/AUDITORY/TACTILE)

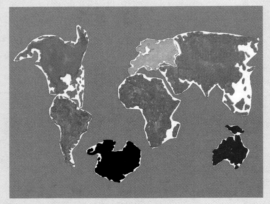

Continents Game

Objective: Identify and locate the oceans and continents on a globe.

Materials: copies of continent shapes (two per child), index cards, scissors, pencils, glue

Trace the outlines of the continents and the oceans onto a sheet of paper so that each shape will fit on an index card. Distribute two copies of the sheet to each child. Have children match the shapes on one of their sheets with the shapes on the globe and write the names of the continents on the shapes. Then have children cut out all the continents on both sheets and glue each one on an index card. Invite pairs of children to use their cards to play "Memory." Suggest to children that they play the game with family members. **(VISUAL/KINESTHETIC)**

From Round Globe to Flat Map

Objectives: Define *globe, continent,* and *equator.* Find the equator and poles on a globe.

Materials: plastic foam balls, markers, colored tape, toothpick flags, scissors, globe

Provide each child with a plastic foam ball and display a globe. Have children work with a partner. Invite them to pretend that the ball they have is the Earth and that they are going to explore it. Have children use a marker to draw the continents and add tape to make the equator and toothpick flags to mark the North and the South Poles.

Suggest that children make up stories to tell each other about their explorations as they draw. Recommend that when drawing each shape they tell which continent they are visiting and how they are traveling through it. As they pretend to cross an ocean to another continent, have them name the ocean they are crossing and what they are using to cross it. Challenge them to use cardinal directions to describe where they are going. As they travel along the equator, have them describe how it feels to be there. Finally, have them pretend they are claiming the North and South Poles for their country as they place each flag and also ask them to describe what it feels like to be there. If children wish, allow them to color in the continents and then the oceans to complete their models of Earth. Suggest that children share their adventures with family members when they take their models home.

(VISUAL/AUDITORY/TACTILE)

3

USING THE LAND

OBJECTIVES

1. Describe how people depend on the land.
2. Identify ways people adapt to and change their environments to meet their needs.
3. Recognize how seasonal changes can affect the land and land use.

VOCABULARY

crop (p. 63)

RESOURCES

Pupil Book/Unit Big Book, pp. 62–65
Write-On Charts 26, 29
Clings
Activity Book, p. 12
Music Audio, "Garden Song"

ACTIVITY CHOICES

Meet Individual Needs

VISUAL LEARNERS Have children find and cut out magazine pictures of unpopulated natural land areas, such as swamps, deserts, river valleys, mountaintops, forests, canyons, or lakeshores. Ask children how they think the land would need to be changed if people wanted to build a new town on these sites. Discuss what people would need that is not there now.

Link to Music

VOCAL/SONG Play the Music Audio "Garden Song" for the class. Invite children to learn and sing the song. This song tells how to make your garden grow. Invite children to take turns singing and pantomiming the actions. Discuss how gardening changes the land.

AUDIO

 Use the UNIT 2 MUSIC AUDIOCASSETTE to hear "Garden Song."

---

1. ACCESS

Invite children to close their eyes and think about the route they took to school today. Then ask if they noticed any changes in and around the community today or recently. Perhaps they saw workers clearing a wooded area, filling in a swamp, or blasting away a rocky hillside. Call on volunteers to describe their observations and to suggest reasons people are changing the land.

Focus on the Main Idea

In this lesson children will observe how people depend on the land as well as how they change the land to meet their needs. Tell children that they will observe how one family has changed and used their land over time.

2. BUILD

Key Content Summary

People have always depended on the land for their basic needs. Over centuries, the land and its features have been altered in many ways to meet the needs of its inhabitants. As children read pages 62–65, ask them to think about how the land is being changed.

Geography

Human-Environment Interactions

Emphasize that people depend on the land for such basics as food, building materials, and clothing. Have children look at the photos, describe the land, and explain what the people are doing. Ask how they know that the photos are from the past.

Q. **What needs do you think Jason's great-grandfather had?**
Responses may include that he needed to earn a living as well as to grow food for his family.

Vocabulary

Point out that *crops* are plants, such as grains, vegetables, and fruit, that people grow to use. Ask children to identify the crop grown in the lesson (wheat). Challenge children to name other crops.

LESSON 3 Using the Land

The children in Jason's class brought pictures and other things from home to help them tell about their families. Jason told the story of how his family has used and changed the land on their farm.

Clearing the land

Plowing the field

62

ACTIVITY CHOICES

Reading Support

USE CONTEXT CLUES As you come to the word *crop*, pause to check understanding. Have children identify clues in the paragraph that help them decide what the word means here.

Meet Individual Needs

ENGLISH LANGUAGE LEARNERS
Ask children to write the names of some crops, each on a separate index card, in their first language. Have them draw the crop on the reverse side of the card and write the word for that crop in English. Use the cards for vocabulary activities.

Harvest time

A long time ago, our farm was covered with trees. My great-grandfather cut down the trees so he could farm the land. A company used the trees to make paper and wood products.

My great-grandfather worked on the farm every day. He worked from early in the morning until it was dark. First, he plowed the field to get it ready for planting. In the spring, he planted wheat seeds in the warm, soft soil. Farming was very hard work.

Rain and sunshine helped the wheat grow tall. In autumn, the **crop** was ready to be harvested. All the workers helped cut the wheat. Everyone celebrated at harvest time!

63

Geography
Human-Environment Interactions
Emphasize that for a good wheat crop, the soil and weather must be right, the seeds must be healthy, and the wheat must be harvested at just the right time.

Q. What might have happened to the wheat planted by Jason's great-grandfather if there had been a drought or a flood? The crop might have been ruined, and people would have had to get their wheat from somewhere else.

History
Innovations Have children use the photos and the information they read to discuss how farming has changed since the days of Jason's great-grandfather. To give a sense of passing time, you may wish to first draw a family tree on the board to show Jason and his sister, their parents, grandparents, and great-grandparents. (See also Unit 6, Lesson 4.) Then discuss how technology—the development of the engine, machinery like the combine in the photo on page 64, and the computer, for example—has helped make farming easier. Encourage children to think about how modern transportation helps farmers get their crops to where they need to go.

WRITE-ON CHARTS

Use WRITE-ON CHART 26 and the Season Clings to make a time line of the seasons to discuss the best times of the year for farming in various areas.

Link to Health

NUTRITION Invite children to bring from home some labels and panels from packages listing ingredients. Suggest products such as cereals, pastas, breads, cookies, and crackers. Have children determine how many contain wheat flour, wheat bran, wheat germ, or wheat kernels. Together, make a poster to show food products containing wheat.

Meet Individual Needs

TACTILE LEARNERS Have children use Write-On Chart 29 and *Long Ago* and *Today* Clings to help them compare and contrast farming today with farming in the days of Jason's great-grandfather.

Economics

Scarcity and Choice Help children determine how many generations of Jason's family have been farming. Explain that in order to keep soil good for farming generation after generation, farmers do certain things. Describe crop rotation and contour plowing for children. Crop rotation is the alternating of crops grown in one field. For example, farmers might grow cotton, which uses a lot of nitrogen, in a field during one season. The next season the farmer might grow soybeans in the field to put back the nitrogen. Contour farming involves plowing furrows along the natural contours of the land to help prevent erosion.

Q. **What do you think would happen if farmers did not take care of their soil ?** Their crops would not grow well.

What do you think would happen to the prices of crops and the products made from them? The prices would go up.

3. CLOSE

Display a picture of a heavily forested area. Then invite children to imagine that they are neighbors of Jason's great-grandfather and that this is what the land they want to farm looks like. Ask children to tell how they would change the land to meet their needs.

My family

Harvesting wheat on our farm

History

Long, long ago, farmers planted wheat in a dry land called Mesopotamia. They used plows pulled by oxen to make rows for the seeds. They dug ditches to carry water to the plants.

64

Farming is different for our family now. We have computers and new machines to help us. But farming is still hard work.

My mother has a job at the television station. She tells what the weather will be. It is very important for farmers to know when it is going to rain.

ACTIVITY CHOICES

Background

COMBINES A crop of wheat has to be harvested as quickly as possible to prevent it from being ruined by bad weather. The combine cuts, threshes, and cleans the wheat in one operation. For thousands of years before the combine was invented, farmers harvested wheat by hand with sickles and scythes.

Extend and Enrich

RESEARCH CROPS Invite children to work in small groups to find out more about other important crops such as corn, rice, beans, and oats. Ask children to select one type of crop and to find out how it grows, where it is grown in the United States, and how it is used. Have the groups share with the class what they learn.

Reteach the Main Idea

IMAGINE LAND USE Ask children to imagine that they are settlers who have come by sea to an unpopulated land. Explain that they have clothing, basic tools and utensils, a variety of plants and seeds from their old land, and a limited supply of food. Have them talk about what the new land is like, what their needs are, and how they will use and change the land to meet their needs.

Our whole family works hard during planting and harvest times. Harvest time is the best time of the year!

I like to watch the machine pour the wheat into the trucks. The wheat is dried and stored in tall buildings called elevators. We sell the wheat to companies that use it to make flour, bread, and pasta.

I love living and working on the farm with my family. But my favorite part of farming is eating all the good foods we get from our land!

Loading the grain

What Do You Know?

1. **How do farmers get the land ready for planting?** They plow the fields.

2. **How do people use or change the land near you?**

65

PUPIL BOOK **OR** UNIT BIG BOOK

Link Literature

Read aloud *The Almond Orchard* by Laura Jane Coats. (Macmillan, 1991) In this story the author explains the operation of an almond orchard over the course of almost a century. Ask children to make a list of the things that changed at the orchard during the story. Have children discuss how the changes helped the people meet their needs at the orchard.

The Almond Orchard

Laura Jane Coats

Check Understanding

The child can
—— describe how people depend on the land.
—— identify ways people adapt to and change their environments to meet their needs.
—— recognize how seasonal changes can affect the land and land use.

Think Critically

Q. **What responsibilities do we have to the land? Why?** Responses should convey that we should take care of the land and conserve resources so that future generations will be able to use the land.

Show What You Know

Performance Assessment Have children work with partners to draw or cut out pictures and use them to create picture stories about how people change the land. Have children use their picture stories to give oral reports.

What to Look For Children's picture stories should reflect the idea that people change the land to meet their needs.

Using the Activity Book Distibute Activity Book page 12. Explain that when arranged in the correct order, the pictures show how the land along a hillside was changed to meet the needs of a family.

Activity Book page 12

HANDS-ON OPTION

The "Hands-On Option" is an alternative way to address all objectives for this lesson or to enrich the content found in the Pupil Book/Unit Big Book.

Our State's Farm and Forest Products

Objective: Describe how people depend on the land.

Materials: United States wall map, state map, reference materials about your state

Display a wall map of the United States and have children locate their state. Then distribute an individual state map to each child. Have children use reference materials to find out what farm and forest products are grown in their state. Instruct them to write the names of the products in the appropriate regions of their maps. **(KINESTHETIC/TACTILE)**

Growing Wheat

Objectives: Describe how people depend on the land. Identify ways people adapt to and change their environments to meet their needs. Recognize how seasonal changes can affect the land and land use.

Materials: drawing paper, crayons, markers

Remind children that the steps in growing products such as wheat have to be done in a certain order, at certain seasons of the year. Have them work with partners to draw the steps in the process of growing wheat, using four sheets of drawing paper labeled *Spring, Summer, Autumn,* and *Winter.* Suggest that children use their books to determine what Jason's family did first, next, and so on. Invite children to share their drawings with classmates. **(AUDITORY/TACTILE)**

Before and After

Objective: Identify ways people adapt to and change their environments to meet their needs.

Materials: drawing paper, crayons, markers, colored pencils, magazines, scissors, glue

Organize children into cooperative groups to make *Before and After* displays. Have children find a magazine picture of an unpopulated area, such as a forest, island, or meadow. Explain that they can develop the land any way they choose: for example, as a town, farm, city, or resort. Children may also choose to leave some of the land undeveloped. One child should record all the changes children plan to make, one or two children should draw pictures to show how the development will look, and the rest of the group should make the display. Have groups share their work with classmates. **(VISUAL/TACTILE)**

4

WHERE DOES OUR FOOD COME FROM?

OBJECTIVES

1. Recognize the many people who work to supply our daily needs.
2. Explain the steps in a flow chart that follows a food product from farm to market.
3. Describe the jobs of workers involved in food processing.

VOCABULARY

flow chart (p. 66)

RESOURCES

Pupil Book/Unit Big Book, pp. 66–69

Activity Book, p. 13

ACTIVITY CHOICES

Community Involvement

This lesson provides a wealth of opportunities for field trips, guest speakers, and demonstrations of behind-the-scenes activities in familiar places. Family or community members whose work involves any of the steps of food processing or sales can help children appreciate the contributions people make to those processes. Possible fieldtrip sites include apple orchards (especially where cider is made), farms, food-processing plants, and container factories. A trip to a grocery store can fill in the ending steps of the process. Many grocery stores also do some of their own preparation and packaging of fresh foods.

Link to Language Arts

WRITE LETTERS Help children generate a list of packaged, canned, and frozen foods they enjoy. Show containers whose labels have addresses where people can write with questions or comments about the food. Invite children to work in groups, with each group writing a letter to one company to request information about its food-processing operation. (Ahead of time, you might want to call toll-free numbers listed on labels to determine which companies have information to send.)

1. ACCESS

As you begin to recite the following rhyme, display a fresh apple and hold a can or jar of applesauce behind your back. At the end of the rhyme, show the applesauce.

> First an apple has to grow.
> Then it will be picked I know.
> But what comes next? What can it be
> That brings my applesauce to me?

Ask children how they think apples get from an apple tree into a can or jar of applesauce. Challenge children to name other foods that are made with apples, such as juice, apple pie, apple butter, and dried apple chips.

Focus on the Main Idea

This lesson introduces the idea of using a flow chart to show what happens to a food product from the time it is grown until it reaches the store. As children follow the process, they learn about the workers who grow, process, transport, and sell our food.

2. BUILD

Key Content Summary

Learning about the processes that bring food products to stores will satisfy children's curiosity and develop awareness of the workers involved.

Visual Analysis

Interpret Pictures Read page 66 and ask children which of the breakfast foods in the picture still look the same as they did when they were grown or picked. Discuss ways the other foods have changed.

Learn from Diagrams As children read the flow chart captions and study the pictures on pages 66–67, be sure they follow the direction of the arrows. Invite volunteers to point out pictures that show workers growing or making food, workers moving food, and workers selling food. Discuss how forms of transportation and other machinery shown in the pictures make the work easier.

Critical Thinking

Invite volunteers to describe the scene inside the cannery. Explain that some workers make juice and some put it into cans and boxes.

Q. **How do you think whole tomatoes are turned into juice?** Tomatoes are cleaned, peeled, crushed, cooked, and strained.

What other foods might come from this cannery? catsup, spaghetti sauce, tomato soup, whole or chopped tomatoes in cans

LESSON 4 Where Does Our Food Come From?

Think about breakfast foods you like to eat. How many people do you think it takes to make that breakfast? Would you be surprised to learn that it takes hundreds?

Many people work to get food from the farm to your table. Some grow or make the food, some move the food, and some sell the food.

Follow the **flow chart**, which shows the path tomatoes take to reach you.

Vegetable farmers plant and care for the tomatoes.

ACTIVITY CHOICES

Reading Support

USE PICTURE CLUES Remind children that a picture can often help a reader figure out a new word. The pictures in the flow chart on pages 66–67 can help children read the accompanying captions. Other photographs in the lesson can serve as aids for reading the remaining text. When children encounter unfamiliar words, suggest that they check nearby pictures for clues.

Meet Individual Needs

ENGLISH LANGUAGE LEARNERS As you point, in turn, to each of the photographs in the flow chart on pages 66–67, ask a *who* or *what* question. Model an answer, leaving out the sentence subject. Have children fill in the subject as they respond in a complete sentence; for example, *Who plants and cares for the tomatoes?* <u>*Vegetable farmers*</u> *plant and care for the tomatoes.* Help children use the correct verb form for each subject as they respond.

Field workers use big machines to harvest the tomatoes.

Truck drivers take the tomatoes to a cannery.

Trains and trucks take tomato juice to markets around the country.

At the cannery, workers make the tomatoes into juice.

67

PUPIL BOOK OR **UNIT BIG BOOK**

Link Literature

Children may think the milk in a carton is no different from the way it comes from the cow. However, even milk is changed before it arrives at the store. Readers will enjoy learning how milk is processed in *Milk: From Cow to Carton* by Aliki. (HarperCollins, 1992) Flow charts show what happens inside the dairy—and inside the cow!

Vocabulary

Ask children to use what they have learned to explain what a *flow chart* is. Then suggest other situations where flow charts would be useful. showing how things are made; instructions for putting something together; directions for doing a job

 ### Geography

Location Focus children's attention on the distance between the tomato juice cannery and the tomato field. Help children conclude that the two must be relatively close so that the tomatoes do not start to spoil on the way and to keep transportation costs down.

Q. **Why would it cost more to move the tomatoes farther away?** You would have to pay for more gas. Also, because it would take longer, you would have to pay more to the people who move them.

Why may canned tomatoes be carried farther away than fresh tomatoes? because they will not spoil for a long time

Critical Thinking

Display the apple and applesauce you used with the rhyme in Access. Ask children to refer to the flow chart on pages 66–67 as a model for naming the steps for turning apples into applesauce. List the steps children mention. Their description should include the following ideas:

• Plant and care for apple trees.
• Pick the apples.
• Take the apples to a factory.
• Make applesauce and put it in containers.
• Take the applesauce to the store.

Productivity and Economic Growth
Read pages 68–69 with children, and have them identify the food items in the picture. Set up a four-column chart. In the first column, children should write the names of foods from the page and others they know about that must be kept cold. In the other columns, children can write names of foods that are frozen, canned, and dried. Challenge children to think of food names that can go in more than one column.

Visual Analysis

Interpret Pictures Discuss and list job titles for the person children see in the picture and have seen at their neighborhood grocery stores. Children's answers may include cashier, manager, bagger, stocker or shelver, meat cutter, baker, cake decorator, and clerk in deli, seafood, or bakery department. Elicit that the people buying food are called customers.

3. CLOSE

Ask each child to write one sentence to tell something he or she learned in this lesson. Some children may wish to share their sentences with the class.

Check Understanding

The child can
— recognize the many people who work to supply our daily needs.
— explain the steps in a flow chart that follows a food product from farm to market.
— describe the jobs of workers involved in food processing.

Foods come from all over the country and around the world. Fresh fruits and vegetables, meat, and milk products must be kept cold as they travel.

Foods may be changed before they are sent to stores. Workers freeze, can, or dry some foods.

68

ACTIVITY CHOICES

Link to Music

MELODY Brainstorm ways to change the song "She'll Be Comin' Round the Mountain" to reflect the five steps in the tomato (or other food) flow chart. Verses might start:
We'll be planting our tomatoes in the field…
We'll be picking our tomatoes in the field…
We'll be driving to the factory in our truck…
We'll be making our tomatoes into juice…
We'll be selling all the juice cans at the store…

After the food gets to the stores, more workers take care of it. Some make sure the food is still fresh. Others put the food where it belongs on the shelves. Other workers check out what you buy and take your money.

The last stop is your family's kitchen. As you enjoy your next meal, thank the many people who helped get it to you!

What Do You Know?

1. Where is tomato juice made? at a cannery
2. What is your favorite breakfast food? Who helps get it to you?

69

Extend and Enrich

DRAW NEW FLOW CHARTS
Invite children to work individually or with a partner to draw a flow chart showing the processing of other food products. Tell children they may break down the process into more than five steps if they wish. Possible end products include peanut butter, pumpkin pie, bread, cherry pie filling, grape jelly, and other canned, frozen, or dried foods.

Reteach the Main Idea

BUILD A FLOW CHART Have children cut apart the five pictures on the Performance Assessment flow chart. Provide square cards on which children can draw arrows. Invite children to shuffle their pieces and reconstruct the flow chart to show how corn is made into cornflakes. Or make a new set of picture or sentence cards, featuring tomatoes or another food, for children to sequence.

Think Critically

Q. **Why are some foods changed before they are sent to stores?** so they do not spoil; because people like to eat foods in different ways; because people don't have time to make many products themselves

In what ways do people depend on other people for food? Farmers need help picking crops, factory workers depend on farmers for food, customers depend on store workers to unpack and sell food, everyone needs transportation workers to move food.

Show What You Know

 Performance Assessment Provide children with art paper and invite them to draw a flow chart titled *From Corn to Cornflakes.* Remind them to draw an arrow from each step to the next.

What to Look For In evaluating children's flow charts, check for correct sequencing of steps based on the flow chart in the text, along with arrows that show how the steps flow from one to another.

Using the Activity Book Mention that many foods go through the process children read about in their books. On Activity Book page 13, children will fill in the missing pictures and captions to complete an oranges-to-orange-juice flow chart.

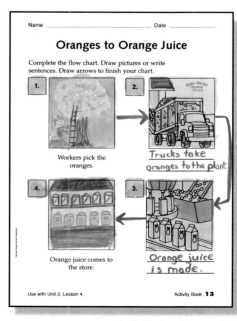

Activity Book page 13

LESSON 4 • 69

HANDS-ON OPTION

Want Ads

Objective: Recognize the many people who work to supply our daily needs.

Materials: classified newspaper section, paper, pencils

Help children list job titles for careers in the food industry. Then display newspaper want ads. Explain that people who need to hire a person for a job put ads in the newspaper. People who want to find a new job read the ads to see what jobs they can choose. Invite children to imagine that they own a food business. Have them write a want ad for a worker they need. Suggest that children name the job, tell what the worker must do, and list any qualifications the worker needs to have. Display the want ads on the bulletin board. **(VISUAL/TACTILE)**

Server Wanted

Take orders.
Serve food with a
    smile.
Must be fast and
    friendly.

Flow Chart for Shoppers

Objective: Explain the steps in a flow chart that follows a food product from farm to market.

Materials: paper, crayons or markers

Invite two volunteers to improvise a skit about grocery shopping. Following suggestions from the audience, the actors can show steps such as making a list, checking coupons, driving to the store, getting a cart, choosing groceries, paying a cashier, loading the car, driving home, and putting groceries away. When the skit is finished, have children make a flow chart to summarize what they saw. You may wish to repeat this activity with other processes, such as receiving, stocking, selling, bagging, and carrying out groceries in a grocery store. **(VISUAL/TACTILE)**

On the Job

Objective: Describe the jobs of workers involved in food processing.

Materials: paper plates, paper cups, food advertisements or magazines, scissors, glue

COOPERATIVE LEARNING Organize the class into groups and ask children to imagine they work in a factory that makes frozen meals. Have children work together to cut out pictures of different kinds of food from food advertisements or magazines, choosing meats, vegetables, and desserts, if possible. Then ask children to decide what steps will be needed to put the meals together, and have them plan an assembly line to accomplish the work. Suggest that children assign one task to each member of the group. Depending on the number of children in each group, the tasks might include taking one plate from a stack, gluing a main course (meat picture) on the plate, and gluing a vegetable picture on the plate. Have children use their assembly line to put together enough meals for each group member to have one to take home. **(KINESTHETIC)**

5

HOW TO MAKE AN APPLE PIE AND SEE THE WORLD

OBJECTIVES

1. Define *resource*.
2. Identify various natural resources.
3. Explain how people depend on resources.

VOCABULARY

resource (p. 71)

RESOURCES

Pupil Book/Unit Big Book, pp. 70–81
Write-On Charts 7, 29, 30
Activity Book, p. 14
Desk Maps
Text on Tape Audio
The Amazing Writing Machine

ACTIVITY CHOICES

Background

THE LITERATURE SELECTION
How to Make an Apple Pie and see the world is an American Library Association (ALA) Notable Children's Book. It is an adventure story that takes a girl to distant and exotic parts of the world in search of the resources she needs to follow the recipe for an apple pie—an excellent example of the relationship between geography and economics and the interdependence of people around the world.

Link to Language Arts

WRITE TO EXPLAIN Have each child choose an item from the chart the class made in Access. Invite children to use encyclopedias and atlases to identify the resources the item was made from and where they might have been found. Have children draw pictures or write a few sentences to tell what they have learned.

TECHNOLOGY

Use THE AMAZING WRITING MACHINE™ RESOURCE PACKAGE to complete this activity.

1. ACCESS

Organize children into small groups, and ask them to make a list of five things they use every day, such as a pencil, a bicycle, or a spoon. Then ask children to think about what these items are made of. Create a class chart as groups describe their items. List the items and the materials children think they are made of. Keep the chart on display for use throughout the lesson.

Focus on the Main Idea

In this lesson children will learn about resources. They will also learn how people depend on these resources.

Tell children that in the story they are about to read, they will look at a number of places around the world. This will help them understand how people everywhere use the land and the resources that come from the land. You may wish to name the countries children will be reading about and help them locate the countries on a globe.

2. BUILD

Key Content Summary

The Earth has an abundance of resources, including land, water, minerals, plants, and animals. Different areas of the Earth have different amounts and kinds of resources. People depend on resources to satisfy their needs.

Vocabulary

Define *resource* as something that is used to produce a good or service. Some resources are natural resources, which are found in nature. Invite children to give examples of natural resources and goods produced by using them. For example, trees are used to make paper; copper, nickel, and silver are used to make coins; soil is used to grow corn; water is used to produce crops.

Visual Analysis

Learn from Pictures Direct children's attention to the picture of the girl in Italy at harvest time, on page 72. Have them identify the resource they see on the page. Children should identify the wheat.

Q. **What other resources do you see in this story?** Responses should include a chicken, a cow, water, sugar cane, apples.

LESSON

5

Learn Geography through Literature

How to Make an Apple Pie and see the world

by Marjorie Priceman

70

ACTIVITY CHOICES

Reading Support

PREVIEWING AND READING THE LESSON Create a word web on the board with *Apple Pie* in the center oval. Have children look at the illustrations and scan the text to add to the web what they need to make an apple pie.

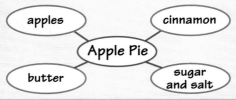

Link to Reading

IDENTIFY THE MAIN IDEA Tell children that the main idea of a selection or paragraph is often stated in the first few lines. Ask children to read the opening lines of the literature selection and to tell the main idea in their own words. Ask them to read to find examples of resources, or things we use from the Earth.

The earth gives us many resources. **Resources** are things people use to make what they need. Find out how you can use the whole world as a supermarket!

Making a pie is really very easy. First, get all the ingredients at the market. Mix them well, bake, and serve. Unless, of course, the market is closed.

In that case, go home and pack a suitcase. Take your shopping list and some walking shoes. Then catch a steamship bound for Europe. Use the six days on board to brush up on your Italian.

If you time it right, you'll arrive in Italy at harvest time. Find a farm deep in the countryside. Gather some superb semolina wheat. An armful or two will do.

Then hop a train to France and locate a chicken.

71

Discuss how people depend on resources to satisfy their basic needs. Mention that all the food we eat comes from plants and animals; our homes are built from trees, stone, and sand; and our clothes are made from cotton and wool.

Q. **How does the girl in the story depend on resources?** She needs the ingredients to make her apple pie.

Movement Point out that the girl in the book is traveling all over the world to get the things she needs to bake her apple pie. Explain that some countries have more resources than others; some environments produce one kind of resource but not another kind.

Q. **Where does the girl travel for each of the ingredients she needs? Why do you think she goes there?** Children should respond that the kurundu tree is found in the rain forest; Vermont produces apples; salt comes from seawater; and so on.

PUPIL BOOK OR UNIT BIG BOOK

AUDIO

Use the UNIT 2 TEXT ON TAPE AUDIOCASSETTE for the literature in this lesson.

Background

RESOURCES Everything the girl needs for her apple pie is produced in the United States except the cinnamon. The spice grows only in such countries as Sri Lanka, India, Brazil, and Jamaica.

Multicultural Link

Invite children to bring in foods from different cultures, such as tofu and baklava, and recipes that are typical of their own cultures. Challenge them to find out where each ingredient comes from.

Culture

Shared Humanity and Unique Identity
Direct children's attention to the picture of the girl in Italy at harvest time, on page 72. Have them identify the resource they see on the page (wheat).

Q. **What are the people in this picture doing?** They are singing and dancing in a wheat field.

How do you think they feel? happy

Tell children that people in all parts of the world celebrate harvest time. Have them tell what they know about the holidays Thanksgiving and Sukkot. Help children understand that both of these holidays were created to celebrate the land and the resources that people can get from the land.

Q. **Why do you think people are happy when they harvest wheat?** People use wheat to make bread and other foods for their families; farmers sell wheat to make money to buy things they need.

72

ACTIVITY CHOICES

Background

CINNAMON This popular spice, which comes from the inner bark of the cinnamon tree, is used mainly in baking and in flavoring candy. Sri Lanka is the principal source of the spice. However, cinnamon trees also grow in Brazil, India, Jamaica, Madagascar, and Martinique. The cinnamon tree grows as tall as 30 feet and has oval leaves and small yellow flowers. Cinnamon trees are pruned so that shoots grow up from the base. The shoots are gathered, and the inner bark is peeled off. As the bark dries, it turns brown and curls up. These curls of bark are sold as cinnamon sticks or ground up and sold as powdered cinnamon.

French chickens lay elegant eggs—and you want only the finest ingredients for your pie. Coax the chicken to give you an egg. Better yet, bring the chicken with you. There's less chance of breaking the egg that way.

Get to Sri Lanka any way you can.

You can't miss it. Sri Lanka is a pear-shaped island in the Indian Ocean. The best cinnamon in the world is made there, from the bark of the native kurundu tree. So go directly to the rain forest. Find a kurundu tree and peel off some bark. If a leopard is napping beneath the tree, be very quiet.

73

Visual Analysis

Interpret Pictures Direct children's attention to the picture of the girl in the boat, on page 73. Ask a volunteer to name the different natural resources the girl is using to sail her boat to Sri Lanka. Guide children to mention the wind that blows the sail, the water beneath the boat, the trees that were used to make the wooden boat, and the cotton that was used to make the sail.

Geography

Movement Have children discuss the different types of transportation the girl uses to gather the ingredients to make her apple pie. Explain that people use many kinds of transportation to move resources around the world.

The girl in the story uses a boat to get cinnamon from Sri Lanka.

Q. **What kind of transportation would you use to get cinnamon from the store?** Responses may include bus, car, taxi, bike, subway, train.

PUPIL BOOK OR UNIT BIG BOOK

Meet Individual Needs

ENGLISH LANGUAGE LEARNERS
If children have difficulty pronouncing *cinnamon*, invite them to work with a partner to list foods that have cinnamon as one of their ingredients. If necessary, guide them to think of cinnamon toast, cinnamon rolls, flan, and apple pie. Then have partners practice writing and saying sentences such as the following: *I like cinnamon toast. Flan is made with cinnamon. You need cinnamon to make apple pie.*

DESK MAPS

Use the DESK MAPS of the world to help children trace the girl's route as they follow the story of her journey.

Understanding the Story

The girl is still on her trip around the world, gathering ingredients for her apple pie. Explain that in each new place she goes to, the girl finds another resource. Invite children to create a two-column chart listing each place she visits and the resource she finds there.

Have children review pages 71–75.

Q. **What ingredients does the girl have so far?** wheat, eggs, cinnamon, milk, salt, sugar

Where did she find each of these ingredients? Italy, France, Sri Lanka, England, the sea, Jamaica

Geography

Regions Point out that the girl travels to different places to get her ingredients because those are the places thought to grow each thing the best. Invite children to work in small groups to discover what food resources are grown in their area, what those resources are used to make, and who buys and sells those resources. Ask groups to share what they learn.

Hitch a ride to England. Make the acquaintance of a cow. You'll know she's an English cow from her good manners and charming accent. Ask her if you can borrow a cup or two of milk. Even better, bring the whole cow with you for the freshest possible results.

Stow away on a banana boat headed home to Jamaica. On your way there, you can pick up some salt. Fill a jar with salty seawater.

When the boat docks in Jamaica, walk to the nearest sugar plantation. Introduce yourself to everyone. Tell them about the pie you're making. Then go into the fields and cut a few stalks of sugar cane.

74

ACTIVITY CHOICES

WRITE-ON CHARTS

Use **WRITE-ON CHART 29** to create a two-column chart on places and the resources we get from them.

Home Involvement

Have children look through cookbooks to find easy recipes that they might try at home. Suggest that they look for recipes that include cinnamon, apples, or other ingredients mentioned in the story. Children may also wish to find and try recipes that come from other countries. Allow children to copy out the recipes to take home. Invite those who make their dishes to report to the class on the results.

Better fly home. You don't
want the ingredients to spoil.

75

Economics

Economic Systems and Institutions
Review with children the different countries the girl has visited in the story. Remind them that different countries have different kinds of resources. Help them understand that some countries have many natural resources while other countries have few.

Q. **If one country has a lot of wheat and another country has none, what could the people of the two countries do?** The people of the country with a lot of wheat could sell wheat to the people of the country that has no wheat.

Geography

Place Direct children's attention to the illustration on page 75. Identify the location as a sugar cane field in Jamaica. Help children locate Jamaica on a globe, and tell them that the weather in Jamaica is very warm and that it rains a lot there. Explain that this kind of weather is just right for growing sugar cane. Guide children to understand that the kind of weather and the amount of water in a country can greatly affect the kind of food resources it can grow.

Background

MILK The milk cows produce is made into butter, ice cream, cheese, yogurt, and many other products. Cows are usually milked in the morning and again in the evening. Most cows are milked by machines, which pump the milk through hoses directly from the cows into a separate milk house. This process helps keep the milk clean. People in some countries use the milk of other animals, such as goats, sheep, camels, reindeer, and water buffaloes.

SUGAR All green plants make sugar, but most of the sugar people use comes from sugar cane. Sugar cane is a tall grass plant that grows best in places where the weather is very warm and rainy. The plant produces stalks 7 to 15 feet tall. These stalks contain a sugary juice from which sugar and syrup are made. Other sources of sugar include sugar beets and corn. Maple syrup and honey are sometimes used instead of sugar.

WRITE-ON CHARTS

A Great Garden
Use WRITE-ON CHART 7 to extend and enrich this lesson. See Teacher's Edition page W21.

Visual Analysis

Learn from Pictures Direct children to examine the illustration on page 76. Point out that the girl is now in an apple orchard in the state of Vermont.

Q. **What resources do you see in this picture?** Responses should include apples, trees, wheat and cinnamon in the bag, the cow and its milk, and the chicken and its eggs.

Guide children to recognize that the land, wind, and sunshine are also resources that people depend on to meet their needs. Open a discussion about what resources were used to build the houses in the background and the ladder the girl is climbing.

Understanding the Story

After children read page 77, invite them to create their own shopping lists for apple pie ingredients. Then ask them to review the story to see if the girl has all the ingredients she needs to make an apple pie.

Q. **What do you think the girl is going to do now?** go home and make her apple pie

76

ACTIVITY CHOICES

Meet Individual Needs

ENGLISH LANGUAGE LEARNERS
Provide children with art supplies, and invite them to draw a separate picture of each of the ingredients listed in the story. Have them make flash cards by cutting out each picture and taping it onto an index card. As children identify each ingredient in the recipe, help them write the name in English on the reverse side of the card. Have children review the cards with a partner who speaks English fluently.

Link to Language Arts

JOURNAL Invite children to write a review of this story in their journals. Have them tell why they liked the story and something they learned from it. Children might also comment on which place in the story they found most interesting. Discuss how reading about people's travels is a way to learn about other places without traveling there in person.

Wait a minute. Aren't you forgetting something? WHAT ABOUT THE APPLES? Have the pilot drop you off in Vermont.

You won't have to go far to find an apple orchard. Pick eight rosy apples from the top of the tree. Give one to the chicken, one to the cow, and eat one yourself. That leaves five for the pie. Then hurry home.

Understanding the Story

Ask children to scan the text on page 77 to find out how many apples the girl takes from the orchard. Children should discover that she picks eight apples.

Q. **How many apples will go in the pie?** five

How many does that leave? three

What does the girl do with the extra apples? She gives one to the chicken and one to the cow, and she keeps one for herself.

Economics

Scarcity and Choice Remind children that everyone on the Earth depends on the same resources. So people should not waste resources but take only what they need. Ask children to take another look at the illustration on page 76.

Q. **How many apples do you think are in the orchard?** Responses will vary.

Why do you think the girl takes only eight apples? That's all she needs for her friends, herself, and her pie; she does not want to waste the apples.

Background

APPLES There are many varieties of apples. They grow in various shades of red, green, and yellow, and the flavor varies from tart to sweet. Apples are one of the most popular fruits. More than half the apples grown (over 2 billion bushels around the world every year) are eaten fresh. Apples can be baked in desserts and used to make apple butter, apple juice, applesauce, apple jelly, and many other products. Apples are 85 percent water and rich in vitamins A and C.

Link to World Languages

OTHER LANGUAGES Children might enjoy hearing the word *apple* in other languages.

pomme (PUHM)—French
ringo (RING•YO)—Japanese
yabloko (YA•bluh•kuh)—Russian
mi´lo (MEE•lou)—Greek
tuffaha (too•FA•hah)—Arabic
mela (MEE•luh)—Italian
apfel (AHP•fel)—German
manzana (man•SAHN•ah)—Spanish
pihnggwo (PING•GWO)—Cantonese

Understanding the Story

The girl is now taking the resources she has gathered on her trip and turning them into the products she needs to make her pie. Guide children to study each picture on pages 78–79. Have them name each resource and the product being made from it.

History

Past to Present Inform children that people could not always buy items like butter and flour at the grocery store. Explain that in the early days of our country, many people had to make their own butter and grind wheat into flour. Help children understand that in some parts of the world, people still must make most of their own foods.

Q. **If you lived on a farm, what could you do to get fresh eggs?** I could raise chickens.

Now all you have to do is mill the wheat into flour,

grind the kurundu bark into cinnamon,

evaporate the seawater from the salt,

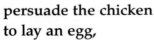

boil the sugar cane,

persuade the chicken to lay an egg,

78

ACTIVITY CHOICES

Background

SALT FROM SEAWATER Seawater is salty because rainwater dissolves minerals on the land, and rivers carry these minerals to the sea. Evaporating seawater (as the girl is doing on page 78) is the oldest method of obtaining salt. Salt that is gathered this way is often called solar salt. Most solar salt is produced in Europe and Asia. Salt that is found in the ground is called rock salt. Huge layers of salt were formed when large parts of the world's oceans dried up millions of years ago. Underground salt deposits are found on every continent in the world.

Background

CHURNING BUTTER No one knows exactly when people first made butter. It is known that people in India churned butter from the milk of water buffaloes as early as 2000 B.C. People in many parts of the world, including the United States, used to make their own butter in churns. A churn is a container with a long paddle. You pour cream into the container and use the paddle to churn, or beat, the cream until little drops of butter start to form. If the cream is churned long enough, it becomes butter and buttermilk. Today factories called creameries make butter and send it to grocery stores for consumers to buy.

milk the cow,

churn the milk
into butter,

slice the apples,

mix the ingredients,
and bake the pie.

While the pie is cooling, invite some
friends over to share it with you.

Remember that apple pie is delicious
topped with vanilla ice cream, which you
can get at the market. But if the market
happens to be closed . . .

79

Recite Ask children to skim the story again. Name a place, and ask for volunteers to tell what resource the girl finds there. Then ask children to name the product the girl makes from that resource. Write the information in a three-column chart on the board or on chart paper. Title the first column *Place*, the second column *Resource*, and the third column *Product*. (Some resources will not have a product to list.) Continue until each ingredient for the apple pie is listed on the chart. Children may wish to consult the two-column chart they started early in the lesson to help them complete this chart.

Kinesthetic Learning

Act Out the Story Invite volunteers to read the story aloud. Other children can act out the parts of the girl and some of the people and animals she meets on her journey around the world. You may wish to reassign roles every two or three pages to give more children an opportunity to participate.

PUPIL BOOK OR UNIT BIG BOOK

Link to Science

OBSERVATION Invite children to take part in making butter in class. Pour a pint of heavy whipping cream into a plastic container with a tight lid. (There should be room for the cream to shake around in it.) Then pass the container around, and allow each child to shake either to a count of 20 or until he or she gets tired. When the butter has formed, allow those who are interested to taste the buttermilk. (Check for allergies to milk products first.) The butter will be sweet butter. Salt some of it, and allow children to sample both kinds on crackers.

Link to Mathematics

MEASUREMENT Write the following recipe for an apple pie filling on the board: 2 cups sliced apples, 1 cup sugar, 1 teaspoon cinnamon, 1/4 teaspoon salt, 2 tablespoons butter. Distribute an assortment of measuring cups and spoons. Ask children to line up the tools to show the amounts of ingredients needed in order from the greatest to the least.

WRITE-ON CHARTS

Use WRITE-ON CHART 30 to create a three-column chart on places, the resources that come from those places, and the products made from those resources.

Visual Analysis

Learn from Pictures   Have children discuss the illustration on pages 80–81.

Q. **What is going on in the picture?** The girl and her friends are eating apple pie.

Help children understand that the people and animals around the table are the characters the girl met on her journey around the world. Suggest that children take another look at the pictures in the story to tell where each person is from.

Q. **Where did the girl meet the boy with the orange shirt and black cap?** He was riding a bicycle in France.

What resource did he help her find? chicken, eggs

Economics

Markets and Prices   Point out that the story is fiction and that most bakers get their ingredients from local markets or food suppliers.

Q. **Do you think you would have trouble finding any of these ingredients where you live? Why or why not?** Probably not; most markets carry these items.

Scarcity and Choice   Discuss the importance of replacing resources that we use. For example, a farmer puts nutrients back into the soil after harvesting to prepare it for next year's planting season. Guide children to understand that we must not waste our resources.

Q. **Why do you think it is important to use resources wisely?** Careful use will make sure that we have enough to last a long time.

3. CLOSE

Have children look through books and magazines to find examples of resources. Ask children to name each resource and tell how people depend on it.

Check Understanding

The child can
___ define *resource*.
___ identify various natural resources.
___ explain how people depend on resources.

80

ACTIVITY CHOICES

Community Involvement

Invite a local baker to visit the classroom to demonstrate making an apple pie. Ask volunteers to write the ingredients on chart paper as the baker uses them in the pie. Have children interview the baker to discover where he or she gets each ingredient. Have volunteers record this information on the chart.

Meet Individual Needs

ADVANCED LEARNERS
Have children use reference books to look up interesting facts about each country the girl visited in the story. Ask them to make a list of the resources each country produces.

YOU CAN EAT IT PLAIN!

What Do You Know?

What resources were needed for the pie?
wheat, kurundu bark, seawater, sugar cane,
chicken, cow, apples

81

PUPIL BOOK OR UNIT BIG BOOK

Extend and Enrich

DIAGRAM TRANSPORTATION
Have children work in groups to list all
the forms of transportation found in
the story. Invite them to make a diagram showing how the girl traveled
from place to place.

Reteach the Main Idea

FIND MAIN IDEAS Review
the major concepts of the literature by asking children to name a
resource the girl in the story goes
in search of and tell how she
prepares it to use in her pie.

Think Critically

Q. **How do people around the world
share resources?** Children should
say that people use resources that
come from many different places.
Countries that have many resources
often sell or trade them to other
countries.

**What can we do to make sure we
have enough resources?** Children
should respond that we need to
save or replace our resources.

Show What You Know

Performance Assessment Ask children to think of something they
use every day. Then have them
invent a story from the object's point of
view, telling what it is made of, where the
resources are found, and why it is important
to its owner. Invite them to write or draw
their story or tell it to a group of classmates.

What to Look For You may assist children in identifying the source of their
objects, but they should be able to describe
the resources used to make it and express
an understanding of their dependence on
resources.

Using the Activity Book Distribute a
copy of Activity Book page 14 to each child.
Invite children to write a few sentences to
describe the things they have at home that
are made from the resources shown.

Name _____ Date _____

Using Resources

Look at the resources on the left. Write about
things at your home that are made from
these resources.

1. chair
   baseball bat
   house

2. water the yard
   fish tank
   drinking water

3. cereal
   popcorn

14 Activity Book   Use with Unit 2, Lesson 5.

Activity Book page 14

HANDS-ON OPTION

Resource Recipes

Objective: Explain how people depend on resources.

Materials: cookbooks, magazines, paper, crayons

Invite children to work with a partner to find or make up a simple recipe. Have them list the ingredients and decide what resource is needed for each one. Children can create pictures to go with their recipes. (TACTILE/VISUAL)

Banana Bread	
flour	wheat stalks
butter	cow
eggs	chicken
water	ocean
sugar	sugarcane stalks
bananas	banana tree

Exploring a Resource

Objective: Explain how people depend on resources.

Materials: paper, crayons or markers

Invite children to work in small groups to explore one resource. Have them think about ways in which people depend upon that resource. Ask children to draw pictures of how people use that resource. (TACTILE/VISUAL)

Compare Resources

Objectives: Define *resource*. Identify various natural resources.

Ask partners to select one of the scenes from the book and describe it. Then have each child find on the page one item that is a natural resource. Ask partners to continue until each child has found a natural resource. (AUDITORY)

Johnny Appleseed

Objectives: Define resource. Explain how people depend on resources.

Materials: tree saplings

Share with children the story of John Chapman—Johnny Appleseed. Chapman planted a large number of apple trees along the early American frontier. He traveled throughout Ohio and Indiana, planting apple orchards as settlers moved west. Legend has it that Chapman gave everyone he met apple seeds or apple saplings; he wore a tin pot for a hat, a coffee sack for a shirt, and no shoes. Invite children to discuss benefits of Chapman's deeds. Then provide a tree sapling for each child or several for the class. (These can often be obtained from your local Soil Conservation Service or Agricultural Extension office.) Help children plant the trees on school property. Discuss with children how planting trees today will help the environment in the future. (AUDITORY)

READ A TABLE

OBJECTIVES

1. Identify the parts of a table.
2. Practice reading a table.
3. Draw logical conclusions about resources and goods from a table.

VOCABULARY

table (p. 82)

RESOURCES

Pupil Book/Unit Big Book, pp. 82–83
Write-On Chart 7
Activity Book, p. 15
Transparencies 5, 20, 21

ACTIVITY CHOICES

Meet Individual Needs

ENGLISH LANGUAGE LEARNERS
Point out that the word *table* has more than one meaning. Help children understand the difference between the table on page 83 and a table they would find at home. Ask children to draw a picture to show each meaning of the word and to write a simple sentence for each picture.

Link to Mathematics

DATA Create a table on the board using the days of the week for the column heads and the names of special school activities, such as gym, music, computers, and art, for the row heads. Ask children to identify on which days of the week they have each special activity and mark an X in the appropriate row and column on the table. Discuss how this table is used to classify information.

TRANSPARENCY

Use TRANSPARENCY 5.

---

1. ACCESS

Ask children to locate the Table of Contents at the beginning of their books. Explain that this is one type of table and that it lists the units and lessons in the order in which they appear in the book. Ask children if they can tell about other types of tables that are used to list information. Call on volunteers to tell where and when they may have seen and used tables and to describe how they were arranged. If children do not suggest it, remind them of how tables can be used to list data in mathematics and science.

Kinesthetic Learning

Ask children to suggest categories of distinguishing characteristics for members of your class. hair color; eye color; color of clothing; right- or left-handedness Use the categories to write column heads on the board. Then invite children to form a human table by lining up under the appropriate heads.

2. BUILD

Visual Analysis

Learn from Tables Have children look at page 83 and identify the table. Invite volunteers to describe how the table is arranged. Help children recognize that this table has columns and rows arranged in a rectangular shape and that symbols and words are used to represent the information about resources.

Q. **How do you know what this table shows?** A title is at the top and the columns and rows are labeled.

How do you read this table? For each resource listed in the left column, you read across the row to find the goods made from it.

Guide children in answering the questions on page 82.

Economics

Scarcity and Choice Focus attention on the row of goods made from oil. Ask children to identify the goods made from this natural resource. Explain that many other goods come from oil, including oil for heating homes, ink for printing books, and wax for making candles. Discuss the consequences of running out of oil and the conservation efforts that can help protect our oil supplies.

Geography

Human-Environment Interactions Focus attention on the four resources. Help children understand that these resources are found in different regions of the United States. Display a United States map that shows rivers and lakes. Show children where the most important deposits of iron ore are found (near Lake Superior in Minnesota and Michigan).

Q. **Why do you think transportation is important?** Transportation takes resources from where they are found to where they are needed.

Chart and Graph Skills

Read a Table

In <u>How to Make an Apple Pie and see the world</u>, you read about things we use from the Earth. You can use a kind of list called a **table** to find out about other important resources.

1 Read the title of the table. What does this table show? goods made from resources

2 What four resources are listed in the table? trees, oil, wheat, iron

3 Name two goods made from wheat. flour, cereal, pasta, pet food

4 What resource is needed to make plastic toys? oil

Think and Do

Some goods are listed more than once in the table. Which goods are made with more than one resource?

82

ACTIVITY CHOICES

Meet Individual Needs

VISUAL LEARNERS Display a map or transparency of the United States to locate Minnesota, Michigan, and Lake Superior. Invite volunteers to find out where the other resources listed on the table can be found. Children can then locate the states or regions on the map.

TRANSPARENCY

Use TRANSPARENCIES 20 and 21 to locate Lake Superior and the surrounding areas.

Goods Made from Resources

Resources	Goods			
trees	furniture	books	medicines	pencils
oil	fuel	plastic toys	pipes	medicines
wheat	flour	cereal	pasta	pet food
iron	paper clips	fire hydrant	pipes	tools

83

Extend and Enrich

MAKE A TABLE Display Write-On Chart 7, and invite small groups of children to choose two or three resources. Have children make a table of goods that come from those resources.

Reteach the Main Idea

PLAY A GAME Invite children to play a game of Resource or Good. Have each child write *resource* on one side of an index card and *good* on the other side. As you name an item from the table on page 83, invite children to hold up the side of the card that describes it. If the item named is a resource, ask volunteers to give names of goods made from it. If the item is a good, have volunteers name the resource(s) it is made from. Repeat the activity several times.

3. CLOSE

Think and Do

Children should identify tools and medicines as goods made from two different resources. Have children who need additional practice reading a table name two goods made from iron.

Review the skill with children by asking the following questions:

Q. **How does a table help you learn?** A lot of information is organized in one place so that you can easily read and understand it.

How is information organized on a table? Information is listed in columns and rows.

Using the Activity Book Distribute copies of Activity Book page 15. Have children follow the directions as they read the table. After children complete numbers 1–4, you may wish to invite pairs of children to discuss various goods that come from their chosen resource and to complete number 5.

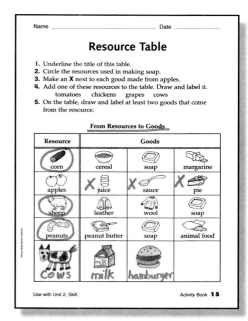

Activity Book page 15

HANDS-ON OPTION

Shopping for Goods

Objectives: Identify the parts of a table. Practice reading a table. Draw logical conclusions about resources and goods from a table.

Materials: Teacher's Edition page 83B, scissors, glue, pencils, crayons

Distribute copies of Teacher's Edition page 83B. Invite volunteers to read aloud the directions and then the names of the stores in the first column. Select one of the rows and ask children to name other kinds of goods that might go in that row. Invite children to select two of the items mentioned and draw them in the last two spaces of that row. If necessary, help children think of a name for their table and tell them to write it in the space provided. Then have children work with a partner to read and answer the questions at the bottom of the page. **(VISUAL/TACTILE/AUDITORY)**

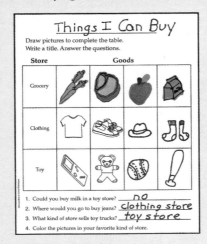

Holiday Traditions

Objectives: Practice reading a table. Draw logical conclusions about resources and goods from a table.

Materials: paper, rulers, pencils or crayons, copies of a table grid (optional)

Invite children to name their favorite holidays and tell how their families celebrate them. Write the names of the holidays on the board. Then have children draw a table to show their three favorite holidays and at least three things they like to do or each of those holidays. Have children trade tables with a classmate, and challenge the classmate to explain to a small group what the owner of the table enjoys most about the holidays.
(TACTILE/VISUAL/AUDITORY)

Favorite Foods

Objectives: Identify the parts of a table. Practice reading a table. Draw logical conclusions about resources and goods from a table.

Materials: cookbooks, posterboard, scissors, glue, markers, copy of the food pyramid (optional)

 Invite small groups of children to look through cookbooks and plan a menu of dishes made with foods all children in the group like. Have each group construct a table to show the ingredients in the dishes they chose. Ask children to write the names of their dishes in the first column and to draw a picture of each dish below its name. Have them write or draw some of the ingredients in the row to the right of each dish. Groups who include apple pie in their menu may want to look back at the story *How to Make an Apple Pie and see the world* for ideas. Post the completed menu tables in the room. Invite children to compare their tables to see how many selected the same dishes and how many different dishes used the same ingredients. Challenge children to evaluate the ingredients in each food to see which are the most healthful.

Then display a copy of the food pyramid. Point out that a healthful meal would include at least one food from each category on the pyramid. Challenge children to determine whether or not their menus are healthful.
(VISUAL/TACTILE/AUDITORY)

Draw pictures to complete the table.
Write a title. Answer the questions.

Store	Goods			
Grocery				
Clothing				
Toy				

1. Could you buy milk in a toy store? _____

2. Where would you go to buy jeans? _____

3. What kind of store sells toy trucks? _____

4. Color the pictures in your favorite kind of store.

Harcourt Brace School Publishers

DEFINE THE PROBLEM

Invite children to study the photos on Pupil Book pages 84–85 and tell what they see. Guide them to connect the picture of the produce market with the store owners who purchase fruit from farmers, the conveyer belt with the factory that makes orange juice, and the supermarket shelf with the people who buy oranges.

Q. What happened to the orange in the top picture? It is frozen; it is covered in ice.

What happens to plants outside after a freeze? They die; they turn brown and rot.

Do you think anyone would buy oranges that are brown and rotten? No, they would not be good to eat.

As you read the text on page 84, explain that Carlos's family sells oranges to make money. Ask a volunteer to tell how the store owner and the juice company also depend on the oranges to make money. Help children understand that all the people who help bring foods to market depend on each other.

Q. Suppose there was a freeze where the Diaz family and others have their orange groves. How might that affect you? There might not be very many oranges at the store for my family to buy.

Guide children to think about how their lives would be different if people did not grow and sell foods.

Q. What would happen if there were no farmers? We would have to grow all of our food ourselves; there would not be enough food for everyone.

❝ PRIMARY SOURCE ❞

Invite a local farmer or someone from your county extension office to come to the classroom. Suggest that children ask questions about the crops grown in your area and how they are affected by the weather.

Solving Problems

What Would Happen If . . .

Carlos Diaz's family owns an orange grove. They sell some of their oranges to stores. They sell the rest to companies that make orange juice.

In a group, talk about what would happen if there were a freeze. A freeze is very cold weather that spoils the oranges.

- What would the freeze do to the Diaz family?
- What would the freeze do to the store owners and the juice company?
- What would the freeze do to people who buy oranges and orange juice?

Show What Would Happen

- Write what each person would say about the frozen oranges.
- Write a newspaper story about the freeze.
- Draw before-and-after pictures to show what a freeze does to the trees and the oranges.

84

ACTIVITY CHOICES

Background

ORANGES Christopher Columbus brought orange seeds to America during his explorations in 1493. However, even in the early 1900s, oranges were still rare and expensive. People ate them only as a special treat on holidays and during celebrations. Today, thanks to improved growing methods, people can enjoy oranges and orange juice all year long. In fact, more than 15 million pounds of oranges are harvested in the United States every year—more than any other fruit.

Link to Science

OBSERVATION Pull a few leaves from a classroom plant and tell children that you are going to put them in the freezer overnight. Bring the leaves to class the following day to show children the effect cold weather has on vegetation. Explain that a freeze happens when the temperature drops below 32°F. Remind children that this is the temperature at which water freezes.

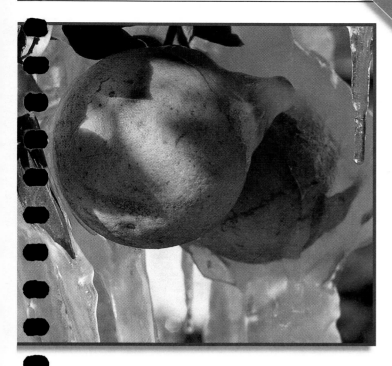

USE PROBLEM-SOLVING SKILLS

Organize children into groups. Suggest that each group choose a person to be the group recorder. Ask the group to study the photos and list ways people use oranges. Then ask them to read and discuss the questions on page 84. After the recorder writes their answers, have them make another list of people who might be affected by a freeze at the Diaz family orange grove.

Q. What would you do if it were your orange grove? try to keep the orange trees warm

Do you think it would be easy or hard to grow oranges? Responses will vary.

SHOW SOLUTIONS

Provide children with paper, pencils, and crayons or markers. Invite groups to read the suggestions on page 84, and allow them to choose one of these ways or some other way to show what happens when there is a freeze. Groups can share their work with the rest of the class.

85

PUPIL BOOK **OR** UNIT BIG BOOK

Meet Individual Needs

ADVANCED LEARNERS Tape a portion of a nightly TV news program to show weather-related problems, such as floods, droughts, or windstorms. Ask children to identify weather and natural disasters that cause problems for farmers. Then have them write about how an event that occurs far away might affect them and their families. For example, tell children that most of the corn grown in the United States comes from Iowa. Ask what might happen if Iowa received very little rain one summer.

Meet Individual Needs

VISUAL LEARNERS Use dominoes to help children understand how one event can start a chain reaction. Draw a line down the middle of a sheet of craft paper. Graph events along the line at one-inch intervals, such as "Oranges Freeze," "Diaz Family Cannot Sell Oranges," "Store Has No Oranges," and "People Cannot Buy Oranges." Place a domino at each point on the line and invite a volunteer to push the first domino over. Have children discuss the results.

Link to Art

ILLUSTRATION Tell children that most oranges in the United States are grown in Florida and California because of the warm weather there. Invite them to research another fruit or vegetable to find out where it is grown. Have children draw a picture of the fruit or vegetable and write below it the name of the state or states in which it is grown.

Demeter and Persephone

The ancient Greeks invented stories to explain why things happen in the world. We call these stories myths, because people today do not believe them. The myth below tells why food is grown at certain times of the year and why the seasons change. As you discuss the story, help children understand the scientific explanation for seasons and the weather patterns that affect crop production.

Demeter was the goddess of the harvest, the gathering of ripe fruits and vegetables. People loved Demeter because she was kind and generous and gave them plenty of food. It was because of her that corn and other grains grew in the fields, and the earth was green.

Demeter had a daughter, called Persephone, whom she loved very much. One day, Hades, the god of the underworld, was riding over the earth, and he saw Persephone. She was so beautiful and friendly that he fell in love with her and asked her to marry him. But she loved her mother and the beautiful earth she lived on, and she didn't want to go with him.

Hades didn't care. He swooped her into his chariot and carried her down into the underworld. Persephone was scared and very unhappy. Oh, how she longed to be with her mother, and run across the bright green fields.

Soon Demeter noticed Persephone was gone, and raised a cry of alarm. Demeter searched and searched for her. Apollo, the god of the sun, told Demeter he had seen Hades carry Persephone off.

Demeter became very sad. She no longer cared for her beautiful earth or the bright yellow grains that were her treasure. She went off by herself to weep for her daughter. And the earth became cold and bare. The golden corn died. Soon the people everywhere became hungry, because they had no grain or fruit to eat.

And so Zeus, the ruler of all the gods, told Demeter that she could get Persephone back from the underworld.

But Hades loved Persephone and didn't want to let her go. So he gave Persephone a special pomegranate, a fruit red on the outside like an apple but full of small fruit-covered seeds on the inside. Because Persephone ate part of the pomegranate, she had to stay in the underworld with Hades for part of every year. And during these months, the earth gets cold, winter comes, and the plants retreat into the earth, just like Persephone. But when Persephone returns from Hades, spring comes and flowers bloom, and Demeter makes the earth bright with her happiness. This, the Greeks thought, is why the earth is cold during the winter, and warmer in the rest of the year.

6

CARING FOR THE EARTH

OBJECTIVES

1. Identify precious resources.
2. Define *conservation*.
3. Draw logical conclusions about the importance of protecting our land and resources.

VOCABULARY

conservation (p. 86)

RESOURCES

Pupil Book/Unit Big Book, pp. 86–89

Write-On Charts 8, 33

Pattern P4

Activity Book, p. 16

The Amazing Writing Machine

Imagination Express: Destination Rain Forest

ACTIVITY CHOICES

Link to Reading

POETRY   Read "Trees" by Sara Coleridge.

The Oak is called the king of trees,
The Aspen quivers in the breeze,
The Poplar grows up straight and tall,
The Peach tree spreads along the wall,
The Sycamore gives pleasant shade,
The Willow droops in watery glade,
The Fir tree useful timber gives,
The Beech amid the forest lives.

Suggest other trees that children might write about to add to this poem, such as birch, dogwood, elm, magnolia, maple, pecan, and redwood.

1. ACCESS

Remind children that a natural resource is a resource found in nature that helps people meet their needs. Help children identify air, water, and land as the most important natural resources. Challenge children to list other resources found in the region where they live. List children's responses on the board.

Focus on the Main Idea

In this lesson children will identify what *precious* resources are and explain why they must be protected. They will learn the meaning of *conservation* and consider what they can do to help. Tell children that in this lesson they will read an interview with a park ranger who helps take care of the Earth.

Link to Language Arts

WRITE A LETTER   Have children write a letter requesting information about how resources can be protected.

Friends of the Earth
1025 Vermont Ave.
Washington, DC 20005-3516

Kids Against Pollution
P.O. Box 22
Newport, NY 13416

Renew America
1400 16th St. NW
Washington, DC 20036

TECHNOLOGY

Use THE AMAZING WRITING MACHINE™ to complete this activity.

2. BUILD

Key Content Summary

The Earth's resources help support life. Plants, animals, water, soil, sunlight, and the air we breathe are all precious resources. For life to continue, we must use our resources wisely.

Geography

Human-Environment Interactions Explain that Ranger Monroe works at Muir Woods National Monument near San Francisco, California. Help children find the approximate location on a map. Then have children look at the photos on the lesson pages. Ask them to describe the land and its features and to identify the resources they see.

Q. What might happen if there were no rangers at the park?
People, plants, and animals might get hurt.

History

People and Events Across Time and Place Explain that Muir Woods National Monument is part of the National Parks System. Explain that the forest was named after the explorer and writer John Muir, who worked to protect forests. Explain that forests are precious because they are home to many plants and animals, are a source of wood, and put oxygen into the air we breathe.

LESSON 6 Caring for the Earth

My name is Nikko and I love trees. I have the largest collection of leaves in my second-grade class. Last week, I talked with a park ranger named Mia Monroe. We talked about conservation. **Conservation** is taking care of resources, such as the forest.

Nikko

Here are some things I found out about the job of a park ranger.

Nikko: Where do you work?

Ranger Monroe: I work in a national park. A national park is a place where the land and animals are protected. Visitors can see many kinds of plants and animals there.

86

ACTIVITY CHOICES

Reading Support

PREVIEW AND PREDICT Explain to children that they are going to read an interview. Ask them to tell what an interview is. Then invite them to scan the pages, looking at the pictures. Explain that the names written at the beginning of many of the paragraphs tell who is speaking. Ask children what questions they might want to ask a park ranger.

Link to Science

INTERDEPENDENCE OF LIFE Explain that carbon dioxide is a gas produced by people and animals when they breathe out. Green plants and trees take carbon dioxide from the air and give off oxygen, which people and animals need to live. Help children draw a picture to illustrate the cycle. Discuss with children what might happen to the Earth if all the trees were cut down.

Link to Art

GRAPHIC ART Display materials about the National Park System in your state. Ask children who have visited any of these sites to share their experiences. Then invite children to create advertisements that would make children in other parts of the country want to come for a visit.

Nikko: What do you like best about being a ranger?

Ranger Monroe: My favorite part of the job is telling children about the plants and wildlife in the forest.

Nikko: What else do you do?

Ranger Monroe: I look for people and animals that might need help. I collect water and soil samples to test. I also make sure that people follow the rules of the park.

87

Civics and Government

Civic Values and Democratic Principles
Explain that when Theodore Roosevelt was President, he invited political leaders, business people, and scientists to an important conference. These people came up with new laws to make sure that our nation's resources are used wisely.

Q. **Why do you think it is important to have laws about how to use resources?** If there were no laws, people might use up or waste our resources.

> **"PRIMARY SOURCE"**
>
> To waste, to destroy, our natural resources, to skin and exhaust the land instead of using it so as to increase its usefulness, will result in undermining in the days of our children the very prosperity which we ought by right to hand down to them amplified and developed.
>
> *President Theodore Roosevelt's Message to Congress [December 3, 1907]*

Vocabulary

Explain that protecting precious resources from being wasted or destroyed is one example of *conservation*. Conservation also means managing and using our resources wisely.

Q. **What are some resources we should conserve, or use wisely? Why?** Responses should include water, oil, trees, animals, soil, air;

PUPIL BOOK OR UNIT BIG BOOK

Link to Mathematics

ADDITION AND SUBTRACTION
Tell children that the average American will use about seven trees a year in products made from trees. Ask children to calculate how many trees they have used so far in their lifetime.

Background

NATIONAL PARK SERVICE The National Park Service is a bureau of the United States Department of the Interior. Its main objective is to conserve and preserve natural wildlife, scenery, and historic sites in more than 350 areas.

WRITE-ON CHARTS

Use WRITE-ON CHART 33 to help children find and mark the approximate location of Muir Woods National Monument and other national parks.

some resources can never be replaced, and some take a long time to be replaced.

What are some ways you can use resources wisely? Responses may include not wasting water, turning off lights, recycling.

Economics

Scarcity and Choice Ask children to review the photos of the forest.

Q. **How do you think this area might look today if it had not been made a national park?** Responses might include that cities and towns, roads and highways, airports and railroads might have replaced the forest.

3. CLOSE

Ask children to form groups of three or four. Invite them to summarize the lesson by creating conservation slogans. Slogans should identify precious resources and explain the importance of protecting them. Invite children to make posters for their slogans and display them around the room.

Check Understanding

The child can
- identify precious resources.
- define *conservation*.
- draw logical conclusions about the importance of protecting our land and resources.

Nikko: What are some of the rules of the park?

Ranger Monroe: People must not litter, pick flowers, or cut down trees. They must not tease or harm the animals. The rules protect the park so everyone can enjoy it.

Nikko: What tools do you use in your job?

Ranger Monroe: I use maps, a compass, and a two-way radio. I also use binoculars to help me watch the forest.

88

Biography

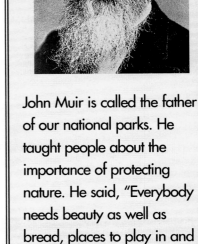

John Muir is called the father of our national parks. He taught people about the importance of protecting nature. He said, "Everybody needs beauty as well as bread, places to play in and pray in, where nature may heal and give strength to body and soul alike."

ACTIVITY CHOICES

Extend and Enrich

WRITE A REPORT Explain that many animals are endangered; that is, all of their kind are at risk of dying off. Provide children with a list of endangered animals. Challenge them to choose one and write a report telling why it is endangered and what people can do to help. Help children express the fact that animals share our planet and its resources, too. Children can draw a picture showing their animal.

Reteach the Main Idea

PLAY A CONSERVATION GAME Play a game of Thumbs Up, Thumbs Down with children. Gather them in a circle, and start the game by stating a rule of the forest, such as *Visitors should remember to bring enough food to feed the animals.* Children must decide if the rule is an example of conservation or not by showing the thumbs up or thumbs down sign. Continue until all children in the circle have stated a rule that is either true or false.

WRITE-ON CHARTS

Reduce, Reuse, Recycle
Use WRITE-ON CHART 8 to extend and enrich this lesson. See Teacher's Edition page W25.

TECHNOLOGY

Use IMAGINATION EXPRESS:™ DESTINATION RAIN FOREST to complete this activity.

Ranger Monroe told me that some park rangers watch the forest for fires. In towers high above the trees, rangers look through binoculars for any sign of smoke.

It is important for visitors and park rangers to work together to keep the forest safe.

Fire tower

What Do You Know?

1. **What is Mia Monroe's job?** park ranger

2. **What questions do you have about conservation?**

89

PUPIL BOOK OR UNIT BIG BOOK

Link Literature

Invite children to read *Rachel Carson* by William Accorsi (Holiday House, 1993), the story of a woman who loved nature and worked to make the Earth a healthful place to live. Ask children to share what they learn from the book.

RACHEL CARSON

written and illustrated by
WILLIAM ACCORSI

Think Critically

Q. **Would you want to be a park ranger? Why or why not?** Children's answers should show that they understand the duties and responsibilities of a park ranger.

How would you explain to someone who is visiting a national park the importance of obeying the rules? Rules protect the animals, plants, and people from harm.

Show What You Know

Performance Assessment Ask children to prepare a list of interview questions they would ask someone who is in charge of taking care of precious resources. Then have children take turns assuming the roles of the interviewer and the person being interviewed.

What to Look For In evaluating children's performances, look for evidence of their understanding of the importance of protecting and conserving precious resources.

Using the Activity Book Invite children to study the scene on Activity Book page 16 and draw a circle around people who are not using the forest wisely. For each circle, have children write on the sign a rule for keeping the forest clean and safe. Children may also wish to color the picture.

Activity Book page 16

HANDS-ON OPTION

A Precious Resource Book

Objective: Draw logical conclusions about the importance of protecting our land and resources.

Materials: magazines, paper, pencils, construction paper, scissors, paste, three-hole punch, yarn

Organize children into small groups, and invite them to find pictures of natural resources in magazines. Have children cut out the pictures and paste them on separate sheets of construction paper. Ask children to list above each picture some ways people use the resource to meet their needs. Have them list below the picture some ways to protect the resource. Help children put the pages together to create a "Precious Resource Book." Children can work together to create a cover for the book. **(TACTILE)**

Public Service Announcement

Objective: Define conservation.

Materials: pamphlets on local conservation programs, audiocassette or video recorder (optional)

Organize children into cooperative-learning groups. Invite them to create one-minute public service announcements that focus on the importance of conservation, ways to practice conservation, where to call or write for information, or how to get involved locally.

Challenge children to be creative and persuasive in their messages. After the group has decided on its message, one child should write the text and one or two children should make props. Another child should time the practices and help cut or add text to make the message one minute long. Invite groups to perform their announcements for the class. If equipment is available, you may wish to record children's performances. **(KINESTHETIC/AUDITORY)**

Conservation Cube Game

Objective: Identify precious resources.

Materials: Pattern P4, paper, crayons, tape

Distribute individual copies of the Conservation Cube Pattern. Invite children to draw a picture of a natural resource in each box of the pattern. Assist them in folding and taping the pattern into a cube. Then organize children into small groups, and invite them to take turns rolling the conservation cubes on a table. Ask them to name some ways to conserve each resource that turns up on the cubes. Expand the game by asking children to name some ways people use the resources to meet their needs. **(TACTILE/VISUAL)**

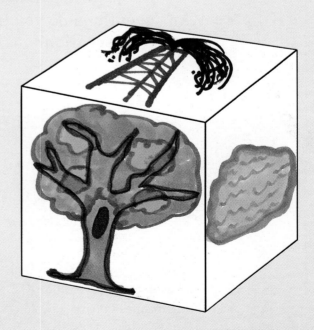

Talking to the Clay

American Indians have always had a special relationship with the Earth. Long ago, it provided everything they needed to live—food, shelter, tools, and medicine. As you read this Catawba tale, have children think about why caring for the Earth is important to Mary Grey.

Mary Grey walked down to the river, carrying her bucket. It was a warm spring day, and the South Carolina hills were bright with sunlight. As Mary walked, she watched for that same yellow color in the riverbank. That color of the sun would show her that she had found the clay she was looking for.

Usually Mary's grandmother went with her to gather clay. But today Mary was going alone for the first time.

Mary kept her eyes open, looking for clay. She could go to the spot her grandmother had shown her, but she wanted to find her own place. She wanted to hear the clay speak to her.

Mary had been only three years old when Grandma Rose started teaching her how to talk to the clay. Her grandmother had just finished making a small round pot. It hadn't yet been put into the fire to harden. Her grandmother put the pot in Mary's hands.

"You feel how this pot is breathing?" Grandma Rose said.

"I feel it breathing," Mary said. And she *had* felt it moving in her hands, *had* felt that it was alive.

A kingfisher darted down from a tree branch and dived into the river just ahead of her. As Mary's eyes followed the bird, she saw a yellow gleam on the bank. Holding the pail tight, she scrambled down the bank and looked. It was clay. She reached out and pulled a little free and squeezed it. It made a round ball in her palm.

Mary put down her bucket and reached into her pocket. She took out a stone that was not a stone. Her uncle, who knew a lot about such things, had told her it was actually a fossil tooth. It came from a big animal called a mastodon, which lived long ago. Mary had found that tooth when she was out walking. It was her favorite thing.

"Clay," Mary said, "I'm glad you let me find you. I want to give this to you. I want you to be my friend for a long, long time."

She dug a hole at the base of the clay bank and placed the stone tooth into it. Then she stood and listened. It seemed as if she could hear a voice, soft and flowing like the sound of the river behind her.

"Thank you," she said. Then she began to fill her bucket with clay.

Discuss how Mary learned about the "talking" clay from her grandmother.

- **How does teaching others about nature help protect the Earth?** When people share what they know, everyone can learn to care.
- **What did Mary give back to the Earth?** an old tooth

MAKING SOCIAL STUDIES REAL

READ AND RESPOND

Geography
Human-Environment Interactions

Have children read pages 90 and 91 and discuss the problem Sabrina and her friends discovered in El Segundo. Invite volunteers to find El Segundo on a map. Allow time for children to explore the subject further by making posters, by reading books, or by writing a letter to Tree Musketeers to find out more about them.

Q. **What are some things that cause pollution?** smoke, gases, chemicals, litter, noise

Lead children in a discussion about why it is important to keep our land and water clean. Children should understand that we need to make our resources last.

Q. **What can you do to help your environment and your community?** Responses may include picking up litter, keeping noise at a reasonable level, and recycling.

Making Social Studies Real

Tree Musketeers

Can kids make a difference? You bet they can! My name is Sabrina. I live in El Segundo, California. My friend and I wanted to help keep the land and water clean. We started a group called Tree Musketeers when we were 8 years old.

United States

El Segundo, California

The Tree Musketeers decided to try to solve a big problem. El Segundo is next to Los Angeles Airport. There is a lot of noise and air **pollution** in our town from the airplanes flying over.

90

ACTIVITY CHOICES

Background

Sabrina Alimahomed is a founder and past president of Tree Musketeers, the nation's first youth environmental group. With adult support the Musketeers plan to make El Segundo a model of what a youth-led organization can accomplish. The Musketeers provide a Memory Tree service, maintain an outdoor community classroom, and hold Arbor Day and Earth Day events.

To contact Tree Musketeers, write 233 Main Street, El Segundo, CA 90245, or call 1-800-473-0263.

We learned that trees could help stop the pollution from coming into El Segundo. We planted a tree and named it Marcie the Marvelous Tree. We have planted more than 700 trees in El Segundo.

What Can You Do?

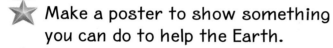
★ Make a poster to show something you can do to help the Earth.

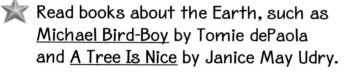
★ Read books about the Earth, such as <u>Michael Bird-Boy</u> by Tomie dePaola and <u>A Tree Is Nice</u> by Janice May Udry.

Visit the Internet at http://www.hbschool.com for additional resources.

91

Vocabulary

Explain environmental pollution to children. Write *air*, *soil*, and *water* on the board and have children suggest ways in which air, soil and water can become polluted. Use a cause-and-effect chain to show how pollution can cause harm. For example, dumping trash in streams causes water pollution, which then kills fish.

Q. **Why is pollution a worldwide problem?** We all breathe air, drink water, and eat food grown in the soil, and pollution can spread out around the world in the air and in the oceans.

Be sure to point out that pollution has been around for a long time but that the increasing population has caused more pollution. Reassure children that there are many laws against pollution and that many organizations are actively working to solve pollution problems. Children can do their share by learning how to reduce pollution.

Background

Earth Day was initiated in 1970, in San Francisco, California, the city of Saint Francis, patron saint of ecology. Now every year on April 22, with the ringing of the United Nations Peace Bell, Earth Day is a global celebration. Some people also observe it on March 21, the first day of Spring (the day of the vernal equinox), or on June 6, World Environment Day.

Link to Health

COMMUNITY HEALTH Invite children to make posters about clean air, water, and soil to remind people of the dangers of pollution. You may wish to arrange for a shopping mall, grocery store, or library to display the posters.

PICTURE SUMMARY

TAKE A LOOK

Remind children that a picture summary is a way to visually represent the main ideas or events in a story. Explain that this summary reviews some of the main ideas in Unit 2.

Visual Analysis

Learn from Pictures Invite children to work individually or with partners to examine the picture summary and to react to its images. Ask children to describe the various images and to suggest what each shows about where we live. Note that the journey's path may begin in the lower left-hand corner and end in the city in the upper right-hand corner.

VOCABULARY BLACKLINES

Distribute the individual word cards for this unit and have children use the words as they discuss the picture summary.

UNIT 2 Review

Picture Summary

Look at the pictures. They will help you remember what you learned.

Talk About the Main Ideas

1. Communities can be different sizes.
2. The Earth has many kinds of land and bodies of water.
3. People change the land.
4. People in towns and on farms depend on each other.
5. Important resources come from the Earth.
6. Conservation helps save resources.

Describe a Character Think of a character who might live in the picture. Tell where the person lives and works. Tell what the person does for fun.

92

ACTIVITY CHOICES

UNIT POSTER

Use the UNIT 2 PICTURE SUMMARY POSTER to summarize the unit.

VOCABULARY CARDS

Have children use the VOCABULARY CARDS for this unit to review key concepts.

Picture Summary Key

Use the picture key to point out some of the illustrations that relate to the list of main ideas. Children will find other examples in the drawing. Help them generalize about the ways people depend on each other and how conservation is important.

SUMMARIZE THE MAIN IDEAS

Ask children to read the summary statements on page 92 and to relate each one to scenes in the picture summary. Lead a class discussion about each scene, and challenge children to offer supporting details for each main idea illustrated. Review the Anticipation Guide statements at the beginning of the unit, on Teacher's Edition page 42.

Help children conclude that people may live in different places but that all people use the Earth to meet their needs.

Sharing the Activity

Provide time for children to complete the Describe a Character activity on page 92. Have children first tell a classmate about the character and then draw pictures to show the character in his or her setting. As children work, invite them to discuss how their pictures are related to the main ideas illustrated in the picture summary.

PUPIL BOOK OR UNIT BIG BOOK

Meet Individual Needs

ENGLISH LANGUAGE LEARNERS
Invite children whose first language is not English to read the summary statements aloud. Ask them to tell how each statement relates to their native country. For example, children might describe the size of their former community as a large city, a suburb, or a small farm town. They can tell whether they lived near a body of water. If children lived on a farm, they might be able to name the farm products grown on the land.

TECHNOLOGY

Use **THE AMAZING WRITING MACHINE™ RESOURCE PACKAGE** to summarize the unit.

USE VOCABULARY

Tell children to write complete sentences that show the meaning of their words. Example: *Corn is an important resource where I live.*

CHECK UNDERSTANDING

❶ A suburb has mostly homes and has more space. A city has taller buildings and is more crowded.

❷ Children should describe a landform (mountain, valley, plain, island) and a body of water (river, lake, ocean).

❸ People can change the land by building or growing things on it.

❹ Children should name people who grow, move, and sell food.

❺ Children should identify a resource and name something that is made from it.

THINK CRITICALLY

❶ Geography tells us how people live in different places. It tells us how people use land and water.

❷ Children might say that they can use resources wisely by not wasting them and by recycling. Other people depend on the Earth, too.

UNIT 2 Review

Use Vocabulary

Choose two words from this list. Use the words in sentences that tell about the place where you live.

conservation
continent
geography
globe
landform
resource

Check Understanding

❶ How is a suburb different from a city?

❷ Name and tell about one landform and one body of water.

❸ How do people change the land?

❹ What workers help get food from farms to our homes?

❺ Tell about something you use from the land.

Think Critically

❶ How does geography help you learn about people?

❷ How can you help take care of the Earth? Why is this important?

94

Apply Skills

Read a Table

Trees		
Kind	**Size**	**Goods**
Maple	50–80 feet	syrup, furniture, boxes, musical instruments
Pecan	90–120 feet	nuts, floors, furniture, indoor walls
Pine	75–200 feet	lumber, turpentine, paint, soap, paper
Oak	40–90 feet	lumber, furniture, barrels, paper, railroad ties
Redwood	200–275 feet	outdoor walls, decks, picnic tables

1 How many kinds of trees are shown on the table?

2 Which tree grows the tallest?

3 Which tree gives us syrup?

Do It Yourself

Make a table. Choose a bird, a fish, an animal, or a flower. Use it as the title of your table. Write two facts about it in your table.

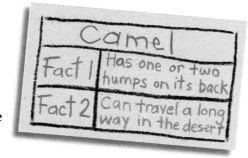

95

Use a Globe

1 north
2 South Pole
3 Europe and Asia
4 Indian Ocean
5 Australia and Antarctica

Apply Skills

Use a Globe

Look at the drawings of the globe and answer these questions.

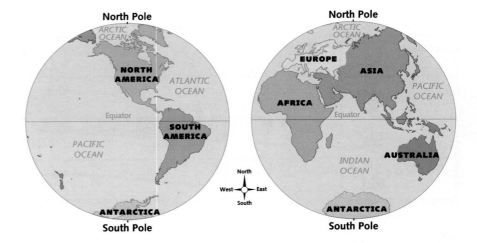

1 Is Europe north or south of the equator?

2 Which pole is in Antarctica?

3 Which two continents join to make up the largest land area?

4 Which ocean is south of Asia?

5 Which continents are completely south of the equator?

96

·········· Unit Activity ··········

Make a Banner

Mountain View

⭐ Draw pictures on the banner that show what the land looks like where you live.

⭐ Show how people have changed the land.

⭐ Find or draw pictures of things that grow on the land and goods made from them.

⭐ Hang up your banner and give it a title.

HARCOURT BRACE

Visit the Internet at http://www.hbschool.com for additional resources.

Read More About It

A New Coat for Anna by Harriet Ziefert. Knopf. Anna's mother finds the resources needed to make Anna a winter coat.

Johnny Appleseed by Steven Kellogg. William Morrow. Legends tell about John Chapman, who planted apple trees for settlers long ago.

Radio Man by Arthur Dorros. HarperCollins. Diego goes with his family from farm to farm to help pick fruits and vegetables.

97

PUPIL BOOK OR UNIT BIG BOOK

UNIT ACTIVITY
Make a Banner

Help children organize their group tasks by suggesting that they make lists of scenes for their banners. Have them plan the placement of the scenes on smaller sheets of paper to use as models for the banners.

READ MORE ABOUT IT

Additional books are listed in the Resource Center on page 42E of this Teacher's Edition.

TAKE-HOME BOOK
Use the TAKE-HOME REVIEW BOOK for Unit 2.

ASSESSMENT
Use UNIT 2 TEST Standard, pp. 19–21. Performance, p. 22.

GAME TIME!
Use GAME TIME! to reinforce the unit.

COOPERATIVE LEARNING WORKSHOP

BON VOYAGE, GEO GEORGIE

Organize the class into groups of four or five children. Tell them they are going to prepare Geo Georgie for a journey. Geo Georgie will need a travel log, a suitcase, and a letter of introduction with special travel instructions. Request volunteers in each group for the following tasks (some tasks may require more than one child).

Materials: Geo Georgie pattern (Pattern P13), writing paper, scissors, paste, stapler, colored crayons or markers, construction paper, cardboard, large envelopes, yarn, plastic bags, United States wall map

Task 1: Color the pattern of Geo Georgie, cut it out, paste it on cardboard, and cut it out again.

Task 2: Write a letter introducing Geo Georgie as a travel companion wishing to see different areas of the country and hoping to collect souvenirs along the way. Brainstorm possible souvenirs, such as travel brochures, postcards, snapshots, pins, flags, patches, stamps, feathers, rocks, shells, or dried plants. The letter should also explain how to make notes in the travel log, telling about the land, people, and resources that Geo Georgie sees.

Task 3: Make a cover for the travel log and fill in Geo Georgie's name and address. Design an itinerary page with spaces for the *date, destination, transportation,* and *sites of interest.* (Note: You will need to make several copies of the itinerary page for each travel log.) Assemble the travel log and staple the pages together.

Task 4: Decorate a large envelope (no smaller than 11 × 14) to look like a trunk or suitcase. Draw stickers for places you know about, imagining Geo Georgie's previous trips. Place Geo Georgie, the travel log, and the letter of introduction in the envelope.

Help children generate a list of people who would make good travel companions for Geo Georgie. They might suggest travel agents, salespeople, flight attendants, truck drivers, or vacationers. Decide on a plan for contacting such people in the community and asking them to take Geo Georgie with them as they travel.

Follow-Up

On a bulletin board, attach a map of the United States to chart Geo Georgie's journeys. Have children use yarn to plot the routes. Souvenirs may also be attached to the bulletin board and connected to their source with yarn (use small plastic bags for bulky items).

What to Look For During ongoing discussion children should exhibit an understanding of the interactions people have within their environments. Children should be able to

▶ describe the Earth by naming its physical features.

▶ state how people's lives are affected by their surroundings.

▶ name resources from the Earth.

▶ use appropriate vocabulary.

REMIND CHILDREN TO:
• Share their ideas.
• Cooperate with others to plan their work.
• Plan and take responsibility for their tasks.
• Show their work.
• Discuss their own and the group's performance.

pages 98A–135B

WE ALL WORK TOGETHER

The major objectives in this unit are organized around the following themes:

UNIT THEMES

▶ **INDIVIDUALISM & INTERDEPENDENCE**
▶ **COMMONALITY & DIVERSITY**

Preview Unit Content

Unit 3 tells the story of the many people who offer goods and services in a community. Children will begin to understand how members of a community depend on these goods and services to meet their many needs. They will recognize important businesses and industries in their communities and examine how different kinds of transportation help distribute goods and services in a community. Throughout the unit children will focus on the choices people make to keep their families healthy, happy, and safe.

You may wish to begin the unit with the Unit 3 Picture Summary Poster and activities. The illustration that appears on the poster also appears on pages 130–131 in the Pupil Book to help children summarize the unit.

UNIT POSTER

Use the **UNIT 3 PICTURE SUMMARY POSTER** to preview the unit.

This program is also available in a **SPANISH EDITION.**

TEACHER'S EDITION	THEMES • Strands	VOCABULARY	MEET INDIVIDUAL NEEDS	RESOURCES INCLUDING ► TECHNOLOGY
UNIT INTRODUCTION **Introduce the Unit** Preview Set the Scene with Literature "**General Store**" by Rachel Field Use the Literature Big Book pp. 98–103A			English Language Learners, pp. 100, 103 Tactile Learners, p. 101	**Pupil Book/Unit Big Book, pp. 98–103** **Write-On Charts** 27, 32 Picture Summary Poster Home Letter Text on Tape Audio Asian Translations Vocabulary Cards *The Rolling Store*
LESSON 1 **Community Services** pp. 104A–105A	**INDIVIDUALISM & INTERDEPENDENCE** • Civics and Government	taxes	English Language Learners, p. 104A Extend and Enrich, p. 105 Reteach the Main Idea, p. 105	**Pupil Book/Unit Big Book, pp. 104–105** **Write-On Chart 9** Activity Book, p. 17 Music Audio, "Workers in Our Town"
SKILL **Use a Pictograph** pp. 106A–107A	**BASIC STUDY SKILLS** • Chart and Graph Skills	pictograph	Tactile Learners, p. 106 Visual Learners, p. 106 Extend and Enrich, p. 107 Reteach the Skill, p. 107	**Pupil Book/Unit Big Book, pp. 106–107** Activity Book, p. 18 Transparency 6 ► GRAPH LINKS
LESSON 2 **People Make Goods** pp. 108A–111A	**INDIVIDUALISM & INTERDEPENDENCE** • Economics • Culture	factory	Visual and Tactile Learners, p. 108 Extend and Enrich, p. 110 Reteach the Main Idea, p. 110	**Pupil Book/Unit Big Book, pp. 108–111** **Write-On Chart 10** Activity Book, p. 19
SKILL **Predict a Likely Outcome** pp. 112A–113A	**BUILDING CITIZENSHIP** • Critical Thinking Skills	prediction	Visual Learners, p. 112A Auditory Learners, p. 112 Extend and Enrich, p. 113 Reteach the Skill, p. 113	**Pupil Book/Unit Big Book, pp. 112–113** Transparency 7 Activity Book, p. 20
LESSON 3 **Goods from Near and Far** pp. 114A–117A	**COMMONALITY & DIVERSITY** • Economics • Geography	trade transportation	Tactile Learners, p. 114A Extend and Enrich, p. 116 Reteach the Main Idea, p. 116	**Pupil Book/Unit Big Book, pp. 114–117** **Write-On Charts 11, 34** Activity Book, p. 21 Vocabulary Cards Desk Maps Music Audio, "Clickety Clack"

23 DAYS

TIME MANAGEMENT

DAY 1	DAY 2	DAY 3	DAY 4	DAY 5	DAY 6	DAY 7	DAY 8	DAY 9	DAY 10	DAY 11	DAY 12
Unit Introduction		Lesson 1		Skill	Lesson 2			Skill	Lesson 3		

TEACHER'S EDITION	THEMES · Strands ·	VOCABULARY	MEET INDIVIDUAL NEEDS	RESOURCES INCLUDING ► TECHNOLOGY
LESSON 4 Makers and Users, Buyers and Sellers pp. 118A–119B	INDIVIDUALISM & INTERDEPENDENCE • Economics	producer consumer	Visual Learners, p. 118A Kinesthetic Learners, p. 118A Auditory Learners, p. 118 Extend and Enrich, p. 119 Reteach the Main Idea, p. 119	**Pupil Book/Unit Big Book, pp. 118–119** Write-On Charts 12, 29 Activity Book, p. 23 Video, Reading Rainbow, *Fox on the Job*
BRAINSTORM Kid Town pp. 120–121A	BUILDING CITIZENSHIP • Critical Thinking Skills • Participation Skills		English Language Learners, p. 120 Visual Learners, p. 121	**Pupil Book/Unit Big Book, pp. 120–121**
LESSON 5 Making Wise Choices pp. 122A–125A	INDIVIDUALISM & INTERDEPENDENCE • Economics • History	wants income	Tactile Learners, p. 122A English Language Learners, p. 122 Extend and Enrich, p. 124 Reteach the Main Idea, p. 124 Auditory Learners, p. 125	**Pupil Book/Unit Big Book, pp. 122–125** Activity Book, p. 24 Vocabulary Cards ► THE AMAZING WRITING MACHINE
SKILL Follow a Diagram pp. 126A–127B	BASIC STUDY SKILLS • Chart and Graph Skills	diagram	English Language Learners, p. 126A Kinesthetic Learners, p. 126 Extend and Enrich, p. 127 Reteach the Skill, p. 127	**Pupil Book/Unit Big Book, pp. 126–127** Activity Book, p. 25 Transparency 8
MAKING SOCIAL STUDIES REAL Biz Kid$ pp. 128–129	BUILDING CITIZENSHIP • Participation Skills	business		**Pupil Book/Unit Big Book, pp. 128–129** ► INTERNET
UNIT WRAP-UP Picture Summary Unit 3 Review Cooperative Learning Workshop pp. 130–135B			English Language Learners, p. 131	**Pupil Book/Unit Big Book, pp. 130–135** Picture Summary Poster Vocabulary Cards Assessment Program, Standard, pp. 23–25 Performance, p. 26 Take-Home Review Book Game Time! ► THE AMAZING WRITING MACHINE

DAY 13	DAY 14	DAY 15	DAY 16	DAY 17	DAY 18	DAY 19	DAY 20	DAY 21	DAY 22	DAY 23
Lesson 4		Brainstorm	Lesson 5			Skill	Making Social Studies Real	Unit Wrap-Up		Unit Test

Multimedia Resource Center

Books

Easy

Lied, Kate. *Potato, A Tale from the Great Depression.* Illus. by Lisa Campbell Ernst. National Geographic Society, 1997. During the Great Depression, a family seeking work finds employment for two weeks digging potatoes in Idaho.

Lyon, George Ella. *Mama Is a Miner.* Illus. by Peter Catalanotto. Orchard, 1994. A young girl pays tribute to her mother's days as a miner.

Paulsen, Gary. *The Tortilla Factory.* Illus. by Ruth Wright Paulsen. Harcourt Brace, 1995. From seed to plant to tortilla, the author describes the workers who plant, prepare, and transport resources.

Rogow, Zack. *Oranges.* Illus. by Mary Szilagyi. Orchard, 1988. It takes the combined labor of many people to bring a single orange from the tree to the table.

Shelby, Anne. *We Keep a Store.* Illus. by John Ward. Orchard, 1990. Everyone in the family helps run a country store.

Average

Bunting, Eve. *A Day's Work.* Illus. by Ronald Himler. Houghton Mifflin, 1994. A newly arrived Mexican immigrant finds work at a daily labor pick-up station in Los Angeles with the help of his young grandson.

Garay, Luis. *Pedrito's Day.* Orchard, 1997. When Pedrito replaces, from his own earnings, money he has lost, his mother decides that he is finally big enough for some of his father's earnings to be used toward buying him a bicycle.

Gibbons, Gail. *Say Woof! The Day of a Country Veterinarian.* Macmillan, 1992. The author describes the day of a veterinarian.

Gibbons, Gail. *Up Goes the Skyscraper!* Macmillan, 1986. Children can follow, in simple text and illustrations, the building of a skyscraper step-by-step.

Hill, Elizabeth S. *Evan's Corner.* Illus. by Sandra Speidel. Puffin, 1993. Needing a place to call his own, Evan is thrilled when his mother points out that their crowded apartment has eight corners, one for each family member.

Kudler, David. *The Seven Gods of Luck.* Illus. by Linda Finch. Houghton Mifflin, 1997. In a Japanese folktale, two poor Japanese children hope to be able to celebrate New Year's Day properly. Because of their kindness, the Seven Gods of Luck help them to do so.

Schotter, Roni. *A Fruit & Vegetable Man.* Illus. by Jeanette Winter. Little, Brown, 1993. Sun Ho watches the artistic fruit and vegetable man, Ruby Rubenstein, at work. Then he begins helping in the store and even offers something new: bean sprouts.

Stewart, Dianne. *The Dove.* Illus. by Jude Daly. Greenwillow, 1993. A visiting dove provides the answer to Grandmother Maloko's financial problems when floodwaters destroy her crops.

Williams, Vera B. *A Chair for My Mother.* Mulberry, 1993. A child, her mother, and her grandmother save dimes to buy a comfortable armchair after all their furniture is lost in a fire.

Williams, Vera B. *Music, Music for Everyone.* Mulberry, 1988. Rosa plays her accordion with her friends in the Oak Street Band and earns money to help her mother with expenses while her grandmother is sick.

Winkleman, Katherine K. *Police Patrol.* Illus. by John S. Winkleman. Walker, 1996. The author describes the activities that take place at a police station and the duties of different types of officers.

Challenging

Chinn, Karen. *Sam and the Lucky Money.* Illus. by Cornelius Van Wright and Ying-Hwa Hu. Lee & Low, 1995. Sam must decide how to spend the lucky money he has received for Chinese New Year.

Daly, Niki. *Not So Fast, Songololo.* Aladdin, 1996. A boy accompanies his grandmother on a shopping trip to the city.

Lewin, Ted. *Market!* Lothrop, Lee & Shepard, 1996. This book looks at the special characteristics of different types of markets around the world.

Mitchell, Margaree King. *Uncle Jed's Barbershop.* Illus. by James Ransome. Simon & Schuster, 1993. Sarah Jean tells about her favorite relative who did his barbering for years without a shop. Finally, as an older man, he is able to open a barbershop.

Williams, Karen Lynn. *Galimoto.* Illus. by Catherine Stock. Lothrop, Lee & Shepard, 1990. Walking through his village, a young African boy finds the materials to make a special toy.

Zimelman, Nathan. *How the Second Grade Got $8,205.50 to Visit the Statue of Liberty.* Illus. by Bill Slavin. Whitman, 1992. The triumphs and setbacks of the second grade are chronicled as the children try a variety of schemes to raise money for a trip to the Statue of Liberty.

LIBRARY

See the **GRADE 2 SOCIAL STUDIES LIBRARY** for additional resources.

Audiocassettes

Slugs at Sea. Music for Little People. The Banana Slug String Band, in a fun and informative way, tells about another world of living things whose home is the ocean. Toll free: 1-800-346-4445

Computer Software

CD-ROM

Exploring Where & Why, Grade 2. Nystrom, Division of Herff Jones, Inc. Mac/Windows. Provides hands-on experiences as children learn about features—including goods and services—of their community. Toll free: 1-800-621-8086

The Factory. Sunburst. DOS, Apple II, Macintosh, and Windows. Spanish version also available. Children experiment with a simulated factory assembly line. Toll free: 1-800-321-7511

Interactive Math Journey. Learning Company. Mac/Windows. A wide range of stories, songs, and activities —including adventures based on trading goods with merchants— further children's understandings about money. (617) 494-1200

Video

Film or VHS Cassettes

Services. Centre Films. Investigates how a house is built. Explores communities where families live and work, focusing on the public places and services of communities. Available on videocassette. Toll free: 1-800-886-1166

Note that information, while correct at time of publication, is subject to change.

A Magical Field Trip to Denver Mint. Aims Multimedia. Rosie O'Flanigan transports three youngsters from their elementary school library to the Denver Mint for an inside view of how money is made. 14 minutes. Toll free: 1-800-367-2467

A Magical Field Trip to the Post Office. Aims Multimedia. Maria is curious as to why stamps are needed, so Rosie O'Flanigan whisks her to the post office to find out about the different jobs and equipment used in posting and delivering mail. 15 minutes. Toll free: 1-800-367-2467

All About Textiles. A guide to educational textile resources. Free.
> American Textile Manufacturers
> Institute
> Communications Division
> 1130 Connecticut Ave., NW
> Suite 1200
> Washington, DC 20036

Consumer Information Catalog. Booklet lists a variety of federal publications available on topics such as food, education, money management, travel, and hobbies. Educators can be put on a mailing list to receive 25 copies or more for their schools. Almost everything is under $2.50; many items are free.
> Consumer Information Catalog
> Pueblo, CO 81009
> (888) 8-PUEBLO

Once Upon a Dime. A comic book about money and the economy. Mail a postcard printed with your name, address, and request. Free.
> Federal Reserve Bank of
> New York
> Public Information Department
> 33 Liberty Street
> New York, NY 10045-0001
> Internet: www.ny.frb.org

Story of Cotton Kit. Teaching packet includes samples of cotton, threads, and fabric; 30 copies of *Story of Cotton, Cotton: From Field to Fabric*, and *Perennial Patriot*. $15.00.
> National Cotton Council of
> America
> P.O. Box 12285
> Memphis, TN 38112

A Study in Shoemaking. Kit of educational materials about how shoes are made.
> Brown Group, Inc.
> Public Relations Student Kit
> 8300 Maryland
> P.O. Box 29
> St. Louis, MO 63166-0029

Linking Social Studies

READING CENTER

Make a Class Pictograph

Materials: books and/or audiocassette stories about money or business (such as *Arthur's Pet Business* by Marc Brown), pictograph on butcher paper with the book titles listed in the left-hand column, happy face stickers, cassette player

Invite children to read or listen to stories about earning, saving, and spending money. When children find a book they enjoy, they add a happy face next to the title of that book on the pictograph. At the end of the unit, discuss the stories and the information on the graph. Ask children to point out which books were liked by the most children and which by the fewest.

Arthur's Pet Business	☺ ☺ ☺
A Chair for My Mother	☺ ☺ ☺ ☺ ☺ ☺ ☺ ☺
The Big Green Pocketbook	☺ ☺ ☺ ☺
A New Coat for Anna	☺ ☺ ☺ ☺ ☺ ☺ ☺
Something Special for Me	☺ ☺ ☺ ☺ ☺ ☺
Evan's Corner	☺ ☺ ☺ ☺
A Fruit and Vegetable Man	☺ ☺ ☺ ☺

MULTICULTURAL CENTER

Make Pottery for a Mexican Feria

Materials: clay, tempera paint, items to create a Mexican *feria* (sandals, baskets, a piñata, paper flowers, bananas and other fruits)

Explain that in Mexico many people sell their goods at outdoor markets, or *ferias*. Ask children to help you create a *feria* by arranging baskets and other goods made in Mexico. Display pictures of Mexican pottery and discuss the colors, shapes, and figures Mexican artists use to decorate their pottery. Then invite children to create clay dishes, cups, and pots. When the clay dries, have children paint colorful designs on their pottery and add the pieces to the *feria* display.

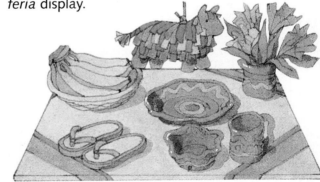

LANGUAGE ARTS CENTER

How to Make a Toy

Materials: paper, pencils, cardboard tubes and boxes, glue, spools, pipe cleaners, buttons, tape, markers, and other materials

Invite children to use the materials to create a toy vehicle, person, piece of furniture, or other toy. As children work, have them keep a picture record of each step in the process of making the toy. Ask children to follow the pictures in their diagram to write a step-by-step explanation of how to make the toy. Display the diagrams, toys, and explanations and have children follow classmates' instructions for building toys.

Across the Curriculum

MATH CENTER

Gingerbread Assembly Line

Materials: clay, gingerbread figure cookie cutter, buttons and beads in assorted colors, paper plates

Invite groups to plan an assembly line for making gingerbread figures. Ask children to decide what the finished product should look like, how many they will make, and who will do each job. Suggest that children place each clay figure on a paper plate that can be passed from one worker to the next. Have each group make a chart telling how many gingerbread figures they made and how many beads or buttons they used for eyes, mouths, noses, and other details. Have children look for number patterns as they compare the charts.

ART CENTER

Set a Goal and Save!

Materials: fabric swatches, assorted art materials, cylindrical oatmeal boxes or empty food containers with plastic lids (such as lemonade mix, baking powder, or cocoa containers)

Discuss items children would like to own and ways they might earn money to buy the items. Then invite children to create a textured picture or sculpture of an item they would like to buy. Suggest that the picture or sculpture be fastened to a container that will be a bank for saving money for the item. Some children may want to build their sculpture around the container. Cut slots in the lids of the "bank" containers and help children fasten their artwork to the container.

HOW TO INTEGRATE YOUR DAY
Use these topics to help you integrate social studies into your daily planning.

READING THEMES	INTEGRATED LANGUAGE ARTS	MATHEMATICS	SCIENCE	ART
Creativity	How to Make a Toy, p. 98G	Gingerbread Assembly Line,	Cause and Effect, p. 112A	Set a Goal and Save, p. 98H
	Journal, pp. 114A, 120, 123	p. 98H	Technology, p. 126	Illustration, pp. 99, 100,
Working Hands	Write a Poem, p. 117	Addition and Subtraction,		108A, 126A
		pp. 104, 111, 123		About the Artist, p. 102
Travel		Data and Graphing, p. 106A		Graphic Art, p. 106
Cooperation		**HEALTH AND PHYSICAL EDUCATION**	**MUSIC**	**WORLD LANGUAGES**
Communicating with Others		Physical Fitness, p. 106A	Vocal, p. 114	Other Languages, p. 114A
Marketplace				

A Story of Buying and Selling

Mr. A makes trucks.

Mrs. B delivers fruit in a truck.

Mr. C sells the fruit in his store.

Mr. A eats lunch at the restaurant.

Mrs. E buys the pies for her restaurant.

Ms. D uses the fruit to make pies.

BULLETIN BOARD

Introduce the concept of producers and consumers by having children create a bulletin board titled *A Story of Buying and Selling.* Relate the following example: *Mr. A's factory makes trucks. Mrs. B bought a truck and uses it to deliver fruit to people like Mr. C, who sells it in his store. Ms. D buys fruit to make pies that she sells to Mrs. E's restaurant, where Mr. A eats lunch.* Invite children to make up, illustrate, and write captions for their own chain story.

Assessment Options

The assessment program allows all learners many opportunities to show what they know and can do. It also provides ongoing information about each child's understanding of social studies.

FORMAL ASSESSMENT

▶ *Unit Review*
(**Pupil Book**, pp. 132–135)

▶ *Unit Assessment*
(**Assessment Program:**
Standard Test, pp. 23–25
Performance Task, p. 26)

STUDENT SELF-EVALUATION

▶ *Individual End-of-Project Checklist*
(**Assessment Program**, p. 6)

▶ *Group End-of-Project Checklist*
(**Assessment Program**, p. 7) for use after cooperative learning activities

▶ *Individual End-of-Unit Checklist*
(**Assessment Program**, p. 8)

INFORMAL ASSESSMENT

▶ *What Do You Know? Questions*
(**Pupil Book**, at end of lessons)

▶ *Think and Do*
(**Pupil Book**, at end of skill lessons)

▶ *Picture Summary*
(**Pupil Book**, pp. 130–131)

▶ *Check Understanding*
(**Teacher's Edition**, in Close, at end of lessons)

▶ *Think Critically*
(**Teacher's Edition**, in Close, at end of lessons)

▶ *Social Studies Skills Checklist*
(**Assessment Program**, pp. 4–5)

PERFORMANCE ASSESSMENT

▶ *Show What You Know*
(**Teacher's Edition**, in Close, at end of lessons)

▶ *Cooperative Learning Workshop*
(**Teacher's Edition**, pp. 135A–135B)

▶ *Performance Task: Money Matters*
(**Assessment Program**, p. 26)

▶ Scoring the Performance Task
Use the *Scoring Rubric for Individual Projects*
(**Assessment Program**, p. 9)

▶ *Scoring Rubric for Group Projects*
(**Assessment Program**, p. 11)

PORTFOLIO ASSESSMENT

Student-selected items may include:

▶ *Hands-On Option,* telephone directory
(**Teacher's Edition**, p. 105A)

▶ *Link to Language Arts,* journal list
(**Teacher's Edition**, p. 114A)

▶ *Using the Activity Book,* diagram
(**Activity Book**, p. 25)

Teacher-selected items may include:

▶ *My Best Work*
(**Assessment Program**, p. 12)

▶ *Portfolio Summary*
(**Assessment Program**, p. 13)

▶ *Portfolio Family Response*
(**Assessment Program**, p. 14)

UNIT 3

Assessment Options

Name _____ Date _____

Unit 3 Test

Vocabulary 5 points each

Write a sentence or draw a picture to tell the meaning of the word.

1. producer Children might describe a producer as a person who makes or grows things that people buy. Drawings might show a factory worker, a carpenter, or a farmer.

2. consumer Children might describe a consumer as a person who buys and uses things. Drawings might show someone buying food, clothing, or other goods. They might also show a person eating food, wearing clothes, or using goods in some other manner.

3. income Children might describe income as money that a person earns for doing work. Drawings might show someone getting paid after completing a job.

4. factory Children might describe a factory as a place where workers make things that people buy. Drawings might show a building, machines, tools, workers, and a product.

5. transportation Children might describe transportation as something that carries people or goods from place to place. Drawings might show vehicles such as airplanes, ships, trains, cars, moving vans, or buses.

6. taxes Children might describe taxes as the money that people must pay a community or government. Drawings might show a person writing a check or giving money to a tax collector.

Harcourt Brace School Publishers

Unit 3 Test   Assessment Program **23**

Name _____

Main Ideas 5 points each

Circle the workers who are paid from tax money.

7.  8. 9.

10. 11. 12.

13. How do factories help communities?

Sample responses: In factories, workers make things that people need, they save consumers the time and work it takes to make things for themselves, they provide jobs for people in the community.

Write <u>yes</u> after each sentence that is true and <u>no</u> after each sentence that is false.

14. To trade means to buy and sell things. ___yes___

15. The United States trades only with Mexico and Canada. ___no___

16. Many countries buy jeans, cars, and other products from us. ___yes___

Harcourt Brace School Publishers

24   Assessment Program   Unit 3 Test

Objectives

- ▶ Describe how community services meet people's needs. (p. 104A)
- ▶ Explain how taxes support community services. (p. 104A)
- ▶ Identify and explain the parts of a pictograph. (p. 106A)
- ▶ Determine availability of selected services in a community. (p. 106A)
- ▶ Describe manufacturing jobs. (108A)
- ▶ Recognize how we depend on people who make goods. (108A)
- ▶ Recognize that some results can be predicted. (p. 112A)
- ▶ Identify the steps in making a prediction. (p. 112A)

- ▶ Predict a likely outcome. (p. 112A)
- ▶ Recognize that countries trade goods with one another. (p. 114A)
- ▶ Identify transportation links that bring goods to a community. (p. 114A)
- ▶ Define *producer* and *consumer*. (p. 118A)
- ▶ Describe how people trade money for goods. (p. 118A)
- ▶ Define *income*. (p. 122A)
- ▶ Recognize that people have unlimited wants but limited resources to satisfy their wants. (p. 122A)
- ▶ Explain the importance of saving money. (p. 122A)

- ▶ Discuss how competition in business creates choices for consumers. (p. 122A)
- ▶ Explain how diagrams help us understand information. (p. 126A)
- ▶ Read a diagram showing how coins are made. (p. 126A)

STANDARD TEST

Name _____

Skills 5 points each

Bicycles Sold Last Week

Monday	🚲 🚲 🚲 🚲 🚲 🚲
Tuesday	🚲 🚲
Wednesday	🚲 🚲 🚲 🚲
Thursday	🚲 🚲 🚲
Friday	🚲 🚲 🚲
Saturday	🚲 🚲 🚲 🚲 🚲 🚲 🚲

🚲 = 1 bicycle

Use the pictograph to answer the questions.

17. How many bicycles were sold on Thursday? _____3_____

18. On which day were the most bicycles sold? ___Saturday___

19. How many bicycles in all were sold last week? _____27_____

20. Complete the diagram about making a kite.

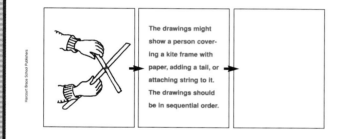

| | The drawings might show a person covering a kite frame with paper, adding a tail, or attaching string to it. The drawings should be in sequential order. | → | |

Unit 3 Test

Assessment Program **25**

PERFORMANCE TASK

Name _____ Date _____

Performance Task

Money Matters

Imagine that your grandmother gave you a gift of ten dollars. Draw one or more pictures to show what you would do with the money. Label your pictures. Then complete the sentence.

Drawings might show a child using money to buy something, saving money by putting it into a bank, or giving money to help a family member or a person in need.

It is smart to use money wisely because Sample response: You can't buy everything you want all at once. If you save some of your money, you'll have more to spend at another time. Besides, you might need to put some money aside for an emergency.

26 Assessment Program

Unit 3 Test

Rubrics

SCORING RUBRICS The scoring rubrics for evaluating individual projects, group projects, and children's presentations may be found in the *Assessment Program,* pages 9–11.

CRITERIA The criteria listed below may be used when looking for evidence of the children's understanding of social studies content and ability to think critically.

▶ *Performance Task: Money Matters* [**Assessment Program,** p. 26]

▶ *Scoring the Performance Task—* Use the *Scoring Rubric for Individual Projects* [**Assessment Program,** p. 9], and look for evidence of the child's ability to:

↳ Demonstrate wise use of money (e.g., by saving some).

↳ Explain the importance of saving money.

↳ Communicate ideas clearly through art and writing.

REMINDER

You may wish to preview the COOPERATIVE LEARNING WORKSHOP on Teacher's Edition pages 135A–135B. Children may complete the activity during the course of the unit.

INTRODUCE THE UNIT

Link Prior Learning

Ask children to discuss what they want to be when they grow up. Write down a variety of occupations on strips of paper and have children take turns drawing them out of a hat. Invite them to role-play their jobs. You may wish to provide costumes or uniforms as props for their role-plays.

Flow Chart

Create a flow chart on chart paper. For the first box, ask children to name a good. For the second box, have them tell how that good is made. For example, is it grown on a farm or made in a factory? Introduce children to the subject of transportation by leading a discussion of how a good gets from where it is made to the market. List transportation suggestions in the *How it gets to you* box. For the fourth box, ask children who might buy the good and how the person would use it.

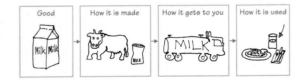

Preview Vocabulary

The vocabulary words listed on page 98 represent the key concepts for this unit. Suggest that children use the words to predict what the main ideas of the unit will be. Ideas for teaching the vocabulary are provided on pages 100 and 101.

UNIT 3 — We All Work Together

Vocabulary

taxes
factory
transportation
producer
consumer
income

98

ACTIVITY CHOICES

Community Involvement

Invite a variety of workers from the community to visit the classroom for a career day. Each worker can speak to the children about his or her job and the goods and services he or she provides for the community. Help children prepare questions they might ask each visitor.

WRITE-ON CHARTS

Use WRITE-ON CHART 32 to create the flow chart.

HOME LETTER

Use UNIT 3 HOME LETTER. See Teacher's Edition pages HL5–6.

99

PUPIL BOOK OR UNIT BIG BOOK

Link to Art

ILLUSTRATION Invite children to draw pictures showing different forms of transportation they have seen in their community. Suggest children share their drawings and tell whether each form of transportation would be used to move people, products, or both. Display children's drawings on a bulletin board titled *Community Transportation*.

AUDIO

Use the UNIT 3 TEXT ON TAPE AUDIOCASSETTE for a reading of this unit.

ASIAN TRANSLATIONS

For students who speak Cambodian, Cantonese, Hmong, or Vietnamese, use the ASIAN TRANSLATIONS for Unit 3. The Harcourt Brace program is also available in a SPANISH EDITION.

Personal Response

Direct children's attention to the photograph on pages 98–99. Discuss the children's costumes. Challenge children to identify the careers the costumes represent.

Q. **Why do you think some workers wear uniforms? How might it help you to know what a police officer's uniform looks like?** Responses might include that uniforms help them do their jobs better. Knowing the uniform makes it easy to spot a police officer when you need one.

Tell children that in this unit they will learn about people who work in their community and in their government. It is important for children to begin to realize that communities are made up of producers and consumers. Point out that many people provide goods and services on which other community members depend.

> ## " PRIMARY SOURCE "
>
> Every culture has proverbs, or common sayings, that offer messages for living. The following English proverbs are included in Ben Franklin's *Poor Richard's Almanac*.
>
> A penny saved is a penny earned.
> A fool and his money are soon parted.
>
> Have children discuss each proverb. Tell them that working hard, saving money, and making wise choices about spending are ideas they will read about in this unit.

Options for Reading

Read Aloud Read each lesson aloud as children follow along in their books. Strategies for guiding children through working with text and visuals are provided with each lesson.

Read Together Have pairs or small groups of children read the lesson by taking turns reading each page or paragraph aloud. Encourage children to use the new vocabulary words as they discuss what they read.

Read Alone Strong readers may wish to read the lessons independently before you read or discuss each lesson with the class.

PREVIEW THE UNIT

Think About Words

Reproduce the following word web as shown:

Help children understand that all the words in the spokes of the web have something to do with working together in the community. Invite children to brainstorm new words related to the words on the chart. To stimulate ideas, read the following context sentences aloud:

> My taxes pay for new roads.
> The factory makes shoes.
> Trucks are one kind of transportation.
> Farmers are producers.
> The consumer is buying bread.
> Lisa saves her income in the bank.

taxes
Money people pay to their government for services.

factory
A place where people make goods.

transportation
Any way of moving people or things from place to place.

100

ACTIVITY CHOICES

WRITE-ON CHARTS

Use WRITE-ON CHART 27 to complete the vocabulary word web.

Meet Individual Needs

ENGLISH LANGUAGE LEARNERS
When you are introducing the vocabulary and discussing the definitions, pair children who speak languages other than English with fluent English speakers. Ask children to pronounce the words carefully and to share ideas about their meanings.

Link to Art

ILLUSTRATION Ask children to draw pictures showing different kinds of transportation they have seen in the community. Then invite children to share their drawings and tell whether each form of transportation is used to move people, products, or both. Display children's drawings on a bulletin board titled *Community Transportation*.

producer

A person who makes or grows something.

consumer

A person who buys and uses goods and services.

income

The money people earn for the work they do.

$ HELP $ WANTED

Responsible teen wanted. Job to include mowing and watering the lawn, weeding the garden, and some painting and light cleanup work. Please call 555-4321 to talk about wages and hours of work.

101

Work with Words

Invite children to turn to pages 100–101 in the Pupil Book. Direct their attention to the words and definitions on the pages. Explain that these words tell the main ideas they will learn about in this unit. Invite volunteers to read each word and its definition aloud. (Note: For additional vocabulary, see the Planning Chart on pages 98C–98D in the Teacher's Edition.) Use the words and the questions that follow to stimulate a general discussion of the new vocabulary.

Q. **What do you think a tax collector does? Does our community have any factories? What other kinds of transportation can you name? Who are the consumers? What are they buying? What is the boy doing to earn money?**

VOCABULARY BLACKLINES

You may wish to reproduce individual copies of the vocabulary words for this unit. They are found in the back of your Teacher's Edition.

VOCABULARY CARDS

Hold up each VOCABULARY PICTURE CARD so that children see the picture side only. Invite children to name the words.

Meet Individual Needs

TACTILE LEARNERS Help children make a simple cone-shaped hat by rolling a sheet of paper and taping it. Ask children to skim through newspapers and magazines to find pictures for the vocabulary words, for example, kinds of transportation, factories, people buying things, and people earning money. Invite children to cut out the pictures and paste them onto their hats.

SET THE SCENE WITH LITERATURE

PREVIEW

Have children turn to pages 102–103. Ask a volunteer to read aloud the title of the poem. Allow children to guess what the poem will be about. Invite children to list different kinds of things that might be found in a general store.

Q. **What type of store would you like to have one day?** Responses might include a grocery store, toy store, bookstore, or video store.

Set the Scene with Literature

Tea

sarsaparilla

Brown Sugar

Calico

white Sugar

102

ACTIVITY CHOICES

Background

ABOUT THE POET   Although Rachel Field (1894–1942) was 10 years old before she could read, she quickly developed a love of languages. After winning a writing contest she went to Radcliffe College and then to New York to work as an editor. At age 36 she became the first woman to receive the Newbery Medal, for *Hitty, Her First Hundred Years*. She wrote many stories, books, plays, and poems. "General Store" was published in a book of poems called *Taxis and Toadstools*, which described her two worlds—New York City and Sutton Island, Maine, where she spent her summers.

Link to Art

ABOUT THE ARTIST   Jane Conteh-Morgan illustrates children's books by using collage. The pieces of paper that she cuts or tears are first painted with acrylics. She adds patterns with brushes, cardboard, stamps, or even sticks. Next, the paper is cut or torn to make shapes. Often she adds small bits of paper with numbers or words cut from magazines. Finally, she arranges the shapes into the final image and glues the pieces to the background paper. Ask children to think of a scene and to illustrate it using a collage of cut-paper shapes.

General Store

by Rachel Field
illustrated by Jane Conteh-Morgan

Some day I'm going to have a store
With a tinkly bell hung over the door,
With real glass cases and counters wide
And drawers all spilly with things inside.
There'll be a little of everything;
Bolts of calico; balls of string;
Jars of peppermint; tins of tea;
Pots and kettles and crockery;
Seeds in packets; scissors bright;
Kegs of sugar, brown and white;
Sarsaparilla for picnic lunches;
Bananas and rubber boots in bunches.
I'll fix the window and dust each shelf,
And take the money in all myself,
It will be my store and I will say:
"What can I do for you today?"

open

103

PUPIL BOOK **OR** UNIT BIG BOOK

READ & RESPOND

Have children follow along as you read the poem. Explain that a general store sells a lot of different items. Tell them that over the years in most places, general stores have been replaced by department stores and supermarkets. Ask children to count the number of items in the poem that would fill the counters and cases. Invite them to tell what they would buy if they went to the general store.

Q. **What would you sell if you owned a general store?** Responses might include bread, fruit, milk, juice, tea, candy, toys, and books.

Point out that a general store is only one kind of business on which community members depend. Remind children that in this unit they will discover people who do many kinds of work.

Meet Individual Needs

ENGLISH LANGUAGE LEARNERS

Create a three-column chart titled *General Store.* Label the columns *How It Looks, What I Will Sell, What I Will Do.* Ask children to use the poem to complete the chart.

HOW IT LOOKS	WHAT I WILL SELL	WHAT I WILL DO
bell over the door	calico	fix window
glass cases	peppermint	dust shelf
wide counters	string	sell things
drawers	tea	
	pots	
	bananas	
	boots	

AUDIO

You may wish to play the TEXT ON TAPE AUDIOCASSETTE for "General Store" as children study the picture.

Link Literature

Children might enjoy beginning the unit with *Up Goes the Skyscraper!* by Gail Gibbons. (Macmillan, 1986) This book provides a step-by-step look at how a skyscraper is built. Ask children to imagine how many workers helped build the school they attend.

Use the

LITERATURE BIG BOOK

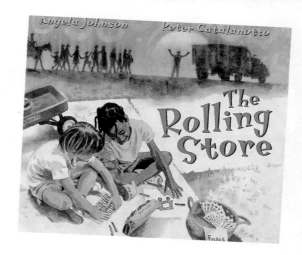

Invite children to read *The Rolling Store* by Angela Johnson. With a lyrical text and beautiful watercolor paintings, this book introduces the concepts taught in Unit 3. A young girl recalls a story told by her grandfather about a vendor's truck that visited rural communities during his childhood days. As the girl and a friend work on their own "rolling store," the story conveys the idea of how members of a community depend on goods and services to meet their many needs.

About the Author and the Illustrator

Angela Johnson has written a number of picture books, including the Coretta Scott King Honor Book *When I Am Old with You*, illustrated by David Soman, and *Julius*, illustrated by Dav Pilkey. She lives in Kent, Ohio.

Peter Catalanotto has painted pictures for books by George Ella Lyon and Cynthia Rylant. He has also written and illustrated four books of his own: *Dylan's Day Out, Mr. Mumble, Christmas Always...*, and *The Painter*. He lives with his family in Doylestown, Pennsylvania.

Reading the Story

Read and discuss the literature to address the following objectives:
1. Recognize that people have wants.
2. Identify people in a community who provide goods and services.
3. Describe how people trade money for goods and services.
4. Recognize the social aspects of trading for goods and services.

Social Studies Connection

Invite children to tell what they learned about goods and services in Unit 1.

Q. **What are some of the things that a family today may want and need?** food, clothing, games, videos, cars

Where do you go to buy things in your community?

Organize children into small groups and have them list items they would like to make and sell in a classroom store. Invite them to reread the story to get ideas. If cardboard boxes are available, provide each group with one that they can decorate to look like the wagon in the story. Children can work in groups to make craft items and then take turns role-playing buying and selling them.

1

COMMUNITY SERVICES

OBJECTIVES

1. Describe how community services meet people's needs.
2. Explain how taxes support community services.

VOCABULARY

taxes (p. 104)

RESOURCES

Pupil Book/Unit Big Book, pp. 104–105
Write-On Chart 9
Activity Book, p. 17
Music Audio, "Workers in Our Town"

ACTIVITY CHOICES

Meet Individual Needs

ENGLISH LANGUAGE LEARNERS
Find or make pictures of the following: teacher, school, police officer, police car, firefighter, fire truck, doctor, nurse, health clinic. Paste each picture onto one side of an index card and write the person's job or the object's name on the other side. Let children become familiar with the flash cards. Then invite them to form pairs to quiz each other. One child should hold up a picture while the other child identifies the job or the object.

Background

TAXES In 1913 the Sixteenth Amendment to the Constitution gave Congress the right to tax the income of the American people. Other important kinds of taxes include property tax and sales tax.

WRITE-ON CHARTS

Special Delivery
Use **WRITE-ON CHART 9** to extend and enrich this lesson. See Teacher's Edition page W28.

1. ACCESS

Introduce the lesson by asking children to think about who, besides their family members, have helped them so far today. If necessary, use questions to help children realize that people such as bus drivers, crossing guards, traffic police, teachers, school aides, and other school staff members all do jobs that help others. Continue by asking children whether they think these people do their jobs for free or for pay.

Focus on the Main Idea

In this lesson children will explore ways in which community services help people meet their needs. Children will discover that education, police and fire protection, and health care are all important community services. They will also learn that these services are paid for with taxes—money collected from the people who live and work in a community. Tell children that in this lesson they will read a news article about how communities pay for services.

2. BUILD

Key Content Summary

Children will learn how communities rely on public services—the necessary work done by teachers, police officers, firefighters, health-care workers, and other public employees. They will also learn that these services are paid for with taxes.

Civics and Government

Political Institutions and Processes
Work with children to create a word web of various public jobs and services. Invite children to explain how each job helps people in a community.

Q. What would happen if we had no teachers, police officers, firefighters, health-care workers, or community leaders? Children might not learn to read, write, and do math; we might have no protection against crime; we might not have anyone to fight fires; sick people might not be cared for; important community jobs might not get done.

Vocabulary

Define *taxes* as money that is paid by people who live and work in a community and that is used to pay community workers and buy things the community needs, such as textbooks, police cars, fire trucks, and hospital supplies.

Q. Why should people pay taxes? So there will be enough money to pay for community services; taxes pay for the services that members of a community share.

3. CLOSE

To summarize the lesson, ask children to provide answers to questions such as *Who would you call to fix a big hole in your street? Who could help you if a stray dog were in your yard?* and *Who would you call if a swing were broken in the park?* Invite children to tell whether they think the workers they would call are paid with tax money.

LESSON 1 Community Services

My class has been learning about how a community pays for its services. We read this article in our weekly news magazine.

Taxes Pay for Community Services

Communities collect money from people who live there. This money is called **taxes**. Taxes are used to pay workers, such as teachers, police officers, and firefighters. Tax money pays our community leaders, too.

Taxes are also used to build schools and to buy police cars and fire trucks. Taxes pay for the care children get at health clinics. Tax money helps a community take care of its citizens.

104

ACTIVITY CHOICES

Reading Support

MAKE PREDICTIONS Tell children that one way to figure out a new word is to use what they know about the sounds the letters stand for and the way the word is used in the sentence. As children read the story, pause before the highlighted word *taxes*. Ask:
• What do you think this word is?
• Does the word you suggested make sense in the sentence?

Link to Mathematics

ADDITION AND SUBTRACTION
Explain to children that a sales tax is extra money people pay when buying goods or services. Invite small groups to play "Market." Provide each group with several items marked from one to three dollars each. Tell children that for every dollar they spend they have to pay five additional cents for sales tax. Begin by asking children questions like *If stickers are one dollar each, and I buy two, how much will I have to pay in sales tax?*

"Tax money helps a community take care of its citizens."

What Do You Know?

1. Who pays taxes?
2. How do taxes help your community?

1. people who live in a community

2. Responses should include various community services supported by taxes.

105

Extend and Enrich

MAKE POSTERS Invite children to imagine they are running a campaign to create new services in their community. Ask them what services they think the community needs and how they will persuade voters to pay taxes for those services. Working alone or in pairs, children can make campaign posters that will persuade voters to pay taxes for those services. Some children may enjoy making campaign speeches as they present their posters to the class.

Reteach the Main Idea

PLAN SERVICES Invite children to imagine that they must start a new community. Help them list what services they might need. Ask children how their community will pay for these services.

AUDIO

 Use the UNIT 3 MUSIC AUDIOCASSETTE to hear the song "Workers in Our Town."

Check Understanding

The child can

—— describe how community services meet people's needs.

—— explain how taxes support community services.

Think Critically

Q. **Suppose your community ran out of money to pay for its services. What might be some solutions to that problem?** Children might suggest raising taxes, having people pay for their own services, or doing without some services.

Show What You Know

Performance Assessment Invite children to write news articles about community services, telling what they are, why they are important, and how they are paid for. Suggest that their articles include both words and pictures.

What to Look For To evaluate children's articles, note whether they list community services such as schools, police and fire departments, and clinics. Also note whether they explain that taxes pay for these services.

Using the Activity Book Invite children to complete Activity Book page 17. Then have children describe the services they drew and tell why these services are important.

Activity Book page 17

LESSON 1 • 105

HANDS-ON OPTION

Directory Assistance

Objective: Describe how community services meet people's needs.

Materials: paper, pencils, drawing paper, crayons, markers, telephone directories

Ask each child to create a directory of telephone numbers of important community services—fire and police departments, hospitals, and the like. Have them get the numbers from a published directory. Invite children to make decorative borders or illustrate their pages with spot art. Suggest that each child write his or her address and phone number on the cover. **(TACTILE/VISUAL)**

Public Helpers

Objective: Describe how community services meet people's needs.

Materials: props such as a stethoscope, a crossing guard's paddle, a police badge, and a cap; cardboard; string; markers

Organize children into groups of three. Explain that they are going to prepare a presentation that will show what they know about public employees in the community. Allow each group to select a public-service job like the ones discussed in this lesson.

Have one member of the group make a prop that can be worn to signify his or her job. Have another group member make and decorate a sign showing the audience the name of the job. Another can prepare one or two sentences that tell how this job helps the community. Children can take turns wearing the sign and the prop and telling the audience about the job. Have groups share their presentations with other classes. **(KINESTHETIC)**

Make a Bulletin Board

Objective: Explain how taxes support community services.

Materials: drawing paper, crayons, markers

Organize children into two groups to brainstorm lists of services that are provided in your community. The first group should list services that are paid for with tax money, and the second group should list services that are not paid for with tax money. Have children make a two-column table of the lists and post it on a bulletin board. They should also add drawings of each service listed. Title the display *Services in Our Community*. **(AUDITORY/VISUAL)**

Skills

USE A PICTOGRAPH

OBJECTIVES

1. Identify and explain the parts of a pictograph.
2. Determine availability of selected services in a community.

VOCABULARY

pictograph (p. 106)

RESOURCES

Pupil Book/Unit Big Book, pp. 106–107

Activity Book, p. 18

Transparency 6

Graph Links

ACTIVITY CHOICES

Link to Mathematics

DATA AND GRAPHING Teach children how to tally. Invite them to practice counting and tallying large quantities, such as the number of children, books, and desks in your classroom. You may wish to teach them the tallying convention of slanting every fifth tally across the previous four.

Link to Physical Education

PHYSICAL FITNESS Demonstrate how to do jumping jacks or arm lifts. Invite children to work in groups of four to tally how many times each child can do the exercise in thirty seconds. Time each session. Have children tally their scores and make a chart to show the results of their group.

TRANSPARENCY
Use TRANSPARENCY 6.

1. ACCESS

Introduce children to the concept of tallying. On the board, tape red, blue, green, yellow, black, and brown crayons in a column, and write the title *Favorite Colors*. Direct each child to come to the board and mark a tally by his or her favorite color. Count the votes aloud and mark a tally for each vote. Invite volunteers to count the tally marks, write the total for each color, and tell which color is the class favorite.

Q. **How many children voted for red? green?** Answers should reflect the tally.

How do you know? You can count the tally marks next to each crayon.

What would it mean if two colors had the same number of votes? The same number of children chose those colors as their favorites.

What would it mean if one color had no tally marks? No one in the class chose it as his or her favorite.

2. BUILD

Vocabulary

Help children recall how symbols are used in reading graphs and maps. Then write the word *pictograph* on the board, and ask children what two words make up this long word. Explain that a pictograph is a *graph* in which each small *picture*, or symbol, stands for one object or one group of objects. Explain that pictographs are used to compare the number of one object to the number of one or more other objects.

Civics and Government

Purposes and Types of Government Have children use the questions on page 106 to discuss the pictograph in the book. To help children begin their own pictographs of community services (see Do It Yourself, page 133), identify local services while listing them on chart paper. Tell them that they can find out how many of each service are in the community by looking in the phone book.

History

Patterns and Relationships Ask children to compare their graphs with the one on page 107. Invite them to explain why each service is important.

Q. **How might pictographs help someone plan a community?** He or she could use them to compare the services a community has with those it needs and with those of other communities.

Use a Pictograph

Mr. Lee's class made a pictograph to show the places that give services in their community. A **pictograph** uses pictures to show numbers of things.

1 Look at the pictograph. How many kinds of services are shown? five

2 Find the Key. What symbol is used to show the number of places that give each kind of service? a building

3 How many schools are there? Count the symbols to find out. four

4 Are there more or fewer fire stations than schools? fewer

Think and Do

Think of another kind of service you could add to the pictograph.

106

ACTIVITY CHOICES

Meet Individual Needs

TACTILE LEARNERS Have children work in pairs to make symbols for objects in the classroom. Invite each child to draw three to five symbols on index cards, using a separate card for each symbol and writing the name of each object on the back of the card. Children can take turns guessing their partners' symbols.

Meet Individual Needs

VISUAL LEARNERS Show children other pictographs, and invite them to describe in their own words the visual information on the pictographs. Help them understand that one pictograph symbol does not always refer to *one* object; it may refer to one group of objects as long as each group has the same number.

Link to Art

GRAPHIC ART Invite each child to pick a favorite symbol and draw it in three different ways. Drawings might vary in color, amount of detail, size, use of words, or even in the image itself. Then invite children to discuss with a partner which versions they like best and why.

Services in Our Community

Bank		
Fire Station		
Hospital		
Post Office		
School		

Key

= 1 service

PUPIL BOOK OR **UNIT BIG BOOK**

Extend and Enrich

MAKE A PICTOGRAPH Work with the children to make a pictograph showing some of the people or the more numerous things in your classroom—students, desks, books, and the like. (See Link to Mathematics on page 106A.) Ask children whether they would like to draw 20 symbols to show 20 things or whether they can think of another way to show numerous items. Help children devise a key in which one symbol equals five items.

Reteach the Skill

EXPLAIN A PICTOGRAPH
Find or make another simple pictograph, and use an overhead projector to show it to the class. Invite children to describe the visual information given in the pictograph and to explain how to read the information.

TECHNOLOGY

Use **GRAPH LINKS** to complete the activities.

3. CLOSE

Think and Do

Children's responses might include health clinics, police stations, public bus stops, parks, libraries, and community centers.

Review the skill with children by asking the following questions:

Q. If your friend had trouble reading a pictograph, what advice would you give? Read the names of the objects on the side of the graph. The symbols next to each name show you the number of those objects. The longest line of symbols shows the highest number. The shortest line shows the lowest number.

What kind of information is good to show on pictographs? Pictographs are good for showing numbers of things and for comparing amounts of things.

Using the Activity Book Distribute copies of Activity Book page 18. Invite children to make a pictograph of the things in their desks or on their work tables by using tally marks or other symbols. Invite children to share their pictographs with classmates.

Activity Book page 18

HANDS-ON OPTION

Take a Poll

Objective: Identify and explain the parts of a pictograph.

Materials: copies of 4-square by 10-square pictograph grids, chart paper

Discuss the kinds of questions that would be good for taking a poll and showing in a pictograph. List on the board or on chart paper questions children mention. Invite each child to choose a question, ask five classmates the question, and design a pictograph to record the results. Remind children to write their questions above their graphs. **(VISUAL/TACTILE/AUDITORY)**

> What is your favorite color?
> What is your shoe size?
> How many pencils do you have in your desk?
>
> In what month is your birthday?
> What is your favorite television show?
> Do you feel happy, sad, mad, or just normal today?
> What kind of pet would you like to have?
> Would you rather go to the zoo or to an amusement park?
> How many people are in your family?
> How many letters are in your first name?

Recycling Day

Objective: Determine availability of selected services in a community.

Materials: 7-square by 10-square pictograph grid mounted on chart paper, crayons or markers, self-stick notes

Invite volunteers whose families recycle to tell about the procedures they follow and on which day the materials they recycle are picked up. Explain that because each city has only a certain number of recycling trucks, the city must use them every day. Make a pictograph to show on which days recycled materials are picked up in each child's neighborhood.

Write the names of the days along the bottom of the pictograph. Give each child a self-stick note on which to draw a truck. Then call one child at a time to the pictograph, and have him or her stick the note in a square of the column that shows the day of the recycling pickup. When all children have affixed their notes, help children interpret the graph. **(VISUAL/KINESTHETIC)**

Button, Button

Objective: Identify and explain the parts of a pictograph.

Materials: a variety of buttons in four different colors, copies of 4-square by 10-square pictograph grids, crayons or markers in colors that match the colors of the buttons, glue (optional)

Give each child a pictograph grid and ten randomly selected buttons. Explain to children that they will sort the buttons and make a pictograph to record the number of buttons of each color. Guide volunteers to explain the steps for completing the graph:

- Give the graph a title.
- On the left-hand side of the graph, show one button for each color of button you name.
- Sort the buttons by color, placing each button in the appropriate square.

Remind children to place the first button of each color in the row beside the color symbol and to work left to right. If children wish to keep their pictographs, suggest that they glue each button in place. Guide children to interpret their graphs by comparing them and answering questions such as these: *Who has the most (name a color) buttons? Who has the fewest? Who has buttons of all four colors? Does anyone have buttons that are all the same color?* **(VISUAL/TACTILE)**

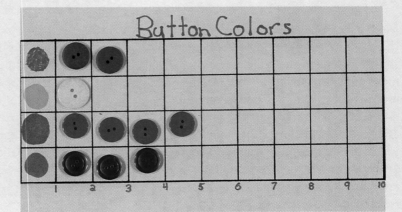

2

PEOPLE MAKE GOODS

OBJECTIVES

1. Describe manufacturing jobs.
2. Recognize how we depend on people who make goods.

VOCABULARY

factory (p. 108)

RESOURCES

Pupil Book/Unit Big Book, pp. 108–111
Write-On Chart 10
Pattern P5
Activity Book, p. 19

ACTIVITY CHOICES

Background

SNEAKERS Today sneakers are part of American fashion, but less than 100 years ago, they did not exist. The process of making sneakers is a long one and requires the work of many people employed in a shoe factory, like the shoe factory featured in this lesson and in the nonfiction book *How Are Sneakers Made?* by Henry Horenstein. It takes many workers to produce a single pair of sneakers, but because they work together, the workers can make over 200 pairs an hour.

INVENTORS African American inventor Jan Ernest Matzeliger (1852–1889) created a machine to "last" shoes, which made it possible to make from 150 to 200 pairs of shoes a day. Although there were machines to cut the shoe leather and shape the sole, *lasting*—shaping the top part of the shoe—could be done only by hand. A skilled laster could produce only 40 to 50 pairs of shoes a day.

1. ACCESS

Ask children to raise their hands if they are wearing sneakers. Then ask them to raise their hands if they are wearing another type of shoe. Invite children to share their ideas about how and where shoes are made. Some children may be familiar with shoemakers in storybooks or shoe-repair shops in real life. Help them understand that today almost all shoes are made by machines, not by hand.

Focus on the Main Idea

In this lesson children will learn about various aspects of manufacturing. They will learn that in a factory, different types of workers must perform different tasks before a product finally can be completed. They will also come to recognize how much we all depend on people who manufacture goods. Tell children that in this lesson they will "visit" a factory where sneakers are made.

Link to Art

ILLUSTRATION Ask children to make a sketch of one of the shoes they are wearing. Allow them to take the shoe off and trace it to get the shape and size as close to the original as they can and then fill in the details. Display sketches during the lesson.

2. BUILD

Key Content Summary

Division of labor allows for specialization in the various jobs needed in the manufacturing process. At the same time, this division prevents workers from participating in the entire process. Nevertheless, without division of labor and assembly lines, most people could not afford many of the products we use today.

Vocabulary

Share the text on page 108, and point out that the word *factory* comes from the Latin word *factor*, which means "maker." Help children understand that a factory is a place where goods are made.

Q. **Why are factories important to a community?** They supply jobs; they make things we need.

Economics

Productivity and Economic Growth Share the text and pictures on pages 109–111. Help children understand that when something is made by hand, one person usually makes the entire object. In a factory people use machines, and each person does only part of the work. Point out the numbered pictures in the text and explain that they show the step-by-step process of manufacturing.

LESSON 2 People Make Goods

Last week Josh's class went on a field trip. You can follow their tour to see how sneakers are made.

1 A sneaker factory is a very busy place. A **factory** is a building in which goods are made. Each factory worker has a special job to do.

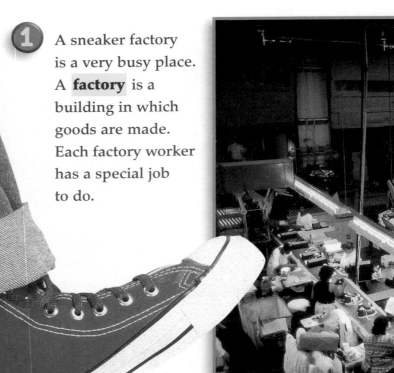

108

ACTIVITY CHOICES

Reading Support

READ AHEAD As children read *People Make Goods,* help them understand the meaning of the highlighted word *factory.* Explain that when they come to a word they do not know, they can read ahead to see if they can get more information. Point out that the words that follow *factory* on this page will help them define this word.

Meet Individual Needs

VISUAL AND TACTILE LEARNERS Invite children to work in the Cards-a-Million greeting card factory. Organize children into groups of five, and have each child perform a different task. One child can obtain raw materials such as construction paper, markers, glitter, stickers, and glue; the second child can fold the construction paper in half; another child can draw a picture on the front of the card; the next child can add stars or glitter to the front; and the fifth child can write a simple saying on the inside, such as Happy Birthday. Help children recognize that each job is an important step toward making the product. Discuss how each group can produce cards quickly and efficiently.

2 The factory buys rubber from countries that are far away. Workers pour melted rubber into molds to shape the sneaker bottoms.

3 Machines cut out the cloth top parts of the sneakers. Then workers sew the parts together.

109

Economics

Economic Systems and Institutions
After children have explored the concept of a sneaker factory, invite them to name other kinds of factories and manufacturing jobs. Prompt children's suggestions by showing pictures of factory-made and handmade objects and asking which objects were made in factories.

Q. **How can you tell whether something was made in a factory?** Items made of plastic, metal, knit cloth, and paper are usually made in factories, and so are most store-bought shoes and clothing. Machines, items that have many parts, and items that come in large quantities are usually made in factories.

PUPIL BOOK OR UNIT BIG BOOK

Link Literature

Invite children to read *The Tortilla Factory* by Gary Paulsen. (Harcourt Brace, 1995) Tracing a tortilla from seed to plant to factory to the dinner table and back to the workers who plant the corn, children will see a continuing cycle of life. Have them focus on the factory in the cycle and the workers who are needed to produce the tortillas. Children might enjoy making simple picture books showing cycles of production for other products of their choice.

Gary Paulsen
THE TORTILLA FACTORY

PAINTINGS BY *Ruth Wright Paulsen*

WRITE-ON CHARTS

Open for Business
Use **WRITE-ON CHART 10** to extend and enrich this lesson. See Teacher's Edition page W31.

Culture

Organizations and Institutions Invite children who know factory workers to share what they know about factory work. Then show children pictures of workers in different types of factories. Ask them to guess whether the work is noisy or quiet, fast- or slow-paced, and simple or complicated.

Q. Would you rather work in a factory or make something by hand? Why? Children might prefer to make things by hand because they would get to make an entire product, they would have more control over their work, and they might be able to work in quieter conditions. They might prefer to work in a factory because they would enjoy working with machines, they would feel proud of being part of a large enterprise, they would have co-workers, and they might earn more money.

3. CLOSE

Ask children to summarize the lesson by dictating sentences to you that describe how work in a factory is organized and to explain why we depend on people who make goods. Record children's responses on chart paper and save for the Reteach activity.

Check Understanding

The child can
—— describe manufacturing jobs.
—— recognize how we depend on people who make goods.

Think Critically

Q. In a factory is it more productive to know one job really well or to try to learn how to perform many jobs? Why? Knowing one job well allows the worker to specialize in one area and help other workers produce more items to sell. It would take longer to make an item if one worker had to make the whole thing.

④ Some workers punch holes in the tops for the laces. Others glue the tops and bottoms together.

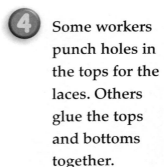

⑤ More workers glue rubber strips around the sneakers.

110

ACTIVITY CHOICES

Extend and Enrich

MAKE A MURAL Invite children to work together to make a giant mural of a factory. Use photos to help children envision the different parts of a factory—the loading dock, where materials are brought to the factory; the shop floor, where workers use machines in the manufacturing process; and the shipping department, where workers take orders for the goods the factory makes. Decide together what the factory in your mural will make.

Reteach the Main Idea

BRAINSTORM To summarize the lesson, display and read aloud the sentences children dictated earlier. Then work with children to brainstorm a list of many types of goods made in factories.

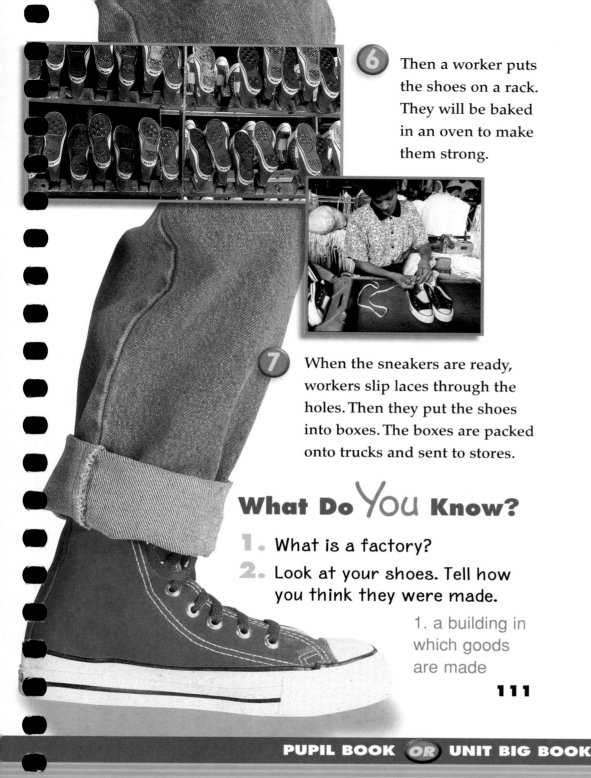

6 Then a worker puts the shoes on a rack. They will be baked in an oven to make them strong.

7 When the sneakers are ready, workers slip laces through the holes. Then they put the shoes into boxes. The boxes are packed onto trucks and sent to stores.

What Do You Know?

1. What is a factory?

2. Look at your shoes. Tell how you think they were made.

1. a building in which goods are made

111

Community Involvement

If possible, invite one or more factory workers to your classroom to talk about what their jobs are like. If no children have relatives or neighbors who work in factories and can come, you might contact a local union or a factory manager to send a representative. Have children prepare questions ahead of time about what they would like to know about working in a factory. Afterward, have the class write a thank-you letter to their guest, telling him or her what they have learned.

Link to Mathematics

ADDITION Present children with this problem: One person can make one item in an hour, but four people can make ten items in an hour. How many can one person make in eight hours? How many can the four people make in eight hours?

Q. **How do factories help people?** Factories provide jobs for people; they make products we might not be able to make ourselves; they provide stores with items to sell.

Show What You Know

Performance Assessment Invite children to draw a series of pictures showing workers making baseball caps or another item of their choice. Suggest children write a caption under each picture to tell what is happening. Have children make books with their pictures and share the books with the class.

What to Look For To evaluate children's drawings and captions, make sure they include both workers and a reasonable process for making baseball caps.

Using the Activity Book Invite children to complete the chart of shirt manufacture on Activity Book page 19 by adding pictures or captions as appropriate. Then have children describe the manufacturing process.

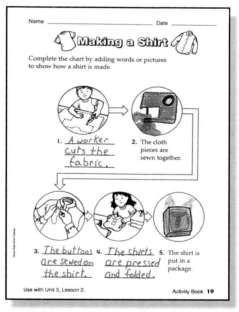

Activity Book page 19

HANDS-ON OPTION

How We Get Canned Corn

Objective: Recognize how we depend on people who make goods.

Materials: Pattern P5, crayons, scissors

Invite children to work in small groups to make accordion books about manufacturing a can of corn. Ask children to brainstorm the steps of manufacturing a can of corn, such as removing the shucks, washing the corn, cutting the kernels off the cob, cooking the corn, putting the corn in a can, and sealing the can. Have children fold their Accordion Box Patterns into six sections and number a section for each step in their process. Then invite them to take turns writing sentences or drawing symbols to represent each step. Allow group members to take turns telling the story of "How We Get Canned Corn" to other groups. **(KINESTHETIC/TACTILE)**

The Story of a Shoe

Objective: Describe manufacturing jobs.

Materials: paper, pencils, drawing paper, crayons, markers

Invite children to write a story from the point of view of a factory-made shoe. The shoe can describe everything that happens to it from the moment its rubber is melted or its leather is cut to the moment that someone puts the shoe on his or her foot. Children might also illustrate their stories, showing things that happen to the shoe as it is made. **(TACTILE/VISUAL)**

Teamwork, Teamwork

Objective: Describe manufacturing jobs.

Materials: bread, peanut butter, jelly, knives, plates, napkins, paper, markers, plastic gloves

COOPERATIVE LEARNING Organize children into groups of four to six. Explain that each group is going to operate as a factory to make peanut-butter-and-jelly sandwiches. Each "factory worker" will have a different job, such as making the sign for each work station, lining up the bread, spreading the peanut butter, spreading the jelly, cutting the sandwiches in half, and cleaning up after the sandwiches are made. Allow each group time to discuss possible ways of organizing the work. Urge children to consider such factors as where items are placed, how many signs are needed, whether all the bread is taken out of the package ahead of time, and who might be best at each task. Each group must make enough sandwiches for all of its members, with each sandwich including the same ingredients and being placed on a plate and cut into halves. Remind children to wash their hands thoroughly and to wear gloves while preparing food. After children have finished making the sandwiches, have each group demonstrate its technique, and invite children to discuss what choices were most efficient. Finally, allow children to eat their sandwiches! **(KINESTHETIC/TACTILE)**

PREDICT A LIKELY OUTCOME

OBJECTIVES

1. Recognize that some results can be predicted.
2. Identify the steps in making a prediction.
3. Predict a likely outcome.

VOCABULARY

prediction (p. 113)

RESOURCES

Pupil Book/Unit Big Book, pp. 112–113
Activity Book, p. 20
Transparency 7

1. ACCESS

Tell children to imagine they are sitting at the kitchen table eating breakfast. On the radio they hear the weatherperson say, "It will probably rain this morning." They look outside the window and see lots of dark, heavy clouds. Suddenly they hear a loud clap of thunder. Ask what they think will happen next.

Q. **How did you know what was going to happen next?** Children can explain that they used clues from the story (the weather forecast, the clouds, the thunder) plus things they already knew (weather forecasts are often accurate; thunder and dark, heavy clouds usually mean rain).

Why is a weatherperson's report sometimes wrong? Sometimes the conditions change suddenly after the weatherperson has already made the report.

ACTIVITY CHOICES

Meet Individual Needs

VISUAL LEARNERS   Display action pictures rich with the potential for things to happen, and invite children to guess what might happen next. Invite them to tell what helped them make their guesses.

Link to Science

CAUSE AND EFFECT   Supply one child with a magnet, another with several paper clips, and still another with a wooden pencil. Ask the class what they think will happen if the magnet is held close to the paper clips and what will happen if the magnet is held close to the pencil. Have children test their predictions. Ask them how they predicted what was going to happen.

TRANSPARENCY
Use TRANSPARENCY 7.

2. BUILD

Vocabulary

Explain that what the weatherperson tells us is a prediction. Define *prediction* as figuring out what you think will happen in the future. A prediction may or may not come true. Invite children to name other people who might make predictions as part of their jobs, such as salespeople and scientists.

Q. **What can people do to make their predictions more accurate?** They can find out as much as possible about what they are predicting.

History

Patterns and Relationships Share with children the text on pages 112–113 and ask them what they think will happen next in the story about Kim. Invite them to share reasons for their thinking. Help them see the story clues that they can use to make their predictions.

Q. **What clues can help you predict what Kim will do?** She wants pink sneakers; her friends all like colored sneakers.

How would knowing more about Kim's past help you? If she usually waits so she can get what she wants, she probably will this time.

Critical Thinking

Guide children through the three steps for making good predictions, listed on page 113. Give them an opportunity to explain their thinking and to compare their predictions with those of classmates.

Predict a Likely Outcome

Kim got money from her aunt and uncle on her birthday. "Thank you," she said. "I'll use it to buy a new pair of shoes."

At the store, the shoe seller asked Kim, "What kind of shoes are you looking for?"

Kim said, "All my friends are wearing bright-colored sneakers. I want pink ones!"

"I am sorry," said the shoe seller. "We have only black sneakers and white sneakers. How would you like a nice pair of sandals?"

What do you think will happen next? What will Kim do? What will the shoe seller do?

112

ACTIVITY CHOICES

Meet Individual Needs

AUDITORY LEARNERS Remind children that doctors use their patients' symptoms to make predictions. Tell children about a child who visits the doctor and complains of a sore throat, cough, and high fever. Ask them what they think the doctor will do next and why. Then tell them the doctor also finds out the child wants to attend a birthday party with other children that afternoon. Ask what they think the doctor will tell the child's parents to do and why.

Role-Play

Invite children to plan and role-play situations like the following: Someone is reading a book while walking, and there's an obstacle in the path. Someone unknowingly drops money and a bystander sees it. Invite children in the audience to make a prediction about what the outcome will be.

You are making a **prediction** when you say what you think will happen next. One way to make good predictions is to follow steps.

1 Read the story. Think about what you know about Kim. What does she want to buy? pink sneakers

2 Look for clues in the story. What does the shoe seller tell her? He offers her sandals instead.

3 Think about what will happen next. Make a prediction. Kim might go to another store. The seller might order what Kim wants.

Think and Do

If a sneaker factory cannot get the rubber it needs to make its shoes, what will happen? Make a prediction.

113

PUPIL BOOK OR **UNIT BIG BOOK**

---

3. CLOSE

Think and Do

Children should predict that there would be a shortage of sneakers, the factory might close, or the factory might use a different material to make soles.

Review the skill with children by asking the following questions:

Q. **Why is it important to make good predictions?** Predictions help us make better decisions about what to do.

Suppose you had to make a prediction, but you did not know what to predict. What would you do? Try to find out more information about the situation. Recall past situations that you could apply.

Using the Activity Book Distribute copies of Activity Book page 20. Invite children to look at each story strip and to draw or write in the last box to predict what will happen next. Have children share their predictions with one another and discuss other possible endings to each strip.

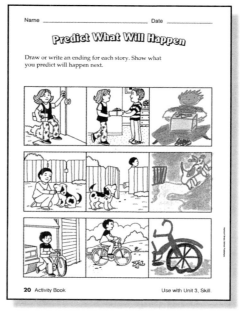

Activity Book page 20

Extend and Enrich

MAKE PREDICTIONS Invite the class to make predictions. They might decide to predict the weather every day for a week, the number of children who will be absent during the week, or the outcome of a sports event. Invite each child to write down his or her predictions and seal them in an envelope. Check them when whatever time period you have chosen is over. Ask children to talk about why some things are more difficult to predict.

Reteach the Skill

PREDICT ENDINGS Supply comic strips that show predictable actions. Cut off the last panel of each strip, and show children the beginning of the story. Invite them to predict what will happen next. Then show them the last panel, and have them compare their predictions with what actually happened. Invite them to discuss how people can make good predictions.

HANDS-ON OPTION

It's So Predictable

Objective: Recognize that some results can be predicted.

Materials: color squares, chart paper, tape

Discuss with children both everyday events and unexpected events that occur in their lives. Invite children to record the events on color squares. Stimulate thinking, if necessary, by mentioning events such as recess, birthdays, fire drills, finding a lost shoe, and Thanksgiving Day. Then prepare a two-column chart with the headings *Predictable* and *Unpredictable*. Make sure each child has at least one event card. Ask each child to tell whether the event on the card is predictable or unpredictable and to explain his or her answer. When the class agrees that an event is either predictable or unpredictable, invite the child holding the card to tape it in the appropriate section of the chart. (VISUAL/AUDITORY)

PREDICTABLE	UNPREDICTABLE
recess	fire drill
birthday	finding a shoe
Thanksgiving Day	

Predicta-Books

Objective: Predict a likely outcome.

Materials: writing paper, construction paper, pencils, stapler

Invite children to write an adventure story. Suggest that they write a draft of the entire story first. Then have them copy the first part of the story on one sheet of paper, stopping at an exciting point. Have them finish the story on another sheet of paper. Help children make blank books by stapling a sheet of paper inside construction-paper covers.

Have children staple the first part of their stories onto the front cover and the ending onto the back cover. Invite each child to read the beginning of his or her story to a partner and then ask the partner to write on the blank page inside the book a prediction about what will happen next. The partner can then read the author's ending on the back cover to confirm or disprove his or her prediction. (VISUAL/TACTILE)

Freeze Frame

Objectives: Identify the steps in making a prediction. Predict a likely outcome.

Materials: toy

Gather three children together and plan the following skit. One child sits on the floor playing with a classroom toy as the others wait "offstage." The child on the floor gets up and walks away, leaving the toy behind. Then the other two children begin walking toward the toy. They are talking animatedly and not looking to see where they are going. Just before the pair reaches the toy, call out "Freeze frame!" and have the actors freeze in position. Invite children in the audience to make predictions about what might happen next, following the steps for making a prediction to explain their reasoning. Then have the actors complete the skit by tripping over the toy, walking around it, or stopping to play with it themselves. Organize the class into small groups and invite them to make up their own skits to perform for the class. Make sure their planning includes a freeze frame and an ending they can perform after the discussion. (VISUAL/AUDITORY/KINESTHETIC)

3

GOODS FROM NEAR AND FAR

OBJECTIVES

1. Recognize that countries trade goods with one another.
2. Identify transportation links that bring goods to a community.

VOCABULARY

trade (p. 114)
transportation (p. 114)

RESOURCES

Pupil Book/Unit Big Book, pp. 114–117
Write-On Charts 11, 34
Vocabulary Blacklines
Vocabulary Cards
Activity Book, p. 21
Desk Maps
Music Audio, "Clickety Clack"

ACTIVITY CHOICES

Meet Individual Needs

TACTILE LEARNERS Provide pairs of children with a variety of objects from different countries, each labeled with its country of origin and concealed in a box or sack. Ask children to select an object with their eyes closed and try to identify it. Ask partners to give hints, telling what the object is used for and, if they know, what country it came from.

Link to Language Arts

JOURNAL Have children start a list of all the things they use that are made in different countries. Remind them to include toys, electronic equipment, food, and clothing. Ask them to list both the item and its country of origin. To find the country of origin of an item, children can examine the item for a label or research the item in an encyclopedia. At the end of the lesson, children might enjoy comparing their lists.

Link to World Languages

OTHER LANGUAGES Invite children who speak other languages to teach their classmates words for items that are imported from their native countries. Children can make a class dictionary naming each object in both English and another language.

1. ACCESS

Begin by displaying a banana and asking children whether they like this kind of fruit. Ask them whether they have a banana plant in their family garden or whether they know of anyone who grows bananas at home. Continue the discussion by asking children where they get bananas. Lead children to trace the banana back to a banana plant. Point out that bananas need very warm and moist weather to grow and that most of the United States does not have that kind of weather. Help children find the countries of Central America on a world map as you tell them that many of the bananas in the United States come from those countries.

Focus on the Main Idea

In this lesson children will explore a range of goods and identify the countries of origin. They will also learn about different modes of transportation used to move goods from one place to another. Tell children that in this lesson they will look at a catalog of goods from around the world and that it was created by another second-grade class.

2. BUILD

Key Content Summary

Because most countries cannot supply all the goods and resources their people want, countries depend on one another to supply these needs through trade. This interdependence reminds people that they benefit from sharing resources. Different modes of transportation, such as trains, planes, ships, and trucks, are used to move these goods from one area to another.

Vocabulary

Share with children the text on page 114 and ask a volunteer to read the definition of *trade*. Have children share experiences with trading—relating what was traded and where they did their trading. Point out that the United States trades goods with many countries around the world. Have children look at a world map and use it to discuss some of the ways these goods can be carried from country to country. Remind children that the way goods are moved from place to place is called *transportation*.

Q. **How is trade between countries like trade between children?**

Children want to make a fair trade; they want to receive something equal to what they give away. It is the same for countries.

LESSON 3
Goods from Near and Far

Countries all over the world trade goods. To **trade** means to buy and sell things. The United States sells cotton, clothing, and food to countries such as China and Mexico. We buy cameras and machines from countries such as Japan and Germany.

Countries use many kinds of **transportation** to move goods. Goods travel by trains, planes, ships, and trucks.

My class has made a catalog of goods we buy from other countries. These goods come from all around the world.

Goods from Other Countries

114

ACTIVITY CHOICES

Reading Support

PREVIEW AND PREDICT Say the words *swap* and *exchange*. Ask children if they know another word that means about the same thing as these two words. Hint that it begins with the letters *tr.* (trade) Invite children to share experiences they have had with trading, telling what they traded and with whom. Then ask children what they think the United States might trade with another country. Read the story to check the ideas.

Link to Music

VOCAL Discuss railroads as a method of transporting goods across land. Then teach children "Clickety Clack." Point out that passenger and freight trains have contributed to the growth of our country for nearly two hundred years.

AUDIO

Use the UNIT 3 MUSIC AUDIOCASSETTE to hear "Clickety Clack."

WRITE-ON CHARTS

Markets Around the World

Use WRITE-ON CHART 11 to extend and enrich this lesson. See Teacher's Edition page W34.

Here is our class catalog. What are some goods we buy from Mexico, Scotland, and Japan?

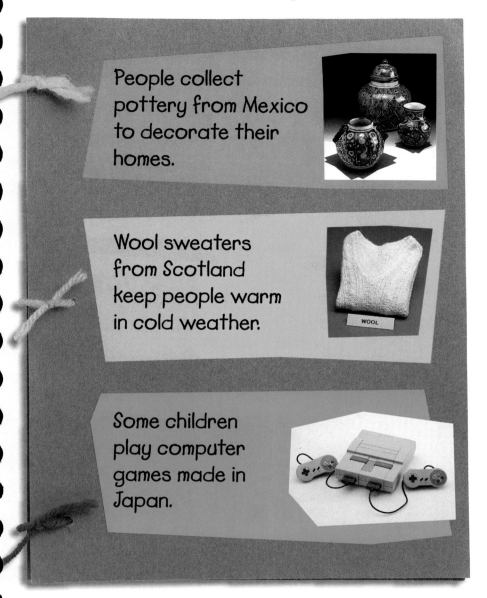

People collect pottery from Mexico to decorate their homes.

Wool sweaters from Scotland keep people warm in cold weather.

WOOL

Some children play computer games made in Japan.

115

VOCABULARY BLACKLINES

Have children choose partners. Provide children with vocabulary cards for *trade* and *transportation*. Invite children to take turns holding up one card at a time while partners say as many related words as they can.

Economics

Interdependence and Income Direct children to study the pictures on pages 115–117. Help them understand that the United States buys goods from other countries and that other countries buy goods that are made here. Invite children to suggest reasons countries trade with one another and list their suggestions on the board or on chart paper. Help children realize that no country can grow or make everything it needs, so all countries depend on one another. Ask children what the goods shown in the catalog tell us about each country's resources.

Q. **Why do you think the United States buys bananas from Costa Rica?** Responses might include that Costa Rica has the right type of weather to grow a lot of bananas and the United States does not; the two countries are close enough for easy transportation.

PUPIL BOOK OR UNIT BIG BOOK

Background

TRADE The United States trades with many countries, but Japan, China, Canada, and Germany are among its most frequent customers and suppliers. Much of this foreign trade is done through international shipping lines, though goods move throughout the country mainly by rail and truck. The United States' main exports include machinery, transportation equipment, chemicals, coal, and agricultural products such as corn, soybeans, and wheat. Major imports include electronic equipment, minerals, and food products such as coffee and seafood.

DESK MAPS

Have children use their DESK MAPS to find countries with which the United States trades.

VOCABULARY CARDS

Provide children with VOCABULARY PICTURE CARDS to use in their Vocabulary activity.

Geography

Regions Have children study the pictures on the catalog cover on page 114. Ask them when each mode of transportation may be used. Point out that different environments require different types of transportation. Invite children to look at a world map as you ask them where people would be most likely to transport goods by train, plane, ship, or truck.

Q. **How do people decide what type of transportation to use?** They think about land routes, water routes, and the weather; they check whether roads or railroad tracks have been built; they also check to see whether the goods being transported last a long time or spoil quickly.

3. CLOSE

Ask children to summarize the lesson by naming a product, the country it comes from, and a means of transportation that could bring it to the United States. Record children's responses on a chart and save for the Reteach activity.

Check Understanding

The child can
____ recognize that countries trade goods with one another.
____ identify transportation links that bring goods to a community.

Think Critically

Q. **Why is it important that countries cooperate and get along?** Countries need one another to meet their needs; if countries did not trade with one another, people in almost every country around the world would not have many of the goods they have now.

Why is trade important to people in the United States? We depend on the goods we import from other countries; many businesses and workers earn money by making goods to export to other countries.

These bananas grew on plants in Costa Rica.

This was made from gold that came from South Africa.

The Netherlands grows tulip bulbs to sell to other countries.

116

ACTIVITY CHOICES

Extend and Enrich

USE A MAP Show the class a map of the region where they live. Together identify how goods are shipped into and out of this area. Discuss the locations of local airports, railroad stations, highways, and waterways. Talk about which goods are transported by each mode of transportation.

Reteach the Main Idea

REVIEW TRADE Read aloud the chart that children created in Close to summarize the lesson. Ask children to explain what this chart tells about trade between countries. Then help children work together to write a definition of the word *trade*.

Sometimes we buy resources from other countries. American workers make goods from the resources. What might they make from these resources?

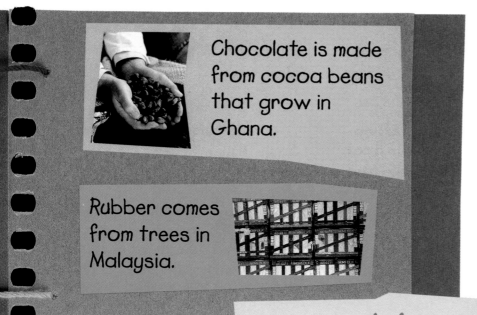

Chocolate is made from cocoa beans that grow in Ghana.

Rubber comes from trees in Malaysia.

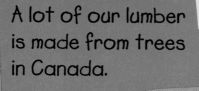

A lot of our lumber is made from trees in Canada.

What Do You Know?

1. How do goods get from other places to the United States?
2. What goods from other countries can you find in your community?

1. trains, planes, ships, trucks

117

PUPIL BOOK **OR** UNIT BIG BOOK

Link to Language Arts

WRITE A POEM After reading aloud "Trucks" by James S. Tippett, guide children in writing class poems about a form of transportation that picks up or delivers goods.

Big trucks for steel beams,
Big trucks for coal,
Rumbling down the broad streets,
Heavily they roll.

Little trucks for groceries,
Little trucks for bread,
Turning into every street,
Rushing on ahead.

Big trucks, little trucks,
In never ending lines,
Rumble on and rush ahead,
While I read their signs.

Performance Assessment Invite children to work together to make their own catalog of goods from around the world. Suggest that each child choose a country and design a page showing one or more goods from that country. Ask children to collect pictures from magazines or catalogs, or to draw their own pictures. Ask for volunteers to design covers. Also, have children discuss the different types of transportation that are needed to ship goods from country to country.

What to Look For To evaluate children's catalog, note whether they show an understanding that some goods are produced in other countries.

Using the Activity Book Ask children to complete Activity Book page 21 by cutting out one product from each person and pasting it in the blank box of the other person. Ask children to write on the lines below each set of goods why they think the children pictured made a good trade.

Activity Book page 21

HANDS-ON OPTION

Trade Fair

Objective: Recognize that countries trade goods with one another.

Materials: magazines, scissors, paste, craft paper, crayons, markers, pens, pencils

COOPERATIVE LEARNING

Invite children to make trading cards showing goods from around the world. Have each child make five trading cards, cutting out and pasting pictures from magazines or drawing their own pictures directly on the cards. Children should work together to research imports and the countries where they are made. Then invite children to organize a trade fair in which they can display their cards and take turns trading their cards with other children. Invite children to discuss why they wanted a new card and how they decided which card to trade for the new one. Ask children whether they felt that they made good trades and why or why not. (KINESTHETIC/TACTILE/VISUAL)

A Product Map

Objective: Recognize that countries trade goods with one another.

Materials: world Desk Maps, drawing paper, markers, crayons, paste, pens, pencils, Write-On Chart 34 (optional)

Provide children with Desk Maps of the world, and invite them to add to the maps by drawing different products that are grown or made in different parts of the world. Alternatively, you could use Write-On Chart 34, inviting children to draw small pictures of products in appropriate places. (TACTILE/VISUAL)

Posters on the Move

Objective: Identify transportation links that bring goods to a community.

Materials: posterboard, markers, crayons

Invite children to create posters showing different ways certain goods can be delivered to stores. Ask them to write a sentence or two for each mode of transportation, telling its advantages and disadvantages. Challenge children to include fanciful means of transportation as well. For example, posters might show an item being delivered by a "product helicopter"—a little rotary blade that attaches to the top of a product and flies the product to a store. After their posters are completed, children might enjoy pretending to be different modes of transportation, such as trains, planes, or trucks. (KINESTHETIC/TACTILE/VISUAL)

4

MAKERS AND USERS, BUYERS AND SELLERS

OBJECTIVES

1. Define *producer* and *consumer*.
2. Describe how people trade money for goods.

VOCABULARY

producer (p. 118)
consumer (p. 119)

RESOURCES

Pupil Book/Unit Big Book, pp. 118–119
Write-On Charts 12, 29
Pattern P6
Vocabulary Blacklines
Activity Book, p. 23
Video, Reading Rainbow, *Fox on the Job*

ACTIVITY CHOICES

Meet Individual Needs

VISUAL LEARNERS Invite children to look through a variety of store catalogs and Sunday advertisements for items people might be interested in buying. Children can cut out the pictures to add to the list of things they have already purchased.

KINESTHETIC LEARNERS Invite children to form pairs and role-play their purchases for the class. If the skit is done in pantomime, let other children guess what has been purchased.

WRITE-ON CHARTS

On the Job
Use WRITE-ON CHART 12 to extend and enrich this lesson. See Teacher's Edition page W38.

VIDEO

Use READING RAINBOW,™ FOX ON THE JOB to meet some young entrepreneurs.

1. ACCESS

Ask children to name some things they have bought recently. List their responses on chart paper and save to be used later in the lesson. Keep the list displayed, but do not explain how it will be used.

Focus on the Main Idea

In this lesson children will read how a class finds ways to make money for a special cause. In the process, they will come to understand the roles of producer and consumer and how money is traded for goods. Tell children they are going to find out how one second-grade class planned a way to raise money to buy a gift for a sick friend.

2. BUILD

Key Content Summary

We depend on producers to make and grow the things we need and to provide services. As consumers, we exchange, or trade, money for goods and services. We can be both producers and consumers.

Vocabulary

Select an item from the list children made in Access, and ask them where the good came from. Help children realize that many people worked to make, ship, and sell the good. Tell children that each of these people is a *producer*, or a person who makes or sells goods or who produces or sells services. A person who buys and uses what a producer makes or sells is called a *consumer*. Emphasize that the children are consumers when they or their families buy the things on the list.

Q. **Why do producers and consumers need each other?** Producers need consumers to buy their goods or services; consumers need producers to make or sell items for them to use or to provide services.

Economics

Interdependence and Income Elicit what the children on pages 118–119 are trying to do and why, who the producers are, and who the consumers are. Then discuss how consumers pay for goods and services.

Q. **Where do consumers get the money they need to pay for the goods and services they buy and use?** They work to earn the money.

What might happen if consumers did not buy the goods or services of certain producers? The producers would not make the money they need to buy the goods and services they need as consumers.

3. CLOSE

To summarize the lesson, distribute the word cards for *producer* and *consumer*, which are in the back of this Teacher's Edition. Invite children to write definitions for both words and give examples of each.

LESSON 4
Makers and Users, Buyers and Sellers

Our school raised money to help a sick classmate. Mandy needs a computer to learn at home. Everyone thought of ways to earn money.

Our class had an arts and crafts sale. We painted pictures and made clay pots to sell. I sold a picture of my dog, Red, for 25 cents. Our teacher said that we were producers. **Producers** make or grow things to sell.

118

ACTIVITY CHOICES

Reading Support

IDENTIFY THE MAIN IDEA
Review the vocabulary words, *producer* and *consumer*, by using a chart like the one shown. As children read, have them record one or more words that help define each key word and give an example of each.

	WHAT IS IT?	WHO IS IT?
producer	person who makes or grows something	farmer growing corn; toymaker building a truck
consumer	person who buys or uses things	man who buys corn; boy who uses toy truck

Meet Individual Needs

AUDITORY LEARNERS
Organize children into small groups to play a game. Display the list made in Access, and invite children to use it for ideas. One player says something like *I am a producer; I grow apples.* The next player might reply, *I am a consumer who buys your apples, but I am also a producer who makes cars.* Children continue in this manner.

We invited our families and friends to the sale. My sister bought two plants for her room. She was a consumer. **Consumers** buy and use things made by producers.

Today our school sent a new computer to Mandy. The money we earned helped buy it for her. The computer will make it easier for Mandy to learn at home.

What Do You Know?

1. What do producers do?

2. When are you a consumer?

1. Producers make or grow things to sell.

2. when you buy and use things made by producers

119

PUPIL BOOK OR UNIT BIG BOOK

Extend and Enrich

ANALYZE PRODUCTS Point to a book and invite children to identify all the kinds of producers needed to make it. List their suggestions on the board. Repeat the process with other classroom objects, such as a computer, a television, a clock, and a flag. Remind them that their school is a consumer because it buys and uses these things.

Reteach the Main Idea

PLAN PURCHASES Direct children back to the list of items they bought. Have them take turns selecting items, telling where they purchased the items and how they made the purchases.

Think Critically

Q. **When are producers also consumers?** when they pay for the supplies they need to make or grow their goods; when they pay for the services and goods they need

Show What You Know

Performance Assessment Have children draw or cut out pictures depicting producers and consumers. Invite children to describe the pictures to their classmates, identifying the producer, the good or service, and the consumer and describing how the consumer trades money for the good or service.

What to Look For Pictures should depict producers providing some product or service and consumers paying for goods or services.

Using the Activity Book Distribute copies of Activity Book page 23. Ask children to draw in the box something that they have bought or used and to then write a brief paragraph telling where and how they purchased it and who produced it. Invite children to share and compare their drawings and paragraphs.

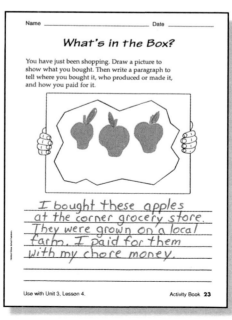

Activity Book page 23

LESSON 4 • 119

HANDS-ON OPTION

A Class Production

Objectives: Define *producer* and *consumer*. Describe how people trade money for goods.

Materials: paper, pencils, drawing paper, crayons, markers

COOPERATIVE LEARNING Invite children to think of ways they could earn money to buy a gift for a friend, support a cause, or buy a needed item for the classroom. Remind the class that producers make money by selling goods or services. Children should decide on goods they could sell (art, plants, baked goods, used objects and books) or services they could provide (washing cars, walking dogs, shining shoes).

Once children have chosen their project, remind them that producers must tell consumers about the good or service they have to sell. Have children brainstorm ways they might advertise their project, such as with invitations to family and friends, flyers to be distributed in the neighborhood, and posters to be put up at school and in the community.

Form groups to work on different parts of the project, such as producing or acquiring the good, displaying it for sale, advertising it, and selling it. Remind children that consumers will trade money for the good or service and that the money the children earn will enable them to buy a gift for a friend, support their cause, or buy something for the classroom.

Finally, carry out the project and use the money for the cause the class has chosen. Afterward, discuss with children what they have learned about the relationship between producers and consumers. **(AUDITORY/KINESTHETIC)**

Producer-Consumer Pairs

Objective: Define *producer* and *consumer*.

Materials: drawing paper, crayons, markers, Write-On Chart 29

Invite children to make side-by-side drawings showing the relationship between producers and consumers. Ask them to draw pairs of producers and consumers, such as a factory worker making a car and a person driving a car, or a farmer growing wheat and a person eating bread. Initiate this activity by inviting the class to brainstorm lists of producers and their products and of consumers and how they use those products. Record the responses on a two-column chart or on Write-On Chart 29, and post the chart prominently for children to refer to as they make their drawings. **(TACTILE/VISUAL)**

A T-Shirt Shop

Objectives: Define *producer* and *consumer*. Describe how people trade money for goods.

Materials: Pattern P6, crayons, markers, blank price tags, tape, play money

Distribute patterns and art supplies. Invite children to create their own designs to be used in a class T-shirt shop. When children have drawn their "designer" T-shirts, have each child decide what dollar amount to charge for his or her shirt, write it on a price tag, and tape the tag to the drawing. Display the completed drawings along the chalkboard ledge. Then invite children to take turns being salespeople and customers, selling and buying the shirts with play money. Ask children to discuss the roles of producers and consumers and tell how consumers trade money for goods. **(KINESTHETIC/TACTILE)**

The Elves and the Shoemaker

Children may enjoy acting out this fairy tale. Use the story to discuss the resources needed to operate a business successfully and the role of producers and consumers in a community.

Once upon a time there lived a poor shoemaker and his seamstress wife. The shoemaker was worried because he had only enough leather to make one pair of shoes. He set out his tools and cut the leather so that he would be ready to work the next day. Then he went to bed. When he awoke, instead of the leather he left the night before, the shoemaker was surprised to find a beautiful pair of brand-new shoes. Later on in the day, a customer came along. He liked the shoes and paid twice the price.

The shoemaker was now able to buy more leather and did as before, this time preparing his materials for two pairs of shoes. The following morning the shoemaker again found perfectly stitched shoes where the leather had been. These were sold at an even higher price. Now the shoemaker left out leather every night. Soon he was able to save a good sum of money. Yet the shoemaker and his wife wondered at their fortune. They decided to hide and watch to find out what happened during the night. Around midnight, two ragged elves crept into the shop and quickly set about making shoes.

Now the shoemaker and his wife felt they must do something to thank their nightly helpers. The shoemaker made each a pair of sturdy boots and his wife sewed them a new set of clothes. They laid out the gifts in the shop and waited once more. The elves were delighted with their surprise and left the shop in their new clothes, never to be seen again.

The shoemaker and his wife continued to make shoes and sew clothes. They grew even more prosperous.

DEFINE THE PROBLEM

Invite children to look at the photograph and tell what materials the children used to create their model town. Guide them to recognize that the children are wearing special clothes.

Q. What does the photograph tell you about the new community the children have created? The new community has streets and roads, a school, a factory, homes, stores, and an apartment or office building.

What do the clothes that the children are wearing show? The children's clothes show some of the community's workers—police officers, bus drivers, and construction workers.

What does the factory produce? The Kid Town factory produces sun visors.

"PRIMARY SOURCE"

Set up opportunities for children to interview city officials and city workers. Remind children that these people help their community. Suggest that children ask questions about what a new community would need. Ask them to use the information on page 120 to create a list of questions prior to the interviews.

Solving Problems

Kid Town

How would you plan a town?

Imagine that you and your classmates are building a new community.

● What goods would your town need?
● What services would it need?
● What kind of factory might help your town to grow?
● Which job would you choose?

Show your ideas.

Plan ways to show your new community.

● Draw a map or make a model of Kid Town.
● Wear special clothes or show tools for jobs in Kid Town.
● Act out consumers using goods and services in your community.
● Draw a picture of something your factory produces.

120

ACTIVITY CHOICES

Meet Individual Needs

ENGLISH LANGUAGE LEARNERS
Provide an opportunity for children who speak the same first language to share ideas about communities and factories. Then have them relate these ideas in English to the rest of the class. Also, children who have lived in another country might enjoy sharing how their community there was like their new community in the United States and how it was different.

Link to Language Arts

JOURNAL Challenge children to research factories in their community or in a nearby city. Have them list the factories and their products in their journals. Children might like to use the information to create a poster showing the goods produced in or near their town.

Background

CITY PLANNER Children might be interested to learn that the job of *city planner* is a real one. Tell them that if they enjoyed this Brainstorm activity, they might like to be a city planner when they grow up. Explain that city planners give advice to leaders on ways to make their communities better. They also plan new neighborhoods and communities where people can live and work.

Kid Town Factory
Sunny Day Visor
Yarn Headband
Soft Beads
Cardboard Brim
Logo or Design

Brainstorm

USE PROBLEM-SOLVING SKILLS

Organize children into several groups. Ask each group to use the questions on page 120 as a guide to plan its own community. Have children list the goods and services their town will need. Then each child can choose a job and write about what his or her duties would be. Children can also discuss the kind of factory that might help their town grow. Remind children to consider the wants and needs of all the people living in the town.

Q. **What kinds of things are produced in factories?** Responses might include toys, clothing, food, tools, cars, furniture, and shoes.

SHOW SOLUTIONS

Provide children with art supplies, drawing paper, craft sticks, small boxes, construction paper, modeling clay, and tools and other props related to various community workers. Invite each group to make a model or a drawing of its new community. Some children might like to dress up to represent their jobs and tell how they help people in the community. Others might enjoy creating diagrams of items produced in the town factory. Allow time for these children to share their diagrams.

121

Role-Play

Organize children into groups of four, and invite them to role-play an assembly line in a factory that makes toy robots. Arrange each group around a table, and give the first child in the line 5 sheets of paper. That child takes one sheet and quickly draws a simple robot head. He or she then passes the paper to the next child and immediately takes another sheet and draws exactly the same head. The second child draws the same body on each sheet he or she receives and passes the paper to the next child, who adds arms. The fourth child adds legs to make their "product" complete. Guide children to understand the importance of teamwork in a factory setting.

Meet Individual Needs

VISUAL LEARNERS Suggest that children look through newspapers, magazines, and books to find photos of neighborhoods and communities. Ask them to look for photos that show both large and small communities. Have them share the photos with the class and discuss the differences and similarities between the communities.

Old Mother Hubbard

Many Mother Goose nursery rhymes will be familiar to children. While they are fun and are sometimes silly, they also carry images that relate to everyday life. Assign the following verses to be recited by volunteers. Children may want to work in teams to recite their verses. Conduct the recital as a round robin, pointing to children or groups of children randomly to offer their selections.

Old Mother Hubbard
Went to the cupboard
To fetch her poor dog a bone;
But when she came there
The cupboard was bare
And so the poor dog had none.

She went to the grocer's
To buy him some fruit;
But when she came back
He was playing the flute.

She went to the tailor's
To buy him a coat;
But when she came back
He was riding a goat.

She went to the hatter's
To buy him a hat;
But when she came back
He was feeding the cat.

She went to the barber's
To buy him a wig;
But when she came back
He was dancing a jig.

She went to the seamstress
To buy him some linen;
But when she came back
The dog was a-spinning.

She went to the cobbler's
To buy him some shoes;
But when she came back
He was reading the news.

She went to the hosier's
To buy him some hose;
But when she came back
He was dressed in his clothes.

After the children have recited several times, discuss the community workers in the rhymes. Invite children to think of other community workers and to write additional verses for "Old Mother Hubbard."

5

MAKING WISE CHOICES

OBJECTIVES

1. Define *income*.
2. Recognize that people have unlimited wants but limited resources to satisfy their wants.
3. Explain the importance of saving money.
4. Discuss how competition in business creates choices for consumers.

VOCABULARY

wants (p. 122)
income (p. 122)

RESOURCES

Pupil Book/Unit Big Book, pp. 122–125
Vocabulary Blacklines
Vocabulary Cards
Activity Book, p. 24
The Amazing Writing Machine

ACTIVITY CHOICES

Meet Individual Needs

TACTILE LEARNERS Bring in coins and currency in several denominations. Invite children to handle the money and describe what makes each denomination different. Together, make a chart listing the names, features, and values of the coins or bills. Then discuss why it is important to be able to tell coins and bills apart. Ask what might happen if coins and bills looked too much alike.

Background

EARLY UNITED STATES CURRENCY In 1785 Thomas Jefferson proposed a system of American tender based on the decimal system, but the first coins were not minted until 1792. Before that time, colonists used many different means of exchange, including barter. Virginians used tobacco as money, New Yorkers traded in beaver skins, Rhode Islanders traded in wool, and South Carolina residents traded in rice. Settlers also had money from their home countries, including Dutch guilders and English pounds sterling. Indians used wampum—white, black, and purple beads made from clamshells and periwinkle—for money. Later, each state made its own coins, which could be used in only that state.

1. ACCESS

Ask volunteers to name something they would like to buy and, if they can, to tell how much it costs. Then ask the class to brainstorm ways children can earn money for the items they would like to buy. Ask children what they do when they do not have enough money to buy everything they want.

Focus on the Main Idea

In this lesson children will explore different ways they can earn and spend money. They will also discuss the benefits of saving money. Tell children that in this lesson they will read about a boy who earns money and must make choices about how to use his money wisely.

2. BUILD

Key Content Summary

Children examine the concept of income and the choices they have about how to use their income. Children also explore trade-offs in their spending decisions and examine why saving money is important.

Economics

Interdependence and Income   To introduce the lesson, share the text on page 122 along with the picture of the boy washing the car. Have children compare their list of how children can earn money with how Jarrod earns money. Point out the value of earning money through personal labor. Introduce the idea of saving by pointing out that in addition to paying for material things and entertainment, money can also be used for future needs and emergencies. Also, show children the photo of the bank book on page 123.

Q. **Why should you save money?** to have enough to buy things that cost a lot; to have enough for special occasions or an emergency

What does it mean to waste money? to buy things when you need money for something more important; to buy something and not use it

LESSON 5 Making Wise Choices

Wants are goods and services that people would like to have. People cannot buy everything they want. They must make choices. Read to see how Jarrod plans to spend his money.

I earn money by washing cars for my neighbors. I also do extra chores at home, such as raking leaves. The money I earn is called **income**.

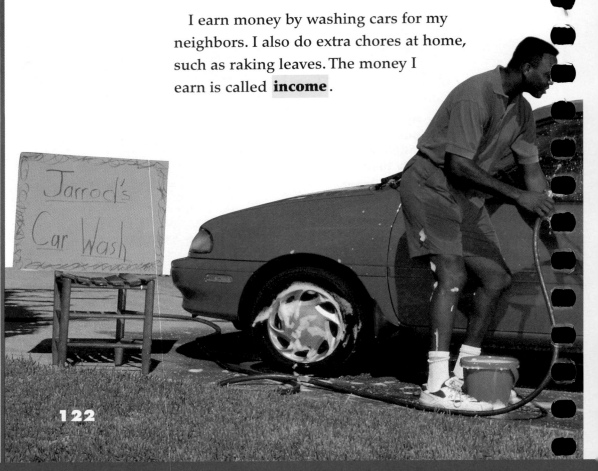

122

ACTIVITY CHOICES

Reading Support

LOOK FOR FAMILIAR WORDS
Pause as children come to the word *income.* Write the word on the chalkboard. Ask children to find two smaller words they already know in this word. (*in* and *come*) Underline the letters for each part. Then help children combine the two words to create the word *income.* Explain that one definition for the word is "money that 'comes in' from working."

Meet Individual Needs

ENGLISH LANGUAGE LEARNERS
Invite children to identify what Jarrod is doing in the first picture. As children say *washing a car,* write *washing cars* on the board. Invite children to read the phrase aloud and to find it in the text. Explain that the phrase is in a sentence that tells how Jarrod earns money—by washing cars for his neighbors. Repeat the process with the second page, focusing on one picture at a time.

I spend some of my income. I keep the money in the bank until I want to spend it. Gran and Pops gave me money on my birthday. I am saving that money for college. I keep it in the bank, too.

Jarrod's Bank Savings

	Deposits
July 7 Money from Gran and Pops for college	$50.00
August 12 Money saved from allowances	$20.00
August 22 Money from lemonade stand and car wash	$35.00

123

PUPIL BOOK OR UNIT BIG BOOK

LESSON 5 • 123

Economics

Scarcity and Choice Share the text and pictures on pages 124–125. Point out that Jarrod named several things he would like to buy. These are Jarrod's *wants*. Wants are things people would like to have. Help children understand the consequences of each of Jarrod's choices (e.g., continued costs for pet care) and stress that consequences like these exist for everyone.

NOTE: Current economic teaching defines *wants* in terms of trade-offs and scarcity and not in contrast to *basic needs*, as defined in Unit 1. For many people, basic needs are among their greatest wants.

Markets and Prices Point out that Jarrod and his mother visited many stores before buying the soccer ball and that the ball they bought was on sale. Explain that a store often lowers its prices on certain goods, or has sales, to get people to shop at that store.

Critical Thinking

Ask children to recall what Jarrod did after he finally decided how to spend his money at the mall. Ask them why Jarrod could get money out of the bank and what happened to his bank account when he withdrew the money to buy the soccer ball.

Q. **Suppose there are two things you want to buy and you only have enough money to buy one of them. What can you do?** You can save money and buy both; you can buy the one you want more and do without the other.

3. CLOSE

Have children summarize what they have learned from this lesson by telling what they think of Jarrod's choice at the mall and explaining why. Ask them to describe how they would have handled the situation.

When I shop, I see many things I want to buy. I make choices about how to spend my money. I do not have enough money yet to buy a new bike. And if I buy a fish tank, I will have to buy fish food every week.

124

I decide to buy a soccer ball. I like to play games with my friends. I will have money left over after I buy the ball. I take the money I think I will need out of the bank.

Mom and I look in different stores. There are many kinds of balls. Some cost more than others. I choose one that is on sale. It has been marked at a lower price to get us to spend our money in that store.

ACTIVITY CHOICES

Extend and Enrich

INTERVIEW ADULTS Invite children to ask adults at home for one reason to spend money and one reason to save it. Ask children to share these answers with the class by writing each answer on a paper leaf. On the bulletin board, draw a large "Spending Tree" and a large "Savings Tree." Tell children to post their leaves on the correct trees.

Reteach the Main Idea

COMPARISON SHOP Organize children into groups of four or five. Give groups a pretend shopping list with four or five items on it. Then provide them with sale circulars from newspapers. Invite children to look through the circulars for the best price of each item on their shopping list. Help them determine where they could get the best buy.

Four major highways and an airport bring many people to Bloomington, Minnesota. It is the home of the largest shopping mall in the United States. Nearly 12 thousand people work at the Mall of America.

Bloomington, Minnesota

United States

Baltimore, Maryland

Baltimore, Maryland, is on the Atlantic Ocean. Ships bring goods into its harbor. In 1896 the oldest shopping mall opened in Baltimore. Today people still shop at Roland Park Marketplace.

Now I think I made a good choice. I have fun playing soccer with my friends.

What Do You Know?

1. Where can you keep money that you save?

2. What do you choose to spend your money on?

1. The bank

PUPIL BOOK OR UNIT BIG BOOK

Meet Individual Needs

AUDITORY LEARNERS Organize children into groups of five or six to play a game of "Round Robin" using this sentence starter: *When I have saved enough money, I will _____.* The first player finishes the sentence, and other players repeat all the things that previous players have said and then add their own ending. When someone makes a mistake, he or she starts a new round.

Community Involvement

Take a field trip to a bank, or invite a bank employee to visit your classroom. Ask children to prepare questions ahead of time, focusing on how saving money is beneficial to individuals and to the community.

Check Understanding

The child can
____ define *income*.
____ recognize that people have unlimited wants but limited resources to satisfy their wants.
____ explain the importance of saving money.
____ discuss how competition in business creates choices for consumers.

Think Critically

Q. **Why do people need incomes?** to pay for the things and services they need and want

Show What You Know

Performance Assessment Supply each child with twenty dollars in play money or counters. Provide catalogs for children to get ideas of ways to use the money. Then have children write what they will buy and why. They should include in their responses what they will do with the remainder of the money.

What to Look For Children should show that they are aware of the value of money and of the importance of savings.

Using the Activity Book Distribute copies of Activity Book page 24. Invite children to set a goal for the money they earn, tell ways to reach the goal, and determine how long it will take to save the money.

Name _____ Date _____

Saving Money

Think of something you would like to buy that costs $20. Imagine that you get $5 a week for doing chores. Think of other ways to earn money. Use the table to make a plan. Write how long it will take you to save the money you need.

Goal To earn $20 to buy _a tennis racket for $15_

Ways I can earn money _$5 a week for chores,_ _save my allowance, do jobs for_ _neighbors, collect + recycle aluminum cans_

Money earned	Money spent

It will take me _3 weeks or less_ to save the money.

24 Activity Book   Use with Unit 3, Lesson 5.

Activity Book page 24

HANDS-ON OPTION

A Money Mural

Objectives: Define *income*. Explain the importance of saving money. Discuss how competition in business creates choices for consumers.

Materials: mural paper, pencils, drawing paper, crayons, markers

 Invite children to create a class mural showing where and how money is spent and saved in their community. As a group, children identify some places they would like to include in the mural, such as a favorite store, a bank, and a movie theater. Then organize children into groups, with each group responsible for drawing one place and the activities that go on there. Below their drawings, children can write captions telling how those activities help their community. **(TACTILE/VISUAL)**

Tale of a Ten-Dollar Bill

Objective: Recognize that people have unlimited wants but limited resources to satisfy their wants.

Materials: paper, drawing materials

Demonstrate how to divide a sheet of paper into three equal sections to represent a comic strip. Point out that a comic strip tells a story quickly and that each of the pictures tells a part of the story. Tell children to draw three pictures that tell a story of how they or their friends might use a ten-dollar bill. Explain how they can use thought bubbles to help the story along. When the comic strips are finished, they can be displayed on a bulletin board or bound in a scrapbook. Then provide time for children to read and enjoy each other's strips. **(TACTILE/VISUAL)**

Save More Now!

Objectives: Recognize that people have unlimited wants but limited resources to satisfy their wants. Explain the importance of saving money.

Materials: magazines, drawing paper, crayons, markers

Invite children to contribute to a list of reasons why saving money is important. Then tell children to imagine they have been hired by a local bank to make posters urging people to save more money. Tell children that their posters should include reasons the class has listed as well as any other reasons they think of. Remind them to use both words and pictures on their posters so their message will be clear. After the posters are completed, organize children into small groups and have them present their work to their group, telling what they have drawn and how it shows that saving is important. **(VISUAL/AUDITORY)**

Skills

FOLLOW A DIAGRAM

OBJECTIVES
1. Explain how diagrams help us understand information.
2. Read a diagram showing how coins are made.

VOCABULARY
diagram (p. 126)

RESOURCES
Pupil Book/Unit Big Book, pp. 126–127
Activity Book, p. 25
Transparency 8

1. ACCESS

Ask children to recall what a bicycle looks like. Then ask how they would go about describing the bicycle to someone who has never seen one. Allow volunteers to share their descriptions with the class. Ask children whether they think this task is hard or easy.

Q. **What would make describing the bicycle easier and more clear?** a drawing or a picture

You may wish to help children recall the use of maps, pictographs, tables, webs, and other graphic organizers that provide visual aids. Tell children that they will learn about another kind of visual in this lesson.

ACTIVITY CHOICES

Meet Individual Needs

ENGLISH LANGUAGE LEARNERS
Help children with limited English understand the concept of a simple drawing representing something more complex. On separate sheets of chart paper, draw simple faces similar to the smiling faces used on round buttons. The faces should show different expressions, such as happy, angry, tired, and sad. Have children interpret each face in turn.

Link to Art

ILLUSTRATION Invite children to once again describe a bicycle, but this time ask them to draw pictures to go with their words. Invite children to compare descriptions with partners. Ask them whether they think it was easier to describe the bicycle with or without the pictures.

" PRIMARY SOURCE "

Bring to class a blueprint of a home or other building, a floor plan for a museum or art gallery, or a surveyor's drawing showing property lines. Ask children to generalize the need for such drawings for planning something new or for understanding how something is laid out.

2. BUILD

Vocabulary

Ask children if they or their parents have ever put something together, such as a model car or a bicycle. Ask if the instructions had pictures showing how to put the object together. Explain that these pictures are *diagrams*, or drawings that show the parts of something or how something is made.

Visual Analysis

Interpret Diagrams Share with children the text on page 126. Ask them to study the diagram and its labels. Invite children to trace with their fingers the lines connecting the labels to the parts of the coin. Help children compare the quarter with a penny, a dime, and a nickel. (Note the smooth edge of a penny to help children understand a reeded ridge.)

Q. **What information does this diagram give?** The diagram shows the parts of a quarter.

What information does it *not* give? It does not give the color of the item or its actual size.

Focus attention on the pictures and text on page 127. Help children understand how each picture shows a step in the minting process.

Q. **How are diagrams useful?** They show how to make something; they show what parts or materials a thing is made of.

How is a diagram different from a picture? A diagram shows only the important parts of an object; a diagram may show the inside of an object, as if the object were cut in half. A picture shows the object just the way it looks.

Chart and Graph Skills

Follow a Diagram

Have you ever wondered how money is made? A **diagram** is a drawing that shows the parts of something or how something is made. This diagram shows the parts of a coin.

reeded ridge
face
U.S. motto
mint date
mint mark
Latin motto ("Out of many, one")
eagle

Look at a penny, a nickel, and a dime. How are they like the quarter? How are they different?

They all have the motto, mint date, and mint mark. They have different pictures on the front and back. The penny and nickel do not have reeded ridges.

126

ACTIVITY CHOICES

Meet Individual Needs

KINESTHETIC LEARNERS Invite a group of children to choose a diagram and arrange their bodies to represent each of the diagram's parts. They might use labels, props, or costumes to make their three-dimensional diagram more clear.

Link to Science

TECHNOLOGY Display diagrams of machines, plants, animals, manufactured objects, or any other objects from magazines, catalogs, or textbooks. Invite each child to choose a diagram and explain it to a partner.

TRANSPARENCY

Use TRANSPARENCY 8.

This diagram shows how coins are minted, or made.

Skills

1 A carving machine carves the design of each side onto a steel stamp.

2 A cutting machine cuts bars of metal into blank coins.

3 A stamping machine stamps the designs on both sides of the blank coins.

4 A counting machine counts the coins into bags to go to the bank.

Think and Do

Design your own coin or paper money. Draw a diagram to show the different parts.

127

PUPIL BOOK OR UNIT BIG BOOK

Extend and Enrich

FOLD PAPER Have children follow written instructions and a diagram for making folded-paper designs (or origami). Ask them to describe how they were able to follow instructions and whether the task could have been made easier in any way.

Reteach the Skill

MAKE A DIAGRAM Invite children to make simple diagrams of something they use, such as a camera, a tape recorder, a telephone, or a video game. Have them explain the parts of their diagrams to partners.

3. CLOSE

Think and Do

Children's diagrams might include some or all of the following parts: a person's face, a date, a motto, and an eagle or other national symbol.

Review the skill with children by asking the following questions:

Q. **What steps do you go through to make a diagram?** Identify each part of something, decide how the parts are put together, draw the object, and draw and label each part.

What steps do you go through to read a diagram? Decide what the diagram is showing, look at the entire object, look at each part, read the labels, and figure out how each part fits with the others.

Using the Activity Book Distribute copies of Activity Book page 25. Have children complete the page by answering questions about the diagram. Then have children share with partners ideas for reading diagrams more effectively.

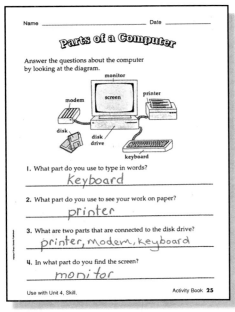

Activity Book page 25

HANDS-ON OPTION

Patent Office

Objective: Explain how diagrams help us understand information.

Materials: assorted art materials such as foam shapes, pipe cleaners, craft sticks; Teacher's Edition page 127B; rubber stamp

Display the art materials and challenge children to use them to design new inventions or to make models of inventions they already use. Explain that inventors protect their inventions by getting patents from the government. A patent shows that the invention is the inventor's idea and keeps other people from making money from his or her idea. Distribute copies of the Patent Application. Ask each child to fill out the application and to show the model and the application to a "patent office clerk" partner. The partner can read the application and explain to the class why a patent should be granted for the invention. After the application has been presented, it can be stamped with the rubber stamp to show that it has been approved and that the patent will be granted. (TACTILE/VISUAL)

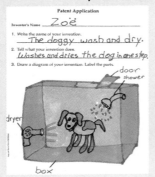

More Diagrams

Objective: Explain how diagrams help us understand information.

Materials: collection of diagrams of common household objects such as videocassette recorders, toys, and appliances

Display the collection of diagrams. Invite children to discuss times when they or adults they know have used diagrams to understand how to use common household objects. Ask children to examine each diagram and read the labels on the parts. Help them conclude that diagrams help people understand how products work and how to repair them. (AUDITORY/VISUAL)

How Things Work

Objective: Explain how diagrams help us understand information.

Materials: paper, pencils

Help children brainstorm a list of everyday objects that have moving parts, such as clocks, radios, cameras, and pencil sharpeners. Invite children to choose an object from the list and draw a diagram of the object. Tell children to draw a line from each part to a blank for a label. Then have partners exchange papers and label the parts of each other's diagrams. Children can use the labeled diagrams to explain to the class how the objects work. (VISUAL/AUDITORY/TACTILE)

How Is It Made?

Objective: Read a diagram showing how something is made.

Materials: reference books, paper, pencils

With children, review the diagram that shows how coins are made. Then invite children to use reference books to find out how one product they use every day is made. Ask children to list or draw the steps that tell how the product is made and to explain the process to the class. (AUDITORY/VISUAL)

How a book is made

Patent Application

Inventor's Name _____

1. Write the name of your invention.

   _____

2. Tell what your invention does.

   _____

3. Draw a diagram of your invention. Label the parts.

Harcourt Brace School Publishers

MAKING SOCIAL STUDIES REAL

READ AND RESPOND

Read aloud pages 128 and 129 and discuss the store in Orlando, Florida, that is run entirely by fifth graders. Explain that BIZ KID$ is part of a social studies class in Florida in which children learn the skills they need to work at a real job. Invite children to tell what they think it would be like to work at BIZ KID$.

Q. What job would you want if you worked at BIZ KID$? Responses will vary depending on the child. (Provide children with a list of possible jobs: greeter, check-out person, salesperson, security guard, and so on.)

Why do people have jobs? to make money so they can buy things they need and want

Invite children to discuss what they would do with the money they made if they worked at BIZ KID$. Provide children with possibilities, such as buy new goods to sell, give some to charity, have a party.

Biz Kid$

One store in Orlando, Florida, is completely run by children. It's called BIZ KID$. Everyone from the greeter to the check-out person is in the fifth grade.

United States

Orlando, Florida

Working at BIZ KID$ is part of a social studies class. The fifth graders are taught how to run a business. A **business** is a place that sells goods or services. At BIZ KID$ students learn how to greet people, count money, sell goods to customers, use a cash register, and get along with other workers.

128

ACTIVITY CHOICES

Background

BIZ KID$ is a store in the Orlando Fashion Square Mall, 3201 East Colonial Drive, Orlando, Florida. This 3,000-square-foot store is unique because it is completely staffed by fifth-grade students. Components of the curriculum include reviewing mock classified ads for job positions, completing a job application, preparing for a job interview, training in customer service and professionalism, technological training on cash terminals, and instruction in basic economic terms such as *customer, profit,* and *supply and demand.* Local business people and educators developed BIZ KID$ to provide a reality-based, hands-on experience. The 10- and 11-year-old students sell real products to real customers in a real retail environment. At the end of the class time, BIZ KID$ expenses such as inventory and rent are paid, and the class votes on how to spend the profits.

Students say that working at BIZ KID$ is fun, and they learn a lot about business, too. Some of the goods fifth graders sell are snacks, first-aid supplies, and Earth-friendly products. At the end of the year, the students decide how they will spend the money they made.

 What Can You Do?

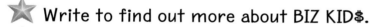 Write to find out more about BIZ KID$.

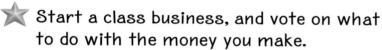 Start a class business, and vote on what to do with the money you make.

Visit the Internet at
http://www.hbschool.com
for additional resources.

129

PUPIL BOOK OR UNIT BIG BOOK

Vocabulary

Define *business* as a store or other establishment that sells, makes, or provides goods or services to consumers. Ask children to list businesses they know about in your community. Help them recognize that a business can be an activity one person or a family does in their home, in a small office or store with a few employees, or in a large company with many workers.

Q. **What does a business need to be successful?** Children might suggest money, workers, resources to make products, advertisements, customers.

Community Involvement

Organize a field trip to a large retail store in your community. Arrange for a broad overview of the various jobs performed in the store such as management, clerking, stocking and display, advertising, and security. Children may enjoy writing job descriptions when they return to class.

PICTURE SUMMARY

TAKE A LOOK

Remind children that a picture summary is a way to visually represent the main ideas or events in a story. Explain that this summary reviews some of the main ideas in Unit 3. Tell children they can trace the path of the dollar bill to see some of the different people in a community who provide goods and services.

Visual Analysis

Learn from Pictures Organize children into small groups. Invite them to examine the picture summary and to react to its images. Ask children to describe the various scenes and to discuss the services and goods they recognize. Have children list people in their communities who help keep them healthy and safe.

VOCABULARY BLACKLINES

Distribute the individual word cards for this unit and have children use the words as they discuss the picture summary.

3 Review

Picture Summary

Look at the pictures. They will help you remember what you learned.

Talk About the Main Ideas

1 Service workers keep people in communities healthy and safe.

2 Workers in factories make many things people need.

3 People trade goods and money for what they want.

4 Producers and consumers need each other.

5 People make choices about how to spend their money.

Think and Draw Think of a job you might want to do someday. Draw a picture that shows the machines or tools you would use.

130

UNIT POSTER

Use the UNIT 3 PICTURE SUMMARY POSTER to summarize the unit.

VOCABULARY CARDS

Have children use the VOCABULARY CARDS for this unit to review key concepts.

Picture Summary Key

Help children follow the arrows to trace the path of the dollar bill, beginning top left:
1. The boy earns a dollar for doing a chore.
2. The boy shops for something he wants.
3. The boy buys what he wants from the store clerk.
4. The store clerk gives the money to the store owner.
5. The store owner deposits the money in the bank.
6. The boy's mother takes money from the family's savings at the bank.

Discuss how money is used to buy goods and services and how producers and consumers depend on each other.

SUMMARIZE THE MAIN IDEAS

Ask children to read the summary statements on page 130 and to relate each one to a specific scene in the picture summary. Lead a class discussion about each scene, and challenge children to offer supporting details for each main idea illustrated.

Suggest that children focus on the people in their communities who help their families meet their needs.

Sharing the Activity

Provide time for children to complete the Think and Draw activity on page 130. Have children discuss what job they would like to have someday and what tools they think they would need to do that job. Invite children to share their drawings.

PUPIL BOOK OR UNIT BIG BOOK

Meet Individual Needs

ENGLISH LANGUAGE LEARNERS
Write the following words on the chalkboard: *dollar bill, goods, service, choice, producer, consumer.* Invite children to work in pairs to write a caption for each illustration in the picture summary. Remind children to start with the first illustration in the top left corner and to follow the path of the dollar bill. Explain that the captions should be only one sentence long and should use the words on the chalkboard. Encourage children to share their captions with the rest of the class.

Link Literature

Children may enjoy reading *How the Second Grade Got $8,205.50 to Visit the Statue of Liberty* by Nathan Zimelman. This story reveals the ups and downs of schemes to raise money for a trip to the Statue of Liberty. Have children compare the class in the story with the class in the lesson.

TECHNOLOGY

Use THE AMAZING WRITING MACHINE™ RESOURCE PACKAGE to summarize the unit.

USE VOCABULARY

❶ transportation
❷ income
❸ factory
❹ producer
❺ consumer
❻ taxes

CHECK UNDERSTANDING

❶ Children might say that taxes pay for teachers, police officers, firefighters, and health-care workers.
❷ Factories save consumers the time and work it takes to make things they need and use.
❸ We can get things we cannot grow or make ourselves. We can also sell products we make.
❹ Children should name a product from another country, the country that produces it, and one way it might be transported to our country.
❺ Consumers must choose how much money to spend and how much to save. They also must decide which things they need or want to buy.

THINK CRITICALLY

❶ When producers such as farmers and factory workers buy things that they need and want, they are consumers, too.
❷ The community could not pay its teachers, police officers, or firefighters. It could not build new schools or roads.

UNIT
3
Review

Use Vocabulary

Which word goes with each box?

consumer   **factory**   **transportation**
producer   **income**   **taxes**

❶ train, ship, truck, airplane

❷ money someone earns

❸ building in which things are made

❹ farmer, baker, quilt maker

❺ buyer and user of products

❻ money people pay to a community

Check Understanding

❶ How do taxes help a community?

❷ Why are factories important to people?

❸ Why do countries trade goods?

❹ Name a product that comes from another country. Tell how it might get here.

❺ Why must consumers make choices about spending money?

Think Critically

❶ Tell how a producer can also be a consumer.

❷ Predict what would happen if people did not pay taxes.

132

Apply Skills

Use a Pictograph

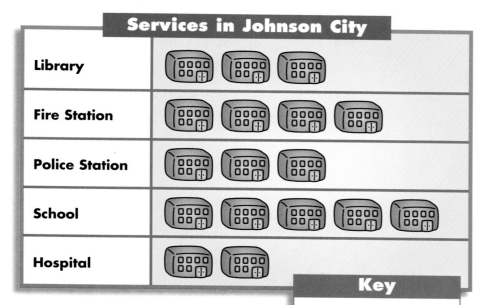

Services in Johnson City

Library	
Fire Station	
Police Station	
School	
Hospital	

Key

= 1 service

1 What kinds of services does Johnson City provide?

2 How many libraries are there?

3 Are there more fire stations or police stations? How many more?

Do It Yourself

Find out how many libraries, schools, hospitals, fire stations, and police stations are in your community. Make a pictograph to show what you found out.

133

APPLY SKILLS

Use a Pictograph
1 libraries, fire stations, police stations, schools, and hospitals
2 three
3 fire stations; one more

Do It Yourself
If children did not make pictographs of your community services, you may wish to have them review the skill here. Help them to find information in the yellow pages and government sections of your phone book.

APPLY SKILLS

Read a Diagram

❶ Abraham Lincoln
❷ eight times (four times in numerals and four times spelled out)
❸ 7
❹ G48476552B

Apply Skills

Read a Diagram

❶ Whose picture is on the five-dollar bill?

❷ How many times is the amount written on one side of the bill?

❸ What is the number of the bank that gave out the money?

❹ What is the serial number of this bill?

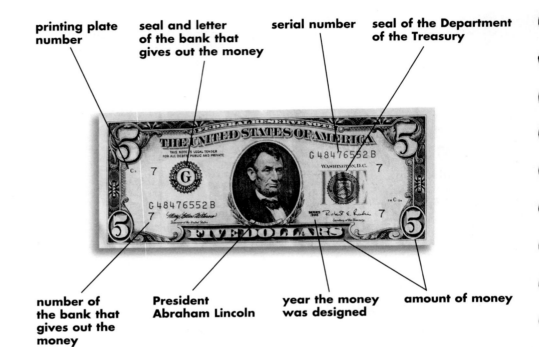

printing plate number

seal and letter of the bank that gives out the money

serial number

seal of the Department of the Treasury

number of the bank that gives out the money

President Abraham Lincoln

year the money was designed

amount of money

134

Unit Activity

Make a Career Day Collage

⭐ Find or draw pictures of workers who make goods and workers who give services.

⭐ Find or draw pictures of the tools workers use or special clothes they wear in their jobs.

⭐ Cut out and paste your pictures to large pieces of construction paper or poster board.

⭐ Hang the collages and talk about workers who make goods. Talk about workers who give services.

Visit the Internet at http://www.hbschool.com for additional resources.

Read More About It

<u>We Keep a Store</u> by Anne Shelby. Orchard. Everyone in a family works together to run a country store.

<u>Market!</u> by Ted Lewin. Lothrop, Lee & Shepard. All around the world, markets sell different kinds of goods.

<u>Music, Music for Everyone</u> by Vera B. Williams. Greenwillow. Rosa and her friends start a band that plays at parties. Best of all, they get paid!

135

PUPIL BOOK OR UNIT BIG BOOK

UNIT ACTIVITY
Make a Career Day Collage

Materials: newspapers, magazines, catalogs, employment or career brochures; scissors; crayons or markers; glue; construction paper or posterboard

In their discussions and through the collages they create, children should exhibit an understanding that people do a variety of jobs requiring different skills and tools. They should recognize a job as a way for a consumer to earn money to buy the things he or she needs from producers of goods and services.

READ MORE ABOUT IT

Additional books are listed in the Resource Center on page 98E of this Teacher's Edition.

TAKE-HOME BOOK

Use the TAKE-HOME REVIEW BOOK for UNIT 3.

ASSESSMENT PROGRAM

Use UNIT 3 TEST
Standard, pp. 23–25.
Performance, p. 26.

GAME TIME!

Use GAME TIME! to reinforce the unit.

COOPERATIVE LEARNING WORKSHOP

SHOP AT A CLASSROOM MARKETPLACE

Invite children to share experiences they have had with shopping in malls, small shops, large markets, outdoor markets, and so on. Have them describe what kinds of items were for sale and how they were displayed. Discuss the different kinds of workers in store—for example, cashiers, stockers, and managers.

Invite children to create a classroom marketplace. Organize them into small groups and explain that each group will make items, decide on prices, create signs, and set up a shop. Provide each child with 10 tokens to represent a week's wages. Guide children as they complete the steps below.

Materials: posterboard, crayons or markers, money or tokens, clay, variety of art and craft materials, labels, small cardboard boxes

Step 1: Children brainstorm a list of items to make, such as refrigerator magnets, paintings, or clay flower vases. They may choose to make multiple copies of one item or a variety of different items for their shop. Children assign roles within their groups and make the items.

Step 2: Children decide on a price for their items, from 1 to 10 tokens. Remind children that if their prices are high, buyers will not purchase the items. Provide sticky labels for children to mark and to attach to the items.

Step 3: Assign each group an area in which to set up its shop. Children name their shops, make signs, and arrange their items.

Step 4: Children take turns visiting each shop and buying items with their tokens. Suggest that the children keep sales records and provide receipts for their customers.

What to Look For In their discussions and through the simulation, children should exhibit an understanding of the people and resources needed to operate a business. Children can

- ▶ identify workers who contribute to the business.
- ▶ describe how the business operates.
- ▶ recognize how the business depends on consumers.
- ▶ explain the importance of money.
- ▶ use appropriate vocabulary.

REMIND CHILDREN TO:
- Share their ideas.
- Cooperate with others to plan their work.
- Plan and take responsibility for their tasks.
- Show their work.
- Discuss their own and the group's performance.

Follow-Up

Invite children to discuss their marketplace experience. You may wish to teach them the following song, sung to the tune of "I've Been Working on the Railroad."

> We've been working in the market
> At our school today.
> Buying and selling in the market
> Things made from paper and clay.
> We found out that it's hard work,
> But we sure had fun.
> We've been working in the market
> And now our work is done.

Role-Play

As children stage the marketplace, you may wish to have them create additional materials and props to use, such as order forms, receipts, and guarantees. Have children suggest scenarios to role-play, such as someone wishing to return an item, or someone requesting an item that is not available. Have children brainstorm ways to solve these problems in the marketplace.

PEOPLE MAKE HISTORY

The major objectives in this unit are organized around the following themes:

UNIT THEMES

▶ **CONTINUITY & CHANGE**
▶ **INDIVIDUALISM & INTERDEPENDENCE**
▶ **COMMONALITY & DIVERSITY**

Preview Unit Content

Unit 4 tells the story of communities over time. Children will examine how events and new technologies in America's history have helped promote change. They will compare ways in which early inhabitants adapted themselves to their environment and study the effects people have had on the environment. Children will also begin to understand that the country and its many communities continue to change today. Children will learn about ordinary and extraordinary individuals who have contributed to our national character and made a difference in people's lives. They should begin to understand how the diverse citizens of a nation can share a common history.

You may wish to begin the unit with the Unit 4 Picture Summary Poster and activities. The illustration that appears on the poster also appears on pages 176–177 in the Pupil Book to help children summarize the unit.

UNIT POSTER

Use the **UNIT 4 PICTURE SUMMARY POSTER** to preview the unit.

Planning Chart

TEACHER'S EDITION	THEMES • Strands	VOCABULARY	MEET INDIVIDUAL NEEDS	RESOURCES INCLUDING ► TECHNOLOGY
UNIT INTRODUCTION **Introduce the Unit** Preview Set the Scene with Literature 📖 **"I Can"** by Mari Evans Use the Literature Big Book pp. 136–141A			English Language Learners, pp. 138, 141	**Pupil Book/Unit Big Book, pp. 136–141** WRITE-ON CHART **Write-On Chart 29** Picture Summary Poster Home Letter Text on Tape Audio Asian Translations Vocabulary Cards *Abraham Lincoln: A Man for All the People*
LESSON 1 **American Indians** pp. 142A–145A	**COMMONALITY & DIVERSITY** • **Geography** • **History**	history shelter	English Language Learners, p. 143 Extend and Enrich, p. 145 Reteach the Main Idea, p. 145	**Pupil Book/Unit Big Book, pp. 142–145** WRITE-ON CHART **Write-On Chart 13** Activity Book, p. 26 Desk Maps Music Audio, "Canoe Song"
SKILL **Read a Time Line** pp. 146A–147A	**BASIC STUDY SKILLS** • **Chart and Graph Skills**	time line	Visual Learners, p. 146A Extend and Enrich, p. 147 Reteach the Skill, p. 147	**Pupil Book/Unit Big Book, pp. 146–147** WRITE-ON CHART **Write-On Chart 26** Clings Activity Book, p. 27 Transparency 9 ► **IMAGINATION EXPRESS: DESTINATION TIME TRIP, USA**
LESSON 2 **We Remember the Past** pp. 148A–151A	**CONTINUITY & CHANGE** • **History** • **Culture**	settler	Advanced Learners, p. 148A English Language Learners, p. 149 Extend and Enrich, p. 150 Reteach the Main Idea, p. 150	**Pupil Book/Unit Big Book, pp. 148–151** WRITE-ON CHART **Write-On Charts 14, 30** Activity Book, p. 28 Desk Maps ► **IMAGINATION EXPRESS: DESTINATION TIME TRIP, USA**
SKILL **Read a History Map** pp. 152A–153A	**BASIC STUDY SKILLS** • **Map and Globe Skills**	colony	Visual Learners, p. 152A English Language Learners, p. 152 Extend and Enrich, p. 153 Reteach the Skill, p. 153	**Pupil Book/Unit Big Book, pp. 152–153** Activity Book, p. 29 Transparency 10 Desk Maps
LESSON 3 **Communities Grow and Change** pp. 154A–157A	**CONTINUITY & CHANGE** • **History** • **Culture**	landmark	Visual and Kinesthetic Learners, p. 154A English Language Learners, p. 154A Extend and Enrich, p. 156 Reteach the Main Idea, p. 156	**Pupil Book/Unit Big Book, pp. 154–157** Activity Book, p. 31 ► **IMAGINATION EXPRESS: DESTINATION TIME TRIP, USA**

24 DAYS

TIME MANAGEMENT

DAY 1	DAY 2	DAY 3	DAY 4	DAY 5	DAY 6	DAY 7	DAY 8	DAY 9	DAY 10	DAY 11	DAY 12
Unit Introduction		Lesson 1			Skill	Lesson 2				Skill	Lesson 3

TEACHER'S EDITION	THEMES • Strands	VOCABULARY	MEET INDIVIDUAL NEEDS	RESOURCES INCLUDING ► TECHNOLOGY
SKILL **Find Cause and Effect** pp. 158A–159A	**BUILDING CITIZENSHIP** • **Critical Thinking Skills**	cause effect	Auditory Learners, p. 158A Tactile Learners, p. 158 Extend and Enrich, p. 159 Reteach the Skill, p. 159	**Pupil Book/Unit Big Book, pp. 158–159** **Write-On Chart 29** Activity Book, p. 32 Transparency 11 ► THE AMAZING WRITING MACHINE
LESSON 4 **People Lead the Way** pp. 160A–163A	**INDIVIDUALISM & INTERDEPENDENCE** • **History** • **Civics and Government**	capital President lawmaker Congress monument	Visual and Tactile Learners, p. 160 Extend and Enrich, p. 163 Reteach the Main Idea, p. 163	**Pupil Book/Unit Big Book, pp. 160–163** **Write-On Charts 15, 27** Vocabulary Cards Activity Book, p. 33 Transparencies 7, 8 Music Audio, "Old Abe"
SKILL **Use a Map Grid** pp. 164A–165B	**BASIC STUDY SKILLS** • **Map and Globe Skills**	route grid	Auditory and Kinesthetic Learners, p. 164A Visual Learners, p. 164 Auditory Learners, p. 164 Extend and Enrich, p. 164 Reteach the Skill, p. 165	**Pupil Book/Unit Big Book, pp. 164–165** **Write-On Chart 31** Activity Book, p. 35 Transparency 12 ► NEIGHBORHOOD MAPMACHINE
BRAINSTORM **History Clues** pp. 166–167A	**BUILDING CITIZENSHIP** • **Critical Thinking Skills** • **Participation Skills**			**Pupil Book/Unit Big Book, pp. 166–167**
LESSON 5 **American Portraits** pp. 168A–173B	**INDIVIDUALISM & INTERDEPENDENCE** • **History** • **Culture**	invention	Auditory Learners, p. 168A Extend and Enrich, p. 172 Reteach the Main Idea, p. 172	**Pupil Book/Unit Big Book, pp. 168–173** **Write-On Charts 16, 29** Activity Book, p. 36 Video, Reading Rainbow, *Alistair's Time Machine*
MAKING SOCIAL STUDIES REAL **Play a Part in History** pp. 174–175	**BUILDING CITIZENSHIP** • **Participation Skills**		Advanced Learners, p. 175	**Pupil Book/Unit Big Book, pp. 174–175** ► INTERNET
UNIT WRAP-UP Picture Summary Unit 4 Review Cooperative Learning Workshop pp. 176–181B			English Language Learners, p. 177	**Pupil Book/Unit Big Book, pp. 176–181** Picture Summary Poster Vocabulary Cards Assessment, Standard, pp. 27–29 Performance, p. 30 Take-Home Review Book Game Time! ► THE AMAZING WRITING MACHINE

DAY 13	DAY 14	DAY 15	DAY 16	DAY 17	DAY 18	DAY 19	DAY 20	DAY 21	DAY 22	DAY 23	DAY 24
	Skill	Lesson 4		Skill	Brainstorm	Lesson 5		Making Social Studies Real	Unit Wrap-up		Unit Test

Multimedia Resource Center

Books

Easy

Beekman, Dan. *Forest, Village, City, Town*. Illus. by Bernice Loewenstein. Crowell, 1982. This book shows how communities, from Indian villages to cities, have changed over the years.

Cowley, Joy. *Gracias, The Thanksgiving Turkey*. Illus. by Joe Cepeda. Scholastic, 1996. Trouble ensues when Papá gets Miguel a turkey to fatten up for Thanksgiving and Miguel develops an attachment to it.

Pryor, Bonnie. *The House on Maple Street*. Illus. by Beth Peck. Morrow, 1987. The author tells about 107 Maple Street and the family that lives there. She also helps us imagine who else has lived near Maple Street in the past 300 years.

Turner, Ann. *Heron Street*. HarperCollins, 1989. Over the centuries, as people settle near the marsh by the sea, herons and other animals are displaced.

Average

Aliki. *A Weed Is a Flower, The Life of George Washington Carver*. Simon and Schuster, 1988. This biography presents the life of a man who, born a slave, became a scientist and devoted his entire life to helping the South improve its agriculture.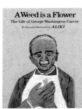

Belton, Sandra. *From Miss Ida's Porch*. Illus. by Floyd Cooper. Four Winds, 1993. On this porch, young and old enjoy exciting stories of Black people who have made a difference.

Brown, Don. *Ruth Law Thrills a Nation*. Ticknor & Fields, 1993. This is a description of the record-breaking flight of a daring woman pilot from Chicago to New York in 1916.

Bruchac, Joseph. *Many Nations, An Alphabet of Native America*. Illus. by Robert F. Goetzl. Bridgewater, 1997. A different group of American Indians is described for each letter of the alphabet.

Greenfield, Eloise. *For the Love of the Game, Michael Jordan and Me*. Illus. by Jan Spivey Gilchrist. HarperCollins, 1997. Two children discover the importance of the human spirit and recognize their similarity to basketball star Michael Jordan.

Keller, Jack. *Tom Edison's Bright Ideas*. Illus. by Lane Yerkes. Steck-Vaughn, 1992. This biography focuses on Edison's research with electricity.

Kent, Zachary. *The Story of Clara Barton*. Childrens Press, 1987. The story of the founder of the American Red Cross is told in this book.

Kessel, Joyce K. *Squanto and the First Thanksgiving*. Illus. by Lisa Donze. Carolrhoda, 1983. Describes how the Indian Squanto taught the Pilgrims how to survive the harsh winter.

Harness, Cheryl. *Young Abe Lincoln: The Frontier Days, 1809–1837*. National Geographic Society, 1996. This book presents the life of this famous President up to age 28.

Lyon, George Ella. *Who Came Down That Road?* Orchard, 1992. A son's questions lead his mother into the past as she lists all the different people, animals, dinosaurs, and even stars that have occupied the place now known as "the road."

Ringgold, Faith. *Dinner at Aunt Connie's House*. Hyperion, 1993. Melody and Lonnie find a surprise of twelve paintings of famous African American women in Aunt Connie's attic, but the bigger surprise is that the paintings can talk.

Swamp, Chief Jake. *Giving Thanks, A Native American Good Morning Message*. Illus. by Erwin Printup, Jr. Lee & Low, 1995. Mohawk children are taught to give thanks for the gifts of the Earth.

Challenging

Adler, David. *A Picture Book of Louis Braille*. Illus. by John and Alexandra Wallner. Holiday House, 1997. This Frenchman, accidentally blinded as a child, originated the raised-dot system of reading and writing. See also other Picture Book biographies.

Dalgliesh, Alice. *The Thanksgiving Story*. Illus. by Helen Sewel. Scribner's, 1988. This Caldecott book tells about a Pilgrim family's struggle to survive in their harsh new homeland.

Greene, Carol. *Mother Teresa, Friend of the Friendless*. Childrens Press, 1983. This biography describes the work of Mother Teresa with the poor of India.

Krull, Kathleen. *Wilma Unlimited*. Illus. by David Diaz. Harcourt Brace, 1996. A biography of the African American woman who overcame crippling polio as a child to become the first woman to win three gold medals in track in a single Olympics.

Leeuwen, Jean Van. *Across the Wide Dark Sea*. Illus. by Thomas B. Allen. Dial Books, 1995. A boy and his family endure a difficult nine-week journey across the ocean and survive the first winter at Plymouth.

LIBRARY

See the GRADE 2 SOCIAL STUDIES LIBRARY for additional resources.

Pinkney, Andrea Davis. *Dear Benjamin Banneker*. Illus. by Brian Pinkney. Gulliver, 1994. This biography of Benjamin Banneker heralds his accomplishments, which include the creation of a wooden clock and his astronomy almanacs.

Tunnell, Michael O. *The Joke's on George*. Illus. by Kathy Osborn. Tambourine, 1993. This book briefly surveys the life of the early American portrait painter Charles Willson Peale and describes an incident involving George Washington.

Audiocassettes

Indian Homes (New Talking Cassette Encyclopedia). Troll Associates. Describes homes of the various groups of American Indians. Toll free: 1-800-526-5289

Let's Read Together. By Jack Hartman. Also available on LP. Themes of caring about others and the world are stressed. Toll free: 1-800-645-3739

Looking Back and Looking Forward. By Ella Jenkins. Also available on LP. Toll free: 1-800-645-3739

Computer Software

Floppy Disk

Discovering America. Davidson. Mac/DOS. Makes history come alive by letting children explore America before it was settled. Includes information about Native American peoples. Toll free: 1-800-545-7677

CD-ROM

People Behind the Holidays. National Geographic Educational Services. Mac/Windows. By learning about the deeds of famous Americans, children see how our country has changed. Toll free: 1-800-368-2728

Note that information, while correct at time of publication, is subject to change.

Video

Film or VHS Cassettes

Everyone Helps in a Community. SVE & Churchill Media. Also available on laserdisc. A farm town in the wilderness grows into a rural town and eventually a busy community. The film contrasts the lives in that early self-sufficient farm town and the lives of people today. It also portrays how a division of labor operates in a community. Toll free: 1-800-829-1900

Hiawatha. Weston Woods Studios. Introduces one of America's favorite poems, "Hiawatha," by Henry Wadsworth Longfellow. Depicts the tradition of the American Indian against a background of authentic Indian music. Toll free: 1-800-243-5020

FREE & INEXPENSIVE MATERIALS

Jamestown-Yorktown Foundation. The following educational materials are available at no cost: *The Jamestown Settlement Museum Teacher's Resource Packet; The Yorktown Victory Center Museum Teacher's Resource Packet*; and an audiovisual catalog. A-V packets concerning the American Revolution and Jamestown are available on loan to teachers for $3, the cost of shipping and handling.
Jamestown-Yorktown Foundation
Education Dept.
P.O. Box 1607
Williamsburg, VA 23187-1607

North American Indians Teaching Packet. Teacher's resource kit includes bibliographies, leaflets, lists of teaching materials available from the Smithsonian, photographs, suggested classroom activities, and information on obtaining Native American pen pals. Single copies free.
National Museum of Natural History
Anthropology Outreach Office
NHB 363, MRC 112
Smithsonian Institution
Washington, DC 20560

Perennial Patriot. Booklet traces cotton growth and the role it plays in the economy. From the days of Jamestown and the birth of the nation to modern day. Up to 30 copies free.
National Cotton Council of America
P.O. Box 12285
Memphis, TN 38112

Postal Pack for Elementary School Students. Curriculum kit includes illustrated activity sheets that teach about postal and transportation history and encourage letter writing and an appreciation of stamps and historic letters. Free.
National Postal Museum
Education Department
2 Massachusetts Avenue
Smithsonian Institution
Washington, DC 20560-0001

The Thanksgiving Primer. Complete 37-page guidebook to recreating the first harvest festival for your family, friends, or church. Includes the evolution of the Thanksgiving tradition, description of the Pilgrims, manners and menus, recipes, bibliography, and more. Single copy $4.95, plus $3.95 shipping and handling.
Plimoth Plantation
Mail Order Department
P.O. Box 1620
Plymouth, MA 02362

Linking Social Studies

ART CENTER

Make a Colonial Town

Materials: large, shallow tray; sod or small plastic trees; plastic farm animals; milk cartons; twigs or straight pretzels; art materials; glue

Cover a sand table or shallow tray with sod or small plastic trees. Ask children to draw or write descriptions of the "forest." Then invite them to remove trees or cut grass to make room for log cabins, corrals, barns, and farm plots. Children can cover milk cartons with pretzels or twigs to create cabins and use miniatures and art materials to add other details to the colonial town. At the end of the unit, ask children to describe the town and to compare their descriptions to the ones they made before they changed the land.

MULTICULTURAL CENTER

Who's Who Calendar

Materials: posterboard, construction paper, markers, biographical reference materials

Provide a list of diverse "people who make history." The list might include Father Junípero Serra, Ellen Ochoa, Benjamin Banneker, Sojourner Truth, Garrett Morgan, Wilma Rudolph, Sacagawea, Chief Joseph, Maya Ying Lin, An Wang. Help children make a large calendar, assigning a different day to each person. Have small groups each choose one person to research. Then children can fill in their person's space on the calendar with a drawing, a fact, or a quote and present a short biographical sketch to the class.

SCIENCE CENTER

Learn About Simple Machines

Materials: pencil sharpener, string or yarn, books, photos of machines such as pulleys, levers, wheels and axles

Provide children with photos of simple machines. Explain that machines help people to push, pull, and lift heavy objects. Remove the cover of a pencil sharpener. Tie string or yarn around the axle of the sharpener and attach a few books to the end of the string. Turn the handle of the sharpener until the books are raised off the ground. Then untie the books and ask a volunteer to pick them up by hand. Challenge children to discuss what life might have been like before people invented machines.

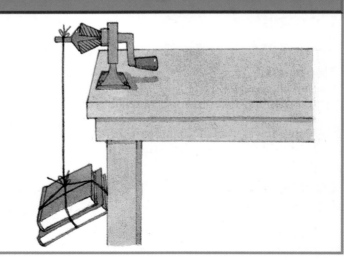

Across the Curriculum

LANGUAGE ARTS CENTER

Write Descriptions for Class Books

Materials: 3-inch metal rings, hole-punched paper or posterboard for pages, strips of lined paper, books and visuals showing colonial life

Invite children to make pages for two class books—one titled *Chores Long Ago* and another titled *Chores We Do Today*. Discuss chores children do at home. Then ask children to look through books showing colonial life for ideas about the chores colonial children might have done. Ask children to make book pages by illustrating and writing descriptions of modern chores and also colonial chores. Suggest children include the tools and materials used to do each chore. Read aloud and compare the completed books.

MATH CENTER

Grid-Tac-Toe

Materials: postcards showing national landmarks, a numbered/lettered 3 × 3 grid with squares slightly larger than postcards, index cards naming squares on the grid by letter and number, checkers

Invite pairs of children to play Grid-Tac-Toe. Children arrange the postcards on the grid and take turns drawing from the stack of index cards. Players must name the building or monument that is in the square indicated on the card. If the answer is correct, the player takes the postcard and places one of his or her checkers on the square. If not, the postcard is left in place, the index card is returned to the bottom of the pile. The first player to have three checkers in a row wins.

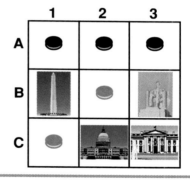 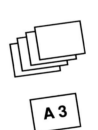

HOW TO INTEGRATE YOUR DAY
Use these topics to help you integrate social studies into your daily planning.

READING THEMES	INTEGRATED LANGUAGE ARTS	MATHEMATICS	SCIENCE	ART
Explorations/ Problem Solving **Life Stories** **Heroes** **Growing and Changing** **Looking Back**	Write Descriptions for Class Books, p. 136H Journal, pp. 139, 144 Write a Narrative, p. 158A Write a Letter, p. 161 Children as Historians, p. 166 Write a Description, p. 168A Write a Report, p. 168 Present Orally, p. 170	Grid-Tac-Toe, p. 136H Quantification, p. 146A Numbers, p. 155 Measurement and Scale, p. 165	Learn About Simple Machines, p. 136G Oceans, p. 155 Observation, p. 168	Make a Colonial Town, p. 136G About the Artist, p. 140 Illustration, pp. 138, 152A Murals, p. 156 Architecture, p. 161 Portraits, p. 169

HEALTH AND PHYSICAL EDUCATION	MUSIC
Play an Indian Game, p. 143 Physical Fitness, p. 164 Growth and Development, p. 169	Vocal/Rhythm, p. 144 Vocal, p. 160A

BULLETIN BOARD

Create a bulletin board titled *Tomorrow's Leaders* and make a grid with yarn. Place each child's photo in one square of the grid. Ask children to write down one way they would like to help their country when they are older and have them "sign" their statements with the letter and number of their square. Place children's statements at the bottom of the bulletin board. Ask children to use the grid to identify who wrote each one.

Assessment Options

The assessment program allows all learners many opportunities to show what they know and can do. It also provides ongoing information about each child's understanding of social studies.

FORMAL ASSESSMENT

▶ *Unit Review*
(**Pupil Book**, pp. 178–181)

▶ *Unit Assessment*
(**Assessment Program:**
Standard Test, pp. 27–29
Performance Task, p. 30)

STUDENT SELF-EVALUATION

▶ *Individual End-of-Project Checklist*
(**Assessment Program**, p. 6)

▶ *Group End-of-Project Checklist*
(**Assessment Program**, p. 7) for use after cooperative learning activities

▶ *Individual End-of-Unit Checklist*
(**Assessment Program**, p. 8)

INFORMAL ASSESSMENT

▶ *What Do You Know? Questions*
(**Pupil Book**, at end of lessons)

▶ *Think and Do*
(**Pupil Book**, at end of skill lessons)

▶ *Picture Summary*
(**Pupil Book**, pp. 176–177)

▶ *Check Understanding*
(**Teacher's Edition**, in Close, at end of lessons)

▶ *Think Critically*
(**Teacher's Edition**, in Close, at end of lessons)

▶ *Social Studies Skills Checklist*
(**Assessment Program**, pp. 4–5)

PERFORMANCE ASSESSMENT

▶ *Show What You Know*
(**Teacher's Edition**, in Close, at end of lessons)

▶ *Cooperative Learning Workshop*
(**Teacher's Edition**, pp. 181A–181B)

▶ *Performance Task: Who's Who?*
(**Assessment Program**, p. 30)

▶ *Scoring the Performance Task*
Use the *Scoring Rubric for Individual Projects*
(**Assessment Program**, p. 9)

▶ *Scoring Rubric for Group Projects*
(**Assessment Program**, p. 10)

▶ *Scoring Rubric for Presentations*
(**Assessment Program**, p. 11)

PORTFOLIO ASSESSMENT

Student-selected items may include:

▶ *Link to Language Arts*, journal
(**Teacher's Edition**, p. 144)

▶ *Link to Mathematics*, chart
(**Teacher's Edition**, p. 146A)

▶ *Using Activity Book*, portrait
(**Activity Book**, p. 36)

Teacher-selected items may include:

▶ *My Best Work*
(**Assessment Program**, p. 12)

▶ *Portfolio Summary*
(**Assessment Program**, p. 13)

▶ *Portfolio Family Response*
(**Assessment Program**, p. 14)

Assessment Options

STANDARD TEST

Name _____ Date _____

Unit 4 Test

Vocabulary 5 points each

Write the word that completes the sentence.

landmark   history   settlers   invention   President

1. Indians lived in America before the first

   _____settlers_____ came on the <u>Mayflower</u>.

2. The story of the missions is part of the

   _____history_____ of California.

3. The seat belt is an _____invention_____
   that has saved lives.

4. The White House is the home of our

   _____President_____.

5. The Washington Monument is

   a _____landmark_____
   in Washington, D.C.

   Draw a picture of the monument.

   > The drawing should show a tall, narrow monument that is pointed at the top.

Unit 4 Test   Assessment Program **27**

STANDARD TEST

Name _____

Main Ideas 5 points each

Write <u>before</u> or <u>after</u> to tell when things happened.

6. The Pilgrims came to America _____after_____
   Columbus came.

7. The Pilgrims began to plan their government

   _____before_____ they landed in America.

Draw a line under each thing that American settlers did to meet their needs.

8. <u>build houses</u>   9. shop for food   10. <u>spin thread</u>

   11. <u>make clothes</u>   12. work in factories

Circle the answer to each question.

13. Who were the first people to live in the
    San Diego area?

    Mexicans   (Indians)   American settlers

14. What can help a city grow?

    (inventions)   fires   floods

15. Who makes our nation's laws?

    the President   (the Congress)

28   Assessment Program   Unit 4 Test

Objectives

- Define *history* as stories of the past. (p. 142A)
- Identify Indians as the first inhabitants of our country. (p. 142A)
- Describe the food, shelter, and clothing of several Native American groups. (p. 142A)
- Identify ways in which Indians helped the Pilgrims. (p. 142A)
- Identify events as occurring before and after a point in time. (p. 146A)
- Sequence a series of events. (p. 146A)
- Use a time line to relate a story. (p. 146A)
- Describe the early history of our country. (p. 148A)

- Recognize the contributions of American settlers. (p. 148A)
- Compare community life now and long ago. (p. 148A)
- Use a history map to identify the 13 colonies. (p. 152A)
- Distinguish between historical and current maps of identical sites. (p. 152A)
- Recognize that names and shapes of places sometimes change. (p. 152A)
- Identify the causes of change in a community. (p. 154A)
- Explain pride in one's community and its past. (p. 154A)
- Identify the causes and effects of certain events. (p. 158A)

- Realize that one cause may have more than one effect. (p. 158A)
- Explore our country's history through its capital. (p. 160A)
- Define the roles of such leaders as President and lawmakers. (p. 160A)
- Name important national leaders. (p. 160A)
- Identify and use a grid to locate places and trace routes on a map. (p. 164A)
- Describe the contributions of famous artists, scientists, educators, and other achievers. (p. 168A)
- Recognize that all citizens are capable of making contributions to society. (p. 168A)

STANDARD TEST

Name _____

Skills

Settlement at Red River

woods
wood pile
settlers' homes
Meeting House
river
woods
garden

Use the map grid to answer the questions. 5 points each

16. What is in B-2? _____ a wood pile

17. In which square is the Meeting House?
_____ C-4

18. How many squares are between the river
and the settlers' homes? _____ 2

Plant Corn   Harvest Corn   Thanksgiving

January February March April May June July August September October November December

Answer the questions about the time line.

19. When did the settlers plant corn? _____ in April

20. How many months did the corn take to grow?
_____ 4

Unit 4 Test   Assessment Program **29**

PERFORMANCE TASK

Name _____ Date _____

Performance Task

Who's Who?

Your class is making a book about "People Who Make a Difference." You have been asked to write about someone you admire to put in the book.

Who would you choose? Sample response: Mary McLeod Bethune

Why do you admire this person? Sample response: She was poor but worked hard to learn and become a teacher.

Write a paragraph telling something interesting about the person you chose.

Sample response: Mary McLeod Bethune had seventeen brothers and sisters.

A white friend told her that Negroes couldn't read. She learned anyway. She started

a college. Even Presidents asked for her help.

30 Assessment Program   Unit 4 Test

Rubrics

SCORING RUBRICS The scoring rubrics for evaluating individual projects, group projects, and children's presentations may be found in the *Assessment Program*, pages 9–11.

CRITERIA The criteria listed below may be used when looking for evidence of the children's understanding of social studies content and ability to think critically.

▶ *Performance Task: Who's Who?* [**Assessment Program,** p. 30]
▶ *Scoring the Performance Task—* Use the *Scoring Rubric for Individual Projects* [**Assessment Program,** p. 9], and look for evidence of the child's ability to:

✔ Recognize the qualities that make people special.
✔ Identify contributions that make a difference in people's lives.
✔ Communicate ideas clearly through writing.

REMINDER

You may wish to preview the performance assessment activity in the COOPERATIVE LEARNING WORKSHOP on Teacher's Edition pages 181A–181B. Children may complete this activity during the course of the unit.

INTRODUCE THE UNIT

Link Prior Learning

Explain that we learn about the past by studying what people have left behind. Ask children to draw objects that might provide clues about the past, for example, books, art, buildings, clothing, and tools. Invite children to share what each item might tell about people who lived long ago.

Outline

Have children scan the unit by reading the lesson titles and looking at the pictures. Invite them to speculate about the main ideas that will be discussed. Help them to prepare an outline using the lesson titles as major headings. Remind children to leave space between items so that they can record information as they read the unit. Then as each lesson is completed, suggest that they return to their outlines to fill in the details.

> Outline
>
> People Make History
>
> A. American Indians
>   1. American Indians lived here first.
>   2. Squanto helps the Pilgrims.
>
> B. We Remember the Past
>
> C. Communities grow and change
>
> D. People Lead the Way
>
> E. American Portraits

Preview Vocabulary

The vocabulary words listed on page 136 represent the key concepts for this unit. Suggest that children use the words to predict what the main ideas of the unit will be. Ideas for teaching the vocabulary are provided on pages 138 and 139.

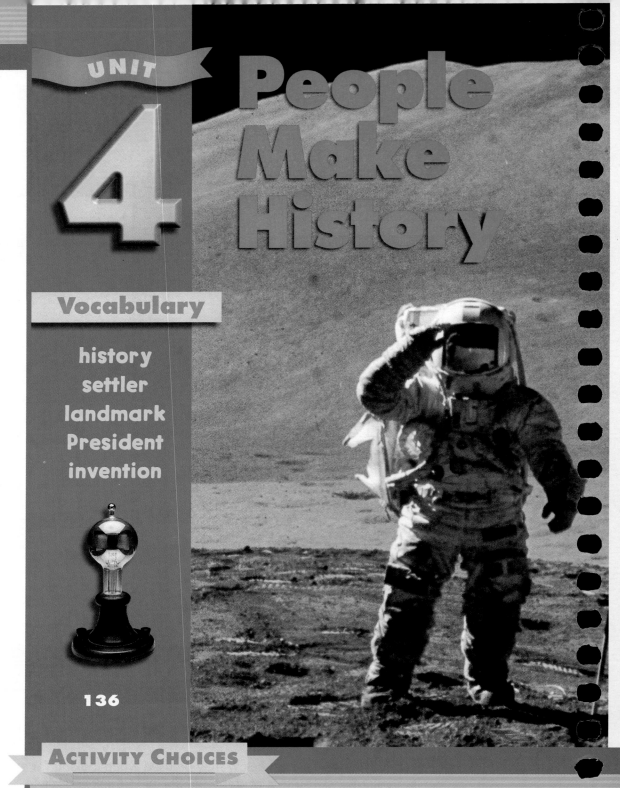

UNIT **4**

People Make History

Vocabulary

history
settler
landmark
President
invention

136

ACTIVITY CHOICES

Community Involvement

Invite a local historian or collector to show children artifacts found in their community. Have children discuss what the objects tell them about the community and how it has changed over time.

HOME LETTER

Use **UNIT 4 HOME LETTER.**
See Teacher's Edition pages
HL7–8.

Personal Response

Direct attention to the photograph on pages 136 and 137. Allow children to discuss what they know about astronauts and space explorations, called missions. Discuss the Lunar Rover (see Background) and discuss what its builders needed to think about as they planned the vehicle.

Q. **What kind of people become space workers and astronauts?** scientists, pilots, and engineers; curious people; brave people

How did space voyages before Apollo 15 help it to be a successful mission? Space workers could take what they learned from earlier missions and use it to plan the next one.

How did Apollo 15 help future missions? Every new mission brings back more information to build on for future missions.

Tell children that in this unit they will learn that many things help make history, especially people . Children will begin to understand the changes brought about by new inventions and new ways of thinking.

> **❝PRIMARY SOURCE❞**
>
> As Neil Armstrong stepped on the moon's surface to plant the American flag, he said, "That's one small step for a man, one giant leap for mankind." Tell children that in this unit they will read about individual achievements that have made a difference in people's lives.

Options for Reading

Read Aloud Read each lesson aloud as children follow along in their books. Strategies for guiding children through working with text and visuals are provided with each lesson.

Read Together Have pairs or small groups of children read the lesson by taking turns reading each page or paragraph aloud. Encourage children to use the new vocabulary words as they discuss what they read.

Read Alone Strong readers may wish to read the lessons independently before you read or discuss each lesson with the class.

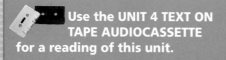
PUPIL BOOK OR UNIT BIG BOOK

Background

THE LARGE PICTURE In May 1961 President John F. Kennedy committed the United States to landing someone on the moon "before this decade is out." Apollo 11 and Neil Armstrong were the first on the moon in 1969. In 1971 the second manned mission shown here, Apollo 15, landed on the moon near Hadley Rille and the Apennine Mountains. It carried a Lunar Roving Vehicle for exploring the moon's surface.

AUDIO

Use the **UNIT 4 TEXT ON TAPE AUDIOCASSETTE** for a reading of this unit.

ASIAN TRANSLATIONS

For students who speak **Cambodian, Cantonese, Hmong, or Vietnamese,** use the **ASIAN TRANSLATIONS** for Unit 4. The Harcourt Brace program is also available in a **SPANISH EDITION.**

PREVIEW THE UNIT

Think About Words

Create a two-column chart on chart paper. Label the first column *Words We Know* and the second column *Words We Learned*. Initiate a discussion about early American history by inviting children to imagine they are the first group of people to live in America. Invite them to brainstorm a list of words associated with people beginning a new nation. Record their responses in the first column. After completing this unit, return to the chart to help children list their new vocabulary words.

Words We Know	Words We Learned
America ships Pilgrims Washington	_____ _____ _____ _____ _____ _____ _____ _____ _____

history

The story of what has happened in a place.

settler

A person who makes a home in a new place.

landmark

A familiar object at a place.

ACTIVITY CHOICES

Meet Individual Needs

ENGLISH LANGUAGE LEARNERS To help children identify and remember the Unit 4 vocabulary words, ask questions about each word. If children cannot recall the name in English, provide two choices. For example: *Which word names a person who first settles in a new place? Is it a President or a settler?*

Link to Art

ILLUSTRATION Ask children to think of a problem they would like to solve. Invite them to draw an invention of their own design that would help solve this problem. Begin by providing an example, such as a wooden leg connected to the back of a chair to prevent children from falling backward and hurting themselves. Ask children to discuss how their inventions would help make life better. Display children's drawings on a bulletin board titled *Inventions Bring Change*.

President

The leader of the United States.

invention

Something that has been made for the first time.

139

Work with Words

Invite children to turn to pages 138–139 in their Pupil Book. Explain that these words tell the main ideas that they will study in this unit. Invite volunteers to read each word and its definition aloud. (Note: For additional vocabulary, see the Planning Chart on pages 136C and 136D in this Teacher's Edition.) To reinforce the meanings of the vocabulary words, read the following sentences aloud, pausing before the blank for children to supply the missing vocabulary word.

1. The story of things that have already happened is called _____. (history)
2. The lightbulb is a famous _____. (invention)
3. George Washington was the first _____ (President) of the United States.
4. People who moved to America to make a home are called _____. (settlers)
5. The Statue of Liberty is a well-known American _____. (landmark)

VOCABULARY BLACKLINES

You may wish to reproduce individual copies of the vocabulary words for this unit. They are found in the back of this Teacher's Edition.

Link to Language Arts

JOURNAL Invite children to write the names of all the Presidents they know. As children work through the lesson, ask them to add any new names to their lists and write what they have learned about each one.

VOCABULARY CARDS

Place the Unit 4 VOCABULARY PICTURE CARDS on the chalkledge, picture-side up. Sing the jingle below to the tune "Row, Row, Row Your Boat." Call on volunteers to name the correct word. When they guess the word, show them the printed word on the opposite side.

Think, think, think with me,
Think about a word.
Listen to what it means: (read definition)
Can you name my word?

UNIT 4

SET THE SCENE WITH LITERATURE

Set the Scene with Literature

PREVIEW

Have children look at pages 140–141. Ask a volunteer to read the title of the poem. Allow children to explain what they think "I Can" means.

Q. **What kind of things "can" you do?** Responses might include ride a bike, read a book, clean my room, help my family.

Have children look at the pictures. Invite them to discuss the activities shown.

Q. **How does what these people do affect the lives of others?** Responses should indicate ways in which people's actions affect others.

140

ACTIVITY CHOICES

Background

ABOUT THE POET Mari Evans was born on July 16, 1923, in Toledo, Ohio. Evans remembers that as a fourth grader she wrote a story that was accepted by her school newspaper. This began her literary career. She was an editor and a teacher during her early years of writing. Since then she has won many awards for her children's stories, poems, and plays, which feature African American experiences.

Link to Art

ABOUT THE ARTIST Melodye Rosales said she first thought of becoming an artist when she found that her toys could not bend and move the way her imagination wanted them to. She started drawing on the back sides of used photocopy paper from her mom's office. Melodye went to art schools and continued to develop her style working for *Ebony Jr.!* She has illustrated many children's books, including the Addy books in the American Girl series. She hopes children find visual enjoyment and excitement in the characters she brings to life on paper. Ask children to draw a character in a scene from their favorite story.

I Can

by Mari Evans
illustrated by
Melodye Rosales

I can
be anything
I can
do anything
I can
think
anything
big
or tall
OR
high or low
WIDE
or narrow
fast or slow
because I
CAN
and
I
WANT
TO!

141

READ & RESPOND

Ask the class to read the poem out loud together. Tell them to stand up each time they say "I Can." Lead children in a discussion about the importance of believing in yourself. Encourage children to share a time when they did something new because they believed they could.

Q. What are some things you want to do when you are older?
Responses might include play baseball or soccer, sing, dance, paint, or cook.

Do you think you can one day?
Yes, I can do or be anything!

Help children understand that this is a country in which there are opportunities for achieving goals for the future and that people's actions are a part of a living history that can affect others.

Meet Individual Needs

ENGLISH LANGUAGE LEARNERS Ask children whose first language is not English to reread the poem. Then write the following sentences on the chalkboard. Invite them to read aloud and complete each sentence frame.
I can be a ____.
I can do a ____.
I can think of something big like a ____.
I can think of something tall like a ____.
I can think of something high like a ____.
I can think of something low like a ____.
I can think of something fast like a ____.
I can think of something slow like a ____.

Link Literature

To show children that many things are possible if you believe in yourself, begin the unit with the book *Ruth Law Thrills a Nation* by Don Brown. (Ticknor & Fields, 1993) This story is about a woman who in 1916 flew from Chicago to New York. Ask children to share what they admire about Ruth Law or someone else who has done something difficult.

RUTH LAW THRILLS A NATION
story and pictures by Don Brown

AUDIO

You may wish to play the TEXT ON TAPE AUDIOCASSETTE for "I Can" and have children think about their own dreams for the future.

LITERATURE BIG BOOK

ABRAHAM LINCOLN
A Man for All the People
A Ballad by Myra Cohn Livingston

Illustrated by Samuel Byrd

Invite children to begin the unit by reading *Abraham Lincoln: A Man for All the People* by Myra Cohn Livingston. Written in ballad form, this book tells the life story of America's 16th President. Readers are introduced to the idea that the actions of significant individuals contribute to our national character.

About the Author and the Illustrator

Myra Cohn Livingston has written or anthologized more than seventy books for children and is the recipient of the Excellence in Poetry Award from the National Council of Teachers of English. Mrs. Livingston lives in Los Angeles, California.

Samuel Byrd lives in Philadelphia, Pennsylvania. He has illustrated a number of picture books, including *Dancing with the Indians* and *A Picture Book of Frederick Douglass*.

Reading the Story

Read and discuss the literature to address the following objectives:

1. Identify Abraham Lincoln as a former President of the United States.
2. Describe major events of Abraham Lincoln's life.
3. Recognize that people and events shape history.

Social Studies Connection

Lead children in a discussion of what they know about Abraham Lincoln.

Q. **What is a president?** A president is a leader of a country.

What do you know about Abraham Lincoln's life? Responses may include that he was born in a log cabin, that he was the President of the United States, that he freed the slaves, that he was President during the Civil War, and that he was shot while watching a play.

List some of the events from the story.
- ▶ Abraham Lincoln grew up in a log cabin.
- ▶ Lincoln became a lawyer.
- ▶ Lincoln was President during the Civil War.
- ▶ Lincoln gave many memorable speeches.

Invite children to reread the story and draw a picture to show one of these events.

1

AMERICAN INDIANS

OBJECTIVES

1. Define *history* as stories of the past.
2. Identify Indians as the first inhabitants of our country.
3. Describe the food, shelter, and clothing of several Native American groups.
4. Identify ways in which Indians helped the Pilgrims.

VOCABULARY

history
shelter

RESOURCES

Pupil Book/Unit Big Book, pp. 142–145
Write-On Chart 13
Desk Maps
Activity Book, p. 26
Music Audio, "Canoe Song"

ACTIVITY CHOICES

Multicultural Link

Descriptions of items on page 143:

POWHATAN: The Powhatans (pow•uh•TANZ) were Eastern Woodlands hunters, fishers, gatherers, and farmers who raised corn, beans, and squash; their shelters were mat-covered multifamily longhouses; deer hides provided their clothing.

CREEK: The Creeks were Eastern Woodlands farmers who raised corn, beans, squash, and sweet potatoes; their houses had mud walls and bark-covered slanted roofs.

NAVAJO: The Navajos were nomadic hunter-gatherers in the South-west; they grew corn and caught small game; their dome-shaped hogans were made of logs covered with earth; they wove woolen clothing.

CHUMASH: The Chumash (CHOO•mash) ate mostly fish and sea animals; their dome-shaped houses were covered with mats made from plants; they wore little clothing; a shaman, or healer, and his ceremonial headdress are shown.

CHINOOK: The Chinooks caught salmon in the rivers of the Pacific Northwest coastal region; their multi-family cedar-plank houses were built partly underground; they wore clothes made of cedar-bark fibers.

1. ACCESS

Many children will be aware that groups of people who today are known as Indians were the first inhabitants of most of what is now the United States. Ask children what they think Indian children of long ago liked to do. Invite children of American Indian descent to share what they know about their heritage.

Have children open their books to pages 58–59. Help children find New Mexico, where April lives, on a United States map. Explain that long ago, Indian groups lived in most of what is now the United States, Canada, Mexico, and South America.

Focus on the Main Idea

In this lesson children will learn that it is from history, or stories about the past, that we know about long-ago times and times not so long ago. They will discover differences among the ways of life of various American Indian groups of the past. Children will also read about how Indians helped the Pilgrims survive in America. As they read about the past in this lesson, they will learn the history of some of the very first Americans.

2. BUILD

Key Content Summary

Stories and information about Indian ways of life build understanding of the term *history* and of the world of the earliest Americans.

Vocabulary

After children have read page 142, write *history* on the board and have a volunteer underline the word *story* that is part of it.

Q. In what way are the words *history* and *story* connected? History is a collection of stories about the past.

Review the meaning of *shelter* as "a place where people live." Ask children how they think historians of many years from now may describe today's foods, shelters, and clothing.

Geography

Human-Environment Interactions

Ask children to examine their Desk Maps of the United States and to share what they know about the weather in different parts of the country.

Q. Why might each Indian group have had its own way of life? They needed the kinds of clothes and homes that suited their own climate; different foods were available in different places.

LESSON 1 American Indians

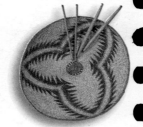

History is made up of the stories people tell about the past. Some stories happened long ago. Others took place even farther back in time.

The history of the American Indians starts long before the United States was a country. We call these people Native Americans because they were the first people to live in what is now America.

Today there are many different groups of American Indians. Each group has its own history and its own way of living. There were many groups of American Indians long ago, too. The table on page 143 shows some groups and the different clothing they wore, foods they ate, and shelters they built. A **shelter** is a place where people live.

142

ACTIVITY CHOICES

Reading Support

PREVIEW IMPORTANT WORDS Invite children to preview pages 142–145 to find important words in the lesson. Explain that these might be words in dark type (*history*, *shelter*), headline words (*American Indians*, *Biography*), or labels, such as those in the table on page 143. List on chart paper the words they suggest. Then discuss the words and practice reading them together. Invite children to add other important words to the list as they read the lesson.

Link Literature

Share the book *Many Nations: An Alphabet of Native America* by Joseph Bruchac. (Bridgewater, 1997) The author and the illustrator reveal the worlds of 26 Indian groups in North America, one for each letter from *A* to *Z*. Ask children to describe each group's food, shelter, and clothing, along with any other details they notice.

WRITE-ON CHARTS

The First Americans

Use WRITE-ON CHART 13 to extend and enrich this lesson. See Teacher's Edition page W41.

Indian Group

Powhatan	Creek	Navajo	Chumash	Chinook

Foods

Shelters

Clothing

143

PUPIL BOOK OR UNIT BIG BOOK

Visual Analysis

Interpret Art Invite children to study the illustration on page 142 to find clues about the way of life of the Indians in the picture. Help them identify the Indians as members of the Powhatan group.

Learn from Tables Remind children that the chart on page 143 is called a *table*. A table lists information in rows and columns. Help children read the names of the Indian groups. Invite volunteers to describe the food, shelter, and clothing of each group. You may wish to contribute details from the Multicultural Link on Teacher's Edition page 142A.

Critical Thinking

Invite children to tell how the kinds of food, shelter, and clothing of the five Indian groups are alike and how they are different. Help them to draw conclusions about reasons for the similarities and differences.

Q. **How did the different Indian groups use the resources around them?** Children may give examples of local foods used by different groups and of homes and clothing made from materials at hand in nature.

Meet Individual Needs

ENGLISH LANGUAGE LEARNERS
Using the table on page 143, say "Show me the Creek Indians," "Show me the Chumash Indians," and so on, and have children point to the corresponding picture in the top row. Then focus on one group at a time and ask children to, for example, point to the Navajo Indians' clothing, then food, and then shelter. As children learn the pattern, invite them to take turns giving directions to one another.

Link to Physical Education

PLAY AN INDIAN GAME Bear Race is an Indian game from the Pacific Northwest. Children race from one line to another. On the word *go*, players put their hands on the ground and bear-walk—moving the right hand and left foot together and then the left hand and right foot. The fastest "bear" may be the winner. Or the judge may choose the best bear-walker instead, showing that how a game is played is more important than speed.

DESK MAPS

Invite children to use their DESK MAPS of the United States as they discuss why the various American Indian groups needed different clothing and ate different kinds of food.

LESSON 1 • 143

Vocabulary

After children have read pages 144–145, explain that *wigwams* are dome-shaped, or rounded, shelters made of wooden poles covered with mats of tree bark. Ask which shelters on page 143 are also dome-shaped. Review *harvest* as the time when crops are gathered from the fields.

History

People and Events Across Time and Place Discuss how the Wampanoags helped the Pilgrims. Include the story of Squanto. Remind children that history can be passed down as written or oral stories. Ask how they first learned about the Pilgrims' Thanksgiving celebration.

HOLIDAY ACTIVITIES

For information and activities related to the Pilgrims and Thanksgiving, see the Holiday Activities section at the back of this Teacher's Edition.

3. CLOSE

Invite volunteers to pretend to be Indian children of long ago. Have the actors use information from the lesson to tell a story about a day in their life. Suggest that some children tell about the Pilgrims or the first Thanksgiving from the point of view of an Indian child.

"The First Thanksgiving" by Jennie Brownscombe

When the Pilgrims moved from Europe to America, they found the Wampanoag Indians already living here. The Wampanoags became the Pilgrims' friends. They taught the Pilgrims how to hunt and fish and to plant crops. The Wampanoags ate mostly corn. They wore clothes made of animal skins and lived in wigwams made of tree bark.

144

Biography

An Indian named Tisquantum, or Squanto for short, helped the Pilgrims and the Wampanoags become friends. Without his help, the Pilgrims might not have lived through their first winter. He taught them the Indian ways of living. Squanto and other Indians joined the Pilgrims for a thanksgiving dinner to celebrate the Pilgrims' first harvest.

ACTIVITY CHOICES

Link to Music

VOCAL/RHYTHM Invite children to learn "Canoe Song" and pretend to be in canoes, "paddling upstream" as they sing the song. You may wish to have children use drums and rattles to tap out the rhythm as they sing.

AUDIO

Use the Unit 3 MUSIC AUDIOCASSETTE to hear "Canoe Song."

Background

SQUANTO Squanto was a Pawtuxet Indian who was captured and taken to Spain as a slave. He then spent some time in England. When he returned to North America, he found that all his people had died of smallpox. He decided to join the colonists at Plymouth and use his English to help them. He served as interpreter for a treaty between the Pilgrims and the Wampanoag leader, Massasoit. He became ill and died after guiding a colonial expedition across Cape Cod.

Link to Language Arts

JOURNAL Remind children that history tells us stories about people who lived before us. Native Americans often passed their stories from parents to children. Point out that we can learn about our history by talking to older people in our own families. Suggest that children ask family members to tell stories about themselves, other relatives, or ancestors. Invite children to record their stories in their journals.

People learn history in different ways. Some read stories written in books. Many American Indians learn their history from stories told aloud. They learn about the past through stories passed from grandparents to parents to children.

What Do You Know?

1. **What Indian group helped the Pilgrims?** the Wampanoags

2. **How can telling stories help people learn history?** People can remember and share their past by passing it on through stories.

145

PUPIL BOOK OR **UNIT BIG BOOK**

Extend and Enrich

SEARCH FOR POCAHONTAS
Many children have seen the animated movie version of the story of Pocahontas, princess of the Powhatan Indians. Suggest that children read a biography of Pocahontas, such as *Pocahontas: Daughter of a Chief* by Carol Greene (Childrens Press, 1988) or *The True Story of Pocahontas* by Lucille Penner (Random House, 1994). Then have them compare the movie version with the true story.

Reteach the Main Idea

PLAY I SPY Use the information from the table on page 143 and the text on page 144 to play a game of I Spy. Model a sample statement, such as "I spy a shelter made of cedar boards" (a Chinook home) or "I spy the Wampanoags' most important food" (corn). Ask the child who gives the correct answer to give the next clue. Allow children to look at their textbooks as they play the game.

Check Understanding

The child can
—— define *history* as stories of the past.
—— identify Indians as the first inhabitants of our country.
—— describe the food, shelter, and clothing of several Native American groups.
—— identify ways in which Indians helped the Pilgrims.

Think Critically

Q. **Why do we use the name *Native Americans* to describe Indians?** because they were the first people to live in this country

Show What You Know

Performance Assessment Provide each child with a 4 × 12- or 4 × 18-inch strip of art paper. Have children use the strip to design a new column about the Wampanoags for the table on page 143.

What to Look For Children's work should include information and art showing that the Wampanoags ate corn, hunted and fished for other foods, lived in bark wigwams, and wore clothes made of animal skins.

Using the Activity Book Challenge children to find the mystery word by completing the puzzle on Activity Book page 26.

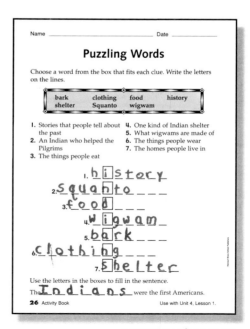

Activity Book page 26

HANDS-ON OPTION

Thanksgiving Then and Now

Objectives: Define *history* as stories of the past. Identify ways in which Indians helped the Pilgrims.

Materials: drawing paper, crayons

Invite children to examine the painting on page 144. Point out that paintings tell stories, and ask children what story from history the picture tells. Then invite children to draw a picture of an event in their own life, such as a favorite birthday party or vacation. The picture should be drawn so that children years from now could look at it and tell its story. Then invite children to show their pictures while other children try to guess their stories. **(VISUAL/TACTILE)**

Long Ago in the Neighborhood

Objectives: Identify Indians as the first inhabitants of our country. Describe the food, shelter, and clothing of several Native American groups.

Materials: found art materials, textbook and other reference books

Help children find out about the group of Indians who once lived in their part of the country by consulting their textbooks and other reference books or by asking a town historian. Have children use found materials to construct a model village to show how the area where they now live may have looked long ago. Children may want to add land features, such as trees or rivers, or clay figures of animals. **(VISUAL/KINESTHETIC)**

The Varied Lives of American Indians

Objective: Describe the food, shelter, and clothing of several Native American groups.

Materials: reference books, United States map, posterboard, crayons or markers

 COOPERATIVE LEARNING Show a United States map, and point out areas where various groups of American Indians lived in the past. Then organize the class into groups, and assign each group the name of an Indian group. Ask each group to research the lives of their Indians, and to design and draw a poster that will help the rest of the class understand their group's customs.

Ask groups to display their posters while they give oral reports on their findings. After all the reports have been given, use the posters to compare the ways of life of the different groups. Children may also enjoy presenting their reports and posters for children from other classes or for family members. **(TACTILE/VISUAL/AUDITORY)**

READ A TIME LINE

OBJECTIVES

1. Identify events as occurring before and after a point in time.
2. Sequence a series of events.
3. Use a time line to relate a story.

VOCABULARY

time line (p. 146)

RESOURCES

Pupil Book/Unit Big Book, pp. 146–147
Write-On Chart 26
Clings
Activity Book, p. 27
Transparency 9
Imagination Express: Destination Time Trip, USA

ACTIVITY CHOICES

Meet Individual Needs

VISUAL LEARNERS Invite children to look through textbooks, newspapers, and periodicals for examples of time lines. Ask children to share and compare the time lines they find. Discuss the similarities and differences among the different time lines. Invite children to note what each time line shows and to identify the time spans and intervals shown on each.

Link to Mathematics

QUANTIFICATION Invite children to brainstorm a list of words that are related to time, such as *minute, hour, day, week, month,* and *year.* Invite children to make a chart telling the number of minutes in an hour, hours in a day, days in a week and in a month, and months in a year. Challenge children to give examples of how they might use these time periods on a time line.

TRANSPARENCY

Use TRANSPARENCY 9.

1. ACCESS

Ask children to name the current month and have a volunteer write it on the board. Then ask children to name the month that will come next. Have a second volunteer write that month on the board to the right of the present month. Follow the same procedure for the month that comes next. Continue by having children name and write all twelve months horizontally in order. Then have children use a yardstick to draw a straight line across the board just above the names of the months. Finally, indicate each month with a short vertical mark on the line. Help children recognize that they have made a time line. Invite children to tell when they celebrate their birthdays and add them to the time line.

Vocabulary

Ask children to define in their own words what a *time line* is. Record their definition on the board and save it.

Q. Where or when have you seen or used a time line before?
Responses might include in science, math, or social studies books, or in magazines.

How do you think time lines are useful? They help you see, understand, and remember the order in which things happened.

2. BUILD

Visual Analysis

Learn from Maps and Time Lines Read the definition of *time line* on page 146, and invite children to compare it with the definition on the board. Help children understand that each picture shows an event from the Pilgrims' voyage from England to America and that it can be used to help tell the Pilgrims' story. Invite children to dictate a sentence or two about each event. Use sentence strips to record their ideas. Offer additional background as needed, and invite children to help you use a map to trace the route of the Pilgrims. Then have children answer the questions as they practice using the time line.

Q. **What does this time line show?** It shows events in the Pilgrims' voyage.

How would you explain how to use the time line? Possible response: I'd move along the line from the first picture on the left to the last picture on the right.

Civics and Government

Civic Values and Democratic Principles Discuss how the people on the *Mayflower* created and signed a document called the Mayflower Compact, in which they agreed to share in setting up a government and promised to obey any laws their leaders would pass.

Chart and Graph Skills

Read a Time Line

A **time line** shows the order in which things happened. This time line tells the story of the Pilgrims.

July 22

Pilgrims sail from Europe to England

September 16

Mayflower sails for America

July	August	September

 How much time is shown on the time line? six months

 In what month did the Mayflower leave for America? September

146

Background

THE PILGRIMS Unable to worship as they wanted in England, many Puritans moved to the Netherlands. After 12 years they decided to leave. In July 1620, they returned to England to join other Puritans who planned to sail to the Virginia colony. On August 15, two ships of Pilgrims set sail but twice turned back because of leaks on one ship, the *Speedwell*. Finally, on September 16, the *Mayflower*—with some passengers from the *Speedwell*—set sail for America, arriving at Cape Cod 65 days later. With winter coming, they decided not to go on to Virginia and instead sailed to a place they called Plymouth.

WRITE-ON CHARTS

Use WRITE-ON CHART 26 and Triangle Clings to re-create a time line of the Pilgrims' voyage to America.

TECHNOLOGY

Use IMAGINATION EXPRESS:™ DESTINATION TIME TRIP, USA to invite children to write about Pilgrims and colonial life in New England.

3 In November the Pilgrims signed a plan for ruling the new settlement. What was it called? the Mayflower Compact

November 21

Mayflower Compact is signed

December 25

Pilgrims land at Plymouth

October	November	December

Think and Do

How many months were the Pilgrims sailing on the <u>Mayflower</u>?

147

Extend and Enrich

PERSONAL-HISTORY TIME LINES Invite children to meet with family members and make a list of events in their lives they consider important with the exact or approximate dates on which those events occurred. Events might be the birth of a brother or sister, learning to ride a bicycle, and starting kindergarten. Have children use their lists to make personal-history time lines from birth to eight years old.

Reteach the Skill

REORDER EVENTS Scramble the sentence strips that children dictated earlier. Then distribute them randomly to volunteers, who will stand at the front of the room. The class then arranges the volunteers with their strips in the correct order. Other volunteers then read the strips in order, telling the story of the Pilgrims' voyage to America.

Q. **What do you think the Mayflower Compact shows about the Pilgrims?** Possible response: They knew how important it was to be able to work together for the good of the group.

3. CLOSE

Think and Do

Children should state that from the time the Pilgrims set sail in September to the time they actually left the ship in December, three months had passed.

Review the skill with children by asking the following question:

Q. **How did this time line help you understand what the Pilgrims did?** Possible response: The time line made it easier to see the order in which events took place and to understand how long it took to reach America by ship at that time.

Using the Activity Book Distribute copies of Activity Book page 27. Have children study the time line and then write about the events shown. Children can then share their writing.

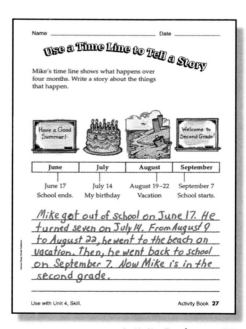

Activity Book page 27

HANDS-ON OPTION

Birthday Time Line

Objectives: Identify events as occurring before and after a point in time. Sequence a series of events.

Materials: large index cards (one per child), markers, twelve long pieces of yarn, tape

Tape a length of yarn along the chalkboard. Have children write their name and birthday on a large index card. Then call children whose birthdays fall in January to the front of the room. Invite children to arrange themselves in order from the first January birthday to the last, with children who are still in their seats helping as necessary. When the class agrees that the group is in the right order, have children tape their cards to the yarn in the same order. Repeat with a new length of yarn for each month of the year. Hang the time lines in order by month around the room or together on one wall of the room if possible. Then ask children questions about when certain events will happen during the year, such as "We will have spring break before April but after February. In what month will we have spring break?" and "Valentine's Day is the day before Jake's birthday (February 15). On what date is Valentine's Day?" **(VISUAL/KINESTHETIC)**

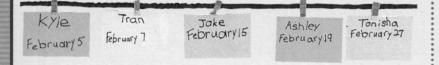

| Kyle February 5 | Tran February 7 | Jake February 15 | Ashley February 19 | Tonisha February 27 |

Looking Forward

Objective: Use a time line to relate a story.

Materials: copies of the classroom calendar for the coming month, one per group; craft paper; markers

Organize the class into four groups, one for each week of the coming month. Include the final days of the month before or the first days of the month after so that each group will have a full seven days with which to work. Record special events taking place in your classroom or in the community on the classroom calendar for the coming month, and then make a copy of it for each group.

Have children work together to reorganize the events in the form of a time line. Then suggest to children that they copy their events and dates onto one long piece of craft paper to make a time line that shows activities for the whole month. Mount the time line in the hall. Then have children use the time line to write newsletters to their families to tell about the important events they will be looking forward to during the month. **(VISUAL/TACTILE/AUDITORY)**

Our School's History

Objectives: Sequence a series of events. Use a time line to relate a story.

Materials: mural paper, crayons or markers

COOPERATIVE LEARNING Write the following job titles on the board: *Researchers, Writers, Artists*. Explain that children will work together to make a time line that shows the history of their school. One group of researchers will use books or encyclopedias to find out about the group or groups of American Indians that lived in their area before their town was built and who may have lived or worked on the property where the school stands now. Another group of researchers will use books, interviews, or artifacts, such as a date on the school building's cornerstone, to find important events in the history of their school. This group will also determine the date when most children in the class entered the school and the date when they will graduate. Writers will be responsible for organizing the information the researchers find and writing it on a time line. Artists will draw pictures, using books and pictures as references, to illustrate events on the time line. Invite children to volunteer to be responsible for one of the jobs. Display the completed time line in the school's lobby so students and visitors can learn more about the school. **(TACTILE/VISUAL)**

2

WE REMEMBER THE PAST

OBJECTIVES
1. Describe the early history of our country.
2. Recognize the contributions of American settlers.
3. Compare community life now and long ago.

VOCABULARY
settler (p. 148)

RESOURCES
Pupil Book/Unit Big Book, pp. 148–151
Write-On Charts 14, 30
Activity Book, p. 28
Desk Maps
Imagination Express: Destination Time Trip, USA

ACTIVITY CHOICES

Role-Play

Organize children into small groups. Explain that they are settlers about to travel to a newly discovered planet. Have one child in each group role-play a reporter and ask the settlers why they want to go to the new planet, what they hope to find there, and what dangers they might face.

Meet Individual Needs

ADVANCED LEARNERS Write the names of the following European explorers on the board: Cabot, Verrazano, LaSalle, Drake, Raleigh, Hudson, Champlain, Magellan, Cortés, Ponce de León, Pizarro, Coronado, and Balboa. Ask children to find out what countries the explorers were from and what part of the Americas each explored. Then have children indicate those areas on a map and report their findings to the class.

DESK MAPS

Have children use their DESK MAPS of the world to chart explored lands.

WRITE-ON CHARTS

Use WRITE-ON CHART 30 to make the KWL chart.

1. ACCESS

Remind children about the first inhabitants of our country, the American Indians. Then help children recall that after explorers like Christopher Columbus arrived in the land we now call the Americas, many people left their homelands to move to this land. Begin a KWL chart, and ask children what they know about the people who came to settle here and what they would like to find out about them. Save the chart for a later activity.

K (What I know)	W (What I want to find out)	L (What I learned)
Some people came from England.	Why did people want to come here?	
Some people came from Spain.	Where did they settle?	
Life was difficult at first.	How was life difficult for them?	
	Did the Indians help them? How?	

Focus on the Main Idea

In this lesson children will continue to explore the early history of our country by observing a reenactment of life in colonial Williamsburg and by then comparing that life with their own lives. Tell children they will visit Williamsburg—a restored colonial village—to see how people lived.

2. BUILD

Key Content Summary

Many Europeans left their countries to settle in this vast land. Although there have been many changes since the first settlers came, much about community life remains the same.

History

Using Historical Evidence Read aloud pages 148–151. Explain that the pictures were taken at Williamsburg, a restored colonial town in Virginia. Emphasize that we can learn about the past by studying what people have left behind—documents, maps, art, buildings, utensils, tools, furniture, clothing, and even folktales.

Culture

Human Relationships Define *settlers* as people who move to start a new community. Invite children to suggest some of the hardships early settlers might have faced, such as bad weather, disease, and lack of food.

Q. **Why do you think the Americas were a good place to settle?**

good land for farming, many trees for houses, animals and fish to eat

You may wish to describe the Pilgrims' arrival in America and have children discuss the changes from life in the early settlement of Plymouth to life later in the more established community of Williamsburg.

LESSON 2

We Remember the Past

As time passed, American Indians saw new communities grow up in America. Compare daily life in one early community with the way you live.

Many years ago people came from other countries to live in America. These early American **settlers** built their own houses and grew their own food. They burned wood to cook food and heat their homes. Families dried, smoked, and salted some foods to store them for the winter. How does your family store food?

growing food

storing food for the winter

148

ACTIVITY CHOICES

Reading Support

USE CONTEXT CLUES Have children pause after they read the first page of the lesson to check for understanding. Ask them if they have ever seen the word *settlers*. Remind them of clues that can help a reader know the meaning of a new word:
- the other words in the sentence
- the pictures on the page

Background

WILLIAMSBURG, VIRGINIA In 1607 Jamestown became the first permanent English settlement. Another settlement, called Middle Plantation, was started nearby. In 1699 it became the capital of the Virginia Colony and was renamed Williamsburg. It soon became a cultural, social, and political center.

Multicultural Link

St. Augustine, Florida, is the oldest United States city. The city was established in 1565 by Spanish explorer Pedro Menéndez de Avilés. The oldest United States house, the Gonzalez-Álvarez House of St. Augustine, is now a national landmark. Because owners from many backgrounds have lived there over the years, the house and its furniture reflect a mixture of different cultures.

Getting clothing was a lot more work back then! Early Americans sheared sheep for wool. They spun the wool into thread. Then they wove the thread into cloth on a loom and made the cloth into clothing. How does your family get the clothes you need?

shearing sheep for wool

spinning wool into thread

weaving cloth

149

PUPIL BOOK **OR** UNIT BIG BOOK

Visual Learning

Interpret Pictures Invite children to describe the scene in each photo.

Q. **What might you learn by visiting the Williamsburg village?** Responses might include how the early settlers lived, what they wore, what tools they used, how they made the things they needed, and what they did for fun.

History

People and Events Across Time and Place Ask children to note similarities between their community and the colonial town in the pictures.

Q. **How is your life like the life of the early settlers?** We have many of the same needs as the early settlers, such as food, clothing, shelter, family, friends, good health, and fun.

How is it different? Most of us do not have to build our own houses, spin wool into thread, make our own clothes, or grow our own food.

Meet Individual Needs

ENGLISH LANGUAGE LEARNERS
Use self-stick notes as labels for the unfamiliar names of objects and activities depicted in the photos. After children learn the words, remove the labels. Then distribute the labels to children and ask them to read each label aloud and place it next to the appropriate object or activity. Children can then use the word in a sentence to tell about the picture.

Link Literature

Encourage children to read *Heron Street* by Ann Turner. (HarperCollins, 1989) They will read how the land experienced many changes over the centuries as people settled near a marsh by the sea. Invite children to discuss what happens as more people move into the area.

Culture

Thought and Expression Explain to children that before printing presses were widely used in America, the colonists got their news from town criers who sang out information on street corners, from news sheets that were posted in public places, and from conversations with people who knew about important events.

3. CLOSE

Return to the KWL chart that children started earlier in the lesson. To summarize the lesson, complete the third column of the chart as children answer their own previous questions about settlers in early America.

Check Understanding

The child can

___ describe the early history of our country.

___ recognize the contributions of American settlers.

___ compare community life now and long ago.

Think Critically

Q. **How would you describe the early history of this country to someone who did not know it?** Children might mention the civilizations of the Indians; the arrival of Columbus; the explorations of America by other people; the arrival of settlers; and the ways settlers had to do everything for themselves, such as building their own homes and towns, growing their own food, and making their own clothing.

Most towns printed a newspaper. The newspaper was one way people learned about their community and the world. How do people get news today?

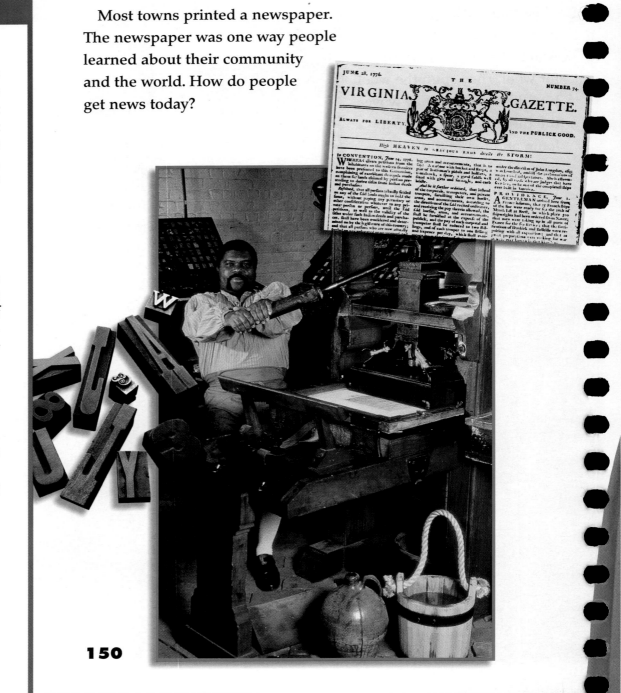

150

ACTIVITY CHOICES

Extend and Enrich

RESEARCH SETTLERS Invite children to find out more about early settlers. Urge them to look for books about Sir Walter Raleigh and Roanoke Island, John Smith and Jamestown, the Pilgrims and Plymouth Colony, the Dutch and New Netherland, and the Swedish and New Sweden. Invite children to share what they learn.

Reteach the Main Idea

COMPARE AND CONTRAST Invite children to refer to the pictures on pages 148–151 and to take turns telling one way their lives are the same as and one way their lives are different from the lives of the settlers.

Early American settlers enjoyed some of the same things we do. They played games with their friends. Families spent time together.

What Do You Know?

1. How did early settlers get food ready to store for winter?

2. Could the early American settlers do what you like to do? Why or why not?

1. They dried, smoked, and salted it.

151

PUPIL BOOK OR UNIT BIG BOOK

TECHNOLOGY

Use IMAGINATION EXPRESS:™ DESTINATION TIME TRIP, USA to explore colonial America.

WRITE-ON CHARTS

What's New, What's Old

Use WRITE-ON CHART 14 to extend and enrich the lesson. See Teacher's Edition page W44.

Would you have liked to live as a settler long ago? Why or why not?
Children may say that life would have been too hard without the conveniences we have today or that life would have been more satisfying and exciting.

Show What You Know

Performance Assessment Organize children into pairs. Ask one child to pretend to be an American settler in Williamsburg and the other to be a modern-day visitor. Have children compare their lives and communities.

What to Look For Look for evidence of the child's general understanding of the differences between the life and times of American settlers and life today, particularly the fact that the settlers had to use different resources to meet their needs.

Using the Activity Book Distribute copies of Activity Book page 28, and invite children to look at the pictures showing aspects of life during America's early history. For each aspect shown, children should draw a picture and write a statement to show a comparable aspect of their own lives. Invite children to share and compare their responses.

Name _____ Date _____

Changes

Draw a picture in each box to show how things have changed. Write a sentence to tell about each picture.

Today we use a computer to write.

Today we use a stove to cook.

Today we ride bikes.

Today we live in apartments.

28 Activity Book   Use with Unit 4, Lesson 2.

Activity Book page 28

HANDS-ON OPTION

Making Succotash and Butter

Objectives: Describe the early history of our country. Compare community life now and long ago.

Materials: Slow cooker, bowl, measuring cup, set of measuring spoons, equal amounts of dried white pea beans and canned corn, salt, pepper, margarine, picture of a butter churn, heavy whipping cream, jar with a lid, crackers

Invite children to make succotash, a mix of beans and corn that early settlers in New England learned to make from the Indians. First, have children rinse the beans, cover them with water, and soak them overnight. Next have children pour the beans into a slow cooker and cook them in water for several hours. Once the beans are soft, have children add the corn, salt, pepper, and margarine. Then stir and enjoy! Point out that the Indians often grew both crops in the same patch and at harvest time would dry and save some of each for the wintertime, when food was scarce.

You may wish to have children make butter to use with the succotash, in place of the margarine. Display a picture of a wooden churn and dasher and explain that by churning—beating or stirring—cream with the dasher, people can turn the cream into butter. Emphasize that first the settlers had to milk cows, wait for the cream to rise to the top of the milk, and then skim off the cream. Invite children to take turns shaking a jar that has been half filled with heavy whipping cream. Ask children to note how long it takes for a lump of butter to form in the jar. Once a large lump has formed, have a child pour the remaining liquid, now buttermilk, into a separate container. Add salt to the butter and ask another child to stir. Add some of the butter to the succotash, and spread the remainder on crackers for children to taste. **(TACTILE/VISUAL)**

A "History" Poem

Objectives: Describe the early history of our country.

Materials: paper and pencils, drawing paper, crayons, markers

 Organize children into cooperative groups to create a "History" poem. Have each group write *HISTORY* vertically down the left margin of a sheet of paper. Challenge children to think of words and phrases beginning with each letter to tell about history and what it means to them. Then have them write their poems on large sheets of drawing paper and decorate the sheets with pictures, cutouts, dates, and facts. Remind children that this kind of poem does not have to rhyme! **(TACTILE/AUDITORY)**

Dear Friends . . .

Objective: Recognize the contribution of American settlers.

Materials: 2/3 cup fresh or frozen berries, 1/2 tsp. salt, 1/2 tsp. vinegar, containers with lids, colander, spoon, writing paper, twigs or feathers

Remind children that settlers learned to use available resources to make many of the things they needed, such as soap, candles, and paper. Point out that they made ink from nuts and berries and used feather quills as pens. Then invite children to make their own ink. Have them place the berries in a colander over a bowl and mash the berries with a large spoon. After children remove the pulp, have them stir the salt and vinegar into the berry juice. Children should repeat the process using different kinds of berries. Then they can imagine they are settlers and can dip twigs or feather quills into the ink and use them to write letters to friends back in England. Have children discuss their experience and comment on the quality and difficulty of this writing process. **(TACTILE/KINESTHETIC)**

READ A HISTORY MAP

OBJECTIVES

1. Use a history map to identify the 13 colonies.
2. Distinguish between historical and current maps of identical sites.
3. Recognize that names and shapes of places sometimes change.

VOCABULARY

colony (p. 152)

RESOURCES

Pupil Book/Unit Big Book, pp. 152–153
Activity Book, p. 29
Transparency 10
Desk Maps

Link to Art

ILLUSTRATION Display historical photographs of your community. If possible, the photos should be of locations the children will easily recognize. Lead a discussion of how the locations have changed. Then invite children to choose a favorite place and create two drawings showing how it might have looked a long time ago and how it looks today.

Meet Individual Needs

VISUAL LEARNERS Organize children into small groups. Provide each group with a box and an assortment of small objects. Ask a volunteer in each group to place 10 to 15 objects in the bottom of the box. Instruct each group to make a simple map showing the arrangement of the objects. Then have children cover their eyes as you remove several objects from each box. Encourage children to use their maps to identify the missing items.

1. ACCESS

Ask children to recall what they know about maps. Review that a map is a special kind of drawing that shows a place from above.

Q. **What are some of the things a map can show?** Possible responses: where things are, how far things are from one another, the size and shape of something, land and water, the names of streets, cities, states, and countries

Arrange objects of different sizes and shapes on the floor. Invite children to draw a map showing the arrangement from above. Rearrange the objects, adding some things and taking others away. Then have children draw a second map showing the new arrangement. Invite them to discuss how the two maps are different and how they are the same. Point out that maps can show how things change.

TRANSPARENCY

Use **TRANSPARENCY 10.**

2. BUILD

Vocabulary

Have children read the introductory text on page 152. Remind them that early American settlers lived in colonies, not in states. Explain that a *colony* is a place ruled by another country. Although the settlers lived in a new land, they had to follow the rules of the country they came from.

Visual Analysis

Learn from Maps   Have children examine the history map and read the text on pages 152–153. Explain that the map shows how this land looked before it was a country. Ask children to describe what they see and to answer the questions in the text. Point out the 13 colonies on the map. Tell children that most of the people who lived in these colonies were from England. Guide children to understand that these 13 English colonies eventually became the United States of America.

Q. **Why do you think the English settlers built their colonies along the Atlantic Ocean?** It was the first place they came to when they got off their ships.

Geography

Location   Ask children to label the East Coast states on their Desk Maps of the United States. Then have them compare the history map on page 153 with their Desk Maps. Name each of the colonies as children study the maps.

Q. **How is the history map different from the United States map?** The history map shows how this land looked long ago, and the map of the United States shows how things look today; the history map shows colonies, and the United States map shows states.

How are the maps the same? They show the same place; some names are the same.

Place   Ask children to locate Massachusetts on both the history map and the map of the United States.

Map and Globe Skills

Read a History Map

Maps can show where places of long ago were. The first English settlers in North America built their colonies along the Atlantic Ocean. A **colony** is a place ruled by another country.

1 What year does this map show?
1773

2 How many English colonies were there?
13

3 In which colony was Jamestown? In which colony was Plymouth?
Virginia; Massachusetts

4 Which colony was the farthest south?
Georgia

Think and Do

● Write these cities on a sheet of paper—Baltimore, Boston, Charles Town, Philadelphia, Williamsburg.

● Find out in which colony each city began. Write the name of the colony next to the city.

152

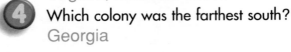

ACTIVITY CHOICES

Background

COLONIAL POPULATION   Most of the people living in the 13 original colonies were English, but even in colonial days, America was diverse. Besides the English and the Native Americans, there were thousands of Dutch, French, Germans, Scotch-Irish, Scots, and Swedes living in the colonies. Although many European countries had settlements and outposts in the New World, the English were the first to live here in large numbers and set up permanent homes.

Meet Individual Needs

ENGLISH LANGUAGE LEARNERS   Provide children with a copy of the map on page 153. Invite them to make flash cards by cutting out each colony and taping it onto an index card. As children identify each colony, help them write the name in English on the back of the card. Invite children acquiring English to review the cards with a partner who speaks English fluently.

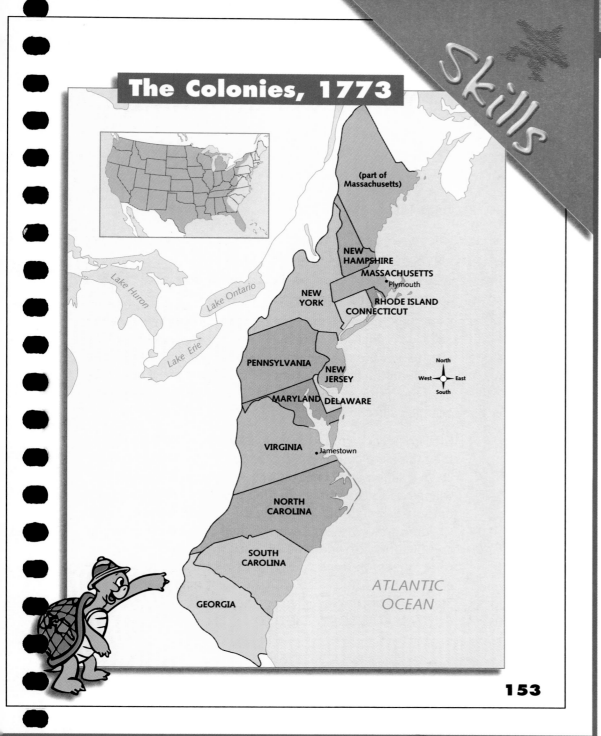

The Colonies, 1773

(part of Massachusetts)

NEW HAMPSHIRE

MASSACHUSETTS
• Plymouth

NEW YORK

RHODE ISLAND

CONNECTICUT

Lake Huron

Lake Ontario

Lake Erie

PENNSYLVANIA

NEW JERSEY

MARYLAND DELAWARE

VIRGINIA
• Jamestown

NORTH CAROLINA

SOUTH CAROLINA

GEORGIA

ATLANTIC OCEAN

North
West — East
South

153

PUPIL BOOK *OR* **UNIT BIG BOOK**

Q. **How has Massachusetts changed since 1773?** It was much bigger and shaped differently when it was a colony.

Have children continue looking for differences and similarities between the history map and the map of the United States.

3. CLOSE

Think and Do

Children's answers should locate Baltimore in Maryland, Boston in Massachusetts, Charles Town in South Carolina, Philadelphia in Pennsylvania, and Williamsburg in Virginia.

Review the skill with children by asking the following questions:

Q. **Which colony was the farthest north?** Massachusetts

What can you learn from looking at this history map? Possible responses: There were 13 colonies in 1773; some of our states were named after English colonies; the first cities were near the ocean.

Using the Activity Book Distribute copies of Activity Book page 29. Have children cut and paste the pictures to turn *Old Town* into *New Town*.

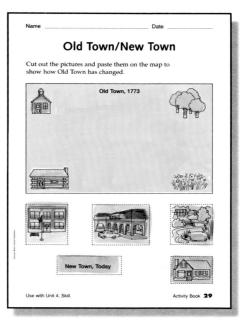

Activity Book page 29

Extend and Enrich

USE A STATE HISTORY MAP
Provide children with both a history map and a current map of their state. Show children how to create a two-column chart titled *Old and New Maps*, with column heads *Same* and *Different*. Have them use the chart to list things that are the same and things that are different on the two maps. Suggest that they check whether the shape or size of their state has changed and whether the names of cities or bodies of water have changed.

Reteach the Skill

USE A HISTORY MAP Challenge children to use the history map on page 153 and their Desk Maps of the United States to determine which present-day states were part of the Massachusetts Colony in 1773. Have children continue comparing the two maps to see what colonies other states were once part of.

HANDS-ON OPTION

The "Hands-On Option" is an alternative way to address all objectives for this lesson or to enrich the content found in the Pupil Book/Unit Big Book.

Colony Diorama

Objectives: Use a history map to identify the 13 colonies. Recognize that names and shapes of places sometimes change.

Materials: shoe boxes, craft materials, glue, scissors, crayons or markers

 Display books, photographs, and other materials about the 13 English colonies. Organize children into four or five groups, and have them choose one of the 13 colonies, using the history map on page 153. Ask each group to use the materials provided to create a diorama about its chosen colony. One child can paint the inside of a shoe box to create a background; other children can add details to the colony, such as people, buildings, and trees. Have children write a short paragraph telling about their colony. **(TACTILE/VISUAL)**

Old and New

Objective: Distinguish between historical and current maps of identical sites.

Materials: current and historical maps of the same location, paper, pencils

Display current and historical maps of the same location. Identify the location that both maps show, and explain that one map shows how the place looked a long time ago and the other map shows how the place looks today. Have children study the two maps and make lists of the similarities and the differences. Discuss with children what they can learn from looking at the history map. **(VISUAL/AUDITORY)**

Future Map

Objective: Recognize that names and shapes of places sometimes change.

Materials: map of the United States, craft paper, crayons and markers

 Organize the class into cooperative groups. Sketch on craft paper for each group an outline of the continental United States, with Alaska and Hawaii on the left side. Then help children recall how they used the history map on page 153 to see how America has changed since 1773.

Challenge each group to create a future map showing how they think the country might be different in the year 2500. Have children draw lines on their maps to indicate the new shapes and sizes of regions. Tell them that they can keep present-day state names or create new ones if they wish. Children may wish to decorate their maps with drawings and pictures. Provide time for each group to share its finished map with the class. Invite other children to compare each group's future map with a current map of the United States and discuss the changes they see. **(VISUAL/AUDITORY/TACTILE)**

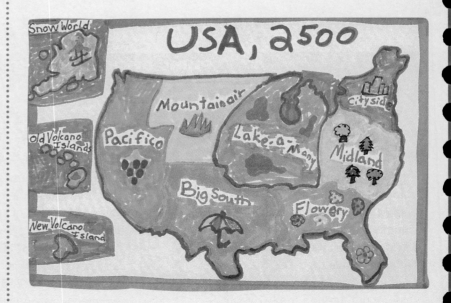

3

COMMUNITIES GROW AND CHANGE

OBJECTIVES

1. Identify the causes of change in a community.
2. Explain pride in one's community and its past.

VOCABULARY

landmark (p. 157)

RESOURCES

Pupil Book/Unit Big Book, pp. 154–157

Pattern P7

Activity Book, p. 31

Imagination Express: Destination Time Trip, USA

ACTIVITY CHOICES

Meet Individual Needs

VISUAL AND KINESTHETIC LEARNERS Invite children to choose a few places and features near the school that they agree make their community special, such as a statue, park, or building. Display a map of the community, and help children locate each place or feature. Then point out the school. Invite children to plan and then trace a route that visitors could take to tour the community, beginning and ending at the school.

Meet Individual Needs

ENGLISH LANGUAGE LEARNERS Pair children acquiring English with fluent English-speakers. Invite them to read aloud together the conversation between Miguel and Grandpa.

Role-Play

Have small groups choose one place along the imaginary community-tour route. Explain that one child will role-play the tour guide and tell what makes that place special, while the other children will role-play tourists asking questions about the place.

1. ACCESS

Begin by asking children to imagine that a group of people from another country is touring the United States and will soon be coming to their community. Invite children to plan a community tour for the visitors. Ask them to identify some natural and human-made features they think make their community special, such as scenic areas and parks, historic buildings and sites, monuments, statues of important people, a zoo or botanical garden, or a museum. List responses on the board. Display a community street map, and have children identify the locations of the places and features.

Q. **Why do you think these places are special or important?** Possible response: The places show something about the community's history and the people who live in the community.

Focus on the Main Idea

As children read the dialogue, they will discover why a boy and his grandfather have pride in their community and its past. Children will also explore how and why communities grow and change. Tell children to think about their own community as they read this conversation between a boy and his grandfather about their city—San Diego, California.

2. BUILD

Key Content Summary

America expanded rapidly as European settlers continued to arrive. As the years passed, forts and settlements grew into villages, villages into towns, and towns into cities. Today, a mix of cultures exists in historic communities like San Diego.

History

Origins, Spread, and Influence Ask volunteers to read pages 154–155 aloud. Discuss that the Spaniards built missions throughout the Southwest between the 1500s and 1800s. Explain that Spanish priests wanted to convert Indians to Christianity. Priests taught Indians how to grow wheat, walnuts, fruit, and oats; how to raise cattle, horses, pigs, and sheep; and how to make certain things, such as leather and woolen goods.

Q. **How do you think the Indians felt when the Spaniards tried to get them to change their faith and give up their ways?**
Responses might include angry and not interested or thankful and interested.

Culture

Shared Humanity and Unique Identity Point out the geography feature on page 155 and the mural on page 156. Remind children that Indians originally lived in the San Diego area and that over time,

ACTIVITY CHOICES

Reading Support

USE PICTURE CLUES Draw a tower on top of a square base. Write the word *landmark* on the base, and ask children to define it. Then have them scan the rest of the story for pictures of landmarks. List the landmarks on the tower. Explain that pictures help us understand what we read.

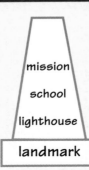

mission

school

lighthouse

landmark

Communities Grow and Change

San Diego is a very old city in California. Join Miguel as he learns how the city has changed and grown.

Miguel: How old is our city, Grandpa?

Grandpa: San Diego began way back in 1769 as a Spanish fort. A priest named Junípero Serra built a kind of church called a mission inside the fort. It was the first mission in California.

Later, Spanish and Mexican settlers came to live at the bottom of the hill below the fort. People can still visit that area. It is called Old Town Historic Park.

San Diego Mission

154

Old Town

Background

SAN DIEGO The landmark Mission San Diego de Alcalá, pictured on this page, began the European settlement of California. Over the last 50 years, San Diego has been one of the fastest-growing cities in the United States. It is now the sixth-largest city in the country. Part of its growth is owed to its natural deepwater harbor, making it an important shipping and military base. San Diego also attracts millions of tourists every year.

Miguel: Walking through Old Town is fun. I like to walk down by the water, too. I can see many kinds of boats sailing in and out of the harbor.

Grandpa: San Diego Bay has been important to our city. In the beginning, trade ships carried goods to and from California. Later, tuna fishing brought canning factories to San Diego. Now, many people have jobs at the Naval Base.

Geography

United States

MEXICO

San Diego, California

San Diego is a city whose neighbor is a country. South of San Diego, California, is the country of Mexico. Many of the Spaniards who settled in California long ago came from Mexico.

155

Spaniards, Mexicans, and English-speaking American settlers came and stayed.

Q. **How do you think having a mix of people affected those who lived in San Diego in the past? Think of their languages, crafts, customs, foods, and building styles.** Groups learned and used what they could from one another. **Why do you think Miguel and his grandfather have pride in their city?** Possible response: Their Spanish or Mexican history played an important part in the growth of San Diego.

"PRIMARY SOURCE"

Invite a local historian to speak to the class. Help children prepare questions about changes in their community. Afterward, have children record in their journals what they learned.

Visual Analysis

Interpret Pictures Ask for volunteers to read pages 156–157 and to describe how San Diego looks today. Review the *landmarks* in this lesson. Emphasize that a variety of things, including new technology, cause communities to grow and change.

PUPIL BOOK OR UNIT BIG BOOK

Link to Mathematics

NUMBERS Have children refer to the text to find out when San Diego began. Have a volunteer write *1769* on the board. Then ask another volunteer to write the current year on the board, above *1769*. Invite children to subtract to find the difference between the two years and to tell how they know which one is more recent.

Multicultural Link

Mention that San Diego was named after a Roman Catholic saint. Explain that some communities are named after land or water features, such as Salt Lake City, Utah; some are named after other places, such as Toledo, Ohio, for Toledo, Spain; and still others are named for their founders, such as Houston, Texas, for Sam Houston. Challenge children to find out how their community got its name.

Link to Science

OCEANS Ask children to look in their science books to read about oceans. Children might research the fish and plant life of an ocean. You may wish to explain how the warm temperatures of the Pacific Ocean near San Diego affect its weather. For example, in 1998 a warm ocean current called El Niño caused heavy rainfall and flooding.

Q. **What new discoveries helped San Diego become a modern city? How?** Responses may include electricity; machines with motors to power them; and increasingly efficient tools, transportation, and communication. All of these have made it easier for people to work and to build, make, grow, and buy what they need.

What other things can cause a community to grow and change? people who come from other places, changes in climate, needs of the people who come to an area, popular tourist attractions

3. CLOSE

Ask children to identify changes that have happened in their community.

Check Understanding

The child can

___ identify the causes of change in a community.

___ explain pride in one's community and its past.

Miguel: Why do so many people visit San Diego?

Grandpa: San Diego is a good place to vacation all year long. There are many parks in the city. Balboa Park has a world-famous zoo, colorful gardens, and museums.

Convention Center

Also, the people of San Diego built a large Convention Center. Groups travel from all over the country to meetings there. Everyone likes to come to a city that has interesting places to visit, good weather, and beautiful beaches.

San Diego Zoo

Mexican Museum mural art

156

ACTIVITY CHOICES

Extend and Enrich

SEQUENCE EVENTS Invite children to list on individual strips of cardboard or posterboard the major events and dates they learned about in the history of San Diego. Ask children to research and record dates of other important events in San Diego history. Then help children arrange the strips across the chalkboard ledge in chronological order.

Reteach the Main Idea

ANALYZE PICTURES Have children take turns choosing one picture from the lesson and telling what kind of change it shows.

TECHNOLOGY

Use IMAGINATION EXPRESS:™ DESTINATION TIME TRIP, USA to explore changes in communities through time.

Link to Art

MURALS Invite groups of children to create murals or paintings to show something special about their own community.

Old Point Loma Lighthouse

Miguel: What is your favorite place, Grandpa?

Grandpa: My favorite landmark is the Old Point Loma Lighthouse. A **landmark** is something people easily see and know as part of the community. The lighthouse is near the Cabrillo National Monument by San Diego Bay. Both landmarks remind us of Juan Rodríguez Cabrillo, who sailed into the bay in 1542. That was more than 200 years before the first mission was built.

Miguel: I like to look out from Point Loma and see our beautiful city. Think how much it has changed!

What Do You Know?

1. From what country were the people who built the first fort and mission in San Diego? Spain

2. What are some landmarks in your community?

157

PUPIL BOOK OR UNIT BIG BOOK

Link Literature

Read aloud *Who Came Down That Road?* by George Ella Lyon. (Orchard, 1992) In this book a son's questions lead his mother into the past as she lists all the different people, animals, dinosaurs, and even stars that occupied the place now known as "the road." Challenge children to tell how the road changed through the years.

Who Came Down That Road?
story by George Ella Lyon • paintings by Peter Catalanotto

Think Critically

Q. **What makes you proud of your community?** Accept responses such as the people, landmarks, and history.

Do you think landmarks like important old buildings should be saved, or should they be replaced with new buildings? Some children may say that old buildings should be saved so people can learn about the past; others may feel that the new is more comfortable or convenient.

Show What You Know

Performance Assessment Have children use this lesson as a model for creating their own imaginary dialogues with a grandparent or other adult, in which they talk about how their community has grown or changed. Children can draw pictures to show changes.

What to Look For Look for evidence of the child's understanding of the kinds of changes that occur in a community.

Using the Activity Book Invite children to imagine they have been asked to design a cover for a book about their community. Explain that the design could show a landmark, a historical figure, or a special feature. Then distribute copies of Activity Book page 31. Invite children to share their cover designs and to explain their choices.

Activity Book page 31

HANDS-ON OPTION

Growing and Changing

Objectives: Identify the causes of change in a community. Explain pride in one's community and its past.

Materials: craft paper, pencils, crayons, markers, magazine pictures, scissors, paste

Cover a wall with craft paper. Draw a river—a thin blue line that snakes from the top of the paper to the bottom. Sketch a simple walled fort or mission in the center, next to the river. Invite each child to add something to the scene to show how the settlement changes as more settlers come and stay. Children might add buildings, roads, bridges, crops, and cattle or sheep. Then have children name the town, create an imaginary history for it, and write the history in a class paragraph. (TACTILE/VISUAL)

Linking Changes

Objective: Identify the causes of change in a community.

Materials: Pattern P7, crayons, markers, pencils, tape

Invite children to work in groups to create a chain that links the past to the present. Ask children to interview older family members to find out about the changes that have taken place in their own community over the years and then to record each change on a pattern strip. Some children may wish to draw pictures to show changes. Have one child use tape to make the first link.

Have the next child put a pattern strip through the link and tape the ends together to form the second link. Continue until all the links have been added. (TACTILE/VISUAL)

Exploring Our Community

Objectives: Identify the causes of change in a community. Explain pride in one's community and its past.

Materials: display table, posterboard, assorted art supplies, scissors, tape, pushpins, glue

Invite children to create a display titled *Our Community*. Ask children to include such resources as postcards, photographs, and drawings of landmarks and special features; pamphlets and brochures from organizations like the chamber of commerce; information gathered from interviews with older residents and members of a local historical society; newspaper articles that highlight historical and cultural events; and even a list of restaurants featuring foods from other cultures. (TACTILE/VISUAL)

FIND CAUSE AND EFFECT

OBJECTIVES

1. Identify the causes of certain events.
2. Recognize the effects of certain actions.
3. Realize that one cause may have more than one effect.

VOCABULARY

cause (p. 158)
effect (p. 158)

RESOURCES

Pupil Book/Unit Big Book, pp. 158–159
Write-On Chart 29
Activity Book, p. 32
Transparency 11
The Amazing Writing Machine

ACTIVITY CHOICES

Meet Individual Needs

AUDITORY LEARNERS Create and record sound effects such as a door slamming; a glass or plate breaking; someone crying, laughing, yelling, or screaming; a dog growling; and an ambulance siren wailing. After you play each sound for the class, invite children to describe what they hear and to suggest a cause-and-effect scenario that may have led to that sound.

Link to Language Arts

WRITE A NARRATIVE Invite children to write story starters in which they set the stage for an adventure. Provide this example: *It was a quiet, breezy summer night and everyone in the family was fast asleep. Suddenly, Tanya sat straight up in her bed and started to laugh.* Ask children to trade story starters and then write a middle and an ending. Invite them to tell what happens and why. Children can then read and discuss their stories, pointing out causes and their effects.

1. ACCESS

Remind children that in Lesson 3 they met Miguel and his grandfather, two people who live in San Diego, California. Ask them to recall that many canning factories moved to San Diego. Ask children whether they remember the reason why. If children do not recall, remind them that tuna fishing was an important industry around San Diego Bay.

Q. **What do you think might happen if tuna could no longer be found near San Diego?** People would lose jobs and move away.

Visual Analysis

Learn from Diagrams Model a cause-and-effect diagram on the board.

Help children find the relationship between the pictures. Then invite them to work in pairs to draw their own examples.

TECHNOLOGY

Use THE AMAZING WRITING MACHINE™ RESOURCE PACKAGE to complete this activity.

2. BUILD

Visual Analysis

Compare Pictures Direct attention to pages 158–159 and read aloud the first paragraph, which defines *cause* and *effect*. Then invite children to compare the picture of San Diego from 1874, on page 158, with the picture of the same area from 1895, on page 159. List children's observations. Emphasize that San Diego grew and thrived as a center for the Pacific Coast cattle-hide trade. New businesses developed, and by 1885 San Diego had its first railroad. Invite children to discuss why they think San Diego grew from a trading center to a railroad stop and eventually to a city. Help them recognize that if a community is to grow and thrive, it must be able to provide for the needs of its people.

Q. **What effect do you think the railroad had?** It made traveling to and from San Diego faster and easier; the railroad brought more people to the area, so new businesses were started that could meet people's needs.

Critical Thinking Skills

Find Cause and Effect

Changes happen for different reasons. What makes something happen is a **cause**. What happens is an **effect**.

1 Look at the first picture. This is how San Diego looked long ago. What was the community like? Children should comment on such things as small size, old houses, few roads.

158

ACTIVITY CHOICES

Home Involvement

Ask children to discuss a news story with their families. Urge them to identify the causes of the events and any other effects of those causes. Suggest that they follow up on the story to see if and how it continues to unfold.

Background

SAN DIEGO During the early 1800s people came to San Diego to trade cattle hides. The port helped San Diego grow as a center for trade, and it became a base for whaling ships. In 1850 San Diego became a chartered city. Ten years later, a businessman named Alonzo Horton developed an area along the east side of the Bay called New Town. The arrival of the railroad in 1885 created another temporary land boom. Today San Diego is a center of health science and medical research activities, as well as a popular convention site.

Meet Individual Needs

TACTILE LEARNERS Display Write-On Chart 29, and label the two columns *Cause* and *Effect*. After children study the two scenes, invite them to list on the chart the cause (the railroad) and its effects. Challenge children to list causes and effects of other historical events they have studied.

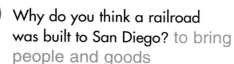
2 Why do you think a railroad was built to San Diego? to bring people and goods

3 The picture below shows San Diego a few years later. What caused the community to grow? As more people arrived, new homes and businesses were built.

Think and Do

What changes do you think you would see in San Diego today? Why?

San Diego from Cor of 5th and Fish Sts.

159

PUPIL BOOK OR UNIT BIG BOOK

Extend and Enrich

ANALYZE NEWS ARTICLES
Provide children with newspaper and magazine articles dealing with current events. Invite children to read an article and then explain to the class what happened and why.

TRANSPARENCY

Use TRANSPARENCY 11.

Reteach the Skill

FIND THE CAUSE Provide children with specific situations, such as a girl being late for school, a fire smoldering in a forest, a NO FISHING sign being posted at a lake, or a sink overflowing. Then have children suggest a possible cause for each situation.

3. CLOSE

Think and Do

Children's responses may include that the city has grown even more because of new businesses and the parks and zoos that attract tourists. They may also comment on signs of modernization in architecture and transportation.

Review the skill with children by asking the following questions:

Q. **How would you explain the difference between cause and effect to a younger child?** Children might explain that a cause is what makes things happen and an effect is what happens as a result. They might also give an example, such as rain as a cause and wet grass as an effect.

Why do you think knowing how to figure out why something happens is important in social studies? It can help us better understand and learn from events in history.

Using the Activity Book Distribute copies of Activity Book page 32. Have children study the causes and then draw the effects. Invite children to write about or tell stories about their drawings.

Activity Book page 32

HANDS-ON OPTION

Why Did It Happen?

Objectives: Identify the causes of certain events. Recognize the effects of certain actions.

Materials: construction paper in light colors, magazines, scissors, glue, crayons or markers

Distribute construction paper, and tell children to fold their sheet in half to make a book. Have them write *Why Did It Happen?* on the front cover and then open the book and write *Cause* on the left half and *Effect* on the right. Invite children to cut out a magazine picture that shows either a cause or an effect and glue it on the appropriate page. Then ask them to draw a picture under the other heading to show an effect of the cause or a cause of the effect. Invite children to share their books with a partner. Suggest that they tell their partner a story to go along with the pictures. **(VISUAL/AUDITORY/TACTILE)**

Cause-and-Effect Charades

Objectives: Identify the causes of certain events. Recognize the effects of certain actions.

Materials: paper, pencil

Write on small strips of paper several causes or effects that can be acted out. Examples might include hitting a ball with a bat, dropping something breakable, or trying to lift something heavy. Prepare enough slips for each child to have one. Have children take turns selecting one of the strips of paper and acting out what is written on it. Other children guess what they are doing and then name either a cause or an effect of that action.

(VISUAL/KINESTHETIC/AUDITORY)

Effect Webs

Objective: Realize that one cause may have more than one effect.

Materials: paper, pencils

With the whole class, create a web to demonstrate how one cause may lead to several different effects. Write a word or phrase that names a familiar action and circle it. Invite children to name things that could happen as a result of the action. In circles attached to lines that radiate from the center circle, record the events children mention. Have children identify the cause and its effects. Once children understand the concept, challenge them to make their own multiple-effect webs. **(TACTILE/VISUAL/AUDITORY)**

Cause-and-Effect Puzzles

Objectives: Identify the causes of certain events. Recognize the effects of certain actions.

Materials: sentence strips, pencils

 Invite children to look back through their social studies textbooks to find important events they have already learned about. Have them write the name of an event or a phrase that describes it at the beginning of the sentence strip and then write a cause of the event. Caution students not to label their cause and effect for this activity. Model how to make an irregular cut to separate the cause from the effect and form two halves of a puzzle. When children have created their puzzles, organize the class into small groups. Have group members mix up all their puzzle pieces. Then have them trade places with another group and reassemble the other group's puzzles. When all the puzzles have been put back together, invite the children who created them to check the answers. **(VISUAL/KINESTHETIC)**

4
PEOPLE LEAD THE WAY

OBJECTIVES

1. Explore our country's history through its capital.
2. Define the roles of such leaders as President and lawmakers.
3. Name important national leaders.

VOCABULARY

capital (p. 160)
President (p. 160)
lawmaker (p. 161)
Congress (p. 161)
monument (p. 162)

RESOURCES

Pupil Book/Unit Big Book, pp. 160–163
Write-On Charts 15, 27
Vocabulary Blacklines
Vocabulary Cards
Activity Book, p. 33
Transparencies 7, 8
Music Audio, "Old Abe"

ACTIVITY CHOICES

Background

CHOOSING A CAPITAL The United States had no permanent capital until 1800. In 1783 Congress decided that the national government should be operated on its own land rather than on land owned by one of the states. In 1791 George Washington chose a site, and in 1800 the government officially moved to the new city of Washington from its temporary home in Philadelphia. You may wish to show on a map Washington's central location relative to the country's boundaries at the time.

Link to Music

VOCAL Invite children to learn the words to "Old Abe" and perform it together. Then repeat the song, substituting the names and deeds of other Presidents the children may know of.

AUDIO

Use the UNIT 4 MUSIC AUDIOCASSETTE to hear the song "Old Abe."

WRITE-ON CHARTS

Use WRITE-ON CHART 27 to create a word web about Washington, D.C.

1. ACCESS

Find out what children know about our nation's capital. Create a word web on the board, with *Washington, D.C.*, in the center. Challenge children to suggest landmarks and special places they have heard of or visited.

famous statues — Washington D.C. — museums
President — capital — White House

Focus on the Main Idea

As children "tour" Washington, D.C., they will discover more about their country's history. They will see where leaders and lawmakers work, and they will visit some monuments honoring different Americans. Tell children they will learn more about the people who have helped lead our country through its many changes.

2. BUILD

Key Content Summary

The historic city of Washington, D.C., is the capital of our nation and the headquarters of our government. It is here that the President leads our nation and Congress passes our nation's laws. It is here that our country honors those who helped make America what it is today.

History

Connections Past to Present to Future
Remind children that the *President* is our country's leader. Ask children to name the President who lives in the White House today and to tell what the President does. Mention that during its history the White House has been destroyed by fire, rebuilt, expanded, and redecorated. Explain that while the White House was changing, our country was changing, too.

Q. How do you think America has changed over the years? There are now fifty states; more people live here now; computers and other machines have made life easier for people.

Civics and Government

Purposes and Types of Government
Help children name members of *Congress* who represent their state. (The names can be found in most telephone directories.) Explain that these *lawmakers* work at the Capitol Building. Point out that the

---

LESSON 4

People Lead the Way

Washington, D.C., is our nation's capital. A **capital** is a city where the leaders of a country work. Come along as we tour this special city in our country's history.

Here is the White House, where the President lives. The **President** is the leader of the United States. Many Presidents have lived in the White House since it was built in 1800. The building has been changed many times. Our country has changed, too.

The White House

160

ACTIVITY CHOICES

Reading Support

USE CONTEXT CLUES Point out the word *capital* in the story. Ask children if they have ever seen this word, and have them tell what it means. (Children may say that a capital is the kind of letter that begins a sentence or a name.) Ask if that meaning makes sense in the sentence. Have children continue reading to find out what a capital of a country is. Help them understand that the word *capital* on page 160 does not mean the same thing as *Capitol* on page 161. *Capitol* refers to a specific kind of building.

Meet Individual Needs

VISUAL AND TACTILE LEARNERS Display Transparencies 7 and 8. Invite children to find Washington, D.C.; identify surrounding states; find their own state; and trace a route between their homes and the nation's capital, naming states they would pass through along the way.

TECHNOLOGY

The internet address for White House for Kids is: http://www.whitehouse.gov/WH/kids/html/kidshome.html.

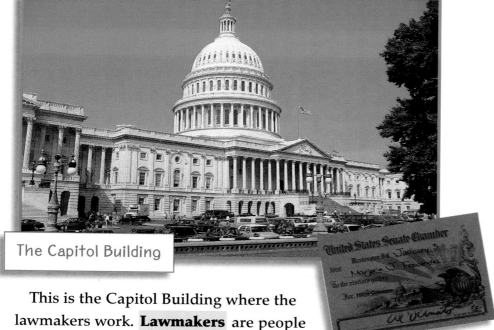

The Capitol Building

This is the Capitol Building where the lawmakers work. **Lawmakers** are people who make the laws of our country. The Capitol Building has had three different domes. The dome is a symbol of our great country.

The **Congress** is the group of lawmakers who work in the Capitol Building. They are some of the leaders who help our country grow and change. They plan ways to keep our country strong.

Congress

161

Capitol is one of the most noticeable structures in Washington because of its architecture and because it is located on a hill.

History

People and Events Across Time and Place Focus attention on page 162 on the monuments honoring Presidents Washington, Lincoln, and Jefferson. Invite children to discuss why monuments were built in honor of these Presidents.

Q. **What makes a person a good leader?** Good leaders are brave, honest, strong, helpful, smart, and willing to do things that have never been done before or that other people won't do.

Patterns and Relationships Direct attention to the photos on page 163 of the Vietnam Veterans Memorial and the Arlington National Cemetery. Explain that over the years many Americans have honored their country by defending it in times of war.

Q. **How do we honor the people who have defended our country in times of war?** by building monuments, having parades, celebrating holidays such as Veterans Day

PUPIL BOOK OR UNIT BIG BOOK

Link to Art

ARCHITECTURE Provide pictures of the Capitol for children to examine. Explain that the Capitol is 287 feet 5 1/2 inches from its base to the top of the Statue of Freedom, 350 feet wide, and more than 750 feet long; covers more than 16 acres; and has 540 rooms. Then invite children to create their own buildings from clay, cardboard, and other art materials, incorporating such features as a dome, pillars, and wings. Display the completed models.

Link to Language Arts

WRITE A LETTER Invite children to write a class letter requesting information and brochures about the nation's capital from the Washington Convention and Visitors Association, 1212 New York Avenue NW, 6th Floor, Washington, DC 20005. Suggest that children ask for information about new national monuments, such as the Roosevelt Memorial and the Korean War Veterans Memorial.

Multicultural Link

Tell children that the Taj Mahal in Agra, India; the Pantheon in Rome, Italy; and Saint Paul's Cathedral in London, England are just a few of the landmarks in countries around the world that have something in common with the Capitol Building. Show children pictures of these buildings and ask them what the buildings have in common. Then invite children to research other famous buildings with domes.

Help children understand that wars have been a tremendous cause of change in our country. Explain that new technologies and medicines have been discovered during times of war. Point out that it was during times of war that many women began to work outside the home because many of the men had gone to war. Tell children that between 1775 and 1991 our nation fought in ten wars. Point out that many lives have been lost in wartime.

3. CLOSE

VOCABULARY BLACKLINES

Distribute the individual word cards for this lesson, which are in the back of this Teacher's Edition. Invite children to summarize the lesson by first writing their own definitions for each word and then using the word cards to summarize what they learned about their country's heritage and the people who have helped to lead the way.

Check Understanding

The child can
____ explore our country's history through its capital.
____ define the roles of such leaders as President and lawmakers.
____ name important national leaders.

This part of the city is called the West Mall. It is not a mall for shopping. People come here to see the monuments. **Monuments** are places or buildings built to honor someone. The Washington Monument and the Lincoln and Jefferson memorials honor three great Presidents. Each one helped lead our country through hard times.

Lincoln Memorial

Thomas Jefferson Memorial

Washington Monument

162

ACTIVITY CHOICES

Background

THREE PRESIDENTS Remind children that George Washington was the first President of the United States, Abraham Lincoln helped keep the country together during the Civil War, and Thomas Jefferson wrote the Declaration of Independence. We celebrate the February birthdays of Washington and Lincoln and the work of all our great Presidents on Presidents' Day, the third Monday of February.

VIETNAM VETERANS MEMORIAL The memorial was designed by Maya Ying Lin, an architecture student. The names of 58,000 American men and women who were killed or missing in the Vietnam War are inscribed on the two 250-foot walls of black granite that compose the memorial. Remind children that we honor all our veterans with a national holiday on November 11.

VOCABULARY CARDS

Use the VOCABULARY PICTURE CARDS for this lesson to play word association with children.

WRITE-ON CHARTS

Meet Me at the Museum
Use WRITE-ON CHART 15 to extend and enrich this lesson. See Teacher's Edition page W47.

People also visit Arlington National Cemetery and the Vietnam Veterans Memorial. These places honor men and women who have died for our country. There are many special places in our country's capital.

Arlington National Cemetery

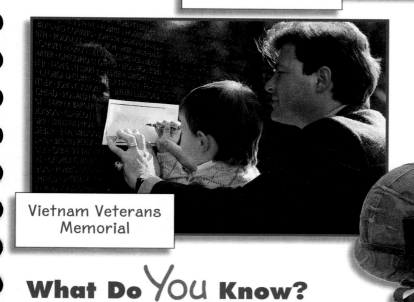

Vietnam Veterans Memorial

What Do You Know?

1. Where does the President of the United States live? the White House

2. How do we remember our country's great leaders? by building monuments and memorials

163

PUPIL BOOK OR UNIT BIG BOOK

Extend and Enrich

RESEARCH Invite children to find out about Pierre-Charles L'Enfant, the French engineer hired by George Washington to design the city of Washington, D.C. Invite children to describe L'Enfant's plan for the nation's capital.

Reteach the Main Idea

LOOK FOR DETAILS Help children form small groups. Invite members of each group to take turns talking about each of the pictures on pages 160–163, giving details about their country, its history, and the people who have helped lead the way.

Think Critically

Q. **What would you tell tourists to see when they visit Washington, D.C.? What would you want to see?** Children should identify specific buildings, memorials, and monuments.

Why is Washington, D.C., important to you and to our country? It is where leaders and lawmakers work to run our country; it has many important buildings and monuments that tell about our history and the people who helped make our history.

Show What You Know

Performance Assessment Invite children to form pairs and pretend to tour the city. Have one child provide background information about one of the landmarks of Washington, D.C., while the other child asks questions.

What to Look For Look for evidence that each child recognizes the significance of the people and sites the pairs discussed.

Using the Activity Book Invite children to cut out the famous landmarks of Washington, D.C., on Activity Book page 33. Then have them paste the landmarks on drawing paper and write a story about a trip to our nation's capital.

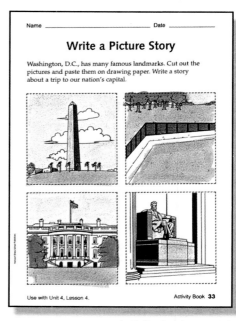

Activity Book page 33

HANDS-ON OPTION

Let's Take a Trip to Washington, D.C.!

Objectives: Explore our country's history through its capital. Define the roles of such leaders as President and lawmakers. Name important national leaders.

Materials: index cards, markers, large sheets of cardboard, scissors, paste, art supplies, game markers, references about and pictures or maps of Washington, D.C.

Organize children into small cooperative groups. Invite each group to design a game that tests players' knowledge of Washington, D.C.; its landmarks, buildings, monuments, and memorials; and the nation's leaders and lawmakers, past and present. Have each group brainstorm a list of questions to ask, such as *Where does the President live? Who is the President of the United States? Where do the lawmakers work?* Then one child can draw or paste appropriate pictures or a map of Washington, D.C., onto a large sheet of cardboard. Another child can complete the game board by drawing a pathway made up of two-inch spaces around the outside of the sheet. A third child can write questions and answers on index cards. Remaining members can make a spinner and game markers and write a set of rules. To play the game, children take turns drawing a card and answering the question. When players answer correctly, they spin to determine the number of spaces they can move their marker. When players answer incorrectly, they do not get to spin. The first player to go around the board is the winner. **(TACTILE/AUDITORY)**

Who's Who in the News?

Objectives: Define the roles of such leaders as President and lawmakers. Name important national leaders.

Materials: current newspapers and magazines, scissors, stapler

Invite children to create a bulletin board display titled *Who's Who in the News?* Ask children to find and cut out pictures of leaders such as the President, the Vice President, Supreme Court justices, Senate and House members, and other Americans who are helping to "lead the way." Invite children to discuss these people's roles and why they are in the news. **(TACTILE/VISUAL)**

Tabletop Models

Objective: Explore our country's history through its capital.

Materials: reference materials about and photographs of Washington, D.C.; cardboard; small boxes; construction paper; clay; paint and brushes; tape; sculpting tools

Invite children to create tabletop models of the buildings and monuments they "visited" during their tour of Washington, D.C. Display the completed models around the room. Then invite children to take turns being tour guides and tourists as they visit the different landmarks. **(TACTILE/KINESTHETIC)**

Skills

USE A MAP GRID

OBJECTIVES

1. Identify and use a grid to locate places on a map.
2. Use a grid and directions to trace routes on a map.

VOCABULARY

route (p. 164)
grid (p. 164)

RESOURCES

Pupil Book/Unit Big Book, pp. 164–165
Write-On Chart 31
Activity Book, p. 35
Transparency 12
Neighborhood MapMachine

ACTIVITY CHOICES

Meet Individual Needs

AUDITORY AND KINESTHETIC LEARNERS When children are not present, hide three objects in the classroom. Then invite children to go on a treasure hunt. Explain that they must look around the room and find three hidden objects without any directions. After the objects are located, hide them again, but this time provide the children with written directions on where to find the hidden objects. For a third search, provide children with a map that has an X marking the hiding place of each item. Have children explain which method made their search the easiest.

WRITE-ON CHARTS

Use **WRITE-ON CHART 31** to practice marking grid squares.

TRANSPARENCY

Use **TRANSPARENCY 12.**

1. ACCESS

Invite children to tell about times when they have used maps. Then invite children to recall some of the buildings they saw on their tour of Washington, D.C. Finally, pretend to be a tourist. Explain that you want to visit the Washington Monument but are not sure where it is.

Q. **How might you help someone find a building or a landmark?**
Accept responses such as by using a map to find out where the monument is located.

Tactile Learning

Help children practice counting squares horizontally and vertically. Distribute copies of a prepared grid. Invite children to locate and color squares as you call out instructions. For example, you might say, "Move right four squares and down three squares. Color that square red." After several squares have been colored, invite children to compare their grids to see if they have followed identical paths.

2. BUILD

Visual Analysis

Learn from Maps Invite children to look at the map on page 165 and describe what they see. Then have them refer to the land-and-water map on pages 54 and 55.

Q. **How would you compare the two maps?** Both have symbols, but the map on pages 54 and 55 does not have numbers, letters, or squares.

What do you think the numbers, letters, and squares are used for? They are used to help find places and to help find ways to get from one place to another.

Vocabulary

Ask a volunteer to read the paragraph on page 164. Then have children explain the meanings of *route* and *grid* in their own words.

Geography

Location Ask volunteers to tell what each symbol on the map represents. Point out that the map shows monuments located on the West Mall in Washington, D.C. Have children describe the grid's arrangement of letters and numbers. Explain that coordinates are usually provided in a map key next to the symbol for the place to be located.

Map and Globe Skills

Use a Map Grid

Maps help visitors to Washington, D.C., find routes to places they want to see. A **route** is a way to travel from one place to another. To help you find places, this map has a set of squares called a **grid**. Each grid square has a number and a letter.

The Reflecting Pool

164

1 Find the Lincoln Memorial. It is in square B-1. In which square is the Washington Monument? B-5

2 In which square is the Vietnam Veterans Memorial? B-2

3 What is in square E-5? Jefferson Memorial

4 In which squares is the Reflecting Pool? B-2, B-3, B-4

ACTIVITY CHOICES

Meet Individual Needs

VISUAL LEARNERS Provide a city map and invite children to find the grid. Have them choose a place on the map and identify its square.

AUDITORY LEARNERS Ask children to make a grid map of your classroom. Partners can take turns giving each other such directions as "Go to G-5."

Link to Physical Education

PHYSICAL FITNESS Create a large grid on the classroom floor. Prepare a set of cards with the number and letter of a square on one side and an activity on the other, such as jumping rope or doing aerobic exercises. Invite children to take turns drawing cards, locating the square, and completing the activity while standing in the square.

Extend and Enrich

MAKE A MODEL AND A MAP Invite children to create a tabletop model of the school neighborhood and to then make a large grid map of their model. Have children use the map to practice identifying places and planning routes from one place to another.

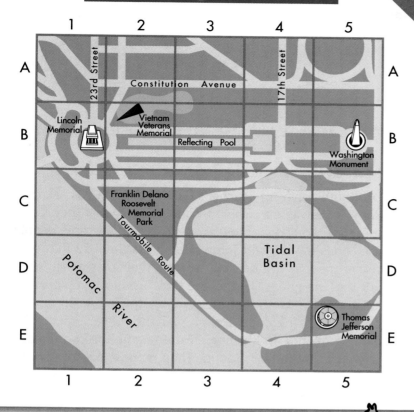

Washington, D.C.

Think and Do

Follow a route. Put your finger in square E-5. Travel up to C-5. Go left to C-2. What park is in the center of the square?

165

PUPIL BOOK OR UNIT BIG BOOK

Reteach the Skill

FIND ROUTES Remind children how you pretended to be a tourist seeking the Washington Monument. Invite children to pretend that you are all walking there from the Vietnam Veterans Memorial. Have them use the grid to find those two locations on the map, and then have them suggest possible routes between the two.

Link to Mathematics

MEASUREMENT AND SCALE
Invite children to use Write-On Chart 31 to map coordinates. Have children write letters along the left side of the grid and numbers along the bottom line of the grid. Explain that to find the correct square, they must find the given letter and count the blocks to the given number. Provide children coordinates and invite volunteers to draw pictures of the items in the squares: A-3, house; D-2, tree; C-4, dog.

Q. **Where are the numbers and letters that name the square where a monument is?** Look for the number at the top or bottom of the column and the letter at the end of the row.

3. CLOSE

Think and Do

After following the route, children should identify the Franklin D. Roosevelt Memorial Park as the park in the center of the square.

Review the skill with children by asking the following questions:

Q. **How is a grid useful?** It makes finding a place on a map fast and easy.

Why does it work? You can use the numbered and lettered squares to find places.

Using the Activity Book Distribute copies of Activity Book page 35, along with pencils and crayons. Have children place the letters A–G along the left side of the grid and the numbers 1–7 along the bottom line of the grid. Have children follow the directions to color a picture on the grid. Invite children to share completed pictures with classmates.

Activity Book page 35

HANDS-ON OPTION

Artifact Search

Objective: Identify and use a grid to locate places on a map.

Materials: play-money coins, one egg carton per pair, tissues or plastic grass

Distribute materials to pairs of children and invite them to construct a site for an archeological dig. Explain that at an archeological dig, people are looking for items that have been buried in the ground for many years. Have each child begin by drawing and labeling a grid with the same number of squares as the egg carton. Suggest that one partner place coins in three sections of the egg carton and mark them on the grid while the other partner hides his or her eyes. Then have the first partner cover each section of the egg carton with a crumpled tissue or plastic grass to hide the coins. The second partner can use an unmarked grid to make guesses about where the coins are hidden. The searcher names the set of coordinates for his or her guess, and the partner who hid the coins consults the marked grid and says yes or no. If the searcher is correct, he or she may dig in that spot for the coin. If incorrect, he or she marks an X at the bottom of the grid. Play continues until all coins have been found. Then partners switch roles and repeat the game. **(VISUAL/TACTILE)**

Neighborhood Places

Objectives: Identify and use a grid to locate places on a map. Use a grid and directions to trace routes on a map.

Materials: paper, crayons, rulers, game pieces

Have pairs of children draw a map of their neighborhood. Suggest that they show roads, buildings, and other landmarks, such as playgrounds, ponds, and trees. Then have children use a ruler to draw horizontal and vertical grid lines over their map. Remind them to label the grid with numbers and letters. Invite children to trade maps with another pair. Partners can then give each other directions for locating a place on the new map and move a game piece to that place. Ask children if they think it would be easier or harder to tell someone how to find something on their map without the grid. **(TACTILE/VISUAL/AUDITORY)**

Secret Code

Objective: Identify and use a grid to locate places on a map.

Materials: Teacher's Edition p. 165B, pencils

Distribute copies of Teacher's Edition page 165B. Ask children if they know what a code is and why they think someone would want to use one. Explain that some people use codes for fun and some people use them so that only certain people will be able to read their messages. Point out that the grid is like the one they used to find places on a map. Tell children that they will use the letters and numbers to read the code and answer the riddle. Practice by naming a letter and having children name the coordinates at which that letter is found. Then name a pair of coordinates and have children tell which letter they represent.

Allow time for children to decipher the code and solve the riddle. Then challenge them to use the code to write a secret message on a separate sheet of paper for a friend to solve. **(VISUAL/TACTILE)**

Secret Code

Use the grid to answer the riddle.
Then use the code to write a message to a friend.

	1	2	3	4	5	
A	H	V	R	M	D	A
B	C	L	U	P	W	B
C	X	Q	A	G	S	C
D	I	E	K	Y	J	D
E	T	N	F	B	O	E
	1	2	3	4	5	

Who planned the capital of the United States?

P I E R R E   C H A R L E S
B-4 D-1 D-2 A-3 A-3 D-2   B-1 A-1 C-3 A-3 B-2 D-2 C-5

L'E N F A N T
B-2 D-2 E-2 E-3 C-3 E-2 E-1

Secret Code

Use the grid to answer the riddle.
Then use the code to write a message to a friend.

	1	2	3	4	5	
A	H	V	R	M	D	**A**
B	C	L	U	P	W	**B**
C	X	Q	A	G	S	**C**
D	I	E	K	Y	J	**D**
E	T	N	F	B	O	**E**
	1	2	3	4	5	

Who planned the capital of the United States?

B-4 D-1 D-2 A-3 A-3 D-2 — B-1 A-1 C-3 A-3 B-2 D-2 C-5

,

B-2 D-2 E-2 E-3 C-3 E-2 E-1

DEFINE THE PROBLEM

Invite volunteers to play the role of detectives as they examine the photos on pages 166–167. Tell them they are looking for clues about history.

Q. **What does each picture tell you about the past?** Many streets are named after important people and places from history; people tell stories about history; cornerstones or wall plaques tell us when old buildings were made; statues tell us about the way people in the past looked and dressed; old houses show us the way people used to live; tombstones tell us when people died.

Help children recognize that there are many ways to find out about our past. Ask them to name other ways they can find out about history.

Solving Problems

History Clues

What can the pictures tell you about history?

Work with a group.

Make a list of the clues you see.

● What clues in each picture tell you about history?
● What other things might give clues about history?

Show your ideas.

Choose a way to show the class your ideas.

● Make up a story about the meaning of one of the clues.
● Role-play solving a history mystery.
● Draw a picture of another clue to history.

166

Link to Language Arts

CHILDREN AS HISTORIANS

Have children compile a "Community History" scrapbook. Guide them to create pages that give general information about when and how the community began. Include a time line of major events (e.g., building of an airport, a bus station, or a railroad; natural disasters; famous visitors). Write a letter to a local newspaper for old copies. Perhaps there are long-time residents of the community who could share old photographs that may be photocopied. Help children research clothes, music, toys, cars, or other artifacts from different times and have them write descriptions or draw pictures of the artifacts. Plan a field trip to a historic neighborhood to view monuments or buildings. Keep the scrapbook on view and encourage children to add artifacts and information about the past and from the present.

HENRY MORGENTHAU JR.
SECRETARY OF THE TREASURY
JAMES A. FARLEY
POSTMASTER GENERAL
LOUIS A. SIMON
SUPERVISING ARCHITECT
GEORGE O. VON NESTA
SUPERVISING ENGINEER
1934

③

④

⑤

JOHN
WOOD
MASSACHUSETTS
CPL
CONTINENTAL LINE
REVOLUTIONARY WAR
1753 · 1830

⑥

167

PUPIL BOOK OR UNIT BIG BOOK

USE PROBLEM-SOLVING SKILLS

Organize children into groups of four to make a list of the clues they see in the pictures. To help them, suggest that they read and answer the questions on page 166. Then ask them to brainstorm ideas about how they could store everyday things to leave clues about their class for people in the future.

Q. **What kinds of things would you choose?** Answers might include a class picture, favorite books, things they have written, or drawings of people and places around the school.

Have children make time capsules. Children might add to them over time. Then, send the capsules home with them to be reopened at their high school graduation.

SHOW SOLUTIONS

Invite children to imagine they found a time capsule with the six photos on pages 166–167. Suggest that each group choose one of the pictures to complete one of the activities on page 166. Allow time for children to share their ideas.

Home Involvement

Invite children and their families to look for clues to history when they are on outings in their neighborhoods or nearby areas. Ask children to keep records or take photographs of their sightings to add to the "Community History" Scrapbook.

Community Involvement

Contact the State Historical Society or a local museum to request materials they may have developed for use in schools. You may wish to plan a field trip to look at artifacts that children can discuss as evidence of the history of your area.

The Legend of Paul Bunyan

Legends are stories passed down through time. They sometimes become part of the history of a people or region. Many times the stories are exaggerated as they are retold. They become tall tales. One favorite American folk hero is Paul Bunyan. Some people believe he really lived. However, the stories about him and his blue ox named Babe are tall tales. Share with children the following tall tale written in rhyme. You may wish to point out Puget Sound on a map of the state of Washington before you tell the story.

Puget Sound

BY HAROLD W. FELTON

One day Paul Bunyan thought his ox
Was going to up and die,
So he picked up a pick and a spade
And a tear drop filled his eye.

And sadly by the sea he dug
A deep hole in the ground,
But Babe got well. The sea surged in.
The hole is Puget Sound.

Help children understand that while history is also a story about our past, it requires facts and evidence to support it. Tall tales and legends are entertaining stories about the past. Children might enjoy choosing someone from history and inventing a tall tale about that person.

5

AMERICAN PORTRAITS

OBJECTIVES

1. Describe the contributions of famous artists, scientists, educators, and other achievers.
2. Recognize that people do not always accept new ideas easily.
3. Recognize that all citizens are capable of making contributions to society.

VOCABULARY

invention (p. 168)

RESOURCES

Pupil Book/Unit Big Book, pp. 168–173

Write-On Charts 16, 29

Pattern P8

Activity Book, p. 36

Video, Reading Rainbow, *Alistair's Time Machine*

The Amazing Writing Machine

ACTIVITY CHOICES

Meet Individual Needs

AUDITORY LEARNERS   Have children imagine that they are the hosts of a radio talk show. Brainstorm with children a list of guests they would choose. Then ask them to write lists of questions for the interviews. Invite them to practice their interviewing skills with partners in radio role-plays.

Link to Language Arts

WRITE A DESCRIPTION   Have volunteers begin a "Who's Who" scrapbook. The entries might be clipped from local and national news sources, or they may be recommended by the class. Each entry might include a picture, a biographical sketch, and a description of the person's accomplishments.

TECHNOLOGY

Use THE AMAZING WRITING MACHINE™ RESOURCE PACKAGE to complete this activity.

WRITE-ON CHARTS

Use WRITE-ON CHART 29 to list famous people the class mentions and reasons those people are famous.

1. ACCESS

Ask children to name famous Americans and Americans they consider special as you list the names in a column on the board. In a second column, list children's explanations of what makes these people famous or special. If necessary, prompt children to include people who have brought about change in our country and in our everyday lives, such as government leaders, scientists, or teachers. Explain that a person does not have to be famous to be special or to do special things. Emphasize that many different Americans have helped make our nation's history.

Focus on the Main Idea

As children tour the "portrait gallery" in the lesson, they will discover some of the scientists, educators, and other special people who have helped shape the United States. Tell children they will read short biographies to learn about seven Americans whose special acts significantly changed life in this country or added to the quality of people's lives.

2. BUILD

Key Content Summary

Many people have made significant contributions to the development of the United States as a nation, often in the face of great opposition. People do not always eagerly accept new ideas and ways.

Visual Learning

Learn from Pictures Ask children to look at the pictures on pages 168–169. Point out the portraits of Thomas Edison and Dr. Charles Drew. Explain that a portrait shows the likeness of a person in a painting, sculpture, drawing, or photograph.

History

People and Events Across Time and Place Focus attention on Thomas Edison. Tell children that Edison was an inventor and that we benefit from many of his inventions today. Define *invention* as "a new object or way of doing something." Have children imagine what life would be like without the electric lightbulb. Then ask how they think the lightbulb changed people's lives.

Q. **Why do you think many people before Edison thought light-bulbs were not a worthwhile idea?** They thought oil lamps and candles were enough; they thought the idea would not work.

LESSON 5 American Portraits

A portrait is a picture or an interesting story about a person. Our country has many people to be proud of. Some are well known. Some are not. Look at and read portraits of seven Americans who have played a part in our history.

Thomas Edison

Some people have changed our lives with their new ideas. When you turn on a light, you can thank Thomas Edison. The electric lightbulb was his invention. An **invention** is a new kind of machine or a new way of doing something. Another of Edison's inventions was the phonograph. It led to the record player, and that led to the stereos and CD players we use today.

168

ACTIVITY CHOICES

Reading Support

PREVIEW AND PREDICT Have each child draw a portrait, or picture, of someone who is important to him or her. Ask children to share their portraits, telling why the person is important. Then read aloud the title of the lesson. Invite children to predict which important Americans they will read about in this story. Keep a list of the predictions to review after you read.

Link to Language Arts

WRITE A REPORT List on the board the names of the following scientists and inventors: Robert Fulton, George Washington Carver, Alexander Graham Bell, Henry Ford, and Maria Mitchell. Provide resource materials, and help children do research on a person from the list. Then invite children to write a report about the person.

Link to Science

OBSERVATION Give each child or small group of children a C or D cell, a flashlight bulb, and a piece of bell wire with the insulation stripped back from both ends. Invite children to experiment with the materials to see if they can make the bulb light up. Explain that Thomas Edison and others worked on ways to make electricity more useful in the home. Challenge children to list all the ways they use electricity at home and in school.

Dr. Charles Drew

You know that you can save your money in a bank. But did you know that blood can be saved in a different kind of bank? When Charles Drew was studying to be a doctor, he learned a lot about blood. He found a way to save blood so it could be used later. Now, when people get hurt and lose blood, saved blood can be used to make them well.

Dr. Drew's invention saved many soldiers' lives during a terrible war. Later he ran the Red Cross Blood Bank. His work is still saving people's lives today.

169

PUPIL BOOK **OR** UNIT BIG BOOK

History

People and Events Across Time and Place Focus attention on Charles Drew. Emphasize that he worked to save the lives of people, especially in emergencies. He discovered ways to store blood for people who have been hurt and need additional blood. He also set up blood banks, where extra blood could be stored.

Q. **Why do you think it is important to be able to store blood?**
Many injured people would die without stored blood.

Link to Health

GROWTH AND DEVELOPMENT
Explain that each time a heart beats, it pushes blood through the arteries. Tell children that this push is called the *pulse*. Have children make a fist with their left hand and use the first two fingers of their right hand to feel the pulse on their left wrist. Then invite children to run in place for a few seconds and then feel how the pulse quickens.

Link to Art

PORTRAITS Invite children to use white paper and a heavy marker to draw a portrait of someone in their classroom, school, or community who they think has done something special. Ask children to label the picture and to write a brief statement telling what the person did.

Community Involvement

Ask a Red Cross volunteer to speak to the class about safety and first aid issues. Review the procedure for using 911 emergency dialing.

VIDEO

Use READING RAINBOW,™ ALISTAIR'S TIME MACHINE to look at the world of inventors.

History

People and Events Across Time and Place Focus attention on Susan B. Anthony and Dr. Martin Luther King, Jr. Ask children to imagine not being allowed to vote because they are part of a group that is considered less intelligent than other people. Then ask children to imagine having to attend a separate school or drink from a different water fountain because of the color of their skin. Ask children to discuss each situation. Explain that many people did not agree with the ideas of Susan B. Anthony and Dr. Martin Luther King, Jr., so it took time to make some important changes.

Q. **Why do you think people opposed the ideas of Susan B. Anthony and Dr. Martin Luther King, Jr.?** They liked things the way they were. They did not understand the changes Anthony and King wanted to make.

How would you persuade someone to allow women to vote or to not judge people based on their skin color? Children might say they would explain how important it is to be fair and treat people equally.

HOLIDAY ACTIVITIES

For information and activities related to Martin Luther King, Jr., Day, see the Holiday Activities section at the back of this Teacher's Edition.

Susan B. Anthony

Some people speak out when laws are unfair. Susan B. Anthony spoke out. She was a teacher who said that our country's laws should be for all Americans. At that time, only men could vote. Her work helped change laws so that women could vote, too. Susan B. Anthony was the first woman shown on American money. Her picture is on the silver dollar.

Dr. Martin Luther King, Jr.

Dr. Martin Luther King, Jr., also worked to make things fair for all Americans. We honor his work with a holiday to celebrate his birthday.

Dr. King was a minister. He believed that people should not be treated differently because of their skin color. Dr. King was a great speaker. Many people followed his ideas for peaceful change. Later they were shocked and sad when Dr. King was shot. Today, people still remember his words.

170

ACTIVITY CHOICES

Link to Language Arts

PRESENT ORALLY Invite children to find out more about the civil rights movement. Ask children to make oral presentations on their findings. Ask them to tell how Dr. Martin Luther King, Jr., influenced the movement.

Sequoyah

Many years ago, a Cherokee named Sequoyah wanted to help his people learn to read and write. But his people did not have an alphabet. So he made up one.

To show how his alphabet worked, Sequoyah wrote some words whispered to him by a stranger. Then he passed the paper to his daughter, Ahyoka, who read the words. The Cherokees were amazed at the "talking leaves." Sequoyah's alphabet was used to write a newspaper for his people. His great invention helped the Cherokees learn many new things.

History

Long, long ago people far away carved marks into clay and stone. Others drew pictures on a kind of paper called papyrus. Later, people called Phoenicians invented an alphabet like the one we use today. As they traveled to other places to trade, they taught writing to the people they met.

171

PUPIL BOOK OR UNIT BIG BOOK

History

People and Events Across Time and Place Focus attention on Sequoyah. Explain that after Sequoyah was exposed to written languages, he wanted to create one for the Cherokee people so that their history could be preserved.

Q. **What might have happened if Sequoyah had not created an alphabet for the Cherokee language?** The history of the Cherokees might not have been written down or saved for the future.

Visual Analysis

Learn from Documents Draw children's attention to the picture of Sequoyah's book on page 171.

Q. **How do we know about Sequoyah's life and accomplishments?** from things that he wrote; from things that other people wrote about him

Help children understand that historians and biographers use different kinds of evidence as they research people's lives and events. Primary sources, such as letters, news articles, interviews, diaries, and books written at the time are some examples.

Multicultural Link

Provide a copy of Sequoyah's alphabet for the class to examine. Have children compare and contrast his alphabet with the alphabet used to write English.

Link to Reading

READ A BIOGRAPHY Remind children that a biography is the life story of a real person. Tell them that *bio* means "life" and *graph* means "write." Have children read a simple biography or read one to them. Afterward, record suggestions for the elements that make up a good biography (e.g., date and place of birth, key events in life, major accomplishments, obstacles overcome, childhood interests). Keep the list posted for reference as children read other biographies or write ones of their own.

Culture

Thought and Expression Have children read pages 172–173. Remind them that in this lesson they have met individuals who have contributed to the safety, welfare, and happiness of others.

Q. **How do people like Arthur Dorros and Kristi Yamaguchi affect people's lives?** They tell us stories; they entertain us; they do things we would like to do.

Have children list some of their favorite writers, artists, musicians, and athletes. Discuss how sharing talents can make a difference in people's lives. Point out how such personalities set examples for everyone to follow. Reread the poem "I Can" at the beginning of this unit.

Q. **Do you have to be famous to make a difference? Why or why not?** Children's responses should focus on the idea that everyone has special talents and dreams, and that we can all make a difference in the lives of other people.

3. CLOSE

Ask children to summarize the lesson by explaining how Thomas Edison, Dr. Charles Drew, Susan B. Anthony, Dr. Martin Luther King, Jr., Sequoyah, Arthur Dorros, and Kristi Yamaguchi helped make a difference in people's lives.

Check Understanding

The child can

____ describe the contributions of famous artists, scientists, educators, and other achievers.

____ recognize that people do not always accept new ideas easily.

____ recognize that all citizens are capable of making contributions to society.

Think Critically

Q. **Why do you think people are sometimes unwilling to accept new ideas at first?** Accept such responses as sometimes people find it too hard to give up old ways, sometimes people are afraid new ways will not work, and sometimes people just do not want change.

172 • UNIT 4

Arthur Dorros

Some people make a difference in our lives because we enjoy their music, art, or stories. Perhaps you have read <u>This Is My House</u>, <u>Abuela</u>, <u>Radio Man</u>, or <u>Isla</u>. These books were written by Arthur Dorros, who is also an artist. He uses both writing and drawing to show how he feels about people and places.

Arthur Dorros enjoys visiting classrooms and helping children find their own stories. He says, "Everyone has stories to tell." He believes that when you tell stories about the world, you can come to know it better. You can also learn more about yourself.

172

ACTIVITY CHOICES

Extend and Enrich

WRITE RIDDLES Ask children to create riddles about famous Americans, giving clues about when they lived and what their contributions were. Then invite children to take turns reading and answering one another's riddles.

Reteach the Main Idea

DESCRIBE PEOPLE Give clues describing the contributions of each person presented on pages 168–173, and invite children to identify and point out the person you are describing.

WRITE-ON CHARTS

"I Have a Dream"

Use WRITE-ON CHART 16 to extend and enrich the lesson. See Teacher's Edition page W50.

Kristi Yamaguchi

Some people do the kinds of things we wish we could do. In 1992, Kristi Yamaguchi won an Olympic gold medal for ice-skating.

When she was very young, Kristi had to wear special shoes to correct a problem with her feet. At age five, she was able to start skating. When she was eight, Kristi entered her first skating contest. Twelve years later, she was the best skater in the world!

Like the speaker in the poem "I Can!" Kristi Yamaguchi believes that children can do or be anything. They just need to have a dream and work hard.

What Do You Know?

1. Name someone who has made a difference in people's lives. What did he or she do?

2. Whose portrait would you add as an American to be proud of?

173

PUPIL BOOK OR UNIT BIG BOOK

Link Literature

Read aloud *Dinner at Aunt Connie's House* by Faith Ringgold. (Hyperion, 1993) This book tells the story of Melody and Lonnie's wonderful discovery of twelve talking portraits of famous African American women. The children are fascinated hearing the women talk about their courageous lives. After reading the story, encourage children to talk about the lives and contributions of the women discussed in the book.

What other Americans do you think deserve special recognition in this lesson? Responses should include famous people who have made positive contributions to America, such as Presidents, and ordinary citizens who have fought for their rights, such as Rosa Parks.

Show What You Know

Performance Assessment Provide children with copies of a silhouette of a head. Invite children to write inside the silhouette several ways that people can contribute to growth and bring about change in their community.

What to Look For Look for evidence that the child recognizes the value of contributions made in the interest of humanity.

Using the Activity Book Distribute copies of Activity Book page 36. Tell children that the National Portrait Gallery, in Washington, D.C., houses portraits of famous Americans like those in the lesson. Invite children to imagine that the National Portrait Gallery is opening a new exhibition about people who are making history today and that the children have been asked to supply the portraits. Invite children to share their portraits and give reasons for their choices.

Activity Book page 36

Biographies

Share the following biographies with children. Explain that these people have made a difference to others both in the United States and around the world. You may want to provide copies of this page so that children can look at the drawings as you read aloud the biographies.

Roberto Clemente
(*kluh•MEN•tay*) (1934–1972) was one of the greatest baseball players in history. He played right field for the Pittsburgh Pirates and helped lead his team to win two World Series victories. Three months before his death, he became the eleventh player in major-league history to get 3,000 hits. Roberto Clemente, who was born in Puerto Rico, died in a plane crash on his way to help people who had been hurt during an earthquake in Nicaragua.

John Glenn (born 1921) was the first American to fly around the Earth in a spaceship. On February 20, 1962, he circled the Earth three times in less than five hours. His spacecraft was named *Friendship 7*. John Glenn's work as an astronaut helped build our country's space program. In 1974 he was elected to the United States Senate. He continued to serve his country by helping to make laws and run the government. At the age of 76, John Glenn returned to space as the oldest American astronaut.

Antonia Novello (born 1944) was the first woman and the first Latina to hold the job of Surgeon General of the United States. She was appointed to the position in 1990. The Surgeon General is a doctor who is in charge of helping Americans be healthy. Antonia Novello was born in Fajardo, Puerto Rico. She studied at the University of Puerto Rico to become a doctor and has worked for many years to help sick children.

Jackie Robinson (1919–1972) was the first African American to play major-league baseball. He was named rookie of the year when he joined the Brooklyn Dodgers in 1947. Jackie Robinson later won the National League's most valuable player award. In 1962 he was elected to the National Baseball Hall of Fame. Thanks to people like Jackie Robinson, children of all races today can play sports or take part in any other activities they choose.

Mother Teresa (1910–1997) was one of the most respected women in the world. As a nun of the Catholic Church, she worked most of her life to help people who were sick and poor. In 1979 she received the Nobel Peace Prize, an award given to people who work to make the world a better place. Mother Teresa lived in India, where she started a group called the Missionaries of Charity. Members of this group now work in more than 90 countries, providing food for the hungry and running shelters for the homeless, hospitals, schools, orphanages, and youth centers.

HANDS-ON OPTION

Portrait Chain

Objective: Describe the contributions of famous artists, scientists, educators, and other achievers.

Materials: crayons, scissors, tape, Pattern P8

Distribute Portrait Chain patterns and ask children to draw in the circles pictures of persons they studied in this lesson or of other famous people. Invite children to cut out the circles and tape them together to form a chain. Display the chain at eye level. Provide extra copies of the pattern, and urge children to draw portraits of special people they learn about in the future and to add those portraits to their chain. **(TACTILE)**

Portraits Come to Life

Objectives: Describe the contributions of famous artists, scientists, educators, and other achievers. Recognize that people do not always accept new ideas easily.

Materials: reference materials, cardboard, tape, costumes, index cards, pencils

COOPERATIVE LEARNING Invite children to write and perform a class play about a tourist who is visiting a portrait museum of famous Americans. Explain that as the tourist looks at the portraits, they come to life, telling who they are and how they helped shape the nation. Organize children into groups of four or five. Ask each group to select one of the special Americans they read about or another person who interests them. Have the members of each group record what they know about the person's struggles and accomplishments and then do research to gather more information. Ask one child in each group to write or tell about the person's life. Two or three children should create a costume and necessary props. The other child can portray the famous person. Children can take turns playing the tourist. **(KINESTHETIC/AUDITORY)**

Inventions in Our Lives

Objectives: Describe the contributions of famous artists, scientists, educators, and other achievers. Recognize that all citizens are capable of making contributions to society.

Materials: pencils, crayons or markers, drawing paper, construction paper, stapler

Invite children to look around the classroom. Ask how they think all the objects in the room came to be. Explain that someone had to invent every item we use: clothing, buttons, zippers, eyeglasses, pencils, and so on. Then tell children that they are going to make a class book of classroom inventions. Ask children to work in pairs to choose an object. Have them draw a picture of it and write a few sentences telling why this object is important in their lives. Invite children to use construction paper for the front and back covers and to staple the pages to make a book. Invite volunteers to design the cover art. Display the book in the class library. **(TACTILE/VISUAL)**

MAKING SOCIAL STUDIES REAL

Social Studies Real

Play a Part in History

READ AND RESPOND

Read aloud pages 174–175 and discuss the history museum at Fort Wilkins, Michigan. Invite volunteers to find Michigan on a map. Help children understand that people go to this museum to see what life was like at Fort Wilkins more than one hundred years ago. Then discuss how local children help museum visitors learn about the past.

Q. **What do the Future Historians do?** They learn about the people who lived in Fort Wilkins a long time ago. Then they dress in costumes and pretend to be those people. They answer visitors' questions about what life was like in Fort Wilkins a long time ago.

How do the volunteers learn to act like children who lived in 1870? They go to a summer camp to learn what life was like for children then.

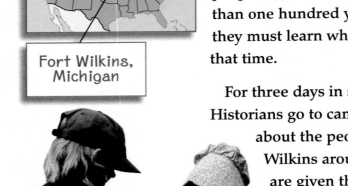

United States

Fort Wilkins, Michigan

174

The history museum at Fort Wilkins, Michigan, is a good place to learn about the past. Children 6 to 18 years old help in the museum. They are called Future Historians. The Future Historians dress in costumes and act like people who lived in Fort Wilkins more than one hundred years ago. To do this, they must learn what life was like at that time.

For three days in summer, the Future Historians go to camp. There they learn about the people who lived in Fort Wilkins around 1870. The children are given the names of real people they will pretend to be.

ACTIVITY CHOICES

Background

FORT WILKINS HISTORIC COMPLEX
Since 1976, the Michigan Historical Center has presented its innovative "role-playing" program to tens of thousands of visitors at Fort Wilkins Historic Complex. This award-winning program involves costumed interpreters who live and act as though it is the summer of 1870.

As members the Future Historians youth association, children ages 7 through 18 become involved not only in historical interpretation techniques, but in volunteer community service, as well. Each participant is assigned a character based on a boy or girl who lived in Fort Wilkins

or in the neighboring community of Copper Harbor in 1870. They receive a manual of information about nineteenth-century games, clothing, household chores, schooling, and recreation.

The children are assigned a college-student mentor who helps them learn to portray children of the period through conversation, chores, and games. The Michigan Historical Center is able to bring a new dimension to its interpretation of life at Fort Wilkins that would not be possible without these young community service volunteers.

Old records and letters give them clues about these people. Old clothing, pictures, and tools tell even more.

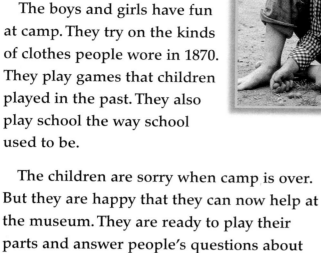

The boys and girls have fun at camp. They try on the kinds of clothes people wore in 1870. They play games that children played in the past. They also play school the way school used to be.

The children are sorry when camp is over. But they are happy that they can now help at the museum. They are ready to play their parts and answer people's questions about the history of Fort Wilkins.

What Can You Do?

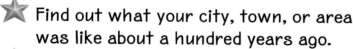 Find out what your city, town, or area was like about a hundred years ago.

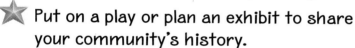 Put on a play or plan an exhibit to share your community's history.

 Visit the Internet at http://www.hbschool.com for additional resources.

175

PUPIL BOOK OR UNIT BIG BOOK

Community Involvement

Invite a representative from a local historical society to speak to the class. Ask the speaker to discuss locations in the community with historical significance. Suggest that children prepare questions in advance about how people lived in their community one hundred years ago.

Meet Individual Needs

ADVANCED LEARNERS Ask children to do research to find out how children in their community lived one hundred years ago. Suggest that they find out what schools were like, what games children played, and what chores children had to do. Children may wish to work in groups to make posters or to role-play scenes that show what life was like in their community a long time ago.

Lead children in a discussion about why museums are important. Children should understand that we can learn a lot about ourselves by studying people from the past.

Q. **What clues do the Future Historians use to find out about the people they will pretend to be?** They use old records, letters, clothing, pictures, and tools.

History

Patterns and Relationships Ask children to think about museums and historical sites in their community. Discuss ways in which these places are like Fort Wilkins. Help children understand why these places are considered important.

Q. **Why are museums and historical sites important to a community?** They help us remember important people, places, and events; they teach us about our past.

Culture

Shared Humanity and Unique Identity Remind children that museums show us how people lived a long time ago. Help children list similarities and differences in the ways of life of the children who lived in Fort Wilkins around 1870 and children today.

Q. **What did children do one hundred years ago that you still do today?** They went to school, played games, and did chores around the house.

How are the lives of children today different from the lives of children one hundred years ago? Children today dress differently and play different games; they learn about different things in school; they watch television, go to movies, and play video games.

> **❝ PRIMARY SOURCE ❞**
>
> If Internet access is available, have children work in groups to gather information on Fort Wilkins State Park and the Copper Harbor community. Then ask each group to give a short report to share its findings with the class.

PICTURE SUMMARY

TAKE A LOOK

Remind children that a picture summary is a way to visually represent the main ideas or events in a story. Explain that this summary reviews some of the main ideas in Unit 4. Tell children they can follow the path on the picture summary to see how our country has grown and changed.

Visual Analysis

Learn from Pictures Organize children into small groups. Invite them to examine the picture summary and to react to its images. Ask children to describe the various scenes and to discuss the many changes America has gone through over the years.

VOCABULARY BLACKLINES

Distribute the individual word cards for this unit and have children use the words as they discuss the picture summary.

UNIT 4 Review

Picture Summary

Follow the pictures. They will help you remember what you learned.

Talk About the Main Ideas

1. American Indians were the earliest people to live in our country.

2. Settlers from other countries built new homes in America.

3. Leaders have shaped our country's history.

4. Communities grow and change.

5. Many different people have helped make America great.

Write About a Hero Choose someone you are proud of. It may be someone you have read about or someone you know. Write about what that person has done. Tell what you can learn from your hero.

176

VOCABULARY CARDS

Have children use the VOCABULARY CARDS for this unit to review key concepts.

UNIT POSTER

Use the UNIT 4 SUMMARY POSTER to summarize unit learning.

Picture Summary Key

SUMMARIZE MAIN IDEAS

Ask children to read the summary statements on page 176 and to relate each one to a specific scene in the picture summary. Lead a class discussion about each scene, and challenge children to offer supporting details for each main idea illustrated. You may wish to have children complete the outlines started at the beginning of the unit, on Teacher's Edition page 136.

Help children focus on the many different people who have lived in America and have helped it to grow.

Sharing the Activity

Provide time for children to complete the Write About a Hero activity on page 176. Invite children to share who their heroes are, either within small groups or with the whole class. Have them discuss what they think makes a person a hero.

PUPIL BOOK OR **UNIT BIG BOOK**

Meet Individual Needs

ENGLISH LANGUAGE LEARNERS

Invite children to restate the main ideas of Unit 4 in their own words. Ask them to use the numbered list and the related illustrations to help them remember what the unit was about. Children who share the same background or native language may wish to work together and discuss each summary statement before presenting their own revised statements to the rest of the class.

TECHNOLOGY

Use the AMAZING WRITING MACHINE™ RESOURCE PACKAGE to summarize the unit.

USE VOCABULARY

1. history
2. President
3. invention
4. settler
5. landmark

CHECK UNDERSTANDING

1. Children might say that early American settlers had to make their own clothes and grow their own food. They did not have modern conveniences such as indoor plumbing and electricity.
2. Children might say that new inventions can cause change. Communities grow and change as more people move into them. Floods, fires, and other disasters can cause change, too.
3. Our country's laws are made by members of Congress in the Capitol Building in Washington, D.C.
4. Children may say that the lightbulb has made it easier to read and travel after dark.

THINK CRITICALLY

1. History is the story of the past. We study history to find out how people lived and what they did. History shows how things change over time.
2. Monuments and landmarks remind us of important events and people. Monuments and landmarks help us learn about the history of a community or country.

UNIT 4 Review

Use Vocabulary

Which word fits the sentence?

settler
invention
President
landmark
history

1. One way to learn about the past is to read _____ books.

2. You can read about _____ Abraham Lincoln.

3. You can learn about Thomas Edison's _____ of the lightbulb.

4. An American _____ had a hard life.

5. San Diego's lighthouse is a _____.

Check Understanding

1. How was the life of an American settler different from your life?

2. What can cause a community to change?

3. Who makes the laws for our country, and where do those people work?

4. Name an invention, and tell how it has changed people's lives.

Think Critically

1. What is history, and why do we study it?

2. Why are monuments and landmarks important to people in a community?

178

Apply Skills

Use a Map Grid

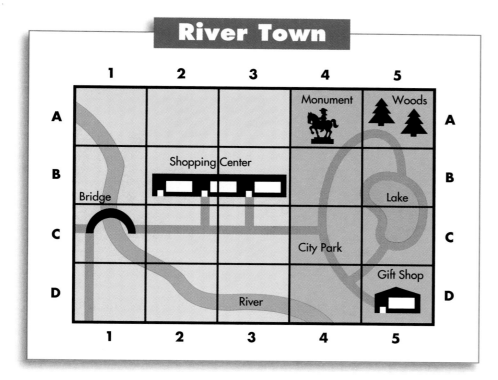

River Town

1   What building is in D-5?

2   In which square is the monument?

3   How many squares are between
the park and the bridge?

179

PUPIL BOOK **OR** UNIT BIG BOOK

APPLY SKILLS

Read a Time Line

❶ twelve months, or one year
❷ February
❸ James Monroe and Thomas Jefferson
❹ in front of George Washington (February 23)

Do It Yourself

For this activity, you may wish to reproduce the time line from the Thinking Organizers section in the back of this Teacher's Edition, or children might enjoy making their own by using different colors of construction paper.

UNIT 4 Review

Apply Skills

Read a Time Line

The time line below shows the birthdays of the first five Presidents of the United States.

| JAN | FEB | MAR | APR | MAY | JUN | JUL | AUG | SEP | OCT | NOV | DEC |

George Washington

James Madison

Thomas Jefferson

James Monroe

John Adams

❶ How much time is shown on the time line?

❷ In what month was George Washington born?

❸ Which two Presidents were born in the same month?

❹ Abraham Lincoln was born on February 12, 1809. Where would you put his birthday?

Do It Yourself

Make a time line to show when people in your family have birthdays.

180

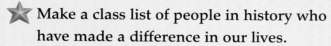

Unit Activity

Make Who's Who Trading Cards

⭐ Make a class list of people in history who have made a difference in our lives.

⭐ Choose a name from the list. Find facts about that person.

⭐ Paste a picture of the person you chose on the front of an index card. On the back of the card, write when and where the person was born. Tell what he or she did.

⭐ Trade cards with your classmates.

Visit the Internet at
http://www.hbschool.com
for additional resources.

Read More About It

<u>Eleanor</u> by Barbara Cooney. Viking. This story about Eleanor Roosevelt explains how she grew up to marry a President and help many people.

<u>The Joke's on George</u> by Michael O. Tunnell. Tambourine. George Washington visits a friend's museum.

<u>Young Abe Lincoln</u> by Cheryl Harness. National Geographic Society. Lincoln's boyhood on the American frontier prepared him to lead his country.

181

PUPIL BOOK **OR UNIT BIG BOOK**

UNIT ACTIVITY

Make Who's Who Trading Cards

Materials: index cards, markers

In their discussions and through the trading cards they create, children should exhibit an appreciation for the contributions made by others to their lives.

READ MORE ABOUT IT

Additional books are listed in the Resource Center on page 136E of this Teacher's Edition.

TAKE-HOME BOOK

Use the TAKE-HOME REVIEW BOOK for Unit 4.

ASSESSMENT

Use UNIT 4 TEST
  Standard, pp. 27–29.
  Performance, p. 30.

GAME TIME!

Use GAME TIME! to reinforce the unit.

COOPERATIVE LEARNING WORKSHOP

MAKE AN INVENTION TIME LINE

Children should work together in small groups to make a time line that includes five inventions that changed people's lives.

Materials for each group: index cards, crayons or markers, paper punch, yarn, poles (dowels)

Select Inventions

Step 1: Have children brainstorm a list of inventions and help them locate reference materials that provide information about them. Discuss what people did before the inventions were available. Help children to understand that most inventions take years to develop before a successful model is presented and that more years pass before the invention becomes commonly used.

Organize children into small groups and distribute materials to each group. Ask children to use the class's list to select five inventions they will include on their time line. Have them write the name and date of each invention on an index card and draw a picture showing the invention. Then ask children to put their invention cards in order by date.

Demonstrate Knowledge

Step 2: As children work, ask them to discuss the information a time line can provide.

Q. **What information can we get from a time line?** A time line shows the order in which things happen.

Present the Project

Step 3: Have children punch a hole in each index card and attach a piece of yarn. Have them tie their invention cards in order of the dates to the pole to create an invention time line. Display the time lines in the classroom.

What to Look For In their discussions and through the time lines they create, children should exhibit the understanding that history is the story of people and events from the past. They should be able to

____ make comparisons between their own lives and life in the past.

____ explain that communities change and grow.

____ identify items from the past.

____ name important figures in American history.

____ use appropriate vocabulary.

Follow-Up

Interested children may want to find out more about other discoveries or inventions and the people who made them. Suggest children choose from the following list of scientists and inventors. Invite children to make time lines or date books to show when the scientists and inventors lived and what their discoveries or inventions were.

Nicolaus Copernicus   Galileo
Isaac Newton   Florence Nightingale
Johannes Gutenberg   James Watt
Samuel Morse   Elisha Otis
Wright Brothers   John Deere
George Eastman   Eli Whitney
Henry Ford   Robert Fulton
Alexander Graham Bell   Garrett Morgan

REMIND CHILDREN TO:
- Share their ideas.
- Cooperate with others to plan their work.
- Plan and take responsibility for their tasks.
- Show their work.
- Discuss their own and the group's performance.

BEING A GOOD CITIZEN

The major objectives in this unit are organized around the following themes:

UNIT THEMES

▶ **CONFLICT & COOPERATION**

▶ **INDIVIDUALISM & INTERDEPENDENCE**

▶ **COMMONALITY & DIVERSITY**

Preview Unit Content

Unit 5 tells the story of the roles and responsibilities of American citizens. Children will focus on the unique characteristics of our country by identifying and discussing state and national symbols, landmarks, and democratic traditions. Children will begin to consider the ways people express conflicting opinions and work together for a common-goal. It will become clear to children that people living in a community are dependent on laws and government to foster cooperation. Children will determine that the foundation of good citizenship is participation in the community.

You may wish to begin the unit with the Unit 5 Picture Summary Poster and activities. The illustration that appears on the poster also appears on pages 212–213 in the Pupil Book to help children summarize the unit.

UNIT POSTER

Use the UNIT 5 PICTURE SUMMARY POSTER to preview the unit.

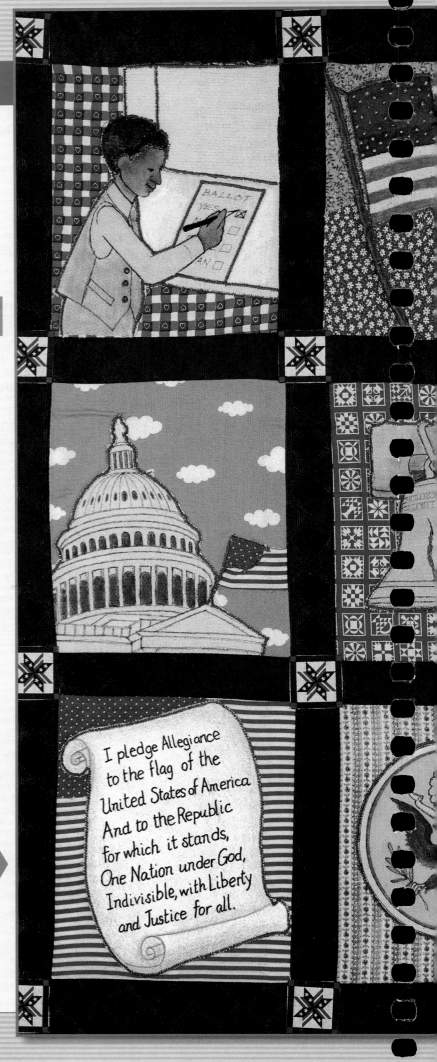

I pledge Allegiance to the flag of the United States of America And to the Republic for which it stands, One Nation under God, Indivisible, with Liberty and Justice for all.

This program is also available in a **SPANISH EDITION.**

TEACHER'S EDITION	THEMES • Strands	VOCABULARY	MEET INDIVIDUAL NEEDS	RESOURCES INCLUDING ► TECHNOLOGY
UNIT INTRODUCTION **Introduce the Unit** Preview Set the Scene with Music "**America**" Use the Literature Big Book pp. 182A–187A			English Language Learners, pp. 184, 187	**Pupil Book/Unit Big Book, pp. 182–187** **Write-On Chart 27** Picture Summary Poster Home Letter Text on Tape Audio Asian Translations Vocabulary Cards *In 1776*
LESSON 1 **Proud Americans** pp. 188A–191A	**COMMONALITY & DIVERSITY** • History • Civics and Government • Geography	holiday motto	Extend and Enrich, p. 191 Reteach the Main Idea, p. 191	**Pupil Book/Unit Big Book, pp. 188–191** **Write-On Charts 17, 30, 39, 40** Activity Book, p. 37 Music Audio, "The Star-Spangled Banner"
SKILL **Make a Choice by Voting** pp. 192A–193A	**BUILDING CITIZENSHIP** • Participation Skills • Critical Thinking Skills	election vote	Extend and Enrich, p. 192 Reteach the Skill, p. 193	**Pupil Book/Unit Big Book, pp. 192–193** **Write-On Charts 15, 31** Activity Book, p. 38 Transparency 13 ► GRAPH LINKS
LESSON 2 **Our Country's Government** pp. 194A–197A	**CONFLICT & COOPERATION** • History • Civics and Government	government judge	Visual Learners, p. 194A Extend and Enrich, p. 196 Reteach the Main Idea, p. 197	**Pupil Book/Unit Big Book, pp. 194–197** **Write-On Charts 18, 26** Activity Book, p. 39 Vocabulary Cards Transparency 14 ► THE AMAZING WRITING MACHINE
SKILL **Find Capitals on a Map** pp. 198A–199A	**BASIC STUDY SKILLS** • Map and Globe Skills	state boundary	Tactile Learners, pp. 198A, 198 Visual Learners, p. 198A Extend and Enrich, p. 198 Reteach the Skill, p. 199	**Pupil Book/Unit Big Book, pp. 198–199** **Write-On Chart 19** Activity Book, p. 40 Transparency 14 Desk Maps Music Audio, "Fifty Nifty United States" ► TRUDY'S TIME AND PLACE HOUSE

21 DAYS

TIME MANAGEMENT

DAY 1	DAY 2	DAY 3	DAY 4	DAY 5	DAY 6	DAY 7	DAY 8	DAY 9	DAY 10	DAY 11	DAY 12
Unit Introduction		Lesson 1			Skill	Lesson 2			Skill	Lesson 3	

TEACHER'S EDITION	THEMES •Strands	VOCABULARY	MEET INDIVIDUAL NEEDS	RESOURCES INCLUDING ▶ TECHNOLOGY
LESSON 3 **Community Government** pp. 200A–201A	**CONFLICT & COOPERATION** • Civics and Government	mayor	Visual and Auditory Learners, p. 200A Extend and Enrich, p. 200 Reteach the Main Idea, p. 201	**Pupil Book/Unit Big Book, pp. 200–201** **Write-On Chart 27** Activity Book, p. 41
SKILL **Understand What People Think** pp. 202A–203A	**BUILDING CITIZENSHIP** • Critical Thinking Skills • Participation Skills			Extend and Enrich, p. 202 Reteach the Skill, p. 203
LESSON 4 **Our Freedoms** pp. 204A–207B	**INDIVIDUALISM & INTERDEPENDENCE** • Civics and Government • History	freedom	English Language Learners, p. 205 Extend and Enrich, p. 207 Reteach the Main Idea, p. 207	**Pupil Book/Unit Big Book, pp. 204–207** **Write-On Charts 20, 29** Activity Book, p. 43 Video, Reading Rainbow, *Amazing Grace*
BRAINSTORM **Getting Along** pp. 208–209	**BUILDING CITIZENSHIP** • Critical Thinking Skills • Participation Skills		Tactile and Auditory Learners, p. 209	**Pupil Book/Unit Big Book, pp. 208–209**
MAKING SOCIAL STUDIES REAL **Kids Voting USA** pp. 210–211	**BUILDING CITIZENSHIP** • Participation Skills			**Pupil Book/Unit Big Book, pp. 210–211** ▶ INTERNET
UNIT WRAP-UP Picture Summary Unit 5 Review Cooperative Learning Workshop pp. 212–217B			English Language Learners, p. 213	**Pupil Book/Unit Big Book, pp. 212–217** Picture Summary Poster Vocabulary Cards Assessment Program, Standard, pp. 31–33 Performance, p. 34 Take-Home Review Book Game Time! ▶ THE AMAZING WRITING MACHINE

DAY 13	DAY 14	DAY 15	DAY 16	DAY 17	DAY 18	DAY 19	DAY 20	DAY 21
Skill	Lesson 4			Brainstorm	Making Social Studies Real	Unit Wrap-Up		Unit Test

Multimedia Resource Center

Books

Easy

Binger, Kilty. *Mary Guy*. Lothrop, Lee & Shepard, 1993. Mary Guy finds a way to make the governor of a tiny Caribbean island repeal his laws prohibiting fun.

Blos, Joan W. *Old Henry*. Illus. by Stephen Gammell. Mulberry, 1987. Henry's neighbors are scandalized that he ignores them and lets his property get run down, until they drive him away and find themselves missing him.

Brandenberg, Franz. *It's Not My Fault*. Illus. by Aliki. Greenwillow, 1980. Children will gain insight into the purpose of rules and laws as they read about a very hectic day in the life of the field mouse family.

Brown, Marc. *Arthur Meets the President*. Little, Brown, 1991. Arthur is a proud American when he wins the essay contest and is rewarded by reading it to the President in Washington, D.C.

Marzollo, Jean. *Happy Birthday, Martin Luther King*. Illus. by J. Brian Pinkney. Scholastic, 1993. A great civil rights leader is introduced.

Marzollo, Jean. *In 1776*. Illus. by Steve Bjorkman. Scholastic, 1994. Words and pictures describe how Americans declared independence from England in 1776.

Popov, Nikolai. *Why?* North-South, 1996. A wordless cautionary tale shows the consequences of conflict.

Average

Bunting, Eve. *Smoky Night*. Illus. by David Diaz. Harcourt Brace, 1994. Bunting makes the Los Angeles riots understandable for children.

Fisher, Leonard Everett. *Stars & Stripes: Our National Flag*. Holiday House, 1993. With the Pledge of Allegiance as accompanying text, this story presents various American flags and gives brief historical information about each.

Fradin, Dennis B. *Voting and Elections*. Childrens Press, 1985. In this photo-essay children will learn how voting and elections work in the United States.

Hathorn, Libby. *Way Home*. Illus. by Gregory Rogers. Crown, 1994. Shane, a homeless boy, pursues a cat, giving readers a realistic view of homeless life in the inner city.

Herold, Maggie Rugg. *A Very Important Day*. Illus. by Catherine Stock. Morrow, 1995. Herold personalizes the experiences of immigrants from thirty-two countries who become American citizens.

Levine, Arthur A. *Pearl Moscowitz's Last Stand*. Illus. by Robert Roth. Tambourine, 1993. Pearl Moscowitz takes a stand when city government tries to chop down the last gingko tree on her street.

Polacco, Patricia. *Chicken Sunday*. Philomel, 1992. To thank Miss Eula, three children sell decorated eggs to buy her a beautiful Easter hat. In the process the children learn a lesson about rules.

Ryan, Pam Muñoz. *The Flag We Love*. Illus. by Ralph Masiello. Charlesbridge, 1996. The meaning of the stars and stripes is conveyed through patriotic verse and beautiful illustrations.

Yoaker, Harry. *The View*. Illus. by Simon Henwood. Dial, 1992. Through a spirit of cooperation, a neighborhood is saved temporarily from the adverse effects of an architectural and environmental disaster.

Zemach, Harve. *The Judge*. Illus. by Margot Zemach. Farrar, Straus & Giroux, 1991. This rhyme about a fiery old judge has a surprise ending.

Challenging

Dalgliesh, Alice. *The Fourth of July Story*. Illus by Marie Nonnast. Simon & Schuster, 1987. The story of our country's birthday offers a look at early America.

Fritz, Jean. *And Then What Happened, Paul Revere?* Coward, McCann, 1973. The story of Paul Revere is told in a humorous way.

Guy, Rosa. *Billy the Great*. Dell, 1994. Billy's parents try to plan his life for him, including his choice of friends, but he has his own ideas.

Greenfield, Eloise. *Rosa Parks*. HarperCollins, 1973. Greenfield tells the courageous story of Rosa Parks.

Maestro, Betsy. *A More Perfect Union: The Story of Our Constitution*. Illus. by Giulio Maestro. Lothrop, Lee & Shepard, 1987. This book describes how the Constitution was drafted and ratified.

Rabin, Staton. *Casey Over There*. Illus. by Greg Shed. Harcourt Brace, 1994. Aubrey's brother, Casey, is fighting in World War I. Aubrey sends a letter to Uncle Sam and gets a response from the President.

Swanson, June. *I Pledge Allegiance*. Illus. by Rick Hanson. Carolrhoda, 1991. This book describes how and why the Pledge of Allegiance was written, how its wording has changed, and precisely what it means.

Van Leeuwen, Jean. *A Fourth of July on the Plains*. Dial, 1997. A story based on an account of a July 4th celebration along the Oregon Trail in 1852, as recalled in the diary of E.W. Conyers.

LIBRARY

See the Grade 2 SOCIAL STUDIES LIBRARY for additional resources.

Audiocassettes

One Voice for Children. Educational Activities. Themes of respect, awareness, listening, caring, and multicultural sensitivity are stressed. Also available on LP. Toll free: 1-800-645-3739

Patriotic and Morning Time Songs. By Hap Palmer. Educational Activities. Also available on LP or CD. Toll free: 1-800-645-3739

Computer Software

CD-ROM

People Behind the Holidays. National Geographic Society. Mac/Windows. Introduces students to people who shaped America. Travel back to meet Christopher Columbus, George Washington, Abraham Lincoln, Martin Luther King, Jr., and others. Includes activity and user's guides, poster and color booklets, and library catalog cards. Toll free: 1-800-368-2728

SimCity. Electronic Arts Direct. Windows 3.1/Mac/DOS. Children are able to design, create, and control a growing city. Children may form city councils; create city maps, city newspapers, and travel brochures; and engage in other activities using the program. Toll free: 1-800-336-2947

ZipZapMap!® USA. National Geographic Educational Services. Mac/Windows/DOS. Children play a geography game in which they place loose pieces correctly on maps. Toll free: 1-800-368-2728

Video

Film or VHS Cassettes

The Respecting Others Game. Alfred Higgins Productions. Jason learns about respecting the rights and belongings of others when Mr. Mac shows him how he would feel if these were taken away from him. He also learns about respecting and appreciating others who are from different cultural backgrounds and those who are handicapped. Children will learn to respect the feelings of others, their rights, and their property. 13 minutes. Toll free: 1-800-766-5353

Taking Responsibility: What's Wrong with Vandalism? Phoenix Learning Group. Clever animation vividly dramatizes to children how to manage their own destructive feelings. By calling on their imaginations to visualize the experiences of vandalism victims, viewers will discover that vandalism always hurts people. 11 minutes. Toll free: 1-800-221-1274

Values and Choices. SVE & Churchill Media. What are honesty and co-operation? How can children identify a value conflict before it occurs and formulate a positive approach? This video offers six school situations that illustrate value dilemmas. No solutions are given, but a great deal of "food for thought" is. 28 minutes. Toll free: 1-800-829-1900

Who Is an American? Educational Activities. Children learn about the "salad bowl" of cultures and that the guarantees of the Bill of Rights apply to all citizens. Toll free: 1-800-645-3739

FREE & INEXPENSIVE MATERIALS

Foundations of Democracy. Series for grades K–12 focuses on the concepts of authority, privacy, responsibility, and justice as fundamental values and principles of a constitutional democracy. Free.
The Center for Civic Education
5146 Douglas Fir Road
Calabasas, CA 91302-1467
1-800-350-4223
E-mail: Center4CIV@aol.com

Historical Documents. Parchment replicas of some of America's most important documents, including Declaration of Independence and Bill of Rights, U.S. Constitution, and "Star-Spangled Banner." 60 cents per copy. Write for a free catalog.
Historical Documents Company
2555 Orthodox St.
Philadelphia, PA 19137

Thought, Word & Deed. Kit to teach children how their actions and attitudes affect others. Kit includes 25-minute video, student worksheets, and teacher's guide. Free.
State Farm Insurance
Public Affairs Department
22 State Farm Drive
Monroe, LA 71208-0010

Traveling Trunk. Trunk includes teacher's handbook that chronicles the 27 years Martin Luther King, Jr., lived in Sweet Auburn, photos, books by Dr. King, Jr., videocassettes, and tapes of his speeches. Call or write to reserve. The only cost is return shipping of the trunk.
Martin Luther King, Jr., National Historic Site
450 Auburn Avenue, NE
Atlanta, GA 30313
(404) 331-5190

Note that information, while correct at time of publication, is subject to change.

Linking Social Studies

MUSIC CENTER

Respond to Patriotic Music

Materials: cassette player; cassette recordings of patriotic songs, marches, and songs of the armed forces; pencils; strips of lined paper; butcher paper divided and labeled Fact and Opinion

Each day, place in the center a different recording of patriotic music. Invite children to listen to the music. Provide strips of lined paper and have children write descriptions and details about what they hear and what they like. Ask children to place each comment under the correct heading to show whether it is a fact about the music or their own opinion. Discuss whether children agree with the placement of each comment.

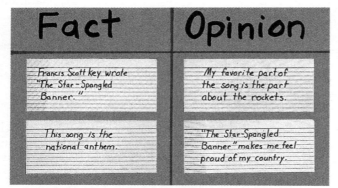

Fact	Opinion
Francis Scott Key wrote "The Star-Spangled Banner."	My favorite part of the song is the part about the rockets.
This song is the national anthem.	"The Star-Spangled Banner" makes me feel proud of my country.

ART CENTER

Stars and Stripes Stamp Art

Materials: potatoes, sponges, or commercial stamps of stars and stripes; red, white, and blue tempera paint; art paper or other items to decorate

Invite children to use the symbols from the national flag to create art to honor their country. Provide stamps and paint in shallow containers and have children create pictures or designs on paper. You may wish to invite children to create and decorate sculptures of small boxes, paper plates, and cardboard tubes or to decorate items they bring from home, such as T-shirts, shoes, caps, or storage boxes. Display the artwork in a classroom area designated as the Stars and Stripes Museum.

READING CENTER

One Student, One Vote!

Materials: books appropriate for reading aloud to children, ballot box, ballots, class list

Invite children to read or look at the books in the center during the week. At the end of the week, invite them to vote for the one they would most like to have you read aloud. Explain to children that one way we make sure each person gets one vote—and only one vote—is to have a person check the list of voters and mark off the names of people as they vote. Assign one child to be in charge of ballots and the voters' list while others count and tally ballots.

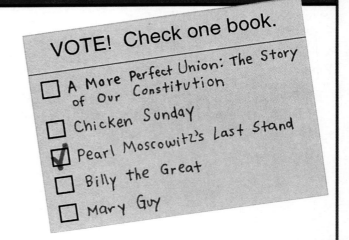

VOTE! Check one book.

- ☐ A More Perfect Union: The Story of Our Constitution
- ☐ Chicken Sunday
- ☑ Pearl Moscowitz's Last Stand
- ☐ Billy the Great
- ☐ Mary Guy

Across the Curriculum

MULTICULTURAL CENTER

World Leader Puzzles

Materials: teacher-made sentence strip puzzles, world map

Ahead of time, prepare two-piece puzzles by cutting word strips in half with matching curves and tongues. Write on one half of each puzzle the name of a country and, on the matching half, what the country's leader is called (United States/President; Saudi Arabia, Spain, Denmark/king; Japan/emperor; Canada/prime minister). Explain that all countries have leaders but that countries have different names for their top officials. Invite children to match pairs of puzzle pieces to find out what different countries call their top leaders. Encourage children to find on the world map each country they learn about.

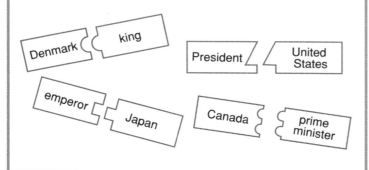

MATH CENTER

Sort and Tally State Flags

Materials: cutouts of the state flags, paper, pencils

Invite children to sort the flags into groups. Suggest that they make up rules to determine which flags would go into each group, such as flags with stars or flags with pictures of animals. After children sort the flags into a group, ask them to tally the number of flags that go in their group and the number of flags that do not. Encourage them to record their rule on one side of a sheet of paper and the tallies on the back. Then suggest that they challenge other children to sort flags according to the rule and to check to see if the tallies match.

HOW TO INTEGRATE YOUR DAY
Use these topics to help you integrate social studies into your daily planning.

READING THEMES	INTEGRATED LANGUAGE ARTS	MATHEMATICS	SCIENCE	ART
Communicating with Others	Missing Words, p. 184 Derivatives, p. 192A Write a Letter, p. 196 Journal, pp. 183, 196, 202A Oral Language, p. 202 Poetry, p. 206	Sort and Tally State Flags, p. 182H Addition and Subtraction, p. 192A	Plants and Animals, p. 188 Observation, p. 202	Stars and Stripes Stamp Art, p. 182G Illustration, p. 182 About the Artist, p. 186 Create Advertisements, p. 204
Cooperation				
Conflict Resolution/ Problem Solving				
Viewpoints		**HEALTH AND PHYSICAL EDUCATION**	**MUSIC**	**WORLD LANGUAGES**
Self and Others		Physical Education, p. 198 Community Health, p. 201	Respond to Patriotic Music, p. 182G Origins, p. 186	Latin, p. 188

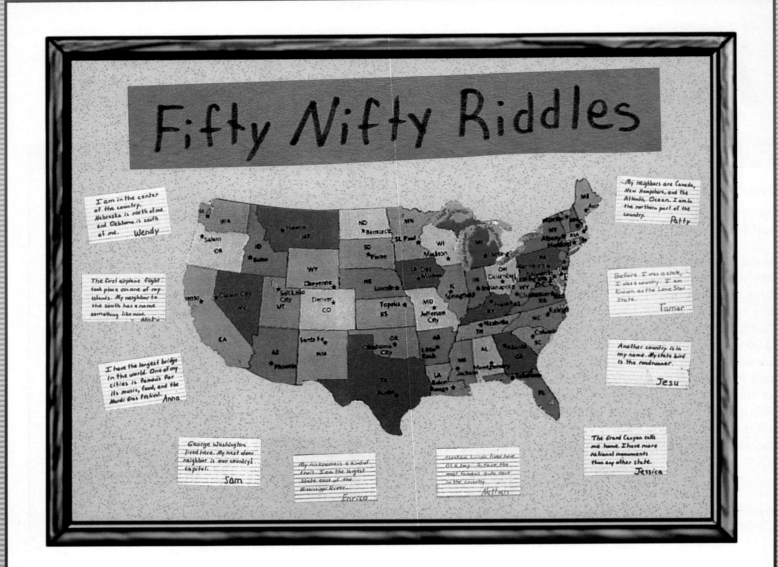

BULLETIN BOARD

Create a bulletin board titled *Fifty Nifty Riddles*. Write the name of each state on a scrap of paper and place it in a hat. Then ask each child to select one of the scraps and to write a riddle telling something about the state. Children who finish may select another state until all fifty have been drawn. Display each riddle with the name of the "riddler." When children think they know the answer to a riddle, they ask the riddler to confirm their guesses.

Assessment Options

The assessment program allows all learners many opportunities to show what they know and can do. It also provides ongoing information about each child's understanding of social studies.

FORMAL ASSESSMENT

▶ *Unit Review*
(**Pupil Book**, pp. 214–217)

▶ *Unit Assessment*
(**Assessment Program:**
Standard Test, pp. 31–33,
Performance Task, p. 34)

STUDENT SELF-EVALUATION

▶ *Individual End-of-Project Checklist*
(**Assessment Program**, p. 6)

▶ *Group End-of-Project Checklist*
(**Assessment Program**, p. 7) for use after cooperative learning activities

▶ *Individual End-of-Unit Checklist*
(**Assessment Program**, p. 8)

INFORMAL ASSESSMENT

▶ *What Do You Know? Questions*
(**Pupil Book**, at end of lessons)

▶ *Think and Do*
(**Pupil Book**, at end of skill lessons)

▶ *Picture Summary*
(**Pupil Book**, pp. 212–213)

▶ *Check Understanding*
(**Teacher's Edition**, in Close, at end of lessons)

▶ *Think Critically*
(**Teacher's Edition**, in Close, at end of lessons)

▶ *Social Studies Skills Checklist*
(**Assessment Program**, pp. 4–5)

PERFORMANCE ASSESSMENT

▶ *Show What You Know*
(**Teacher's Edition**, in Close, at end of lessons)

▶ *Cooperative Learning Workshop*
(**Teacher's Edition**, pp. 217A–217B)

▶ *Performance Task: Proud to Be an American!*
(**Assessment Program**, p. 34)

▶ Scoring the Performance Task
Use the *Scoring Rubric for Individual Projects*
(**Assessment Program**, p. 9)

▶ *Scoring Rubric for Group Projects*
(**Assessment Program**, p. 10)

▶ *Scoring Rubric for Presentations*
(**Assessment Program**, p. 11)

PORTFOLIO ASSESSMENT

Student-selected items may include:

▶ *Meet Individual Needs*, booklet
(**Teacher's Edition**, p. 194A)

▶ *Link to Language Arts*, journal
(**Teacher's Edition**, p. 196)

▶ *Hands-On Option*, letter
(**Teacher's Edition**, p. 201A)

Teacher-selected items may include:

▶ *My Best Work*
(**Assessment Program**, p. 12)

▶ *Portfolio Summary*
(**Assessment Program**, p. 13)

▶ *Portfolio Family Response*
(**Assessment Program**, p. 14)

STANDARD TEST

Name _____ Date _____

Unit 5 Test

Vocabulary 5 points each

Write a word to complete the diagram.

judges votes government freedom mayor

1.

President · Supreme Court · Congress

The Branches of Our

government

2.

Places and the People Who Work There	
White House	President
Capitol	lawmakers
Supreme Court	judges

3.

Community Leaders

City Council · School Board

mayor

4.

Election Day → People mark ballots. → Votes are counted. → A leader is chosen.

5. Choosing our own leaders + Making our own laws = _____ Freedom

Unit 5 Test   Assessment Program **31**

STANDARD TEST

Name _____

Main Ideas 5 points each

Answer the questions.

6. How many branches does our government have? _____ 3

7. In what building does our President live? _____ the White House

8. Who makes the laws for our government? _____ Congress

9. In what building are the laws made? _____ the Capitol Building

10. Who tells whether a law is fair? _____ the Supreme Court

Draw two symbols of our country.

11.   12.

Drawings might show the American flag,
the Statue of Liberty, the bald eagle.

List three things people do to help their community.

13. Sample responses: vote, get along with one another,

14. help make the community beautiful, write letters, work

15. together to make the community a better place to live, help others

32 Assessment Program   Unit 5 Test

Objectives

- ▶ Identify ways Americans honor their country. (p. 188A)
- ▶ Identify symbols of America. (p. 188A)
- ▶ Recognize and recite or sing the Pledge of Allegiance, the national motto, and the national anthem. (p. 188A)
- ▶ Describe the contributions of famous Americans. (p. 188A)
- ▶ Recognize that voting is one way to choose leaders. (p. 192A)
- ▶ Explain the idea of one person, one vote. (p. 192A)
- ▶ Describe what determines a winning vote. (p. 192A)

- ▶ Identify the three branches of our country's government. (p. 194A)
- ▶ List the main responsibility of each branch of government. (p. 194A)
- ▶ Describe the role of judges in solving problems. (p. 194A)
- ▶ Define *boundary*. (p. 198A)
- ▶ Identify states and their capitals. (p. 198A)
- ▶ Use cardinal directions to describe locations on a map. (p. 198A)
- ▶ Identify how governing bodies such as school boards and city councils affect our lives. (p. 200A)

- ▶ Describe the need for good government and the role citizens play in achieving it. (p. 200A)
- ▶ Distinguish fact from opinion. (p. 202A)
- ▶ Recognize the rights of people to hold different opinions. (p. 202A)
- ▶ Explore the idea of freedom in America. (p. 204A)
- ▶ Identify freedoms that United States citizens enjoy. (p. 204A)
- ▶ Identify people who have worked for freedoms. (p. 204A)
- ▶ Recognize that people can use their freedoms to make a difference. (p. 204A)

STANDARD TEST

Name _____

Skills 5 points each

Complete the sentences.

16. One state that shares a boundary with

California is _____ Arizona or Nevada _____ .

17. The map symbol for the capital of our country

is a star inside a circle. The symbol for a

state capital is _____ a star _____ .

18. The direction you would travel from Carson City to

the capital of Colorado is _____ east _____

Tell whether the sentence is a <u>fact</u> or an <u>opinion</u>.

19. Many people visit Arizona. _____ fact _____

20. Arizona is too hot. _____ opinion _____

Unit 5 Test   Assessment Program   **33**

PERFORMANCE TASK

Name _____   Date _____

Performance Task

Proud to Be an American!

Draw a picture to show something you do to honor
your country. Label your drawing. Then tell why you
are proud of your country.

Drawing might show a child celebrating Independence Day,

pledging allegiance to the flag, or singing the national anthem.

☆ I am proud of my country because Sample responses: My country

stands for good things, it helps its citizens, it is strong and protects us from

attacks, it is a beautiful country, people from many countries live together in

our country, we have freedom.

_____ .

34   Assessment Program   Unit 5 Test

Rubrics

SCORING RUBRICS The scoring rubrics for evaluating individual projects, group projects, and children's presentations may be found in the *Assessment Program*, pages 9–11.

CRITERIA The criteria listed below may be used when looking for evidence of the children's understanding of social studies content and ability to think critically.

▶ *Performance Task: Proud to Be an American!* [**Assessment Program**, p. 34]
▶ *Scoring the Performance Task*—Use the *Scoring Rubric for Individual Projects* [**Assessment Program,** p. 9], and look for evidence of the child's ability to:

✔ Understand how people honor our country (pledge allegiance to the flag, sing the national anthem, celebrate Independence Day, etc.).
✔ Give reasons for being proud of our country.
✔ Communicate ideas clearly through art and writing.

REMINDER

You may wish to preview the performance assessment activity in the COOPERATIVE LEARNING WORKSHOP on Teacher's Edition pages 217A–217B. Children may complete this activity during the course of the unit.

INTRODUCE THE UNIT

Link Prior Learning

Organize children into groups of two or three. Invite the groups to role-play ways in which people honor their country. If necessary, provide children with examples, such as singing the national anthem, raising the American flag, saying the Pledge of Allegiance, and keeping the environment clean.

Anticipation Guide

Find out what children know by having them categorize the following statements as true or false. Then discuss what they are interested in learning more about.

1. _____ Citizens are each allowed two votes in elections.

2. _____ Good citizens obey traffic laws.

3. _____ The United States government has three branches.

4. _____ The Bill of Rights makes sure we have our freedoms.

5. _____ Everything people say is fact.

Preview Vocabulary

The vocabulary words listed on page 182 represent the key concepts for this unit. Suggest that children use the words to predict what the main ideas of the unit will be. Ideas for teaching the vocabulary are provided on pages 184 and 185.

UNIT 5

Being a Good Citizen

Vocabulary

vote
government
judge
mayor
freedom

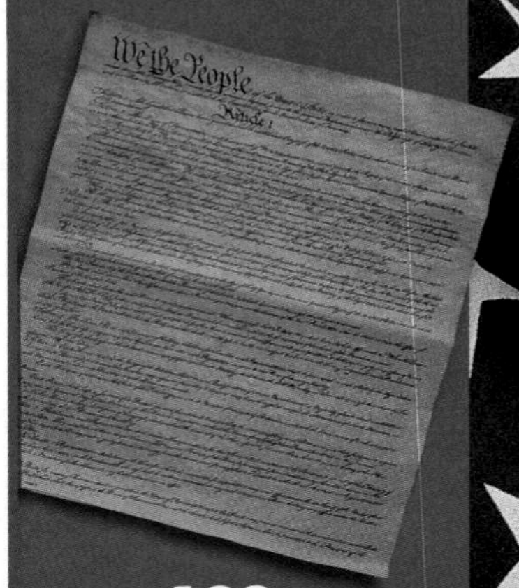

We the People

182

ACTIVITY CHOICES

Community Involvement

Arrange a field trip to your state capitol, where children can visit with state representatives and other officials. If this is not possible, invite a representative of your state or local government to address your class.

Link to Art

ILLUSTRATION Invite children to draw a picture of themselves honoring their country and its symbols. Encourage them to write about why they honor their country this way. Invite children to share their drawings with the class.

HOME LETTER

Use UNIT 5 HOME LETTER. See Teacher's Edition pages HL9–10.

PUPIL BOOK OR UNIT BIG BOOK

Link to Language Arts

JOURNAL Have children keep a daily record of the things they learn about being good citizens. At the end of the unit, ask children to write a paragraph in their journals telling "Why I Am a Good Citizen."

AUDIO

Use the **UNIT 5 TEXT ON TAPE AUDIOCASSETTE** for a reading of this unit.

ASIAN TRANSLATIONS

For students who speak Cambodian, Cantonese, Hmong, or Vietnamese, use the **ASIAN TRANSLATIONS** for Unit 5. The Harcourt Brace program is also available in a **SPANISH EDITION.**

Personal Response

Direct children's attention to the photo on pages 182–183. Discuss the reasons people honor their country. Then invite children to name the ways the United States is being honored by the children in the photo.

Q. **In what ways do you honor our country each day?** Responses may include raising the flag, pledging allegiance, singing patriotic songs, being a good citizen.

Tell children that in this unit they will learn about their government and about the rights and responsibilities of American citizens. They will discover that good citizens participate in the community.

> **"PRIMARY SOURCE"**
>
> In a letter to James Madison, March 2, 1788, George Washington wrote, "Liberty, when it begins to take root, is a plant of rapid growth." Tell children as they study this unit to think about how, for more than 200 years, Americans have built a free country that depends on the continued participation of all its citizens.

Options for Reading

Read Aloud Read each lesson aloud as children follow along in their books. Strategies for guiding children through working with text and visuals are provided with each lesson.

Read Together Have pairs or small groups of children read the lesson by taking turns reading each page or paragraph aloud. Encourage children to use the new vocabulary words as they discuss what they read.

Read Alone Strong readers may wish to read the lessons independently before you read or discuss each lesson with the class.

PREVIEW THE UNIT

THINK ABOUT WORDS

Reproduce the following word web:

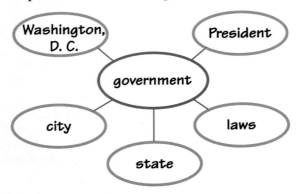

Write the word *government* in the middle of the web. Invite children to suggest words that have to do with what they think *government* means. Help them understand that government is the authority over our nation, states, and communities. To help them think of words to add to the web, you may wish to use the following questions:

Q. **Who helps us take care of our country? our state? our community? What kinds of things do they do? Have you ever seen a government building? Where was it?**

vote

A choice that gets counted.

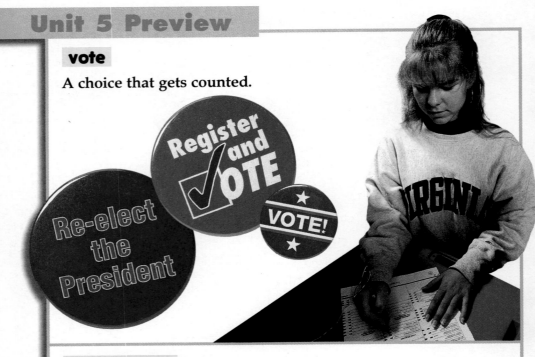

government

A group of people who make the laws for a community or a country.

184

ACTIVITY CHOICES

WRITE-ON CHARTS

Use WRITE-ON CHART 27 to complete the vocabulary web.

Link to Language Arts

MISSING WORDS Write the following sentences on chart paper. Ask children to copy each sentence and fill in the missing word. As you proceed through each lesson, ask children to tell whether their answers were correct.

There are three branches of our ____.

People ____ in an election.

Not everyone in the world enjoys ____.

A ____ is another name for a justice.

The ____ is a city leader.

Meet Individual Needs

ENGLISH LANGUAGE LEARNERS
As you discuss the words on the pages and ask follow-up questions, allow children who speak the same first language to sit together in small groups and share ideas about their meanings. Then have them relate these ideas in English to other children.

judge

Someone who works as a leader in court.

mayor

The leader of a city or town.

freedom

The right of people to make their own choices.

185

PUPIL BOOK OR UNIT BIG BOOK

VOCABULARY CARDS

Display the word side of the five **VOCABULARY PICTURE CARDS** for Unit 5 on the chalk ledge. Invite volunteers to hold up a card for the rest of the class to see and use the word in a sentence.

WORK WITH WORDS

Invite children to turn to pages 184–185 in their Pupil Book. Then direct their attention to the words and their definitions on the pages. Explain that these words tell the main ideas that they will learn in this unit. Invite volunteers to read aloud each word and its definition. Add the words to the web if they have not been suggested. (Note: For additional vocabulary, see the Planning Chart on pages 182C–182D in this Teacher's Edition.) Use the words and the questions that follow to stimulate a general discussion of the new vocabulary.

Q. **Have you ever voted? What were you voting for?**

> **Some people who work in the government make laws. What do you remember about laws?**

> **How is the judge in this photo different from other judges you may have seen?**

> **Why do you think communities need leaders such as a mayor?**

> **Read the definition for *freedom*. What kinds of choices do you make?**

VOCABULARY BLACKLINES

You may wish to reproduce individual copies of the vocabulary words for this unit. They are found in the back of your Teacher's Edition.

SET THE SCENE WITH MUSIC

PREVIEW

Have the class look at pages 186–187. Ask children to read aloud the title of the song. Encourage them to share things they know about America, such as places they have visited, historical information, or things they like about their country. Explain that people have written many songs and poems about our country to express their love for America and the appreciation they have for the beauty of this land.

Q. **Why do people write songs about America?** to show their love for their country, to tell the history of America, to tell why America is a great country, to be patriotic

Set the Scene with 𝄞 Music

186

ACTIVITY CHOICES

Link to Music

ORIGINS Introduce children to patriotic music, such as "You're a Grand Old Flag," "Yankee Doodle," and the marches of John Philip Sousa. Organize a parade and invite children to sing and march along with the music.

Background

"AMERICA" The melody of "America" is actually the melody of the British national anthem, "God Save the Queen." The origin of the music is obscure but it is thought to have been first composed in the late 1500s. The melody became so popular in Europe that a variety of lyrics were written to accompany it. In 1832 Samuel F. Smith, a U.S. citizen, wrote the words of "America" to be sung to the British tune.

Link to Art

ABOUT THE ARTIST Byron Gin's art is a combination of printmaking techniques. He carved the statue, island, and clouds out of linoleum then inked and pressed them onto paper. For the sky and water, he used a monoprint method of ink on glass. To finish the piece, he used colored pencils. Children can practice block printing using potatoes or apples.

America

by Samuel F. Smith
illustrated by Byron Gin

My country, 'tis of thee,
Sweet land of liberty,
of thee I sing;
Land where my fathers died,
Land of the pilgrims' pride,
From every mountainside
Let freedom ring.

My native country, thee,
Land of the noble free,
Thy name I love;
I love thy rocks and rills,
Thy woods and templed hills;
My heart with rapture thrills
Like that above.

187

PUPIL BOOK **OR** UNIT BIG BOOK

READ & RESPOND

Ask children to sing the song aloud with you. Lead a discussion about the purpose of the song. Explain that songs and poems are good ways for people to share their feelings about other people and places. Challenge children to pick out the words that let them know the author loved his country.

Q. **If you wrote a song about your country, what would it say?** Responses might mention the beauty of the country, freedom, fun, pride, respect, and love for the country.

Find the words that mention something about being free. liberty, freedom, free

Why do you think freedom is mentioned so often? The writer may have considered freedom one of the best things about America.

Meet Individual Needs

ENGLISH LANGUAGE LEARNERS
After children sing the song about America, solicit information from children who are learning English about their countries such as names of traditional songs, how people dress, weather conditions, customs, and holidays. Then invite them to sing and teach the class a song they know.

Link Literature

Invite children to begin the unit by reading *Happy Birthday, Martin Luther King* by Jean Marzollo. (Scholastic, 1993) This book provides an introduction to Martin Luther King, Jr., and his accomplishments. He worked hard to bring peace and freedom to all people. Ask children to tell about someone they know who helps other people.

Use the
LITERATURE
BIG
BOOK

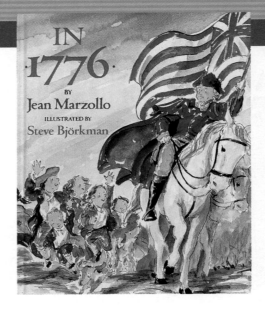

IN 1776
BY
Jean Marzollo
ILLUSTRATED BY
Steve Björkman

Invite children to begin the unit by reading *In 1776* by Jean Marzollo. In lively rhyming text, this book provides a strong foundation for future learning. Through important events and concepts in American history, it introduces readers to the idea that democracy is an ongoing process.

About the Author and the Illustrator

Jean Marzollo lives with her husband and two sons in Cold Spring, New York. She has written many books for parents and children. Among her favorites are history books and biographies for young readers. She is the author of *In 1492* and *Happy Birthday, Martin Luther King*.

Steve Björkman lives in Irvine, California. His three children along with many other readers have enjoyed his playful illustrations in such books as *In 1492, I Hate English* (an ALA Notable Book), and *This Is the Way We Go to School*.

Reading the Story

Read and discuss the literature to address the following objectives:

1. Describe the early history of our country.
2. Identify the Declaration of Independence.
3. Discuss famous Americans and how they made a difference.
4. Recognize the freedoms that all Americans have.

Social Studies Connection

Help children to brainstorm what they know about the early history of the United States.

Q. **Why is the Fourth of July an important holiday?** It's our country's birthday; America declared its independence from England; Americans celebrate their history.

List some of the historical events from the story.

▶ King George refuses to free the colonies.
▶ The American Revolution begins at Lexington and Concord.
▶ Thomas Jefferson helps to write the Declaration of Independence.
▶ George Washington becomes the first President.

Invite children in small groups to read about one of these events or some other event of the period. Then ask each group to role-play a scene for the class.

1

PROUD AMERICANS

OBJECTIVES

1. Identify ways Americans honor their country.
2. Identify symbols of America.
3. Recognize and recite or sing the Pledge of Allegiance, the national motto, and the national anthem.
4. Describe the contributions of famous Americans.

VOCABULARY

holiday (p. 188)
motto (p. 188)

RESOURCES

Pupil Book/Unit Big Book, pp. 188–191
Write-On Charts 17, 30, 39, 40
Pattern P9
Activity Book, p. 37
Music Audio, "The Star-Spangled Banner"

ACTIVITY CHOICES

Background

INDEPENDENCE DAY On July 4, 1776, the Second Continental Congress made the United States an independent nation by signing the Declaration of Independence. The Declaration was based on the philosophy that all people have natural rights and that a government has the right to rule only if it has been granted that right by the people. The day of the signing of the Declaration is considered the birthday of our nation and is celebrated as Independence Day, or the Fourth of July. However, Independence Day has not always been celebrated as a national holiday. The states, led by Pennsylvania, made it a legal holiday about 100 years after the signing of the Declaration of Independence.

1. ACCESS

Share "Fourth of July" by Marchette Chute and invite children to compare their Fourth of July experiences with those mentioned in the poem.

> Fourth of July, Fourth of July.
> That's when the flag goes waving by.
> And the crackers crack, and the popguns pop,
> And the big guns boom and never stop.
> And we watch parades, and listen to speeches,
> And picnic around on all the beaches.
> And it usually rains, and it's always hot;
> But we all like Fourth of July a lot.

Focus on the Main Idea

In this lesson children will explore the meaning of patriotism. Certain people who were important in the early days of the country will be introduced, as will various symbols associated with our country. Children will learn about and recite the Pledge of Allegiance, the national motto, and the national anthem of the United States. Tell children that in this lesson they will see what a class like theirs does to honor America.

Multicultural Link

If any children in your class have lived in countries other than the United States, invite them to share information about holiday celebrations in those countries. Have children compare those celebrations with their celebration of Independence Day.

NOTE: You may have some children who, because of religious or other beliefs, choose not to participate in certain celebrations or in pledging allegiance to the flag. This behavior should not be judged as a lack of good citizenship.

2. BUILD

Key Content Summary

Understanding the symbols of patriotism helps preserve the story of this nation's past and builds appreciation for the rights people enjoy as citizens of the United States.

Vocabulary

Define *holiday* as a special day set aside to honor some person or event. Explain that the Fourth of July is a national holiday, a special day celebrated by the whole country.

Q. **What other national holidays can you name?** Columbus Day, Presidents' Day, Memorial Day, Labor Day, Thanksgiving, Martin Luther King, Jr. Day, Veterans Day

HOLIDAY ACTIVITIES

For information and activities related to Independence Day, preview the Holiday Activities section at the back of the Teacher's Edition.

History

Connections Past to Present to Future
Focus attention on pages 188–189. Explain that another name for the Fourth of July holiday is Independence Day. Point out that for many years our country was ruled by Great Britain and that American leaders

LESSON 1
Proud Americans

Americans sing "America" on the Fourth of July. The Fourth of July is our country's birthday. Our community celebrates this special day, or **holiday**, with a parade. Did you know that the United States is more than 200 years old?

We like to honor our country during the school year, too. We decorate our room with balloons. We hang a banner with our country's motto, In God We Trust. A **motto** is a saying that people try to live by.

188

ACTIVITY CHOICES

Reading Support

PREVIEWING AND PREDICTING
Read the lesson title with children and begin an idea web. Have them suggest what they think the lesson might be about. Next have children scan the pictures on pages 188–191 and add to the web.

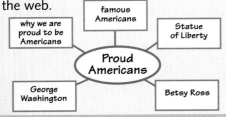

Link to World Languages

LATIN Allow children to examine several coins to find the words *E Pluribus Unum*. Share the meaning of the Latin words ("out of many, one") and the idea that they represent (out of thirteen colonies, one nation). Explain that Latin is no longer a spoken language, but that many spoken languages have words based on Latin. In fact, almost half of all English words in current use are of Latin origin.

Link to Science

PLANTS AND ANIMALS Invite volunteers to find out what a bald eagle looks like, why it is called *bald*, where it lives, what it eats, how it raises its young, and whether or not it is considered an endangered species.

E Pluribus Unum is a motto that is on our money. The Latin words mean "out of many, one." We are one country of many different people.

Our country has many symbols. My class is making a bulletin board. We will show pictures of our country's symbols, such as the Statue of Liberty, the White House, and the bald eagle. One famous leader named Benjamin Franklin wanted the turkey to be America's bird. Our country's lawmakers chose the eagle instead.

189

PUPIL BOOK **OR** UNIT BIG BOOK

Link Literature

Invite children to read *I Pledge Allegiance* by June Swanson. (Carolrhoda, 1991) Point out that this book describes how and why the Pledge of Allegiance was written, how its words changed over the years, and precisely what the pledge means. You may wish to use Write-On Chart 39 to help children review the Pledge of Allegiance.

WRITE-ON CHARTS

Traits of a Good Citizen
Use WRITE-ON CHART 17 to extend and enrich this lesson. See Teacher's Edition page W53.

declared independence on July 4, 1776. Explain that this is why Americans celebrate the Fourth of July.

Civics and Government

Patriotic Identity Explain that a *motto* is a saying that reminds people of an important idea. Identify the national motto as In God We Trust. Tell children that this has been our motto for only 40 years, but that many of our earliest settlers came here for religious reasons. Point out that *E Pluribus Unum* is another well-known motto for this country.

 Geography

Human-Environment Interactions On a U.S. map, help children find places where some famous American landmarks are located.

- the Statue of Liberty in New York Harbor
- the Capitol Building in Washington, D.C.
- Mount Rushmore in South Dakota
- the Gateway Arch in St. Louis, Missouri
- the Alamo in San Antonio, Texas
- the Golden Gate Bridge in San Francisco, California

Visual Analysis

Interpret Pictures Have children name and describe the pictures on the bulletin board.

Q. **Why are these pictures symbols of our country?** Mount Rushmore—the faces of four great U.S. Presidents are carved in the mountain; eagle—our national bird; Statue of Liberty—has welcomed countless immigrants entering the U.S.; George Washington—our first President; the White House—home of the First Family; Franklin Roosevelt, John F. Kennedy, Thomas Jefferson, Benjamin Franklin, Harriet Tubman —other well-known Americans

❝PRIMARY SOURCE❞

The Liberty Bell was first hung in 1753 with a Biblical inscription that reads, "Proclaim Liberty throughout all the Land unto all the Inhabitants Thereof."

History

People and Events Across Time and Place Encourage children to examine the pictures on pages 190–191. Tell them that these children are playing the parts of some people who did important things for the United States many years ago. Ask them to look at the pictures and identify any people or symbols that look familiar to them. Then share the text on pages 190–191. Discuss the historical significance of Betsy Ross, Francis Scott Key, Thomas Jefferson, and George Washington, and the symbolism of the Liberty Bell and the Great Seal.

Q. **Why were George Washington and Thomas Jefferson important in the history of our country?** They were very important in starting our country. Washington led the fight for independence and was elected the first President. Jefferson helped write the Declaration of Independence and was elected the third President.

Civics and Government

Patriotic Identity Tell children the story in the Background note of how Francis Scott Key wrote "The Star-Spangled Banner." Then teach them to sing the anthem.

Q. **Why do Americans usually stand when "The Star-Spangled Banner" is played?** out of respect for the flag; to show patriotism

3. CLOSE

Invite children to name ways they honor America. List their suggestions on chart paper and save them to be used in the Reteach part of the lesson.

Check Understanding

The child can
—— identify ways Americans honor their country.
—— identify symbols of America.
—— recognize and recite or sing the Pledge of Allegiance, the national motto, and the national anthem.
—— describe the contributions of famous Americans.

UNIT 5

Ms. Carroll's class is having a play. The children in the play are dressed as people in American history. They tell us about other American symbols.

I am Betsy Ross.

I sewed the first American flag. Our flag is red, white, and blue. Each star stands for one of the states in our country. The stripes stand for the first 13 states in the United States.

I am Francis Scott Key.

I wrote our country's anthem. An anthem is a song that honors something. The anthem of the United States is about the American flag. It is called "The Star-Spangled Banner."

190

ACTIVITY CHOICES

WRITE-ON CHARTS
Use WRITE-ON CHART 40 to help children discuss the lyrics of the national anthem.

AUDIO
Use the UNIT 5 MUSIC AUDIO-CASSETTE to hear "The Star-Spangled Banner."

Background

"THE STAR-SPANGLED BANNER" During the War of 1812, British ships attacked American troops at Fort McHenry, near the Baltimore harbor. Francis Scott Key, a lawyer from Washington, D.C., observed the attack while being held overnight on an enemy warship. The sight of the United States flag still flying in the morning inspired him to write a poem. That poem, "The Star-Spangled Banner," was soon set to music, and was made the official anthem of the United States in 1931.

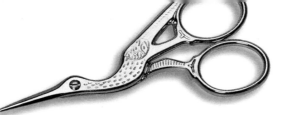

I am Thomas Jefferson.

In 1776 I wrote the Declaration of Independence that helped start the United States. People showed their love for the new country by ringing the Liberty Bell every Fourth of July. In 1835 the Liberty Bell cracked.

My name is George Washington.

I was the first President of the United States. You can see my picture and the Great Seal of the United States on a one-dollar bill. The Great Seal is on important papers, too.

What Do YOU Know?

1. **What is our country's motto?** In God We Trust
2. **How do you show pride in your country?** show respect for our flag, sing our national anthem, say the Pledge of Allegiance

191

Extend and Enrich

RESEARCH Tell children that there are rules and customs that tell us how and when we should display the American flag. Invite interested children to ask at home about those customs or to look them up with the help of a librarian or another adult. Invite children to share their findings with the class.

Reteach the Main Idea

MAKE A CHART Make a three-column chart or use Write-On Chart 30, labeling one column *People*, one *Places*, and one *Things*. Display the list of ways to honor America made during the Close of this lesson. Ask children to help you sort these ways into the appropriate columns.

Think Critically

Q. **Why do Americans honor their country?** People in our country have many rights and freedoms. Many people have worked hard to make sure we have these rights and freedoms. Some have even lost their lives to protect them.

Show What You Know

Performance Assessment Have children create a bulletin board display like the one in the lesson and title it *Proud Americans*. They might create 3-D models of some American symbols or cut out and display newspaper and magazine articles and pictures that reflect the celebration of national holidays or visits to historic landmarks and national monuments.

What to Look For In evaluating the bulletin board display, look for children's recognition of the significance of American symbols, historic buildings, historic people, and different ways Americans celebrate.

Using the Activity Book Invite children to complete Activity Book page 37 by filling in the blanks with words, phrases, or sentences. Point out that there is more than one correct way to complete each sentence. Have children share their completed pages with partners and compare answers.

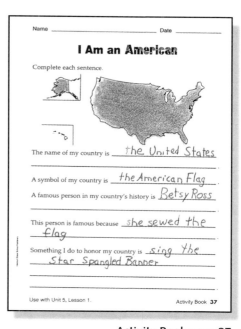

Activity Book page 37

LESSON 1 • 191

HANDS-ON OPTION

Famous Americans

Objectives: Identify ways Americans honor their country. Describe the contributions of famous Americans.

Materials: research materials, paper, pencils

Point out that one way Americans honor their country is by learning about people who have contributed to its history. Organize children into cooperative groups to research one of these famous Americans: Betsy Ross, Francis Scott Key, George Washington, Thomas Jefferson, Benjamin Franklin, Paul Revere, Benjamin Banneker, Phillis Wheatley, or Molly Pitcher. Have each group select a member to record the group's findings in an idea web. **(VISUAL)**

Symbol Stands

Objective: Identify symbols of America.

Materials: Pattern P9, crayons, scissors, tape

Invite children to work in small groups to make symbol stands for their desks. Ask each group to brainstorm a list of American symbols. Then provide the Symbols Stand Pattern to each child. Have each child choose a symbol from the list and draw it onto the top section of the pattern. Ask children to cut out the patterns and fold them into stands. Help them tape their stands onto their desks. Invite children to tell classmates how their symbols represent America and what the symbols mean to most Americans. **(TACTILE)**

Primary Source: Letter

Objective: Describe the contributions of famous Americans.

Materials: paper, pencils, envelopes

Copy the following letter excerpt. Make five copies and insert each letter in an envelope.

> August 19, 1785
>
> Dear Peter Carr,
>
> He who permits himself to tell a lie once, finds it much easier to do it a second and third time, till at length it becomes habitual.
>
> From,
>
> Thomas Jefferson

Arrange children into five small groups and recall with them who Thomas Jefferson was. Tell them that Thomas Jefferson wrote letters to his friends and that many of his letters have been saved. Explain that you have copied a sentence from one of his letters. Distribute a copy to each group and have them read the letter, write in their own words what Thomas Jefferson meant, and explain what the sentence tells us about Thomas Jefferson. Invite each group to share their work with the class. **(TACTILE/VISUAL/AUDITORY)**

Choral Readings

Objective: Recognize and recite or sing the Pledge of Allegiance, the national motto, and the national anthem.

Invite groups of children to choose the pledge, the motto, or the anthem to practice choral reading. Help them write response scripts in their own words that explain or paraphrase parts of the original text. Each group should form two sides and take turns reciting and responding. **(AUDITORY)**

MAKE A CHOICE BY VOTING

OBJECTIVES

1. Recognize that voting is one way to choose leaders.
2. Explain the idea of one person, one vote.
3. Describe what determines a winning vote.

VOCABULARY

election (p. 192)
vote (p. 192)

RESOURCES

Pupil Book/Unit Big Book, pp. 192–193
Write-On Charts 15, 31
Activity Book, p. 38
Transparency 13
Graph Links

ACTIVITY CHOICES

Link to Mathematics

ADDITION AND SUBTRACTION
Give children various oral problems to solve, like the following: *Eight children chose show* A *as their favorite television show,* 6 *chose show* B, *and* 14 *chose show* C. *How many children in all chose a favorite show?* Discuss the practice of "polling" to find out what's on the minds of American citizens.

Link to Language Arts

DERIVATIVES Write *vote* and *elect* on the board. Ask children to brainstorm a list of other words they can make from these roots, such as *voter, votes, voting, elected,* and *election.* Invite them to talk about how to form each word, what each word means, and how to use the words in sentences.

WRITE-ON CHARTS

Use **WRITE-ON CHART 31** to record and tally the favorite television show of the class.

TRANSPARENCY

Use **TRANSPARENCY 13.**

1. ACCESS

Tell children that you would like to see which television show is the favorite of the class. Invite them to brainstorm the names of several popular shows as you list them on the board, assigning each one a letter. Pass to each child one small piece of paper on which to write the letter of the show that is his or her favorite from among those listed. Have children fold the pieces of paper in half and insert them into a shoe box that you pass around. Invite several children to help announce the choices and tally them on the board. Beside the name of each show, write the number of children who chose it. At the top of the list, write the total number of children who made choices. Encourage children to tell what they can learn from the numbers in the list.

Q. **How can we figure out which television show is the most popular with this class?** Add the papers for each show. The show with the greatest number of papers is the most popular.

2. BUILD

Vocabulary

Have children read the introductory text on page 192. Explain that to *vote* means to make a choice known. Define *election* as a time when people make choices by voting. Point out that in an election each person votes once and that the choice that receives the most votes wins.

HOLIDAY ACTIVITIES

For information and activities related to Election Day, see the Holiday Activities section at the back of the Teacher's Edition.

Civics and Government

Political Institutions and Processes
Share the photos and the rest of the text on pages 192–193. Ask children to answer the questions in the text. Explain that most government leaders are elected. Point out that in some places, people vote using machines rather than paper ballots.

Q. **What happens to people's votes on Election Day?** They are counted, and the winners are decided by the highest number of votes.

Make a Choice by Voting

In our country, leaders like George Washington and Thomas Jefferson are chosen in an **election**. Here is how an election works.

Today is election day at Lincoln Elementary School. Each class will choose someone to send to a special student meeting. In an election, people **vote** to choose the person who will do a job for them.

1

When people vote, they think about who will do the best job. What choice do these children have?

Tina or Jake

192

2

One way to vote is to mark a piece of paper called a ballot. Each person may vote only once. How does the girl above show her choice? Why does she mark only one name on the ballot? She has only one vote, which she marks for Jake on the ballot.

ACTIVITY CHOICES

Community Involvement

Display a picture of a voting machine and explain how it works. If possible, arrange for children to explore an actual voting machine and look at actual ballots. Contact the voter registrar's office for sample ballots or mock election materials.

Home Involvement

Suggest that children ask older family members about their experiences of voting and the kinds of things for which they have voted. If possible, have children accompany family members to the polls for a firsthand look at the process.

Extend and Enrich

TALLY VOTES Set up an election in which the class chooses its favorite zoo animal or similar favorite. Ask children to decide upon the candidates or choices. Then help them prepare ballots. Encourage children to discuss the choices before they vote. Provide a box in which children can place their ballots. When everyone has voted, help children tally the votes to determine the winner.

3

How will the children decide who wins?

They counted the votes. The one with the most votes wins.

4

All voters agree to accept the winner.

Think and Do

Make a list of the reasons you would vote for someone in an election.

193

Reteach the Skill

VOTE FOR A CLASS PET Invite children to pretend that they are going to vote on the best pet for a classroom. Provide three choices, such as a hamster, a gerbil, and a fish. Then suggest that children make a list of pros and cons for each pet to help them decide which choice is the best. Provide children with ballots and allow time for them to vote. Help a volunteer count the votes and then share the results. Tell children that the animal with the highest number of votes wins.

TECHNOLOGY

Use **GRAPH LINKS** to complete this activity.

Rights and Responsibilities Select a classroom job, like that of class treasurer, and have children list the qualities they think a child should have to do that job. Explain that all voters have the responsibility of learning about the candidates' qualifications for the job before deciding how to vote. Point out some poor reasons for casting a vote for a person, such as liking the person's looks.

Q. **How can voters get ready for elections?** listen to speeches, read newspapers, watch television

3. CLOSE

Think and Do

Children's answers should indicate that they would vote for a person if they think he or she would do a good job.

Review the skill with children by asking the following question:

Q. **Suppose we want to choose a school mascot. How would voting help us decide which one to choose?** Voting would tell us which mascot more children like.

Using the Activity Book Distribute copies of Activity Book page 38. Have children count the ballots and determine where the class will go on their trip.

Activity Book page 38

LESSON 1 • **193**

HANDS-ON OPTION

Campaign Posters

Objectives: Recognize that voting is one way to choose leaders. Describe what determines a winning vote.

Materials: posterboard, crayons, markers

 Divide the class into four or five groups. Have each group imagine that its members are organizing a campaign to elect a class leader. Invite them to invent a name for their candidate. Then have them brainstorm a platform on which their candidate will run. Ask them to make a list of issues they think are important to the class and qualities needed to lead the class. Challenge the groups to write slogans for their candidates' campaigns. Then have each group create a poster for its candidate that illustrates its slogan or campaign issues. You may wish to hold a secret ballot to vote for the best campaign poster. **(AUDITORY/TACTILE)**

Take a Vote!

Objective: Explain the idea of one person, one vote.

Materials: Write-On Chart 15, chart paper

Review the lesson on Washington, D.C., in Unit 4 and Write-On Chart 15 about the Smithsonian Institution. Help children list on chart paper some places they would like to visit in the nation's capital. Ask the class to vote first to choose the top three favorites and then vote again to choose the overall class favorite. Use the voting process to make clear that each person can vote only once in an election and that one vote can sometimes make the difference to a candidate's or on an issue's winning. **(AUDITORY)**

The Voting Center

Objective: Describe what determines a winning vote.

Materials: shoe box, paper, posterboard

Set up an interactive voting center in the classroom similar to the one shown here. Hang a poster in the voting center titled *Vote of the Day, by. . .* Have children take turns being responsible for determining what the class should vote on each day. The volunteer should complete the phrase by writing his or her name at the top of a sheet of paper, writing a voting question, and hanging the paper in the voting center. The volunteer can draw pictures to illustrate the vote, or he or she might want to display things from home to show what will be voted on, such as pictures of musicians or sports figures, toys, or foods. At the end of each day, count the votes and display the results. **(TACTILE)**

Vote of the Day, by:

Kara

Vote for your favorite sport:

Baseball   Basketball   Kickball

★ VOTING QUESTION	RESULTS
What's your favorite color?	Blue
Should pizza be served more often in the lunchroom?	Yes
What should our classroom mascot be?	A tiger
What is your favorite sport?	

2

OUR COUNTRY'S GOVERNMENT

OBJECTIVES

1. Identify the three branches of our country's government.
2. List the main responsibility of each branch of government.
3. Describe the role of judges in solving problems.

VOCABULARY

government (p. 194)
judge (p. 196)

RESOURCES

Pupil Book/Unit Big Book, pp. 194–197
Write-On Charts 18, 26
Vocabulary Blacklines
Vocabulary Cards
Activity Book, p. 39
Transparency 14
The Amazing Writing Machine

ACTIVITY CHOICES

Meet Individual Needs

VISUAL LEARNERS Invite children to make a booklet titled *Rules and Laws*. Ask children to draw and label two pages each for rules at school, rules at home, and laws. Bind the pages and invite children to read the booklet in pairs.

TRANSPARENCY

Use **TRANSPARENCY 14** to locate Washington, D.C.

TECHNOLOGY

Invite children to watch Congress in action on C-SPAN, a television cable service. C-SPAN in the classroom is a free membership service for educators. To join, call 1-800-523-7586.

1. ACCESS

Help children recall what they learned about Washington, D.C., in Unit 4. Display pictures of the White House, the Capitol Building, and other landmarks in Washington, D.C. Invite children to name the places they recognize and tell what they know about them. Help children locate the nation's capital on a map.

Focus on the Main Idea

In this lesson children will be introduced to the basic structure of the federal government. They will identify the three branches of government and list the purpose of each branch. They will focus on the role of judges in government. Tell children they will see a mobile, made by other children, that shows how the different parts of government share responsibilities.

2. BUILD

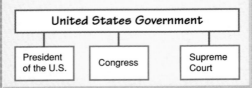

Key Content Summary

The United States government is divided into three branches that make and carry out the laws of our country. The Constitution describes the jobs of each branch and the role of our government.

Vocabulary

Define *government* as the people who make and carry out laws. Tell children that this lesson is about the national government, the government for the whole country.

History

People and Events Across Time and Place Share the text on page 194. Invite children to tell what they know about the Constitution. Tell children that the original of the Constitution is on display at the National Archives in Washington, D.C. Explain that the Constitution was written to tell how our government should be organized and run.

LESSON

2 Our Country's Government

My class is learning about the people who make laws and lead our country. These groups of people are our **government**.

The Constitution is the highest law in our country. It protects all the people of the United States. The Constitution tells about the three branches, or parts, of our government. Each branch has its own job to do. We are making a mobile to show the branches of our government.

The President is in one branch of our government. The President leads our country. The President chooses people to help and to give advice. They work together in the White House. Do you know the name of our President?

194

ACTIVITY CHOICES

Reading Support

IDENTIFY THE MAIN IDEA As you read the lesson with children, create a chart to show the branches of the government. You might want to include on your chart a picture and a label for each branch.

United States Government		
President of the U.S.	Congress	Supreme Court

Background

THE CONSTITUTION The United States Constitution was written in 1787 and accepted in 1788. It separates federal powers into three distinct branches—no one more powerful than the others. The Constitution has been amended only 27 times.

THE NATIONAL ARCHIVES The National Archives and Records Administration stores records dating back to 1774, including the Declaration of Independence and the Constitution. All records are available to the public.

Congress is another branch of government. Members of Congress make new laws. These lawmakers come from communities all over the country. They vote for the laws they think we need.

195

PUPIL BOOK OR UNIT BIG BOOK

Link Literature

Read aloud the book *A More Perfect Union: The Story of Our Constitution* by Betsy and Giulio Maestro. (Lothrop, Lee & Shepard, 1987) This book tells of the birth of the Constitution and the adoption of the Bill of Rights. After reading the book, work with children using Write-On Chart 26 to make a time line depicting the events that led up to the signing of the document.

VOCABULARY CARDS

Invite partners to use the lesson VOCABULARY PICTURE CARDS to challenge each other to use each word in a sentence.

❝PRIMARY SOURCE❞

The Constitution begins with the Preamble:

We the people of the United States, in order to form a more perfect Union, establish justice, insure domestic tranquillity, provide for the common defense, promote the general welfare, and secure the blessings of liberty to ourselves and our posterity, do ordain and establish this Constitution for the United States of America.

Civics and Government

Political Institutions and Processes Ask for volunteers to read the text on pages 194 and 195 and to describe the first two branches of government. Ask children to tell what the name of the current President is and what they know about the work the President does. Point out that the people who work in the President's office make sure that laws are obeyed. Explain that Congress has two houses—the Senate and the House of Representatives. Tell children that the people of each state select people to represent them in Congress, and that all the laws for the United States are made by the people who serve in Congress.

Q. **How is the job of a lawmaker different from that of the President?** A lawmaker makes and passes laws. The President makes sure those laws are obeyed.

Vocabulary

Explain to children that a *judge* is someone in government who decides what laws mean and whether laws have been broken. Tell them that there are judges at all levels of government but that in this lesson they will be learning about nine special judges, called *justices*, who work in Washington, D.C.

VOCABULARY BLACKLINES

Distribute the individual word cards for the lesson, which are in the back of the Teacher's Edition. On the back of each card, children should write a description of the word on the front.

Civics and Government

Political Institutions and Processes Share the photos and text on pages 196–197. Tell children that these nine people are the judges, or justices, who make up the Supreme Court—the third branch of the federal government. Explain that it is their job to make sure the laws passed by Congress agree with the United States Constitution. They also decide whether laws have been enforced fairly. Explain that these justices are not elected but are chosen by the President and approved by the Senate. They serve for their lifetimes or until they wish to retire.

Q. **What qualities do you think a judge should have?** fairness, good listening skills, intelligence

Why do you think there is an odd number of justices on the Supreme Court? When they vote, there cannot be a tie.

3. CLOSE

Ask children to summarize the lesson by telling what they know about the jobs of the President, Congress, and the Supreme Court. Invite them to tell which branch of government they would like to work in and why.

The Supreme Court is also a branch of our government. It is the highest court in the United States. A court is where judges work. **Judges** tell us if laws are fair and decide if laws have been broken.

Supreme Court Building

196

History

Parthenon

The people of Greece built this temple more than 2,000 years ago. The Supreme Court is much newer. It was built in 1936. How does the Supreme Court building look like the Parthenon?

ACTIVITY CHOICES

Extend and Enrich

CHORAL READING Write on the board the Preamble to the Constitution. (See "Primary Source" on page 195.) Explain that the Preamble is the opening part of the Constitution and that it explains why early leaders wrote the Constitution. Then lead the class in a choral reading of the Preamble.

Link to Language Arts

JOURNAL Ask children to imagine they are grown up and can choose to be President, a member of Congress, or a Supreme Court justice. Ask them to record in their journals which they would choose to be and why.

WRITE A LETTER Help children find out the names of their senators and representatives. Invite children to write letters to those leaders, inquiring about what they are doing in Congress.

TECHNOLOGY

Use **THE AMAZING WRITING MACHINE™** to complete the writing activities.

There are nine judges in the Supreme Court. They are called justices. Sandra Day O'Connor was the first woman to be a Supreme Court justice.

The President, the Congress, and the Supreme Court are in Washington, D.C. All three branches of the government work together to lead our country.

What Do You Know?

1. **Who makes the laws in our country?** Congress

2. **Why is it important to have good leaders?** They help us make our country a good place to live.

The Supreme Court Justices

Ruth Bader Ginsburg

William H. Rehnquist

Anthony M. Kennedy

David H. Souter

John Paul Stevens

Sandra Day O'Connor

Clarence Thomas

Stephen G. Breyer

Antonin Scalia

197

PUPIL BOOK OR UNIT BIG BOOK

Reteach the Main Idea

MATCH THE BRANCHES Prepare a set of three index cards labeled *President*, *Congress*, and *Supreme Court*. Prepare a second set of cards to describe the main job of each branch of government, such as *leads the country*, *makes laws*, and *decides if laws are fair*. Scramble the cards and have children match each branch of government with the main job it does.

WRITE-ON CHARTS

The People's Government
Use WRITE-ON CHART 18 to extend and enrich this lesson. See Teacher's Edition page W56.

Check Understanding

The child can
—— identify the three branches of our country's government.
—— list the main responsibility of each branch of government.
—— describe the role of judges in solving problems.

Think Critically

Q. **Why do you think there is more than one person responsible for making and carrying out laws in our government?** The job is too big for one person; it has too much power for one person; the laws will be fairer.

Show What You Know

 Performance Assessment Ask children to create their own mobiles to illustrate the three branches of government. Invite them to draw their own pictures or cut them from newspapers and magazines.

What to Look For To evaluate children's mobiles, note whether they include at least one thing to represent each branch of the government and whether all items are organized by the branch they represent.

Using the Activity Book Invite children to complete the puzzle on Activity Book page 39 by reading the clues and referring to the words in the word box.

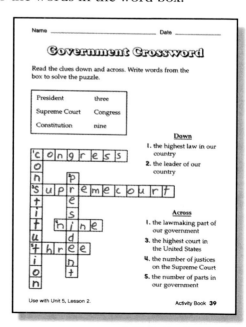

Activity Book page 39

HANDS-ON OPTION

Help Wanted

Objectives: Identify the three branches of our country's government. List the main responsibility of each branch of government.

Materials: research materials, paper, pencils

Organize children into three cooperative groups to research the three branches of government. Assign each group a different branch. Help children brainstorm a list of questions they might answer in their research, such as *What are the President's jobs? Where does the President live? Who can run for President? How long does the job last? What are the jobs of lawmakers in Congress? Where do senators and representatives live? Where do they work? What are the names of the nine justices on the Supreme Court? Where do they live and work? How long have they served?* Then ask children within the groups to select specific questions to research. They might present their findings in the form of want ads, which can be shared with the class. **(TACTILE)**

Help Wanted

Wanted: President of the United States.

Must be a native U.S. citizen, age 35 or over.

Must be able to live in Washington, D.C. and work long hours.

Duties include

You Be the Judge

Objective: Describe the role of judges in solving problems.

Materials: paper, pencils, craft sticks, crayons, markers, glue

Invite children to make craft-stick puppets of judges. Then ask children to recall the story of "The Three Bears" and to list the things Goldilocks did. (She went into the bears' house uninvited, she ate their food, she broke a chair, she slept in a bear's bed, and she ran away when the bears found her.) Invite children to work in small groups to create finger plays in which they judge Goldilocks's actions. Have them decide whether they think Goldilocks broke any laws. Suggest to children that they share their group's decisions with the class. **(AUDITORY/KINESTHETIC/TACTILE)**

In the News

Objectives: Identify the three branches of our country's government. List the main responsibility of each branch of government.

Materials: newspapers, news magazines

Create a bulletin board display titled *In the News* with the following headings: *The President, The Congress, The Supreme Court.* Invite children to skim through news magazines and daily newspapers for photos and reports of our government at work. Suggest that children clip these photos and reports and post them on the bulletin board under the appropriate heading. **(TACTILE/VISUAL)**

Skills

FIND CAPITALS ON A MAP

OBJECTIVES

1. Define *boundary*.
2. Identify states and their capitals.
3. Use cardinal directions to describe locations on a map.

VOCABULARY

state (p. 198)
boundary (p. 198)

RESOURCES

Pupil Book/Unit Big Book, pp. 198–199

Write-on Chart 19

Activity Book, p. 40

Transparency 14

Desk Maps

Music Audio, "Fifty Nifty United States"

Trudy's Time and Place House

ACTIVITY CHOICES

Meet Individual Needs

TACTILE LEARNERS Provide children with a puzzle map of the United States. You might make your own puzzle by mounting a United States map on posterboard and cutting apart the states. As children put the puzzle together, they can learn the names, sizes, shapes, and locations of the states.

VISUAL LEARNERS Provide children with maps showing the states and their capitals. Then invite children to play the game "What's My Capital?" with partners. Children take turns naming a state and having a partner name and point out the capital of that state.

AUDIO

Use the UNIT 5 MUSIC AUDIOCASSETTE to teach children the song "Fifty Nifty United States."

DESK MAPS

Use United States DESK MAPS to help children locate and learn the different shapes of the 50 states.

1. ACCESS

Explain to children that our country is divided into 50 areas of land called *states*. Invite children to locate and name as many states as they can, using their Desk Maps. Write the states' names on the board as they are given. Then teach children the song "Fifty Nifty United States." After learning the song, children may be able to add to the list. Encourage children to share anything they know about the states. They might share their experiences in states they have visited or tell about favorite teams or athletes who play in certain states.

Q. **How would you describe your state to someone who lived in another state?** Children's responses might include the location of the state, the geography, something about the people, and any landmarks and points of interest.

Help children recall that Washington, D.C., is our nation's capital. Remind them that a *capital* is a city where a government is located. Point out that each state has a capital city. Ask children to name the capital of their state. Use the list of state names on the board to prompt children to name any other state capitals they know.

2. BUILD

Vocabulary

Have children use their fingers to trace the outlines of their own state and neighboring states on the map. Explain that the outline of each state is its boundary. Point out that a *boundary* shows where one state ends and another begins. Explain that a map helps people know where boundaries are located.

Geography

Location Share with children the text on pages 198–199. Remind them that one way people find things on a map is by using a compass rose. Have children respond to step 3. Lead children to understand that if they are facing north, south is behind them, east is to their right, and west is to their left. Explain that by pointing north, a compass rose acts like a real compass. Have children identify each direction on the map, using this rule.

Q. **What would you do if the compass rose only showed which way is north?** All you need to know is north. South is always the opposite direction, east is to the right as you face north, and west is to the left as you face north.

Find Capitals on a Map

Our country has fifty **states**. This map of the United States shows the boundary of each state. A **boundary** is the line around a state. It shows where the state begins and ends. Each state also has a capital city for its own government.

1 Find the map key. What symbol stands for a state capital? Find your state on the map. What is its capital city? What is the name of our country's capital?
The state capital symbol is a star. Washington, D.C., is **198** our country's capital.

Map Key

⊛ National capital
★ State capital
— Boundary

ACTIVITY CHOICES

Meet Individual Needs

TACTILE LEARNERS Invite partners to play a game in which one child silently chooses a place on the map and guides the partner to it with directions such as *Move your finger north from Texas to North Dakota, go west to the next state, and move to the capital city of that state.* The partner must follow the directions to identify the chosen place.

Link to Physical Education

PHYSICAL EDUCATION Label the walls in your classroom to indicate *north, south, east,* and *west.* Go over the directions with children. Then play a game of "Simon Says," using the directions in your commands. For example, you might give commands such as these: *Simon says face north and hop. Simon says face east and march in place. Simon says face west and touch your toes.*

Extend and Enrich

MAKE A FACT BOOK Invite children to do research and create a class book titled *Fun Facts About the Fifty States.* They might include the names of state capitals, birds, and flowers; facts about population and land; and unusual and interesting facts.

TRANSPARENCY

Use **TRANSPARENCY 14.**

2 Find the compass rose at the bottom of the map. Remember, a compass rose gives the directions on a map.

3 Point to your state on the map. Tell what is north, south, east, and west of your state. What is the capital of each of your neighbor states?

United States

Think and Do

Find Georgia. What is the capital of the state that is west of Georgia?

199

Reteach the Skill

FIND CAPITALS Display Transparency 14. Help children identify north, south, east, and west on the map. Invite volunteers to trace the outline of the United States with their fingers. Then ask them to point to states in each direction. Review the definition of *capital* and call attention to the capital symbol on the map. Ask for a volunteer to locate your state and name the capital city. Then name other states, having children locate them on the map and identify the capital cities.

WRITE-ON CHARTS

State Flags
Use WRITE-ON CHART 19 to extend and enrich this lesson. See Teacher's Edition page W59.

TECHNOLOGY

Use TRUDY'S TIME AND PLACE HOUSE to reinforce finding directions.

3. CLOSE

Think and Do

Children should recognize that Montgomery is the capital of the state west of Georgia.

Review the skill with children by asking the following questions:

Q. **What is the location of your state?** Children should use cardinal directions in their responses and describe the state's location in relation to the entire country, neighboring states, or bodies of water.

What is the name of a state you have visited or would like to visit? What is the name of its capital city?

What is the name of our nation's capital? Describe its location. Washington, D.C., is our capital. It is in the eastern part of the United States. It is east of Virginia, west of Maryland, and south of Pennsylvania.

Using the Activity Book Distribute copies of Activity Book page 40. Have children answer the questions, using the compass rose as a guide.

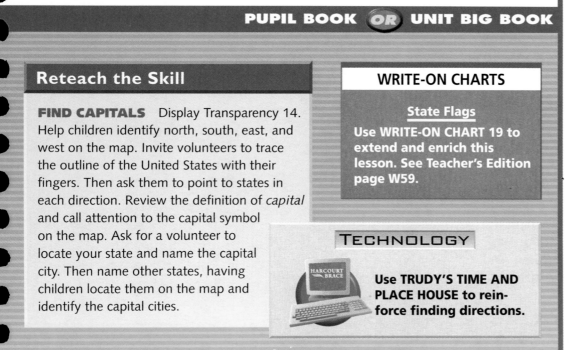

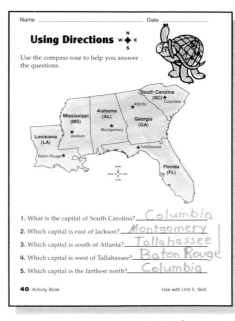

Activity Book page 40

HANDS-ON OPTION

A New Country

Objective: Define *boundary*.

Materials: Pattern P1, crayons or markers

Organize children into cooperative groups. Invite each group to use the Puzzle Pattern to draw and color a map of a make-believe country. Explain that each puzzle piece can be a state in their new country. Tell them to outline each piece with a dark marker to represent that state's boundary. Remind groups to name their new country and its states. Children might also like to name and show the location of state capitals and identify state birds and flowers. Invite a volunteer from each group to trace the outlines of the states with a finger as he or she shares the completed map with the class. (TACTILE/VISUAL)

On the Map

Objectives: Identify boundaries. Identify states and their capitals. Use cardinal directions to describe locations on a map.

Materials: slips of paper, paper bag, United States wall map showing the states and their capitals

Write the letters *N*, *S*, *E*, and *W* on slips of paper—enough for each child to have one—and place them in a paper bag. Display a wall map of the United States showing the states and their capitals. Ask each child to reach into the bag and pull out a letter. Have children take turns approaching the map and identifying a state that is in the north, south, east, or west, depending on the letter drawn. Help children read the names of the states they choose and the capitals.

(AUDITORY/KINESTHETIC)

Classroom Directions

Objective: Use cardinal directions to describe locations.

Materials: compass, craft paper, crayons, markers

Introduce children to a compass, and allow them to become familiar with it. Help them locate true north in the classroom, and invite them to make a large sign that says *North* to mark that end of the room. Then help children locate south, east, and west in the classroom, and have them create and place other direction signs. Show them how the compass compares with the compass rose on a map. Children can use their direction signs to play a game of "I Spy," using the words *north, south, east,* and *west* to describe where objects are in the room.
(KINESTHETIC/TACTILE/VISUAL)

A Compass Rose Garden

Objective: Use cardinal directions to describe locations on a map.

Materials: United States wall map, drawing paper, crayons or markers

Show children several examples of a compass rose. Then invite them to design their own compass roses. Encourage them to be creative, but remind them to include the letter labels *N*, *S*, *E*, and *W* for North, South, East, and West. Arrange their compass roses around a United States wall map, each with its north end pointing up. Title the display *A Compass Rose Garden*. Challenge volunteers to describe the locations of states and state capitals, using the compass roses for reference. (AUDITORY/TACTILE/VISUAL)

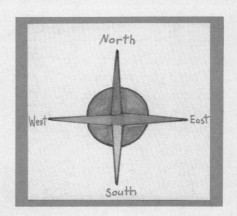

3

COMMUNITY GOVERNMENT

OBJECTIVES

1. Identify how governing bodies such as school boards and city councils affect our lives.

2. Describe the need for good government and the role citizens can play in achieving it.

VOCABULARY

mayor (p. 201)

RESOURCES

Pupil Book/Unit Big Book, pp. 200–201

Write-On Chart 27

Activity Book, p. 41

ACTIVITY CHOICES

Meet Individual Needs

VISUAL AND AUDITORY LEARNERS Invite children to watch and listen to news broadcasts on television and radio. Encourage them to watch for news about the local government. Ask children to share with the class what they learn about local government in action.

WRITE-ON CHARTS

Use WRITE-ON CHART 27 to organize a government word web.

Home Involvement

Encourage children to accompany a family member to a local community meeting, like a Parent-Teacher Association or ward meeting. Invite children to report their impressions of what was accomplished at the meeting.

Community Involvement

Invite a member of your local school board to visit the class to talk about his or her job or to take the class to visit the city or town hall for a meeting with the mayor or another government leader. Prepare children by discussing the kinds of questions they might ask.

1. ACCESS

Begin a word web by writing *government* in the center circle. Ask children what groups help lead or govern their community. Write *United States government*, *state government*, and *city government* or *local government* and any other groups they suggest.

Q. **Why do people need local governments as well as the United States government?** The United States government makes laws for the whole country. Local governments make laws about things that affect only local communities.

Focus on the Main Idea

In this lesson children will explore local governments. They will see how citizens can initiate changes, and they will study the role of local ruling bodies such as school boards and city councils. Tell children that in this lesson they will see how the citizens of one community got a new playground.

2. BUILD

Key Content Summary

A persuasive letter provides an example of how citizens can initiate change in a community.

Civics and Government

Purposes and Types of Government
Read pages 200–201. Ask children to explain what the people had to do to get a new playground.

Q. **Why do you think they asked a lot of people to sign the letter?**
so that the school board would see that many people wanted a new playground

Describe for children several types of community leaders. Explain that a school board is a group of elected citizens that makes decisions about things that affect the schools in a community; that in cities and towns with a *mayor*, it is the mayor's job to lead the people and enforce the laws of the community; and that city or town councils are made up of men and women who make the laws for a community.

3. CLOSE

Ask children to summarize the lesson by telling in their own words how citizens of a community can make a difference.

LESSON 3 Community Government

Citizens can work together to make changes. Last year our school needed a new playground. We wanted to use an empty lot near the school. Maya's dad helped us write a letter. We asked our teachers, parents, and neighbors to sign it.

1. This is the empty lot.

2. Maya's dad helped us write a letter.

3. People signed the letter.

200

ACTIVITY CHOICES

Reading Support

READ AHEAD As children read the lesson, help them with the meanings of unfamiliar words, such as *mayor*, by asking them to continue reading. Explain that often they can learn the meanings of new words by reading the sentences that follow.

Extend and Enrich

ROLE-PLAY If possible, display a diagram detailing how the local government is organized and listing some responsibilities of each person or group. Then assign children roles like news reporter, council member, and citizen. Have them role-play news conferences in which local leaders tell how their decisions will affect the community.

Link Literature

Read aloud *Pearl Moscowitz's Last Stand* by Arthur A. Levine. (Tambourine, 1993) In this story Pearl takes a stand when the city government tries to chop down the last gingko tree on her street. Invite children to discuss ways citizens can take a stand on issues.

Noel's mom gave the letter to the school board. The school board held a meeting. Many people came to the meeting to listen and speak. The school board voted to buy the empty lot.

Citizens worked together to build the playground. The mayor started the job. The **mayor** is one of our city leaders.

My teacher says we are lucky to live in the United States. Citizens can make changes in their schools, communities, states, and country.

4. The school board voted.

5. The mayor started the job.

What Do You Know?

1. Who are some community leaders? mayor, school board

2. How can you work with your leaders?

PUPIL BOOK OR UNIT BIG BOOK

Reteach the Main Idea

SUMMARIZE NEWS ARTICLE Display a local newspaper clipping that tells about the school board, the city council, or a local government agency. Summarize the article and discuss how each group can affect children.

Link to Health

COMMUNITY HEALTH List on the board local leaders like the following: police chief, fire chief, health inspector, safety director, and environmental inspector. Help children investigate the jobs of these workers to find out how they protect citizens.

Check Understanding

The child can
—— identify how governing bodies such as school boards and city councils affect our lives.
—— describe the need for good government and the role citizens can play in achieving it.

Think Critically

Q. **What would happen if the citizens of a community did not like the decisions made by the school board or city council?** The citizens could vote the leaders out of office or write them letters or make phone calls.

Show What You Know

Performance Assessment Have children write a letter to the principal to persuade him or her to make a change in their school.

What to Look For To evaluate children's letters, note whether they clearly stated a realistic situation they would like to see changed, included how they would like it changed, and gave persuasive reasons why it should be changed.

Using the Activity Book Distribute Activity Book page 41. Tell children that school boards have a set amount of money— a budget—with which to work. Have children write a letter describing one of their choices and their reasons for making it.

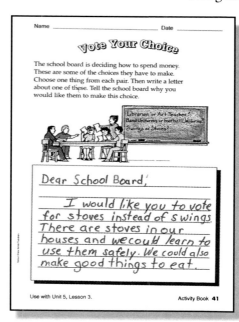

Activity Book page 41

HANDS-ON OPTION

Government in Action

Objective: Describe the need for good government and the role citizens can play in achieving it.

Materials: local telephone directory, paper, pencils

Help children find listings for various departments of the city or town government in the local telephone directory. Talk about the departments listed and the services they provide. Suggest that children make a list of names and phone numbers for services they have benefited from in the past or think they might benefit from in the future to place in their journals. **(TACTILE/VISUAL)**

Government Scrapbook

Objective: Identify how governing bodies such as school boards and city councils affect our lives.

Materials: newspapers, scissors, paste or tape, construction paper

Provide children with local newspapers and help them find and clip out articles about the local government, including articles about the mayor, city council, and school board. Children can mount the articles on construction paper and put the pages together to make a scrapbook. **(TACTILE/VISUAL)**

The Campaign Trail

Objectives: Identify how governing bodies such as school boards and city councils affect our lives. Describe the need for good government and the role citizens can play in achieving it.

Materials: posterboard, markers

 Suggest that children pretend some of their classmates are candidates for mayor, school board members, or other local offices. Organize children into cooperative groups to make campaign posters for the candidates. Encourage groups to create slogans for each candidate and to list campaign promises. Point out to children that they should keep in mind everything they have learned about voting and leadership qualities. **(TACTILE/VISUAL)**

Kids Take Action

Objective: Describe the need for good government and the role citizens can play in it.

Materials: paper, pencils

Present children with a real or hypothetical community issue, such as community leaders' wanting to turn a city swimming pool into a parking lot or the school board's wanting to hold school on Saturdays. Invite children to write a letter to persuade community leaders or the school board not to follow through with their plans. **(AUDITORY/TACTILE)**

Skills

UNDERSTAND WHAT PEOPLE THINK

OBJECTIVES

1. Distinguish fact from opinion.
2. Recognize the rights of people to hold different opinions.

RESOURCES

Pupil Book/Unit Big Book, pp. 202–203
Activity Book, p. 42
Transparency 15
The Amazing Writing Machine

1. ACCESS

Read the following statements one at a time to the class:

George Washington was the first President of the United States.
The United States is the best country in the world.
There are three branches to our nation's government.
The White House is the nicest building in Washington, D.C.

After you read each sentence, ask children whether the statement can be proved.

Q. Why can we not prove these statements: *The United States is the best country in the world; the White House is the nicest building in Washington, D.C.?* because they tell how a person thinks or feels, and people think and feel differently

ACTIVITY CHOICES

Link to Reading

READ A BIOGRAPHY Ask the school librarian to provide age-appropriate biographies of people who played important roles in forming our nation and government. Invite children to choose biographies and present oral reports on the people they read about. Encourage children to include information about the person that can be proved, as well as their thoughts and feelings about the person and his or her accomplishments.

Link to Language Arts

JOURNAL Ask children to choose their favorite of something, such as a favorite food, sports team, or color. Invite them to write a paragraph in which they try to persuade the reader to adopt the same favorite. Encourage children to be descriptive and use specifics, including statements that can be proved and others that cannot.

TECHNOLOGY

Use THE AMAZING WRITING MACHINE™ RESOURCE PACKAGE to complete the writing activity.

2. BUILD

Critical Thinking

Explain that a *fact* is a statement that is true or tells something that has actually happened. Point out that an *opinion* is what a person thinks or feels about something. Have children read the text and answer the questions on pages 202–203.

Q. **How can you tell the difference between the facts and the opinions in Mr. Wilson's letter?** The facts, such as *I live in the building next to the empty lot*, can be proved. The opinions cannot be proved because they are based on Mr. Wilson's feelings.

Culture

Thought and Expression Open a discussion about the importance of being able to have and express opinions. Introduce the importance of learning new facts to help form or change opinions. Invite children to tell about times when they changed their minds because they had learned something new.

Q. **Why might someone's opinions be different from yours?** People's opinions are based on what they know and feel, and not all people know the same things or feel the same way about things.

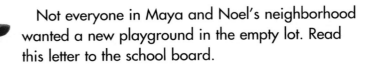

Critical Thinking Skills

Understand What People Think

Not everyone in Maya and Noel's neighborhood wanted a new playground in the empty lot. Read this letter to the school board.

April 12, 1999

Dear Members of the School Board,

I live in the building next to an empty lot. The lot has been for sale for many months. I know that you want to buy it for a playground. I think that is a bad idea. Children make too much noise. I think they will also leave trash on the ground. I hope you will put your playground somewhere else. Thank you.

Sincerely,
John Wilson

202

ACTIVITY CHOICES

Link to Language Arts

ORAL LANGUAGE Write words such as dogs, colors, fruits, and sports on index cards or slips of paper. Place the cards in a box or paper bag. Ask volunteers to select a card and read what it says. Have each volunteer make up two statements about the subject on the card. One statement should be a fact and the other should be an opinion. Ask classmates to categorize the statements.

Link to Science

OBSERVATION Invite children to observe something in your classroom, such as plants or classroom pets. Ask them to list or tell their observations. Then discuss which are facts and which are opinions.

TRANSPARENCY

Use TRANSPARENCY 15.

Extend and Enrich

EVALUATE ADVERTISEMENTS Organize children into small groups and give each group a food advertisement. Ask group members to make a list of facts mentioned in the ad and to tell where they could check them. Then ask them to list the opinions mentioned in the ad.

People often have strong feelings about things. They want others to listen to their ideas. Sometimes they tell facts, or true statements. Sometimes they give opinions. Opinions tell what people think. People often have different opinions.

1 Read Mr. Wilson's letter. What does he feel strongly about?

2 What facts does he give about the empty lot?

3 What opinions does he have about children? How can you tell?

Think and Do

- Work with a partner.
- Write your own letter to the school board.
- Give two facts and two opinions about why the playground should be built on the empty lot.

203

PUPIL BOOK OR UNIT BIG BOOK

Reteach the Skill

WRITE FACTS AND OPINIONS
Invite children to each write one sentence stating something they know about their school and one stating something they think about their school. Display a sign that says *Facts* and one that says *Opinions*. Ask children to read their sentences aloud and to post the sentences under the appropriate signs.

Home Involvement

Ask children and family members to watch a favorite television commercial together. Suggest that they list and discuss the facts and opinions it contains. Invite children to share what they learn.

Q. **How can citizens express their opinions in our country?** by voting, by writing and calling lawmakers, by speaking out at government meetings, by writing to newspapers and magazines

3. CLOSE

Think and Do

Invite children to give facts and opinions about why the playground should be built. Ask children how they could prove the facts.

Review the skill with children by asking the following questions:

Q. **Which of these is a fact and which is an opinion?** *Our classroom has six windows. I think our classroom is the cheeriest room on the floor.* **How do you know?** The first sentence is a fact; we can count the windows to prove it. The second sentence is an opinion because it tells what somebody thinks.

Using the Activity Book Distribute copies of Activity Book page 42. Have children write *fact* or *opinion* next to each sentence. Then have them write a fact and an opinion of their own about their state or local community.

Name _____ Date _____

Fact or Opinion

Write **fact** or **opinion** for each sentence

1. Pennsylvania is one of the 50 states.
   fact
2. Pennsylvania is the best state to visit.
   opinion
3. The city of Philadelphia is in Pennsylvania.
   fact
4. You can see the Liberty Bell in Philadelphia.
   fact
5. The capital of Pennsylvania is Harrisburg.
   fact
6. If you visit Pennsylvania, you should go by airplane.
   opinion

Write a fact and an opinion about your state or community

Fact: _Oranges grow in Florida._

Opinion: _It is the best state!_

42 Activity Book   Use with Unit 5, Skill.

Activity Book page 42

HANDS-ON OPTION

Express Your Opinions Book

Objective: Recognize the right of people to hold different opinions.

Materials: heavy drawing paper, crayons or markers, colored pencils, newspapers, magazines, scissors, glue

Organize children into cooperative groups, and invite each group to create an "Express Your Opinions" book. Ask each group to brainstorm ways people in the United States can express their opinions, such as by writing letters and making speeches. Each group member should make one page for the book. Some can draw pictures of people expressing opinions. Others can cut out from magazines and newspapers pictures of people expressing their opinions. One child can design the cover for the book, and another can collect and bind the pages. Place each group's book in the reading center for children to review. (TACTILE/VISUAL)

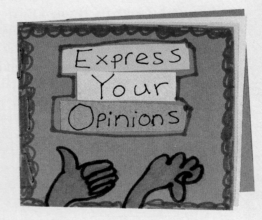

Is That a Fact?

Objective: Distinguish fact from opinion.

Materials: drawing paper, crayons or markers

Invite children to draw pictures of something they like, such as a favorite sport, animal, food, or person. Ask them to write on the back of their paper three facts and three opinions about the subject of the drawing, such as *I have a fish* and *I have the best fish*. Invite partners to play a game in which one child holds up his or her drawing and reads either a fact or an opinion. The other child then categorizes the statement as opinion or fact. (AUDITORY/TACTILE)

Fact or Opinion?

Objective: Distinguish fact from opinion.

Materials: sentence strips, large envelopes, pencils

Organize children into groups of five, and provide each group with ten sentence strips and an envelope. Ask each group to choose a topic, such as a favorite book, vacation spot, or television show, and write the name of the topic on the outside of the envelope. Then have children write five opinions and five facts about the topic on the sentence strips. Tell them to place the sentence strips in the envelopes and trade envelopes with another group. Children can take turns pulling a sentence strip from the envelope, reading it aloud, and deciding whether the statement is a fact or an opinion. (AUDITORY/TACTILE)

OUR FREEDOMS

OBJECTIVES

1. Explore the idea of freedom in America.
2. Identify freedoms that United States citizens enjoy.
3. Identify people who have worked for freedoms.
4. Recognize that people can use their freedoms to make a difference.

VOCABULARY
freedom (p. 204)

RESOURCES
Pupil Book/Unit Big Book, pp. 204–207
Write-On Charts 20, 29
Activity Book, p. 43
Video, Reading Rainbow, *Amazing Grace*

ACTIVITY CHOICES

Background

ATHENS, GREECE Many scholars consider Athens, Greece, to be the birthplace of democracy. Democracy began to develop in ancient Greece as early as 500 B.C. In fact, the word *democracy* comes from the Greek words *demos*, which means "people," and *kratos*, which means "rule" or "authority." When the people of Athens adopted a new constitution around 508 B.C., their new political system provided every qualified citizen with a chance to help run the city government. People were given the right to choose their leaders in annual elections. They could also vote to get rid of bad leaders. However, democracy in ancient Athens differed in major ways from democracy today. All citizens voted directly rather than by electing representatives to vote for them.

THE BILL OF RIGHTS Ten amendments, or changes, were officially added to the Constitution on September 25, 1791. These amendments make up the Bill of Rights. They guarantee us certain freedoms, such as freedom of speech, freedom of religion, and freedom of the press.

1. ACCESS

Ask each child to name his or her favorite place to eat and to tell why it is his or her favorite. Remind children that they have just stated opinions.

Q. **How would you feel if someone told you it was against the law to tell what you think?** I would be worried. I would think it was unfair.

What do we have in the United States that allows us to tell what we think? a fair government; good laws

Explain to children that in some countries people are not allowed to tell what they think. Point out that in the United States we are allowed to tell what we think about anything because of the Bill of Rights.

Focus on the Main Idea

In this lesson children will learn about the meaning of freedom. They will discover what some of our freedoms are, that some freedoms are given by the Bill of Rights, and why these freedoms are important to us. They will also learn about people who have helped others gain certain freedoms.

2. BUILD

Key Content Summary

Discovering the freedoms that we have today will help children appreciate the people who have fought for our freedoms in the past. Children will also come to realize that these freedoms are as important to citizens of the United States today as they were when the Bill of Rights was added to the Constitution.

Vocabulary

Define *freedoms* as the rights people have to do the things they want to do, as long as they don't interfere with the freedoms of others. Point out that we often refer to our freedoms as our rights.

Q. **What are some of the things you enjoy choosing to do?** I enjoy choosing what to eat and wear, what to watch on television, and what to play with my friends. I can choose to play soccer or take music lessons.

Civics and Government

Patriotic Identity Ask volunteers to each read aloud one of the picture captions on pages 204–205. Point out that these are four of the freedoms listed in the Bill of Rights. Organize children into small groups. Ask each group to list these four freedoms and then to list under each at least one way the freedom lets them do

LESSON 4 Our Freedoms

People in our country have many freedoms. **Freedoms** are the rights people in the United States have to make their own choices. Patrick Henry was a famous leader who helped our country get its freedoms long ago. He loved freedom so much that he said, "Give me liberty or give me death!" Liberty is another word for freedom.

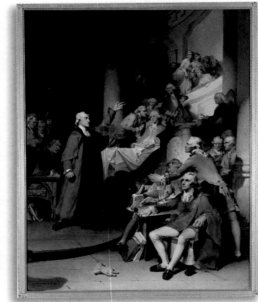

"Patrick Henry Before the Virginia House of Burgesses" by Peter F. Rothermel

204

Patrick Henry helped get the Bill of Rights added to the Constitution. The Bill of Rights lists the freedoms that Americans have.

> Freedom of speech

ACTIVITY CHOICES

Reading Support

PREVIEW AND PREDICT Read aloud the title *Our Freedoms* and write those words in the middle of a word web. Invite children to name people or things they associate with those words. Allow them to scan the pictures on pages 204–207 while they add to the web.

Link to Art

CREATE ADVERTISEMENTS Tell children that people use their freedom of speech when they advertise products they want to sell. Invite each child to create a poster advertising a favorite product. Remind children that an advertisement should tell or show at least one reason why other people should buy that product.

Right to meet peacefully

Freedom of religion

Freedom of the press

Americans have enjoyed these freedoms for more than 200 years. The Constitution says that the government can never take them away.

205

PUPIL BOOK OR UNIT BIG BOOK

Meet Individual Needs

ENGLISH LANGUAGE LEARNERS

Have children use each of the four captions about freedoms to make grab bags. Help them glue a label to each bag and then find or draw pictures to put in the bags. The children can then work together to empty and refill the bags, categorizing the pictures correctly.

WRITE-ON CHARTS

Use **WRITE-ON CHART 29** to help children make a two-column chart titled *People Who Made a Difference*.

things they want to do. Invite the groups to share their lists with the class.

History

People and Events Across Time and Place Organize children into pairs. Provide a variety of biographies of the same famous person who has made a difference in some way to our country. (See the list of biographies under *Primary Source* below.) Invite each pair to read one biography and then to write questions an interviewer might ask the famous person. Have pairs take turns role-playing for the class an interview with the famous person.

Connecting Past to Present to Future Point out that we have freedoms today because men and women of the past worked to gain them. Create a two-column chart titled *People Who Made a Difference*. Ask children to name as many people as they can, such as Patrick Henry, Susan B. Anthony, and Rosa Parks, who worked for our freedoms. List these names in the first column. In the second, record what each person did. If necessary, have children reread the lesson, or provide encyclopedias for them to gather more information.

"PRIMARY SOURCE"

The following biographies provide first-hand information about a variety of people who worked for freedoms and who made a difference.

A Picture Book of Benjamin Franklin by David Adler, Holiday House, 1990.

A Picture Book of Martin Luther King, Jr. by David Adler, Holiday House, 1989.

I Am Rosa Parks by Jim Haskins, Dial Books, 1997.

Patrick Henry, Voice of the American Revolution by Louis Sabin, Troll Books, 1985.

Minty, A Story of Young Harriet Tubman by Alan Schroeder, Dial Books, 1996.

Civics and Government

Rights and Responsibilities of Citizens
Ask children to think about how they might be able to use their freedoms to make a difference in the world.

Q. How can you make a difference? help take care of the Earth and the animals; write to the President and to members of Congress to ask for help with laws; tell others when you think they are doing something wrong; do good things to help other people

As children brainstorm ways people today can help others and work with the government, record their responses on the board. Then invite each child to choose one of the ways and draw a picture to illustrate it.

Visual Analysis

Interpret Pictures Look at the "Freedom Is . . ." banner on page 207.

Q. What does freedom mean to these children? happiness, sharing, having the same rules

How do you know? by looking at the pictures and words on their banner

3. CLOSE

Ask children to summarize the lesson by telling in their own words what they know about our freedoms.

Check Understanding

The child can
—— explore the idea of freedom in America.
—— identify freedoms that United States citizens enjoy.
—— identify people who have worked for freedoms.
—— recognize that people can use their freedoms to make a difference.

Rosa Parks

Sometimes people help us remember what our freedoms are. A woman named Rosa Parks reminded us that the same freedoms belong to all Americans. Rosa Parks worked to help change things for African Americans. She said, "I was just one of many who fought for freedom."

Both Patrick Henry and Rosa Parks shared how they felt about freedom. Today many young people learn about their freedoms in school.

206

Biography

Rosa Parks grew up on her grandparents' farm in Alabama. As she became older, she saw that African Americans were not treated fairly. She did not think people should be kept apart by skin color. Later, she and her husband worked with groups to stop this. One day a bus driver said she must give up her seat to a white person. Rosa Parks would not do it. Unfair laws were changed because she believed in her freedom.

ACTIVITY CHOICES

WRITE-ON CHARTS

Let Freedom Ring
Use WRITE-ON CHART 20 to extend and enrich this lesson. See Teacher's Edition page W62.

VIDEO

 Use READING RAINBOW,™ AMAZING GRACE to examine the freedom to follow one's dream.

Link to Language Arts

POETRY Ask children to think about what freedom means to them and why it is important to have freedom. Then invite them to write poems about freedom. Remind them that a poem need not rhyme.

Our class made a banner to explain what freedoms mean to us. We all wrote on the banner. One girl wrote, "Freedom is having the same rules for everyone." Our banner was hung at City Hall for everyone to share.

What Do You Know?

1. **Where is the Bill of Rights written?** in the Constitution
2. **What do our freedoms mean to you?**

207

PUPIL BOOK OR UNIT BIG BOOK

Extend and Enrich

MAKE A BOOK Invite each child to create a book called "Our Freedoms." Have children make a separate page about each freedom. Suggest that they also include at least one page about someone who worked for our freedoms in the past. Then have them create a cover and bind their pages into a book. Display the finished books in the reading corner.

Reteach the Main Idea

LIST FREEDOMS Organize children into small groups. Assign each group one of the four freedoms discussed in the lesson. Have groups write the freedom at the top of a sheet of paper. Then ask them to think of ways they use their freedom and to record their ideas. Invite groups to share their lists and discuss how these freedoms make their lives better.

Think Critically

Q. **What are some of the freedoms we have as citizens of the United States?** freedom of speech, freedom of religion, freedom of the press, freedom to meet peacefully

Which freedom is most important to you? Why? Answers will vary but should include one of the freedoms discussed in the lesson.

Show What you Know

Performance Assessment Invite groups of children to make their own "Freedom Is . . ." banners similar to the one on page 207. Provide each group with craft paper, art materials, and, if possible, magazines or catalogs that contain pictures of some of the people who worked for our freedoms in the past. Display children's completed banners in the hall.

What to Look For Each child's contribution should indicate that he or she understands what freedom means. Children may have included pictures of people who worked for our freedoms.

Using the Activity Book Distribute copies of Activity Book page 43. Ask children to read all the sentences before they select the words to fill in the blanks. You may wish to have a volunteer read each sentence aloud. Suggest that children cross out words as they are used.

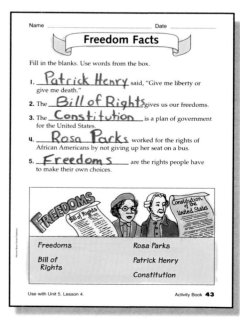

Activity Book page 43

HANDS-ON OPTION

The "Hands-On Option" is an alternative way to address all objectives for this lesson or to enrich the content found in the Pupil Book/Unit Big Book.

Class Newspaper

Objectives: Explore the idea of freedom in America. Identify freedoms that United States citizens enjoy.

Materials: 11 x 17 sheets of paper; old newspapers, magazines, and catalogs; crayons or markers; glue; scissors

COOPERATIVE LEARNING Remind children that one of the freedoms we are given in the Bill of Rights is freedom of the press. Organize children into cooperative groups, and assign each group a part in creating a class newspaper. One group might write class news, another group might report on school news, a third group might do a cartoon and joke section, a fourth group might write an editorial section about the concerns of the class and what they want to do about them, a fifth might do an advice column, and a sixth might do a review column telling about their favorite and least favorite movies, television shows, books, music, and games. You may also want to select one group to be the newspaper's editors and have them help you lay out the pages and put the paper together. Suggest that children look at several newspapers. Then have each group plan its section and divide up the tasks. Some of the children should find information and write the articles while others draw or find pictures to use in their section. Compile the completed sections in a newspaper format and make a copy for each child. Children may also want to distribute copies of their newspaper to children in other classrooms. **(TACTILE/VISUAL/AUDITORY)**

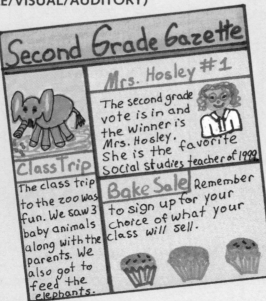

Freedom Train

Objectives: Explore the idea of freedom in America. Identify freedoms that United States citizens enjoy.

Materials: picture of a train; construction paper, crayons, markers, tape

Display a photo or drawing of a train, and invite each child to draw a train car on a sheet of construction paper. Ask children to write and complete the following sentence below their drawings:

I am free to _____.

Guide them to complete the sentence with a freedom they enjoy as an American citizen. Help children tape their train cars together, end-to-end, along a wall to form a Freedom Train. Children can take turns pointing out and discussing with the class the freedoms they chose. **(AUDITORY/TACTILE/VISUAL)**

Who Am I?

Objectives: Identify people who have worked for freedom. Recognize that people can make a difference.

Materials: paper, pencils, encyclopedias or books containing short biographies of famous Americans

Invite pairs or small groups of children to make up "Who Am I?" riddles about people who have worked for freedom.

Example:

I helped add the Bill of Rights to the Constitution.
I said, "Give me liberty or give me death."
Who am I?

Children can also write riddles about Americans who have made a difference in other ways. Invite them to read their riddles aloud for others to answer. **(AUDITORY)**

Let Freedom Ring!

Objectives: Explore the idea of freedom in America. Identify freedoms that United States citizens enjoy.

Materials: construction paper, crayons or markers, scissors

Remind children that they learned about the Liberty Bell in Lesson 1 and that *liberty* is another word for *freedom*. Invite a volunteer to tell the story of the Liberty Bell. (If necessary, refer children to Pupil's Book page 191.) Then have each child draw and cut out a large liberty bell, using the photo on Pupil's Book page 204 as a model. Ask children to write on their bells one or more of the freedoms they learned about in this lesson. (AUDITORY/KINESTHETIC/TACTILE)

Freedom Press Conference

Objectives: Explore the idea of freedom in America. Identify freedoms that United States citizens enjoy.

Materials: index cards, pencils

Invite children to role-play a press conference about freedom. Explain that at a press conference someone gives radio, television, and newspaper reporters information about something important. At this press conference government leaders will talk about freedoms. Assign half of the class to be government leaders and half to be reporters for the different media. Provide children with index cards. Ask the government leaders to write short paragraphs on their cards, explaining the different freedoms. The reporters take notes on their cards as the leaders read their paragraphs aloud during the conference. You may wish to allow the reporters to question the leaders. After the conference, the reporters can summarize the leaders' speeches from their notes, as if reporting the news. You may wish to invite another class to attend the press conference. (AUDITORY/KINESTHETIC/TACTILE)

Make a Difference

Objectives: Explore the idea of freedom in America. Identify freedoms that United States citizens enjoy. Recognize that people can use their freedoms to make a difference.

Materials: paper, pencils, posterboard

Point out that all people can make a difference if they use their freedoms to make things better. Organize the class into small groups, and ask children to think of some changes they would like to see in their school or community—for example, new playground equipment or a new park. Then have each group brainstorm a list of actions they could take that would help get that change made. Guide children to realize that the freedom of speech gives them the right to talk to other people, to write letters, and to make posters; and the freedom to meet peacefully gives them the right to hold meetings and to organize events. Have each group choose and follow through with one action from its list— for example, writing a letter or making a poster. Encourage them to share their finished work with the class. You may want to select one of the projects and help children present it to the school board or the city council. (AUDITORY/TACTILE)

DEFINE THE PROBLEM

Invite children to look at the pictures and recognize the conflict between the boy and the girl. Help children clearly define both sides of the argument. Ask them to think of reasons to defend each of the positions.

Q. **What problem are the children having?** The boy is cutting in line in front of the girl and telling her she cannot play kickball with the boys.

Why are the children arguing about who can play kickball? The girl wants to play kickball but the boy does not want girls to play.

USE PROBLEM-SOLVING SKILLS

Organize children into small groups. Suggest that they choose one person in each group to serve as the group recorder. Ask them to read the questions on page 208. Then encourage the groups to brainstorm ideas on how the problem of who can play kickball might be solved. Ask the recorder to list the possible solutions. Then have the children in the group choose the solution they think would work best.

Q. **What would be a fair solution? What would be an unfair solution?** A fair solution would be to let everyone play. An unfair solution would be for the boys not to let the girl play.

ACTIVITY CHOICES

Solving Problems

Getting Along

Work with a group. Talk about the children's different opinions.

● Why does each child think he or she is right?
● How can the children solve their problem?

What Would You Do?

Choose a way to show the class your ideas.

● Draw a cartoon.
● Act out your way to solve the problem.
● Write a story.

This is a boys' game. Go away.

208

Background

CONFLICT RESOLUTION Children often experience conflict at school. They may tease or bully during play. Helping children to gain insight into their behavior and to find ways for resolving their differences will develop the skills they need to cope with conflict as an adult.

Additional sources:

Peace Education Foundation
1900 Biscayne Blvd.
Miami, FL 33132; 1-800-749-8838

Consortium on Peace Research Education and Development

4260 Chain Bridge Road
George Mason University
Fairfax, VA 22030; (703) 993-2405

National Institute for Dispute Resolution
1726 M Street NW, Suite 500
Washington, DC 20036; (202) 466-4764

Children's Creative Response to Conflict
Box 271, 521 North Broadway
Nyack, NY 10960; (914) 353-1796

Educators for Social Responsibility
23 Garden St.
Cambridge, MA 02138; (617) 492-1764

You can't get in front of me. I was here first.

You can't make me!

3

209

SHOW SOLUTIONS

Provide paper, pencils, and crayons or markers. Invite groups to read the suggestions on page 208, and allow them to choose one of these ways or some other way to show their solutions. Groups can share their solutions with the rest of the class.

Auditory Learning

Listen to a Poem Read aloud "The Quarrel" by Eleanor Farjeon.

I quarreled with my brother,
I don't know what about,
One thing led to another
And somehow we fell out.
The start of it was slight,
The end of it was strong,
He said he was right.
I knew he was wrong!

We hated one another.
The afternoon turned black.
Then suddenly my brother
Thumped me on the back,
And said, "Oh, come along!
We can't go on all night—
I was in the wrong."
So he was in the right.

Ask children to tell how the quarrel described in the poem is like quarrels they have had with a sibling or friend. Discuss what the narrator means when he or she says, "'I was in the wrong.' So he was in the right."

Meet Individual Needs

TACTILE AND AUDITORY LEARNERS
Provide each child with the Finger Puppets Pattern (P10). Invite children to create finger puppets of children similar to themselves and their friends. Have them talk about ways to end quarrels and fights. Ask them to think of situations they know of, they have experienced, or they have seen on television. Then have children present finger-puppet plays showing ways to end the conflicts. Encourage them to vary the outcomes in some instances by using a mediator.

Role-Play

Have children suggest other situations in which conflict might arise, such as property use or ownership, sports conduct, manners, and adherence to class rules.
[CAUTION: Children should not engage in personal accusation.]
Invite volunteers to act out the situations while other class members advise them on ways to resolve their issues.

READ AND RESPOND

Read aloud pages 210–211 and discuss the Kids Voting USA program at Winship Magnet School in Macon, Georgia. Explain that children at this school are learning skills they need to be good citizens when they grow up. Allow time for children to explore the subject more by discussing different ways people can take an active part in their government.

Q. Why is voting important? Voting gives citizens choices.

How are school elections the same as government elections? In both, people choose leaders, each person gets one vote, and the winner gets the most votes.

Discuss election day with children. Invite them to share things they have seen on television, such as election results, candidates' speeches, advertisements, or people at polling places. Explain that election day is very exciting for many people, because on this day they can help make decisions about what will happen in their communities and their country.

Q. How could you decorate your classroom for election day? Responses may include posting symbols of the United States, such as a bald eagle, the American flag, drawings or photos of past Presidents, or the Statue of Liberty.

66 PRIMARY SOURCE 99

Interview Arrange for children to interview someone from the election commission or voter registration office about the local election process. Provide sample ballots for children to study before the interview. After the interview children can give their addresses and learn which polling places they would go to on election day.

Kids Voting USA

United States

Macon, Georgia

At Winship Magnet School in Macon, Georgia, children of all ages are learning how to be good citizens. They know that citizens must take an active part in their government.

Every year teachers Laney Sammons and Jeannie Waters work with second graders on activities that teach good citizenship. The children use ideas from a project called Kids Voting USA. They plan school elections, learn about their community government, and even go with their parents to vote on election day. Jeannie Webb Hodges, the principal at Winship, says "When the children talk about voting at home, their parents get excited, too."

210

ACTIVITY CHOICES

Background

Developed by teachers for teachers, the Kids Voting USA Curriculum© models democratic practices at the classroom level through cooperative learning structures, group problem solving, and active, child-centered experiences. Typical lessons involve role-plays, craft activities, and classroom elections. Students from kindergarten through high school can participate in exciting activities about the election process and then cast ballots alongside older family members in local, state, and national elections. Children vote on the same issues as adults by using an easy-to-follow ballot. The votes are counted by volunteers, and the results are reported by the news media just as official results are. The goal of the program is that each child, through firsthand experience, develops information-gathering skills that aid in critical decision making. The objective of the Kids Voting USA Curriculum© is to show the value of voting.

As the children learn about voting, they also learn about finding information, solving problems, and making decisions. They have fun decorating their classrooms for voting day. In one classroom a life-size eagle reminds children of the symbols of the United States.

After the children vote, they wear their "I Voted" stickers proudly. With the voting habits they have learned, these young citizens will grow up to be active members of their community and country.

Building Citizenship

What Can You Do?

- Find out how citizens sign up to vote in your community.
- Make posters to remind people to vote.

Visit the Internet at http://www.hbschool.com for additional resources.

History

Connecting Past to Present to Future
A voting machine is a mechanical device for recording and counting votes at an election. Some election districts in the United States use computerized voting machines. The computer totals all votes for each candidate or issue and prints out the results. The United States was the first country to conduct elections by machine.

Holiday Activities

For information and activities related to election day, see the Holiday Activities section at the back of the Teacher's Edition.

PUPIL BOOK OR UNIT BIG BOOK

Meet Individual Needs

ENGLISH LANGUAGE LEARNERS Provide an opportunity for children who speak the same first language to share ideas about voting and elections. Then have them relate these ideas in English to the rest of the class.

Link to Language Arts

JOURNAL Ask children to imagine that they are old enough to vote on election day. Invite them to record in their journals some of the things they would like to vote about. Remind children that on election day, people vote to decide important issues as well as to choose their leaders.

Meet Individual Needs

ADVANCED LEARNERS Challenge children to research and identify important issues in their communities that will be voted on in the next year.

Technology

Visit the Internet at **http://www.hbschool.com** for additional resources.

PICTURE SUMMARY

TAKE A LOOK

Remind children that a picture summary is a way to visually represent the main ideas or events in a story. Explain that this summary reviews some of the main ideas in Unit 5. Help children recognize that they are looking at a picture of a citizenship quilt showing symbols and landmarks and people expressing their rights as Americans.

Visual Analysis

Learn from Pictures Organize children into small groups. Invite them to examine the picture summary and to react to its images. Ask children to describe the various pictures on the quilt and to discuss the symbols, landmarks, and rights they recognize. Ask children to list other objects, places, and activities they associate with America.

> **VOCABULARY BLACKLINES**
>
> Distribute the individual word cards for this unit and have children use the words as they discuss the picture summary.

UNIT
5
Review

Picture Summary

Look at the pictures. They will help you remember what you learned.

Talk About the Main Ideas

1. Americans honor their country and its history.

2. We elect people to be the leaders of our country.

3. The United States government has three branches.

4. States and communities have governments, too.

5. Americans have many freedoms.

Tell a Story Make up a story about a trip to our country's capital or your state's capital. Tell what you saw and who you met there.

212

I pledge Allegiance to the flag of the United States of America And to the Republic for which it stands, One Nation under God, Indivisible, with Liberty and Justice for all.

ACTIVITY CHOICES

UNIT POSTER

Use the UNIT 5 PICTURE SUMMARY POSTER to summarize unit learning.

VOCABULARY CARDS

Have children use the VOCABULARY CARDS for this unit to review key concepts.

Picture Summary Key

1. Voter
2. American Flag
3. Community Leader
4. Constitution
5. Capitol
6. Liberty Bell
7. Freedoms
8. Supreme Court
9. Pledge of Allegiance
10. Great Seal of the United States
11. Statue of Liberty
12. White House

SUMMARIZE THE MAIN IDEAS

Ask children to read the summary statements on page 212 and to relate each one to a specific drawing in the picture summary. Lead a class discussion about each patch on the quilt, and ask children to offer supporting details for each main idea illustrated.

Review the Anticipation Guide at the beginning of the unit, on Teacher's Edition page 182. Recall with students which statements they marked as *true* or *false*. Discuss what was learned about these statements and invite children to indicate whether each statement is true or false based on what they have learned.

Help children recognize how our country's character is defined in its national symbols, landmarks, and democratic traditions.

Sharing the Activity

Provide time for children to complete the Tell a Story activity on page 212. Ask children to discuss what symbols and landmarks they saw on their trips. Invite children to share their stories in small groups or with the whole class.

PUPIL BOOK OR UNIT BIG BOOK

Meet Individual Needs

ENGLISH LANGUAGE LEARNERS Pair children who are learning English with children who are fluent in the language. Provide each pair with a set of large index cards and ask them to copy the five summary statements. Encourage children to read each statement to his or her partner and then draw a related picture on the opposite side. Children may wish to use the illustrations on the Picture Summary as a guide or draw an original one.

TECHNOLOGY

Use the AMAZING WRITING MACHINE™ RESOURCE PACKAGE to summarize the unit.

UNIT 5
REVIEW

USE VOCABULARY

❶ A mayor is a leader of a city.
❷ A judge works in a court.
❸ A person can vote one time in each election.
❹ Our government has three branches.
❺ Americans have the freedom to worship as they please.

CHECK UNDERSTANDING

❶ Americans celebrate Independence Day, pledge allegiance to the flag, and sing the national anthem.
❷ The Constitution is the highest law in our country. It tells about the branches of our government.
❸ Children might respond that our government leads our country, helps protect us, or works to make our country a better place to live.
❹ Children might say that the Supreme Court, or the justices, decide whether laws are fair.
❺ People help our government by voting, by obeying laws, and by getting along with one another.

THINK CRITICALLY

❶ Children might say that the eagle is a good symbol because it is big and strong and free.
❷ Answers might include the mayor, city council, and school board.
❸ Good citizens help their government and work together to make their community a better place to live.

UNIT
5
Review

Use Vocabulary

Use the word in the box in your answer.

❶ Is a **mayor** a leader of a city, state, or country?

❷ Where does a **judge** work?

❸ How many times can each person **vote** in an election?

❹ How many branches does our country's **government** have?

❺ What is one **freedom** Americans have?

Check Understanding

❶ How do Americans honor their country?

❷ What is the Constitution?

❸ How does our government help us?

❹ Who decides if laws are fair?

❺ How do people help their government?

Think Critically

❶ Do you think the bald eagle is a good symbol for our country? Explain.

❷ Who are some leaders in your community?

❸ What are some things that good citizens do?

214

Apply Skills

Find Capitals on a Map

Five States

Map Key
★ State capital
— Boundary

1. Name two states that share a boundary.
2. What is the capital of Tennessee?
3. In which direction is Tennessee from Kentucky?
4. In which direction would you go to get from Richmond to Frankfort?

Do It Yourself

Make a map of your state and its neighbors.

Add the capitals.

Draw a compass rose.

Write two questions about finding capitals.

215

APPLY SKILLS

Find Capitals on a Map

1. Children can name any two neighboring states.
2. Nashville
3. south
4. west

Do It Yourself

Have children share their maps in groups to check the spelling of state names and to compare placement of capitals. Invite them to exchange their projects and answer the questions about finding capitals.

PUPIL BOOK OR UNIT BIG BOOK

APPLY SKILLS

Understand What People Think

You may wish to pair children for this activity. After teams have shared their opinions, invite them to give and support their opinions in writing.

Make a Choice by Voting

Discuss how American citizens can work alone or in groups through their representatives to suggest new laws. You may wish to extend this activity to include a school-wide campaign and election by your class.

Apply Skills

Understand What People Think

1 Name something you have strong feelings about.

2 Give one fact and one opinion about the thing you named.

Make a Choice by Voting

In 1996 Massachusetts passed a law naming its state dessert. The idea for the law came from a group of school children. They wanted Boston cream pie to become the state dessert. Lawmakers voted—and agreed with their idea!

Work with your classmates to choose a snack for your state or city. Take a vote to decide the class favorite.

216

·········Unit Activity··········

Make Ballot Boxes

Work in small groups to make ballot
boxes for all the classrooms in your school.

 List ideas from the group for ways to decorate your box.

 Vote to decide which idea or ideas to use.

 List the jobs that need to be done and who will do them.

 Give your box to another class. Tell them what your class
has learned about voting.

Visit the Internet at
http://www.hbschool.com
for additional resources.

Read More About It

<u>Billy the Great</u> by Rosa Guy. Delacorte. Two families find a way
to work out their problems and become good neighbors.

<u>The Flag We Love</u> by Pam Muñoz Ryan. Charlesbridge. This
poem explains the meaning of the flag through our history.

<u>A Very Important Day</u> by Maggie Rugg Herold.
Morrow. On a snowy day in New York, 219 people
from 32 countries become new American citizens.

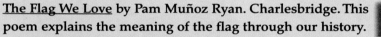

217

UNIT ACTIVITY
Make Ballot Boxes

Materials: cardboard boxes, construction
paper, crayons, markers, scissors, tape

Use this activity to emphasize getting along
as part of good citizenship in cooperative
groups. Review the voting process as children work to decide on the plan for their
group's box.

READ MORE ABOUT IT

Additional books are listed in the Resource
Center on page 182E of this Teacher's
Edition.

TAKE-HOME BOOK
Use the TAKE-HOME REVIEW BOOK for Unit 5.

ASSESSMENT PROGRAM
Use UNIT 5 TEST Standard, pp. 31–33. Performance, p. 34.

GAME TIME!
Use GAME TIME! to reinforce this unit.

COOPERATIVE LEARNING WORKSHOP

MAKE A POCKET SCRAPBOOK

Children should work together in small groups to compile newspaper articles, magazine pictures, and their own writing and drawing for a pocket scrapbook of things that show good citizenship.

Display some pictures of American symbols and discuss the fact that showing pride in one's country is one aspect of being a good citizen.

Materials for each group: pictures of symbols of the United States, newspapers, magazines, drawing paper, paper lunch bags, crayons or markers, scissors, glue, posterboard, hole punch, yarn

Identify Symbols of America

STEP 1: Organize the class into small groups and describe the activity. Help children hole punch the left side of the bags and invite them to insert in the bags the pictures and other items they have collected. Suggest that as they look for items to add to their scrapbooks, children ask themselves: How do other people show good citizenship?

Demonstrate Knowledge

STEP 2: As children work, ask them to discuss ways people can show pride in their country.

Q. **What are some ways people can show they are proud to be Americans?** Examples may include showing respect for our flag, singing the national anthem, and celebrating Independence Day.

Present the Project

STEP 3: Have children make a posterboard cover for their scrapbooks. Suggest that they include the title *Good Citizen Scrapbook* and symbols of America on their covers. Help them bind the covers and lunch bags together with yarn. Encourage groups to share their scrapbooks with the class. You may wish to have children add items to the scrapbooks as they find them.

What to Look For In their discussions and through the scrapbooks they create, children should exhibit an understanding of the ways Americans can show good citizenship. They should be able to

► identify several symbols of America.
► explain why it is important to vote.
► name ways people show good citizenship.
► describe how our country is governed.
► list some of the freedoms citizens enjoy.
► use appropriate vocabulary.

REMIND CHILDREN TO:
• Share their ideas.
• Cooperate with others to plan their work.
• Plan and take responsibility for their tasks.
• Show their work.
• Discuss their own and the group's performance.

6

PEOPLE IN TIME AND PLACE

The major objectives in this unit are organized around the following themes:

UNIT THEMES

▶ **CONTINUITY & CHANGE**
▶ **COMMONALITY & DIVERSITY**

Preview Unit Content

Unit 6 tells the story of the people who built our country. Children will read how pioneer families changed the land. They will see that many Americans' ancestors came from other countries, contributing to the diversity of our population. Through the study of a family history, children will recognize the role parents and grandparents play in developing family traditions. Children also will read about family and community celebrations in our country and around the world and compare the elements of all. Finally, the importance of communication using words, symbols, and pictures will be discussed as children come to recognize the importance of working together for the future of the world.

You may wish to begin the unit with the Unit 6 Picture Summary Poster and activities. The illustration that appears on the poster also appears on pages 266–267 in the Pupil Book to help children summarize the unit.

UNIT POSTER

Use the **UNIT 6 PICTURE SUMMARY POSTER** to preview the unit.

Planning Chart

TEACHER'S EDITION	THEMES • Strands	VOCABULARY	MEET INDIVIDUAL NEEDS	RESOURCES INCLUDING ▶ TECHNOLOGY
UNIT INTRODUCTION **Introduce the Unit** Preview Set the Scene with Literature **"Pride"** by Alma Flor Ada Use the Literature Big Book pp. 218A–223A			English Language Learners, pp. 220, 223 Visual Learners, p. 221	**Pupil Book/Unit Big Book, pp. 218–223** **Write-On Chart 27** Picture Summary Poster Home Letter Text on Tape Audio Asian Translations Vocabulary Cards *Homeplace*
LESSON 1 **People on the Move** pp. 224A–227A	**CONTINUITY & CHANGE** • History • Geography • Economics	pioneer	Advanced Learners, p. 225 Extend and Enrich, p. 227 Reteach the Main Idea, p. 227	**Pupil Book/Unit Big Book, pp. 224–227** **Write-On Chart 21** Activity Book, p. 44
LESSON 2 Learn Culture through Literature **Winter Days in the Big Woods** by Laura Ingalls Wilder pp. 228A–239A	**COMMONALITY & DIVERSITY** • History • Geography • Economics • Culture		English Language Learners, pp. 229, 233, 235 Visual Learners, pp. 229, 231 Advanced Learners, pp. 231, 236 Kinesthetic Learners, p. 236 Extend and Enrich, p. 238 Reteach the Main Idea, p. 239	**Pupil Book/Unit Big Book, pp. 228–239** **Write-On Charts 29, 33** Activity Book, p. 45 Music Audio, "When I First Came to This Land" Text on Tape Audio
LESSON 3 **A World of People** pp. 240A–243A	**COMMONALITY & DIVERSITY** • Culture • Geography • History	ancestor	Tactile Learners, p. 241 Extend and Enrich, p. 242 Reteach the Main Idea, p. 242	**Pupil Book/Unit Big Book, pp. 240–243** **Write-On Charts 22, 34** Activity Book, p. 46 Vocabulary Cards Video, Reading Rainbow, *The Lotus Seed* ▶ **THE AMAZING WRITING MACHINE**
SKILL **Use a Bar Graph** pp. 244A–245A	**BASIC STUDY SKILLS** • Chart and Graph Skills	bar graph	English Language Learners, p. 244A Auditory Learners, p. 244A Advanced Learners, p. 244A Extend and Enrich, p. 244 Tactile Learners, p. 245 Reteach the Skill, p. 245	**Pupil Book/Unit Big Book, pp. 244–245** Activity Book, p. 47 Transparency 16 Desk Maps ▶ **THE AMAZING WRITING MACHINE** ▶ **GRAPH LINKS**

24 DAYS

TIME MANAGEMENT

DAY 1	DAY 2	DAY 3	DAY 4	DAY 5	DAY 6	DAY 7	DAY 8	DAY 9	DAY 10	DAY 11	DAY 12
Unit Introduction	Lesson 1				Lesson 2			Lesson 3		Skill	Lesson 4

TEACHER'S EDITION	THEMES •Strands	VOCABULARY	MEET INDIVIDUAL NEEDS	RESOURCES INCLUDING ▶ TECHNOLOGY
LESSON 4 **A Family History** pp. 246A–251A	CONTINUITY & CHANGE • Culture • Geography		English Language Learners, p. 247 Tactile Learners, p. 248 Advanced Learners, p. 249 Extend and Enrich, p. 251 Reteach the Main Idea, p. 251	**Pupil Book/Unit Big Book, pp. 246–251** Activity Book, p. 48 Desk Maps ▶ THE AMAZING WRITING MACHINE
LESSON 5 **Community Celebrations** pp. 252A–255A	CONTINUITY & CHANGE • History • Culture	custom	Extend and Enrich, p. 254 Reteach the Main Idea, p. 255	**Pupil Book/Unit Big Book, pp. 252–255** Write-On Chart 23 Activity Book, p. 49 Vocabulary Cards
SKILL **Learn from Artifacts** pp. 256A–257A	BASIC STUDY SKILLS • Reading and Research Skills	artifact	Kinesthetic Learners, p. 256A Advanced Learners, p. 256 Extend and Enrich, p. 257 Reteach the Skill, p. 257	**Pupil Book/Unit Big Book, pp. 256–257** Write-On Charts 24, 27 Activity Book, p. 50 Transparency 17
LESSON 6 **One for All, All for One** pp. 258A–261A	COMMONALITY & DIVERSITY • Culture • Geography	communication	Extend and Enrich, p. 260 Reteach the Main Idea, p. 260	**Pupil Book/Unit Big Book, pp. 258–261** Write-On Chart 26 Clings Activity Book, p. 51 Music Audio, "The World Is a Rainbow"
SKILL **Act on Your Own** pp. 262A–263B	BUILDING CITIZENSHIP • Participation Skills	independence	Extend and Enrich, p. 263 Reteach the Skill, p. 263	**Pupil Book/Unit Big Book, pp. 262–263** Write-On Chart 32 Activity Book, p. 52 Transparency 18 Music Audio, "Unsung Heroes"
MAKING SOCIAL STUDIES REAL **Prairie Peace Park** pp. 264–265	BUILDING CITIZENSHIP • Participation Skills		English Language Learners, p. 264	**Pupil Book/Unit Big Book, pp. 264–265** ▶ INTERNET
UNIT WRAP-UP Picture Summary Unit 6 Review Cooperative Learning Workshop pp. 266–271B			English Language Learners, p. 267	**Pupil Book/Unit Big Book, pp. 266–271** Picture Summary Poster Vocabulary Cards Assessment Program, Standard, pp. 35–37 Performance, p. 38 Take-Home Review Book Game Time! ▶ THE AMAZING WRITING MACHINE

DAY 13	DAY 14	DAY 15	DAY 16	DAY 17	DAY 18	DAY 19	DAY 20	DAY 21	DAY 22	DAY 23	DAY 24
		Lesson 5		Skill	Lesson 6		Skill	Making Social Studies Real	Unit Wrap-up		Unit Test

Multimedia Resource Center

Books

Easy

Chocolate, Debbi. *Kente Colors*. Illus. by John Ward. Walker, 1996. A rhyming description of the kente cloth costumes of the Ashanti and Ewe people of Ghana and portrayal of the symbolic colors and patterns.

Dorros, Arthur. *Tonight Is Carnaval*. Dutton, 1991. There is great excitement high in the Andes Mountains of Peru as everyone gets ready for the festival.

Hudson, Wade. *I Love My Family*. Illus. by Cal Massey. Scholastic, 1993. At a joyous family reunion, relatives sing, dance, eat lots of food, and pose for a family picture.

Johnston, Tony. *Yonder*. Dial, 1988. A plum tree changes in the passing seasons, as do the lives of a three-generation farm family.

Moss, Marissa. *In America*. Dutton, 1994. Walter's grandfather tells the story of immigrating to America from a village in Lithuania.

Rattigan, Jama K. *Dumpling Soup*. Illus. by Lillian Hsu-Flanders. Little, Brown, 1993. A young Hawaiian girl tries to make dumplings for her family's New Year's celebration.

Rylant, Cynthia. *When I Was Young in the Mountains*. Illus. by Diane Goode. Dutton, 1992. The author describes her childhood with her grandparents in the Appalachian Mountains.

Average

Castañeda, Omar S. *Abuela's Weave*. Illus. by Enrique O. Sanchez. Lee & Low, 1993. A girl and her grandmother weave beautiful tapestries to sell at the market in Guatemala.

Friedman, Ina R. *How My Parents Learned to Eat*. Houghton Mifflin, 1984. An American sailor courts a Japanese girl and each tries, in secret, to learn the other's way of eating.

Ketner, Mary Grace. *Ganzy Remembers*. Illus. by Barbara Sparks. Atheneum, 1991. Ganzy tells her daughter, granddaughter, and great-grand-daughter stories about her childhood on a farm years ago.

Levinson, Riki. *Soon, Annala*. Orchard, 1993. While eagerly awaiting the arrival of her two younger brothers from the old country, Anna tries to speak more English and less Yiddish.

McCurdy, Michael. *Hannah's Farm: The Seasons on an Early American Homestead*. Holiday House, 1988. Seasonal changes dictate daily activities on a nineteenth-century farm.

Nye, Naomi Shihab. *Sitti's Secrets*. Illus. by Nancy Carpenter. Four Winds, 1994. Although there are thousands of miles between Mona and her grandmother, Sitti, they remain true neighbors forever.

Polacco, Patricia. *The Keeping Quilt*. Simon and Schuster, 1988. A home-made quilt ties together the lives of four generations of a Jewish family.

Reynolds, Marilynn. *The New Land, A First Year on the Prairie*. Illus. by Stephen McCallum. Orca, 1997. This book tells the adventures of a family's travels by boat, train, and wagon to their new homestead.

Wallner, Alexandra. *Laura Ingalls Wilder*. Holiday House, 1997. A biography of the well-known author of *The Little House on the Prairie* describes the pioneer experiences that provided the basis for her writing.

Waters, Kate, and Madeline Slovenz-Low. *Lion Dancer: Ernie Wan's Chinese New Year*. Photos by Martha Cooper. Scholastic, 1990. Children have a chance to see Ernie's preparation and excitement as he performs his first lion dance on the Chinese New Year.

Wing, Natasha. *Jalapeño Bagels*. Illus. by Robert Casilla. (Athenium, 1996) For International Day at school, Pablo brings something that reflects the cultures of both his parents.

Zelver, Patricia. *The Wonderful Towers of Watts*. Tambourine, 1994. Illus. by Frane Lessac. This book describes how an Italian immigrant built three unusual towers in his backyard in the Watts neighborhood of Los Angeles.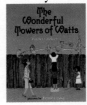

Challenging

Dragonwagon, Crescent. *Home Place*. Illus. by Jerry Pinkney. Aladdin, 1993. While out hiking, a family comes upon the site of an old house and finds some clues about the people who once lived there.

Kuklin, Susan. *How My Family Lives in America*. African American, Asian American, and Hispanic American children describe their families' cultural traditions.

Maestro, Betsy. *Coming to America, The Story of Immigration*. Illus. by Susannah Ryan. Scholastic, 1996. From Native Americans to the present, this book tells the history of people moving to America.

LIBRARY

See the Grade 2 SOCIAL STUDIES LIBRARY for additional resources.

Miller, William. *Zora Hurston and the Chinaberry Tree*. Illus. by Cornelius Van Wright and Ying-Hwa Hu. Lee & Low, 1994. Zora Hurston's father tells her to wear dresses and read the Bible. But her mother teaches her to climb a chinaberry tree.

Oberman, Sheldon. *The Always Prayer Shawl*. Illus. by Ted Lewin. Boyds Mills, 1994. This book tells the story of a czarist Russian boy's immigration to the United States, his growing up, and his appreciation for his heritage.

Turner, Ann. *Dakota Dugout*. Illus. by Ronald Himler. Macmillan, 1989. A woman describes her experiences living with her husband in a sod house on the Dakota Prairie.

Audiocassettes

Around the World in Dance. Henry "Buzz" Glass and Rosemary Hallum, Ph.D. Also available on LP or CD. Toll free: 1-800-645-3739

Holiday Songs Around the World. Also available on LP or CD. Toll free: 1-800-645-3739

Hopping Around from Place to Place. Ella Jenkins with the Chicago Children's Choir. Also available on LP. Toll free: 1-800-645-3739

Computer Software

Floppy Disk

The Graph Club. Tom Snyder Productions, Inc. Children work in groups to gather, sort, and classify information. They represent this information in either a bar, line, circle, or picture graph. Also available on CD-ROM. Toll free: 1-800-342-0236

Note that information, while correct at time of publication, is subject to change.

CD-ROM

Explorapedia: World of People. Microsoft. Windows. This program covers science, technology, art, education, and industry for children 6 to 10. Toll free: 1-800-376-5125

Family Tree Maker. Brøderbund. Mac/Windows. This program will organize and print out family tree charts. Toll free: 1-800-474-8840

Nigel's World: Adventures in World Geography. Davidson. Mac/DOS. Nigel, the fearless Scotsman, travels the world snapping pictures of fascinating people, places, and monuments. Toll free: 1-800-545-7677

Picture Atlas of the World. National Geographic Educational Services. Mac/Windows/DOS. This multimedia atlas provides maps, photos, music, languages, statistics, and other reference materials for countries around the world. Toll free: 1-800-368-2728

Video

Film or VHS Cassettes

Different and the Same: That's Us! Alfred Higgins Productions. This film fosters respect and appreciation for physical and cultural differences and similarities. 14 minutes. Toll free: 1-800-766-5353

Molly's Pilgrim. Phoenix Learning Group. This is a live-action adaptation of the book by Barbara Cohen. 24 minutes. Toll free: 1-800-221-1274

Creative Exchange. Program for teaching communication, sponsored by Hallmark, Crayola, Scholastic, and the U.S. Postal Service. Includes

20-page resource guide with cross-curricular lesson plans, book suggestions, and art techniques. Free. Toll free: 1-800-HALLMARK

Geography Awareness Week (Nov. 16–22). Teacher's packet contains color posters, maps and map activities, and teacher's handbook. Order item #XY88701997ES. $4 for 1–9 packets, $3 for 10–19 packets. Make check payable to the National Geographic Society.
> National Geographic Society
> P.O. Box 98190
> Washington, DC 20090-8190

Geography Education Newsletter. The quarterly Geography Education Program newsletter UPDATE provides news, product reviews, classroom ideas, teacher profiles, and reproducible lesson plans. Free subscription.
> National Geographic Society
> Geography Education Program
> P.O. Box 98190
> Washington, DC 20090-8190

Skipping Stones Magazine. A nonprofit children's magazine brings together children from all over the world by sharing their writing, artwork, photos, and more. "Pen Pals Wanted" pages in each issue. Send written request, 4 stamps, and $1.
> Skipping Stones Magazine
> Dept. HB98
> P.O. Box 3939
> Eugene, OR 97403-0939

You, Me, & Others. This instructional package provides 20-page teacher's guide and reproducibles for teaching K–2 children about heredity. Available from your local chapter of the March of Dimes. Free.

Linking Social Studies

LANGUAGE ARTS CENTER

Write a Class Family Ties Book

Materials: construction paper, ribbon, class book pages (blank), colored pencils, chart paper

Have children brainstorm about what "ties" a family together. Discuss family traditions, favorite foods, and unique cultural traits. Talk about how grandparents and other older family members help families learn about their heritage. Invite children to suggest a list of special things grandparents and grandchildren can do together. Have each child write and illustrate a story about something special he or she has done with a grandparent or some other older family member. Ask volunteers to decorate a cover for a class *Family Ties* book and bind the stories together for classroom display.

ART CENTER

Chinese Egg Painting

Materials: white eggs, push pins, small bottle caps, glue, watercolors and fine paintbrushes

Many cultures decorate eggs. The Chinese have been painting delicate designs on eggs for thousands of years. Help children puncture and remove enough shell from the wide end of the eggs to drain the insides. (You may wish to save and cook the eggs.) Once each egg is dry, glue its open end to a lid or similar base stand. Invite children to paint pictures on their eggs. Share examples of Asian art to show the use of space, color, and natural subjects. Children may first gently trace their designs in pencil, taking care not to puncture the shell.

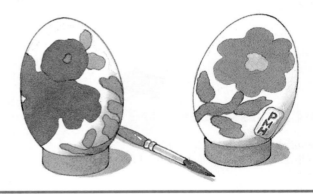

MULTICULTURAL CENTER

Musical Tour of the Americas

Materials: cassette player, cassette recordings of music from countries in the Americas, rhythm instruments, journals

Each day, provide in the center some music from one of the countries in the Americas. Post the name of the country and, if possible, provide postcards, pictures, or books from that country. Invite children to listen to the recording and to keep time to the music on a rhythm instrument. Encourage children to write journal entries describing the instruments and the rhythms they hear and to tell what they like about the music.

Across the Curriculum

READING CENTER

A Reading Passport to the World

Materials: variety of rubber stamps, inkpad, folk-tales and fairy tales from other countries

Explain to children how travelers use passports to visit other countries. Discuss how reading can be almost like a visit to another place and invite children to make a "reading passport." List the titles of the folktales and fairy tales that are available in the center and the name of the country from which each story comes. Have children fold and staple half-sheets of 8 1/2 x 11-inch paper to create their passports. Each time they read a story, children can stamp their passport with one of the rubber stamps and write under the stamp the name of the country they "visited."

MATH CENTER

Graphing Diversity

Materials: laminated wall graph, self-adhesive notes

Invite children to participate in showing diversity through a daily class graph. Each day, post a question next to the wall graph and have children add to the bar a self-adhesive note that represents their answer to the question. Graph topics might include school activities, eye color, favorite holidays, birth-places, and leisure activities. The graph should offer four or more possible response categories and a bar for "other." Allow time to discuss the results of each graphing activity and allow those who responded in the "other" category to explain their responses.

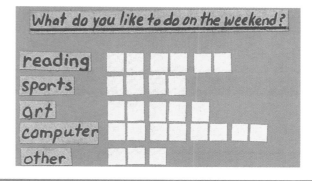

HOW TO INTEGRATE YOUR DAY
Use these topics to help you integrate social studies into your daily planning.

READING THEMES	INTEGRATED LANGUAGE ARTS	MATHEMATICS	SCIENCE	ART
Self and Others	Write a Family Ties Book, p. 218G	Graphing Diversity, p. 218H	Weather, p. 231	Chinese Egg Painting, p. 218G
Changes	Write a Letter, p. 219	Abacus, p. 246	Tools, p. 256A	About the Artist, p. 222
Holidays	Journal, pp. 220, 241, 247, 252A, 258, 262	Data and Graphing, p. 262		Graphic Art, p. 240A
Near and Far	Write to Analyze, p. 244			Picture Time Line, p. 247
Communicating with Others	Interviewing, p. 262A			Mural, p. 262
				Create Sculptures, p. 265

HEALTH AND PHYSICAL EDUCATION	MUSIC	WORLD LANGUAGES
Nutrition, p. 230	Sing a Song, p. 220	Other Languages, p. 248
	Vocal/Song, p. 228	Chinese Writing, p. 249
	Musical Instruments, p. 236	
	Music for a Purpose, p. 260	

BULLETIN BOARD

Create a bulletin board titled *Let's Celebrate!* Display a world map. Around the map display photos or drawings of items associated with different celebrations from around the world. Cluster the items under the name of the related holiday. Then put pins in the countries where the holidays originated and connect them to the holiday with yarn. Ask children to examine the photos and to name celebrations in which they participate.

Assessment Options

The assessment program allows all learners many opportunities to show what they know and can do. It also provides ongoing information about each child's understanding of social studies.

FORMAL ASSESSMENT

▶ *Unit Review*
(**Pupil Book**, pp. 268–271)

▶ *Unit Assessment*
(**Assessment Program:**
Standard Test, pp. 35–37,
Performance Task, p. 38)

STUDENT SELF-EVALUATION

▶ *Individual End-of-Project Checklist*
(**Assessment Program**, p. 6)

▶ *Group End-of-Project Checklist*
(**Assessment Program**, p. 7) for use after cooperative learning activities

▶ *Individual End-of-Unit Checklist*
(**Assessment Program**, p. 8)

INFORMAL ASSESSMENT

▶ *What Do You Know? Questions*
(**Pupil Book**, at end of lessons)

▶ *Think and Do*
(**Pupil Book**, at end of skill lessons)

▶ *Picture Summary*
(**Pupil Book**, pp. 266–267)

▶ *Check Understanding*
(**Teacher's Edition**, in Close, at end of lessons)

▶ *Think Critically*
(**Teacher's Edition**, in Close, at end of lessons)

▶ *Social Studies Skills Checklist*
(**Assessment Program**, pp. 4–5)

PERFORMANCE ASSESSMENT

▶ *Show What You Know*
(**Teacher's Edition**, in Close, at end of lessons)

▶ *Cooperative Learning Workshop*
(**Teacher's Edition**, p. 271A–271B)

▶ *Performance Task: Wish You Were Here!*
(**Assessment Program**, p. 38)

▶ Scoring the Performance Task
Use the *Scoring Rubric for Individual Projects*
(**Assessment Program**, p. 9)

▶ *Scoring Rubric for Group Projects*
(**Assessment Program**, p. 10)

▶ *Scoring Rubric for Presentations*
(**Assessment Program**, p. 11)

PORTFOLIO ASSESSMENT

Student-selected items may include:

▶ *Show What You Know,* quotation
(**Teacher's Edition**, p. 227)

▶ *Hands-On Option,* passport
(**Teacher's Edition**, p. 243A)

▶ *Link to Language Arts,* journal
(**Teacher's Edition**, p. 247)

Teacher-selected items may include:

▶ *My Best Work*
(**Assessment Program**, p. 12)

▶ *Portfolio Summary*
(**Assessment Program**, p. 13)

▶ *Portfolio Family Response*
(**Assessment Program**, p. 14)

STANDARD TEST

Name _____ Date _____

Unit 6 Test

Vocabulary 5 points each

For each word below, draw a picture and write the meaning.

artifact   ancestor   communication   custom

1. [ ]   Children might write that an artifact is something that is made and used by people. Drawings might show pottery, jewelry, a statue, an arrowhead, or a tool.

2. [ ]   Children might write that an ancestor is someone in a family that lived long ago. Drawings might show a person whose appearance or surroundings suggest an earlier time.

3. [ ]   Children might write that communication is sharing ideas with others. Drawings might show a person talking on a telephone, writing a letter, listening to the radio or television, or speaking directly with someone.

4. [ ]   Children might write that a custom is a way of doing something. Drawings might show fireworks, a piñata, seven candles, chopsticks, a parade, or a costume.

STANDARD TEST

Name _____

Main Ideas 6 points each

5. What can you learn from older family members?

   family history, customs

Write <u>yes</u> or <u>no</u> to answer the questions.

6. Do all people have the same needs? ____yes____
7. Do all people have the same customs? ____no____
8. Do all people have the same feelings? ____yes____
9. Are all our ancestors from England? ____no____
10. Are all Americans special in some ways? ____yes____

Use these words to complete the table.

   Kwanzaa   Cinco de mayo   Epiphany   Chinese New Year

Holiday Customs

Holidays	Customs
11. Epiphany	parade from a church, diving for a cross, dancing, seafood
12. Chinese New Year	parade with a dancing dragon, paper lanterns, duck, rice
13. Kwanzaa	candles, stories, dancing, drums, ham, sweet potato pie
14. Cinco de mayo	parade with riders on horses, guitars, piñatas, candy, toys

Objectives

- ▶ Describe the role of pioneers in the settlement and growth of our country. (p. 224A)
- ▶ Identify types of transportation used to move people to and across the United States. (p. 224A)
- ▶ Describe the life of a pioneer family. (p. 228A)
- ▶ Compare the ways people got their food long ago with the ways people get their food today. (p. 228A)
- ▶ Explain how weather affected pioneers. (p. 228A)
- ▶ Appreciate the diversity of a community's population. (p. 240A)

- ▶ Recognize that many Americans' ancestors came from other places. (p. 240A)
- ▶ Explain the importance of knowing about other people. (p. 240A)
- ▶ Identify the purpose and parts of a bar graph. (p. 244A)
- ▶ Recognize that every family has its own history. (p. 246A)
- ▶ Explain the pattern of a family tree. (p. 246A)
- ▶ Appreciate the value of learning from family members. (p. 246A)
- ▶ Describe family, ethnic, and religious customs. (p. 252A)

- ▶ Discuss the origins of various holidays and celebrations. (p. 252A)
- ▶ Draw conclusions about a people's lifeways from observing an artifact representing their culture. (p. 256A)
- ▶ Recognize that people use communication to work together to create a safer, more healthful planet. (p. 258A)
- ▶ Describe ways people can protect the quality of life in their communities. (p. 258A)
- ▶ Identify examples of acting independently. (p. 262A)
- ▶ Recognize that independent action can affect other people. (p. 262A)

STANDARD TEST

Name _____

Skills 4 points each

Our Favorite Activities							
Baseball							
Soccer							
Skiing							
Skating							
Reading							
Swimming							

0   1   2   3   4   5   6   7

Use the bar graph to answer the questions.

15. Which activity did the most children choose?

_____ soccer _____

16. Which activity was chosen by the same

number of children as baseball? ___ reading ___

17. Which activity was chosen by the fewest

children? _____ skiing _____

Tell two things the artifact shows about life long ago.

18. Sample responses: People used bows

and arrows for hunting; they hunted

deer; they made and used vases; they

19. liked to draw pictures.

_____

_____

Unit 6 Test   Assessment Program **37**

PERFORMANCE TASK

Name _____ Date _____

Performance Task

Wish You Were Here!

Imagine that you are a new settler somewhere in America. You are writing a letter to a friend who lives where you used to live. Draw a picture of your new home. Then complete the letter.

The drawing should show a simple dwelling made of natural materials, such as stone, logs, sod, or clay.

Sample response:

Dear _____ Jeremy _____,

Here I am in _____ Spring Valley _____.

My life has really changed! Let me tell you what

it's like to live here. We live in a log cabin that I helped

Dad build. There is a big fireplace in it. We use it for cooking

food and for keeping warm on cold days. Everyone in the

family works very hard here. But we love this place! The hills

and the rivers are beautiful.

_____

Your good friend,

Nan

38   Assessment Program   Unit 6 Test

Rubrics

SCORING RUBRICS The scoring rubrics for evaluating individual projects, group projects, and children's presentations may be found in the *Assessment Program,* pages 9–11.

CRITERIA The criteria listed below may be used when looking for evidence of the children's understanding of social studies content and ability to think critically.

▶ *Performance Task: Wish You Were Here!* [**Assessment Program,** p. 38]

▶ *Scoring the Performance Task—* Use the *Scoring Rubric for Individual Projects* [**Assessment Program,** p. 9], and look for evidence of the child's ability to:

↙ Identify the changes families experience when they move to a new place.

↙ Describe the way pioneer settlers lived.

↙ Communicate ideas clearly through writing.

REMINDER

You may wish to preview the performance assessment activity in the COOPERATIVE LEARNING WORKSHOP on Teacher's Edition pages 271A–271B. Children may complete this activity during the course of the unit.

INTRODUCE THE UNIT

Link Prior Learning

Ask children to work in pairs, asking each other about special events at home and telling interesting stories about older family members. Allow time for children to share what they learn in small groups. Explain that people can learn a lot by talking to others. Tell children that in this unit they will learn many things about families who live both near and far away.

Word Web

Create two word webs, with *Near* in the center of one and *Far* in the center of the other. Invite children to use a map or a globe to locate countries that are near the United States and countries that are far away. Help them write the name of each country in the appropriate web.

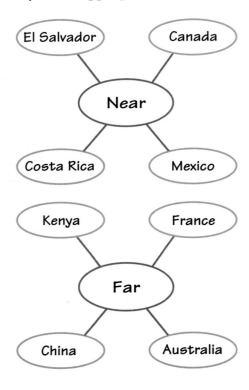

Preview Vocabulary

The vocabulary words listed on page 218 represent the key concepts for this unit. Suggest that children use the words to predict what the main ideas of the unit will be. Ideas for teaching the vocabulary are provided on pages 220 and 221.

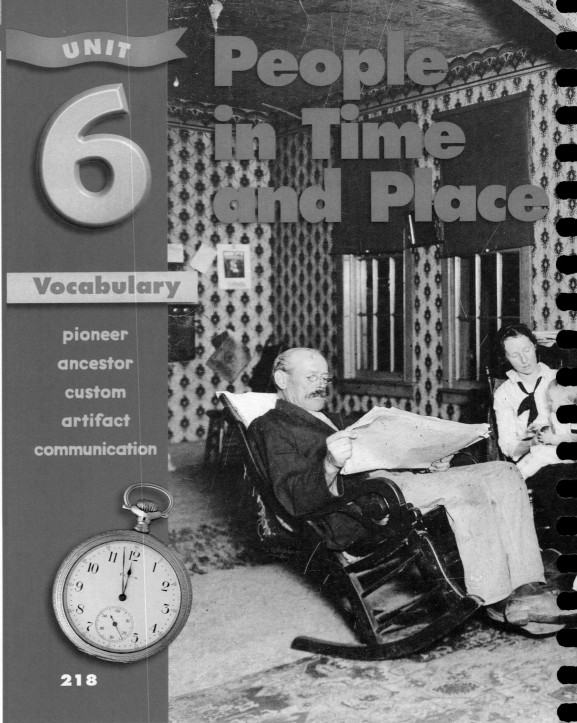

UNIT 6

People in Time and Place

Vocabulary

pioneer

ancestor

custom

artifact

communication

218

ACTIVITY CHOICES

Community Involvement

Identify a few people in the community whose ancestors immigrated to America or were some of America's first inhabitants. Invite these people to visit the class and to share their personal histories. Help children prepare questions to ask the visitors about their ancestors and countries.

WRITE-ON CHARTS

Use WRITE-ON CHART 27 to create word webs about countries near and far.

HOME LETTER

Use UNIT 6 HOME LETTER. See Teacher's Edition pages HL11–12.

219

PUPIL BOOK *OR* **UNIT BIG BOOK**

Have children comment on the family in the photo.

Q. **Is this photo old or new? Why do you think so?** old, because of the way they are posing; because it is not in color.

Why do you think people keep family portraits? so they know where they came from; so they know who their relatives are; so they can see how they have changed.

Tell children that in this unit they will learn how family histories connect people through time and from place to place. Children will discover that people who have moved to the United States have brought their histories and customs with them.

❝PRIMARY SOURCE❞

Laura Ingalls Wilder said she wrote her stories because "I wanted the children now to understand more about the beginnings of things, to know what is behind the things they see—what it is that made America as they know it."

Options for Reading

Read Aloud Read each lesson aloud as children follow along in their books. Strategies for guiding children through working with text and visuals are provided with each lesson.

Read Together Have pairs or small groups of children read the lesson by taking turns reading each page or paragraph aloud. Encourage children to use the new vocabulary words as they discuss what they read.

Read Alone Strong readers may wish to read the lessons independently before you read or discuss each lesson with the class.

Link to Language Arts

WRITE A LETTER Many countries have embassies in large cities such as San Francisco and New York or in Washington, D.C. From your local library, obtain embassy addresses for countries mentioned in this unit or other countries your children may be interested in learning about. Children can write to the embassies for information. Keep brochures, maps, and other materials in a global center for the children to use as references throughout the unit.

AUDIO

Use the **UNIT 6 TEXT ON TAPE AUDIOCASSETTE** for a reading of this unit.

ASIAN TRANSLATIONS

For students who speak **Cambodian, Cantonese, Hmong,** or **Vietnamese,** use the **ASIAN TRANSLATIONS** for Unit 6. The Harcourt Brace program is also available in a **SPANISH EDITION.**

PREVIEW THE UNIT

Think About Words

Organize children into small groups, and have them categorize the following statements as true or false. Ask children to record their answers on paper.

1. _____ <u>Pioneers</u> moved across the country looking for new places to build homes.
2. _____ The <u>ancestors</u> of many Americans came from other countries.
3. _____ A <u>custom</u> is something you do a different way each time.
4. _____ <u>Artifacts</u> tell us about people and how they live.
5. _____ People in different countries cannot <u>communicate</u> with one another.

pioneer

A person who first settles in a new place.

ancestor

Someone in a family who lived long ago.

custom

A way of doing something.

220

ACTIVITY CHOICES

Meet Individual Needs

ENGLISH LANGUAGE LEARNERS
Give children time to add the new words to their vocabulary notebooks. Remind them to copy the definition or draw pictures for the words that they are not sure of. Then invite them to look back through their books as a review. Partners may wish to tell each other what they have learned about their new English words.

Link to Language Arts

JOURNAL Ask children to choose one of the unit vocabulary words and use it in a KWL chart. Children should write everything they know about the word in their journals. Then they should write one thing they would like to know about that word. Remind them to refer to their journals when their word is introduced in a lesson and add something they learned.

Link to Music

SING A SONG Sing the following verse to the tune "The Muffin Man," each time substituting a different vocabulary word. At the end of each verse, ask children to read or tell the definition.

Oh, do you know what *ancestor* means, *ancestor* means, *ancestor* means?

Oh, do you know what *ancestor* means? Now tell me what you know.

artifact

An object that is made and used by people.

communication

Sharing ideas with others.

221

Work with Words

Invite children to turn to pages 220–221 in their Pupil Book. Then direct their attention to the words and their definitions on these pages. Explain that these words tell the main ideas of Unit 6. Call on volunteers to read each word and its definition aloud. (Note: For additional vocabulary, see the Planning Chart on pages 218C–218D in this Teacher's Edition.) Then reread the true-false statements from the previous page. Ask children to use what they learned about the meaning of each word to find out if their answers were correct.

> **VOCABULARY BLACKLINES**
>
> You may wish to reproduce individual copies of the vocabulary words for this unit. They are found in the back of your Teacher's Edition.

PUPIL BOOK OR UNIT BIG BOOK

VOCABULARY CARDS

Display the unit VOCABULARY PICTURE CARDS. Ask children to identify the three words that tell about things that came before. (*pioneers, ancestors, artifacts*)

Meet Individual Needs

VISUAL LEARNERS Ask children to write one of the unit vocabulary words and its definition in the center of a sheet of drawing paper. Encourage them to draw or cut out and paste pictures from newspapers or magazines that are examples of that word. For example, for the word *communication*, children might show people talking, a television set, a letter, a computer, and a walkie-talkie.

SET THE SCENE WITH LITERATURE

PREVIEW

Ask children to turn to pages 222–223. Have a volunteer read aloud the title *Pride*. Encourage children to share their thoughts about the word. Ask them to consider whether they think it is good or bad to be proud.

Q. **What are some things that might make us feel proud?**
Responses might include doing well in school, helping someone else, learning to read, being a good friend, helping your parents.

Set the Scene with **Literature**

Pride

by Alma Flor Ada
illustrated by Gerardo Suzan

Proud of my family
proud of my language
proud of my culture
proud of my race
proud to be who I am.

222

ACTIVITY CHOICES

Background

ABOUT THE POET Alma Flor Ada was born in Camagey, Cuba, and lived in Spain and Peru before coming to the United States. She is a professor of multicultural education at the University of San Francisco and has had many children's books published in Spain, Mexico, Argentina, and Peru. Her first book was *The Gold Coin* (Atheneum, 1991), illustrated by Neil Waldman. Dr. Ada has four children and lives in San Mateo, California with her husband.

Link to Art

ABOUT THE ARTIST Gerardo Suzan lives in Torreón, a small city in northern Mexico. Suzan enjoys working on picture books for children around the world, creating scenes that connect with reality but at the same time portray a whimsical element of fantasy. He works with acrylic paint because he can add colors and textures. For this poem he said, "I thought about working with textures of sand, just as if I had worked on the walls of old village houses in my country." Invite children to mix substances (sand, oatmeal, flour) with paint or adhere materials (glitter, rice, confetti) to wet paintings to give their illustrations different textures.

Orgullo

por Alma Flor Ada
ilustrado por Gerardo Suzan

Orgullosa de mi familia
Orgullosa de mi idioma
Orgullosa de mi cultura
Orgullosa de mi raza
Orgullosa de ser quien soy.

223

PUPIL BOOK OR UNIT BIG BOOK

Ask a volunteer to read the poem aloud. Then invite the class to read it aloud together until they can read it chorally. Help children realize that it is important to be proud of who they are. Language, culture, race, and family all help make us who we are. Encourage children to share something that makes them feel proud.

Q. **What would make your family proud of you?** Answers might include good grades, kindness, honesty, willingness to help others.

Meet Individual Needs

ENGLISH LANGUAGE LEARNERS After reading the poem, help children understand that each one of them belongs to a family and shares a language, culture, and race with a larger group of people. Focus on the phrase *proud of my race*. Explain that there are several meanings of the word *race*. Read each definition and ask children to identify the correct meaning in this poem.

race—a contest of speed, as between runners, swimmers, or cars

race—a group of people that share the same features, such as hair and skin color

Link Literature

To show children that pride in one's family and culture is important, begin the unit with the book *Tonight Is Carnaval* by Arthur Dorros. (Dutton, 1991) This story is about a young boy who looks forward to the *carnaval* that is celebrated in his South American town. Ask children to tell about a celebration such as a state fair or carnival that is important to their community.

AUDIO

You may wish to play the **TEXT ON TAPE AUDIOCASSETTE** for "Pride" as children study the picture.

LITERATURE BIG BOOK

HOMEPLACE

by Anne Shelby

illustrations by
Wendy Anderson Halperin

Invite children to begin the unit by reading *Homeplace* by Anne Shelby. Detailed illustrations and easy-to-read text help children recognize people's dependence on one another and on their environment. Just as a family photo album connects a child with his or her ancestry, *Homeplace* uses the age-old art of storytelling to introduce readers to the concept that families are always growing and changing.

About the Author and the Illustrator

Anne Shelby lives on a farm near Oneida, Kentucky. She has written three other picture books: *We Keep a Store*, illustrated by John Ward, and *What to Do About Pollution…* and *Potluck*, both illustrated by Irene Trivas.

Wendy Anderson Halperin lives with her family in South Haven, Michigan. The first book she illustrated was *Hunting the White Cow* by Tres Seymour. It was a *School Library Journal* Best Book of 1993, a 1994 ALA Notable Book, and the winner of the honor book award in the Marion Vannett Ridgeway Competition.

Reading the Story

Read and discuss the literature to address the following objectives:

1. Recognize how early settlers met their needs.
2. Identify ways people change and use their environment to meet their needs.
3. Explain the importance of working together.
4. Discuss a family history.

Social Studies Connection

Ask children to tell what they know about how the land and homes looked when the United States was first settled and how both have changed over time.

Q. **What are some reasons a family might want to make changes to the place in which they live?** Children's responses may include one or more of the following ideas: families get larger; people want to use new inventions in their homes; not everyone likes the same things.

List on the board or on chart paper some changes that occurred in this story.

▶ The homeplace grew from a log cabin to a large farmhouse.
▶ The women changed their ways of doing chores.
▶ New and faster transportation methods were developed.

Organize children into small groups. Ask each group to create a time line to show the changes in a particular item in this story. Have children draw small pictures to show, for example, how the changing house, the farm tools and machinery, or the baby's bed looked in each time period.

1

PEOPLE ON THE MOVE

OBJECTIVES

1. Describe the role of pioneers in the settlement and growth of our country.
2. Recognize that people came from many places to live in the United States.
3. Identify types of transportation used to move people to and across the United States.

VOCABULARY

pioneer (p. 224)

RESOURCES

Pupil Book/Unit Big Book, pp. 224–227
Write-On Chart 21
Activity Book, p. 44

ACTIVITY CHOICES

Home Involvement

If any children in your class have lived in countries other than the United States, suggest that they talk with their families about why they came to this country and how they chose this community. Ask children to share with classmates what they learn.

"PRIMARY SOURCE"

Share the following firsthand accounts of immigrants' experiences.

I Was Dreaming to Come to America: Memories from the Ellis Island Oral History Project by Veronica Lawlor. Viking, 1995.
If Your Name Was Changed at Ellis Island by Ellen Levine. Scholastic. 1993.

1. ACCESS

Sing with children the traditional American song "I've Been Working on the Railroad." Ask whether people have always been able to travel across the country by train. Have children suggest types of transportation people might have used for moving long distances before trains were invented. Then invite children who have moved to tell the locations of their old and new homes and the kinds of transportation they used to move themselves and their belongings.

> I've been working on the railroad, all the live-long day.
> I've been working on the railroad, just to pass the time away.
> Can't you hear the whistle blowing? Rise up so early in the morn;
> Can't you hear the captain shouting, "Dinah, blow your horn!"

Focus on the Main Idea

In this lesson children will encounter the pioneers who traveled from the East to clear the land and "open up" the West. Then they will meet immigrants who arrived in the United States from many other parts of the world. Along the way, children will explore the forms of transportation that made these moves possible.

Multicultural Link

The population of the United States is becoming more ethnically diverse. Immigrants from all over the world have come to live here. Some have come for religious freedom, some to escape wars or persecution, and some to build better lives for themselves and their families. From 1820 to 1990, about 37 million immigrants came to the United States from Europe, 13 million came from Latin America, 6 million came from Asia, 300,000 came from Africa, and 150,000 came from Australia and New Zealand.

2. BUILD

Key Content Summary

Through discussion of the pioneer movement, the immigration surge, and the contribution of transportation to both, children will begin to understand and appreciate the diversity of our country. Children will also recognize the common feelings and experiences of people from all parts of the world as they settled and moved across a new and strange country.

Vocabulary

Remind children that settlers are people who make the first homes in a new place. Define a *pioneer* as one of the first people to settle in a new place. Point out that pioneers are often doing something that is dangerous or difficult.

History

Origins, Spread, and Influence Invite children to read pages 224–225 aloud. Discuss what it would be like to travel a long distance with all your belongings. Point out that the pioneers had no roads to follow. The settlers who came later followed paths or trails that had been made by the pioneers or explorers who went before them.

Q. What might have been difficult or dangerous about the pioneer journeys you read about on page 224? People could get sick or hurt and not be able to get help; they might run out of food or water; weather could be bad; wagons might break down.

Geography

Location Invite partners to scan the text on pages 224–225 and search for place names. Remind children to look for capital letters at the beginnings of names. Compile a class list of the locations on chart paper. Using United States and world maps, help children locate Spain, England, the Atlantic and Pacific oceans, the areas in the United States known as the West and the East, and the states of California, Nebraska, and Utah.

LESSON 1
People on the Move

Remember that settlers came to live in America long ago. People from Spain settled in the West. English settlers built communities in the East. There was a lot of land in between that was not settled.

Then people from the East began to move across the country as pioneers. A **pioneer** is a person who first settles in a new place. The pioneers traveled on foot, on horseback, and in wagons. They crossed rivers, plains, and mountains. They started farms and ranches and built towns all across the land.

"Pioneers of the West" by Helen Lundeberg

224

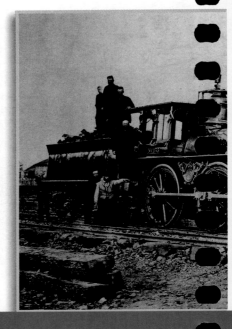

ACTIVITY CHOICES

Reading Support

FIND MAIN IDEA AND DETAILS
Write the lesson title, "People on the Move," on chart paper and ask children what they think it might mean. Explain that the title gives the main, or most important, idea of a lesson and that sentences that tell more about the main idea are called details. Pause as you progress through the pages to have children identify details about people on the move. List children's ideas on the chart.

WRITE-ON CHARTS

Be a Pioneer
Use Write-On Chart 21 to extend and enrich this lesson. See Teacher's Edition page W65.

More pioneers moved across the country. Soon trains brought the things that the communities needed. They also brought more people.

Some people started businesses. Communities built schools and churches. Some towns grew into cities. In time every part of the country was settled, from the Atlantic Ocean to the Pacific Ocean.

The first railroad to cross the country was built 130 years ago. One group of workers started from Sacramento, California. Another group started from Omaha, Nebraska. The tracks met in Promontory, Utah. Now people could travel by train all the way across the continent.

225

Background

RAILROADS The United States government provided land for the world's first railroad to cross a continent. Workers, including thousands of Chinese immigrants, built the railroad eastward from California. Thousands of European immigrants worked westward from Nebraska. One of the hardest jobs was crossing the Rocky Mountains and the Sierra Nevada. Where the tracks met, a golden spike was driven to join them on May 10, 1869, at Promontory Point, Utah.

Meet Individual Needs

ADVANCED LEARNERS Ask children to design a transportation time line. Time lines might include drawn or cutout pictures of various vehicles used for westward expansion or might center on the development of railroads only. Guide children in finding reference materials such as *Trains and Railroads* by Sydney Wood. (Dorling Kindersley, 1992) Time lines can include dates or simply be a sequence of labeled pictures.

Visual Analysis

Interpret Pictures As children examine the photographs on pages 224–225, help them identify ways that people traveled across the country to new homes. Ask children to imagine themselves in the place of a person in one of the photographs.

Q. **How might you be feeling? What would you be thinking about the choices your family has made?** Children might describe feelings of fear, excitement, adventure, or independence. They might say that they would look forward to starting a new life or that because they would be the first people to settle in a new place, they would have more choices about what kind of business to start and where to live.

Economics

Interdependence and Income Discuss the importance of the railroad in the growth of settlements. Explain that people liked to live where trains could bring them goods they needed. So settlements on railroad lines grew into towns.

Q. **What kinds of things do you think the trains carried to the new communities across the country?** food, lumber, animals, coal, oil for lanterns, new settlers

History

People and Events Across Time and Place Read with children the text on pages 226–227. Help children understand that for the people who came to the United States, traveling across a huge ocean for many weeks was not easy. In addition, having enough money for the trip did not mean they could be sure of staying here. Everyone who arrived in this country— men, women and children alike—had to answer certain questions and pass a physical examination.

Q. **What do you think are some reasons people traveled long distances to come to the United States?** They wanted a chance for a good job and a better life; they wanted to live in a country at peace; they believed life would be easier here.

Geography

Location Display a world map and a map of the United States. Invite volunteers to locate the countries of Russia, Turkey, and Poland. Then help them find Ellis Island in New York Harbor and Angel Island in San Francisco Bay. Lead a discussion about possible routes people from these countries might have traveled and on which coast of the United States they would have landed.

Visual Analysis

Interpret Pictures Point out that the people in the large photograph are carrying boxes and bags.

Q. **What do you think these travelers brought with them?** Children might suggest family treasures, clothing, dishes, food, photographs, jewelry.

3. CLOSE

Invite children to summarize the lesson by telling about the two groups of "people on the move" described in the text. Invite them to speculate about which might have been more difficult—the long journey across the United States or starting a new life in a new place—and to give reasons for their answers.

Check Understanding

The child can
—— describe the role of pioneers in the settlement and growth of our country.
—— recognize that people came from many places to live in the United States.
—— identify types of transportation used to move people to and across the United States.

Think Critically

Q. **How was transportation important in the settlement of our country?** Answers will vary but should include the idea that horses, wagons, trains, and ships were needed not only to move people to and across the country but also to take them supplies they needed to build communities.

Many people moved from place to place in the United States. People also came from other places around the world to live in this new country. They sailed here on big ships. In the East the ships landed at Ellis Island. In the West they landed at Angel Island.

In both places the new people had to tell why they wanted to move to the United States. Doctors also made sure they were healthy.

Read what some children thought about coming to a strange new land.

226

Ellis Island

ACTIVITY CHOICES

Background

ELLIS ISLAND Ellis Island and Liberty Island, site of the Statue of Liberty, lie near each other in New York Harbor. Ellis Island is named for the man who owned it in the 1700s. Immigrants got off their ships and waited on Ellis Island to find out whether they would be allowed into the United States. Ninety-eight percent of all immigrants were accepted, but some, including criminals and those with infectious diseases, were not. More than 12 million immigrants passed through Ellis Island in the 60 years before it closed in 1954. The busiest years were between 1918 and 1924. Ellis Island reopened in 1990 as a national historic site. Visitors to its museum can see actual passports, clothing, toys, and old photographs. They can also hear recorded memories of those who entered the country there. The American Immigrant Wall of Honor contains 200,000 names of immigrants to this country.

Golda Meir from Russia

"Going to America then was almost like going to the moon. We were all bound for places about which we knew nothing at all and for a country that was totally strange to us."

Eleven-year-old from Turkey

"I couldn't read, I couldn't write, I couldn't speak. I had never been to school in my life until I came here, on account of the war over there. But I picked it up. I picked it up very good, thank God."

Helen Cohen from Poland

"When I was about 10 years old I said, 'I have to go to America.' I was dreaming about it. And I was dreaming, and my dream came true. When I came here, I was in a different world. I'm free. I'm just like a bird. You can fly and land on any tree and you're free."

What Do You Know?

1. How did the pioneers travel across America? on foot, on horseback, in wagons, and later by train

2. How would you feel about moving to another country?

227

Performance Assessment Invite children to pretend they are pioneers or immigrants. Ask each child to write a brief "quotable" description of his or her feelings about the journey.

What to Look For Evaluate children's descriptions to note whether they thoughtfully described their feelings about the trip.

Using the Activity Book Distribute copies of Activity Book page 44. Ask children to read the directions aloud. Have them complete the ticket information and then draw a picture of themselves showing the type of transportation they would use.

Activity Book page 44

Extend and Enrich

EXPLORE EXPRESSIONS Invite children to reread Helen Cohen's quotation. Discuss the way Helen spoke of a bird flying free to express her happiness. Ask children to imagine they are leaving the homes they love and moving to a new country far away where they do not know the language, the customs, or any people. Have them create a diary page of one of their first experiences in their new country. Invite children to share their diaries by reading them aloud.

Reteach the Main Idea

DISCUSS JOURNEYS Organize children into small groups. Ask each group to pretend its members are a pioneer family traveling across the United States or an immigrant family arriving from another country. Have groups discuss where they are coming from, their reason for traveling, where they are going, and their way of travel. Group members should also make a list of supplies they will need for their journey. Then invite groups to share the information about their journey.

Background

GOLDA MEIR This girl from a poor family in Kiev, Ukraine, grew up to become the leader of Israel. Her family immigrated to the United States, to Milwaukee, Wisconsin, in 1906 when she was eight. In 1921 she moved to Palestine, now Israel. Meir worked to establish Israel as a free Jewish nation. After Israel declared its independence in 1948, Golda Meir held many official jobs in the new country's government. She was Israel's prime minister from 1969 to 1974.

HANDS-ON OPTION

Before-and-After Pictures

Objective: Describe the role of pioneers in the settlement and growth of our country.

Materials: drawing paper; crayons or markers; magazine pictures of virgin forests, mountains, and prairies (optional)

Show pictures of forests or have children imagine how land looks before people cut down trees and other plants to build homes and make roads. Have children fold a sheet of drawing paper in half and draw "Before" and "After" pictures. In the Before picture, children can show how a place in the United States looked when the pioneers first saw it. In the After picture, they can show how it looked after the settlers had built a town. **(VISUAL/TACTILE)**

Sing a Journey

Objective: Identify types of transportation used to move people to and across the United States.

Materials: chart paper

Sing the song "I've Been Working on the Railroad" with children again to familiarize them with its four sections. Then tell them that they are going to help make up a song to this tune about the way early settlers traveled to this country. Start off the song with "We're off across the ocean on a . . . ," inviting children to supply a suitable ending, such as *big boat*. Write this line on chart paper, and add a second line: "Such a long, long way!" Then ask children for suggestions to fill out the rest of the first section of the tune, focusing on reasons for and feelings about the journey.

Where the tune changes ("Dinah, won't you blow"), start children off on a new chart page with "Going to take our . . . ," and have them complete that section as a list of possessions settlers would be likely to take. When the tune changes again ("Someone's in the kitchen with Dinah"), start a third chart page with "Here's what we'll do when we get there," and have children make up lines about what settlers would need to do. Begin the section that corresponds to "Fee, fi, fiddle-ee-i-o" with "Oh, my, we're so glad we came!" on a fourth page, and have children tell why the settlers are glad to be in their new land.

Sing the whole song through with children, and then divide the class into groups. Challenge each group to follow the pattern on the chart pages and make up a song for one of the ways pioneers traveled across the country. For example, children might begin: "We're off to California [in a wagon, on the railroad, by a stagecoach]." Invite groups to perform their songs for the class, adding actions to dramatize them if they wish. **(AUDITORY/TACTILE)**

Make a Primary Source

Objectives: Recognize that people came from many places to live in the United States. Identify types of transportation used to move people to and across the United States.

Materials: beige paper, pencils

Help children understand that when immigrants and pioneers left home, they often had to leave people they loved. Have children imagine that they are immigrants. Have them write a letter to someone in their old home describing their journey to their new home. To give the letter an aged look, have them fold their letter as if it had been in an envelope and wrinkle it. **(TACTILE)**

Dear Grandma,

We're here at last! The trip was long and hard. We slept in a big, dark room with many other people. The ship was cold and the waves made it bounce all the time. But when we saw the Statue of Liberty we forgot all that. We can't wait to start our new life. I miss you.

Love,
Greta

2

WINTER DAYS IN THE BIG WOODS

OBJECTIVES

1. Describe the life of a pioneer family.
2. Compare the ways people got their food long ago with the ways people get their food today.
3. Explain how weather affected pioneers.

RESOURCES

Pupil Book/Unit Big Book, pp. 228–239
Write-On Charts 29, 33
Activity Book, p. 45
Music Audio, "When I First Came to This Land"
Text on Tape Audio

ACTIVITY CHOICES

Background

THE AUTHOR Laura Ingalls Wilder wrote a series of books in which she shares her adventures as a pioneer child. She tells how her family traveled by covered wagon across the Midwest and then settled in the Big Woods in Wisconsin.

AUDIO

 Use the UNIT 6 TEXT ON TAPE for the literature in this lesson.

1. ACCESS

Ask children if they have ever made cookies. If they have, ask them where they got the ingredients to make the cookies. Explain that while most of the items probably came from a grocery store or supermarket, some people grow or raise many food items themselves.

Focus on the Main Idea

Lesson 1 discussed how settlers moved across the country and started farms and ranches. In this lesson children will read about the pioneers, the very first settlers. They will read about how one pioneer family met its needs for food, shelter, and entertainment. As children look at the daily lives of the members of this family, invite them to think about which ways of doing things remain the same today and which have changed over time.

Community Involvement

Help children make a connection to the past by arranging for a guest speaker to demonstrate cooking utensils from long ago. Ask the guest to bring, if possible, a butter churn, an iron kettle, antique ladles, toasting forks, husking pins, and corn graters. Local historical societies, antique dealers, museum curators, and other community agencies are good resources for speakers.

2. BUILD

Key Content Summary

"Winter Days in the Big Woods" is part of the autobiography *Little House in the Big Woods* about the childhood of a pioneer girl named Laura Ingalls. Laura lived with her family in a little house in the Big Woods of Wisconsin. As winter approached, Laura and her family worked to get the little house ready for the cold days ahead. By the time the winter snows began to fall, Laura and her family were warm and cozy in their log house.

Auditory Learning

Read Expressively Have children take turns reading aloud. Explain that as they read, they should use their voice to show how the characters feel.

History

People and Events Across Time and Place Tell children that long ago, people traveled across the United States looking for lands where no one yet lived. Many families, like Laura Ingalls's, made the dangerous trip across the wilderness in covered wagons. Usually, several families traveled together, helping one another along the way and sharing their food and other supplies.

Q. **Why do you think the Ingalls family decided to make this dangerous trip?** to make a better life with a home and land of their own

LESSON **2**

Learn Culture through Literature

WINTER DAYS IN THE BIG WOODS

by Laura Ingalls Wilder
illustrated by Renée Graef

228

ACTIVITY CHOICES

Reading Support

PREVIEW AND PREDICT Discuss what Laura and her family are doing on the first page of the story. Explain that pioneer families did not have refrigerators. Ask children to suggest foods the pioneers ate and ways they kept the food from spoiling. Make a diagram of children's responses.

Can It

tomatoes
beans
pumpkin
beets

Dry It

buffalo
beef
turkey
pork

Link to Music

VOCAL/SONG Invite children to learn and then sing "When I First Came to This Land," an American ballad about settling this country.

AUDIO

Use the UNIT 6 MUSIC AUDIOCASSETTE to hear "When I First Came to This Land."

Once upon a time, a little girl named Laura lived in the Big Woods of Wisconsin in a little house made of logs.

Laura lived in the little house with her Pa, her Ma, her big sister Mary, her baby sister Carrie, and their good old bulldog Jack.

Winter was coming to the Big Woods. Soon the little house would be covered with snow. Pa went hunting every day so that they would have meat during the long, cold winter.

Ma, Laura, and Mary gathered potatoes and carrots, beets and turnips, cabbages and onions, and peppers and pumpkins from the garden next to the little house.

229

Geography

Location The "Big Woods" in this story are in the state of Wisconsin. Assist children in locating Wisconsin on a map or globe.

Q. **What kind of winter weather do you think this state has?** very cold and snowy

Visual Analysis

Interpret Pictures Ask children to describe the house in the picture. Help them understand that the spaces between the logs were filled in with clay, moss, or mud.

Q. **How do you think the house was heated?** by burning logs in a fireplace

How is the Ingallses' log cabin like your home? How is it different? Children may mention a variety of similarities and differences.

Background

BUILDING A HOME Pioneers built cabins from logs 12 to 15 feet long. One person alone could not lift the heavy logs, so neighbors gathered to help. House-raising was one of the many ways pioneer families helped one another. Discuss with children ways families today help one another.

WRITE-ON CHARTS

Use WRITE-ON CHART 33 to help locate Wisconsin.

Meet Individual Needs

ENGLISH LANGUAGE LEARNERS Invite children to make flash cards by drawing or cutting out pictures of vegetables, including those mentioned on page 229. Help them label each picture in English. Invite children to review the cards with a partner who speaks English fluently.

VISUAL LEARNERS Help children visualize various features of a pioneer homestead by having them make a map showing the log cabin and areas where these things might be found: garden, barn, woodpile, forest, and fenced areas for pig, cow, and chickens. Ask children to explain their arrangement.

Geography

Human-Environment Interactions
Help children understand that pioneers depended on having the right weather to grow their food. Focus attention on the first sentence on page 230.

Q. **Why do you think pioneer families picked their vegetables before winter comes?** The snow would kill the plants; they need the food to eat during the winter.

Then construct a chart showing weather requirements for various vegetables, such as carrots, cabbages, beets, and pumpkins. Have children write *yes* or *no* to indicate whether or not the vegetables need the kind of weather shown.

	☀	🌧	❄❄
Carrots	yes	yes	no
Cabbages	yes	yes	no
Beets	yes	yes	no
Pumpkins	yes	yes	no

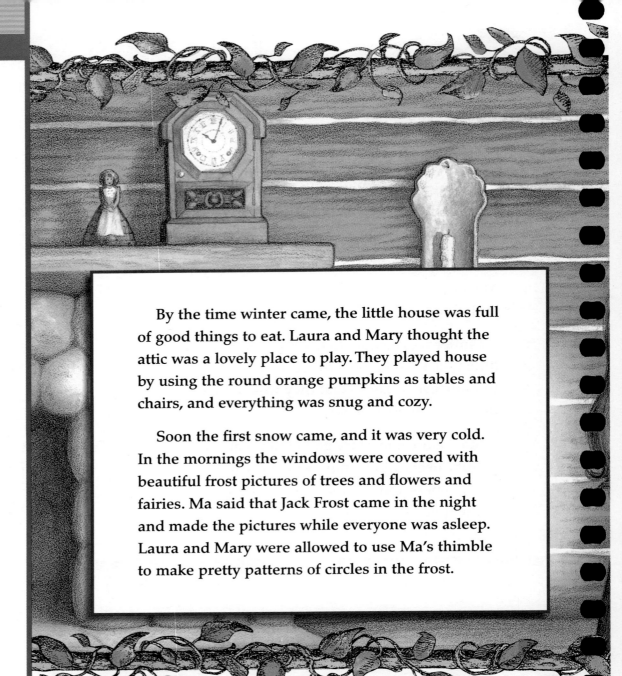

By the time winter came, the little house was full of good things to eat. Laura and Mary thought the attic was a lovely place to play. They played house by using the round orange pumpkins as tables and chairs, and everything was snug and cozy.

Soon the first snow came, and it was very cold. In the mornings the windows were covered with beautiful frost pictures of trees and flowers and fairies. Ma said that Jack Frost came in the night and made the pictures while everyone was asleep. Laura and Mary were allowed to use Ma's thimble to make pretty patterns of circles in the frost.

230

ACTIVITY CHOICES

Link to Health

NUTRITION Help children understand the simple food needs of early pioneers. Review the basic food groups—breads and cereals, fruit and vegetables, meat, and dairy. Then discuss ways in which settlers could find or grow foods to meet their nutritional needs. Ask children to make charts showing the kinds of foods settlers ate in each food group. You may wish to comment on the limitations in their diet because of food storage and preparation methods.

231

Understanding the Story

Children may recall that Laura and Mary used Ma's thimble to scratch pictures in the frost. Tell children that a *thimble* is a small metal cap that fits over the finger. It is used to push a needle through heavy material when sewing. If possible, bring in a thimble for children to try on.

Economics

Interdependence Tell children that pioneer families depended on one another for some of their needs. Point out that farmers today supply the needs of many people across the country.

Q. **If there had been a huge crop of carrots, what might a farmer from long ago have done with them?** Can the carrots for use later; sell them to or trade them with other families; feed them to the cattle.

What might a farmer today do with a crop of carrots? A farmer might sell the carrots at a roadside stand or sell them to a food processing factory.

Meet Individual Needs

ADVANCED LEARNERS Tell children that when people wake to find frosty designs on their windows, they often say that Jack Frost has been there in the night. Ask children how they think the story of this make-believe character got started. Invite interested children to research the history behind the name.

VISUAL LEARNERS If possible, let children watch a portion of a television newscast that shows weather-related problems such as floods, droughts, or blizzards. Discuss with them the problems these natural disasters cause for farmers today. Ask children how they think such weather affected the pioneers.

Link to Science

WEATHER Invite children to choose a fruit or vegetable and find out how that food is grown. Tell children that early farmers recorded in almanacs the best times for planting and harvesting different foods. Help children work with calendars to chart the times to grow the foods they chose. Discuss the weather conditions that help and hinder good crops and their harvests.

History

Connections Past to Present Explain that pioneer men, women, and children did outdoor and indoor chores every day from the time the sun came up to the time it went down. The children often helped pick crops, grind corn, wash clothes, take care of animals and babies, sew, and do other tasks. Ask children to compare the pioneer children's lives with their own lives today.

Q. **What chores do you do?** Children may say they make their beds, empty the dishwasher, feed the dog, or do other simple chores.

Critical Thinking

Ask children to reflect on the chores and responsibilities of pioneer children.

Q. **In what ways was everyday life hard for pioneer children?** Children had to work nearly all day; they had very little time to play; they had to help their families make or grow the things they needed or wanted.

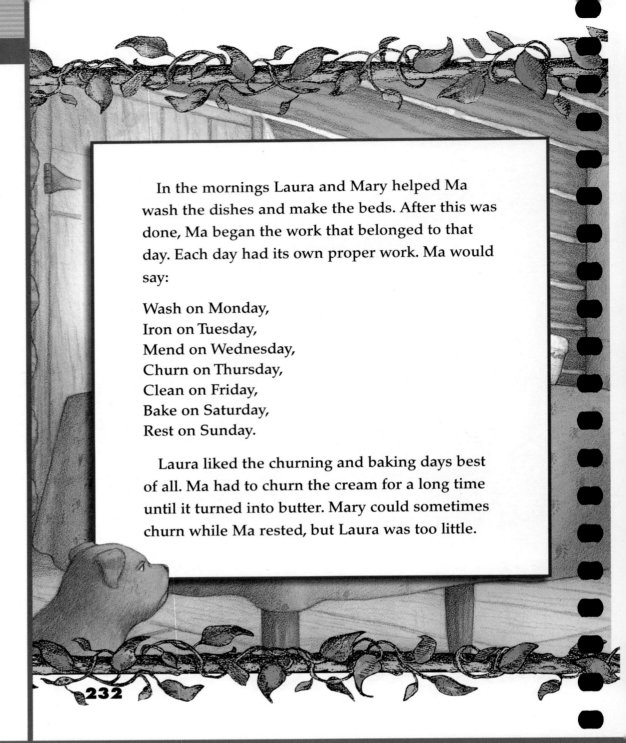

In the mornings Laura and Mary helped Ma wash the dishes and make the beds. After this was done, Ma began the work that belonged to that day. Each day had its own proper work. Ma would say:

Wash on Monday,
Iron on Tuesday,
Mend on Wednesday,
Churn on Thursday,
Clean on Friday,
Bake on Saturday,
Rest on Sunday.

Laura liked the churning and baking days best of all. Ma had to churn the cream for a long time until it turned into butter. Mary could sometimes churn while Ma rested, but Laura was too little.

232

ACTIVITY CHOICES

Reading Support

READ AHEAD As children read the list of daily chores, they may come across some unfamiliar words, such as *churn*. Tell children to read ahead to discover the meaning of the word.

Background

SCHOOLS Children may be interested to know that many pioneer children went to school. Some children were taught at home by their parents. Some settlements had small schoolhouses with a schoolteacher. Either way, most pioneer children had lessons only in the winter, when there were fewer chores to be done.

233

PUPIL BOOK **OR** UNIT BIG BOOK

Understanding the Story

Ma and the girls had specific chores for each day of the week. Review the chores mentioned on page 232. List separately chores children are familiar with and chores they are not familiar with. Review the lists, explaining chores such as mending and churning.

Critical Thinking

Help children think about the advantages and disadvantages of settling in the wilderness.

Q. **What do you think would happen if someone in the family did not churn the butter, bake the bread, and grind the corn each day?** The family would not have food to eat.

How would having another family living nearby change life for the pioneers? Neighbors would be able to share chores, trade food and other things they needed, and have friends.

How do you think pioneers may have felt when other families settled near them? Responses should include both the advantage of being able to share responsibilities and the disadvantage of having to share the land.

Meet Individual Needs

ENGLISH LANGUAGE LEARNERS

Explain that the word *iron* has more than one meaning.
1. It is a strong metal.
2. It is the name of an object made of metal that is heated and used to press wrinkles out of clothes.
3. It is the action used to press the wrinkles out of clothes.

Have children draw a picture to show each meaning. Then ask children to define the word as it is used in the story.

Visual Analysis

Interpret Pictures Invite children to look at the furniture in the pictures on pages 234–235.

Q. **How do you think this pioneer family got the furniture for their log cabin?** They may have made it, bought it, or traded for it.

Where could they get the wood to build the furniture? They could cut down trees from a nearby forest.

Geography

Human-Environment Interactions Tell children that pioneer women made beautiful quilts to keep their families warm on cold winter nights. The quilts were made from scraps of worn-out clothes and leftover yarn. Pioneers were very good at recycling and reusing items.

Q. **What did Laura and Mary make?** little loaves of bread from leftover bread dough and cookies from cookie dough

---

"PRIMARY SOURCE"

You may wish to share with children *Pioneers* by Martin W. Sandler. (HarperCollins, 1994). It includes more than 100 photographs and illustrations from the Library of Congress, bringing the frontier to life in all its danger, its struggle, and its adventure.

234

ACTIVITY CHOICES

Background

SEWING Making clothes was a job that took a long time. Some pioneer families kept a sheep or two, from which they got wool. Families who lived where cotton would grow often grew some. Pioneer women used spinning wheels to twist the fibers of wool or cotton into wool yarn or cotton thread. Then they wove the yarn or thread into woolen or cotton cloth. They used the cloth to make shirts, pants, dresses, and capes. If possible, ask someone from your community to demonstrate how yarn or thread is spun using a spinning wheel.

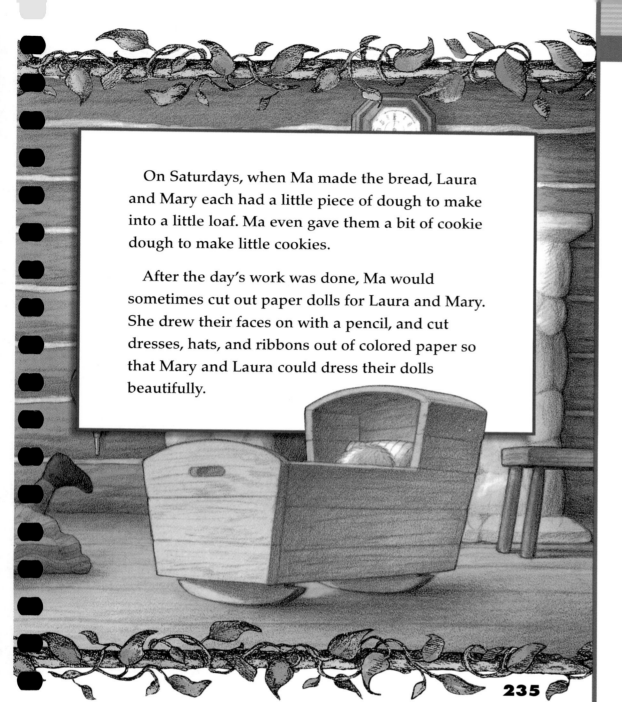

On Saturdays, when Ma made the bread, Laura and Mary each had a little piece of dough to make into a little loaf. Ma even gave them a bit of cookie dough to make little cookies.

After the day's work was done, Ma would sometimes cut out paper dolls for Laura and Mary. She drew their faces on with a pencil, and cut dresses, hats, and ribbons out of colored paper so that Mary and Laura could dress their dolls beautifully.

235

Understanding the Story

Children may recall that Ma cut out paper dolls for Laura and Mary. Reread the part of the story on page 235 that describes how the dolls were made. Then invite children to make paper dolls for each character in the story and use the dolls to act out the story.

Economics

Interdependence Ask children to think of things they need or want. Discuss whether we always get what we want, and why or why not. Then ask if children of long ago might have had these same wants, and why or why not.

Q. **Where would you go to get these things today? How would children of long ago have gotten them?**

You may wish to record children's responses on a chart similar to the one shown here.

Long Ago	Today
I want a doll.	I want a doll.
We might make paper dolls.	We might buy one at the toy store.

PUPIL BOOK OR UNIT BIG BOOK

Meet Individual Needs

ENGLISH LANGUAGE LEARNERS

Use small self-stick notes to make labels for objects in the picture, such as the rocker, paper dolls, lamp, and clock. Place the notes beside the corresponding pictures on the page. Let children remove the labels when they can identify the objects in English.

WRITE-ON CHARTS

Use WRITE-ON CHART 29 to create the "wants" chart.

History

Origins, Spreads, and Influence Ask children to look at the pictures in the story or in reference books to find ways pioneer families lighted their homes.

Q. **How did the pioneers light their homes?** with candles, oil lamps, fires in their fireplaces

Why do you think these ways might be hard to use? Each had an open flame that was dangerous and had to be carefully watched; pioneers had to make candles, clean oil lamps, and cut wood for fireplaces.

What do people use to light houses today? People use electricity for lamps and other kinds of lights.

Understanding the Story

Ask children to reread the part on page 237 where Pa comes home and then study the picture on page 236.

Q. **How do you think Pa felt when he came in at night? Why did he feel this way?** He was probably very tired from working so hard.

What was one way Pa relaxed and had fun? He played the fiddle and sang with the girls.

Why do you think that nearly all of the things the family did inside the house took place in front of the fireplace? It was the warmest place in the house, and it gave the most light.

236

ACTIVITY CHOICES

Meet Individual Needs

KINESTHETIC LEARNERS Children may enjoy clapping their hands and tapping their feet to the rhythm of the song "Yankee Doodle."

ADVANCED LEARNERS The pioneers had to be able to do many jobs in order to meet the needs and wants of their families. Invite children to list all the job titles a pioneer could have been given, such as carpenter, musician, logger, hunter, farmer, preacher, and teacher.

Link to Music

MUSICAL INSTRUMENTS Tell children that pioneers taught themselves to play such instruments as mouth organs, fiddles, banjos, guitars, and pianos. Sometimes they used household items such as washboards and washtubs, metal spoons, pots and pans, jugs, and carved wooden whistles to make music. Invite children to make musical instruments using metal, glass, rubber bands, cardboard containers, and other items they choose. Create a classroom "jug band" to play some old favorite folk tunes, such as "The Old Gray Mare," "If I Had a Hammer," and "My Bonnie Lies Over the Ocean."

But the best time of all was at night, when Pa came home. He would throw off his fur cap and coat and mittens and call, "Where's my little half-pint of sweet cider half drunk up?" That was Laura, because she was so small.

Sometimes Pa would take down his fiddle and sing. Pa would keep time with his foot. Laura and Mary would clap their hands to the music when he sang:

"Yankee Doodle went to town,
He wore his striped trousies,
He swore he couldn't see the town,
There was so many houses."

237

PUPIL BOOK OR UNIT BIG BOOK

Link Literature

Share with children *Laura Ingalls Wilder*, a biography of the woman who wrote *Little House in the Big Woods*. Children will learn more about Laura's childhood on the American frontier, her days as a farm wife, and her career as an author.

Thought and Expression Ask children if they know the song "Yankee Doodle." Tell them that it is a song that was first sung long ago. Invite children to join you in singing the song as it appears in the story or the more popular version shown here.

Yankee Doodle
Yankee Doodle went to town
A-riding on a pony,
Stuck a feather in his cap
And called it macaroni.
Yankee Doodle keep it up,
Yankee Doodle dandy.
Mind the music and the step
And with the girls be handy.

Culture

Shared Humanity and Unique Identity Help children develop an appreciation of different cultural backgrounds by inviting them to share songs they sing with their families.

3. CLOSE

Ask children to summarize the lesson by describing the life of a pioneer family and telling how the family was affected by weather conditions.

Check Understanding

The child can
___ describe the life of the pioneers.
___ compare the ways people got their food long ago with the ways people today get their food.
___ explain how weather affected pioneers.

Think Critically

Q. What jobs did the pioneers have to do before winter came? They had to harvest their crops, can and dry food to eat, chop plenty of wood for the fireplace, and make sure their house would be warm in the cold weather.

How do you think the pioneers felt when they saw the first signs of spring? happy that warm weather was coming; glad they had made it through the winter

Show What You Know

Performance Assessment Invite children to imagine they are pioneers who live where few others live. They have to take care of themselves. On the board or on chart paper, begin the chart shown below. Then ask children to copy and complete it to show things they would do by themselves and things they would need to depend on others for.

We Do It Ourselves	We Depend on Others for It
grow our food	build our house
make our clothes	

Other times Pa would tell stories. When Laura and Mary begged him for a story, he would take them on his knees and tickle their faces with his long whiskers until they laughed out loud. His eyes were blue and merry.

238

ACTIVITY CHOICES

Extend and Enrich

INVENTIONS Remind children of the lantern that filled the Ingallses' home with light. Invite children to list eight items we use today that were not yet invented when Laura Ingalls was a child. Then ask children to write a sentence for each item on their list, describing what a pioneer family used instead. Have children take turns sharing one item from their list and reading their sentence aloud.

Outside it was cold and snowy, but the little log cabin was snug and cozy. Pa, Ma, Laura, Mary, and Baby Carrie were comfortable and happy in their little house in the Big Woods.

What Do You Know?

What did Laura's family do for fun?
played games, read, and played music

239

Reteach the Main Idea

MAKE A CHART Organize children into small groups, and ask each group to make a large three-column chart with the headings *Homes, Food, Play*. Have children write sentences that tell what they learned about the lives of the pioneers. In the first column, children should describe a pioneer home—how it was made and what it looked like inside. In the second column, children should describe how families got their food and what they ate. In the last column, children should tell what families did for fun. Invite children to read their sentences to other groups.

What to Look For In evaluating the chart, look for ideas that show children understand that the early settlers had to plant gardens and hunt to meet nearly all of their needs for food, clothes, and shelter and most of their wants. Make sure children understand that as settlers began to live closer together, they were able to share, trade, and buy a few items.

Using the Activity Book Have children complete Activity Book page 45. Ask them to choose a vegetable from the story and draw pictures in the boxes to show the steps in growing and preparing the vegetable to be winter food. Then have children number the boxes to show the correct order of the steps.

Activity Book page 45

HANDS-ON OPTION

Plan a Garden

Objectives: Describe the life of a pioneer family. Compare the ways people got their food long ago with the ways people get their food today.

Materials: drawing paper, crayons or markers

Remind children that pioneers had to grow the ingredients of the things they liked to eat. Ask children to imagine that they are pioneer children whose parents have asked them what they would like for their dinners in the coming year. Distribute drawing paper, and invite children to draw on one side one or more of their favorite dinners and desserts. Point out that these should be simple meals that a pioneer family could have made. Then ask them to turn over their paper and draw a fence around the edge. In the garden they have created, they should draw each kind of food their family would need to grow to prepare the dishes they drew. Invite children to share their menu-and-garden plans with classmates. **(VISUAL/TACTILE)**

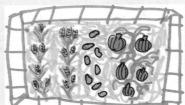

Pioneer Calendar

Objectives: Describe the life of a pioneer family. Explain how weather affected pioneers.

Materials: drawing paper, pencils, crayons or markers, chart paper (optional)

Direct children to fold a sheet of drawing paper from bottom to top and then from bottom to top again so that they have four rows. Help them fold or rule the page vertically to form three columns. Ask children to trace the folds and rules with crayons or markers so that they have twelve boxes. Then have children label the months on their calendars. Next, ask children to think of all the things a pioneer family might want to remember when to do. These could include both chores and celebrations. Have children

note as many "reminders" as they can on their calendars, trying to have at least one item for every month. Children can add seasonal and other decorations to their calendars and display them on a bulletin board. **(VISUAL/TACTILE)**

January	February	March	April
fix fence make candles	cut ice for storage	finish quilt	dig garden
May pull weeds	**June** make jam	**July** 4th of July picnic	**August** make pickles store hay
September harvest corn	**October** prepare meat for storage	**November** chop wood	**December** ice skate on pond

Classroom Quilt

Objective: Describe the life of a pioneer family.

Materials: fabric scraps, stapler

COOPERATIVE LEARNING Remind children that pioneer women cut squares of fabric from worn-out clothing and sewed them together to create decorative quilts. Ask children to bring in a piece of their outgrown clothing. (Provide fabric scraps for those who do not bring in their own.) Cut the fabric into same-size squares. Arrange the squares on a bulletin board to create a colorful quilt pattern, and staple them in place. Invite each child to point to his or her square and share a memory of the piece of clothing it came from. **(TACTILE)**

3

A WORLD OF PEOPLE

OBJECTIVES

1. Appreciate the diversity of a community's population.
2. Recognize that many Americans' ancestors came from other places.
3. Explain the importance of knowing about other people.

VOCABULARY

ancestor (p. 241)

RESOURCES

Pupil Book/Unit Big Book, pp. 240–243
Write-On Charts 22, 34
Pattern P11
Activity Book, p. 46
Vocabulary Cards
Video, Reading Rainbow, *The Lotus Seed*
The Amazing Writing Machine

ACTIVITY CHOICES

Link to Art

GRAPHIC ART Invite children to make family heritage plaques. Give each child a piece of scrap wood. Have children trace their pieces of wood on drawing paper and cut out the shapes. Then ask children to write their last names on the papers in large letters. Invite them to decorate the letters with things that are important to their families. Have children glue their papers to their wood scraps to create name plaques, and display the plaques.

Community Involvement

Invite a person from another country to speak to the class about life in his or her homeland. Help children prepare a list of questions before the visit.

1. ACCESS

Explain that a person's last name can sometimes tell something about his or her family. A surname may tell what country the family is from or what occupation the family's ancestors held. For example, *Hoopers* and *Coopers* once put hoops on barrels; *Smiths* were blacksmiths; *Goldsmiths* worked with gold; *Johnson* was the son of John. Names beginning with *Mc* or *Mac* are usually Scottish; names beginning with *O'* are usually Irish; names ending with *-son* or *-sen* are often Scandinavian; and names ending with *-ski* or *-sky* may be Polish or Russian. Invite children to share any clues their surnames reveal about their family histories.

Focus on the Main Idea

In this lesson children explore the concept of ancestors. They come to understand that many Americans' ancestors are from other countries and that this contributes to the diversity of the population of the United States. Children also examine the importance of learning about other people.

2. BUILD

Key Content Summary

People from many different countries come to live in the United States, giving our country a diverse population. It is important to learn about others so that we can understand them and be friends and so that we can appreciate them as sources of our country's rich heritage.

Culture

Thought and Expression Invite children to read the text and look at the photos on pages 240–241. Discuss how Antonio is communicating with the children in the class. Point out that in addition to music he uses language, facial expressions, and pictures to communicate. Help children understand that listening to music, watching dance, looking at art and architecture, and reading literature all help us learn more about a culture.

Q. **How is music a language we can all understand?** Music can make us feel things without words.

Vocabulary

Remind children that many families came to the United States long ago from other countries. Introduce the word *ancestor* by directing children's attention to the definition on page 241.

LESSON

A World of People

Many people come from other countries to live in the United States. Join these children as they meet a new friend. See what they learn about him and about one another.

Today we have a special visitor in our classroom. His name is Antonio. He is from Italy. Antonio has brought pictures of his family and his school. He likes to read books, just as we do. His books are written in the Italian language. Antonio is learning to speak English. He plays his violin for us because music is a language we can all understand.

240

ACTIVITY CHOICES

Reading Support

READ AHEAD As children read, help them to pronounce the word *ancestors* and tell them to continue reading the rest of the sentence. Ask them to tell what words in the sentence helped them figure out the meaning of *ancestors*. (*people in our family who lived before us*) Explain that reading the words that follow a new word may help them learn what it means.

Role-Play

Invite children to tell others something about themselves by pantomiming something they like to do. Allow other children to guess the activities being pantomimed.

VOCABULARY CARDS

Pass around the VOCABULARY PICTURE CARD for *ancestor,* and invite each child to share something about his or her ancestry.

Antonio is Tina's cousin. Tina's ancestors came from Italy. **Ancestors** are people in our families who lived before us. The ancestors of many Americans came from other countries. Some of them moved here hundreds of years ago. Others have been here only a short time.

Chad's ancestors came here from Africa long ago. Emily's family moved here from Poland when she was a baby. Cam Linh and her family just moved here from Vietnam.

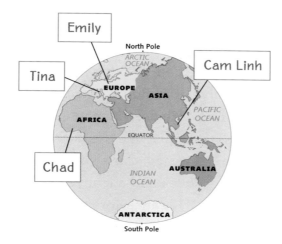

Our Ancestors

241

PUPIL BOOK OR UNIT BIG BOOK

Meet Individual Needs

TACTILE LEARNERS Help children locate Italy, Poland, Vietnam, and the continent of Africa on a globe or on Write-On Chart 34. Have them trace a path from each place to the United States with their fingers. Children who know their ancestors' homelands may wish to repeat the activity from those countries.

Link to Language Arts

JOURNAL Invite children to use their journals to record what they think it would be like—or what it was actually like—to move to a new country.

TECHNOLOGY

Use THE AMAZING WRITING MACHINE™ to complete this activity.

PRIMARY SOURCE

Invite families to send to school non-breakable items that tell something about their ancestors or their cultures, such as photos, toys, musical instruments, clothing, or food containers. Create a display of the items.

Geography

Movement As children locate the areas of the world from which ancestors came, help them to identify the kinds of things that would be different in those areas. food, clothing, climate, language, religion, entertainment Discuss what happens when people with different cultures move to another country.

Q. **What problems might newcomers to our country have when they first arrive?** speaking the language; finding foods they enjoy; getting used to the weather, if it is different

Auditory Learning

Play Music Find and play recordings of folk songs or musical instruments from other countries. Allow children to compare the sounds to music they enjoy. Explain that all countries have different kinds of music, traditional and popular. Help them to understand that taste in music is personal but that people are influenced by the kind of music they hear as they are growing up.

Kinesthetic Learning

Folk Dance Teach a folk dance to the class. Discuss how dances have been passed from generation to generation.

Q. **Why do you think dancing is a popular form of entertainment?** It's fun; people can get together; it's good exercise; it makes people proud of who they are.

Visual Analysis

Interpret Pictures If possible, display a patchwork quilt for children to examine. Then direct attention to the text and pictures on pages 242–243, and ask children to describe the quilt. Ask volunteers to explain how the United States is like a large quilt.

Q. **What do the children's quilt squares show about their families and ancestors?** Children should note that each square tells about the artist's family. For example, one child's ancestor was a Pilgrim; one child's family celebrates Jewish holidays.

History

Connections Past to Present to Future Explain that some people know what countries their ancestors came from, but others do not. Emphasize that we are all Americans regardless of when our ancestors came to this country and which countries they came from. Point out that the first Americans, the American Indians and Arctic peoples of Alaska, were here before other groups began to arrive.

Culture

Shared Humanity and Unique Identity Point out that all cultures have things in common with other cultures and things that are unique. Work with children to make a list comparing features of the cultures they have observed.

Q. **What can we learn from people who have moved here from other countries?** different ways of doing things; new stories, songs, games, and foods

3. CLOSE

Explain that children are going to "pack" a suitcase with the things they have learned about in the lesson. Have children write or dictate sentences about the origins of their ancestors or of someone else in their community. Invite children to tape their sentences onto a suitcase shape made of construction paper. Tape a label to the suitcase that says *Going to America.* Save it for the Reteach activity.

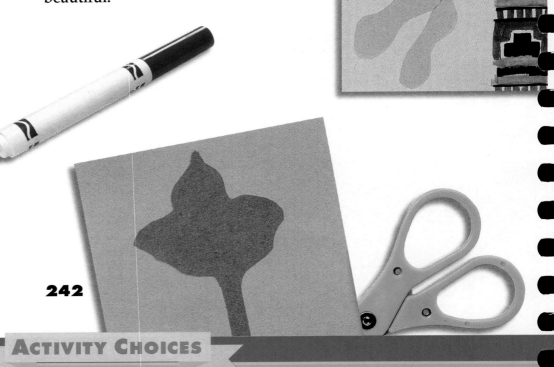

Our class is making a quilt. We have made patches that tell about our families. Mine shows Grandma, me, and my bicycle. Grandma is from Ireland, so I drew a shamrock on my patch. Bobby is from Canada. He drew a maple leaf on his patch, just like the one on the Canadian flag. Carla's patch has ballet shoes and a Hopi Indian design. Her ancestors were some of the first Americans.

Our teacher says the United States is like a big quilt. Each patch is different, but together the pieces are strong and beautiful.

242

ACTIVITY CHOICES

Extend and Enrich

RESEARCH ELLIS ISLAND Display a picture of the Statue of Liberty. Explain that the statue was a gift from the people of France when our country was 100 years old. Tell children that since that time, the Statue of Liberty has greeted people who have come to the United States by boat and have landed at Ellis Island. Provide resources, such as *Watch the Stars Come Out* by Riki Levinson, and invite children to find out more about Ellis Island.

Reteach the Main Idea

LEARN ABOUT CULTURES Invite children to "unpack" the *Going to America* suitcase by reading the sentences. Help them recognize that Americans' ancestors came from many different places and that it is important to learn about members of other cultures in the community.

Our quilt helps us know more about one another. That makes it easier to be friends.

What Do You Know?

1. Where do many Americans' ancestors come from?

2. Why is it important to learn about other people?

243

PUPIL BOOK OR UNIT BIG BOOK

WRITE-ON CHARTS

The Americas
Use WRITE-ON CHART 22 to extend and enrich this lesson. See Teacher's Edition page W68.

VIDEO

Use READING RAINBOW,™ THE LOTUS SEED to discover how a Vietnamese girl carried her traditions to her new home.

Check Understanding

The child can
— appreciate the diversity of a community's population.
— recognize that many Americans' ancestors came from other places.
— explain the importance of knowing about other people.

Think Critically

Q. **How can we help people who have just moved here from other countries?** We can help them feel welcome, find their way, and learn about our way of life, and we can express an interest in theirs.

Show What You Know

Performance Assessment Help children locate on a wall map the countries their ancestors came from and mark them with pushpins. Then invite them to mark the countries of ancestors of other people in their community.

What to Look For To evaluate children's map of ancestors, note whether they recognize that most people have ancestors from other countries.

Using the Activity Book Invite children to write their own Recipe for America on Activity Book page 46 by completing the card. Suggest that looking at a globe may help children choose countries. Invite children to read their "recipes" aloud.

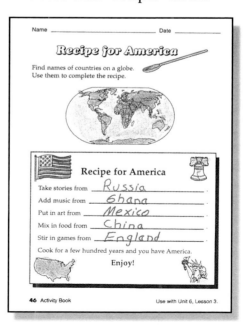

Activity Book page 46

HANDS-ON OPTION

Making Musical Instruments

Objective: Explain the importance of knowing about other people.

Materials: audio recorder and recordings of musical selections from several countries; materials for making musical instruments, such as coffee cans with lids, paper tubes, oatmeal boxes, and beans; art paper and other materials

 Play several musical selections, and invite children to describe how the music makes them feel. Call attention to the different instruments used in the selections. Point out that instruments such as guitars, flutes, and drums are played in the music of many cultures. Challenge children to use the materials you provide to create their own new musical instruments. Then organize children into cooperative groups to play their instruments. Designate one child in each group to be the bandleader. Give children time to practice and then invite the groups to play their instruments for the class. Discuss with children how music can help us get to know the people of other cultures and why it is important to learn about other people. **(AUDITORY/KINESTHETIC/TACTILE)**

Traveling Abroad

Objective: Recognize that many Americans' ancestors came from other places.

Materials: Pattern P11, pencils, globe

Ask children to tell what countries their ancestors came from, if they know. Then invite them to imagine that they are going to travel to the countries of some of their ancestors. Explain that when people travel to other countries, they must have passports with their names, dates and places of birth, and signatures on them. Provide a Passport Pattern to each child, and invite children to fill out the passports as indicated. Have them fold the passports so that the word *Passport* appears on the front cover. Invite children to write on the inside of their passports the names of the countries they plan to visit. Help children locate on a globe the countries they are traveling to, and discuss the routes they might take to get there. **(KINESTHETIC/TACTILE)**

We Learn from Others

Objective: Appreciate the diversity of a community's population.

Materials: stones or beans that are painted on one side, pie plates

Explain that we can learn about other people through the songs, stories, and games they enjoy. Lead small groups of children in playing an American Indian game called Stone Toss. Players take turns tossing stones onto a pie plate, trying to get them to land painted side up. Challenge children to predict how many of their stones will land painted side up. When children have finished the game, invite them to share a game, story, or song that they enjoy playing with friends or family members. **(AUDITORY/KINESTHETIC)**

USE A BAR GRAPH

OBJECTIVES
1. Identify the purpose and parts of a bar graph.
2. Use a bar graph to show where children's ancestors came from.

VOCABULARY
bar graph (p. 244)

RESOURCES
Pupil Book/Unit Big Book, pp. 244–245
Activity Book, p. 47
Transparency 16
Desk Maps
The Amazing Writing Machine
Graph Links

1. ACCESS

Arrange groups of like objects, such as pencils or coins, for children to count. Write on the board the names of the objects. Next to each name, record the number of items children counted in that group.

Q. **What other ways can you think of to show the number of objects in a group?** charts and graphs

Remind children that a pictograph is a type of graph that compares the number of objects in several groups by using symbols, or pictures, to stand for the objects. Invite children to make a pictograph, using the pencils, coins, and other objects they counted earlier.

2. BUILD

Visual Analysis

Learn from Graphs Read the text on pages 244–245 with children. Make sure children recognize that the graph categories are continents, not countries. Help them understand that most people in the United States have ancestors from more than one country. Help them recognize that the children who made the chart included only the ancestors of which they were aware. Call attention to the *Not Sure* category, and explain that some people don't know where their ancestors came from. Then model for children how to interpret a bar graph.

Auditory Learning

Ask children to name their ancestors' countries as you keep a tally. Then, on chart paper, create a class graph similar to the one on page 245. Ask children to interpret the graph, prompting them by asking questions such as *Which country did the most ancestors come from?* Save the graph for the Reteach activity.

Vocabulary

Ask children to reread the definition of a bar graph on page 244. Explain that a bar graph uses bars to show numbers of things.

Q. **Where might you see a bar graph** in newspapers, magazines, schoolbooks

---

Use a Bar Graph

Our class quilt tells about our ancestors. We also made a bar graph to show how many of our ancestors came from each part of the world. A **bar graph** is a kind of drawing that shows numbers of things.

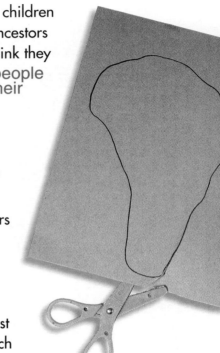

1 Look at the bar graph. The children listed the continents their ancestors came from. Why do you think they added <u>Not Sure</u>? Some people may not know where their ancestors came from.

2 Find Africa on the graph. What number does the bar reach? How many children have ancestors from Africa? five

3 Four children have ancestors from the same continent. Which continent is that? North America

4 Compare the bars. From which continent did the most ancestors come? From which continent did the fewest come? Europe; Australia

244

ACTIVITY CHOICES

Link to Language Arts

WRITE TO ANALYZE Invite children to work in pairs to find examples of bar graphs in magazines and newspapers. Have them cut out one graph and mount it onto a sheet of paper. Ask partners to compose two questions that can be answered by interpreting the graph, and write them below the graph. Have them write the answers on the back of the paper. Invite children to switch graphs with another set of partners and use the graphs to answer each other's questions.

TECHNOLOGY

Use THE AMAZING WRITING MACHINE™ to complete this activity.

Extend and Enrich

CREATE GRAPHS Invite children to name their favorite musical instrument, such as guitar, violin, piano, harmonica, or drum. Record the kinds of instruments on the board, and place a tally mark beside the one each child chooses as his or her favorite. Use the information to create a bar graph on chart paper. Ask children questions that help them to interpret the graph, such as which instrument was chosen by the most children and which by the fewest.

TECHNOLOGY

Use GRAPH LINKS to complete this activity.

Our Ancestors

Skills

	0	1	2	3	4	5	6	7
Africa								
Asia								
North America								
South America								
Europe								
Australia								
Not Sure								

Think and Do

Work with classmates to make a bar graph. List foods from different countries. Then use the bars to show the number of children who like each food.

245

PUPIL BOOK OR UNIT BIG BOOK

Meet Individual Needs

TACTILE LEARNERS Invite children to tell where their ancestors came from. Then help children use world desk maps to locate the continents and countries they have named. You may wish to have children trace with their fingers a route for getting from that country to the United States.

Reteach the Skill

READ A GRAPH Review with children the graph they made about their own ancestors. Model how to interpret the graph by looking at the information it gives: the names of the countries from which the ancestors came and the numbers of people who came from each country. Help children identify and compare the number of people each bar represents.

3. CLOSE

Think and Do

Children's graphs should list foods from other countries and use colored bars to show how many children like each food named on the graph.

Review the skill with children by having them describe the parts of a bar graph. Children should mention that a bar graph is a chart that uses bars to show numbers of things and that each bar is labeled to show what it stands for. They should also mention that the length of the bar tells the number of things it stands for.

Q. When are bar graphs helpful?
when you need to show or compare numbers of things

Using the Activity Book Discuss the information on Activity Book page 47 about how a group of children's ancestors arrived in America. Ask children to complete the bar graph using the information about the means of transportation. Ask children to check one another's work.

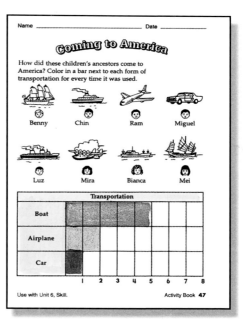

Activity Book page 47

UNIT 6 • 245

HANDS-ON OPTION

Floor Graph

Objectives: Identify the purpose and parts of a bar graph. Use a bar graph to show where children's ancestors came from.

Materials: masking tape, drawing paper, colored construction paper, crayons or markers, self-stick notes

Organize children into cooperative groups to help make a class bar graph showing where their ancestors came from. Help one group of children use masking tape to mark off a bar graph on the floor with seven columns and seven rows. The rectangles in each row should be about the same size as a sheet of construction paper. Ask a second group to draw and label the six continents that appear on page 245, each on a different-colored sheet of construction paper. Ask children to draw a question mark on a seventh sheet of drawing paper to represent the category *Not Sure*. They will place each drawing in front of a row on the bar graph. Ask a third group to write the graph title, *Class Ancestors*, on drawing paper. This group can also write the numbers 0–7 on self-stick notes and place one below each vertical line on the graph. Display stacks of colored construction paper, and ask each child to choose a sheet matching the color of the continent from which his or her ancestors came. The child should then place the sheet of construction paper in the proper place on the graph. Challenge volunteers to interpret the results and to point out the different parts of the bar graph.
(KINESTHETIC/TACTILE/VISUAL)

Around the World Games

Objective: Identify the purpose and parts of a bar graph.

Materials: reference books, drawing paper, markers, crayons

Invite small groups to create bar graphs of games from different countries. Begin by asking children to list games and do research to find out the country of origin for each game. When the lists are complete, suggest that children take a survey of classmates to find out which game is their favorite. Then have group members work together to tally the results and show them on a bar graph. Ask children to write a question below their graph that can be answered by interpreting the results, for example, *How many people*
in our class like Mancala best?* Have them write the answer on the back of their paper. Display the finished bar graphs, and challenge children to answer the questions by interpreting the graphs.
(AUDITORY/KINESTHETIC/TACTILE/VISUAL)

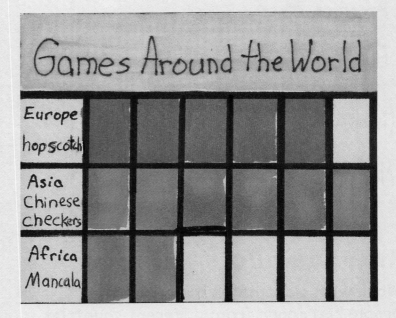

Foods of the World

Objective: Identify the purpose and parts of a bar graph.

Materials: craft paper; one-inch squares of red, green, orange, and blue construction paper; tape

List the following foods and their origins down the left-hand side of a sheet of craft paper: Barbecue/United States; Spaghetti/Italy; Frankfurters and Sauerkraut/Germany; and Fried Rice/China. Use red, green, orange, and blue markers to write the names of each food. Draw a bar graph on the paper, making each food the beginning of a row. Display the graph on a bulletin board and title it *Foods I Like.* Provide one-inch squares of colored construction paper in stacks of red, green, orange, and blue. Then invite children to study the graph and choose the meal they would most like to eat. Guide them to mark their choices by pinning the corresponding colored square in the appropriate row. Have children challenge each other by asking questions that require interpreting the graph.
(AUDITORY/TACTILE/VISUAL)

4

A FAMILY HISTORY

OBJECTIVES

1. **Recognize that every family has its own history.**
2. **Explain the pattern of a family tree.**
3. **Appreciate the value of learning from family members.**

RESOURCES

Pupil Book/Unit Big Book, pp. 246–251
Activity Book, p. 48
Desk Maps
The Amazing Writing Machine

ACTIVITY CHOICES

Home Involvement

If possible, enlist the help of children's family members as you begin the study of family history. If cultural and family items were sent to school for Lesson 3, children may wish to reexamine the display. Ask family members to help now by answering children's questions about family members of the past and present, family memories and stories, and skills and traditions that have been passed down through the generations. Since children will also study photos on a family tree, this may be a good time for family members to look through their photograph albums with children, introducing people whose faces are unfamiliar to them.

1. ACCESS

Read aloud "Four Generations" by Mary Ann Hoberman below. Explain that a *generation* is the group of all people who are growing up at about the same time. Children and their parents are in two different generations. Ask what the poem's title means. Lead children in a discussion about what the poet is saying about her family now and in the past.

> Sometimes when we go out for walks,
> I listen while my father talks.
>
> The thing he talks of most of all
> Is how it was when he was small
>
> And he went walking with *his* dad
> And conversations that they had
>
> About *his* father and the talks
> They had when *they* went out for walks.

Focus on the Main Idea

Remind children that history is true stories about the past. In this lesson children will learn that each family has its own history. Children will meet an American family with a Chinese background and learn about its family tree. They will see that families do many of the same kinds of things, even though they may do them in different ways.

Background

CHINA As children learn about family history through the story of the Chiang family of California, they are also introduced to ways in which the family reflects its Chinese heritage. In this lesson they will learn that China's population is larger than any other country's. About one out of every five people in the world live in China. In area, only Canada and Russia are larger than China. China's name for itself is *Zhongguo* or "Middle Country." In ancient times Chinese people thought of themselves as the center of the world, both in culture and location.

2. BUILD

Key Content Summary

Through the example of one family and its heritage, children will discuss things that all families share—love and knowledge passed from one generation to another, memories of the past, and special traditions.

Culture

Shared Humanity and Unique Identity
Tell children that they will meet a boy who is about their age and his family. Write *Bryan Chiang* (CHANG) on the board and pronounce the name. Invite children to preview the pictures and captions on pages 246–247. After children have read each paragraph, ask them to summarize what they now know about Bryan's family history.

Have children who have lived in the same place all their lives tell what they like and do not like about that place. Ask children who have moved to share their likes and dislikes about the different places they have lived.

Visual Analysis

Interpret Pictures Focus on the word *Chinatown* in the caption on page 246. Explain that *Chinatown* is a nickname for neighborhoods in many towns where people of Chinese background live, work, and play together. The Chinatown in this picture is a community within the large city of San Francisco.

LESSON 4

A Family History

Every family has a history. Babies are born, and then they grow up. As grown-ups they may marry and have children of their own. Some people move far away to live in another part of the world. Others stay in the same place all their lives. Each family has a past. Every family has a story to tell.

Seven-year-old Bryan Chiang was born near San Francisco, California. He has lived in the same house all his life. His grandparents, who live near him, were born in China. They moved to the United States a long time ago to find a better life.

Bryan Chiang and his family in Chinatown

246

ACTIVITY CHOICES

Reading Support

PREVIEW AND PREDICT Read the lesson title with children, and invite them to begin an idea web. Have them tell what they might learn in a lesson about a family's history. Next, have children look at the pictures on pages 246–251 and read the captions. Add new ideas to the web.

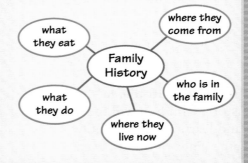

Link to Mathematics

ABACUS If a real abacus is available, allow children to examine it. Point out the columns of beads that slide up and down on rods and the crosswise bar that divides it into upper and lower sections. Tell children that the top beads each stand for five; those below each stand for one. Starting on the right side of the abacus, each column has a place value: ones, tens, hundreds, and so on, just as written numbers do.

When Bryan visits his grandparents' house, he can see things that came from China. He likes to use the abacus. People in China have used this tool for thousands of years. With it they can add, subtract, multiply, and divide without using a pencil and paper.

Bryan's grandfather learned to use an abacus when he was Bryan's age. Later he brought the abacus with him to the United States. For many years he used it in his business to add up his customers' bills.

Bryan's grandfather explains how an abacus works.

Bryan's father works in a bank. He uses a computer.

247

Geography

Location Help children locate San Francisco and China on a world map. Ask children to identify the ocean that lies between the two places.

Movement Invite a volunteer to trace a China-to-California route on a world map. Ask what types of transportation people might use to travel between the two places.

Q. **Why might people moving from China to the United States be more likely to settle in the western part of the country than in the eastern part?** It is closer to the place where they come into this country; they could live near others who had come from China.

Visual Analysis

Interpret Pictures Direct children's attention to the family photographs on page 247.

Q. **What do these pictures tell us about members of Bryan's family?** Both Bryan's grandfather and father use machines to work with numbers. His grandfather uses an abacus, and his father uses a computer.

Link to Language Arts

JOURNAL Ask children to interview someone in their family about something that person liked to do as a child or something he or she learned to do from another family member. Have children record their interviews in their journals and share what they learned.

TECHNOLOGY

Use THE AMAZING WRITING MACHINE™ to complete this activity.

Link to Art

PICTURE TIME LINE Provide materials children can use to construct family time lines. Ask children to think of four or five events that they can represent with colorful cutouts and arrange in sequence on a long sheet of art paper. Children can write labels or captions for their symbols and also add dates if they wish. Picture ideas might include a rattle for the birth of a child, a bone for a new puppy, or a car or plane for a family trip.

Meet Individual Needs

ENGLISH LANGUAGE LEARNERS Use the photographs in the lesson to promote discussion about the history of Bryan's family and of families in general. Progress through the pictures, having children read the captions as they are able. Ask them to point out details in the photographs and explain what is happening. Extend the discussion to include things many families do the same way.

Geography

Regions Rotate a globe and point out the land areas first on one side of the Earth and then on the other. Identify the half of the globe that shows Asia, Europe, Africa, and Australia as the Eastern Hemisphere of the world. Rotate the globe. Have children locate the United States and identify it as being in the Western Hemisphere. Review the names and locations of continents children have studied.

Tactile Learning

Trace a Route Read the text on pages 248–249 with children. Then invite volunteers to locate China in the Eastern Hemisphere on the globe and trace the route Bryan's grandparents would have taken from China to the United States in the Western Hemisphere.

Visual Analysis

Learn from Diagrams Focus attention on the pictures on pages 248–249. Help children understand how photographs can teach us about our past. Point out that the diagram on page 249 shows how people in a family are related to one another. Have children put their finger on the "trunk" and trace a tree shape around the edges of the pictures. Ask children to find Bryan's picture and then name the other family members from the bottom up.

Q. **Why else might this drawing be called a family tree?** The two sides look like branches; parts of it seem to grow off other parts.

Sometimes Bryan's grandparents show him photographs from China. Many of these show family members who lived a long time ago. He sees pictures of his great-grandparents and of his grandparents when they were young.

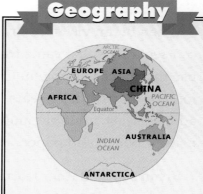

Geography

China is a country in the half of the world called the Eastern Hemisphere. It is on the continent of Asia. China has the most people of any country in the world—more than one billion.

The photographs from China help Bryan understand his family history.

248

ACTIVITY CHOICES

DESK MAPS

Use the DESK MAPS of the world to reinforce the Geography sections of this lesson.

Link to World Languages

OTHER LANGUAGES Invite children who speak other languages to teach their classmates the words for family members, such as *mother, father, aunt, uncle, grandmother*, and *grandfather*. Show volunteers how to draw a simple family tree. Help them label each person's name in each language.

Meet Individual Needs

TACTILE LEARNERS Ask children to trace Bryan's family tree with a finger as they study it closely. Invite children to trace up each side of the tree separately and then use a finger on each hand to move up the two sides at once, one generation at a time. Have them read the names in each generation. You might also work downward from the top, having children point to both people in each couple and then bring their fingers together to find each couple's child(ren).

One way people learn about their family history is by making a family tree. A family tree is a drawing that shows family members, their parents' family members, and so on over many years.

Bryan's
Family Tree

Lew Yau Siew
1887-1968
劉有笑

No Photo

Chiang Yen Kok
1847-1930
蔣恩國

Yen Liu Tan
1900-1955
袁柳春

Kwong Han Kong
1896-1984
鄺漢光

Chiang Lum Hai
(Tommy)
1919-
蔣林海

Kwong Mook Lan
(Lillian)
1929-
鄺木蘭

Lau Sui Man
1915-1970
劉瑞文

Luk Ngai Ching
(Lillian)
1923-
陸毅貞

Chiang Kee Yick
(John)
1949-
蔣其益

Lau May Kay
(Maggie)
1952-
劉美姬

Chiang Chee Wah
(Julia)
1987-
蔣智華

Chiang Chee Keit
(Bryan)
1990-
蔣智傑

249

Link to World Languages

CHINESE WRITING Each figure in Chinese picture writing is called a character. Each character stands for a word or part of a word, not just a sound. Some symbols can be combined to make a new word. For example, the word for *bark* is a combination of the characters for *mouth* and *dog*. Most Chinese words have only one syllable. The Chinese language can also be written in our alphabet so that we can read Chinese names and places.

Meet Individual Needs

ADVANCED LEARNERS Invite children to find books, magazines, pictures, or other information about countries that are part of their backgrounds or family histories. Alternatively, you may wish to have them research states in our country where they or other family members have lived. Ask children to compile their information on posters, using the Geography box about China on page 248 as a model.

Culture

Human Relationships Continue to explore the information on Bryan's family tree. Point out that the pictures of Bryan and his sister are side by side and connected to a line that joins their parents' pictures. Discuss some of the following points and questions as you proceed.

- Bryan's father's side of the family forms the left branch of the tree. His mother's family forms the right branch. Have children find Bryan's father and mother, their parents, and Bryan's father's grandparents.
- Explain that this family tree includes four generations. Discuss how Bryan is related to the row of people above his parents (his grandparents) and to the people on the top row (his great-grandparents).

Q. **Why do you think Bryan's mother's grandparents do not appear on the tree?** There may be no pictures of them.

Visual Analysis

Interpret Diagrams Point out that Bryan's name is written in the Chinese language under his picture. Ask children to compare Chinese and English versions of family members' names. Explain that the drawings at the bottom of the boxes are the same names in Chinese writing.

Then write on the board the first and last name of a class member and a sibling with the same last name. Have children notice the matching last names. Focus on Bryan's and Julia's Chinese names and note how the first parts of the names match. Explain that in China, family names are written first.

Q. **Why is Bryan's mother's family name different from his, Julia's, and their father's?** It is the name she had before she got married.

What do you think the dates under the pictures mean? years of birth and death

Critical Thinking

Read pages 250–251 with children. Lead a discussion about the kinds of things Bryan and his sister are learning about their family's history from the older members of their family.

Q. **How are older family members important to us?** We learn about our family history from them. Stories, traditions, and customs are handed down by our parents and grandparents.

How might Bryan's or anyone's family tree spread around the world? Children may grow up, move, and raise families in other places in the world.

Culture

Thought and Expression Ask children to share their experiences with wonton soup or other ethnic foods. Discuss places in your community where people can eat or buy foods that are different from the ones they are used to. Explain that to make money to support themselves, some people who are new to this country open restaurants or stores to sell food they learned to prepare in the countries they came from. These businesses give people from many cultures a way to learn to enjoy each other's foods.

3. CLOSE

Ask children to review the photo captions on pages 246–251 and then summarize the lesson by telling how parents, grandparents, and ancestors are important in their lives.

Check Understanding

The child can

____ recognize that every family has its own history.

____ explain the pattern of a family tree.

____ appreciate the value of learning from family members.

Think Critically

Q. **Why do you think older family members like to teach you things?** They love you and want you to know how to do things; they want you to be proud of your family; they want to pass on special family stories.

Bryan loves to eat Chinese food. Sometimes his grandfather lets him help make a meal. When Bryan's father was a boy, his grandfather taught him to cook. Now Bryan's grandfather is teaching Bryan how to make wonton soup, one of Bryan's favorite foods. Bryan says, "My grandpa is a good teacher as well as a good cook."

To make wonton for the soup, Bryan puts meat filling in the center of a piece of dough. Then he wets the edges of the dough, folds them over the filling, and presses them together.

Bryan carefully pinches the wonton to keep the filling inside.

250

ACTIVITY CHOICES

Link Literature

Children will appreciate Pablo's multicultural problem solving in the book *Jalapeño Bagels* by Natasha Wing. (Atheneum, 1996) Many children will identify with Pablo's blended background. After reading the book, children might enjoy inventing their own tasty treats by combining foods and flavors from different cultures.

Multicultural Link

Explain that many of the foods cooked in different countries are nearly the same, though they may have different names. Help children list foods that, like wontons, are made with dough—for example, ravioli and tortellini (Italy), pierogi (Poland), pelmeni (Russia), pasties (Western Europe), samosa (India), and noodles and dumplings (Germany).

Bryan is proud of his Chinese background. He and his sister, Julia, are learning to speak Chinese. Bryan and Julia can write their names in Chinese letters called characters. They have learned many things about their family's history.

Bryan likes to think about how his family tree first started to grow, far away in China. Now the tree is larger, with branches in the United States, too. He wonders how big his family tree will grow in the future.

What Do You Know?

1. Where did Bryan's grandparents come from? China

2. What can you learn from your grandparents? Responses should reflect something from a family's history.

251

 Performance Assessment Invite children to write a picture story about a family they know. Suggest that they draw and label pictures about a place where they live or have lived, work someone does at home or at a job, something they have learned how to do from a family member, and a favorite meal.

What to Look For To evaluate the booklets, look for children's own versions of activities that Bryan's family shares.

Using the Activity Book Distribute Activity Book page 48 and ask children to write about things that older family members have taught them how to do or say.

Activity Book page 48

PUPIL BOOK OR UNIT BIG BOOK

Extend and Enrich

COMPARE NOW AND LONG AGO Have children recall that Bryan's father and grandfather both use mathematics, although in different ways. Invite children to tell how things in their own families were done in earlier generations and how they are done now. For example, children may compare how people traveled, the kinds of schools they attended, the foods they ate, and the ways they communicated over long distances. Children may wish to compile the information in book form, showing the ways of earlier generations on the left-hand page and the ways of today on the right-hand page.

Reteach the Main Idea

CONSTRUCT A FAMILY TREE Cut out small paper rectangles and give 12 to each child. Have children write the names of Bryan's family members on the rectangles and arrange them on construction paper to reconstruct Bryan's family tree. Have children glue down the names and draw lines to show how the people are connected. Invite children to discuss what they have learned about Bryan's family history as they work.

HANDS-ON OPTION

Generations Time Line

Objective: Appreciate the value of learning from family members.

Materials: drawing paper, pencils, crayons or markers, children's encyclopedia

Ask children to interview family members to find the names and approximate birth years of a parent, a grandparent, and, if possible, a great-grandparent. Have them organize the names and dates on a time line, beginning with the oldest family member and working toward the right. Tell children to finish by writing their own name and birth date. Help them use reference books or information from family members to name a historical event that occurred while each family member on the time line was growing up. Have children add the name of the event to the time line. Children may want to use drawings of the family members and events. Invite children to share their time lines, telling what questions they would like to ask each family member about the historical event he or she experienced. **(VISUAL/AUDITORY/TACTILE)**

My Own Family Tree

Objective: Explain the pattern of a family tree.

Materials: construction paper, self-stick notes, markers

Have children design their own family tree. Give children self-stick notes and have them write the name of a family member on each one. Suggest that children limit their tree to brothers, sisters, parents, and grandparents, but accept any people they want to include. Have children arrange the notes and draw lines to show connections between family members. **(VISUAL/TACTILE)**

Family Treasures

Objectives: Recognize that every family has its own history. Appreciate the value of learning from family members.

Materials: paper bag or shoe box, drawing paper, art supplies, magazines and newspapers

 Organize children into small groups to create a family history treasure box. Ask group members to imagine they all belong to the same family. Each child should represent a member of the family, covering at least three generations. Give each group a bag or box and have members fill the box with items that represent their different generations. For example, "grandparents" may wish to create a passport that allowed them to travel to the United States. "Parents" may show a photo of a new baby. Allow children to use real items or to find pictures in newspapers or magazines. When the boxes are filled, invite each group to present its family story for the rest of the class by telling what each item is and explaining what part it played in their family history. **(TACTILE/AUDITORY)**

5

COMMUNITY CELEBRATIONS

OBJECTIVES

1. Identify special days celebrated in the community.
2. Describe family, ethnic, and religious customs.
3. Discuss the origins of various holidays and celebrations.

VOCABULARY

custom (p. 252)

RESOURCES

Pupil Book/Unit Big Book, pp. 252–255
Write-On Chart 23
Pattern P12
Activity Book, p. 49
Vocabulary Blacklines
Vocabulary Cards
The Amazing Writing Machine

ACTIVITY CHOICES

Link to Language Arts

JOURNAL Ask children to describe in their journals some part of their family's celebration of a holiday. For example, children might write about how to make a holiday decoration, prepare a special dish, or play a holiday game.

TECHNOLOGY

Use THE AMAZING WRITING MACHINE™ RESOURCE PACKAGE to complete this activity.

Community Involvement

Invite representatives from groups who organize community celebrations, such as festivals or parades, to speak to the class about some of the customs that are part of them.

1. ACCESS

Remind children that a celebration honors something, such as a birthday or a holiday. Invite children to share ways they celebrate special times with their families. Ask children to name the days or events they celebrate and tell what they usually do in celebration.

Focus on the Main Idea

In this lesson children explore the customs involved in a variety of community celebrations. They share some family customs and identify special days celebrated in their community. Tell children that in this lesson they will read about five festivals that are celebrated in different communities.

2. BUILD

Key Content Summary

Many families and communities honor important events with special customs. These customs may include parades, feasts, festivals, and parties.

Vocabulary

Share the text on pages 252–253. Introduce the word *custom* by calling attention to the definition on page 252. Explain that a custom is something that is done the same way each time. Have children name the customs discussed on these two pages. Invite children to share some of their family customs, such as Thanksgiving dinner or New Year's parties.

VOCABULARY BLACKLINES

Provide partners with the vocabulary card for *custom*. Have children take turns holding up the card while their partners describe customs in their families or communities.

History

Connections Past to Present to Future
Explain that many family customs are connected to community celebrations. These celebrations may be held to honor someone special in the community, to commemorate a special event or holiday, or to observe a

---

Community Celebrations

In some communities, families celebrate special holidays. They may wear colorful costumes and eat tasty foods. They may dance and sing songs passed down from their ancestors. Our class made a scrapbook of some of these special times.

Chinese New Year

For several days during Chinese New Year, people wish each other "Gung Hay Fat Choy" or "Happy New Year." You can see bright-red decorations everywhere. People eat spring rolls and duck with rice stuffing. These are old Chinese customs. A **custom** is the way people usually do things. Another favorite custom is carrying paper lanterns through the streets behind a dancing dragon.

252

ACTIVITY CHOICES

Reading Support

RELATE WORDS Pause as you come to the word *custom* in the story. Say the word *tradition*, and describe how the two words are related. Then ask children to suggest other synonyms. Children may find it helpful to substitute one of the synonyms for *custom* as they read.

custom
tradition
habit
routine
way

VOCABULARY CARDS

Use the VOCABULARY PICTURE CARD for *custom* to spark a discussion about local customs.

Cinco de mayo

On May 5, Mexican Americans watch parades with riders on beautiful horses. The smell of tortillas, burritos, and tamales fills the air. This is Cinco de mayo. It is a fiesta, or feast, that reminds us of the freedom Mexicans fought for long ago.

Everyone loves dancing and singing to the music of the guitars and horns. Children have fun trying to break piñatas. The piñatas are stuffed with fruits, candies, and toys.

253

PUPIL BOOK OR UNIT BIG BOOK

religious occasion. Some community celebrations originated in other countries and were brought to the United States by immigrants.

Culture

Shared Humanity and Unique Identity Share the text on pages 254–255. Ask children to name any similarities among the celebrations in the lesson, such as dancing, music, foods, and decorations. Point out that many communities celebrate similar events that are common the world over, such as harvest festivals or end-of-winter festivals.

Q. **What other events might be celebrated in communities around the world?** birthdays, the new year, other seasonal festivals

History

Patterns and Relationships Ask children to think about special celebrations held in their community. Discuss ways in which they are similar to the ones in the lesson. Help children identify the reasons these events are celebrated in their community and reasons for other commonly celebrated events, such as birthdays, the new year, and harvest times.

Q. **Why are celebrations important to a community?** They help people remember important events; they bring people closer together; they are fun.

Multicultural Link

Many cultures celebrate harvest festivals. It was the harvest festivals of African peoples that inspired the creation of the African American holiday Kwanzaa. Help small groups find facts about harvest festivals, such as those in Israel and Greece or those celebrated in the United States by Native Americans. Then have groups make posters illustrating the festivals they found.

WRITE-ON CHARTS

Celebrations Around the World
Use WRITE-ON CHART 23 to extend and enrich this lesson. See Teacher's Edition page W71.

3. CLOSE

Invite children to summarize the lesson by playing a clapping game. Seat children in a circle. Begin a rhythm by having children pat their laps once and clap twice. Then model the game for children by saying *custom* as they pat their laps. On the claps, name a family custom or a special day celebrated in the community, such as Cinco de mayo. Invite children to take turns naming a custom or celebration as the class continues the rhythm.

HOLIDAY ACTIVITIES

For information and activities related to Rosh Hashanah, Kwanzaa, Chinese New Year, and Cinco de mayo, see the Holiday Activities section at the back of the Teacher's Edition.

Check Understanding

The child can
— identify special days celebrated in the community.
— describe family, ethnic, and religious customs.
— discuss the origins of various holidays and celebrations.

Kwanzaa

At the end of December, many African American families celebrate Kwanzaa. On each of the seven days, a candle is lit. The first day is Umoja, which means unity, or togetherness.

Kuumba is the sixth day. People wear colorful African clothing, tell old stories, and dance to African drums.

The last day is the Karamu, or feast. Black-eyed peas, ham, apple salad, corn bread, sweet-potato pie, and other delicious dishes are served.

Juneteenth

Some African Americans celebrate another holiday called Juneteenth. On June 19 they remember the day in 1865 when slaves in Texas were given their freedom. Families gather at parades and picnics to tell stories about their history. Many people give thanks for their freedom by singing the hymn "Lift Ev'ry Voice."

"Lift ev'ry voice and sing
Till earth and heaven ring,
Ring with the harmonies of Liberty."

254

ACTIVITY CHOICES

Background

JUNETEENTH On June 19, 1865, the two-and-a-half-year-old Emancipation Proclamation was read in Galveston, Texas. Freed slaves began to hold a celebration of this important day each year, which came to be called Juneteenth. Similar to the Fourth of July, this commemoration is often called Freedom Day or Emancipation Day. It was declared an official state holiday in Texas in 1979. Juneteenth is a day not only to remember the struggles of slavery, but also to celebrate unity, spiritual strength, and culture.

GREEK EPIPHANY The Epiphany celebration in Tarpon Springs, Florida, is held in early January. Epiphany comes from a Greek word meaning "to show oneself." Sponsored by St. Nicholas Greek Orthodox Cathedral, the celebration commemorates the baptism of Jesus.

Extend and Enrich

PLAN A CELEBRATION Invite children to create a celebration for their class. Remind children of some of the reasons for celebrations. Help children establish customs for their celebration. What type of food will be served? What type of costumes will be worn? What type of decorations will be used? When the planning is complete, allow children to hold their celebration, and invite family members or other classes to attend.

Greek Epiphany

For almost 100 years Greeks in Tarpon Springs, Florida, have celebrated the Feast of the Epiphany. January 6 is an important holiday of the Greek church. Families parade from the church to Spring Bayou for the blessing of the water. A cross is thrown into the water, and young men dive after it. The one who finds it wins honor.

A glendi, or festival, follows with dancing and music and plenty of seafood to eat. Thousands of visitors come to Tarpon Springs every year for this exciting Greek festival.

What Do You Know?

1. What group celebrates Kwanzaa? African Americans

2. How does your family or community celebrate special times?

255

PUPIL BOOK OR UNIT BIG BOOK

Reteach the Main Idea

READ A CALENDAR Use a 12-month calendar or one of the group-made calendars on page 255A to review holidays celebrated in their community throughout the year. Invite children to add family celebrations to the calendar and describe them.

Link to Reading

IDENTIFY THE MAIN IDEA Have children form small groups, and assign each group one page from the lesson. Suggest that group members first read the pages to themselves and then work together to determine the main ideas.

Think Critically

Q. **What is your favorite family or community custom? Why?** Children might say celebrating a birthday, exchanging gifts at Christmas, or watching fireworks on the Fourth of July.

Show What You Know

Performance Assessment Ask children to write a paragraph about a celebration in their community. Have them include the date, if they can, and describe family and community customs that are part of the celebration. Invite children to illustrate their descriptions.

What to Look For To evaluate children's descriptions, note whether they identified and described a community celebration and customs associated with that celebration.

Using the Activity Book Distribute copies of Activity Book page 49. Ask children to identify each holiday represented. Invite children to name a celebration in their community in the last box and draw some symbols of it.

Activity Book page 49

HANDS-ON OPTION

Greeting Cards

Objectives: Identify special days celebrated in the community. Describe family, ethnic, and religious customs.

Materials: greeting cards, construction paper, crayons, markers, scissors, glue

Display a variety of greeting cards for such celebrations as Valentine's Day, St. Patrick's Day, and Hanukkah. Discuss with children family customs and community festivals in their area. Then invite children to select celebrations and create greeting cards for someone who celebrates it. Show children how to make the cards by folding pieces of construction paper in half. Invite them to use crayons, markers, or paper cutouts to decorate their cards. Suggest that they write messages on both the outside and the inside of their cards. Display children's work on a bulletin board titled *Greetings!* (TACTILE/VISUAL)

Holiday Windsocks

Objective: Identify special days celebrated in the community.

Materials: Pattern P12, crayons, glue, scissors, yarn

Encourage children to discuss special days celebrated in their community. Then invite children to choose a holiday and create a holiday windsock. Provide children with copies of the Holiday Windsock Pattern, and invite them to decorate their windsocks with colors and symbols of the holiday. Ask children to cut out the top and the strips, glue the top together, and then glue the strips to the top. When the glue has dried, children can attach yarn to the top of the windsock to use as a handle. Then help children organize a parade of community festivals in which they can display their windsocks. (KINESTHETIC/TACTILE/VISUAL)

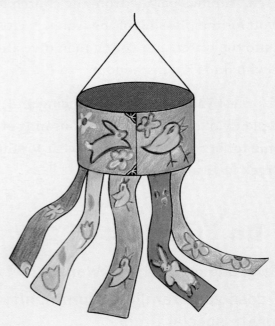

Holiday Calendars

Objectives: Identify special days celebrated in the community. Discuss the origins of various holidays and celebrations.

Materials: blank 12-month calendars made by ruling sheets of chart paper into 12 squares; pencils; crayons

 Organize children into cooperative groups to create holiday calendars. Have children brainstorm holidays celebrated in each month, and record their ideas on the board. Provide each group with a blank calendar. Suggest that one child write the name of each holiday in the appropriate square. Have other children illustrate the holidays. Still others can find out why these holidays are celebrated and write a sentence or two in the appropriate square. Display children's calendars in the classroom. (TACTILE/VISUAL/AUDITORY)

LEARN FROM ARTIFACTS

OBJECTIVES

1. Define *artifact*.
2. Draw conclusions about a people's life-ways from observing an artifact representing their culture.

VOCABULARY

artifact (p. 256)

RESOURCES

Pupil Book/Unit Big Book, pp. 256–257
Write-On Charts 24, 27
Activity Book, p. 50
Transparency 17

ACTIVITY CHOICES

Meet Individual Needs

KINESTHETIC LEARNERS Bury a variety of tools—different for each group—in a tub of sand. Invite small groups to go on an "archaeological dig" to uncover tools that represent modern culture. Have each group member trace or draw the tool he or she has "excavated" and write a sentence or two about the tool and the people who use it. Help the children of each group staple their pages together to make a booklet. Hang the booklets on a bulletin board titled *What Tools Can Tell Us.*

Link to Science

TOOLS Many artifacts are the tools of past cultures. Arrange a field trip to a museum to look at tools from ancient cultures, or show a documentary about an archaeological dig. Discuss with children what scientists can learn about a culture from the tools people leave behind.

1. ACCESS

Place a variety of tools—such as a screwdriver, wrench, and fingernail clipper (nothing with sharp edges or points)—in a box or tub. Invite children to take turns selecting a tool and telling something about the type of worker who might use it. Then remind children of the ways of life of the different American Indian groups they learned about in Unit 4. Help children recall that some groups were hunters and gatherers while others were farmers. Ask children what kinds of tools were needed for these different ways of life.

Q. **What might you learn about people by looking at their tools?**
what kinds of work they did, what kinds of resources they used, where they lived (in the woods, near water, on ice)

WRITE-ON CHARTS

Learning About Ourselves and Others

Use WRITE-ON CHART 24 to extend and enrich this lesson. See Teacher's Edition page W74.

2. BUILD

Vocabulary

Write the word *artifact* on the board. Tell children that an artifact is an object made by people for use in their daily lives.

Q. **Why are artifacts important?** They give clues about the lives of the people who used and made them.

Visual Analysis

Learn from Artifacts Direct children's attention to the photos on pages 256–257. Then read the text with children. Guide them to realize that the objects in the photos are artifacts of different groups of American Indians. Help children answer the questions on page 256.

History

Evidence Point out that most of the artifacts pictured were used in special ceremonies of the Native American tribes.

Q. **What clues do the artifacts provide about the beliefs of each Indian culture?** Children should make a connection between the purpose of the artifact and the culture's beliefs: Hopis and Indians of the Northwest Coast have great respect for their ancestors; Plains Indians are farmers and are thankful for good harvests; Navajos believe that ceremonies can heal the sick.

Reading and Research

Learn from Artifacts

Celebrations are important to Native American people, too. The objects in the photos were made to be used in celebrations. Objects made by people are called **artifacts** . Artifacts help us learn about the lives of the people who make them.

1 Look at the artifacts and read about them. Describe each artifact. How do you think each one is used?

2 What materials do the Indians use to make the objects?

3 What can you tell about the Hopis by looking at the kachina doll?

4 What can you tell about the Plains Indians from their artifact?

256

The Hopis carve kachina dolls from wood to teach children the ways of their people.

ACTIVITY CHOICES

Background

KACHINAS In the religion of the Pueblo Indian tribes of present-day Arizona and New Mexico, a *kachina* (kuh•CHEE•nuh) is an ancestral spirit. The Hopi (HO•pee), one of these tribes, believe that these ancestral spirits live half the year in Hopi villages and the other half in underground spirit dwellings. The carved, wooden kachina dolls represent the kachina spirits.

Background

TOTEMS The Indians of the Northwest Coast, such as the Haida (HY•duh), Tlingit (TLING•kit), and Tsimshian (CHIM•shee•uhn), have traditionally erected the massive carved posts called totem poles to commemorate important events, to delineate national boundaries, and to honor their ancestors. The carvings depict family histories and show the various spirits who guided a family's ancestors.

Meet Individual Needs

ADVANCED LEARNERS Invite children to bring in, draw, or make a wide range of artifacts from the past and the present to create a class museum. Children can act as tour guides to tell classroom visitors interesting facts about each artifact and the people who made it.

TRANSPARENCY

Use TRANSPARENCY 17.

The Plains Indians use rattles made from gourds to celebrate good harvests.

The Navajos believe sand paintings help sick people in healing ceremonies.

Cornhusk masks are used by the Iroquois in celebrations.

Some Indians of the Northwest Coast honor their ancestors with totem poles carved from tree trunks.

Think and Do

Draw a picture of an artifact that might tell someone about you.

257

Extend and Enrich

STUDY ARTIFACTS Show children artifacts or pictures of artifacts from various American Indian groups. As children examine each artifact, guide them to draw conclusions about the group of people who created it. Ask about such topics as what the article was used for, what it reveals about the people who used it, and what questions the artifact raises in the children's minds.

Reteach the Skill

CREATE A WORD WEB Review pages 256–257 with children. Use Write-On Chart 27 to create a word web for the word *artifact.* As children tell what an artifact is and what it can be used for, record their responses in the chart.

Culture

Thought and Expression Invite children to note further details about the artifacts, such as shape, type of decoration, color, and the materials used to make them, such as sand, leather, and wood. Challenge children to make connections between the environment in which the Indians lived and the resources they used to make the artifacts.

3. CLOSE

Think and Do

Children's pictures should reflect some aspect of their lives, such as where they live or what they like to do.

Review the skill with children by asking the following question:

Q. **How can learning about past cultures help us today?** We can see how much the world has changed; we can feel pride in our heritage; we can understand the history and customs of different people.

Using the Activity Book Distribute Activity Book page 50 to each child. Ask children to draw a picture of an artifact they use today that would help people of the future learn about them and their culture. Then ask children to answer the question on the lines provided. Invite them to share their answers and drawings with classmates.

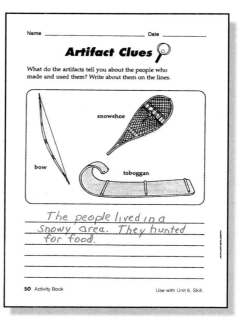

Activity Book page 50

HANDS-ON OPTION

Sand Paintings

Objectives: Define *artifact*. Draw conclusions about a people's lifeways from observing an artifact representing their culture.

Materials: sand, powdered tempera, plastic containers, 6" x 6" squares of cardboard, pencils, markers, glue

Invite children to create a Navajo sand painting like the one on page 257. In advance, mix sand and powdered tempera in plastic containers. Provide each child with a cardboard square on which to draw a design. Guide children to trace the parts of their design they want one color with glue and pour the colored sand over the glued area. They can repeat this process for each color. When the paintings are dry, invite children to display their work on the chalk ledge or in a special display area. Ask children what they think people in the future might learn about their class by looking at their sand paintings. **(TACTILE/VISUAL)**

Artifact Mobiles

Objective: Draw conclusions about a people's lifeways from observing an artifact representing their culture.

Materials: clothes hangers, yarn or string, scissors, tape, drawing paper, markers, crayons, magazines

Challenge children to brainstorm a list of tools they use. Point out that items such as a toothbrush, fork, and pencil are artifacts. Invite them to draw pictures or look through magazines to find pictures of some of the items on their artifact lists. Provide each child with a clothes hanger and several lengths of string or yarn. Children can cut out their drawings and pictures, tape them to one end of a piece of string, and then attach each artifact to their hanger. Display their artifact mobiles around the room. **(TACTILE/VISUAL)**

Class Totem Poles

Objective: Draw conclusions about a people's lifeways from observing an artifact representing their culture.

Materials: cardboard tubes, cardboard squares, construction paper, magazines, scissors, glitter, crayons or markers, glue, modeling clay (optional)

 Invite children to work together in cooperative groups to create totem poles for the class. Provide photos or drawings of real totem poles for children to study. Then provide each group with a cardboard tube from a roll of paper towels. Ask a child in each group to make a base for the totem by gluing the tube to a flat, cardboard square. Other children can draw pictures, cut photos from a magazine, or cut shapes out of construction paper to decorate the totem poles. Remind children that the Indians of the Northwest Coast used totem poles to commemorate important events and to honor their ancestors. Challenge children to decorate their totem poles to tell something about the people in their class. As an option, you might have children shape a top for their totem poles out of modeling clay. Display the finished totem poles in the classroom or hallway. **(KINESTHETIC/TACTILE/VISUAL)**

Lesson

6

ONE FOR ALL, ALL FOR ONE

OBJECTIVES

1. Recognize that people use communication to work together to create a safer, more healthful planet.
2. Describe ways people can protect the quality of life in their communities.
3. Explain how people around the world are connected.

VOCABULARY

communication (p. 261)

RESOURCES

Pupil Book/Unit Big Book, pp. 258–261

Write-On Chart 26

Clings

Activity Book, p. 51

Music Audio, "The World Is a Rainbow"

The Amazing Writing Machine

ACTIVITY CHOICES

Link to Reading

POETRY Read aloud the poem "You and I" by Mary Ann Hoberman, and invite children to tell how people who live in different parts of the world are alike and how they are different.

Only one I in the whole wide world
And millions and millions of you,
But every you is an I to itself
And I am a you to you, too!
But if I am a you and you are an I
And the opposite also is true,
It makes us both the same somehow
Yet splits us each in two.
It's more and more mysterious,
The more I think it through:
Every you everywhere in the world is an I;
Every I in the world is a you!

1. ACCESS

Remind children of the artifacts they learned about earlier. Review with them that people also tell about themselves through different types of art. Prompt children to discuss other things people express through art, such as their concerns, their cultures, and their ideas about the world. Record children's ideas on the board.

Focus on the Main Idea

In this lesson children begin to understand the importance of the idea of a global community. They learn that people around the world share many problems and interests. Children also discover that people around the world are connected through various means of communication. Tell children they will be looking at posters that boys and girls around the world made to show how to keep the world a good place to live.

2. BUILD

Key Content Summary

People around the world are connected by shared interests, needs, and concerns. We use communication to meet our needs and to tell one another our interests and concerns. When we communicate, we discover that people in other places are much like us and that we can work together to make the world a safer and a more healthful place.

Visual Learning

Learn from Posters Invite children to look at the posters and read the text on pages 258–261. Discuss how children's concerns are like the ideas on the posters.

Q. **Why is it important to know what other people think?** so we can get along with others, so we can solve our problems, so we can learn more about other people and see that we are alike

Culture

Shared Humanity and Unique Identity Ask children how the posters show the needs, wants, and concerns of people everywhere. Help children understand that people, no matter where they live, what color their skin is, or what language they speak, all want the same things: a healthful, safe, and peaceful world.

LESSON 6 One for All, All for One

People around the world have many of the same needs. They share the same feelings about what makes life good. People everywhere think about how to keep safe and healthy and how to get along with others.

Some children in other countries made posters to show how to keep our world a good place to live. How are their ideas like yours?

Henrik Kaurin
Age 8
Sweden

Use the earth as you need it.

258

ACTIVITY CHOICES

Reading Support

USE PICTURE CLUES Children may be unfamiliar with the names of the countries in the captions. Help them understand that the words name countries other than the United States. Have children look at each arrow and identify the continent it points to. Then help them read the names of the countries in the captions.

Link to Language Arts

JOURNAL Each day for a week, ask children to write one of their concerns and at least one way that problem could be solved.

TECHNOLOGY

Use The AMAZING WRITING MACHINE™ to complete this activity.

PEACE IS Good BECAUSE HOMES don't get destroyed.

Mirna Hamady
Age 8
Abu Dhabi,
United Arab
Emirates

Daniel Vargas
Age 7
Costa Rica

We have to keep the water clean.

259

Multicultural Link

Point out that before people communicate, they usually greet each other. Share with children the following words of greeting from around the world:

Hola (OH•lah)—Spanish
Konnichiwa (koh•NEE•chee•wah)—Japanese
Ti Kanis (tee•KAH•nees)—Greek
Nee How Ma (NEE•HOW•MAH)—Mandarin
Yatahey (yah•tah•HAY)—Navajo
Guten Tag (goo•tin TAHG)—German
Jambo (JOHM•boh)—Swahili
Bonjour (bohn•ZHUR)—French

Q. **What do the posters tell you about children in other places?** Children everywhere are much the same; we all want, need, and think about the same things.

Vocabulary

Have children read page 261. Explain that *communication* refers to ways people send messages or information to other people. Point out that people constantly communicate with one another.

Geography

Human-Environment Interactions
Point out that advances in scientific technology have made it easy for people to communicate with one another around the world. Mention such innovations as the fax machine, the computer modem, and the Internet.

Q. **How many ways can you give a message to a friend?** speak to the person, call the person on the phone, write a note, type a note on a computer, leave a message on an answering machine, use sign language

How does communication help make the world a safer and more healthful place? People can talk about ways to solve problems. They can share ideas for taking better care of the environment, getting rid of crime, and making our lives easier.

Culture

Human Relationships   Read to children the following Mother Goose nursery rhyme.

> Mollie, my sister, and I fell out,
> And what do you think it was all about?
> She loved coffee, and I loved tea,
> And that was the reason we couldn't agree.

Help children understand that the global community is like a family. At times not everyone can agree. Discuss how communication and understanding can bridge differences.

3. CLOSE

To summarize the lesson, write on chart paper the sentence *People around the world communicate by* _____. Invite volunteers to complete the sentence. Record their responses and display the chart in the classroom.

Check Understanding

The child can

____ recognize that people use communication to work together to create a safer, more healthful planet.

____ describe ways people can protect the quality of life in their communities.

____ explain how people around the world are connected.

Kevyn Loggins
Age 7
Germany

Peace is at my friend's house. She lets me hold her ♥ rabbit and I say thank you very much. friendship makes peace.

Natalie Madi
Age 6
Lebanon

Peace begins with me by playing nicely in the game.

260

ACTIVITY CHOICES

Extend and Enrich

USE SIGN LANGUAGE Demonstrate, or have a person from the community demonstrate, the use of braille and American Sign Language as forms of communication. Teach children to sign a simple phrase or to sign a song as they sing it.

Reteach the Main Idea

ILLUSTRATE A CHART Invite children to join you in making a chart about ways people around the world communicate. Ask children to find pictures in magazines to represent each suggestion for the chart. Ask them to tell partners how the pictures match the statements.

Link to Music

MUSIC FOR A PURPOSE Teach children the song "The World Is a Rainbow" from the Unit 6 Music Audiocassette, and discuss its meaning. Then provide children with crepe paper streamers of different colors. Invite children to do a Rainbow Dance as they sing, waving the streamers to the rhythm of the song.

The children made these posters to communicate their feelings. **Communication** is the sharing of ideas. When people get to know one another, they can work together to solve problems.

John Oh
Age 7
South Korea

What Do You Know?

1. Name a problem children around the world care about.

2. What are some ways people communicate with each other?

1. Answers might include peace, health, the environment.

2. Children should list writing and a variety of communication technologies. They could also mention the arts—painting, music, and dance.

261

Link Literature

Read aloud *Sitti's Secrets* by Naomi Shihab Nye. (Four Winds, 1994) This story of two very different cultures highlights the bond between a girl and her grandmother. After you read, discuss ways that Mona and her grandmother might have kept in touch with each other.

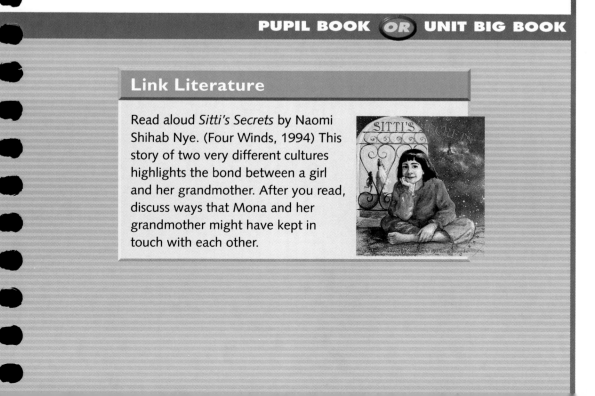

Think Critically

Q. **How are people around the world much the same?** They all need to feel safe; they want to take care of the environment and make the world a better place.

What are some ways you can help keep our planet a healthful and safe place to live? by picking up litter and recycling; by helping people in the neighborhood; by working with other people to make changes

Show What You Know

Performance Assessment Invite children to create posters showing ways to make the world a better place to live. Ask them to illustrate their posters with pictures clipped from magazines or with their own drawings. Help children write captions for their posters. Then display the posters in the cafeteria or another common area of the school.

What to Look For Children's posters should demonstrate their knowledge of the ways people can work together to make the world a safer and more healthful place to live.

Using the Activity Book Have children study the poster on Activity Book page 51. Then invite them to complete the page by telling what they think the message of the poster is.

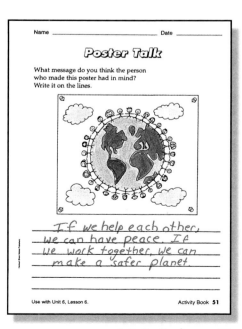

Activity Book page 51

LESSON 6 • 261

HANDS-ON OPTION

Communication Time Line

Objectives: Recognize that people use communication to work together to create a safer, more healthful planet. Explain how people around the world are connected.

Materials: Write-On Chart 26 and Triangle Clings, drawing paper, pencils, crayons, markers, reference materials

Use Write-On Chart 26 and Triangle Clings to model for children how to create a time line. Then organize children into cooperative groups, and have each group create a communication time line on drawing paper. Help children use reference materials to find out when the telephone, the radio, television, the computer, and other major methods of communication were introduced. One group member can draw the time line and add the dates and communication methods, and the others can illustrate the methods. As children share their time lines, prompt them to discuss how these innovations have made it easier to communicate around the world. Display the time lines in the classroom or a hallway. **(TACTILE/VISUAL)**

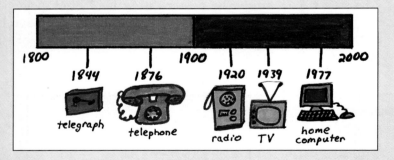

Sing a Song for a Better World

Objectives: Recognize that people use communication to work together to create a safer, more healthful planet. Describe ways people can protect the quality of life in their community. Explain how people around the world are connected.

Materials: paper, pencils

Help children review ways they can help make their community and the world safer and more healthful to live in. Remind children that people everywhere have many of the same basic needs and similar feelings about what makes life good. Then organize children into cooperative groups to create songs about how to make the world a better place. Challenge groups to write lyrics about ways people's needs can be met and how the world can be made a safer, more healthful place. Have one member of each group write down the song, and have other members illustrate it. You might suggest that children write new lyrics to a familiar tune, such as "Twinkle, Twinkle, Little Star," "The Farmer in the Dell," or "The Itsy Bitsy Spider." After groups have practiced singing their songs, invite them to add movements and perform the songs for the class. Add the song sheets to your class songbook. **(AUDITORY/KINESTHETIC)**

Skills

ACT ON YOUR OWN

OBJECTIVES

1. Define *independence*.
2. Identify examples of acting independently.
3. Recognize that independent action can affect other people.

VOCABULARY

independence (p. 262)

RESOURCES

Pupil Book/Unit Big Book, pp. 262–263
Write-On Chart 32
Activity Book, p. 52
Transparency 18
Music Audio, "Unsung Heroes"
The Amazing Writing Machine

ACTIVITY CHOICES

Link to Language Arts

INTERVIEWING Help children list people who have helped make a difference in their school, such as active teachers, parents, and school volunteers. Invite partners to choose one person from the list and write several questions to ask this person about his or her work at school. Arrange for children to interview the people they have selected.

Link Literature

Read aloud *Zora Hurston and the Chinaberry Tree* by William Miller. (Lee & Low, 1994) This beautifully illustrated story tells about an incident in the childhood of African American writer Zora Hurston. Hurston's mother taught her to "reach for the newborn sky" and "always jump at the morning sun."

After you have read the story, ask children to think of other phrases that mean to try for the best, for example, "go for the gold."

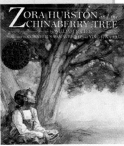

TRANSPARENCY

Use TRANSPARENCY 18.

1. ACCESS

Review the actions of people such as César Chávez, Jimmy and Rosalynn Carter, or Rachel Carson (Write-On Chart 16). Remind children that their contributions to society helped make the world a better place in which to live. Guide children to recognize that these people went ahead and acted on their own to change our world for the better.

Q. **Why do you think some people feel that they have to act on their own to solve problems?** They may feel that an important change needs to be made and that no one else is going to do it.

Vocabulary

Explain that *independence* means "the ability and willingness to act on your own." Tell children that Rachel Carson wrote a book informing people about how pesticides harm our environment. Because of her efforts, people around the world began working to preserve the environment. Eventually, laws were written to protect the Earth's water, air, and land. Help children brainstorm a list of ways to act independently to make a change, for example, by writing letters, making phone calls, making posters, and talking with the teacher.

Q. **When might you decide to act on your own?** when you feel that a change is needed and you want to let others know how you feel

2. BUILD

History

People and Events Across Time and Place Discuss how César Chávez organized a farm workers' union that helped migrant farm workers get better wages and working conditions. Many people joined in Chávez's struggle to change labor laws in the United States.

Q. What kinds of things can be done independently, and what kinds of things are better done with a group? One person can tell others about a problem by writing letters, making phone calls, and making posters. Groups of people are needed for making big changes, such as changing laws.

Visual Analysis

Learn from a List Read aloud the steps for acting independently on page 263. You may also wish to review the strategies for solving problems in Unit 1 on page 30. Choose a community problem, such as broken playground equipment at the park, and have children follow the steps for acting independently to tell how they would solve the problem. Record children's responses on the board.

Act on Your Own

Many children are interested in helping their communities. When Kristina Swartwout was nine years old, she saw a problem in her town of Ashland, Oregon. Cars were not stopping for children at crosswalks. Kristina wrote a letter to the Ashland newspaper. The mayor of Ashland read the letter and made Kristina a member of the Traffic Safety Commission.

Acting on your own is showing **independence**. Kristina's independent act helped make her community safer for everyone.

Dear Editor,

262

ACTIVITY CHOICES

Link to Mathematics

DATA AND GRAPHING Point out that carefully researched information can be helpful in explaining your actions. Explain that Rachel Carson researched the effects of different chemicals on the environment so that she could present accurate information on pesticides.

Link to Art

MURAL Divide a large sheet of craft paper. Ask children to create a mural that shows community problems on the left and on the right, people acting independently and in groups to solve these problems.

Link to Language Arts

JOURNAL Ask children to think of a problem in their community that they would like to see solved, such as a lack of bike paths or playgrounds. Invite them to write in their journals what they would like to do about the problem.

TECHNOLOGY

Use THE AMAZING WRITING MACHINE™ to complete this activity.

Kristina followed these steps:

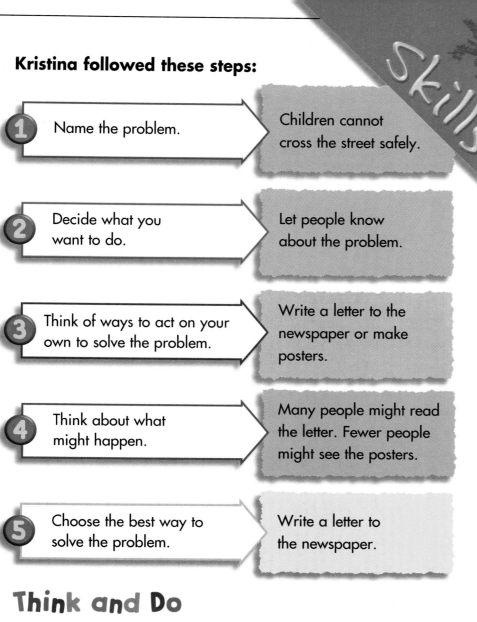

1. Name the problem. → Children cannot cross the street safely.

2. Decide what you want to do. → Let people know about the problem.

3. Think of ways to act on your own to solve the problem. → Write a letter to the newspaper or make posters.

4. Think about what might happen. → Many people might read the letter. Fewer people might see the posters.

5. Choose the best way to solve the problem. → Write a letter to the newspaper.

Think and Do

Think of a problem and write a plan for solving it.

263

Extend and Enrich

Make available some children's magazines that provide examples of "Kid Heroes." Lead children in a discussion about what makes someone a hero. Invite children to make an award to present to someone in the school who has overcome a difficult personal problem, has achieved a goal, has received an honor, or has solved a problem in the school or the community. Then have children submit nominations for the Kid Hero award.

Reteach the Skill

Have children reread page 263. Help them use the flow chart on Write-On Chart 32 to record the steps for solving a problem. Then reread the chart with children, and ask them why each step is important.

AUDIO

Use the UNIT 6 MUSIC AUDIOCASSETTE to hear the song "Unsung Heroes."

Q. When a person acts independently, does she or he affect only himself or herself? Why or why not? Many independent actions, good and bad, affect the lives of many people.

3. CLOSE

Think and Do

Children's plans should include, in the correct order, the five steps to be followed in solving a problem.

Review the skill with children by asking the following questions:

Q. Why is it important to care about your community and be willing to act on your own? so you can help make your community a better and safer place; so you can make changes that no one else is working on

Is acting independently always better than acting with a group? No, some big changes can be made only by working with a group.

Using the Activity Book Distribute copies of Activity Book page 52, and challenge children to identify the problem in the picture. Then have children follow the problem-solving steps from the lesson to find a solution for the problem.

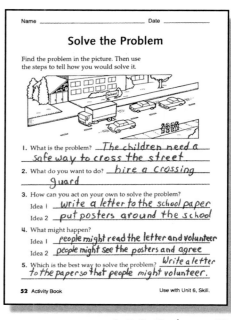

Activity Book page 52

HANDS-ON OPTION

A Group Effort

Objectives: Identify examples of acting independently. Recognize that independent actions can affect other people.

Materials: paper, pencils, art supplies

Organize children into cooperative groups, and have each group list problems in their community or school that they would like to see solved, such as lack of crosswalks, clean-up efforts, and playground facilities. Suggest that one child interview classmates, faculty, and administration to find out which issue people consider the most important. After children have decided on one issue, ask other children to write a plan for solving the problem. The plan should include, in the correct order, the five steps listed on page 263. Suggest that everyone review the plan and choose the best solution. Then ask children to work together to make posters, write letters, or complete other tasks decided upon. If possible, help children implement their plan and track the results throughout the school year. **(AUDITORY/KINESTHETIC/TACTILE)**

Independence Posters

Objectives: Define *independence*. Identify examples of acting independently. Recognize that independent actions can affect other people.

Materials: posterboard, crayons, markers

Invite children to create posters showing different ways people can act independently. Ask them to write a sentence or two for each drawing, telling what the problem is, what the person is doing to solve the problem, and what the results might be. After the posters are completed, children might enjoy performing a short skit to act out what their posters show. **(KINESTHETIC/TACTILE/VISUAL)**

Making a Difference

Objectives: Identify examples of acting independently. Recognize that independent actions can affect other people.

Materials: current newspapers and magazines, scissors, stapler

Invite children to create a bulletin board display titled *People Who Make a Difference.* Ask them to find and cut out pictures of people who work to solve some of our country's problems. As children place the photos on the bulletin board, have them explain what these people do and how their actions affect other people.
(AUDITORY/TACTILE/VISUAL)

An Old Man and a Boy

Tell children that they can learn about other cultures from folktales. They will also discover that people everywhere have similar ideas. Read the following East African folktale.

A long time ago there was a land called "Wells," because it had a lot of water wells. People and animals drank water from the wells. But, during the dry season, the water level was always low because of lack of rains.

One day, an old man found a boy sitting next to a well and asked him, "What are you waiting for while sitting next to the well?"

The boy answered, "I am waiting for the well to be full of water so that I can drink from it."

The old man then told him, "Child, if you don't kneel down to drink, you will only drink when the rains come."

Discuss the advice given by the old man to the boy.

- **Why did the boy need to act independently?** The problem of getting water from the well could not be solved without the boy taking action.

Help children understand that one of their greatest resources is within themselves.

MAKING SOCIAL STUDIES REAL

READ AND RESPOND

Tell children that Lincoln is the capital of Nebraska. Invite volunteers to find Lincoln, Nebraska, on a map. Explain that near Lincoln there is a special park with exhibits that help children and adults discover the importance of world peace. Read aloud pages 264–265, and discuss Prairie Peace Park. Allow time for children to explore the subject more by brainstorming words they think of when they hear the word *peace*.

Q. **What does the World Peace Mural in Prairie Peace Park make you think about?** Guide children to give the following responses: friendship, happiness, cooperation.

Why do you think artists from 29 countries were asked to work together on the mural? to show that people from different countries can get along and work together

MAKING Social Studies Real

United States

Lincoln, Nebraska

Prairie Peace Park

Long ago, wagon trains carried settlers from many countries across the prairies of the United States. Today, people from around the world come together outside Lincoln, Nebraska, at Prairie Peace Park. Here children can discover how important it is to get along with our world neighbors.

In the Children's Maze, ideas for a safe and peaceful world are found in paintings from children around the world. As visitors walk through the maze, they can use rubber stamps to show that they reached each of the ten stations.

Children's Maze

264

ACTIVITY CHOICES

Background

Around 2,000 people attended the opening of Prairie Peace Park on June 11, 1994. This educational, environmental park covers almost 30 acres along Interstate 80 just west of Lincoln, Nebraska, at Exit 388. The park offers a place where children's visions about peace are brought to life. It uses the human body and the prairie itself as models for new ideas about how people can live together in peace and develop a much better

world. Prairie Peace Park is one of four peace museums in the United States. This unique park was designed and built by volunteers and is supported entirely by donations and admission fees. All the staff work without pay.

To contact Prairie Peace Park, write to P.O. Box 95062, Lincoln, NE 68509; call (402) 795-2144; or e-mail Peace.Ink@ispi.net.

Meet Individual Needs

ENGLISH LANGUAGE LEARNERS
Provide an opportunity for children who speak the same first language to share ideas about world peace. Then have them relate these ideas in English to the rest of the class.

In Children's Sculptures, visitors can see the sixteen winning sculptures from the Children's Peace Statue Project. The sculptures give meaning to the park's motto Where Children's Visions Come to Life.

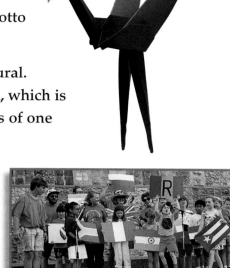

Also interesting is the World Peace Mural. Artists from 29 nations carved the mural, which is made from clay marked by the footprints of one thousand people.

Prairie Peace Park has more mazes, maps to walk on, videos, and computer games for all to enjoy. Children can also go to Peace Camp there. The park's director, Don Tilley, and his volunteers say, "Give children the right view of the world, and they will give us peace."

What Can You Do?

⭐ Make a peace mural for your school.

⭐ Talk to people from other countries to find out who they are and what they care about.

Visit the Internet at http://www.hbschool.com for additional resources.

265

Lead children in a discussion about the importance of getting along with friends and neighbors. Have children list some of the ways they work together in class. Guide them to understand that people around the world need to get along, too.

Q. **What are some of the rules for getting along in class?** Children may mention one or more of the following: lining up to go outside, raising a hand to speak, sharing toys and games, taking turns, not pushing, not fighting, not calling names.

" PRIMARY SOURCE "

If possible, have children use the Internet to find out more about Prairie Peace Park. The Web site is http://www.igc.apc.org/PeacePark. Invite children to look up information about the exhibits to see, mazes to explore, and games to play at the park.

Background

WORLD PEACE MURAL
This mural at Prairie Peace Park was created in Flagstaff, Arizona, during May of 1993 by more than 40 artists from 29 nations around the world. About 1,500 people pressed their feet into the clay to create the foot-prints. The clay was then fired in the largest wood-fired kiln in North America. When sculpted, the mural measured 10 feet by 80 feet.

CHILDREN'S SCULPTURES
The 16 sculptures in this exhibit were inspired by the true story of Sadako Sasaki, a 12-year-old girl from Japan who died as a result of the nuclear bombing of Hiroshima. Her story is described in the exhibit. Sculptors helped each of the 16 young artists to develop a sculpture from the poster he or she created as part of a national contest.

Link to Art

CREATE SCULPTURES Organize children into groups. Provide them with art supplies, and ask them to use what they have learned from reading about Prairie Peace Park to create their own world peace sculptures. Display the finished sculptures, and allow children to act as guides while other classes walk through their peace museum.

PICTURE SUMMARY

TAKE A LOOK

Remind children that the picture summary is a way to visually represent the main ideas or events in a story. Explain that this summary reviews some of the main ideas in Unit 6. Tell children they are looking at the photo album of a family in which the grandparents were immigrants.

Visual Analysis

Learn from Pictures Organize children into small groups. Invite them to examine the picture summary and to react to its images. Ask volunteers to choose a photo from the summary and to discuss what they think the people in the picture are doing. Have children compare the activities in the pictures with activities they have seen in other family albums.

VOCABULARY BLACKLINES

Distribute the individual word cards for this unit and have children use the words as they discuss the picture summary.

UNIT
6
Review

Picture Summary

Look at the pictures. They will help you remember what you learned.

Talk About the Main Ideas

1. People have moved from place to place in our country.

2. People from many different countries live in the United States.

3. People find out about themselves by learning their family history.

4. Groups of people celebrate holidays with special customs.

5. People everywhere care about peace, cooperation, and a healthy world.

Make Puppets Make a stick puppet of someone in your family or someone you know. Then work with a partner. Use your puppets to describe a family custom or an interesting fact about the family.

266

ACTIVITY CHOICES

UNIT POSTER

Use the UNIT 6 PICTURE SUMMARY POSTER to summarize the unit.

VOCABULARY CARDS

Have children use the VOCABULARY CARDS for this unit to review key concepts.

Picture Summary Key

The picture album shows three generations of a family. Grandparents arrive in the United States, become citizens, and raise a family. Children can follow the growth of their son (in glasses) through a wedding, military career, and the birth of his own children. Numbers in the key correspond to the main ideas, all of which show the family history (number 3).

SUMMARIZE MAIN IDEAS

Ask children to read the summary statements on page 266 and relate them to the picture summary. Lead a class discussion about each photo in the album. Then ask children to offer supporting details for each main idea illustrated. Review the word web made at the beginning of the unit, on Teacher's Edition page 218. Suggest that children focus on how people of different backgrounds can work together to solve the world's problems.

Sharing the Activity

Provide time for children to complete the Make Puppets activity on page 266. Organize children into small groups and invite them to put on a puppet show about their families.

PUPIL BOOK or UNIT BIG BOOK

Meet Individual Needs

ENGLISH LANGUAGE LEARNERS

Write each summary statement as a question on chart paper as shown below. Ask children to read and answer them using what they have learned.

1. Why do people in our country move?
2. What different countries do people who live here come from?
3. How can you learn about yourself?
4. What special customs and holidays do people celebrate?
5. How can people show they care about peace, cooperation, and a healthy world?

TECHNOLOGY

Use **THE AMAZING WRITING MACHINE:™ RESOURCE PACKAGE** to summarize this unit.

USE VOCABULARY

Sample responses:
1 piñata; seven candles
2 Pilgrim
3 arrowhead; spinning wheel
4 great-grandfather
5 talking on the telephone; writing a letter

CHECK UNDERSTANDING

1 Pioneers moved to new lands and built communities.
2 Children might name any country.
3 Families share their histories by keeping records with photographs, telling stories, remembering customs, and celebrating special holidays.
4 We learn about people's customs and beliefs as we find out about their holidays.
5 Sharing ideas lets us know one another better and helps us solve problems.

THINK CRITICALLY

America is made up of people whose ancestors came here from many other countries. Like the different patches of a quilt, their different ways make America strong. Learning about their customs helps us get along with them.

UNIT 6 Review

Use Vocabulary

Give another example to help explain each word.

Word		Examples	
1. custom		Fourth of July parade	
2. pioneer		an explorer	
3. artifact		an old cooking pot	
4. ancestor		great-grandmother	
5. communication		writing a letter	

Check Understanding

1 How did pioneers help our country grow?

2 The ancestors of Americans came from many countries. Name three of these countries.

3 How do families share their history?

4 What can we learn about people from their holidays?

5 Why do people need to communicate?

Think Critically

How is America like a big quilt? How does that make America strong?

268

Apply Skills

Use a Bar Graph

The bar graph shows how many children would like to visit each place.

Places We Would Like to Visit	0	1	2	3	4	5	6	7
Animal Park in Africa								
Castles in Europe								
Rain Forest in South America								
Kangaroo Ranch in Australia								

 1 What choices did the children have?

2 Which place was chosen by the most children?

3 Which place was chosen by the fewest children?

Do It Yourself

Make a bar graph to show how long families have lived in your community. Ask classmates to find out when their families first moved to your area. Make bars to show less than 10 years, 20 years, 30 years, 40 years, and more than 50 years.

269

APPLY SKILLS

Use a Bar Graph

1 African animal park, European castles, South American rain forest, Australian kangaroo ranch

2 South American rain forest

3 Australian kangaroo ranch

Do It Yourself

Model how to organize the side and bottom of the graph. You may use Write-On Chart 31 for whole group instruction or have individual children record the data on the Thinking Organizer graphs copied from the back of the Teacher's Edition.

APPLY SKILLS

Learn from Artifacts

An arrowhead tells you something about a tool that people might have used to hunt animals for food. Arrowheads were chipped and shaped from stones. Today people use machine-made bows and arrows and rifles to hunt.

Made from wood and ridged metal, a washboard was used for scrubbing clothes by hand. Today many people have automatic washing machines for their laundry.

UNIT
6
Review

Apply Skills

Learn from Artifacts

What might you learn from looking at this arrowhead?

What might you learn from looking at this washboard?

Choose one of the artifacts above.
Work with a partner to find answers to these questions about your artifact.

• How was it made?

• How was it used?

• What does it tell you about the user?

• How is it like something you know about today?

Tell about something you use today that may be called an artifact in the future.

270

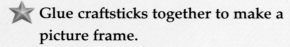

·········Unit Activity·········

Make a Picture Frame

⭐ Glue craftsticks together to make a
picture frame.

⭐ Decorate your picture frame.

⭐ Ask for a photograph or draw a
picture of your family or a relative.
Tape it to the picture frame.

⭐ Make a name and date tag to tape to the back
of the picture. Hang your picture at home.

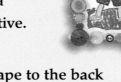

Visit the Internet at
http://www.hbschool.com
for additional resources.

Read More About It

<u>The New Land, A First Year on the Prairie</u> by
Marilynn Reynolds. Orca. The author describes her
grandparents' pioneer life.

<u>Family Pictures</u> by Carmen Lomas Garza. Children's Book
Press. An artist paints and writes about family customs.

<u>The Keeping Quilt</u> by Patricia Polacco. Simon & Schuster.
A homemade quilt is handed down in a Jewish family.

271

PUPIL BOOK OR UNIT BIG BOOK

UNIT ACTIVITY
Make a Picture Frame
Materials: craft sticks; decorating materials
such as buttons, bows, glitter, stickers; glue

In their discussions and through the pictures they frame, children should recognize
that family portraits are part of the record
of a family's history.

READ MORE ABOUT IT

Additional books are listed in the Resource
Center on page 218E of this Teacher's
Edition.

TAKE-HOME BOOK

Use the TAKE-HOME REVIEW
BOOK for UNIT 6.

ASSESSMENT

Use UNIT 6 TEST
Standard, pp. 35–37.
Performance, p. 38.

GAME TIME!

Use GAME TIME! to reinforce
the unit.

COOPERATIVE LEARNING WORKSHOP

MAKE A "WORLD OF PEOPLE" MURAL

Children should work together in small groups to make a paper-doll mural showing a variety of people involved in various activities, such as helping others, communicating with others, and enjoying celebrations. Murals should include photos, magazine pictures, words, and small artifacts.

Materials for each group: large paper-doll shapes cut from craft paper, crayons or markers, scissors, glue, magazines, construction paper

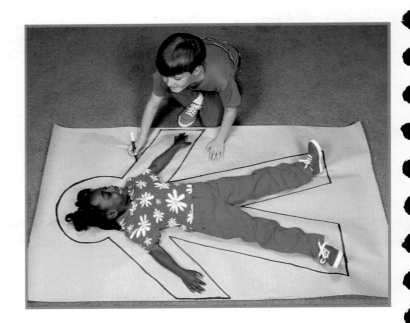

Describe People

STEP 1: Show children a large paper-doll cutout and ask them how you could make it look like every person in the world. Guide them to realize that people look different, live in different places, speak different languages, eat different foods, and celebrate different holidays. Then have children describe ways in which people are alike—for example, in needing food, shelter, and clothing. Organize children into small groups and explain that they will make a mural that shows how people all over the world are alike and different. Provide each group with a large paper-doll cutout and other materials.

Demonstrate Knowledge

STEP 2: As children work, ask them to discuss how people all around the world are alike and different.

Q. **What is the same about celebrations all over the world?** Celebrations honor people and events. Many celebrations include food, dancing, games, and other customs.

Present the Project

STEP 3: On the board, draw a representation of the globe. Have children hold up their paper dolls as they share them with the class. Display children's work under a banner with the title *World of People*.

What to Look For In their discussions and through the murals they create, children should exhibit the understanding that the world is made up of diverse peoples. They should be able to

▶ name places where many Americans' ancestors are from.
▶ explain why it is important to learn about other people.
▶ describe a variety of family and community celebrations.
▶ list ways people can help others by volunteering.
▶ use appropriate vocabulary.

REMIND CHILDREN TO:
• Share their ideas.
• Cooperate with others to plan their work.
• Plan and take responsibility for their tasks.
• Show their work.
• Discuss their own and the group's performance.

Glossary

A

ancestor
Someone in a family who lived long ago. My **ancestor** came to America from England. (page 241)

artifact
An object that is made and used by people. This bowl is an Indian **artifact**. (page 256)

B

bar graph
A picture that shows how many or how much. This **bar graph** shows the states one family has visited. (page 244)

boundary
A line that shows where one state ends and another begins. The red line shows the **boundary** between Indiana and Ohio. (page 198)

business
A place where people make or sell goods or give services. My family started a TV repair **business**. (page 128)

C

capital
A city in which government leaders meet and work. Washington, D.C., is the **capital** of the United States. (page 160)

cause
A person or thing that makes something happen. Lightning was the **cause** of the fire. (page 158)

citizen
A member of a community. Pedro is a **citizen** of the United States. (page 32)

city

A large community where people live and work. New York City is the largest **city** in the United States. (page 24)

compass rose

Arrows on a map that show directions. The **compass rose** shows which way is north, south, east, and west. (page 28)

colony

A place that is ruled by another country. Virginia was the first English **colony** in America. (page 152)

Congress

Our country's lawmakers. The **Congress** of the United States meets in the Capitol Building. (page 161)

communication

Sharing ideas with others. Many people use telephones for **communication**. (page 261)

conservation

Working to save resources or make them last longer. Forest rangers teach us about the **conservation** of trees. (page 86)

community

A place where people live and the people who live there. The **community** I live in is a big city. (page 21)

consumer

A person who buys and uses goods and services. This **consumer** is buying food for a picnic. (page 119)

continent

One of the largest bodies of land on the Earth. We live on the **continent** of North America. (page 60)

country

A land and the people who live in that land. The United States is one of three **countries** in North America. (page 32)

crop

A kind of plant that people grow for food or other uses. Corn is an important **crop** in the United States. (page 63)

custom

A way of doing something. Eating with chopsticks is a **custom** in many Asian countries. (page 252)

desert

A dry place. Very little rain falls in a **desert**. (page 51)

diagram

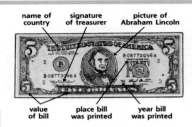

A drawing that shows the parts of something. The **diagram** shows the parts of a five-dollar bill. (page 126)

direction

North, south, east, or west. The sign tells us in which **direction** to go. (page 28)

effect

Something that happens from a cause. The forest fire was the **effect** of a lightning strike. (page 158)

election

The time when people vote. The **election** for President is held in November. (page 192)

freedom

The right of people to make their own choices. Americans have the **freedom** to worship as they please. (page 204)

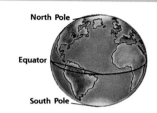

equator

A line on a map or globe that is halfway between the North Pole and the South Pole. The weather at the **equator** is hot. (page 61)

geography

The study of the Earth and its people. Maps show something about the **geography** of a place. (page 48)

factory

A place where people make goods. This **factory** makes shoes. (page 108)

globe

A model of the Earth. We find places on our classroom **globe**. (page 60)

flow chart

A chart that shows the order in which things happen. The **flow chart** shows how to make a kite. (page 66)

goods

Things that people make or grow. People who play soccer buy these **goods**. (page 26)

government

A group of people who make the laws for a community or a country. There are people from each state in the United States **government**. (page 194)

grid

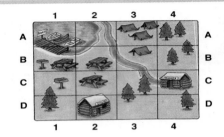

Lines that cross one another to form boxes. The lines of a **grid** can help you find places on a map. (page 164)

group

A number of people doing an activity together. This **group** is making music. (page 14)

history

The story of what has happened in a place. This picture book is about the **history** of our country. (page 142)

holiday

A time to celebrate. The Fourth of July is an American **holiday**. (page 188)

income

The money people earn for the work they do. I am saving part of my **income** to buy a computer. (page 122)

independence

The freedom of people to choose their own government and make their own laws. On the Fourth of July, we celebrate our country's **independence**. (page 262)

invention

Something that has been made for the first time. The first lightbulb was an important **invention**. (page 168)

island

Hawaii

Land that has water all around it. The state of Hawaii is made up of many **islands**. (page 52)

landmark

A familiar object at a place. The Alamo is a Texas **landmark**. (page 157)

judge

Someone who works as a leader in court. The **judge** ruled that Mrs. Page had broken the law. (page 196)

law

A rule that everyone must follow. The **law** says cars must stop at a stop sign. (page 25)

lake

A body of water that has land all around it. The people who live around the lake enjoy fishing. (page 53)

lawmaker

A leader who makes laws. Many **lawmakers** work in our state capital. (page 161)

landform

A kind of land. Mountains, hills, and plains are **landforms**. (page 50)

leader

A person who helps a group plan what to do. A principal is the **leader** of a school. (page 16)

map

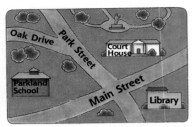

A drawing that shows where places are. We can find the library on the **map**. (page 23)

map key

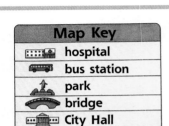

A list of the symbols on a map. The **map key** tells what the symbols on a map stand for. (page 28)

mayor

The leader of a city or a town. The **mayor** meets with the lawmakers of our community. (page 201)

monument

Something set up to honor someone or something. This **monument** honors George Washington. (page 162)

motto

A word or short saying that tells a feeling or an idea. Our country's **motto** is "In God We Trust." (page 188)

mountain

The highest kind of land. There is snow on these **mountains**. (page 50)

needs

Things people cannot live without. Food, clothing, and a place to live are **needs**. (page 18)

neighborhood

A small part of a community. Our **neighborhood** has a fruit and vegetable market. (page 18)

O

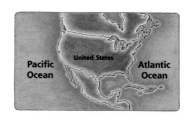

ocean

A very large body of salty water. The Pacific **Ocean** is west of the United States. (page 52)

pollution

Anything that makes the air, land, or water unclean. Throwing garbage into a lake or river causes **pollution**. (page 90)

 P

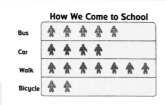

pictograph

A picture that uses symbols to show numbers of things. This **pictograph** shows how the children in one class come to school. (page 106)

prediction

Something a person says will happen. Tom's **prediction** is that it is going to rain. (page 113)

pioneer

A person who leads the way into land that has not been settled. Many **pioneers** traveled west in covered wagons. (page 224)

President

The leader of the United States. George Washington was our country's first **President**. (page 160)

plain

Land that is mostly flat. Our farm is on a **plain**. (page 51)

producer

A person who makes or grows something. Factory and farm workers are **producers**. (page 118)

R

resource

Something people use that comes from the Earth. Wood is an important **resource**. (page 71)

river

A long body of water that flows through the land. The Mississippi River is the longest **river** in the United States. (page 53)

route

A way to go from one place to another. The map shows the **route** to Grandma's house. (page 164)

rule

Something you must or must not do. A good **rule** for home and school is "Put things away after using them." (page 16)

S

services

Jobs people do that help others. Firefighters, police officers, and teachers provide **services**. (page 27)

settler

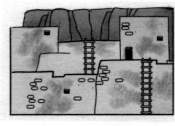

A person who makes a home in a new place. **Settlers** from many countries built homes in the West. (page 148)

shelter

A place to live. Some American Indians built their **shelters** from clay. (page 142)

state

California

A part of our country. The United States has fifty **states**. (page 198)

suburb

A community near a city. We live in a **suburb** of Chicago. (page 49)

symbol

A picture that stands for something real. A square is a **symbol** for a store on this map. (page 28)

T

table

Lists of things in groups. This **table** shows my best friends. (page 82)

taxes

Money people pay to their government for services. This man's **taxes** will pay for community services. (page 104)

time line

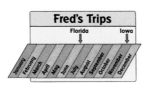

A line that shows when things happened. This **time line** shows when Fred took trips this year. (page 146)

trade

To give money, goods, or services to get something in return. Mary wants to **trade** her book for Nancy's. (page 114)

transportation

Any way of moving people or things from place to place. Airplanes are one kind of **transportation**. (page 114)

V

valley

Low land between hills or mountains. A small river runs through the **valley**. (page 50)

vote

A choice that gets counted. The person who gets the most **votes** is the winner. (page 192)

W

wants

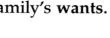

Things people would like to have. A new car is one of my family's **wants**. (page 122)

Index

Credits

Photo Credits:
Key: (t) top; (b) bottom; (l) left; (r) right; (c) center

Thinking Organizers

Many methods may be used to organize ideas and concepts. The contents of these pages are intended to act as guides for that organization. These copying masters may be used to help children organize the concepts in the lessons they have read. They can also be used to help children draw conclusions and make inferences about the material they are studying.

Contents

THE POWERFUL IDEAS
THEMES AND STRANDS OF SOCIAL STUDIES

Commonality and Diversity

Interaction Within Different Environments

Continuity and Change

OUR WORLD
Geography
History
Civics and Government
Economics
Culture

Individualism and Interdependence

Conflict and Cooperation

THE FIVE THEMES OF GEOGRAPHY

Location

★ Where is a place located?
★ What is it near?
★ What direction is it from another place?
★ Why are certain features or places located where they are?

Place

★ What is it like there?
★ What physical and human features does it have?

Human–Environment Interactions

★ How are people's lives shaped by the place?
★ How has the place been shaped by people?

Movement

★ How did people, products, and ideas get from one place to another?
★ Why do they make these movements?

Regions

★ How is this place like other places?
★ What features set this place apart from other places?

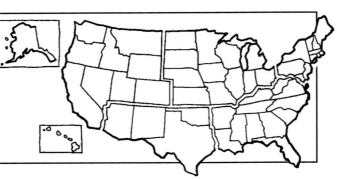

ASK YOURSELF SOME HISTORY QUESTIONS

What happened?

When did it happen?

Who took part in it?

How and why did it happen?

CURRENT EVENTS

Summary of an Important Event:

Who:

What:

When:

Where:

How:

Prediction

What do I think will happen next?

Personal Reaction

My reaction to the event:

Harcourt Brace School Publishers

MY SOCIAL STUDIES JOURNAL

The most important thing I learned was...

Something that I did not understand was...

What surprised me the most was...

I would like to know more about...

Harcourt Brace School Publishers

READING GUIDE

K	What I **K**now

W	What I **W**ant to Know

L	What I **L**earned

Harcourt Brace School Publishers

UNDERSTAND THE MAIN IDEA

MAIN IDEA

SUPPORTING DETAIL

SUPPORTING DETAIL

SUPPORTING DETAIL

SUPPORTING DETAIL

TELL
FACT FROM OPINION

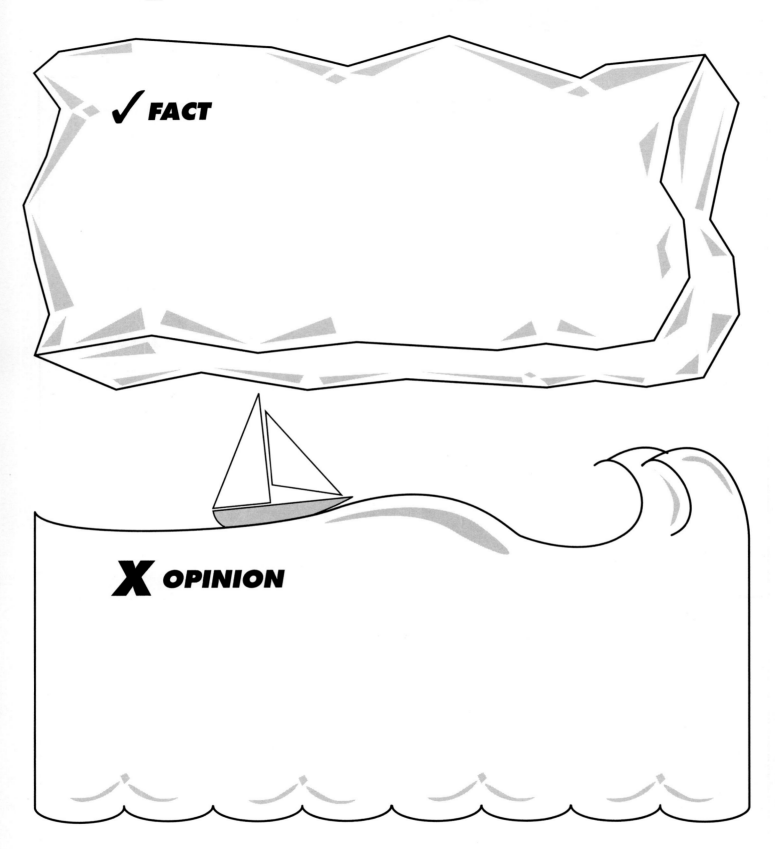

✓ **FACT**

✗ **OPINION**

CAUSE AND EFFECT

EFFECT

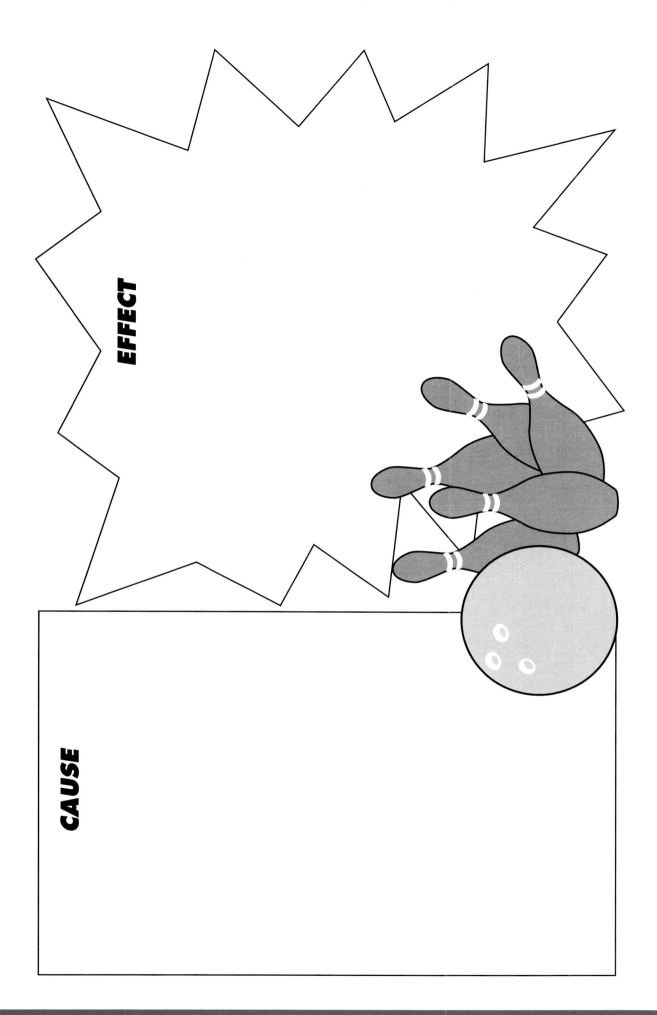

CAUSE

COMPARE AND CONTRAST

Information About "A"	Information About "B"

Harcourt Brace School Publishers

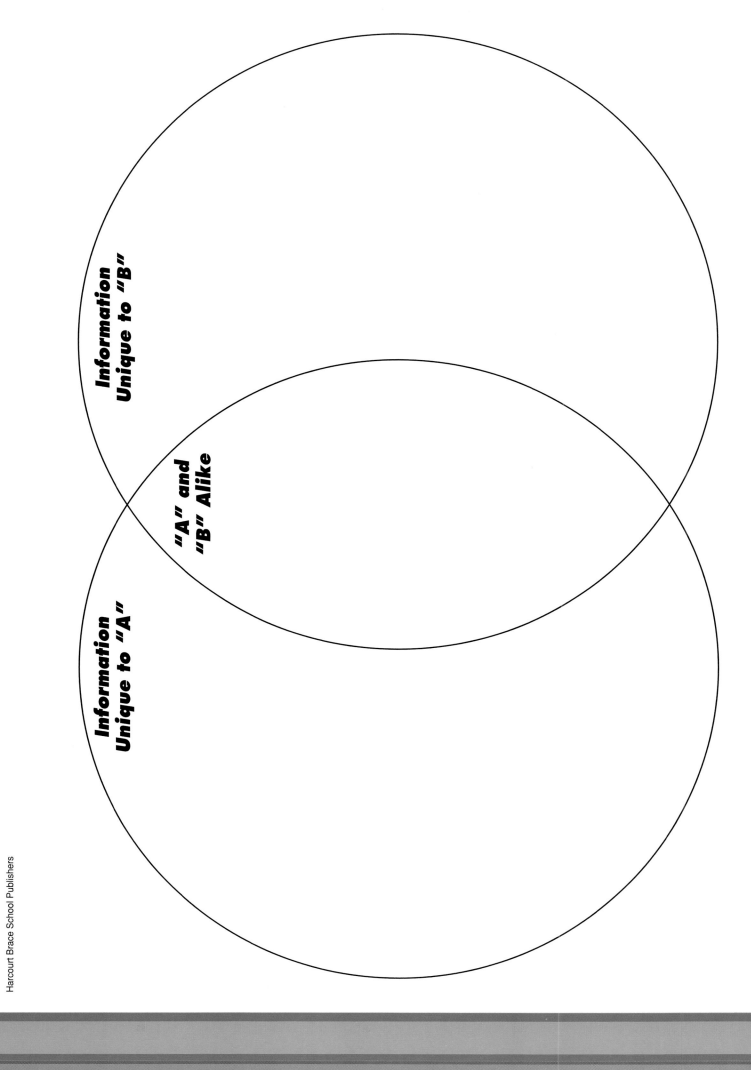

Information
Unique to "B"

"A" and
"B" Alike

Information
Unique to "A"

Harcourt Brace School Publishers

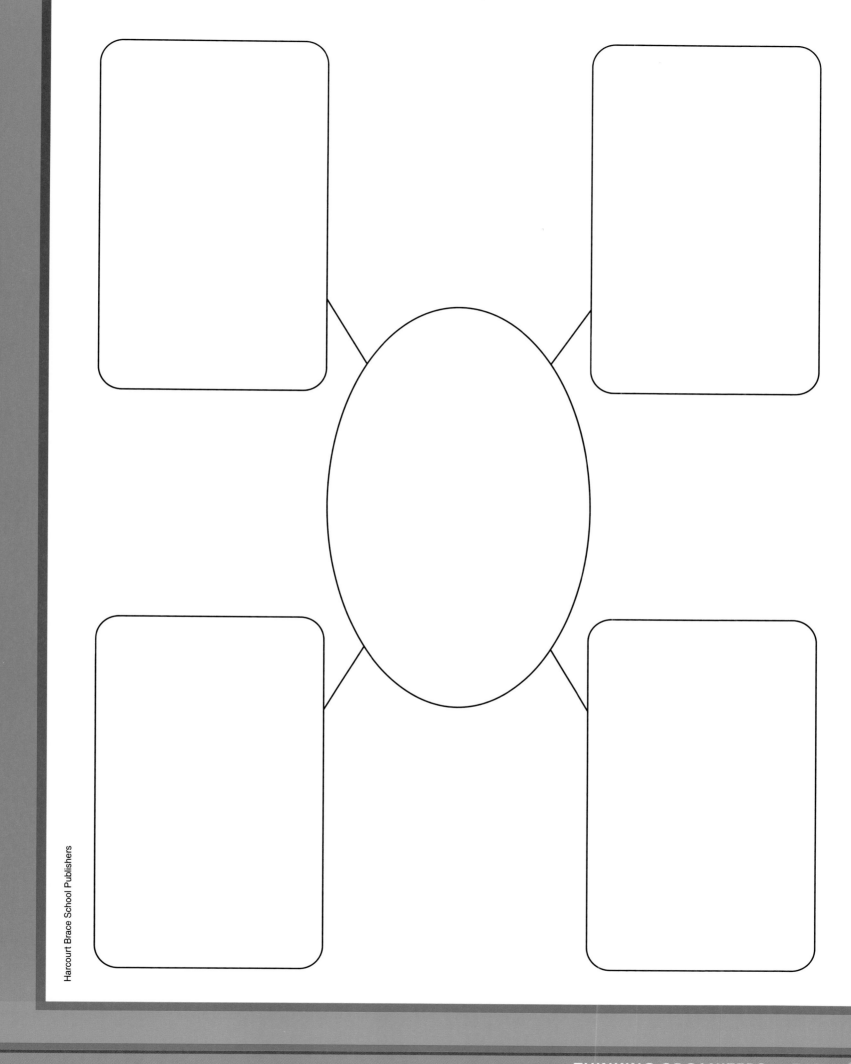

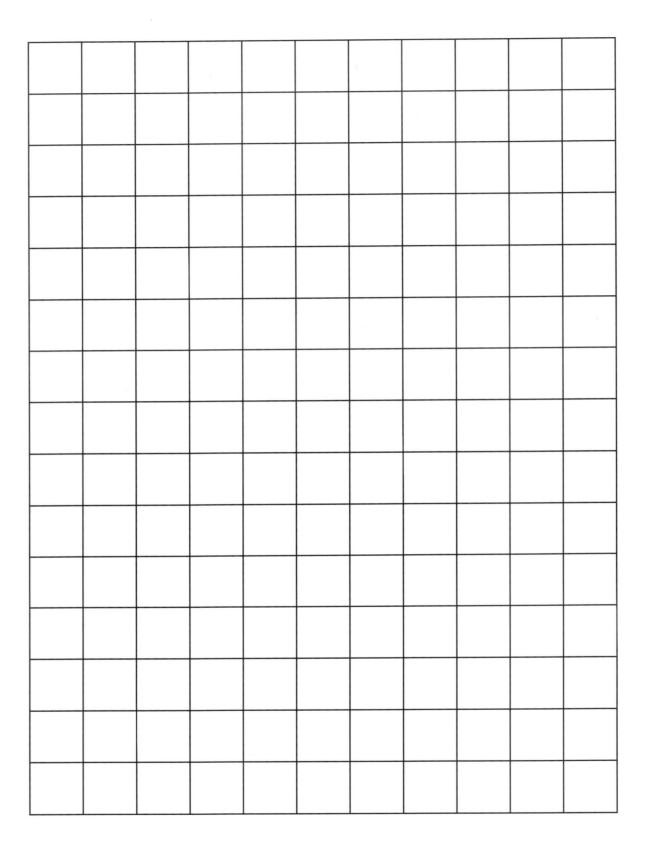

Harcourt Brace School Publishers

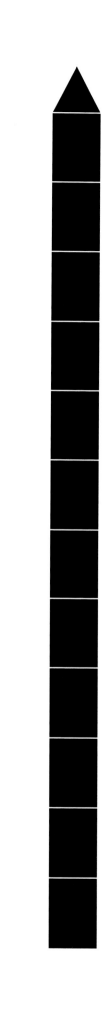

THE UNITED STATES

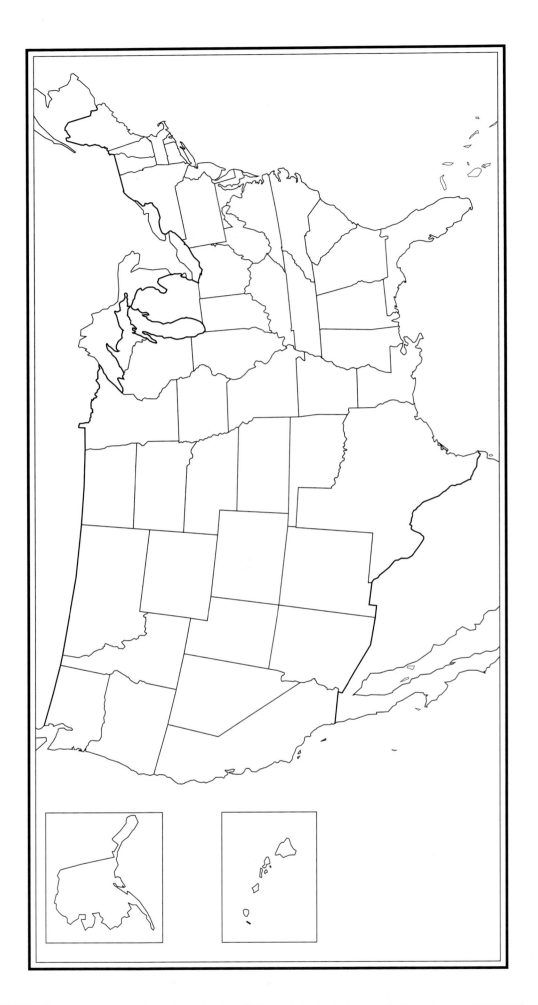

NORTH AMERICA

THE WORLD

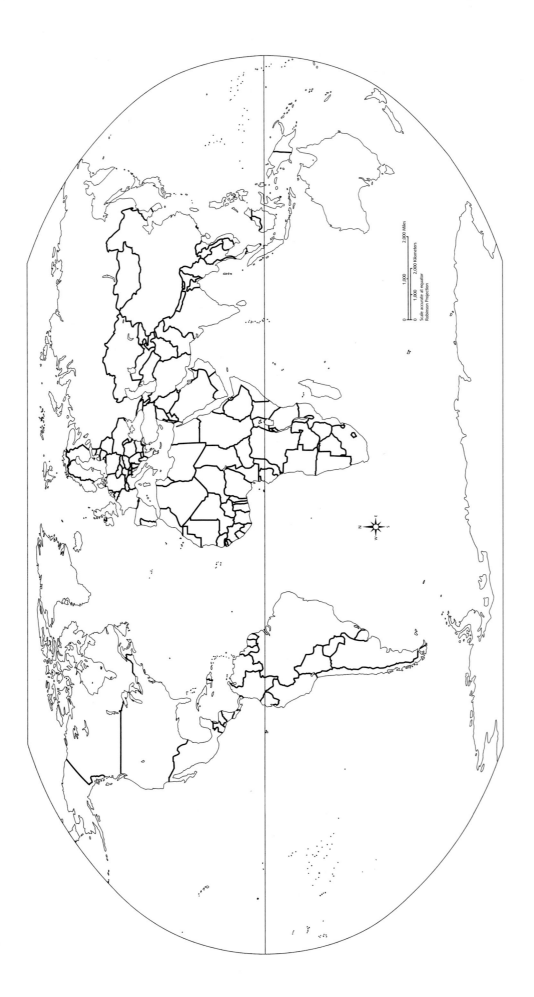

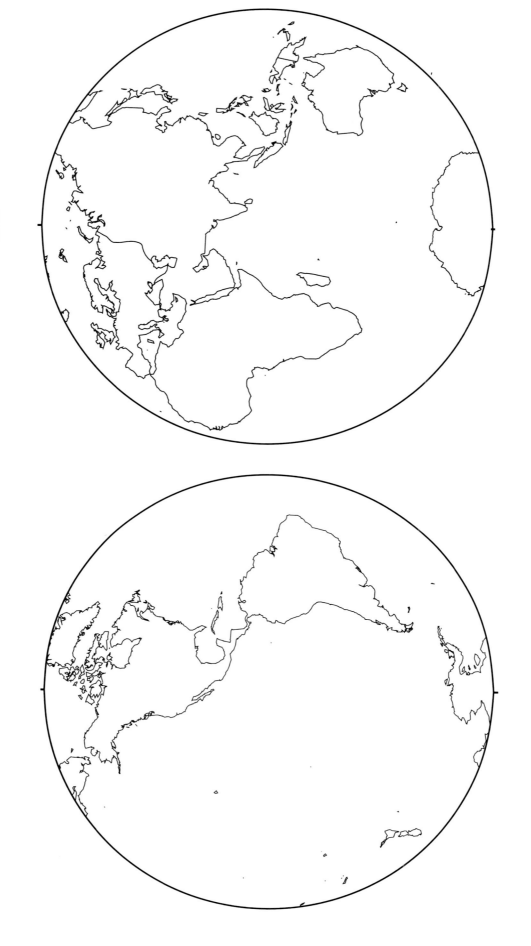

EASTERN HEMISPHERE

WESTERN HEMISPHERE

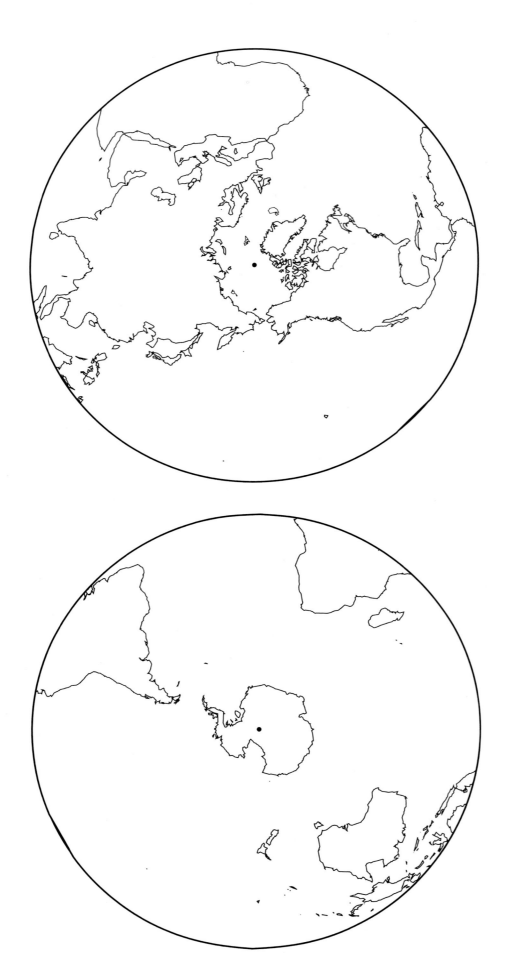

NORTHERN HEMISPHERE

SOUTHERN HEMISPHERE

Activity Patterns

The reproducible patterns in this section are for use with the activities described in the Hands-On Option pages of your Teacher's Edition lesson plans. You may also want to use the patterns to create other activities appropriate for children in your class.

Contents

SCHOOL PUZZLE

GOODS AND SERVICES WHEEL

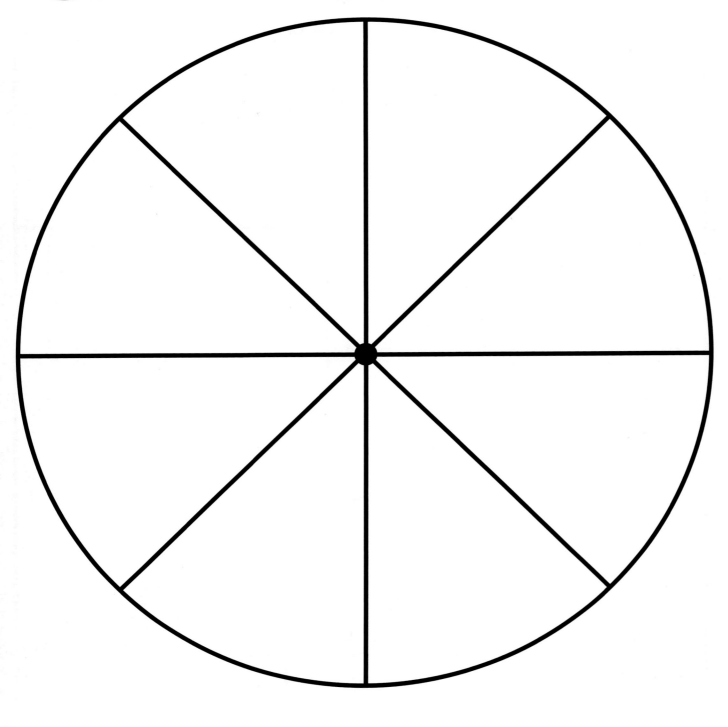

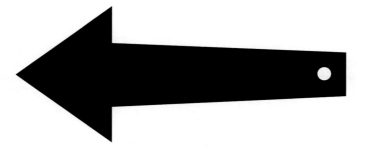

Harcourt Brace School Publishers

CULTURAL FILMSTRIP

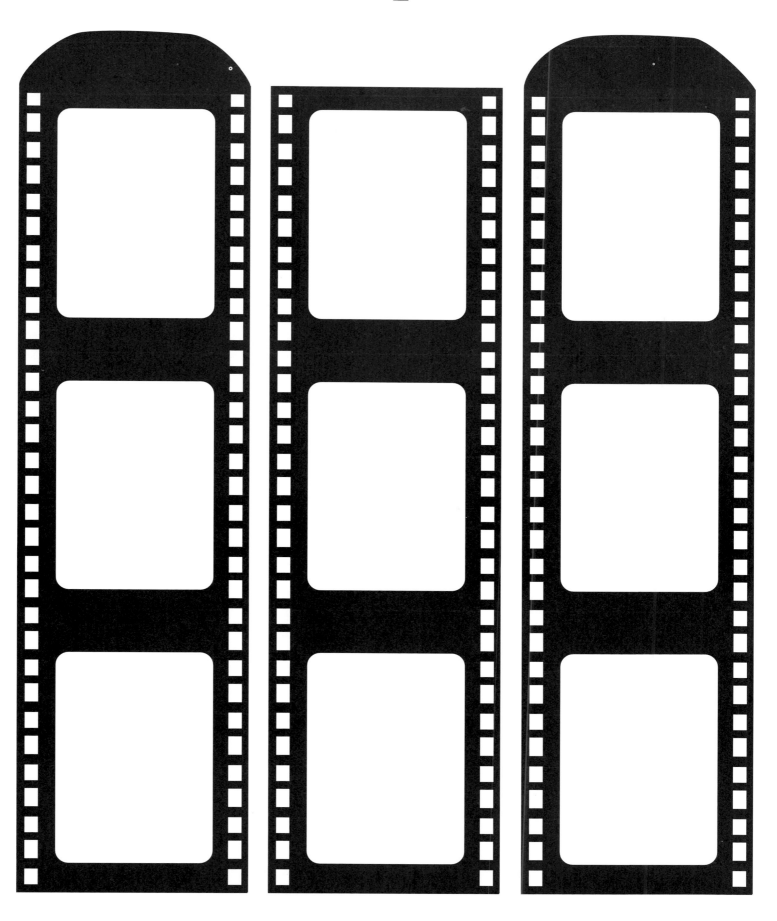

CONSERVATION CUBE

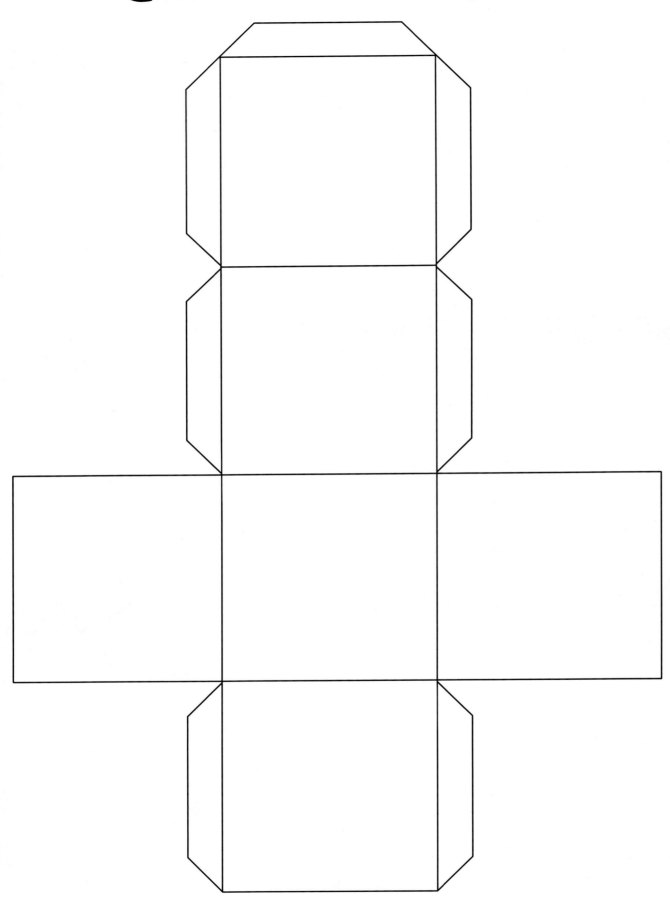

Harcourt Brace School Publishers

ACCORDION BOOK

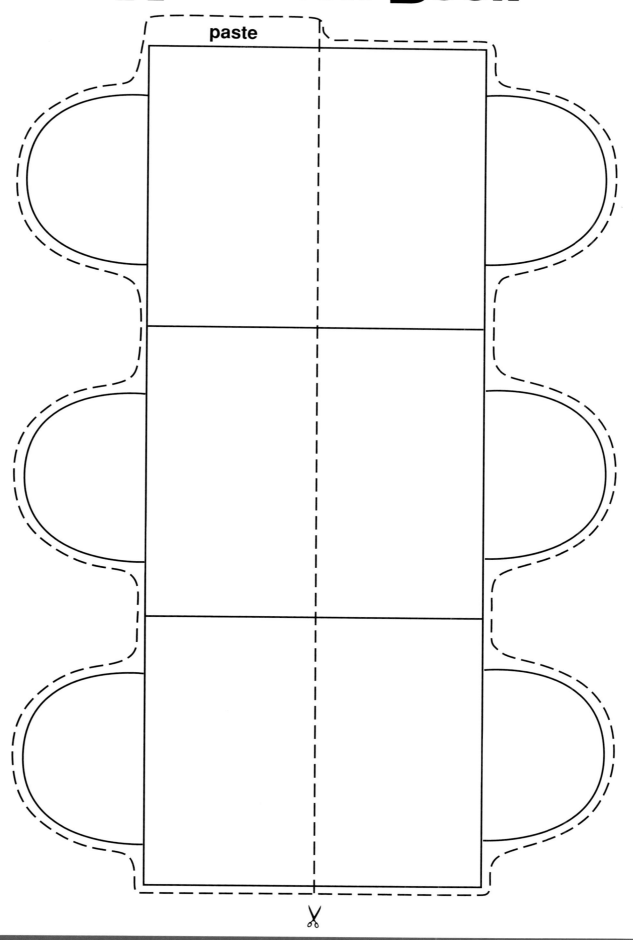

paste

DESIGN A T-SHIRT

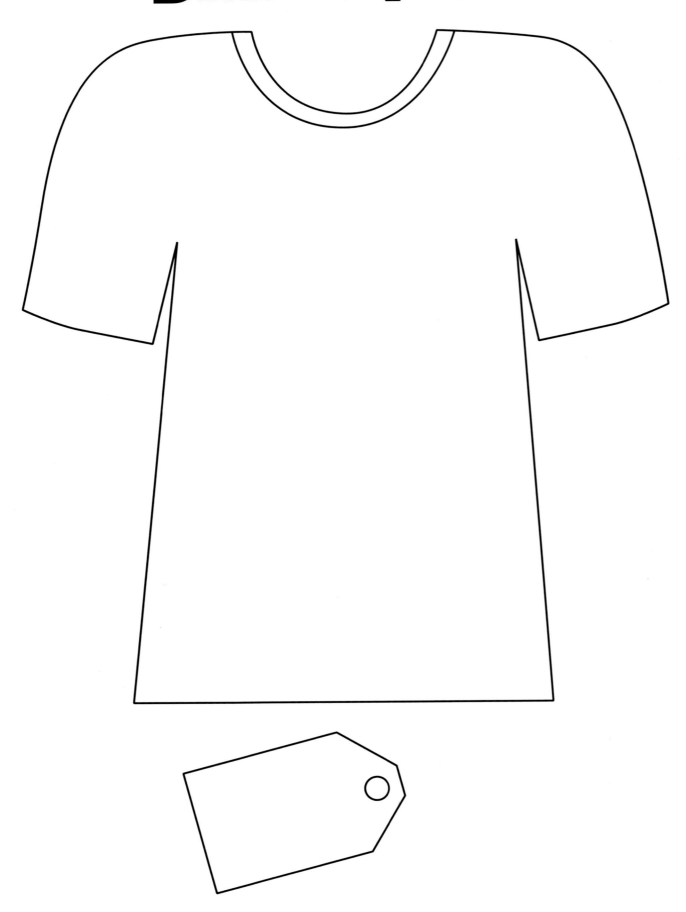

CAUSE-AND-EFFECT CHAIN

Tape here

Tape here

Tape here

Tape here

PORTRAITS CHAIN

Symbols Stand

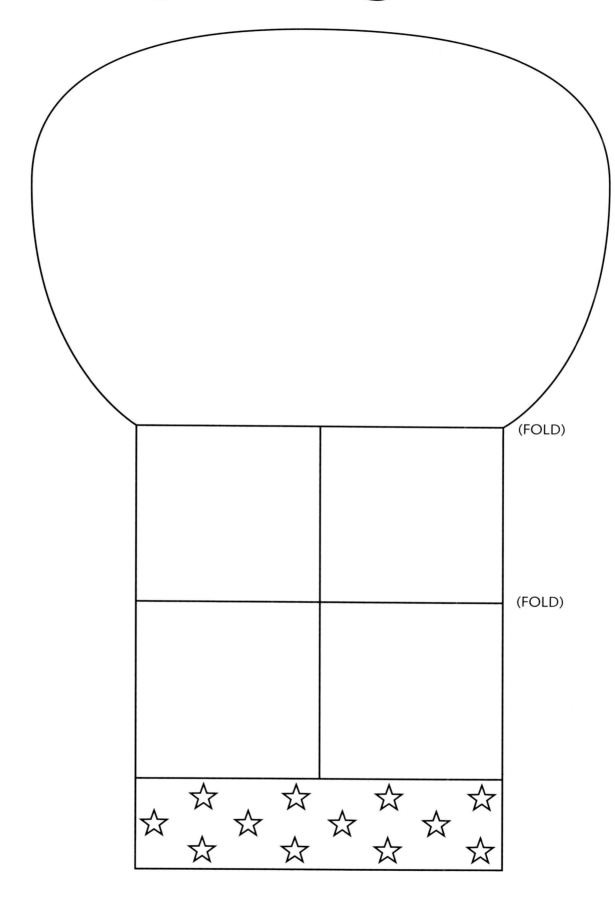

(FOLD)

(FOLD)

FINGER PUPPETS

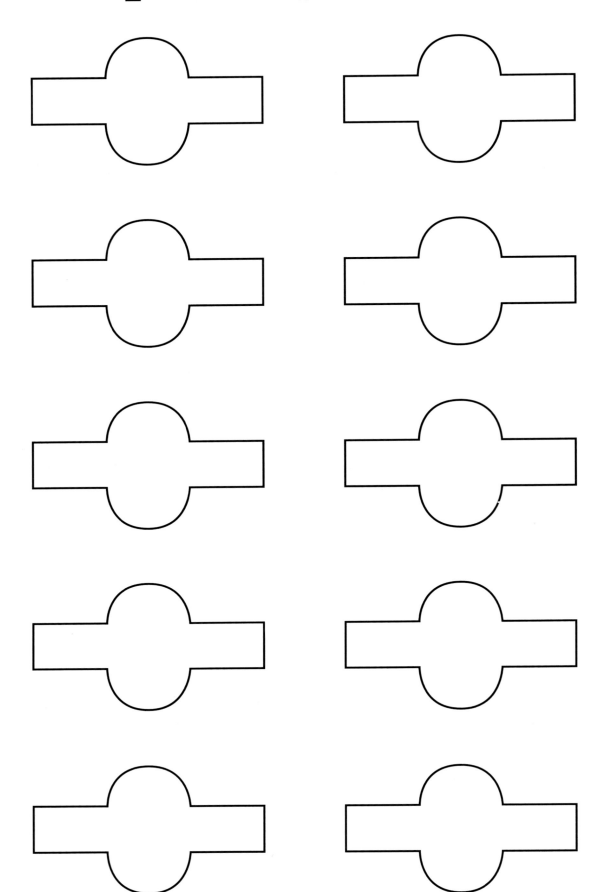

Harcourt Brace School Publishers

TRAVEL PASSPORT

Name _____

Date of Birth _____

_____
Month   Day   Year

Place of Birth

_____

_____
State   Country

_____
Signature

PASSPORT

United States of America

✂ -

Name _____

Date of Birth _____

_____
Month   Day   Year

Place of Birth

_____

_____
State   Country

_____
Signature

PASSPORT

United States of America

Harcourt Brace School Publishers

Holiday Windsock

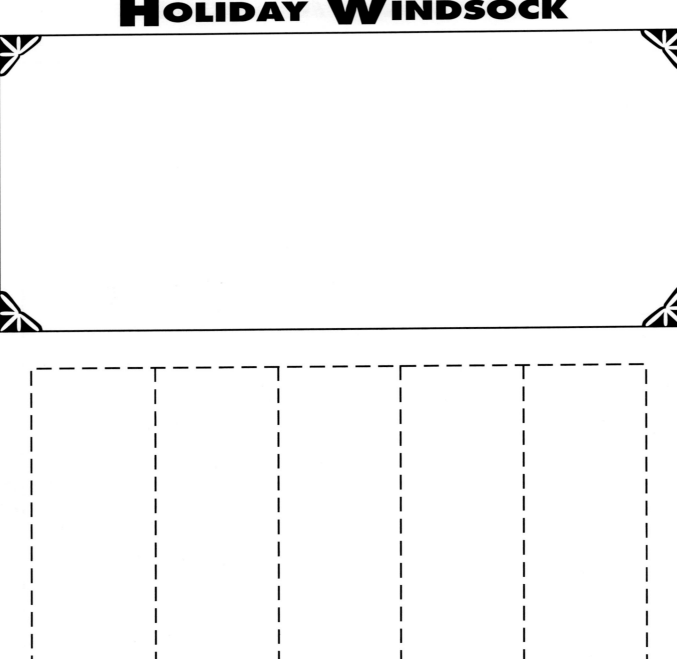

GEO GEORGIE

Vocabulary
Blacklines

This reproducible section will help you create word cards for the vocabulary found at the beginning of each lesson in your Teacher's Edition. Throughout the lesson plans you will find suggestions for using the vocabulary cards with the children. In addition, they may be used to preview the unit, to build vocabulary notebooks , to assist children with language difficulty or English language learners, and to review vocabulary at the end of the unit. Use blank cards to add vocabulary to meet the special needs of your class.

alike	different
citizen	direction
city	goods
community	group
compass rose	law
country	leader

map	rule
map key	safety
needs	services
neighborhood	symbol

city	flow chart
conservation	geography
continent	globe
crop	island
desert	lake
equator	landfill

landform	resource
mountain	river
ocean	suburb
plain	table
pollution	valley
recycle	weather

business	pictograph
consumer	prediction
diagram	producer
factory	product
income	taxes
market	tool

trade	wants
transportation	

capital	history
cause	invention
colony	landmark
Congress	lawmaker
effect	machine
grid	monument

museum	shelter
President	time line
route	volunteer
settler	

boundary	holiday
Constitution	judge
election	mayor
flag	motto
freedom	state
government	vote

Harcourt Brace School Publishers

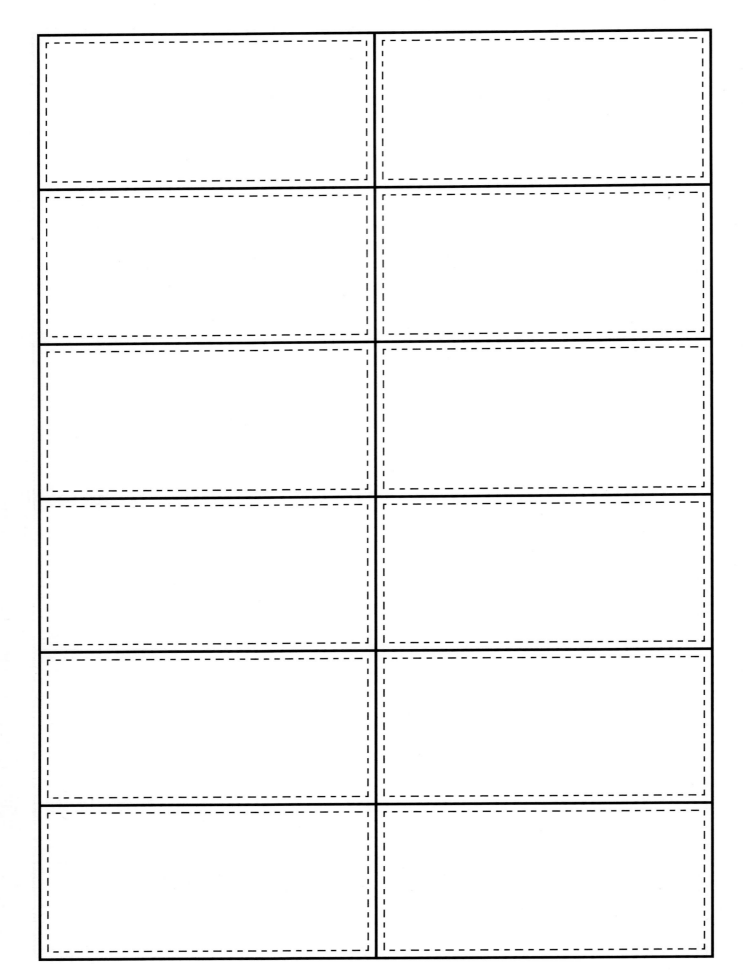

ancestor	custom
artifact	hemisphere
bar graph	independence
communication	pioneer
cooperation	

Holiday Activities

At appropriate times of the year, the holiday backgrounds and activities provided in this section can be used to reinforce concepts discussed in your social studies program. The holiday activities explore a variety of individual and community celebrations. They can prompt discussion of the commonality and diversity of the traditions and cultures found in our country.

Contents

LABOR DAY

LABOR DAY is a special day to honor workers and their contributions to the community. Labor Day is celebrated on the first Monday in September throughout the United States. Many people do not have to work on this day. They may spend the day resting or enjoying the day off with their families. Many people watch parades, go on picnics, attend sports events, or join in recreational activities that they enjoy.

- President Grover Cleveland signed a bill in 1894 to make Labor Day a national holiday.
- Children have a "job" to do, too—it is to go to school.
- Workers in Puerto Rico, Canada, Australia, and in many parts of Europe celebrate Labor Day, too.

Make a Uniform Graph

Explain that some people wear special clothes in their jobs. Police officers and forest rangers wear uniforms so people will know who they are and what their jobs are. Firefighters wear special clothes to protect them when they fight fires.

Ask children to think about people who wear special clothes in their jobs and people who do not. Have children draw pictures of the workers. Then help them create a picture graph to compare the number of people who do wear uniforms with the number who do not. A sample graph follows.

Workers Help Each Other

> ### You Will Need:
> several cardboard boxes (different sizes)
> tempera paint and large brushes
> masking tape, glue, stapler
> red construction paper rectangles to
>   be used as bricks
> brown-paper-bag squares to be used as shingles

Invite children to look at buildings and houses around your school. Make a list of the people who worked together to create the buildings, including:

    architect—designs the house and draws the plans
    general contractor—buys materials and hires builders
    carpenter—builds the frame of house
    bricklayer—puts bricks on house
    roofer—puts shingles on roof
    painter—paints the inside and outside of the house

Assign student architects to work together to discuss, design, and draw plans for a cardboard-box building. Ask children to choose a general contractor to "hire" workers. Then watch as workers follow the architects' plans for constructing the building. If necessary, help the general contractor resolve disputes and answer workers' questions.

Sing a Labor Day Song

Sing "Whistle While You Work" with children. Interested children may want to whistle the tune, too. Invite children to sing other working songs, such as "People in the Neighborhood," "I've Been Working on the Railroad," and "Parents Are People."

Rosh Hashanah

ROSH HASHANAH is the Jewish New Year. The holy day occurs during September or October and begins the holiest time of the Jewish year. During Rosh Hashanah people may attend services and commit themselves to God and to doing good deeds during the year ahead.

Many Jews send New Year's cards to their friends and families. Jewish families often gather in their homes to share food and blessings.

- Some Jews observe the holiday for two days, while others observe it for one.

- Special foods may be eaten. Raisins, apples dipped in honey, and honey bread stand for sweetness in the coming year. The traditional bread, or *challah*, is round and often has raisins. The round bread represents the year's cycle.

- Ten days after Rosh Hashanah begins, Yom Kippur is observed. It is the most sacred Jewish holiday and is the climax of the holy season.

Create a "Sweet" New Year

Invite children to prepare some of the traditional foods for the Jewish New Year celebrations.

Yeast Rolls

(For a "Smooth" Year)

1. Roll a handful of prepared yeast dough into a ball.

2. Be sure the roll is round and smooth.

3. Bake as directed on the package.

Stuffed Apples

(For a "Sweet" New Year)

1. Core an apple.

2. Cut the apple in half lengthwise so that each half has a well where the core was.

3. Fill each well with dates.

4. Pour honey on top and eat.

Draw a New Year Symbol

Tell the children that the *shofar* is a symbol of the Jewish New Year, Rosh Hashanah. The shofar is a ram's horn that is blown to mark the beginning of the holy day and the new year. Ask children to think about how they celebrate the new year, whether it is in a synagogue with the blowing of the shofar or something quite different. Invite children to draw pictures to show symbols for their celebrations.

Make a New Year Card

Invite children to make greeting cards on folded construction paper by combining their New Year symbol drawings with written messages. Explain that Jewish New Year cards usually have wishes for peace and good health to family and friends. Children may paste their symbol drawings on the folded paper or they may redraw their symbols. Suggest that children think about their messages before writing them on the card.

COLUMBUS DAY

Christopher Columbus was an explorer for Spain who sailed across the Atlantic Ocean. He was looking for a shorter route to use in trading valuable goods with the Indies. Columbus landed on an island in the Bahamas. Instead of finding a new trade route, Columbus discovered a new continent that lay between Europe and Asia. This continent was North America.

Three hundred years after Christopher Columbus arrived in the Americas, people in the United States decided to name a holiday in his honor. COLUMBUS DAY is a national holiday celebrated on the second Monday in October. It is celebrated with parades and speeches. Government offices and many businesses are closed.

- Calendars traditionally show October 12 as Columbus Day.
- When Columbus landed in the New World, he believed that he had reached the Indies, so he called the people that he met *Indians*.
- On Columbus's first voyage, he sailed with three ships, the *Niña*, the *Pinta*, and the *Santa María*.

Read a Compass

Explain that a *caravel* is a sailing ship like the ones used by Columbus on his first voyage. It was a wooden ship with tall masts and many sails. The shape of the boat was different from that of modern ships. But sailors on the caravels used compasses, just as crews of modern ships do, to help determine directions. Columbus and his men probably relied on a small compass.

Provide a handheld compass and invite children to identify directions of objects in the classroom. Help them familiarize themselves with the compass first.

1. Find north, south, east, and west on the face of the compass.
2. Turn the compass in any direction, and then let it go. The needle will always come to rest pointing north.
3. Walk south, east, and west, using the compass to identify the direction.

Dream a Dream

As a child, Christopher Columbus may have dreamed of sailing to some faraway place. Ask children what they dream of doing when they grow up. Then invite them to write about their dreams.

Rhyme a Fact

Invite children to tap their hands on their knees or their desks to create a rhythm as you say this rhyme together:

In fourteen hundred ninety-two,

Columbus sailed the ocean blue.

Help children write at least two more lines for the rhyme that tell other facts about Columbus's voyage. Invite children to perform the completed rhyme for the class.

He made the long and dangerous trip on the <u>Santa María</u>, his ship.

ELECTION DAY

The first Tuesday after the first Monday in November is **ELECTION DAY** in the United States. This is a day set aside for Americans to vote. Every four years on this day, people vote for a President to lead the United States. Election Day is also the time when adults vote on issues that affect their state and city.

The first known secret vote was held in Athens, Greece. After a trial, each judge dropped a round stone into a box to indicate his vote. A white stone meant "innocent." A black stone meant "guilty." Today people in the United States vote by marking ballots or by using voting machines. Each machine is in a private booth.

- Women have not always been allowed to vote. A long time ago, it was believed that men should make all of the decisions about government. Today, women not only vote, they run for and get elected to government positions.

- Citizens must be at least eighteen years old to vote in the United States.

Make a Choice

Explain that one of the freedoms Americans enjoy is the freedom to choose leaders and to help make choices about issues that affect them. Invite children to think about choosing a leader for their class. Ask them to consider what they would want a leader to do.

Talk about the people and issues. Remind children to discuss both sides. Then have children advertise their opinions by making posters or campaign signs. Interested students may want to give campaign speeches, too.

Cast a Ballot

You Will Need:

Ballot Pattern
hole punch
refrigerator box (optional)

Explain that voters in the United States go to polling places to vote. The polling places might be churches, schools, or other buildings where voting booths have been placed. The voting booth provides a private place for the voter to mark his or her ballot.

Invite each child to fill out a ballot. Have children fill in the issues or names of people they are voting on in your class election. Set up a private voting booth in the classroom, such as an empty refrigerator box. Encourage children to go into the booth, one at a time, and mark their vote(s) on the ballot by making a hole beside the name or issue with a hole punch. After everyone has voted, count the ballots and celebrate with the winners.

Sing an Election Day Song

Invite children to join you in singing a traditional song that is often sung during campaigning and at election time.

For He's a Jolly Good Fellow

For he's a jolly good fellow, (sing 3 times)

Which nobody can deny. (sing 3 times)

For he's a jolly good fellow, (sing 3 times)

Which nobody can deny!

ELECTION DAY BALLOT

Office/Position

Names

Issue or Rule

Choice

VOTE

THANKSGIVING

THANKSGIVING is a holiday that celebrates a harvest in America a long time ago.

Many people left Europe in the 1600s looking for a new life in the Americas. One group, the Pilgrims, left England to find a place where they could worship as they wished. They sailed across the ocean on a ship called the *Mayflower* and landed in North America at a place they called Plymouth. Here they worked to clear the land, build houses, and make a new life.

During the first winter in Plymouth, half of the settlers died. In the spring an Indian named Squanto helped those who survived plant corn and barley. Their fall harvest was a success, so the Pilgrims held a feast to give thanks to God and to thank the Indians. The Pilgrims shared the feast with their new friends, the Wampanoag Indians.

Today families gather at Thanksgiving to share good things to eat and to give thanks for the good things in their lives.

- Turkey is a traditional Thanksgiving food. People at the first Thanksgiving feast ate wild turkey, but they also enjoyed other meats including venison, duck, goose, lobster, and clam.
- President Abraham Lincoln made Thanksgiving a national holiday in 1863.
- Schools, banks, government offices, and most businesses are closed on Thanksgiving Day.

Learn a Pilgrim Game

Invite children to play a version of stool ball, a game Pilgrim children may have played while on the *Mayflower*.

You Will Need:

rubber playground ball

stool or chair

How to Play:

1. Form two equal teams.
2. One team will stand behind a line and roll the ball to try to hit the stool.
3. The other team will defend the stool by catching the ball before it hits the stool and rolling it back to the team behind the line.
4. When the stool is hit, the team gets a point. Then the teams switch positions.

Compare Grains

Explain that the Pilgrims did not know about corn when they landed in Plymouth. Corn was not grown in England, where they came from. The Indians introduced them to corn, showing them how to grow it and how to cook it and use it in baking.

Provide corn bread muffins for children to sample. (CAUTION: Check records for allergies first.) Have them compare them to other kinds of muffins by color, texture, smell, and taste.

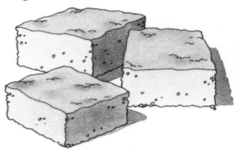

Sing a Turkey Song

Sing the song "Five Fat Turkeys." Have children take the parts of the five turkeys. Instruct the "turkeys" to "fly out" of the tree to find new hiding places at the appropriate point in the song.

Five Fat Turkeys
A Traditional Song

CHRISTMAS AROUND THE WORLD

For many people, CHRISTMAS is a religious holiday honoring the birth of Christ. Christmas customs vary from family to family and are based on traditions brought by ancestors from other countries.

In the United States, many Christians go to church on Christmas Eve for a special ceremony in which they welcome the day when Christ was born. On Christmas morning, some children hurry to see if Santa Claus has left them special gifts. In many homes, families and friends come together to eat and to exchange gifts.

Homes are often decorated with holly, ivy, and evergreen trees as reminders of the beauty of nature. Houses and shops may be trimmed with outdoor lights, and festive music may be played.

Christmas is celebrated in many countries. The holiday signifies the spirit of peace and goodwill.

- For nine days before Christmas, people in Mexico celebrate *las posadas*. They join in a search for a safe place for the infant Jesus. According to custom, they are turned down every night except the last night, Christmas.

- In Holland, children fill their wooden shoes with hay for St. Nicholas's horse. In the morning, the hay is gone and their shoes are filled with treats.

- In the windows of Norwegian homes, burning candles welcome travelers to enter for food and shelter.

Sing International Songs

Point out that most families who celebrate Christmas like to sing Christmas songs. Join children in singing favorite Christmas songs. Include some songs that were brought over from other countries.

Germany	"O Christmas Tree (*O Tannenbaum*)"
England	"The Twelve Days of Christmas"
United States	"Jolly Old Saint Nicholas"

Las Posadas Play

Explain that in Mexico, *las posadas* plays are enacted for several nights before Christmas. These show Mary and Joseph's journey to Bethlehem and their search for a resting place.

Set out simple props and invite children to use them when reenacting *las posadas*. Interested children may wish to enact the ending of the story with the birth of the baby Jesus.

International Christmas Tree

Ask children to share experiences with Christmas and to name symbols such as reindeer, stars, angels, bells, and Santa Claus. Explain that children in other countries celebrate in different ways, with different symbols. In Mexico, children play a game with piñatas. Children in England burn special holiday Yule logs. The custom of decorating trees began in Germany. In Brazil, Papa Noel brings presents. In Norway, animals are given special treats.

Provide reference material, and invite children to research symbols of Christmas around the world. Have them draw pictures of the symbols on tagboard circles. Hang these as ornaments on a tree in the room.

KWANZAA

KWANZAA is a holiday observed by many African Americans to celebrate family, community, and culture. The festival was first observed to celebrate the first fruits of the winter season.

Today the holiday begins on December 26 and lasts for seven days. Each day during the celebration, families gather, light a candle, and talk about one of the seven important ideas, or *principles*, of the African American culture. Kwanzaa is also celebrated with dancing, singing, reading poetry, and feasting. Some families exchange gifts, too. Kwanzaa is a time to celebrate the achievements of African Americans.

- The seven principles of the African American culture are *unity*, *self-determination*, *collective work and responsibility*, *cooperative economics*, *purpose*, *creativity*, and *faith*.
- On the last day of Kwanzaa, many communities gather for a feast called *karamu*.

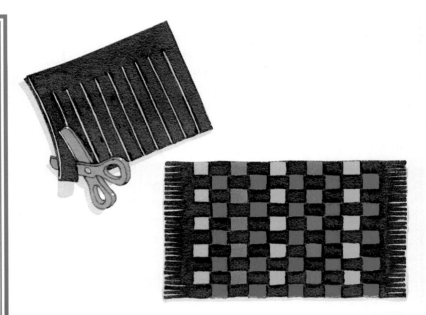

1. Fold black construction paper in half. Cut slits about 1 inch apart, starting at the folded edge, and cutting up to about 2 inches from the edge of the paper.

2. Weave colored strips through the slits in the black paper. Begin each row in opposition (first one under, second over, and so on). Colored strips should follow this order: yellow, green, red, green. Repeat to fill.

3. Cut fringe along the side edges. You may want to laminate the placemats for durability.

Talk with a Community Volunteer

Point out that many African Americans in the community work to improve life for others. Invite a community volunteer who works in a hospital, feeds the homeless, or performs another important volunteer job to visit your class. Ask the person to describe his or her work and to help children recognize ways in which they might help others.

Kwanzaa Placemat

Discuss kente (KEN•tay) cloth with the children. Explain that many years ago, the colorful, striped cloth was worn by kings in the West African country of Ghana. Invite children to weave Kwanzaa placemats to look like kente cloth.

You Will Need:

large sheets of black construction paper

scissors

long strips (about 1″ wide) of yellow, green, and red construction paper.

Perform an African Rhythm

Explain that during Kwanzaa celebrations, people share traditional African foods, songs, dances, and folktales. Some Africans and African Americans have special ways of making music with their bodies. They may clap their hands; clap their shoulders, sides, and legs; click their tongues; and stamp their feet.

Challenge children to improvise an African rhythm, using body music alone. Then have them use drums and shakers to accompany the rhythm.

CHINESE NEW YEAR

The **NEW YEAR** is the happiest holiday of the year for the Chinese and is celebrated by Chinese all over the world. The Chinese preserve their traditions through their holidays, especially this most important one.

The New Year festival begins in late January (or early February) and lasts for fifteen days. During the celebration, people have parades, dragon dances, and fireworks. Homes may be decorated with banners, brightly colored decorations, and signs that express good wishes. Families often gather for dinners that include fish and rice. It is a time to wish others well and to forgive past grudges.

- The Chinese New Year festival is filled with traditions and symbols.
- The color red is a symbol of happiness. Many houses are decorated with red and many people dress in red for the occasion.
- The dragon is a symbol of royalty. Dragons are seen in parades and on banners made for the holiday.
- The New Year celebration ends with a Lantern Festival. Those who march in the parade carry lighted lanterns.

"Light" a Chinese Lantern

Explain that during the Festival of Lanterns, people carry lighted lanterns. The streets are also decorated with lanterns of all colors, sizes, and shapes. Invite children to make Chinese lanterns to decorate your room.

You Will Need:	
Lantern Pattern	scissors
glue	yellow tissue paper
yarn	

1. Fold the pattern on the solid line.
2. Cut along the dotted lines.
3. Unfold and roll the lantern. Glue dot A to dot A. Glue dot B to dot B.
4. Crumple yellow tissue paper and slide it inside the lantern.

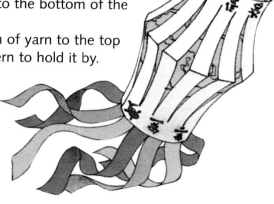

5. Cut tissue paper streamers and glue them to the bottom of the lantern.
6. Tie a length of yarn to the top of the lantern to hold it by.

Create a Chinese Dragon

Explain that children carrying a huge dragon usually lead the Dragon Dance. The dragon may be very long with as many as one hundred people carrying it. Invite children to make a dragon as follows: Paint a large box to create the head of the dragon. Use bright colors. Add glitter, feathers, tissue "scales," or other decorative materials to it. Attach a sheet or a long piece of mural paper to the head of the dragon. Decorate the "body" to match the head.

March in the Parade

Invite children to celebrate the Chinese New Year! Organize a parade and invite others to watch. Your parade can include lantern carriers, children to carry the dragon and perform a Dragon Dance, and musicians to play triangles, finger cymbals, and wooden flutes.

CHINESE LANTERN

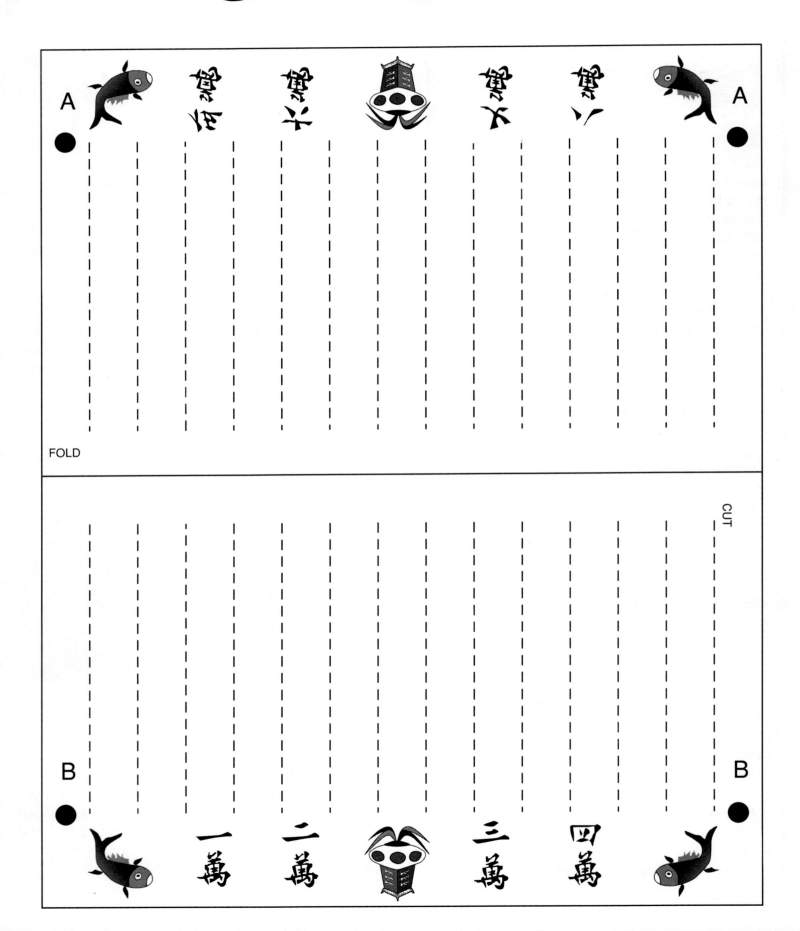

FOLD

CUT

A

A

B

B

Harcourt Brace School Publishers

 **MARTIN LUTHER KING, JR., DAY** is one of our country's newest holidays. It honors a man who was very important in helping America understand that everyone should be treated equally.

Dr. King was born in Atlanta, Georgia, on January 15, 1929. One day when he was a minister in Montgomery, Alabama, an African American woman was arrested because she refused to give her seat on the bus to a Caucasian man. Dr. King organized the people in his neighborhood to protest the unfair treatment of the woman on the bus. Many people refused to ride the buses for 381 days.

Martin Luther King, Jr., continued to speak out against the poor treatment of the African American people. He organized a historic march to the White House. At the Lincoln Memorial he gave a famous speech calling for freedom for all.

On April 4, 1968, Dr. King was assassinated. Today we celebrate his birthday by remembering his work for equal opportunity.

- On the third Monday in January each year, people honor Dr. King for what he did for our country.
- Many neighborhoods celebrate Martin Luther King, Jr., Day with picnics, parades, and marches.

Qualities That Count

Have children find pictures of Martin Luther King, Jr., in magazines, newspapers, and library books. Talk about the pictures and discuss what children think Dr. King was like from his actions.

Invite children to name other people they admire and identify the qualities or achievements that make those people special. List the names of the people and their qualities on chart paper.

Invite children to share ideas for developing personal characteristics like those listed on the chart paper.

Fair Play

Explain that Dr. King worked to create a world in which everyone would be treated fairly and would obey the same rules. Ask children what they think the words *fair* and *unfair* mean.

Copy the pattern pieces on the next page. Ask children to cut out the pieces, staple the pages together to make a minibook, and draw pictures on each of the book pages to show scenes of fairness and unfairness.

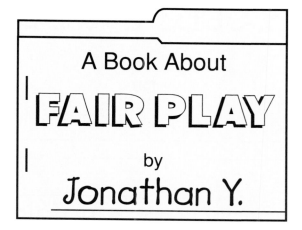

Dream Keepers

Explain that Martin Luther King, Jr., had a dream that all people would get along with each other. He had a dream that there would be no more unfairness in the world. He shared his dreams in his famous freedom speech at the capital.

Invite children to use puppets to act out scenes that show ways of solving problems peacefully. You might present scenarios such as the following:
- In the middle of a game on the playground, an older boy takes your soccer ball.
- A girl you know cuts in line in front of you at lunch.
- Your classmates say you run too slowly and they don't want you on their team.

Friendship Bracelets

You Will Need:
colored braid in 12-inch lengths small beads (optional)

Invite children to braid friendship bracelets to give to persons they do not know well. Ask children to find out all they can about their new friends.

Fair Play Book

A Book About FAIR PLAY

by

_____

fair

unfair

fair

unfair

fair

Harcourt Brace School Publishers

EASTER

EASTER is one of the two most important holidays for Christians. The holiday is a time to celebrate the resurrection of Jesus Christ after he died on a cross.

Easter is observed at the beginning of spring, in March or April. For many, the holiday is a time to think about new life associated with the season. Flowers bloom, birds and insects hatch, bears and cubs come out of dens in which they have been hibernating for the winter, and the Earth comes to life again.

People participate in many customs during the Easter season. Some popular traditions include parades and carnivals, dyeing and hunting for Easter eggs, wearing fancy hats, watching plays that tell the Easter story, and sharing an Easter feast with family and friends.

- Colored eggs are part of the Easter customs. Eggs have long been a symbol of the universe and of new life.

- The Easter Bunny comes from an old Egyptian belief that the rabbit is a symbol of spring because its babies are born during this season.

- Many people plant flower gardens and vegetable gardens at Easter.

- To celebrate Easter, an egg-rolling contest is held for children at the White House.

Write to the President

Explain that each year, the President of the United States holds an Easter party on the lawn of the White House in Washington D.C. Invite children to write to the President to find out more about the event. Here are some questions they might want answered.

- What events are held?

- Who is invited?

- How many eggs are hidden?

- Who dyes the eggs?

Decorate Eggs

Explain that in Russia and Ukraine, decorated eggs are given as Easter gifts. Beautiful eggs were created by Karl Fabergé, the czar's jeweler, who decorated them with gold and jewels. Today, the fancy eggs are collected as art treasures.

Invite children to make their own Fabergé eggs. Have children glue art materials on eggs to create interesting scenes. Suggest that children give their eggs to someone special.

You Will Need:

boiled or plastic eggs
craft glue
beads, jewels, glitter, sequins, thin gold braid

Plant a Garden

Explain to children that although Easter is a religious holiday, it is also a festival of spring and hope and of new life after the cold winter. Invite children to celebrate the new life that spring brings by planting a garden. Provide the following directions: Put a spoonful of rich soil in each cup of an egg carton. Plant carrot, radish, or flower seeds in each cup. Keep the carton in a light place and water the soil every day. Watch as the seeds sprout into new life in your classroom.

CINCO DE MAYO

 **CINCO DE MAYO**, which means "the fifth of May" in Spanish, is a national holiday in Mexico. It is also celebrated by Mexican Americans in the United States to honor the defenders of Mexican freedom.

On May 5, 1862, French troops attacked the city of Puebla, Mexico. The Mexican army did not have nearly as many men or weapons as their attackers but fought hard to defeat them. The victory was especially impressive because the Mexicans defeated the French in only four hours.

People celebrate Cinco de mayo with religious services, patriotic speeches, parades, fireworks, Mexican music, dancing, Mexican foods, games, and mock battles that tell the story of the Mexican army in its fight with the French army long ago.

- Most Mexican celebrations for Cinco de mayo include lively fiestas, or fairs. The fiestas may take place in the center of town. Musicians, singers, and dancers may perform. Artists and cooks may sell their goods.

- Each May 5 in Puebla, Mexico, a mock battle is staged to remember and celebrate the victory over the French army in the Battle of Puebla.

Cook Corn Snacks

Explain that tortillas are the basic bread of Mexico. The thin, flat pancakes were originally baked on flat stones, but are now baked on griddles. Make corn tortillas for snack time or for your classroom fiesta. (CAUTION: Check records for allergies first.)

You Will Need:
2 cups finely ground cornmeal
1 1/2 cups warm water

Mix ingredients and form small balls. Roll them between sheets of waxed paper until they are thin and round. Cook on a hot griddle until brown on both sides. You may want to serve the warm tortillas with butter, cinnamon sugar, or refried beans.

Create a Mexican Mural

Invite children to help create a colorful mural similar to the ones created by Mexican artists for Cinco de mayo fiestas.

Copy the pattern on the next page for each child. Have children study the design, which was inspired by ancient Mexican paintings. They can color in the design with felt-tip markers, craft paints, or glitter pens. They may want to add yarn to outline parts of the design or to fill in small areas. Have children place four completed designs together to create the full pattern. Arrange and glue the completed patterns on mural paper to create a festive panel for the classroom door or bulletin board.

Cinco de mayo Mural

1/4 OF PATTERN

Harcourt Brace School Publishers

Independence Day

On July 4, 1776, American leaders signed the Declaration of Independence. The document announced that Americans would no longer be ruled by the king of England. July 4 became a very important day to all Americans, because it meant freedom and independence. This date has been celebrated ever since as the birthday of the United States.

On **INDEPENDENCE DAY**, today, people still celebrate the freedom that we enjoy. There are parades with marching bands, Boy Scouts and Girl Scouts, war veterans, floats, and waving flags. Americans may dress in red, white, and blue and listen to patriotic speeches, gather to hear the Declaration of Independence read aloud, and watch fireworks in the park.

- The Declaration of Independence was adopted on July 4, 1776, but it was not actually signed until August 2 of that year.

- The 56 men who signed the Declaration of Independence did not use a pen. They dipped a turkey feather, or quill, into an inkwell and used the tip to write on the document.

Freedom Speech

Explain that the Declaration of Independence announced our freedom from England. It also stated that people have certain rights. They have the right to gather, the right to speak freely, and the right to worship as they wish. Discuss other rights and freedoms Americans have.

Invite children to decorate a podium (or box) with red, white, and blue fabric. Ask volunteers to stand at the podium and speak to the class. Have them tell what freedom means to them and why it is important.

Focus on the Flag

Point out that America was made up of only 13 colonies when the Declaration of Independence was signed more than 200 years ago. Remind children that today the United States is 50 states united into one free country.

Take children to the school library to look for pictures of the flag that represented the 13 original colonies. Have them compare it to the flag we fly today and discover

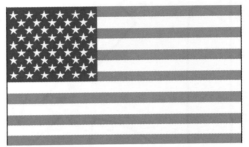

how the flags are alike and how they are different. Ask children to find out what the stars and stripes represent.

Then provide red, white, and blue construction paper and gold gummed stars, and invite children to make models of each flag. Hang their flags proudly in your room as your class celebrates this important day in our country's history.

Raise a Patriotic Voice

Set out red, white, and blue streamers, American flags, and star-studded banners. Invite children to wave them to the rhythm of patriotic music such as "You're a Grand Old Flag," "America," or "Stars and Stripes Forever."

Home Letters

These home letters offer a way of linking the children's study of social studies to the children's family members. There is one letter, available in both English and Spanish, for each unit. The focus for each letter is an activity or activities that children and family members can share.

Contents

Social Studies

Dear Family Members,

Our class is beginning a new social studies unit, called "We Belong to Many Groups." We will find out that our schools, families, neighborhoods, communities, and country are all groups to which we belong. We will learn how members of a group work together and how different groups depend on one another. You can help your child get ready for this unit by doing the following activities. As you talk together, make notes that your child can share with our class.

Family Activity

Take a walk with your child around your neighborhood or another part of your community. Have your child list the shops and other businesses your family uses. Tell your child that these businesses help the neighborhood and the community grow.

_____

_____

_____

_____

Help your child find your neighborhood on a map of your community. Then find your community on a state map, your state on a map of the United States, and the United States and your state on a world map or globe.

Family Reading

Choose a book to share about people and groups you can find in cities. You might read *The Day of the Rainbow* by Ruth Craft or *Taxi! Taxi!* by Cari Best. After you read, invite your child to talk about the people and the groups that are part of a community.

_____

_____

_____

_____

Thank you for supporting our social studies program.

Sincerely,

HARCOURT BRACE

Social Studies

Queridos familiares,

Nuestra clase está comenzando una nueva unidad de estudios sociales titulada "Pertenecemos a muchos grupos". Vamos a aprender que formamos parte de los siguientes grupos: la escuela, la familia, los vecindarios, las comunidades y nuestro país. Aprenderemos cómo los miembros de un grupo trabajan juntos y cómo los diferentes grupos dependen unos de otros. Usted puede ayudar a que su hijo(a) se prepare para esta unidad mediante las siguientes actividades. Mientras conversan, tomen notas para que su hijo(a) las comparta con la clase.

Actividad familiar

Vaya de paseo con su hijo(a) por su vecindario u otra parte de su comunidad. Pídale que haga una lista de las tiendas u otros negocios que su familia utiliza. Explíquele que estos negocios ayudan a que el vecindario y la comunidad crezca.

_____

_____

_____

_____

Ayude a su hijo(a) a encontrar su vecindario en un mapa de la comunidad. Después, encuentren su comunidad en un mapa del estado; su estado en un mapa de Estados Unidos; y a Estados Unidos en un mapa del mundo o en un globo terráqueo.

Lectura familiar

Escoja un libro que trate sobre personas y grupos que se encuentran en ciudades. Pueden leer *The Day of the Rainbow* de Ruth Craft o *Taxi! Taxi!* de Cari Best. Después de la lectura, anime a su hijo(a) a hablar sobre las personas y los grupos que forman parte de una comunidad.

_____

_____

_____

_____

Gracias por apoyar nuestro programa de estudios sociales.

Sinceramente,

Harcourt Brace School Publishers

HARCOURT BRACE

Social Studies

Dear Family Members,

Our class is beginning a new social studies unit, called "Where We Live." We will be learning about the land and its resources. We will find out how the land around us affects our lives and how we use the resources the land produces. You can help your child get ready for this unit by doing the following activities. As you talk together, make notes that your child can share with our class.

Family Activity

Talk with your child about the geography of your area. What kinds of land and water are near you? What type of weather do you have in your community? Take your child for a walk or a drive and observe how people are using and changing the land.

_____

_____

_____

_____

Conserve water for a month. Try simple water-saving steps such as turning off the water while brushing your teeth, using a timer for shorter showers, and placing a brick in the tank of your toilet. Also, when waiting for tap water to heat up, place a bucket or bowl under the faucet and use the cold water you save to water plants, wash cars, or water pets.

Family Reading

Choose a book to share about the land. You might read *Stringbean's Trip to the Shining Sea* by Vera B. Williams or *Across the Blue Mountains* by Emma Chichester Clark. After you read, invite your child to compare the land in your community with the land mentioned in the book.

_____

_____

_____

_____

Thank you for supporting our social studies program.

Sincerely,

HARCOURT BRACE

Social Studies

Queridos familiares,

Nuestra clase está comenzando una nueva unidad de estudios sociales, titulada "Donde vivimos". Vamos a aprender cómo la tierra a nuestro alrededor afecta nuestras vidas y cómo usamos los recursos naturales que la tierra produce. Usted puede ayudar a que su hijo(a) se prepare para esta unidad mediante las siguientes actividades. Mientras conversan, tomen notas para que su hijo(a) las comparta con la clase.

Actividad familiar

Hable con su hijo(a) sobre la geografía de su zona. ¿Cerca de qué tipos de terreno y cuerpos de agua viven ustedes? ¿Qué tipo de clima tienen en su comunidad? Vaya de paseo con su hijo(a), ya sea caminando o en coche, y observen cómo las personas usan y modifican la tierra.

_____
_____
_____
_____

Ahorre agua durante un mes. Traten de tomar medidas simples para ahorrar agua, tales como cerrar la llave de agua mientras se lavan los dientes, usar un reloj para ducharse más rápido y colocar un ladrillo en el tanque del inodoro. También, cuando esperen a que se caliente el agua de la llave, pongan un recipiente bajo la llave y usen el agua fría que ahorraron para regar las plantas, lavar coches o para darles de beber a sus mascotas.

Lectura familiar

Escoja un libro que trate sobre la tierra. Pueden leer *String-bean's Trip to the Shinning Sea* de Vera B. Williams o *Across the Blue Mountains* de Emma Chichester Clark. Después de la lectura, anime a su hijo(a) a comparar el terreno de su comunidad con el que se mencionó en el libro.

_____
_____
_____
_____

Gracias por apoyar nuestro programa de estudios sociales.

Sinceramente,

Dear Family Members,

Our class is beginning a new social studies unit, called "We All Work Together." We will be learning about goods and services and the people who produce them. We will find out how the people of a community depend on each other to provide goods and services, and how people make wise choices. You can help your child get ready for this unit by doing the following activities. As you talk together, make notes that your child can share with our class.

Family Activity

Hold a "product" hunt in your house to find out where different products are manufactured. Have your child check food labels to find out where different foods are produced. Then have him or her check clothing tags to see where clothing is manufactured. Have your child make lists of the places.

_____

_____

_____

_____

Help your child start saving money. The savings can be kept in a "piggy bank" or an actual bank savings account. Suggest that your child choose something he or she wants to buy as a goal for saving.

Family Reading

Choose a book to share about jobs or workers in our country. You might read *Uncle Jed's Barbershop* by Margaree King Mitchell or *Oranges* by Zack Rogow. After you read, invite your child to talk about how some of the things in your home are produced or manufactured.

_____

_____

_____

_____

Thank you for supporting our social studies program.

Sincerely,

Queridos familiares,

Nuestra clase está comenzando una nueva unidad de estudios sociales titulada "Todos trabajamos juntos". Vamos a aprender sobre los bienes y servicios y sobre las personas que los producen. Averiguaremos cómo las personas en una comunidad dependen entre sí para proporcionar bienes y servicios, y cómo las personas toman buenas decisiones. Usted puede ayudar a su hijo(a) a prepararse para esta unidad mediante las siguientes actividades. Mientras conversan, tomen notas para que su hijo(a) las comparta con la clase.

Actividad familiar

Busque productos en su casa para averiguar dónde se fabrican. Pida a su hijo(a) que mire las etiquetas de los paquetes o latas de comida para averiguar dónde se producen. Luego, pídale que mire etiquetas de ropa para ver dónde se fabrican. Pida a su hijo(a) que haga una lista de estos lugares.

_____

_____

_____

_____

Ayude a su hijo(a) a ahorrar dinero. Los ahorros se pueden guardar en una alcancía o en una cuenta de banco. Como incentivo para ahorrar sugiera que piense en algo que le gustaría comprar.

Lectura familiar

Escoja un libro que trate sobre trabajos o trabajadores en su país. Pueden leer *Uncle Jed's Barbershop* de Margaree King Mitchell o *Oranges* de Zack Rogow. Después de la lectura, anime a su hijo(a) a hablar sobre cómo se fabrican o se producen las cosas en su casa.

_____

_____

_____

_____

Gracias por apoyar nuestro programa de estudios sociales.

Sinceramente,

Harcourt Brace School Publishers

Social Studies

Dear Family Members,

Our class is beginning a new social studies unit, called "People Make History." We will be learning about the change and growth brought about by technology, the environment, and people. You can help your child get ready for this unit by doing the following activities. As you talk together, make notes that your child can share with our class.

Family Activity

Share the history of your community with your child. Point out historic sites and landmarks, and visit a local museum.

_____

_____

_____

_____

Tell your child about someone you admire from history. Share why you think this person was important to history. Then have your child draw a picture of that person, showing something he or she did.

Family Reading

Choose a book to share about the changes people experience over time. You might read *Heron Street* by Ann Turner or *A Weed is a Flower, The Life of George Washington Carver* by Aliki. After you read, invite your child to talk about how the people in the books reacted to the changes in their lives.

_____

_____

_____

_____

Thank you for supporting our social studies program.

Sincerely,

Harcourt Brace School Publishers

Queridos familiares,

Nuestra clase está comenzando una nueva unidad de estudios sociales titulada "La gente hace la historia". Vamos a aprender acerca de los cambios y el crecimiento causados por la tecnología, el medio ambiente y las personas. Usted puede ayudar a su hijo(a) a prepararse para esta unidad mediante las siguientes actividades. Mientras conversan, tomen notas para que su hijo(a) las comparta con la clase.

Actividad familiar

Comparta la historia de su comunidad con su hijo(a). Señale cuáles son algunos monumentos históricos y visiten un museo local.

_____

_____

_____

_____

Hable con su hijo(a) sobre un personaje de la historia que usted admira. Diga por qué cree que esa persona fue importante para la historia. Luego, pida a su hijo(a) que haga un dibujo de esa persona, en el que muestre algo de lo que hizo.

Lectura familiar

Escoja un libro sobre los cambios que la gente ha sufrido a través del tiempo. Pueden leer *Heron Street* de Ann Turner o *A Weed is a Flower, The Life of George Washington Carver* de Aliki. Después de la lectura, anime a su hijo(a) a hablar sobre cómo las personas reaccionaron a los cambios en sus vidas.

_____

_____

_____

_____

Gracias por apoyar nuestro programa de estudios sociales.

Sinceramente,

Dear Family Members,

Our class is beginning a new social studies unit, called "Being a Good Citizen." We will be learning how good citizens honor their country. We will find out about the branches of our country's government and the different kinds of local government. You can help your child get ready for this unit by doing the following activities. As you talk together, make notes that your child can share with our class.

Family Activity

Talk about voting. Then make a family decision, such as what to have for dinner or what to do this weekend, by voting.

_____

_____

_____

_____

Have your child draw a picture showing something that represents our country or a way to honor our country. He or she may think of drawing the flag, a bald eagle, or someone singing the National Anthem.

Family Reading

Choose a book to share about being a good citizen. You might read *The View* by Harry Yoaker or *Old Henry* by Joan W. Blos. After you read, invite your child to talk about how people can be good citizens.

_____

_____

_____

_____

Thank you for supporting our social studies program.

Sincerely,

HARCOURT BRACE

Social Studies

Queridos familiares,

Nuestra clase está comenzando una nueva unidad de estudios sociales, titulada "Cómo ser buenos ciudadanos". Vamos a aprender cómo los buenos ciudadanos honran a su país. Averiguaremos sobre las diferentes ramas en el gobierno de nuestro país y los diferentes tipos de gobiernos locales. Usted puede ayudar a su hijo(a) a prepararse para esta unidad mediante las siguientes actividades. Mientras conversan, tomen notas para que su hijo(a) las comparta con la clase.

Actividad familiar

Hable sobre el voto. Luego, voten para tomar una decisión familiar como por ejemplo, lo que van a cenar o lo que van a hacer este fin de semana.

_____

_____

_____

_____

Pida a su hijo(a) que dibuje algo que represente a nuestro país o una manera de honrar a nuestro país. Puede dibujar la bandera, un águila o alguien cantando el himno nacional.

Lectura familiar

Escoja un libro que trate sobre cómo ser un buen ciudadano. Pueden leer *The View* de Harry Yoaker u *Old Henry* de Joan W. Blos. Después de la lectura, anime a su hijo(a) a hablar sobre cómo las personas pueden ser buenos ciudadanos.

_____

_____

_____

_____

Gracias por apoyar nuestro programa de estudios sociales.

Sinceramente,

HARCOURT BRACE

Social Studies

Dear Family Members,

Our class is beginning a new social studies unit, called "People in Time and Place." We will be learning how our country was settled by people from many different countries. We will find out about how people and their celebrations make our communities interesting and how people in communities and around the world are connected. You can help your child get ready for this unit by doing the following activities. As you talk together, make notes that your child can share with our class.

Family Activity

Talk about celebrations that are unique to your community. Do you have a festival that makes your community special? Make plans to attend such a celebration or festival.

_____

_____

_____

_____

Share your family history with your child. Look at photographs and family heirlooms. Discuss customs, beliefs, and traditions that have been passed down in your family.

Family Reading

Choose a book to share about cultures. You might read _Ganzy Remembers_ by Mary Grace Ketner or _How My Parents Learned to Eat_ by Ina Friedman. After you read, invite your child to talk about the fact that people are people everywhere.

_____

_____

_____

_____

Thank you for supporting our social studies program.

Sincerely,

Harcourt Brace School Publishers

HARCOURT BRACE

Social Studies

Queridos familiares,

Nuestra clase está comenzando una nueva unidad de estudios sociales, titulada "Nuestros vecinos cerca y lejos". Vamos a aprender cómo personas de diferentes nacionalidades poblaron nuestro país. Averiguaremos cómo las personas y sus festejos hacen nuestras comunidades interesantes y cómo las personas en las comunidades y alrededor del mundo están conectadas. Usted puede ayudar a su hijo(a) a prepararse para esta unidad mediante las siguientes actividades. Mientras conversan, tomen notas para que su hijo(a) las comparta con la clase.

Actividad familiar

Hablen sobre los festejos que se celebran únicamente en su comunidad ¿Hay algún festival que hace especial a su comunidad? Haga planes para ir a uno de esos festejos o festivales.

_____

_____

_____

_____

Comparta la historia de su familia con su hijo(a). Miren fotografías y recuerdos familiares. Conversen sobre las diferentes costumbres, creencias y tradiciones que han pasado de generación en generación.

Lectura familiar

Escoja un libro que trate sobre culturas. Pueden leer *Ganzy Remembers* de Mary Grace Ketner o *How My Parents Learned to Eat* de Ina Friedman. Después de la lectura, anime a su hijo(a) a hablar sobre el hecho de que las personas son personas en toda partes.

_____

_____

_____

_____

Gracias por apoyar nuestro programa de estudios sociales.

Sinceramente,

Harcourt Brace School Publishers

Write-On Charts

The Write-On Charts provide an opportunity to extend and enrich lessons in the Pupil's Edition. The following Write-On Chart lessons provide instructional strategies, activities, and ideas for using the charts.

Contents

TEACHING TIPS
Using the Write-On Charts

The Write-On Charts and their accompanying lessons can be used to introduce children to the Grade 2 Social Studies curriculum, extend and enrich the content in the Grade 2 Pupil Edition, and provide graphic organizers and outline maps for whole-class discussion. Using both the Pupil Edition and the Write-On Charts can help your children gain the skills and confidence necessary for becoming independent learners.

Extending and Enriching Lessons (Charts 1–24)

Use these Write-On Charts and their accompanying lessons to extend and enrich the units in the Grade 2 Pupil Edition. There are four Write-On Charts provided for each unit. The lessons in this Teacher's Edition provide questioning strategies, critical thinking questions, and activity choices.

Chart	Title	Unit/Lesson	TE Page
1	Meeting Needs Now and Long Ago	1/2	20
2	The Laws We Live By	1/3	25
3	Signs of Safety	1/Brainstorm	31
4	Children of the World	1/4	33
5	Home, Sweet Home	2/1	51
6	A World of Water	2/1	53
7	A Great Garden	2/5	75
8	Reduce, Reuse, Recycle	2/6	88
9	Special Delivery	3/1	104A
10	Open for Business	3/2	109
11	Markets Around the World	3/3	114
12	On the Job	3/4	118A
13	The First Americans	4/1	142
14	What's New, What's Old	4/2	151
15	Meet Me at the Museum	4/4	162
16	"I Have a Dream"	4/5	172
17	Traits of a Good Citizen	5/1	189
18	The People's Government	5/2	197
19	State Flags	5/Skill	199
20	Let Freedom Ring	5/4	206
21	Be a Pioneer	6/1	224
22	The Americas	6/3	243
23	Celebrations Around the World	6/5	253
24	Learning About Ourselves and Others	6/Skill	256A

Using the Graphic Organizers (Charts 25–32)

These Write-On Charts can be used in a variety of ways. The time line and the graph can be used to provide additional practice during skills lessons and at other times when children apply the skills. The web, Venn diagram, and tables can be used to help children organize concepts in the lessons they have read. Suggestions for when to use the organizers are provided in this Teacher's Edition in the lessons that accompany the Pupil Edition.

Chart	Title
25	Calendar
26	Time Line
27	Web
28	Venn Diagram
29	Two-Column Table
30	Three-Column Table
31	Graph
32	Flow Chart

Using the Maps (Charts 33–38)

The outline maps can be used at any time to show the location of a city, state, country, or continent. Children can also color the maps, to show the features of a place or region, the expansion or movements of people, or the products of a state or country. Suggestions for when to use the maps are provided in this Teacher's Edition in the lessons that accompany the Pupil Edition.

Chart	Title
33	United States Map
34	World Map
35	Western Hemisphere Map
36	Eastern Hemisphere Map
37	North America Map
38	South America Map

1
MEETING NEEDS NOW AND LONG AGO

Meet Individual Needs

ENGLISH LANGUAGE LEARNERS
Provide old pictures and modern pictures of products. Pair children with native-English speakers who can point to the pictures and model saying *today* and *long ago*. Ask the helpers to point to various things on the pictures and have the learner acquiring English identify it as a product of today or of long ago.

Home Involvement

Invite children to talk with their grandparents, other older members of their families, or elderly neighbors about what it was like in their neighborhood or community years ago. Suggest children ask these people what changes they have seen in the way families live, in what they do for fun, and in the things they buy.

Link to Science

TECHNOLOGY Suggest children find pictures of items or list names of items that use electricity. Then ask them to find pictures of items or list items that were used before electricity was available, for example, a candle for light or a washboard for scrubbing clothes.

OBJECTIVES

1. Compare families and neighborhoods today with those from the past.
2. Recognize that more goods and choices are available today.

VOCABULARY

alike
different

RESOURCES

Write-On Chart 1
Clings
Activity Book, p. 53
The Amazing Writing Machine

1. ACCESS

Invite children to brainstorm a list of places to shop. If children have trouble naming places, suggest they think about where their clothes came from, where they bought their school supplies, and where the food they ate for lunch was purchased. Then ask children where they think their grandparents and great-grandparents shopped to meet their needs. Add these to the list and save it for the Build section.

Q. **Do you think it was easier or harder for your grandparents and great-grandparents to purchase things from stores? Why?** Harder; because there were fewer stores, and items were harder to transport.

Focus on the Main Idea

In this lesson children will compare and contrast two commercial areas—one from today and one from long ago. They will point out that goods and choices are different today than they were in the past. Tell children they are going to compare what it was like to live in a neighborhood years ago with what it is like today.

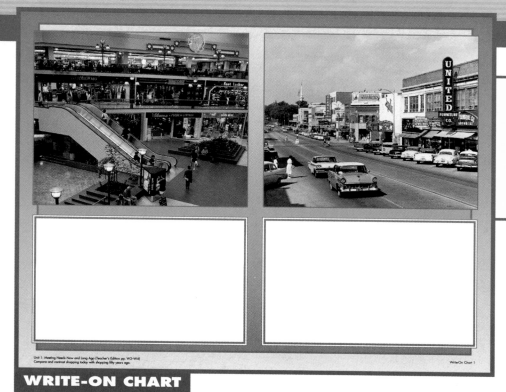

Unit 1: Meeting Needs Now and Long Ago (Teacher's Edition pp. W2–W4)
Compare and contrast shopping today with shopping fifty years ago.

Write-On Chart 1

WRITE-ON CHART

2. BUILD

History

Connections Past to Present to Future   Ask children to describe the scenes on Write-On Chart 1 and to identify which represents today and which represents long ago. Have a volunteer use a dry-erase marker to write the labels *today* and *long ago* on the appropriate pictures or use the clings to do the same. Then have them identify and list the things in each picture that characterize it as being from today or long ago.

Q. **What kinds of things might you have bought if you shopped on this street years ago?** food, clothes, books, tools

   What might you buy in a shopping mall today that you could not have bought years ago? power tools, video games, computers, electrical appliances

Invite children to fill in the columns on the Chart to compare the stores of today with the stores of long ago. Label one column *Alike* and the other column *Different*. Remind children that *alike* means "the same" and *different* means "not the same." Invite children to list ways the old stores and ones of today are alike and ways they are different.

Kinesthetic Learning

Form Compare and Contrast Lines   Invite children to make stickers for the types of stores listed in the Access section. Distribute one sticker to each child, and ask children to place the stickers on their shirts. Invite children to create a human mall. Ask children with stickers of stores that would not be in a modern mall to step out. Then ask the children who stepped out to create an old-time downtown. Invite children to compare and contrast the stores in the modern mall with those in the downtown area of the past.

ACTIVITY CHOICES

Background

In the past people might get what they needed in a general store, a five-and-dime, or from a traveling peddler. Today more choices are available. You can even shop by phone from television.

DEPARTMENT STORES   have many different departments which sell hard goods (furniture and appliances) and soft goods (clothes and sheets). The first U.S. department stores were established in the 1860s.

DISCOUNT STORES   sell a variety of products at discounted prices. These stores came on the scene in 1945 after World War II ended.

CATALOGS   Richard W. Sears began selling watches by mail in 1886. In 1887 he hired Alvah C. Roebuck to repair the watches. Together they formed Sears, Roebuck and Company in 1893. They began selling many types of products by mail-order catalog.

Link to Language Arts

WRITE A DESCRIPTION   Suggest that children describe their neighborhood in the future. What will transportation, communication, housing, recreation, and so on be like?

TECHNOLOGY

Use THE AMAZING WRITING MACHINE™ RESOURCE PACKAGE to complete this activity.

Extend and Enrich

MAKE A PICTURE FILE Have children clip pictures from magazines of items that help meet our needs today. Invite children to place each clipping in an envelope and seal it. Tell them to imagine they can mail the envelope to the future so others can see how our needs were met today. Place the envelope in a shoe box marked "Future" and invite children to share them with other classes.

Reteach the Main Idea

LABEL PICTURES Write either *Long Ago* or *Today* on several self-stick notes. Display books that contain historical and modern-day pictures of things such as homes, travel, communication, clothing, or recreation. Ask children to look at each picture, discuss what it shows, and put the appropriate self-stick note on the picture.

Link to Health

NUTRITION Explain to children that all foods will spoil if they are not preserved. When foods spoil, they are no longer safe to eat. Very long ago people usually preserved foods by drying, salt curing, and fermenting them. By the 1700s people were starting to use methods of preservation, such as canning. In 1851, cold storage was improved with the invention of a machine for making ice. Clarence Birdseye developed the first modern quick-freezing process, which led to advances in freezing foods.

3. CLOSE

Ask children to summarize the lesson by naming things they might find in their neighborhood today that would not have been there long ago.

Check Understanding

The children can
—— compare families and neighborhoods today with those from the past.
—— recognize that more goods and choices are available today.

Think Critically

Q. **If you lived in your neighborhood long ago, what activities could your family have done for fun that you could still enjoy today?** play games, go for a walk, read aloud together, sing songs

Why are more things available today than long ago? More things have been invented.

Show What You Know

Performance Assessment Invite children to imagine and role-play what it might have been like to live years ago on a farm or in a community with one general store compared to what it is like today in a modern community. Children might plan and present skits to show people shopping in each situation.

What to Look For Children's role-plays should reflect an understanding that more goods and choices are available to families today.

Using the Activity Book Distribute copies of Activity Book page 53. Have children look at the pictures in each box. Tell children to compare grocery shopping years ago with grocery shopping today and write about each. Allow children time to talk in small groups about their comparisons.

Activity Book page 53

2

THE LAWS WE LIVE BY

OBJECTIVES

1. Distinguish between rules and laws.
2. Discuss how community laws are made.
3. Recognize that breaking laws has consequences.

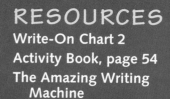

RESOURCES

Write-On Chart 2
Activity Book, page 54
The Amazing Writing Machine

ACTIVITY CHOICES

Community Involvement

Invite a city council member or commissioner to visit the classroom and talk about how laws are made in your community. Prompt children to ask the guest why these laws are necessary.

Link to Health

SAFETY AND FIRST AID Provide a number of household items that list precautions, and discuss laws that require labels such as age specifications on toys, the fire retardancy of fabrics in pajamas, and keep-out-of-reach-of-children warnings on cleaning products. Show children where to find the labels. Ask children to discuss why the precautions are listed and how they help protect people.

1. ACCESS

Ask children to share with the class what they recall from earlier discussions about rules and laws. Review the idea that rules and laws help us live together and interact in ways that are healthy, safe, fair, and polite and that laws are rules for a community that are written down for all to follow.

Q. **Why are laws important to your community?** Without laws, some people might hurt other people and other people's property.

Paraphrase a newspaper article about local lawmakers and an issue of interest to the class, or show children a videotape of a broadcast of a city council meeting or school board meeting. Use one of these to prompt a discussion of laws and the people who make them.

Focus on the Main Idea

In this lesson children will explore the difference between rules and laws and the need for and the existence of laws in a community. They will role-play a city council meeting at which possible laws will be suggested and discussed. Tell children that in this lesson they will have a chance to see how laws are made.

Children describe what they see in the picture and tell what they think people are doing at the meeting. Children decide on laws they think would be good for a community and write them on the chart.

WRITE-ON CHART

Meet Individual Needs

ADVANCED LEARNERS Help children think through a typical day and recognize the ways laws affect them. Make a list of the laws they suggest. For example: *rode school bus* (driver had to have license and follow traffic laws.) Then prepare a bulletin board entitled *Laws in Our Lives*. Create the following heads: *Health, Safety, Order, Respect for People and Property*. Invite each child to illustrate one of the laws and display the art under the correct heading on the bulletin board.

Background

LAWMAKING Every community in the world has laws. In the United States we practice *representative democracy*, in which representatives—chosen by the people—make decisions about the laws of a community, a state, or the nation. Representatives consider public comment on a proposal and debate the merits of the issue. They then make a decision on whether the proposal should become a law.

2. BUILD

Civics and Government

Purposes and Types of Government Point out that rules are made for small groups of people, such as those playing a game or those attending a school. Laws are made for all people in a community. Help children understand that city leaders, like those at the city council meeting in the photo, decide what laws to pass. Point out that people in a community elect city leaders as well as express their opinions about the laws they want.

Q. **How are laws and rules alike?** They state what people can and cannot do.

Rights and Responsibilities Help children understand that laws are made for the good of the people. Point out that some laws are made to protect the health and safety of the people. Other laws are made to maintain order or to protect property. Help children recall laws of their community that fall into these categories.

Remind children that just as there are consequences for breaking the rules at school, there are consequences for breaking the laws in a community. Police officers, judges, and other officials help make sure laws are followed and violators are punished.

Role-Play

Organize children into small groups. Ask each group to role-play a city council and decide whether to make laws on questions such as *Should people riding bicycles wear helmets?* and *Should people be allowed to honk car horns in the city?* Have a representative from each group record its laws on the Write-On Chart and explain why the law is important.

3. CLOSE

Ask children to summarize the lesson by explaining the difference between rules and laws and giving an example of each. Have them tell why the law they give as an example is important in the community and how it was probably made.

Check Understanding

The child can
—— distinguish between rules and laws.
—— discuss how community laws are made.
—— recognize that breaking laws has consequences.

Think Critically

Q. **Why would members of a city council want to know how people in the community think and feel about issues?** Laws affect the people in the community. People should have a say in those laws because people choose city council members to represent them.

Why should everyone in a community follow laws? so people will be safe and so the community will be fair to everyone

Show What You Know

Performance Assessment Ask children to choose a proposed law to defend: *The city park should close at sundown* or *Walkers should only cross the road at crosswalks*. Ask them to write a letter to the council explaining why they think the proposal should be a law.

What to Look For Children's letters should show that they understand the difference between simple rules and laws and that they understand that laws are meant for the protection of all the people in the community.

Using the Activity Book Distribute copies of Activity Book page 54. Invite children to examine the picture and circle the people who are engaged in appropriate behaviors. Then ask children to write laws to match the good behaviors.

Name _____ Date _____

☆ Making Laws ☆

Circle each person who is following a safety law.
Write laws to match the pictures you circled.

Laws
Bike riders must wear helmets.
Do not litter.
Use a leash to walk dogs.
Do not burn leaves.

54 Activity Book   Use with Write-On Chart 2.

Activity Book page 54

Extend and Enrich

ANALYZE A LAW Remind children that laws carry consequences if they are broken; a person who is caught driving over the speed limit may have to pay a fine or be put in jail. Point out that although the penalties for breaking most laws are fines or jail sentences, some communities design punishments to fit the crimes. For example, someone responsible for damaging property may have to repair what was damaged. Ask children to think of a law in their community and a suitable punishment for breaking it.

Reteach the Main Idea

SIMULATE LAWMAKING Present children with a situation that involves a problem in a community. For example: "The intersection of Third Street and Green Road was not a busy one until many new houses were built on Third Street. Now many families live there. Children walk to and from school. They ride their bicycles. There is much more traffic. Many cars speed along Green Road and through the intersection." Invite children to identify the problem, recommend a law to fix it, and explain why people should follow the law.

Link to Language Arts

JOURNAL Invite children to write their concerns about crime. Explain that such groups as police departments, community crime stoppers, and neighborhood watch groups work to combat crime.

TECHNOLOGY

Use THE AMAZING WRITING MACHINE™ to complete this activity.

3

SIGNS OF SAFETY

ACTIVITY CHOICES

Link to Language Arts

JOURNAL Invite children to record in their journals all the signs and symbols they see in a given day. To get them started, you might take them on a walk around the school and point out some signs.

Meet Individual Needs

AUDITORY LEARNERS Point out that many symbols, such as flags and stop signs, are visual. Others involve sounds. Make a tape of some common auditory symbols, like a police, fire, or ambulance siren; the bells of an ice-cream truck; and the busy signal on the telephone. Discuss how some sounds, such as elevator bells and street-crossing signals, help people who are visually challenged. Invite children to listen to the tape, identify the symbols, and tell what they stand for.

Background

SYMBOLS Symbols play an important role in international communication. For example, every branch of science has a system of symbols. In math, Greek letters and other symbols form an abbreviated language. And since the 1930s many countries have been working to create a traffic-sign system that can be understood worldwide.

OBJECTIVES

1. Recognize common safety symbols.
2. Compare and contrast the meaning of safety and information symbols.
3. Understand the usefulness of rules and order.

VOCABULARY
safety

RESOURCES
Write-On Charts 3, 29
Clings
Activity Book, p. 55

1. ACCESS

Describe the meaning of *symbol* as a picture that stands for something else. Display the following objects or pictures of objects: an American flag, a stop sign, a no-smoking sign. Ask children to identify each symbol and tell what it stands for.

Q. **Why do some signs use symbols instead of words?** Possible responses: It is easier to understand a picture; some people cannot read English.

Focus on the Main Idea

In this lesson children will learn about signs and symbols as communication tools. They will recognize common safety symbols within a city scene, understand how the symbols relate to rules and order, and compare the meanings of different safety and information symbols. Tell children they will learn about signs and symbols that will help keep them safe.

Unit 1: Signs of Safety (Teacher's Edition pp. W8–W10)
Find examples of signs and symbols for information and safety.

Write-On Chart 3

WRITE-ON CHART

Children identify all the signs and symbols on the chart and tell how they help people in a community.

Geo Georgie Clings (optional)

2. BUILD

Critical Thinking

Ask children to review signs and symbols they see in their community, such as school-crossing signs, stop signs, and signs for bicycle lanes. Discuss what each symbol means and how the sign or symbol helps to convey laws or information. Have children tell which signs help maintain order and safety in the community and which give information.

Vocabulary

Define *safety* as freedom from harm or danger. Invite children to discuss situations or places in which safety is a concern, such as riding a bicycle, swimming or other sports, construction sites or electrical repair work, and dealing with unfamiliar foods and medicine.

Visual Analysis

Interpret Pictures Encourage children to describe what they see on Write-On Chart 3. Invite volunteers to circle or place Geo Georgie Clings on specific signs and symbols and tell what they mean. Have them tell how the information and warnings help people.

Q. **How do signs help keep order and safety in a community?**
They remind people of laws that protect them.

Invite volunteers to name other signs with which they are familiar. Have children create a two-column chart headed *Safety Signs* and *Information Signs*. Ask them to draw in the correct column the signs they have learned about.

ACTIVITY CHOICES

Role-Play

Discuss emergencies and the use of 911 as a way of getting help. Provide pairs of children with play telephones, and let them take turns role-playing 911 calls. One child can be the person calling 911, and the other can be the dispatcher. Remind callers to speak slowly and clearly, to give their names and addresses, and to state the problems.

Link to Art

ILLUSTRATION Ask children to create signs using symbols rather than words. Tell them that their signs can be about safety or health laws or can give information but that they should be different from the ones talked about in the discussion. Suggest children share their signs with one another.

Extend and Enrich

MAKE SIGNS Ask children to work in groups to create signs. The signs can show symbols without words for classroom or school rules, or they can provide information for new students. Allow children to select the signs they feel are best for conveying the information and to post them in appropriate places throughout the school and classroom.

Reteach the Main Idea

MAKE A SAFETY CHART Invite children to look through magazines and newspapers to find pictures of safety and informational symbols. Have them cut out and paste the pictures onto a sheet of paper and label them *Safety* or *Information*. Ask children to identify each symbol and tell how it helps them be safe or gives them information they need to know.

Multicultural Link

Extend your discussion to symbols as a means of communicating to people who speak other languages. You might share books like *Symbol Art: Thirteen Squares, Circles*, and *Triangles from Around the World* by Leonard Everett Fisher, which explains symbols used around the world, or *Handtalk: An ABC of Finger Spelling and Sign Language* by Remy Charlip and Mary Beth Miller, which introduces finger spelling and sign language.

3. CLOSE

Ask children to summarize the lesson by describing safety and information symbols and by telling how those symbols help maintain law and order in a community.

Check Understanding

The child can
 recognize common safety symbols.
 compare and contrast the meaning of safety and information symbols.
 understand the usefulness of rules and order.

Think Critically

Q. **What does it mean when a symbol has a line drawn through it?** You should not do what the symbol shows.

What are some signs you have seen with lines drawn through them? No Smoking, No Passing, No Pets.

What happens when someone steals a safety or information sign or destroys it by painting over it? People who need the information that the sign gives will not have it. They could get hurt or lost. It costs the community money to replace the sign.

Show What You Know

Performance Assessment Have children create Safety First posters promoting some aspect of safety discussed in the lesson.

What to Look For Evaluate children's posters for evidence that they understand the importance of signs in keeping order and keeping people safe.

Using the Activity Book Distribute copies of Activity Book page 55. Have children identify the symbols on the page and write which ones remind people of safety laws and which ones give information. Suggest children take the completed page with them when walking or riding around their community so they can check off the symbols they see.

Activity Book page 55

4

CHILDREN OF THE WORLD

OBJECTIVES

1. Describe and compare communities around the world.
2. Compare family responsibilities in various cultures.

RESOURCES

Write-On Chart 4
Clings
Activity Book, p. 56
Music Audio, "One Light, One Sun"

ACTIVITY CHOICES

Home Involvement

Ask children to share any collections they have that relate to people in other countries, such as coin collections, stamp collections, or collections of dolls dressed in clothing from different countries. Tell children it is important that they get permission from their families before bringing in a valuable collection.

1. ACCESS

Introduce the lesson by asking whether children have ever lived in or traveled to another country. Invite them to share their experiences or to share what books, television, and movies have taught them about living in another country. Have children identify the country they are talking about and find it on a map. Encourage them to tell how life in that country was different from and similar to life here.

Q. **What do you think people mean when they say "It's a small world"?** People all over the world have many things in common. We can travel to other countries and can communicate with people in other countries easily.

Focus on the Main Idea

In this lesson children will explore ways people around the world are alike and ways they are different. Tell children that in this lesson they will see pictures of children from different countries. The pictures provide clues to children's lives and family responsibilities. The children in your class will compare their own lives with those of the children in the photos.

Link to Reading

READ ALOUD To introduce the lesson, you may wish to share a story that deals with the theme of diversity and commonality, such as *The Chalk Doll* by Charlotte Pomerantz or read aloud "Like Me" by Lois Lenski.

All around the world
there are children like me.
In many strange places
they happen to be.
They eat and they sleep,
they run and they play;
They work and are helpful
day by day.
Their dress and their food
may seem very queer,
Their homes too are different
From those I know here.
But all round the world
they are still just like me,
In living and giving,
good friends are we.

Unit 1: Children of the World (Teacher's Edition pp. W11–W13)
Compare and contrast the lives of children in four different countries.

Write-On Chart 4

Children compare the children in the pictures with the children in this country.

Dot Clings (optional)

ACTIVITY CHOICES

Background

KENYA is a tropical country where most people live in rural farm settlements. In the growing cities people live in small stone and cement homes. Some Kenyans decorate their household utensils and make colorful beaded jewelry. Many tourists visit Kenya's wildlife parks.

GREECE is surrounded by water so fish is a common food (note hanging squid). Sponges are also a product of the sea. Religious icons are often displayed in homes. Many Greeks enjoy folk dancing.

CHINA has more people than any other country. Many live in crowded cities. Rice and vegetables are common foods eaten with chopsticks. Boats provide transportation along China's rivers and coast. The artistic style of writing is called calligraphy. The pipa is an instrument that has been played in China for nearly two thousand years.

MEXICO was settled by the Spanish whose influence is reflected in its arts and architecture. Mexican food is often spiced with peppers. The ornately decorated hats are called sombreros. The skull in the picture was made for the Day of the Dead, a festive holiday at the end of October when ancestors are honored.

AUDIO

Use the **UNIT 1 MUSIC AUDIOCASSETTE** to hear the song "One Light, One Sun."

2. BUILD

Culture

Shared Humanity and Unique Identity   Ask children to look at the pictures on Write-On Chart 4. Explain that those children are about their same age but that each comes from a different country. Point to each child and tell whether that child comes from Kenya, Greece, Mexico, or China. Or, give clues about the four countries, and ask children to guess which country belongs with each group of pictures. Tell children that the items pictured show something about the ways the children live.

Invite volunteers to use dry-erase markers to circle ways that they are like those children and ways they are different. You may wish to use the red and blue Dot Clings as labels. Help children identify elements of culture to compare, such as music, food, dance, transportation, art and architecture, and religion.

Q. **Imagine you could meet one of these children. What would you do together?** Some might say they would like to play sports or listen to music—something they have in common with one of the children. Others might say they want to learn more about a child—play a game or sport they have never played.

Kinesthetic Learning

Role-Play   Invite children to take turns role-playing one of the pictured children. Have them introduce themselves to classmates and tell a little about themselves.

3. CLOSE

Invite children to think of a question they would like answered by one of the children on Write-On Chart 4. Provide reference materials on the four countries featured, and have children work with partners to research the answer to their questions. Then ask partners to present their questions and findings to the class.

Check Understanding

The child can
—— describe and compare communities around the world.
—— compare family responsibilities in various cultures.

Think Critically

Q. **Imagine that you are being featured on the Write-On Chart. What items would you include in your photos to show others about your life in America?** Children should recognize that items such as food, clothing, homes, and hobbies are evidence of a way of life.

Why do people who live in other countries sometimes dress differently from you? Climate and the availability of materials may be factors. Traditional dress is frequently worn for celebrations because the people are proud of their heritage.

Show What You Know

Performance Assessment Have children create pages for a book about the children on the Write-On Chart or others of their choice. Tell them to write sentences such as *I am like José because . . .* or *I am different from José because . . .* Have children create a page for each child on the Write-On Chart. Compile children's pages into one class book called *We Are All Alike; We Are All Different.*

What to Look For Children should show similarities based on things all people have in common and differences based on culture or geography.

Using the Activity Book Distribute copies of Activity Book page 56. Invite children to meet Nu Dang, a boy from Bangkok, Thailand. Help children find Thailand on a world map or a globe. Then have them look at the pictures to find out about Nu Dang's way of life. Ask them to write a story to tell what they have found out about Nu Dang.

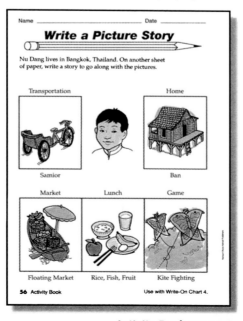

Activity Book page 56

ACTIVITY CHOICES

Extend and Enrich

RESEARCH A FOREIGN COMMUNITY Organize the class into cooperative groups. Help each group select one community in another country to research. After they have selected a leader and recorder, the rest of the group should search for information about how people live their daily lives, what their homes look like, and what they do for recreation. Have children draw pictures and write sentences to tell about life in the foreign community they choose. Display children's work on a bulletin board titled *Communities Around the World*.

Reteach the Main Idea

MAKE A CULTURAL GRAB BAG Fill a brown paper bag with pictures and artifacts that illustrate a variety of cultural backgrounds. You might include, for example, a foreign language newspaper or magazine, a pair of chopsticks, and a food wrapper or empty container. Ask children to take turns reaching into the bag and selecting something. After they identify the item, have them tell how it is similar to and different from something they use.

Link Literature

Share the book *All in a Day* by Mitsumasa Anno et al. (Philomel, 1988) The book highlights differences and similarities in the lives of eight children in cities around the world. Encourage children to compare and contrast their own lives with the lives of the children in the book.

5

HOME, SWEET HOME

ACTIVITY CHOICES

Meet Individual Needs

KINESTHETIC LEARNERS Take children on a walk around the neighborhood or on a bus tour of the community to observe the different kinds of homes and the landscapes that surround them. Invite them to record their observations of the homes and landscapes they see by drawing pictures and making notes.

Link to Language Arts

JOURNAL Ask children to draw a picture of any kind of house at the top of a journal page. Then ask them to write a story called "Home, Sweet Home" about an imaginary family who lives in the house. Children should include details about what the house looks like, where it is, and how the house meets the needs of the family. Invite children to share their stories with the class.

TECHNOLOGY

Use IMAGINATION EXPRESS:™ DESTINATION NEIGHBORHOOD to complete this activity.

OBJECTIVES

1. Identify and describe various kinds of homes.
2. Explain how environment is a factor in choosing or constructing a shelter.

VOCABULARY
weather

RESOURCES
Write-On Chart 5
Clings
Activity Book, p. 57
Vocabulary Blacklines
Transparencies 23, 24
Imagination Express: Destination Neighborhood
The Amazing Writing Machine

1. ACCESS

Write *Home, Sweet Home* on the board and ask children if they have ever heard the phrase before. Call on volunteers to explain what it means. Then read aloud the following poem:

Home, Sweet Home
Home, sweet home,
I really like my home.
I go to school each day,
But home is where I play.
What fun to be back home!

Q. **In what ways are all our homes alike?** They protect us against bad weather and dangers and provide us with a place to eat, sleep, and be with our families.

Focus on the Main Idea

In this lesson children will explore various kinds of homes. They will discover how environment, including landforms and weather conditions, account for differences among them. Tell children that this lesson will give them a look at how people live in the United States and around the world.

Children use dry-erase markers to describe homes in photo captions.

Land and Water/Weather Clings (optional)

2. BUILD

Visual Analysis

Learn from Pictures Ask children to describe what they see on the chart. Explain that the photos on the chart show some of the different kinds of homes found around the world. Call on volunteers to write a caption under each home and tell something about the setting in the photo.

Q. **Why do you think there are so many different kinds of homes?** People like and need different things; the land, weather, and resources are different in different places.

Vocabulary

Explain that homes protect people from weather and danger. Help children understand that *weather* means the condition of the air outdoors at any time and place.

> ### VOCABULARY BLACKLINES
>
> Invite children to use the word card *weather* as they name different kinds of weather and different kinds of homes.

Critical Thinking

Direct children's attention to the house on stilts. Emphasize that the types of homes people build depend mainly on the weather, the land, and the building materials that are available. You may wish to have children place the appropriate Land and Water/Weather Clings on each shelter.

Q. **What does the house on stilts tell you about the land and the weather?** It probably rains a lot, causing the body of water to overflow often.

ACTIVITY CHOICES

Multicultural Link

Explain that years ago American Indians of the plains migrated from place to place following buffalo. Each time they moved, they carried their tepees and belongings with them. Cut a piece of string sixty feet long, and arrange it in a circle on the floor. Explain that this was about how much space the Plains Indians had in their tepees. Have children list things they think they would need for different seasons of the year. Ask children if all their belongings could fit in that space. Discuss how an Indian family could live in such a small space.

TRANSPARENCY

Use TRANSPARENCIES 23 and 24 to locate each shelter.

Meet Individual Needs

ADVANCED LEARNERS Challenge children to find out about other kinds of shelters. Ask them to describe each shelter and draw a picture. Children should also do research to find out where each type of shelter is found and what it is made of. Possible choices for investigation include adobes, igloos, houseboats, beach huts, and mobile homes.

Link to Language Arts

WRITE TO COMPARE AND CONTRAST Ask children to compare and contrast two kinds of homes on the chart, such as a farmhouse and a condominium. Have children use a Venn diagram to record how the shelters are different and how they are alike. Remind them to include details about the environment as well.

TECHNOLOGY

Use THE AMAZING WRITING MACHINE™ RESOURCE PACKAGE to complete this activity.

Building Background: Homes

From the mud and thatch dwellings of many African countries to the condominiums of New York City, homes vary around the world. Some of the variation is caused by differing geography and available natural resources.

1. **Mauritanian Sahara: Nomad Encampment** Tents are common residences for nomadic people. Nomads are people who travel from place to place in order to make a living. The portability of tents works well with their lifestyles. Tent-dwelling nomads are found all over the world but primarily in Africa, the Arabian Peninsula, Australia, India, and Southeast Asia.

2. **Alaska: Log Cabin** Log cabins were a popular form of shelter among early settlers in the United States forest regions. Settlers built log cabins because the logs for building them were easy to obtain from the surrounding forests. The simplest cabins were built with round logs with notches cut near the ends. Spaces between the logs were filled with stones or thin boards and sealed with mud. Different varieties of log cabins were introduced in this country as settlers from different European countries arrived.

3. **Cooks Bay, Mooréa near Tahiti: Stilt House** Stilt houses are common in the Pacific Islands, Indonesia, and the Philippines and other areas with much swampland. The houses are elevated to provide protection from moisture on the land and flooding.

4. **Roosevelt Island, New York: Manhattan Park Condominiums** Condominiums are multifamily dwellings similar to apartments, except that each housing unit is owned rather than rented. The owners own in common all the halls, stairways, grounds, and recreational facilities used by the condo dwellers.

5. **Topsham, Vermont: Farmhouse** Farmhouses are built in rural areas and may have various shapes, forms, and materials.

6. **Urumchi Grasslands in Northwestern China: Sod House** Sod houses are built with walls of sod, or turf. Sod houses are found mainly on open plains, where there are few trees to supply lumber for building.

7. **Amsterdam, Holland: Prinzen Gracht Canal House** Houses built along canals are often row houses, which are lines of identical houses joined together at the sides by common walls. They are found in Venice, Amsterdam, San Antonio, and other places where there are canals.

3. CLOSE

Ask children to summarize the lesson by identifying what can be learned about people by looking at where their homes are built and the materials they use to build them. Responses should indicate a knowledge of environment, weather, ways of life, and personal taste.

Check Understanding

The child can
—— identify and describe various kinds of homes.
—— explain how environment is a factor in choosing or constructing a shelter.

Think Critically

Q. **Why might someone choose to live in a mobile home? Who might choose to live in an apartment?** A person who moves around a lot or lives in an area where other homes are not available might choose a mobile home. A person who lives in a city might choose an apartment.

How might the number of people living in an area affect the kind of homes that are available? If there are a lot of people and very little land, there will probably be more apartments and condominiums than houses.

Show What You Know

Performance Assessment Provide drawing paper and pencils, crayons, or markers. Invite children to be architects and design a house that fits its surroundings. Ask them to describe how it will be suitable for the people who will live there.

What to Look For Children should be able to identify different kinds of shelters and demonstrate how environmental factors, such as climate and the land, help determine the kinds of shelters people build.

Using the Activity Book Distribute a copy of Activity Book page 57 to each child. Tell children to draw a line from each home to the environment in which it belongs. Afterward, ask children to explain their decisions. Discuss which houses might be suitable for more than one environment.

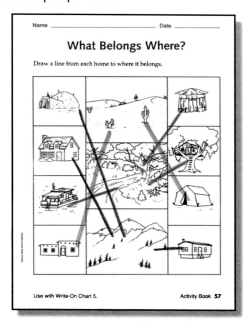

Activity Book page 57

Extend and Enrich

BUILD A HOME Provide cardboard boxes and lids, straw, craft sticks, poster paper, and art supplies. Challenge children to make a variety of homes. When children finish their construction, have them display together structures that belong in similar environments.

Reteach the Main Idea

PLAY A GAME Invite groups of children to play "Where Do I Live?" Children take turns giving clues about a kind of house for others to guess. For example, "I live in a place that is tall with many windows. Lots of other people live there, too. You would find this place in a city. Where do I live?" Children may wish to refer to the Write-On Chart for ideas.

6
A WORLD OF WATER

ACTIVITY CHOICES

Meet Individual Needs

KINESTHETIC AND VISUAL LEARNERS Take children on a walk through the school building to look for ways water is used. If possible, walk through the cafeteria, building maintenance office, nurse's office, and the faculty and art rooms. Then invite children to make a mural titled *Water, Water, Everywhere* showing pictures of ways water is used.

Link to Language Arts

JOURNAL Have children interview people who work in the school or neighborhood to find out how they depend on water to do their jobs. Have children write their questions and responses in their journals and draw pictures of the people at work.

Link to World Languages

OTHER LANGUAGES Teach children the word for water in the following languages:

Spanish	*agua*	(AH•gwah)
German	*wasser*	(VAH•ser)
French	*eau*	(OH)
Japanese	*mizu*	(MEE•ZOO)
Russian	*voda*	(vah•DAH)

Invite children who know other languages to share the word for water.

OBJECTIVES

1. Describe how people depend on water.
2. Identify ways people can conserve water.

RESOURCES

Write-On Chart 6
Clings
Activity Book, p. 58
Music Audio, "I Saw Three Ships Come Sailing By"

1. ACCESS

Invite children to tell what they do before they come to school in the morning. As children respond, make two lists on the board. In one column, write activities which require the use of water. Write items which do not require water in the second column. Have children review the two lists.

Q. **What do you need in order to do all the things in the first column?** water

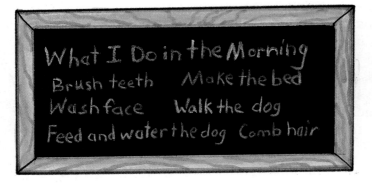

Focus on the Main Idea

In this lesson children will explore ways in which all living things use water. They will learn ways to conserve water. Tell children that in this lesson they will learn how important water is in their everyday lives.

Unit 2: A World of Water (Teacher's Edition pp. W18–W20)
Identify the many uses for water.

Write-On Chart 6

WRITE-ON CHART

2. BUILD

Visual Analysis

Interpret Pictures Ask children to describe the scene on Write-On Chart 6. Help them identify it as an urban setting.

Q. **What clues help you know this is a city?** Responses might include apartment building, city street.

Write the word *water* in the center of a word web and explain that water can be used in many ways. Write the categories *homes*, *to grow food*, *play*, and *transportation* on spokes extending from the center.

Critical Thinking

Direct children's attention to the city scene. Have volunteers use dry-erase markers or Clings to circle ways people are using water. As children identify ways, write their responses under appropriate categories on the word web.

Q. **What are some other ways people use water?** Responses might include to water crops and animals, to put out fires, to wash clothes.

Discuss why everyone should learn ways to save and protect water. Create a chart to list ways people save water and ways people waste water.

Q. **What can you do to protect and care for water?** Don't waste water; keep it clean.

ACTIVITY CHOICES

Home Involvement

Ask children to place a pan under a running faucet when they wash their hands. Then have them pour the water into a measuring cup. Have them record in their journals the amount of water used. They should then repeat the activity, turning off the water while they use soap. Invite children to share their journal entries telling how much water they saved.

Meet Individual Needs

ADVANCED LEARNERS Provide a rainfall map of the United States and explain that rain does not fall in the same amounts all over the Earth. Invite children to study the map to discover areas in which rain is plentiful and areas in which it is not. Ask children to draw pictures to show an area with a lot of rain and an area that gets little rain.

Meet Individual Needs

KINESTHETIC AND AUDITORY LEARNERS Invite children to listen to "I Saw Three Ships Come Sailing By" on the Unit 2 Music Audio. Suggest that they learn the words and sing along. Then ask them to think of other songs or rhymes about water ("Rain, Rain, Go Away," "It's Raining, It's Pouring"), or have them make up their own. Suggest that children add sound effects to their songs and perform them for the class. Invite children to write and illustrate their songs for a class songbook.

Extend and Enrich

MAKE A LIST Suggest that children think about areas of the country where water is not plentiful or about times when little rainfall leads to shortages of water. Challenge them to make a list of the ways they can limit the use of water every day in a "Save Water" campaign.

Reteach the Main Idea

KEEP A LIST Ask children to keep a list of all the ways they use water or come in contact with water in one day. Review their lists with them to make sure they recognize how essential water is in their daily lives.

AUDIO

Use the **UNIT 2 MUSIC AUDIOCASSETTE** to hear the song "I Saw Three Ships Come Sailing By."

3. CLOSE

Ask children to summarize the lesson by recalling ways water is used to satisfy people's needs.

Check Understanding

The child can
— describe how people depend on water.
— identify ways people can conserve water.

Think Critically

Q. **In what ways would water be important to the following people?**
- **a farmer**   • **an athlete**
- **a fisher**   • **a city water-worker**

Children's responses should mention the use of water for crops, health, recreation, and business and employment.

Show What You Know

 Performance Assessment Have children create posters that illustrate why we should protect our precious water supplies. Invite the children to write slogans for their posters. Arrange a school-wide display of the posters.

What to Look For Children should show important ways in which people depend on water.

Using the Activity Book Distribute a copy of Activity Book page 58 to each child, and invite children to write about or draw ways they use water at home, at school, and at play.

Activity Book page 58

7
A GREAT GARDEN

OBJECTIVES

1. Classify information about resources found in the United States.
2. Recognize the relationship between geographical land features and the resources found there.

RESOURCES

Write-On Charts 7, 27
Activity Book, p. 59
Transparency 14
Desk Maps
The Amazing Writing Machine

ACTIVITY CHOICES

Meet Individual Needs

VISUAL LEARNERS Provide magazines and craft paper. Invite children to make their own word webs by writing the word *resources* in the center of a circle on a sheet of paper. Have them cut out pictures of resources from the Earth and glue them around the word *resources*.

AUDITORY LEARNERS Invite children to play Name a Resource. Explain that they will take turns naming natural resources for each letter of the alphabet, except the letter *x*. Invite the first child to name a resource that begins with the letter *a*, such as apples. The next child then names a resource that begins with *b*, and so on through the alphabet.

1. ACCESS

Begin a word web with the word *resources* as the center word. Ask children to name the resources they read about in *How to Make an Apple Pie and see the world*. Then ask them to name other resources they have learned about and add them to the web.

Q. **What resources do we have in our community?** Children should suggest local resources. Add these resources to your word web if they are not already written there.

Focus on the Main idea

In this lesson children will identify and classify a variety of resources found in the United States. They will discuss the relationship between resources and where they are found. Tell children that in this lesson they will use a map to learn more about the country's resources.

WRITE-ON CHARTS

Use WRITE-ON CHART 27 to create a resources word web.

Unit 2: A Great Garden (Teacher's Edition pp. W21-W24)
Name resources and locate them on the United States map.

Write-On Chart 7

WRITE-ON CHART

Have children label each state. Then use a dry-erase marker to draw a line from each resource to a state where it can be found.

![ACTIVITY CHOICES banner]

Background

USING PAGE 111 Provide clues about the resources from Building Background on page 111. Have children identify on Write-On Chart 7 photos of each resource as it is mentioned.

Meet Individual Needs

TACTILE LEARNERS Ask children to look over the resources listed earlier on the word web and classify them in categories, such as livestock, fruits, vegetables, grains, lumber. Then invite children to create a large mural of a map of the United States. Help them draw an outline of the map and create symbols for each resource on Write-On Chart 7. Then invite them to draw the resources directly on the mural or construct them out of heavy paper and paste them to the mural where the resource can be found. Display the completed resource mural on the classroom wall.

DESK MAPS

Use the DESK MAPS of the United States as an alternative to the mural in the resource map activity.

TRANSPARENCY

Use TRANSPARENCY 14 to help children label the chart with state names.

2. BUILD

Visual Analysis

Learn from Maps Ask children to describe the map on Write-On Chart 7. Help children identify it as a map of the United States. Point to each state on the chart, and help volunteers use a dry-erase marker to label each state. You may wish to display a United States map with state names as a reference.

Critical Thinking

Direct children's attention to the various resources that appear around the border of Write-On Chart 7. Ask children to name each resource as you point to it. Explain that these are some of the major resources found in the United States. Provide information about each resource. (See page W23.) Then have children draw a line from the resource to the state or states which are the leading producers of that resource. Leading producers are mentioned in each paragraph and in parentheses.

Q. **Why do you think certain crops are grown in some states, but not in others?** Children should mention differences in climate and types of land.

Geography

Movement Point out the rivers and lakes on a map. Have a volunteer trace the rivers and outline the lakes. Ask children if they can identify these bodies of water. Responses should include the Mississippi River and the Great Lakes. Ask children to name resources found in these areas. Discuss how important transportation is to the farmer and the consumer.

Q. **How might a Minnesota wheat farmer get his crop to a buyer in Louisiana?** by boat on the Mississippi River

What other forms of transportation are used by farmers? trucks and trains

Building Background

1. **Grapes** grow well in climates that have warm to hot, dry summers and mild winter temperatures. California produces about 90 percent of the grape crop. (New York, Pennsylvania, Michigan)

2. **Pine trees** grow in a variety of climates but grow best in sandy, rocky soil. (Washington, Oregon, Alaska, northern California)

3. Washington grows more **apples** than any other state. Melted snow from the mountains irrigates Washington's valleys, making the soil ideal for apple orchards. (Michigan, New York, California, Pennsylvania, Virginia, North Carolina)

4. Broilers (**chickens** 5–12 weeks old) are the leading farm product in Arkansas. (Georgia, Alabama, North Carolina, Mississippi)

5. Most **tobacco** grows best in a warm climate and in carefully drained and fertilized soil. North Carolina is the leading tobacco-producing state. (Kentucky, Tennessee, South Carolina, Virginia, Georgia)

6. The oldest and richest **deciduous tree** forests in North America are found in the central Appalachian Mountains. (Kentucky, Tennessee, Virginia, North Carolina)

7. **Dairy cattle** farming exists in every state. Wisconsin leads the states in milk production, producing about 3 billion gallons per year. (California, New York, Minnesota, Pennsylvania)

8. About three-fourths of the **corn** crop is grown in the Corn Belt. Iowa and Illinois are the leading producers. (Indiana, Michigan, Minnesota, Missouri, Nebraska, Ohio, South Dakota, Wisconsin)

9. With its hot, dry climate and fertile soil, Texas leads the Cotton Belt states in the production of **cotton**. (Alabama, Arizona, Arkansas, California, Georgia, Louisiana, Mississippi, Missouri, New Mexico, North Carolina, Oklahoma, South Carolina, Tennessee)

10. **Peanuts** grow mainly in warm regions with a lot of sunlight and rainfall and a frost-free growing period of four to five months. Georgia produces nearly half of the annual peanut crop. (Alabama, North Carolina, Texas, Virginia)

11. Most **beef cattle** graze on open grassland unsuitable for growing crops. Texas leads the states in number of beef cattle. (Kansas, Nebraska, Oklahoma, Missouri)

12. **Potatoes**, the world's most widely grown vegetable, are grown in almost every state. (Idaho, Washington, Maine, Oregon, Wisconsin)

13. California leads in **lettuce** production, with nearly 70 percent of the commercial crop. Certain varieties of lettuce grow nearly year-round in the state's cool valleys. (Arizona, Florida, Colorado, New York)

14. Most **sheep** are raised west of the Mississippi River. Texas is the leading sheep-raising state. (California, Wyoming, Colorado)

15. More **oranges** are harvested each year than any other fruit. Florida produces about 80 percent of the crop. (California, Arizona, Texas)

16. Many varieties of **wheat** are planted in different areas throughout the year, depending on the climate. Kansas leads the states in wheat production. (North Dakota, Montana, Oklahoma, Washington)

17. **Tomatoes** grow best in areas with fertile soil, lots of sunshine, and a long growing season. California produces three-fourths of this commercial fruit crop. (Florida, Ohio, Michigan)

18. **Celery** requires a long growing season and moist, fertile soil. California and Florida are the top producers of celery.

19. **Carrots** can survive cool winters and summer heat. However, they grow best in deep, rich, sandy soil. California is a top producer.

ACTIVITY CHOICES

Meet Individual Needs

AUDITORY LEARNERS Invite children to play a resource game by giving a clue about each resource, such as *The state of New York has many dairy farms that produce milk and milk products for nearby cities. From what resource does milk come?* Ask a volunteer to draw a circle around the resource with a dry-erase marker.

Link to Health

NUTRITION Invite children to brainstorm a list of fruits and vegetables grown in the United States. Ask volunteers to research the nutritional values of the fruits and vegetables on the list. Suggest they look in their health books and the encyclopedia. Display a food pyramid. Discuss the recommended servings of fruits (2–4 servings) and vegetables (3–5) they should have each day. Then invite children to help you make a fruit or vegetable salad.

Link to Language Arts

JOURNAL Invite children to describe their favorite foods and to name the resources from which they come.

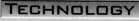

TECHNOLOGY

Use THE AMAZING WRITING MACHINE™ to complete this activity.

Extend and Enrich

RESEARCH RESOURCES Organize children into small groups. Invite each group to choose a different resource, such as rice, sorghum, soybeans, hogs, grapefruit, peaches, strawberries, or nuts, and research its history. Suggest that children write the information in their journals and include any facts they consider interesting and important for their classmates to know. Children can prepare a poster and read aloud their journal reports. Suggest that they begin by looking in the encyclopedia or an almanac for information.

Reteach the Main Idea

MATCH RESOURCES Write each of the following words on an index card: *animal, fruit, vegetable, grain,* and *tree.* Place the cards face down. Display Write-On Chart 7. Ask a child to choose one card, read it aloud, name a resource on the chart that belongs in that category, and identify one state where it can be found. Return the card to the pile. Continue until each child has taken several turns.

3. CLOSE

Ask children to look through magazines to find examples of resources from the United States. As children work, ask each child to name a resource and tell where it can be found.

Check Understanding

The child can
> classify information about resources found in the United States.
> recognize the relationship between geographical land features and the resources found there.

Think Critically

Q. **What kinds of resources are found in the United States?** The United States has many resources, including livestock, fruits, vegetables, grains, and trees.

Why do you think it is important for a country to have many resources? Children might respond that having many resources helps a country meet the needs of its citizens without having to depend on other countries.

Show What You Know

Performance Assessment Invite each child to create a page for a resource catalog. Assign each child a resource. Ask children to draw a picture of their resource on drawing paper. Then have them find out and write where the resource can be found and what products are made from that resource. Compile the pages into a book that can be added to the Science Center.

What to Look For Children should demonstrate an understanding of where resources come from and what they are used to make.

Using the Activity Book Distribute copies of Activity Book page 59. Tell children to write each of the words at the bottom of the page in the correct category. Then have them draw lines to connect the goods with the resources they come from.

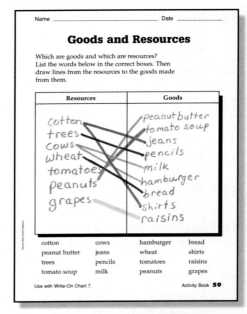

Activity Book page 59

8

REDUCE, REUSE, RECYCLE

OBJECTIVES

1. Recognize that there are many ways we can protect resources.
2. Understand that reducing, reusing, and recycling are ways to conserve resources.

VOCABULARY

recycle
landfill

RESOURCES

Write-On Chart 8
Clings
Activity Book, p. 60

ACTIVITY CHOICES

Community Involvement

Invite a representative from a local recycling center to talk to children about the different ways people can recycle in the community. Have children prepare questions ahead of time about what things to collect, why and how to sort the items, what happens at the recycling plant, and how materials are reused. Afterward, children can discuss what they learned about recycling and then set up a recycling center in the classroom, the cafeteria, or the playground or in another school area.

Link to Music

VOCAL Invite children to sing these words to the tune of "Row, Row, Row Your Boat":

Pick, pick, pick it up.
Lend a helping hand.
Merrily, merrily, merrily, merrily,
Cleaning up the land!

Children can form groups to sing a round.

1. ACCESS

Write the word *conservation* on the board, and review with children what it means. Ask children how the park ranger in Lesson 6, Caring for the Earth, helps conserve and protect the natural resources in the national park. Discuss how she educates visitors about the plants and wildlife, cares for animals that are hurt, collects water and soil samples for testing, makes sure visitors obey the rules, and watches for forest fires.

Q. **What are some things you can do to help conserve and protect the resources in your school or community?** Put things in the trash instead of littering, pick up litter, recycle, use water wisely.

Focus on the Main Idea

In this lesson children will explore ways to conserve and protect resources. They will learn about the importance of reducing, reusing, and recycling materials. Tell children that as they follow a trail through the mountains and forests and by the ocean, they will decide what to do with the litter and trash they find along the way.

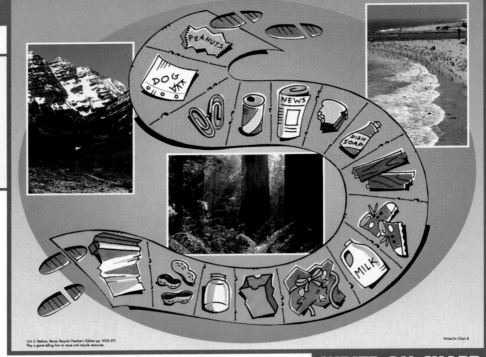

Children flip a coin to determine whether to move one space (heads) or two (tails), and they use a dry-erase marker to show where they are on the trail.

Dot Clings (optional)

Background

LANDFILLS If enough land is available, landfills are probably the cheapest way to dispose of solid waste. Refuse is spread in thin layers and compacted by bulldozers. When the compacted materials reach a depth of approximately ten feet, clean soil is spread over the refuse and compacted. Proper contouring of the land, compacting, and drainage engineering minimize the possibility of pollution.

Link to Science

RECYCLING AND RENEWAL
Have children bury some of the trash they collected, such as a meat tray, paper bag, plastic lid, or can, in a dirt-filled terrarium and observe what happens over the next month or two. Also, have them add fruit and vegetable peels. Place the terrarium near a sunny window and make sure the soil is moist. Have children record and discuss their observations.

2. BUILD

Vocabulary

Explain that one thing we can do to conserve resources is to recycle. Define *recycle* as a way to clean and reuse materials.

Q. **What are some things that we can recycle?** paper, wood, plastic, cans, glass, tires

Visual Analysis

Interpret Pictures Ask children to identify, describe, and compare the landscapes on Write-On Chart 8. Then focus attention on the trail, and ask children to identify the different kinds of litter and trash. Emphasize that the food, for example, will break down quickly in the soil but that the aluminum foil and the can will take a very long time to break down.

Q. **How would you feel about seeing litter and trash everywhere if you visited one of the places pictured? Why?** Children may say they would be upset or angry because the trash is spoiling the land and could hurt the animals.

Vocabulary

Ask children what they think happens to the garbage that sanitation workers collect. Define the vocabulary word *landfill* as the place where garbage can be dumped and allowed to break down.

Tactile Learning

Play a Game As children play the game and move along the trail, ask what they would do with each piece of trash or litter to help keep their country beautiful.

Q. **Why do you think it is important to recycle, reduce, and reuse things?** to help save our resources

3. CLOSE

Ask children to summarize the lesson by naming some of our resources. Then ask them to look again at Write-On Chart 8 and tell whose responsibility it is to protect our precious resources.

Check Understanding

—— recognize that there are many ways we can protect resources.

—— understand that reducing, reusing, and recycling are ways to conserve resources.

Think Critically

Q. **What would you say to a friend who tosses an aluminum can on the ground at the park or playground?** *"Please put your can in a trash can or take it home so it can be recycled."*

If you were a lawmaker, would you vote for a law that makes everyone sort trash so that it can be recycled? Why or why not? Possible responses might include that if we do not all recycle, we could run out of important resources.

Show What You Know

 Performance Assessment Invite children to create flyers or brochures to show what people can do to conserve and protect resources and the environment.

What to Look For Children should be able to identify reducing, reusing, and recycling certain items such as glass, plastic, paper, and aluminum as ways to help conserve and protect resources.

Using the Activity Book Distribute copies of Activity Book page 60. Invite children to identify the three items on the page. Then ask them to write sentences telling how they might reduce, recycle, or reuse each item. When children have completed the page, invite them to share and compare their ideas.

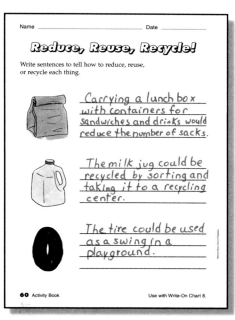

Name _____ Date _____

Reduce, Reuse, Recycle!

Write sentences to tell how to reduce, reuse, or recycle each thing.

Carrying a lunch box with containers for sandwiches and drinks would reduce the number of sacks.

The milk jug could be recycled by sorting and taking it to a recycling center.

The tire could be used as a swing in a playground.

60 Activity Book   Use with Write-On Chart 8.

Activity Book page 60

Extend and Enrich

WRITE A STORY Invite children to imagine they are a can, a plastic lid, a glass bottle, or a cellophane wrapper that has just been tossed on the ground by someone picnicking near a forest stream. Ask them to write a story telling what happens to them. Have children illustrate their stories and then read them aloud to the class.

Reteach the Main Idea

ANALYZE A CHART Return to Write-On Chart 8, and have children discuss how they would sort the trash and litter for recycling.

Home Involvement

Suggest that children talk with family members about the importance of conserving and protecting resources. Ask them to keep a log of the things they as a family do to help. Invite children to share their logs with classmates.

Link to Reading

READ FOR A PURPOSE Suggest that children read nonfiction books about environmental awareness to find out more about what they can do to participate. They might also enjoy three fiction stories about clever characters who find interesting ways to recycle "garbage": *Galimoto* by Karen Lynn Williams, *Stay Away from the Junkyard* by Tricia Tusa, and *Round-and-Round Again* by Nancy Van Laan.

9

SPECIAL DELIVERY

ACTIVITY CHOICES

Community Involvement

Arrange to take children to a post office to speak with a postmaster and to observe various postal operations. Help children prepare questions ahead of time about stamps; ZIP Codes; the jobs of different postal workers; the ways mail is collected, sorted, and delivered; and the other services a post office provides. When you return to the classroom, invite children to share what they learned.

Link to Language Arts

WRITE A LETTER Invite each child to write a letter to a family member or friend who lives in another town, city, or state. Ask children to recall the parts of a letter—the heading, greeting, body, closing, and signature—and how to capitalize and punctuate each one correctly. When children have completed their letters, have them write the mailing address and return address on an envelope. Remind them to include the ZIP Code. Children can then stamp and mail their letters.

TECHNOLOGY

Use THE AMAZING WRITING MACHINE™ to complete this activity.

OBJECTIVES

1. Identify a post office as a government agency.
2. Trace the process for getting and delivering mail.
3. Describe how businesses depend on the postal service.

RESOURCES

Write-On Chart 9

Clings

Activity Book, p. 61

Music Audio, "The Postman"

The Amazing Writing Machine

1. ACCESS

Invite children to recall the steps it takes to make tomato juice and to get it from the farm to consumers. Emphasize the importance of each person's job and what happens when there is a breakdown at any point in the process. Have volunteers list the steps on the board as they are identified. Then display an addressed envelope or package that was delivered to you at school by the United States Postal Service. Ask children to tell how they think it got to you from the person who sent it.

Q. What kinds of things do you get in the mail? birthday cards, letters, invitations, thank-you notes, magazines, packages

Focus on the Main Idea

In this lesson children will begin to explore the United States Postal Service, how it operates, and how it connects businesses and their customers. Tell children that they will trace the path of mail through the postal system from its origin to its destination.

Children trace the route of a letter from the mailbox to its final destination.

Mail is:
1. stamped, mailed, and collected.
2. "culled," or sorted by size.
3. postmarked at a canceling machine.
4. sorted at computers and grouped by ZIP Code.
5. transported to its destination.
6. sorted by local ZIP Codes.
7. delivered.

Mail Cling (optional)

WRITE-ON CHART

2. BUILD

Economics

Economic Systems and Institutions   Direct attention to the mailboxes on Write-On Chart 9, and ask children to tell what they are and how people use them. Emphasize that mailing is just the first of many steps needed to get letters and packages to their final destinations. Explain that it is the job of the United States Postal Service, a government agency, to collect, sort, and deliver the billions of pieces of mail that people and businesses mail each year. Invite children to use the chart to describe each step in getting mail to its destination. Have children circle or place the Mail Cling on each number as you list the steps in the box above. Tell children that using ZIP Codes has helped speed up the process of sorting and delivering mail and that to mail a letter or package, a person must pay postage. Then have children recall the cannery they discussed earlier.

Q. **How is the postal service like the cannery we visited in Unit 2?**
Both have special jobs to do; both provide something important; both depend on transportation and communication.

Interdependence and Income   Point out that the postal service is an important link between businesses and consumers. Invite children to suggest ways a department store, for example, might use the postal service. Help them recognize that businesses depend on the mail to advertise, to bill customers, to receive payments from customers, and sometimes to deliver goods to customers.

Continue by explaining that before the invention of the telephone, the postal system was the only organized way people had to communicate over long distances.

ACTIVITY CHOICES

Background

PONY EXPRESS   The pony express was established in 1860 to relay mail along the 1,966-mile trail between St. Joseph, Missouri, and Sacramento, California. The journey took riders ten days or less, which was faster than by boat or stagecoach. There were 190 pony express stations between the two cities. A rider would mount a horse at one station, carry the mail ten to 15 miles to the next station, change horses, and continue riding for a total of 75 miles or more before being replaced by the next rider. The rider would carry the mail day and night, no matter what the weather.

Link to Art

GRAPHIC ART Point out that United States postage stamps were first issued by Congress in 1847 and that by 1855 mail would not be delivered without them. Have children bring canceled stamps from home. Invite them to talk about the pictures on the stamps. Children can then use the stamps to create a collage.

Extend and Enrich

INTERVIEW BUSINESS PEOPLE
Invite children to interview business people they know to find out how the businesses depend on the United States Postal Service. Have children report their findings to the class.

Reteach the Main Idea

SEQUENCE POSTAL DELIVERY
Make sets of labels on large index cards for the steps in the process of getting mail from the sender to its destination. Give a set to each group of children. Have them arrange the labels in order and then tell what happens during each step.

Link to Reading

READ FOR A PURPOSE Invite children to read *The Post Office Book: Mail and How It Moves* by Gail Gibbons to add more details to the process of mail handling by the U.S. Postal Service.

AUDIO

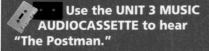 Use the UNIT 3 MUSIC AUDIOCASSETTE to hear "The Postman."

---

3. CLOSE

Ask children to summarize the lesson by pretending they are a letter that a child has just written to a friend and by telling the steps the letter goes through to be delivered. Invite the "letters" to tell about some of the other mail they meet along the way.

Check Understanding

The child can
—— identify a post office as a government agency.
—— trace the process for getting and delivering mail.
—— describe how businesses depend on the postal service.

Think Critically

Q. **Why do you think so many people have different jobs and special machines at the post office?** Postal workers have to be very organized to handle so much mail.

Imagine you are about to open a store in your community. How might you use the postal service? to mail advertisements announcing the opening, to let customers know about sales and specials, to bill customers, to send payments to utility companies, to send goods that people buy

Show What You Know

Performance Assessment Assign each row a ZIP Code. Have each child address an envelope to a classmate in another row and "mail" the letter in a class mailbox. Then have children take turns collecting the mail and taking it to a table designated "post office," where they sort the mail by ZIP Code. Then have a letter carrier for each ZIP Code deliver the envelopes.

What to Look For Children should show an understanding of how the postal service collects, sorts, and delivers mail.

Using the Activity Book Distribute copies of Activity Book page 61. Invite children to address the envelope and then number the pictures to show the steps a letter will go through to reach its destination.

Activity Book page 61

10
OPEN FOR BUSINESS

OBJECTIVES

1. Understand how small businesses work.
2. Describe how consumers influence the availability of goods and services.
3. Recognize how people can put their special talents to work.

RESOURCES

Write-On Chart 10
Clings
Activity Book, p. 62

Community Involvement

Invite a small-business person or craft-worker into your classroom to talk about his or her work. Help children prepare questions ahead of time about how the person learned to do the work, how prices are set for the things that are sold, what the person likes most about his or her work, and what some of the problems are that the person faces in his or her work.

1. ACCESS

Invite children to pretend they are each about to open their own business. Define *business* as a store or other establishment that sells, makes, or provides goods or services to consumers. Ask children to tell what kind of business they plan to open and operate and to explain why they chose the particular business.

Q. What might you need to open and operate a real business?

Responses may include goods and services that people want or need, a place to run the business, a way to advertise, and money to pay the costs of running the business.

Record children's ideas on chart paper and save.

Focus on the Main Idea

In this lesson children will begin to explore what it takes to run a business and how the costs of running a business affect prices and profits. Children will also have an opportunity to demonstrate how they as customers can affect prices and profits.

Link to Art

GRAPHIC ART Display a variety of logos representing different local businesses. Have children examine each logo and discuss what it communicates about the business. For example, the logo may show the product the business produces or the location of the business. Explain that a logo helps people remember a business, so it is a very important way for the producer to communicate with the consumer. Then invite children to create a logo for the business they plan to open. To announce the opening of their businesses, children should create ads in which they incorporate their logo designs. Display the completed ads. Point out that advertising is an important aspect of running a business.

Children use counters to bid for sale items in a simulated auction. Volunteers write the price each item sells for.

Circle Clings (optional)

Unit 3: Open for Business (Teacher's Edition pp. W31–W33)
Describe small businesses and bid on items for auction.

Write-On Chart 10

ACTIVITY CHOICES

Multicultural Link

Bring in pictures or examples of other cultures' arts and crafts that can be purchased in specialty shops selling imported goods. Invite children from different cultures to bring items from home as well. Ask children to speculate about the kind of skill that is needed to make each item. Some children may want to do further research to write a report or give a talk about a particular craft.

Background

HANDMADE VERSUS FACTORY-MADE Today handmade arts and crafts are usually more expensive than factory-made items because it usually takes longer to make something by hand than by a machine. Years ago almost all manufactured items were handmade, but today most are factory-made. Now people can afford more items, but the quality of the items has changed. Because fewer people today are skilled at arts and crafts, handmade items often seem more special.

2. BUILD

Economics

Markets and Prices Have children identify the kinds of businesses on the chart and the items those businesses sell. Point out that there are costs to running a business. Ask what the costs might include, and add children's responses to the chart you started in Access. Help children recognize that in addition to paying workers and buying materials, there are the costs of rent, water, electricity, gas, telephone, decorating and maintaining the store, taxes, and advertising. Have them distinguish between established businesses and those conducted temporarily or part-time from people's homes.

Q. **Which do you think costs more to run, the map and globe store or a yard sale? Why?** The map and globe store costs more because the owner has more expenses.

How do you think the store owner's costs affect the price you pay for a globe? The price of a globe includes part of the store owner's cost.

Point out the potter. Explain that some people, like potters, work for themselves because they have special interests or talents. Ask what special interest the antique dealer might have. Emphasize that no matter what the business, it will not succeed without a demand for its goods or services.

Q. **What can happen if consumers do not want a certain good or service any longer or if the prices are too high?** The owner could lose money and go out of business.

On the chart, draw a circle or place a Circle Cling around one of the items for sale. Then invite children to participate in an auction. Have them use counters to bid, or make offers, on the item. The highest bidder gets to buy the item. Repeat the activity with each item. Review the final prices for all four items, emphasizing how customers create the demand for goods.

3. CLOSE

Ask children to summarize the lesson by telling what a person wanting to open a video game store would have to know about running a small business.

Check Understanding

The child can

—— understand how small businesses work.

—— describe how consumers influence the availability of goods and services.

—— recognize how people can put their special talents to work.

Think Critically

Q. **How would you explain the effect consumers can have on a business?** If many people want, need, or demand a certain good, its price might go up; if people no longer want or need a certain good, its price might go down.

What special talents and interests do you have that you might put to work one day? Responses may include a musical or an artistic ability, an interest in books and videos, and an interest in cooking and baking.

What advice would you give someone who wants to start a small business but who has never been in business before? Think about all the costs; think about what special talents you have; find out what consumers want and need.

Show What You Know

Performance Assessment Invite children to pretend they are arts-and-crafts workers with their own small businesses. Ask them to draw pictures of four items they might make and sell. Have children name their businesses and write advertisements for the items.

What to Look For Children should show an understanding of the kinds of concerns affecting the owners of small businesses.

Using the Activity Book Distribute copies of Activity Book page 62. Invite children to name the diner they would like to open and then fill in a business plan. Have them list their costs, the customers who would buy their products, and where they would open the business.

Activity Book page 62

Extend and Enrich

LIST BUSINESSES Invite children to use local newspapers and the yellow pages to make a list of the different kinds of businesses in their community.

Reteach the Main Idea

HOLD AN AUCTION Have another auction, this time using items that children have drawn, including pictures of services they might perform. Afterward, discuss what seems to determine an item's price.

ACTIVITY CHOICES

11

MARKETS AROUND THE WORLD

Meet Individual Needs

VISUAL LEARNERS Write the names of different kinds of markets, such as *flea market, supermarket, farmers' market,* and *fish market,* on individual posterboard or construction paper strips, and pin them across the top of a bulletin board. Then, one at a time, hold up pictures depicting goods and services that appeal to children. As each is identified, have children name the kind of market where it can be purchased and pin the picture under the correct market name on the bulletin board.

Community Involvement

Take children on a field trip to an unusual market, like a bazaar, an outdoor farmers' market, or a specialized market. Ask them to look for things they do not usually see where their family ordinarily shops. After returning to the classroom, help children list those things and talk about how the market is different from the kinds of markets they frequent.

OBJECTIVES

1. Define *market*.
2. Compare and contrast markets around the world.

VOCABULARY

market
product

RESOURCES

Write-On Chart 11
Clings
Vocabulary Blacklines
Activity Book, page 63
Transparencies 23, 24

1. ACCESS

Write the word *market* on the board. Help children define *market* as any place where people come together to buy and sell goods and services. Invite children to suggest words or phrases that include the word *market*, such as *supermarket, fish market, farmers' market,* and *flea market,* and then have them suggest other kinds of stores. Write the words on the board. Then play "To Market, To Market, What Kind of Market?" Begin by telling children that you want to buy a fresh lobster, a dozen clams, a pound of shrimp, and some flounder. Ask children to name the kind of market where these items can be purchased. (fish market, seafood department of a supermarket) Then invite children to take turns naming goods and services they would like to buy, and have the class identify the kind of market where each of the goods or services is sold.

Q. **Why do we need markets?** We need markets so people can buy and sell things. Because many goods and services are available in one market, consumers can shop more easily.

Focus on the Main Idea

In this lesson children will learn that markets are found around the world. In the process they will come to a better understanding of what a market is. Tell children that in this lesson they will see how people in different parts of the world use the marketplace.

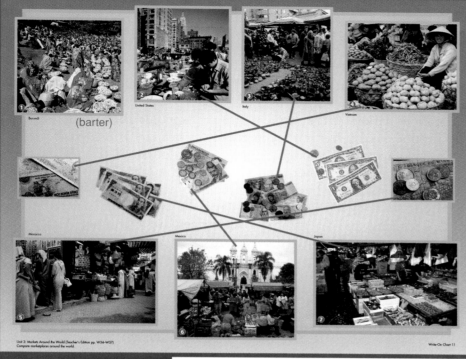

(barter)

WRITE-ON CHART

Children identify markets in different countries. They match currency to the markets where it might be used.

Flag Clings (optional)

2. BUILD

Visual Analysis

Compare Pictures   Invite children to describe the different markets on Write-On Chart 11, noting the various goods and services, the activities of the people, and whether the markets are in the United States or in other countries. Help the children place an appropriate Flag Cling on each country. Emphasize that a market can be anywhere that a buyer and a seller get together to trade goods and services.

Q. **How do you think people got what they needed before there were markets?** They grew or made what they needed or perhaps traded with nearby relatives or neighbors.

Economics

Interdependence and Income   Point out that in some markets, consumers do not use money to get what they want. Explain the concept of bartering, helping children compare and contrast bartering with paying for *products* with money. Invite them to give examples of times when they or their families bartered to get goods or services.

Q. **When might bartering work better than using money?** when two people each have something the other wants

Help children match the currency on the chart with its country.

Culture

Shared Humanity and Unique Identity   Emphasize that going to market is often a social event, because it gives people a chance to exchange ideas and share news.

ACTIVITY CHOICES

Link to World Languages

OTHER LANGUAGES   Have children who know other languages teach the class the words for *market*, such as *mercado* in Spanish and *marché* in French. Invite them to describe the products found in those markets and how people pay for the goods and services there. Suggest that if they have coins or bills from another country, they might bring them in to show to the class and teach classmates the names of the money.

Role-Play

Invite children to set up their own market and role-play what happens there. Help them agree on the type of market, what goods or services are sold, what type of money is used, and whether bartering is allowed. They can use empty food boxes as props. After their role-play, ask them to discuss what they learned about markets.

Meet Individual Needs

VISUAL LEARNERS   Display a globe, world map, or Transparencies 23 and 24. Help children find the city, state, or country of each market shown on Write-On Chart 11.

Multicultural Link

Many large cities have markets that represent various cultures within the community. Cities such as New York, San Francisco, and Chicago all have areas called Chinatown. In these areas Chinese American merchants have shops and restaurants. Customers can buy authentic Chinese food, Chinese clothes, and other products unique to the Chinese culture. Chinatown is only one example of the many cultural markets in the United States. Other markets represent cultures from Germany, Italy, Mexico, Korea, Vietnam, and so on.

Link to Art

SCULPTURE   Provide children with salt dough or clay of varying colors, paints, crayons, cardboard, craftsticks, tape, toothpicks, construction paper, tools for sculpting, and fine-tip markers. Invite children to make a tabletop model of a market that includes a variety of booths or stands displaying many of the kinds of goods sold at a market. Suggest they add action figures to represent people involved in buying and selling.

Build Background

Markets Around the World   Markets around much of the world have not changed much over the centuries. A market may be a roadside stand or an outdoor market where farmers and craftspeople rent stalls to display their produce and wares. In some countries farmers run regular delivery routes, bringing fresh produce right to the doorsteps of customers. In developing countries farmers and craftspeople might simply set up business in gathering places by spreading their crops and wares on blankets on the ground. In such countries market day is a social as well as a commercial event. Bartering and bargaining over prices are common. Market-day activities are often the only break people have from their routines and labor.

1. **Burundi**   The women are carrying baskets of manioc (cassava) roots to a market in Burundi, the small east-central African country at the northern end of Lake Tanganyika. Other crops grown and sold in Burundi are sweet potatoes, corn, beans, peas, bananas, coffee, cotton, and tea.
2. **New York, New York**   Residents and tourists alike enjoy shopping for new and used goods at street flea markets.
3. **Rome, Italy**   An Italian flea market along a cobblestone street is a wonderful place for tourists and residents to meet and look over such items as old copper and brass pots and pans.
4. **Dalat, Vietnam**   A favorable climate and plentiful water make Vietnam a good place for growing crops, particularly rice. These women are selling vegetables.
5. **Fez, Morocco**   Shoppers dressed in long jalabas and veils walk along a narrow city street lined with small, wall-less shops and stalls selling jewelry, baskets, and other goods.
6. **Guadalajara, Mexico**   Pottery, baskets, and clothes are just some of the things that can be purchased at an outdoor market on a Sunday in Guadalajara.
7. **Tsukiji, Japan**   Japan has a large-scale fishing industry with fleets in all the oceans and catches more fish than any other country. Fish is the main source of protein in the Japanese diet.

3. CLOSE

VOCABULARY BLACKLINES

To summarize the lesson, provide children with word cards for the terms *market, product, producer, and consumer*. Have children use each word in a sentence.

Check Understanding

The child can
—— define *market*.
—— compare and contrast markets around the world.

Think Critically

Q. **If you were to travel to a different country to visit its markets, what could you learn about the people, their ways, and their country?**

Responses may include the kinds of foods they eat; the way they dress; their language and money; the music, toys, and games they enjoy; and the kinds of arts and crafts they create.

Show What You Know

Performance Assessment Have children form groups to select two markets pictured on Write-On Chart 11 and to compare and contrast them in a role-play. Tell them one of the markets should be similar to ones they have in their community and the other should be a kind they are not familiar with.

What to Look For Children should choose a supermarket or fish market to contrast with an outdoor market or possibly a bazaar. Their role-playing should show evidence that they exchange money for or barter for goods and that the money is appropriate to the market. It might also acknowledge incidental differences, like shopping carts, paper bags, and packaging.

Using the Activity Book Distribute copies of Activity Book page 63, and invite children to go shopping at the Kids' Flea Market. Have them list what they bought and tell why.

Activity Book page 63

ACTIVITY CHOICES

Reteach the Main Idea

ASK QUESTIONS Ask for a volunteer to write on the board the definition of a *market*. Then ask children *When you go to a grocery store to buy two apples, are you in a market?* or *If a farmer were to sell apples at a stand, would that be a market?* Have children make up other examples to ask each other.

Extend and Enrich

COMPARE MARKETS Provide children with magazines and other reference materials, and invite them to find pictures of markets in the United States and around the world. Encourage them to compare and contrast these markets with each other and with the ones on Write-On Chart 11. Then have children share their findings with the rest of the class.

Link Literature

Children may enjoy reading *A Fruit & Vegetable Man* by Roni Schotter. (Little, Brown, 1993) In this story, Sun Ho watches Ruby Rubenstein, an artistic fruit and vegetable man, at work. When Sun Ho begins helping in the store, he suggests they sell something new—bean sprouts. Invite children to discuss where their families buy fruits and vegetables and to describe how the fruits and vegetables are arranged.

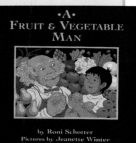

12

ON THE JOB

ACTIVITY CHOICES

Home Involvement

Invite children to ask adults and older siblings at home about the jobs they do and the tools they use. Encourage children to share this information in class when listing jobs and related tools.

Meet Individual Needs

KINESTHETIC LEARNERS Organize children into teams to play a game of "Charades" in which one team must guess the job that a member of an opposing team is acting out. Ask children to use jobs that have been talked about so far in the lesson.

OBJECTIVES

1. Explore jobs and related job tools.
2. Link choice of job to special interest, talent, or family legacy.

VOCABULARY
tool

RESOURCES
Write-On Chart 12
Clings
Activity Book, p. 64

1. ACCESS

Invite children to brainstorm jobs held by people they know. If necessary, tell children to ask those who hold jobs at home what jobs they do and how they do them. Invite children to predict what jobs they will do when they become adults and to tell why they made those predictions.

Q. **How do you think people decide what jobs to do?** Accept responses such as choosing a job based on interest, talent, family legacy, friends' jobs, and pay.

Focus on the Main Idea

In this lesson children will learn about the different kinds of jobs people do and the tools and talents people need to do their jobs. Tell children that in this lesson they will match jobs with the tools used in those jobs.

oxygen mask

micro- scope

stetho- scope

camera

football gear

computer

tool belt

Unit 3: On the Job (Teacher's Edition pp. W38-W45)
Match jobs and the skills and tools needed to perform them.

Write-On Chart 12

WRITE-ON CHART

Children will use dry-erase mark- ers to draw appropriate tools for each job pictured.

Tool Clings (optional)

2. BUILD

Culture

Human Relationships   Invite children to identify and write captions for the jobs that are pictured on the Write-On Chart. Explain that workers often use tools to do their jobs more easily and more quickly. Define *tool* as any instrument used in doing work. Ask children to show the tools each worker uses, either by drawing the tools in the box provided or by using the Tool Clings.

Q. **How do tools help workers do their jobs?** Workers can do jobs more quickly and more easily; fewer workers are needed to finish a job.

What tools help you do your job as a student? pencils, mark- ers, computers, rulers

Shared Humanity and Unique Identity   Invite children to guess why people choose their jobs and to discuss how special interests or talents— physical skills, math abilities, artistic talents, inquisitive natures—family or friends, and the amount of pay might affect the choice. Invite children to talk about the kinds of jobs they might like to do. Ask them to tell what attracts them to their choices.

Q. **What kinds of jobs might a person with a curious nature choose?** scientist, mechanic, antique dealer, astronaut, teacher, researcher **a person with good physical skills?** dancer, gymnast, gym teacher, fitness trainer, construction worker

Why is it important to like your job? Responses might include that you would enjoy going to work, you would do your job well, and you would be happy.

You may wish to have children revisit the opening photograph in Unit 3 on pages 98–99 to discuss the skills and tools of each worker pictured.

Extend and Enrich

CAREER TALK Invite a career counselor to talk about the kinds of training needed for jobs children think they would like to do. After the talk, have children list on a chart the ideas they learned. Title the chart *Jobs for Us* and display it in a special Careers Corner.

Reteach the Main Idea

DISCUSS TOOLS Bring in a number of tools, such as a saw, a piece of chalk, a crossing guard's paddle, and a shovel. Invite children to tell what kind of job might be done with each tool and to share what they know about that job. Ask children to tell if they would be interested in any of these jobs and to explain why or why not.

HOLIDAY ACTIVITIES

For information and activities related to Labor Day, see the Holiday Activities section at the back of the Teacher's Edition.

3. CLOSE

Invite a volunteer to choose a Tool Cling. Call on another child to identify from the Write-On Chart the worker who uses that tool. The second child can call on another to tell how this worker might use the tool on the job. Repeat the process until all jobs and tools are matched.

Check Understanding

The child can
—— explore jobs and related job tools.
—— link choice of job to special interest, talent, or family legacy.

Think Critically

Q. **What advice would you give a friend who is trying to choose a job?** Children might suggest telling a friend to think about his or her interests and talents, to ask questions of many different kinds of workers, and to read about different jobs.

In what jobs might workers use a computer? Secretaries and other people who work in offices might write letters and keep information on computers; teachers might plan lessons on computers; scientists do research on computers.

Show What You Know

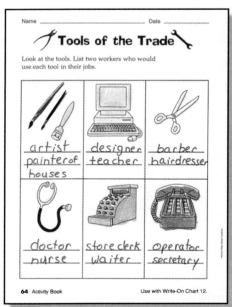

Performance Assessment Organize children into two groups—one to recall various jobs and the other to recall various tools discussed in class. Have each child select a job or a tool, write its name on a card, and attach the card to his or her clothing. Have the children mingle to match up workers with tools. Ask them to explain why they matched as they did and why some could not match.

What to Look For Most jobs and tools that have been discussed during class should be represented and matched.

Using the Activity Book Distribute copies of Activity Book page 64. Invite children to examine the tools and list any workers they can think of who would use each tool. Invite children to share their work with a partner.

Name _____ Date _____

✏ Tools of the Trade

Look at the tools. List two workers who would use each tool in their jobs.

artist painter of houses	designer teacher	barber hairdresser
doctor nurse	store clerk waiter	operator secretary

64 Activity Book   Use with Write-On Chart 12.

Activity Book page 64

13

THE FIRST AMERICANS

OBJECTIVES

1. Describe an aspect of the early history of our country by telling about a Native American culture.

2. Compare daily life for a group of early Americans to that of the present day.

RESOURCES

Write-On Chart 13

Clings

Activity Book, p. 65

Music Audio, "Canoe Song"

The Amazing Writing Machine

Imagination Express: Destination Ocean

ACTIVITY CHOICES

Multicultural Link

Tribes with strong similarities are grouped into *culture areas*. Those culture areas and some of their tribes were as follows:

FAR NORTH: Athabaskan, Cree, Inuit, Ottawa

EASTERN WOODLANDS: Algonkin, Cherokee, Chickasaw, Chippewa, Choctaw, Creek, Delaware, Iroquois, Natchez, Powhatan, Seminole, Shawnee, Wampanoag

PLAINS: Arapaho, Assiniboine, Blackfoot, Caddo, Cheyenne, Comanche, Crow, Kiowa, Mandan, Omaha, Osage, Pawnee, Sioux

NORTHWEST COAST: Chinook, Haida, Kwakiutl, Makah, Nootka, Tlingit

CALIFORNIA-INTERMOUNTAIN: Cayuse, Chumash, Flathead, Klamath, Kutenai, Nez Perce, Paiute, Pomo, Shoshone, Ute, Yakima

SOUTHWEST: Apache, Hopi, Navajo, Papago, Pueblo, Yaqui, Yuma

MIDDLE AMERICA: Aztec, Maya, Toltec

1.ACCESS

Ask children to name the first Americans. Emphasize that many different groups of American Indians live throughout North and South America. Explain that they lived here many, many years before any other people came. Then read aloud these verses from "Indian Children" by Annette Wynne.

Where we walk to school each day
Indian children used to play—
All about our native land,
Where the shops and houses stand.

Only wigwams on the ground,
And at night bears prowling round.
What a different place today
Where we live and work and play!

Make sure children recognize that today the descendants of early American Indians live throughout the United States, many on reservations—land that they own.

Focus on the Main Idea

Tell children that in this lesson they will study a painting to see what life was like for one group of early Americans.

TECHNOLOGY

Use IMAGINATION EXPRESS:™ DESTINATION OCEAN to invite children to write about the Chumash people of California.

Children describe the activities and label types of food, clothing, tools, and shelter used by tribes of the Eastern Woodlands.

Circle and Geo Georgie Clings (optional)

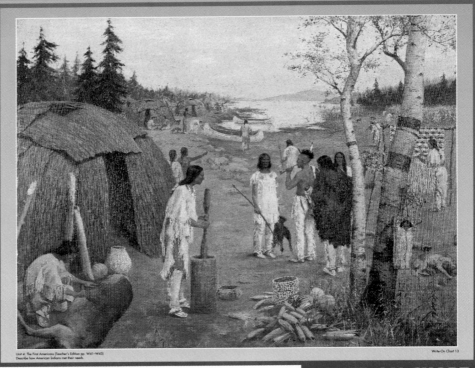

ACTIVITY CHOICES

Background

TRIBES OF THE EASTERN WOODLANDS Indians of the Eastern Woodlands hunted, gathered, and farmed. They lived in villages surrounded by palisades—walls of sharpened tree trunks. Their planting fields lay outside the walls. They grew corn, beans, and squash; gathered nuts, berries, wild fruits, greens, and shellfish; caught fish; and hunted birds, deer, beaver, bear, and porcupine. They ate the meat of these animals and used the skins for robes, capes, blankets, and other clothing. The painting by A. A. Jansson shows daily life among the Algonkins. It hangs in the American Museum of Natural History.

Link to Reading

WRITE A BOOK REVIEW Invite children to read a Native American legend or a book about American Indians. Then ask them to write book reviews suggesting why their friends might enjoy reading these books.

TECHNOLOGY

Use THE AMAZING WRITING MACHINE™ RESOURCE PACKAGE to complete this activity.

2. BUILD

Geography

Human-Environment Interactions Invite children to describe the setting shown on the Write-On Chart, noting the hills, forests, water, and vegetation. Explain that the picture shows the Eastern Woodlands, a region that once extended from the Great Lakes to what is now the Carolinas and Tennessee, and from the Atlantic Ocean to the Mississippi River. Ask for a volunteer to point out the region on a wall map. Emphasize that although there are several kinds of land in this region—coast, lakes, mountains, and valleys—much of it was once covered by forest.

Q. **Why do you think the forest was important to the Indians?**
They used the trees to build homes, canoes, weapons, tools, and utensils; wood was used for fuel; the forest was home to many animals the Indians needed.

Why were the rivers, lakes, and ocean important? They provided food, transportation, and water.

History

People and Events Across Time and Place Explain that the people in the picture belong to an American Indian tribe of the Eastern Woodlands. Ask children to describe the Indians' clothing, food, utensils, tools, and weapons as well as the activities they are doing. Have volunteers use a dry-erase marker or clings to circle the items and activities. Invite children to take turns placing Geo Georgie Clings on items we use or activities we do today. Have them describe how what we use or do today is like or different from each item or activity.

Q. **How are your needs like those of the people in this picture?**
Responses may include the need for food, clothing, shelter, education, and love.

3. CLOSE

Have the class form two groups. Challenge one group to identify ways the daily lives of early Eastern Woodland Indians were like the daily lives of Americans today. Challenge the other group to name ways daily life then was different from daily life now.

Check Understanding

The child can
—— describe an aspect of the early history of our country by telling about a Native American culture.
—— compare daily life for a group of early Americans to that of the present day.

Think Critically

Q. **Would you want to have lived in the times of early Americans? Why or why not?** Responses might include that although life was more difficult back then, it would have been exciting.

Do you think life was most difficult for woodland tribes, desert tribes, or tribes that lived in cold climates? Why? Accept all reasonable responses as children cite such factors as weather, lack of trees, and fewer places to grow food.

Show What You Know

Performance Assessment Help children form small groups of four to six. Assign each group a topic, such as food, clothing, shelter, or jobs. Ask each group to create a chart entitled *Today and Long Ago*, listing examples of their topic from the past and present.

What to Look For Children should be able to give examples of food, clothing, shelter, or jobs from today and long ago.

Using the Activity Book Give each child a copy of Activity Book page 65. Invite children to list ways their daily lives are similar to and different from the daily lives of the two early American children pictured. Have children begin by drawing pictures of themselves in the right-hand space at the top of the page. When children have completed the page, invite them to share and compare their lists.

Activity Book page 65

Extend and Enrich

RESEARCH TRIBES Have children form small groups, and assign each group a tribe from a different region. Have each child research an aspect of tribal life, such as food, clothing, customs, shelter, games, or transportation. Each group can then organize the information and present it to the class.

Reteach the Main Idea

PRESENT ORALLY Direct children's attention to the Write-On Chart and invite them to imagine that they are in the scene. Have each child tell something about his or her life as an early American Indian.

Meet Individual Needs

ADVANCED LEARNERS Write the words *wigwam* and *longhouse* on the board, and explain that each was a type of shelter used by some early American Indians. Challenge children to find out more about wigwams, longhouses, and other types of shelter that American Indians used. Have children draw pictures or make models of each type of shelter.

Link to Music

VOCAL/RHYTHM Invite children to learn "Canoe Song." Have them form pairs and pretend to be in canoes, "paddling upstream" as they sing the song. You may wish to have children use drums and rattles to tap out the rhythm as they sing.

AUDIO

Use the UNIT 4 MUSIC AUDIOCASSETTE to hear "Canoe Song."

14

WHAT'S NEW, WHAT'S OLD

Meet Individual Needs

VISUAL/AUDITORY/TACTILE LEARNERS Gather a variety of old kitchen utensils and display them on a table. Challenge children to guess what they are and how they were used. As a variation, briefly describe how each item was used while children guess which utensil you are talking about. Ask children to identify items people use today to complete the same tasks. Then invite children to try using the old utensils.

Link to Language Arts

JOURNAL Invite children to think about all the chores they do at home and the equipment they use to do them. Then have children interview parents and grandparents to find out what equipment they used to do the same chores when they were children. Ask children to write about their findings in their journals.

TECHNOLOGY

Use THE AMAZING WRITING MACHINE™ to complete this activity.

OBJECTIVES

1. Describe how technologies have changed.
2. Identify the effects of technology on our lives.

VOCABULARY
machine

RESOURCES
Write-On Chart 14
Clings
Activity Book, p. 66
The Amazing Writing Machine

1. ACCESS

Ask children to recall how American Indians and early settlers traveled from place to place and to describe some challenges and obstacles they faced along the way. Then invite children to discuss how families today move from one part of the country to another.

Q. **Why do you think it is easier for people today to travel?**
Responses might include that we have cars, trucks, trains, planes, paved roads, bridges, and tunnels, and we can stop at stores, restaurants, and motels along the way.

In what other ways do you think our lives are easier? We have better tools, machines, and equipment to help us do our work; we do not have to grow all our own food or make all our own clothes; we have faster ways to communicate, like the telephone and fax; we have more free time.

Focus on the Main Idea

In this lesson children will explore changes in technology and will examine how technology has affected our lives. Tell children they will see how some machines and appliances have changed over the years and they will find out how these machines have changed our lives.

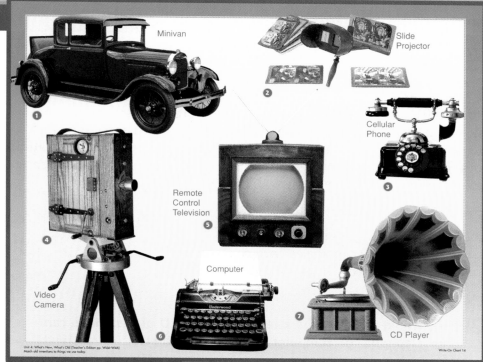

Minivan

Slide Projector

Cellular Phone

Remote Control Television

Video Camera

Computer

CD Player

Underwood

Unit 4: What's New, What's Old (Teacher's Edition pp. W44-W46)
Match old inventions to things we use today.

Write-On Chart 14

WRITE-ON CHART

Invite children to identify the machines that were used long ago. Then, next to each old machine, children should draw a picture of or write the name of the modern machine that we use instead today.

Word Clings (optional)

2. BUILD

Visual Analysis

Interpret Pictures Invite children to identify and describe each machine on Write-On Chart 14 and to explain how it is used. Then invite them to draw or write the name of a modern machine we use instead of each old machine. Children can use Word Clings to correctly label each photo or drawing as one from long ago or from today.

Q. **Why is** *What's New, What's Old* **a good title for this chart?** because we are comparing machines from the past with ones we use today

Vocabulary

Write the word *machines* on the board. Define machines as devices that have moving parts and are used for doing work. Point out that all machines do work, even those used for activities that are fun. Invite children to brainstorm a list of machines and then organize them into categories, such as office, home, garage, farm, communication, and transportation.

History

People and Events Across Time and Place Ask children to think about how people traveled before the automobile became available.

Q. **How do you think the first automobiles changed people's lives?** They made it easier and faster to travel.

Connections Past to Present to Future Discuss the impact of the other early machines, focusing on how they improved over the years, how they affect people's lives today, and how they may change in the future.

ACTIVITY CHOICES

Meet Individual Needs

ENGLISH LANGUAGE LEARNERS
Invite children to make word flash-cards by drawing or cutting out pictures of different kinds of machines and taping them onto individual cards. As children identify each machine, help them write its name and a brief description of what the machine does in English on the reverse side. Invite children acquiring English to review the cards with a partner who speaks English fluently.

KINESTHETIC LEARNERS Invite children to demonstrate how to use each item on the chart by miming an activity in which the item is used and perhaps by also making an appropriate sound. Challenge the class to guess what each child is doing and which item he or she is using.

Community Involvement

Arrange to take children on a field trip to a museum where they can learn about old and new technology.

Extend and Enrich

MAKE A TIME LINE Invite children to work in groups to trace the history of a machine, such as the washing machine, iron, stove, toilet, refrigerator, sewing machine, or camera. Have them find out how the machine has changed over time and then help them make a time line to show significant changes.

Reteach the Main Idea

TRACE CHANGES To help children recognize how technology affects their lives, have volunteers choose one modern machine and describe all the ways people's lives would be different if that machine did not exist.

3. CLOSE

Ask children to look through books in the library for scenes of people of the past doing such jobs as guiding animals pulling a covered wagon, plowing a field with a horse-drawn plow, cooking over an open fire, or splitting logs. Have children identify the machine or tool being used and then tell how the same job is done today.

Check Understanding

The child can
—— describe how technologies have changed.
—— identify the effects of technology on our lives.

Think Critically

Q. **How would you describe a television, car, CD player, video camera, telephone, or computer to an early settler?** Children might respond that a telephone is a special machine that lets people talk to each other whenever they want and wherever they are.

Which modern machine would you not want to do without? Why? Possible response: the computer, because it can be used to communicate, learn, play games, and even watch movies and listen to music

Show What You Know

Performance Assessment Invite children to choose a machine from the chart and then create an advertisement for it that will capture the attention of potential customers—past or present—by showing how the machine will change their lives.

What to Look For Children should be able to show how using the machine will affect the buyer's life. Their ads may also incorporate concrete examples of at least one way the technology has changed.

Using the Activity Book Distribute copies of Activity Book page 66. Ask children to identify what is going on in each picture. Then invite children to choose one activity and draw a picture to show the appliance or machine people use to do the same work today. Allow children to share and compare their drawings and discuss how technology has changed people's lives.

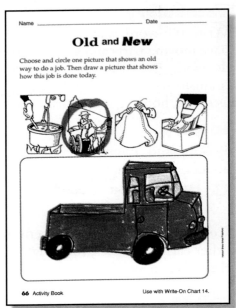

Activity Book page 66

15

MEET ME AT THE MUSEUM

OBJECTIVES
1. Recognize that people and events shape history.
2. Explore our country's heritage through the Smithsonian Institution.

VOCABULARY
museum

RESOURCES
Write-On Chart 15
Clings
Activity Book, p. 67

Meet Individual Needs

VISUAL AND AUDITORY LEARNERS Invite children who have collections to bring them for "Show and Tell." Ask children to tell why they enjoy collecting and the special meaning the items hold for them.

Background

THE SMITHSONIAN INSTITUTION In 1829 British scientist James Smithson left his fortune to the United States to found "an establishment for the increase and diffusion of knowledge among men." In August 1846 the United States Congress created a museum called the Smithsonian. It is governed by a board made up of the Vice President of the United States, the chief justice, three senators, three representatives, and nine citizens. The Smithsonian has grown from one building, the Castle, to a large complex of institutes and facilities, most of which are in Washington, D.C. The Smithsonian preserves and exhibits objects representing American history, the arts, aeronautics and space exploration, science and technology, and natural history. It is also involved in scientific research and exploration and produces a variety of publications.

1. ACCESS

Ask children whether they have any special items they like to collect or save, such as sports cards, dolls, miniature cars, or souvenirs from trips. Explain that while individuals often collect things that have special meaning, so do groups of people, such as our country's government. These special collections are often placed on display for everyone to enjoy.

Q. **Why would a country want to preserve and display certain items?** so that its people can remember the past and the people who did great things.

Focus on the Main Idea

Children will continue to explore their country's heritage as they "tour" several museums—each a part of the Smithsonian Institution in Washington, D.C. Tell children they will discover that Washington, D.C., has many museums to explore, each showing something about the people and events that helped shape our country.

Unit 4: Meet Me at the Museum (Teacher's Edition pp. W47–W49)
Match exhibits to the museums where they would be seen.

Write-On Chart 15

WRITE-ON CHART

Children will identify museums in the Smithsonian and tell where certain exhibits might be displayed.

Star Clings (optional)

ACTIVITY CHOICES

Meet Individual Needs

KINESTHETIC LEARNERS Invite children to bring in objects similar to those that might be in the various museums of the Smithsonian so they can set up a classroom museum. As an alternative, choose one type of exhibit, such as toys, and invite each child to bring in one item for an exhibit.

Link to Science

ENVIRONMENT Discuss the term *natural history*. Explain that items in a natural history museum are often displayed in exhibits that look like their natural settings. Then have children create a shoe-box diorama for an insect or other animal by drawing and coloring a background on the inside of the box and placing objects from nature inside.

2. BUILD

Visual Analysis

Learn from Pictures Define *museum* as a place where a collection of important objects is kept. Tell children that museums often display items related to science, art, or history. Explain that the map on Write-On Chart 15 shows where several museums in Washington, D.C., are located and that they are part of a group of museums called the Smithsonian Institution. Ask children how many museums are on the map and have them describe each photograph.

Q. **What do you think the photographs stand for?** They stand for the kinds of things you can see in each museum.

Explain that the Castle was the original Smithsonian and is now used as an office building. Then say the name of each building—the Castle, Museum of Arts and Industries, Hirshhorn Museum and Sculpture Garden, National Air and Space Museum, Museum of Natural History, National Museum of American History, and National Gallery of Art. Give children clues about each museum and have them find and label it on the Write-On Chart. Then invite volunteers to draw a line from each exhibit pictured to the museum where it is housed. You may wish to have children place a Star Cling on each museum as they identify it.

History

People and Events Across Time and Place Emphasize how the Smithsonian can help us learn about the people and events that shaped our nation.

Q. **Why do you think Amelia Earhart and her plane are important?** She tested new planes and new ways to fly so that we could improve them.

3. CLOSE

Ask children to summarize the lesson by inviting them to explain what the Smithsonian Institution is and why it is important to the people of America.

Check Understanding

The child can
—— recognize that people and events shape history.
—— explore our country's heritage through the Smithsonian Institution.

Think Critically

Q. **Which museum would you want to visit? Why?** Accept all reasonable responses, such as the National Museum of American History because it shows how people in America used to live.

What items or activities of today do you think might be shown in future exhibits as our contributions to our country's heritage? Accept all reasonable responses, such as computers and faxes; people working to save the environment; music; or models of modern buildings.

Show What You Know

Performance Assessment   Have children look through magazines and cut out three pictures—one to reflect an important recent event, one to show an object that is important to our culture, and one to honor people who are making history today. Challenge children to explain which museums exhibits honoring these people, objects, or events would be displayed in and why.

What to Look For   Children should be able to recognize people, objects, and events that are shaping our nation today.

Using the Activity Book   Distribute copies of Activity Book page 67. Ask children to draw a picture of something they would like to see added to the Museum of Natural History, the National Museum of American History, or the National Air and Space Museum as an example of our heritage, our people, or current events.

Activity Book page 67

Extend and Enrich

CATEGORIZE PICTURES   Provide magazines, such as *Smithsonian*, and ask children to choose pictures that interest them. Then invite the class to categorize the pictures into areas of interest, with each area representing a different kind of museum.

Reteach the Main Idea

CATEGORIZE EXHIBITS   Provide children with the following list and ask them to identify the museum on the Write-On Chart in which each item is probably displayed:

Alexander Graham Bell's first telephone (National Museum of American History); Elias Howe's first sewing machine (National Museum of American History); a dinosaur exhibit (Museum of Natural History); sculptures and paintings (Hirshhorn Museum); *Skylab* space station (National Air and Space Museum)

Community Involvement

Take children to a museum in your community. Arrange to have the curator speak with children about how exhibits are chosen, assembled, and cared for. When you return to class, invite children to discuss what they learned about museums.

16

"I HAVE A DREAM"

Link to Science

CAUSE AND EFFECT Invite a volunteer to drop a pebble into a pond, a puddle, or a container of still water. Point out the way the ripples spread outward all the way to the water's edge. Present the analogy that one person's actions, however small, can spread to affect many others, including people that person has never met.

Link to Health

DISEASE PREVENTION AND CONTROL Guide children to realize that some people work for the good health of others in their communities. Explain that certain diseases, such as measles, mumps, and polio, can spread quickly throughout a community. Tell children that many such diseases can be prevented by immunizing people against them. Ask children to check with family members whether their immunizations are up-to-date. If so, children could create and wear a button proclaiming, "I'm immune! No disease for me!"

OBJECTIVES

1. Explore ways to maintain or improve the quality of life.
2. Identify individuals who have made contributions to our country and the world.

VOCABULARY
volunteer

RESOURCES
Write-On Chart 16
Clings
Activity Book, p. 68
Music Audio, "Together"

1. ACCESS

Help children recall the American Portraits lesson in this unit. Remind them of the people discussed in that lesson and how they changed history. Refresh their memory of Dr. Martin Luther King, Jr., and the work he did to obtain civil rights for all Americans. Read aloud or, if possible, play a recording of Dr. King's speech "I Have a Dream." Explain that Dr. King's dream of equality of all people helped him continue to work toward that goal even when he faced hardships.

Q. **How did Dr. King work to make his dream come true?** He led peaceful marches; he talked to people about his ideas.

Focus on the Main Idea

In this lesson children will learn about the following famous people who, by following their dreams, worked or are working to make the world a better place in which to live: César Chávez, Rachel Carson, Rosalynn and Jimmy Carter, Christa McAuliffe, Louis Braille, and Maya Angelou. Children explore ways to make life better in their own communities, their country, and the world. Tell children that they will learn about the dreams of some famous people who have worked to make the world a better place in which to live.

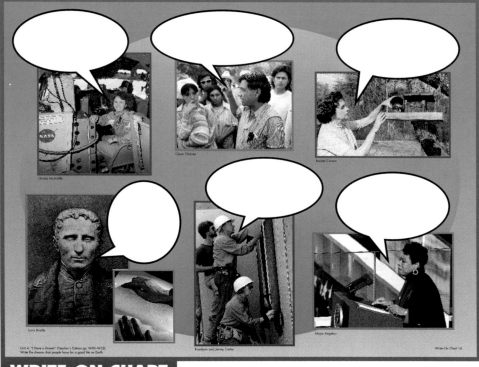

Children use a dry-erase marker to fill in the speech balloon above each person with words that summarize that person's dream for making the world a better place.

Geo Georgie Clings (optional)

2. BUILD

Vocabulary

Draw attention to Rosalynn and Jimmy Carter by circling their picture or using a Geo Georgie Cling as a pointer. Ask children what they think the people in this picture are doing. Explain that Jimmy Carter is a former President and that he and his wife do volunteer work with Habitat for Humanity, an organization that builds houses for the poor. He said that we "share with them the responsibility of finding a better future. Then let them do their work and have control over what goes on." Define *volunteer* as someone who works to help others without being paid.

Q. **In what ways can you volunteer to help your community?**
pick up litter, visit older people, or join a group—such as the Boy Scouts or Girl Scouts—that helps others.

History

People and Events Across Time and Place   Explain that other people have worked to make life better for people. One at a time, direct attention to César Chávez, Rachel Carson, Christa McAuliffe, Louis Braille, and Maya Angelou. Use information from Background to describe their contributions to society. Then invite volunteers to write words in the speech balloons to summarize each person's dream.

Civics and Government

Rights and Responsibilities of Citizens   Point out that ordinary citizens, such as many of the people on the Write-On Chart, can accomplish extraordinary things if they have a dream for the future and work to make it come true. People can use their skills and work hard to make life better for everyone.

ACTIVITY CHOICES

Background

CÉSAR CHÁVEZ   Chávez worked to help migrant farm workers win fair wages and safe working conditions. He said, "The fight is never about grapes or lettuce. It is always about people."

RACHEL CARSON   Carson inspired environmental protection measures against pesticides. She said, "The history of life on earth has been a history of interaction between living things and their surroundings."

CHRISTA MCAULIFFE   NASA chose McAuliffe to be the first teacher to travel in space. She died in the explosion of the *Challenger* space shuttle. She believed that children are part of a living history and should participate. She said, "I touch the future. I teach," and she asked her students to "Reach for the stars!"

LOUIS BRAILLE   Braille, a French educator who was blind, invented the braille alphabet, which many people who are blind use for reading and writing.

MAYA ANGELOU   Angelou is a novelist, poet, singer, dancer, actress, editor, and civil rights activist. Her writings stress courage, perseverance, and self-acceptance. She said, "When you volunteer to do something for the community, it is important that you understand you're doing it for yourself."

Extend and Enrich

HELP VOLUNTEERS Help children research various volunteer organizations in their community. Then invite children to select an organization and develop a class project to help that organization. For example, children could plan a fund-raising event to help the local Humane Society.

Reteach the Main Idea

MATCH PEOPLE AND THEIR DEEDS In a column on the board, write the names of the people pictured on Write-On Chart 16. In another column and in a different order, write a brief summary of each person's philosophy or accomplishments. Help children match each name to the summary. Invite a volunteer to draw a line connecting the two.

AUDIO

Use the Unit 6 MUSIC AUDIOCASSETTE to hear the song "Together."

3. CLOSE

Ask children to summarize the lesson by naming other people who help the community, such as volunteers, teachers, and government workers.

Check Understanding

The child can
____ explore ways to maintain or improve the quality of life.
____ identify individuals who have made contributions to our country and the world.

Think Critically

Q. **How does helping others help us?** It makes us feel good about ourselves; it makes life better for everyone; the people you help might help you someday.

What special things have the people on the Write-On Chart done? They have had dreams and have worked to make the world a better place.

Show What You Know

Performance Assessment Invite children to choose a "dreamer" and write a speech for that person. If children need help, suggest the following: Florence Nightingale, Chief Seattle, Mary McLeod Bethune, Roberto Clemente, Jonas Salk, or Mother Teresa.

What to Look For Children should be able to identify their chosen person's dream and how that person went about making his or her dream a reality.

Using the Activity Book Ask children to complete Activity Book page 68 by adding details to the person to create a self-portrait. Then ask children to fill in the speech balloon by describing their dream for making the world a better place.

Activity Book page 68

17

TRAITS OF A GOOD CITIZEN

OBJECTIVES

1. Identify the traits of a good citizen.
2. Recognize that all Americans have rights and responsibilities as citizens.

RESOURCES

Write-On Chart 17
Clings
Activity Book, p. 69
Choices, Choices: Taking Responsibility

1. ACCESS

Ask children to describe where they live. Write their responses on the board. Probe for varied responses that include the local community, town or city, state, and country. Remind children that they can be part of more than one community.

Focus on the Main Idea

In this lesson children will recognize that being a citizen means being a member of various communities and having certain rights and responsibilities. They will study examples of good and bad citizenship and distinguish between the two. Tell children that in this lesson they will meet some good community members and some who are not so good.

ACTIVITY CHOICES

Background

UNITED STATES CITIZENSHIP
People born in the United States are automatically United States citizens. They are called *native citizens*. Naturalization is the legal process by which a foreign-born person becomes a United States citizen. To become a naturalized citizen, a person must have lived in the United States for five years, be at least 18 years old, have good moral character, be loyal to the United States, understand English, know the history of the United States and how the United States government works, and take an oath of allegiance to the United States. Naturalized citizens and native citizens have the same rights except one—a naturalized citizen cannot become President or Vice President of the United States.

Meet Individual Needs

ADVANCED LEARNERS Ask children to list the characteristics they think make a good citizen of the classroom. Elicit from children responses such as *shares with others, obeys classroom rules*, and *respects others and their property*. Review the list of responses, and ask children which traits would apply to being a good citizen of their local community.

Children identify the people who are being good citizens and the people who are not being good citizens. Volunteers complete the sentence telling something a good citizen does.

Triangle and Star Clings (optional)

WRITE-ON CHART

Role-Play

Invite children to role-play each of the situations pictured on the Write-On Chart in which people are acting as good citizens. Then invite them to create a skit for each of the pictures in which people are not practicing good citizenship. These skits should show the opposite behavior from that pictured on the chart. In both cases, have children tell at the end of their skits how good citizenship improves a community.

Meet Individual Needs

AUDITORY LEARNERS Read aloud, one at a time, good and bad citizenship behaviors. For example, your list might include voting, littering, stopping at a stop sign, and parking a bicycle in a neighbor's driveway. Invite children to categorize each action as good or bad citizenship and to tell how the examples of poor actions can be improved.

2. BUILD

Critical Thinking

Introduce Write-On Chart 17, and tell children the people pictured are citizens of local, state, and national communities. Explain that a good citizen works with others to make these communities better places to live. Have children brainstorm ways people can show good citizenship. Then invite them to describe what they see in each picture. Ask children to indicate, using a dry-erase marker or Triangle and Star Clings, whether the person is being a good citizen or not being a good citizen. Invite volunteers to complete sentences in the write-in box by describing things good citizens would do.

Q. **What can the people who are not being good citizens do to become good citizens?** They can obey the traffic laws, throw their trash in a basket, and respect others' property.

Civics and Government

Rights and Responsibilities of Citizens Direct children's attention to the people on the Write-On Chart who are not being good citizens. Ask children why those people's behavior is not considered "good." Explain that though we have rights and freedoms as citizens of the United States, we also have responsibilities, such as respecting the rights and property of others.

Q. **What can you do to be a responsible citizen?** follow rules, treat everyone fairly, set a good example

3. CLOSE

Invite children to nominate a boy and a girl as Good Citizens of the Week. Have nominators explain why they made the choices they did. List good-citizenship qualities on the board as they are mentioned. Complete the process by allowing children to vote for the candidate they feel best fits the description on the board.

Check Understanding

The child can
____ identify the traits of a good citizen.
____ recognize that all Americans have rights and responsibilities as citizens.

Think Critically

Q. **Why is voting a way to be a good citizen?** It is a way to make sure that people get the leaders and the laws that they want.

Why should all people be good citizens? If all people were good citizens, everyone would be treated with respect, everyone would get along more peacefully, and our communities would be better and safer places to live.

Show What You Know

Performance Assessment Provide children with newspapers, and ask them to skim for photos and headlines that illustrate examples of good and bad citizenship. Have children cut these out and display them on a chart or bulletin board that has been divided into two parts, one titled *Good Citizens* and the other *Not-So-Good Citizens*.

What to Look For Children should be able to distinguish acts of good citizenship from acts of not-so-good citizenship.

Using the Activity Book Distribute copies of Activity Book page 69. Have children unscramble the letters to spell words that describe acts of good citizenship. Then have them match the words and pictures by writing each letter in the appropriate box.

Activity Book page 69

Extend and Enrich

INTERVIEW CITIZENS Invite children to conduct interviews with adults they know to find out about other responsibilities Americans have as citizens. Children can compile their findings into one list that might include responsibilities such as serving on a jury, responding to the United States census, running for office, taking care of the environment, and serving in the armed forces.

Reteach the Main Idea

IDENTIFY BEHAVIORS On separate pieces of paper, write examples of good and poor citizenship. Have children select one piece of paper at a time from a box and tell whether the behavior is that of a good citizen or not. Record children's responses. Ask children to explain their reasons.

TECHNOLOGY

Use CHOICES, CHOICES:™ TAKING RESPONSIBILITY to explore fairness and personal responsibility.

18

THE PEOPLE'S GOVERNMENT

ACTIVITY CHOICES

Link to Art

SHAPE AND PATTERN Ask children to choose a familiar object to draw, such as a pen or a pencil sharpener, and to label the parts. Ask children to write directions that will help the diagram explain how to operate or put together the object. When children are finished, allow them to share their diagrams with the class.

Meet Individual Needs

TACTILE LEARNERS Provide plastic figures of people or clay for children to create their own figures of people who belong to their families, clubs, or sports teams. Invite children to arrange the figures to illustrate the structure of these organizations.

OBJECTIVES

1. Read a diagram showing the structure of government and how its powers are balanced.
2. Recognize how the government represents Americans.

RESOURCES

Write-On Chart 18
Clings
Activity Book, p. 70

1. ACCESS

Ask children to think of a time when they got a new toy or model that had to be put together. Have them tell how they knew what to do. Display a set of directions containing a diagram for putting together a toy. Elicit the idea that the words and the diagram explain how to put the toy together. Remind children that a diagram is a drawing or plan that explains how to do something, how something operates, or how the parts of something are related. For example, a family tree is a diagram that explains how the members of a family are related. You may wish to review diagramming skills in Unit 3.

Focus on the Main Idea

In this lesson children will build on what they previously learned about the three branches of the United States government. They will identify each branch and its function using an organizational diagram. Tell children that in this lesson they will study a diagram that shows how our government works.

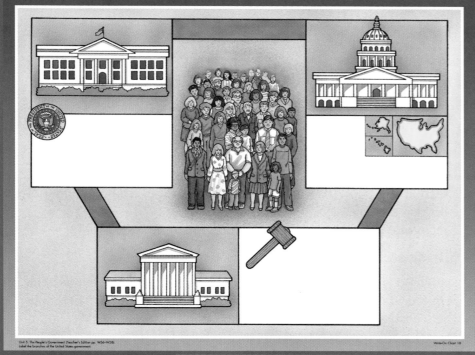

Unit 5: The People's Government (Teacher's Edition pp. W56-W58)
Label the branches of the United States government.

Write-On Chart 18

Children and teacher label the branches of government and list the responsibilities of each branch.

Star Clings (optional)

2. BUILD

Visual Analysis

Learn from a Diagram   Remind children that in Lesson 2, they learned about the three branches of the United States government. Explain that the diagram on Write-On Chart 18 will help children better see how our government works. Ask children to name the three branches of the United States government and tell how they know which is which on the diagram. Discuss the significance of each of the images on the diagram. Conclude by asking volunteers to label on the diagram each of the branches of government.

Civics and Government

Political Institutions and Processes   Brainstorm with children the various jobs, duties, and functions of the people in each of the branches of the government. As each idea is mentioned, help a volunteer record it in the box on the Write-On Chart. Ask children questions concerning the responsibilities of each branch and have them place a Star Cling on the appropriate branch. For example, *Who would say that someone did not get a fair trial? Who would pass a law to give money for studying space? Who would talk to the leader of another country?* Emphasize that our government starts with the people who elected its members.

Q. **How do ordinary citizens play a part in government?** by voting for people to represent them; by finding out about government by reading and talking; by writing letters to or calling lawmakers in Congress to tell how they feel about things

Background

CONGRESS   Congress consists of two houses: the Senate and the House of Representatives. Their primary task is to make laws, but they also approve federal appointments and treaties, conduct investigations, propose constitutional amendments, confirm Presidential election results, impeach and try federal officials, and review the conduct of their own members.

THE PRESIDENT   The President has seven basic roles: chief executive, commander in chief, foreign policy director, legislative leader, party head, popular leader, and chief of state. The President enforces federal laws, treaties, and federal court rulings; develops federal policies; prepares the national budget; and appoints federal officials.

SUPREME COURT   The Supreme Court is the highest court in the land. Its basic duty is to determine whether federal, state, and local governments are acting according to the Constitution. The Court has nine members, who decide cases requiring interpretation of the Constitution and those having to do with federal laws and treaties. The Court also decides disputes in which the United States or two or more states are involved.

Extend and Enrich

RESEARCH GOVERNMENT JOBS

Tell children there are many people who help the President lead the country. Invite children to find out about the jobs of the Vice President, Cabinet members, and ambassadors and share their findings with the class.

Reteach the Main Idea

PIECE TOGETHER A DIAGRAM

Write the name of each branch of the United States government on an 8 1/2 × 11 inch sheet of paper. On smaller pieces of paper, write the names of corresponding buildings, symbols, and job descriptions. Allow children to manipulate these papers into an arrangement that depicts the organization of the three branches. Periodically ask children to explain why they put a piece of paper where they did.

3. CLOSE

Ask children to summarize the lesson by telling how the United States government works for Americans.

Check Understanding

The child can

___ read a diagram showing the structure of government and how its powers are balanced.

___ recognize how the government represents Americans.

Think Critically

Q. **Why do you think the writers of the Constitution divided the United States government into three equal parts?** so they could help each other; so they could share responsibilities of government

In a famous speech, Abraham Lincoln talked about government "of the people, by the people, for the people." What do you think he meant? We vote for our leaders and they make the laws we want.

Show What You Know

 Performance Assessment Have children draw a simple diagram to illustrate the balance of power within the three branches of the United States government.

What to Look For Children should identify the three branches of government, showing that they have equal power but separate responsibilities.

Using the Activity Book Distribute copies of Activity Book page 70. Have children cut out the blocks and, on a separate sheet of paper, create an organizational chart of their school. Remind children that the person with the most authority goes at the top and the ones with the least authority go at the bottom. **Note:** You may have to adjust this activity if your school's management structure is different.

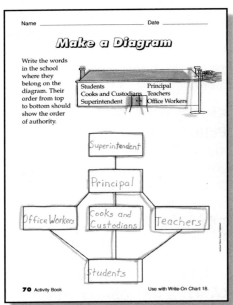

Activity Book page 70

19

STATE FLAGS

OBJECTIVES

1. Explain the significance of flags used as symbols.
2. Explore the symbolism used on state flags.

VOCABULARY

flag

RESOURCES

Write-On Charts 19, 26
Clings
Pupil Book/Unit Big Book, pp. A4–A5
Activity Book, p. 71
Music Audio, "There Are Many Flags"

1. ACCESS

Play "There Are Many Flags" or another song about the national flag, and invite children to sing along. Point out that this song refers to the United States flag—a symbol of our country. Ask children to recall what they learned in Lesson 1 about the flag and other symbols of our country. Review the meanings of the stars and the stripes.

Q. **Where are some places you might see the United States flag?**
outside public buildings such as the post office, library, and court-house; at school; in a parade

Focus on the Main Idea

In this lesson children will review the significance of flags as symbols and will explore the symbolism depicted on state flags. Tell children that in this lesson they will identify the state flag of each of the 50 states. Then they will create their own flag to represent their school or local community.

ACTIVITY CHOICES

Background

FLAGS There are many kinds of flags besides national flags. Among them are those representing states, cities, clubs, and schools. Most flags use one or more of these basic colors—red, white, blue, green, yellow, black, purple and orange. The colors are often symbols, such as red for bravery, white for purity, and blue for loyalty. Many state flags display the state's seal and symbols that represent important industries in the state. Among other symbols used on state flags are symbols of agriculture, commerce, industry, and hard work. The number of stars on a flag may indicate the order in which the state joined the union.

AUDIO

 Use the UNIT 5 MUSIC AUDIOCASSETTE to help children learn "There Are Many Flags."

Home Involvement

Invite children and family members to look for flags as they go about their daily business. Children might record their sightings in a notebook. Invite them to sketch or write a few words to describe each flag they see and to note where they see it.

Children identify each state and its flag. They write each state capital's name beneath the appropriate state flag.
Geo Georgie Cling (optional)

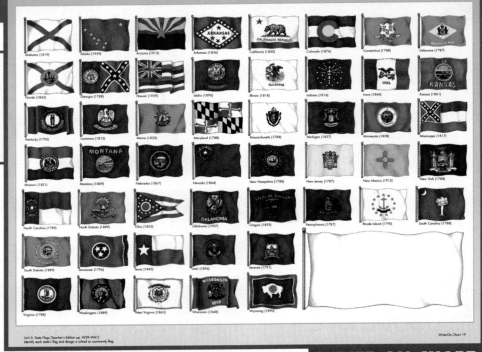

ACTIVITY CHOICES

Link to Language Arts

GRAMMAR, MECHANICS, USAGE
Point out that the flags on the chart are positioned in alphabetical order according to state name. Practice alphabetizing state names with the class. Provide children with lists of five states and ask them to alphabetize the names. Allow children to check each other's work using the chart for reference.

Meet Individual Needs

TACTILE LEARNERS Provide real flags for children to examine. Ask them to describe the colors and the symbols on each. Suggest that they touch each color as they name it and that they trace the shapes with their fingers. Discuss the symbolism used on each flag.

ADVANCED LEARNERS Help children make a time line on mural paper or Write-On Chart 26 to show when each of the 50 states was admitted into the union. Children can make pictures of the state flags to cut and paste onto the time line in order.

Background

ALASKA'S FLAG Children might be interested to hear that using Ursa Major (the Big Dipper) on Alaska's state flag was the idea of a thirteen-year-old boy from Chignik, Alaska. Benny Benson's design was adopted in 1927.

2. BUILD

Visual Analysis

Compare Pictures Direct children's attention to the Write-On Chart. Explain that each state in the United States has its own flag. Ask children to open their books to pages A4–A5 for reference, or display a wall map of the United States that has the state names filled in.

Q. **Why do you think states have flags?** to act as symbols of state government; to stand for and honor the state

Ask for a volunteer to place Geo Georgie on your state flag or to circle it. Ask questions such as *What color is the flag? What do the pictures on it show?* and *What do you think the pictures stand for?* Invite volunteers to choose another flag on the map and tell how it is like their state flag. Discuss what the symbols on the other state flags might mean. As children discuss each flag, ask for a volunteer to write the name of that state's capital below the flag on the Write-On Chart.

Q. **How are the state flags alike? How are they different?** Many flags have the colors red, white, and blue. Many have stripes. Some flags have pictures on them, but others don't.

Invite children to take turns giving clues about different flags on the map. Once a classmate guesses a flag, have him or her circle the correct flag or place the Geo Georgie Cling on it. Then invite children to create a flag to represent their school or local community. Help children develop symbols that represent the school or local community and the people who live and work there.

3. CLOSE

Ask children to summarize the lesson by telling why states have patriotic symbols such as flags.

Check Understanding

The child can
—— explain the significance of flags used as symbols.
—— explore the symbolism used on state flags.

Think Critically

Q. **Pick a symbol often used on state flags. Why do you think it is used so often?** Children should be able to recognize symbols on various flags. Their responses should make logical connections between the symbol and the important quality it stands for.

Show What You Know

Performance Assessment Provide children with paper and crayons or markers, and ask them to design a flag that represents themselves. Encourage them to develop one or more symbols for the flag that tell something about themselves.

What to Look For Children should show an understanding of symbols as pictures that represent something else. The symbols they choose should in some way reflect their personalities, backgrounds, and likes or dislikes.

Using the Activity Book Distribute copies of Activity Book page 71 to each child. If necessary, explain how the code works—each number stands for the letter above it. After children decode the state names, you might suggest that they find the corresponding flags on Write-On Chart 19.

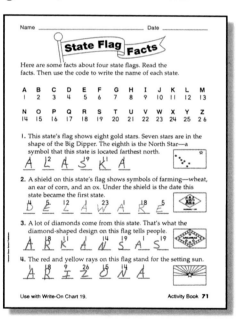

Activity Book page 71

Extend and Enrich

FOLD FLAGS Tell children that as a symbol of our country the United States flag should be honored. Explain that one way we honor the flag is in the way we care for it. When not in use, the flag should be folded in a special way—the way used in the military. The flag should be folded twice lengthwise, forming a long strip. Then, starting at the striped end, it should be folded into a series of triangles. Provide children with sheets of paper to practice this traditional method of folding. You may wish to invite someone from a local military unit, veterans' organization, or scouting organization to demonstrate the folding and discuss flag etiquette.

Reteach the Main Idea

PLAY "I SPY" Display Write-On Chart 19, and play a game of "I Spy" with children. Provide clues such as *I spy a flag that is red, white, and blue. It has one white star on it.* Call on a child to find and circle the flag. Help children identify the name of the state that the flag represents. Then discuss the symbols on the flag.

Multicultural Link

Display flags or pictures of flags representing the countries of origin of children in your class who were born outside the United States. Discuss the symbols on the flags, and have children compare the symbols with those on the United States flag. You may wish to have children make replicas of these flags and display them on the bulletin board.

20
LET FREEDOM RING

Background

THE BILL OF RIGHTS Soon after the Constitution was approved by the states, ten amendments were added. These changes are called the Bill of Rights. This bill ensures that all Americans have the following rights and freedoms: 1. freedom of religion, speech, and the press and the right to meet peacefully to complain of government wrongdoing; 2. the right to bear arms; 3. freedom from the military taking over one's home; 4. freedom from search and seizure without probable cause; 5. freedom from imprisonment without indictment by a grand jury, from being tried twice for the same crime, and from being made to witness against oneself; 6. the right to have a speedy trial and to have defense counsel; 7. the right to a trial by jury in civil cases; 8. freedom from excessive bail and from cruel and unusual punishment; 9. basic human rights and freedoms not enumerated in the Bill of Rights; 10. all powers not specifically given to the federal government are granted by the Bill of Rights to the individual states or to the people directly.

OBJECTIVES

1. Appreciate freedoms that United States citizens enjoy.
2. Recognize that our basic freedoms are protected by the Bill of Rights.

VOCABULARY

Constitution

RESOURCES

Write-On Charts 20, 27
Activity Book, p. 72
The Amazing Writing Machine

1. ACCESS

Remind children that the Constitution is the framework for our government. Ask children to recall what they learned in Lesson 2 about the United States Constitution. Write their responses on the board in a simple word web centered on the word *Constitution*.

Q. **Why do you think the United States Constitution has lasted for over 200 years?** Early leaders wrote it so that it would work for all Americans, no matter when they lived.

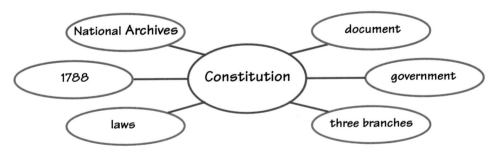

Focus on the Main Idea

Through a series of photos depicting Americans enjoying some of their freedoms, children will develop an awareness that they also enjoy these freedoms and are protected by the Bill of Rights. Tell children that in this lesson they will learn about a part of the Constitution called the Bill of Rights, which outlines the freedoms Americans enjoy.

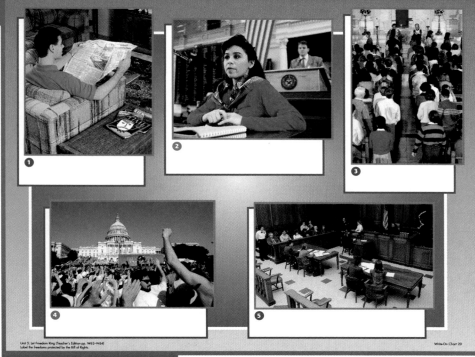

Unit 5: Let Freedom Ring (Teacher's Edition pp. W62–W64)
Label the freedoms protected by the Bill of Rights.

Write-On Chart 20

WRITE-ON CHART

Children identify the freedoms pictured and label them with a dry-erase marker.

2. BUILD

Visual Analysis

Learn from Pictures Ask children to describe each picture on the Write-On Chart and identify the freedom it illustrates. Call on volunteers to use a dry-erase marker to label the freedoms. Point out that although some people may take these freedoms for granted, there are places in the world where people do not enjoy such freedoms. Discuss the Bill of Rights and the freedoms it guarantees for all United States citizens.

Q. **Why do you think freedom is important to Americans?** People are happier when they are free; we fought for freedom a long time ago; freedom has made our country strong and important in the world.

History

People and Events Across Time and Place Continue to discuss why these freedoms are important to Americans and what our people have done to gain and keep them. Point out that every child in the class who is not a Native American came from another country or has parents, grandparents, or other ancestors who came from another country. One of the reasons many people came here was to enjoy freedoms they did not have in their native lands.

ACTIVITY CHOICES

Link to Art

PHOTOGRAPHY Invite children to photograph or find pictures of people engaged in tasks such as going to school, reading a book, or shopping. Display the photos on a bulletin board titled *Let Freedom Ring*. Invite children to write captions describing the freedoms reflected in the photos.

Meet Individual Needs

ENGLISH LANGUAGE LEARNERS Point to each picture on the Write-On Chart and model for children a simple phrase to describe what the picture shows, such as *people praying, people meeting, people speaking*. Then ask children to point to the pictures and describe in their own words what is happening.

Link to Language Arts

JOURNAL Have children record in their journals some of the things they do during one day. Then have them review their entries, thinking about how their activities reflect freedoms and rights protected by the Bill of Rights.

TECHNOLOGY

Use THE AMAZING WRITING MACHINE™ to complete this activity.

Extend and Enrich

RESEARCH ACTIVE CITIZENS

Provide a list of people or groups who used their freedoms to make changes in our country; for example: Linda Brown and her parents, who sued the Topeka Board of Education for the integration of schools; Dorothea Dix, who led the drive to build state hospitals for the mentally ill and improve prison conditions; and Eleanor Roosevelt, who worked to improve living conditions for the disadvantaged in this country. Invite children to research and report to the class about a person or group like these.

Reteach the Main Idea

WEB FREEDOMS Make a word web on the board, or use Write-On Chart 27, and write *Freedoms* in the center. Invite children to name freedoms they and other Americans enjoy. Record their responses in the web. Then discuss with children what the freedoms are and why they are important to them.

Multicultural Link

Tell children that one reason many people have come to live in America is for religious freedom. As a result, many religions are represented in the United States. The largest religion in the nation is Christianity, which includes Catholicism, the Protestant religions, and Mormonism. Some other religions represented are Judaism, Islam, and Buddhism.

3. CLOSE

Ask children to take turns describing a freedom and telling why it is important to him or her.

Check Understanding

The child can
____ explore the idea of freedom in America.
____ identify freedoms that United States citizens enjoy.
____ recognize that our basic freedoms are protected by the Bill of Rights.

Think Critically

Q **What does *freedom of speech* mean?** that people can express their opinions without being hurt or thrown in jail if others disagree. You may wish to discuss the limits of free speech to prevent slander—false or damaging speech.

How does being able to express different opinions help a country? People understand things better when they hear different opinions. When people understand better, they can make choices that better help their country.

Show What You Know

Performance Assessment Invite children to write a paragraph, poem, or story showing what freedom means to them. Allow children to freely choose a medium of expression.

What to Look For Children's expressions should show an understanding of the freedoms and rights that United States citizens enjoy.

Using the Activity Book Distribute copies of Activity Book page 72. Invite children to draw lines to match each freedom with the picture that illustrates it.

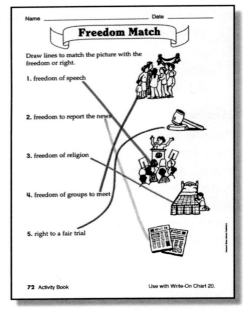

Activity Book page 72

21

BE A PIONEER

OBJECTIVES

1. Recognize that people and events shape history.
2. Identify ways that people adapt to and change their environment.

RESOURCES

Write-On Charts 21, 28
Clings
Activity Book, p. 73
Transparencies 20, 21, 22
The Amazing Writing Machine

1. ACCESS

Direct children's attention to a map of the United States. Explain that early settlers lived mostly along the coasts. Point out that most of the country was not yet settled by Europeans and was occupied by American Indians. However, settlers soon began to move inland to find new places to live.

Q. How do you think people learned about new lands to settle?
Responses might include that people heard about the lands from explorers or traders.

Why do you think people wanted to move? Children might suggest that people wanted land, adventure, or more space.

Focus on the Main Idea

In this lesson children will explore what life was like for pioneers as they forged westward across the continent. Tell children that they will pretend to be pioneers, traveling along the Oregon Trail on a 2,000-mile journey that will take nearly six months.

ACTIVITY CHOICES

Background

WESTWARD MOVEMENT During the first of two great westward migrations between 1760 and 1850, thousands of pioneers struggled across the Appalachian Mountains, pushing the United States frontier to the Mississippi River valley. By the 1840s, news of great forests and fertile lands in what is now Oregon had sparked a second migration.

THE OREGON TRAIL Travelers to the West usually gathered in St. Louis, Missouri, and traveled by steamboat on the Missouri River to Independence, Missouri. From there, they organized themselves into wagon trains to cross the prairies to Fort Kearny, Nebraska. Then they traveled on the Platte River to Fort Laramie, Wyoming. They followed the North Platte River and crossed the Rocky Mountains to the Green River valley at Fort Bridger, Wyoming. Then, they turned northwest to Fort Hall, Idaho, and followed the Snake River to Fort Boise, Idaho. They crossed the Blue Mountains and traveled down the Columbia River to Fort Vancouver and the Willamette Valley of Oregon. The journey took six months and was a test of strength and endurance.

Children list or draw things they would take as pioneers on a journey in a covered wagon.

Weather Clings (optional)

Pioneer Supplies

Food (flour, sugar, salt, bacon)
Household goods (iron stoves, pots and pans, beds and bedding, furniture, clothing)
Tools (axes, knives, nails, rope)
Animals (horses, mules, cattle, oxen)

Unit 6: Be a Pioneer (Teacher's Edition pp. W65-W67)
Draw things you might need if you were a pioneer.

Write-On Chart 21

WRITE-ON CHART

ACTIVITY CHOICES

Meet Individual Needs

TACTILE LEARNERS Display a map of the United States and help children trace the Oregon Trail. Point out that much of the trail followed the rivers, and invite children to speculate why.

TRANSPARENCY

Use TRANSPARENCIES 20, 21, and 22 to trace the Oregon Trail.

Link to Mathematics

COMPUTATION AND ESTIMATION Explain that wagon trains traveled between 15 and 20 miles a day, stopping only at noon and at night. Help children estimate and then compute how far a caravan could have traveled in a week and in a month at 15 miles a day and at 20 miles a day.

Meet Individual Needs

VISUAL LEARNERS Draw a Venn diagram on chart paper, or use Write-On Chart 28, and invite children to compare lives of the pioneers with the lives of people of today. Have them add to the chart as they learn about pioneers.

2. BUILD

Vocabulary

Define *pioneers* as the men, women, and children who traveled across the country, settling the lands from the Appalachian Mountains to the Pacific Ocean. Ask children how else we might use the word *pioneer*. Explain that sometimes people use the word *pioneer* to refer to someone with a new idea or to someone who breaks new ground in art, music, science, or human relations.

History

People and Events Across Time and Place Ask children to describe and identify the covered wagon on Write-On Chart 21. Help them recognize that many pioneers packed their belongings in covered wagons such as the one pictured and made long and dangerous journeys across America with other families in wagons. Point out that pioneers lived different lives in the homes they left than they did in their new homes in the wilderness. Discuss ways the pioneers changed the lands they settled.

Critical Thinking

Explain that pioneers traveled through unfamiliar land. Emphasize that when they reached their destinations, there were no restaurants, stores, motels, paved roads, detailed maps, repair shops, or homes for them. Invite children to think about what the pioneers might have taken with them on their journeys. Have volunteers record the items on the chart as children list them. Then place different Weather Clings on the chart, one at a time, and ask children to tell how each type of weather might have affected the pioneers' journeys.

3. CLOSE

Read aloud the poem "Old Log House" by James S. Tippett. Invite children to summarize the lesson by telling about the lives of the pioneers.

On a little green knoll
At the edge of the wood
My great great grandmother's
First house stood.
The house was of logs
My grandmother said
With one big room
And a lean-to shed.
The logs were cut
And the house was raised
By pioneer men
In the olden days.

I like to hear
My grandmother tell
How they built the fireplace
And dug the well.
They split the shingles;
They filled each chink;
It's a house of which
I like to think.
Forever and ever
I wish I could
Live in a house
At the edge of a wood.

Check Understanding

The child can

——— recognize that people and events shape history.

——— identify ways that people adapt to and change their environment.

Think Critically

Q. **What words and phrases would you use to describe the character of the pioneers?** Children might say *brave, strong, hardworking,* and *daring.*

In what ways do you think the pioneers were like the Pilgrims? Both groups traveled west, settled in new lands, and faced great dangers.

Show What You Know

 Performance Assessment Invite children to write paragraphs persuading people to move to and settle in the West.

What to Look For Children's paragraphs should reveal the adventuresome spirit of the pioneers and the changes they made in our country.

Using the Activity Book Distribute copies of Activity Book page 73, and invite children to pretend they are pioneers writing a letter to a relative in the East. Have them describe their experiences, using the information they learned during the lesson.

Name _____ Date _____

A Letter from the West

Write to a friend or family member back home.
Tell about your wagon journey west.

June 12 ___, 1841

Dear Sarah
Today we saw a herd of buffalo! We ride for hours each day. The prairie is beautiful.

Love,
William

Use with Write-On Chart 21. Activity Book **73**

Activity Book page 73

Extend and Enrich

PLAN FUTURE TRAVEL Invite children to make a list of all the things they would want to take with them if they were part of a pioneer family from the future, going to spend a year in a space station. After they have completed their lists, tell children they can take only half of the things they listed. Challenge them to explain their choices.

Reteach the Main Idea

THINK CRITICALLY Ask children what they think would be the hardest part of a pioneer's life.

Link to Reading

CREATE A SKIT Invite children to read such books as *Going to Town* and *Dance at Grandpa's* from a series by HarperCollins adapted from the Laura Ingalls Wilder books. Then have readers create skits about pioneers.

Link to Language Arts

JOURNAL Ask children to share any experiences they may have had with moving a long way from their homes. Then invite them to write in their journals about how they felt about moving or how they would feel if they were moving away.

TECHNOLOGY

 Use THE AMAZING WRITING MACHINE™ to complete this activity.

22

THE AMERICAS

Meet Individual Needs

TACTILE LEARNERS Duplicate outline maps of the Western Hemisphere, and mount them on posterboard. Ask children to cut out the countries to create map puzzles. Invite partners to work together to reassemble their map puzzles.

Link to Art

COLOR Invite children to explore the use of color on maps and globes. Show them a map or globe, and remind them that blue usually stands for water and green for land. Then give each child a paper plate. Have children paint their plates blue and allow them to dry. Then give each child a copy of a map of the Western Hemisphere. Have children mix yellow and blue to paint the land areas green, let them dry, cut them out, and glue them to their paper plates.

Multicultural Link

Mexico and Central and South America are populated by descendants of native Indians, Africans, and Spaniards. Large groups of the population are mestizos, mixtures of Europeans and Indians. The languages, art and music, and customs of these cultures add to the uniqueness of the Western Hemisphere.

OBJECTIVES

1. Identify neighbors of the United States in the Western Hemisphere, using a map or a globe.
2. Recognize the ways in which neighboring countries depend on one another.

VOCABULARY

hemisphere
cooperation

RESOURCES

Write-On Chart 22
Clings
Activity Book, p. 74
Transparency 23
Trudy's Time and Place House

1. ACCESS

Ask children to name ways neighbors interact with one another and to share experiences they have had with neighbors. Guide children to realize that neighbors often visit one another, help one another, and borrow things from one another.

Q. **Why is it important to know your neighbors?** Visiting neighbors is fun; neighbors can help you; you can learn from your neighbors.

Focus on the Main Idea

In this lesson children identify countries that are neighbors of the United States. They recognize ways neighboring countries interact with and depend on one another. Tell children that in this lesson they will use a map to locate the neighbors of the United States and learn about ways countries depend on one another.

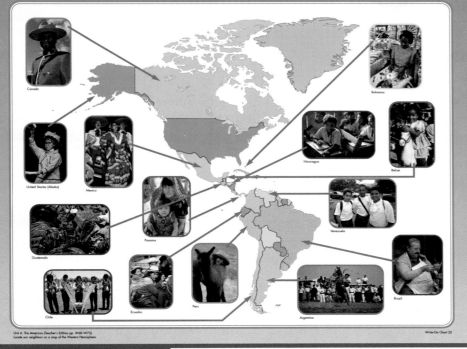

Children label each country on the map and identify the country in which each person pictured lives.

Flag Clings (optional)

2. BUILD

🌐 Geography

Location Explain that the map on Write-On Chart 22 shows one side of a globe. Remind children that a globe is a model of the Earth. Ask volunteers to use a globe to identify the seven continents, the oceans, and the North and South poles. Help children locate North America, Central America, and South America; identify this side of the globe as the Western Hemisphere. Define *hemisphere* as half of a globe.

Human-Environment Interactions Point out the United States on the map, and identify the surrounding countries as neighboring countries. Ask volunteers to place Flag Clings on the map to represent each country. Explain that the people pictured on the chart live in these countries. Then provide information from Background about the countries shown. Invite children to use a dry-erase marker to draw a line from each person to his or her country.

Lead children in a discussion of how people in our country relate to and cooperate with our country's neighbors. For example, we visit one another's countries; we help one another in times of need; we welcome people who move to our country from neighboring countries; we trade goods and services with one another.

Q. **Why are our neighboring countries important to us?** Children might say that neighbors help us in disasters and trade goods with us.

ACTIVITY CHOICES

Background

CANADA Second-largest country in the world; most like our own.

ALASKA (U.S.) Largest state of the United States; home to several Arctic peoples.

MEXICO Some of the oldest Indian cultures live in this mountainous country.

PANAMA A narrow country whose canal connects the Atlantic and Pacific oceans.

GUATEMALA Colorful clothing identifies the different Indian groups; gives us the chicle used in chewing gum.

CHILE Has the driest deserts and the second-highest mountain range in the world; "skinny" country, as long as the United States is wide.

ECUADOR The equator crosses this large exporter of bananas and cacao.

PERU Once the center of Spanish power in South America; also home to the Inca Empire hundreds of years ago.

BAHAMAS Columbus sailed into the clear shallow waters of these coral-surrounded islands off the coast of Florida.

TECHNOLOGY

Use TRUDY'S TIME AND PLACE HOUSE to explore geography.

Background

NICARAGUA Volcanic ash has contributed to its fertile soil; earthquake-prone.

BELIZE English-speaking country; large coral reef teems with tropical fish.

VENEZUELA The world's highest waterfall, Angel Falls, is found in this leading oil-producing country.

ARGENTINA Gauchos herd roaming cattle and horses on the sprawling pampas.

BRAZIL Amazon River flows through rich rain forests; largest country of South America.

Extend and Enrich

MAKE A GUIDEBOOK Invite children to work in small groups to create a guidebook to the Western Hemisphere. Each group should choose a different country and create a fact page for it. Invite children to illustrate their pages with the flag and other symbols of their chosen countries. Suggest that the class choose an artist to create a cover before you bind the guidebook.

Reteach the Main Idea

CONNECT COUNTRIES Use a large map to review the countries of the Western Hemisphere. Help children identify the United States. Provide pieces of string of various lengths. Invite a volunteer to select a piece of string and tack one end of it to the United States and the other end to a neighboring country. Ask the volunteer to name the country at the other end of the string.

TRANSPARENCY

Use TRANSPARENCY 23 to review the countries in the Western Hemisphere.

3. CLOSE

Use a globe or a map of the Western Hemisphere to help children summarize the lesson by locating and naming the countries in the Western Hemisphere. Review with children ways in which neighboring countries interact with one another.

Check Understanding

The child can
   identify neighbors of the United States in the Western Hemisphere, using a map or a globe.
   recognize the ways in which neighboring countries depend on one another.

Think Critically

Q. **What might happen if two countries were not good neighbors?** People might not help each other in disasters; they might go to war with each other.

Why does it make sense for countries to trade goods with their neighbors? It is easier to move goods between countries that are close together.

Show What You Know

Performance Assessment Provide reference materials on the Western Hemisphere. Then have each child choose a country he or she would like to have as a partner. Explain that the children should choose countries that are neighbors of the United States and should name one thing that the United States does to get along with the people of that country. Ask children to identify, by writing or drawing, two things that are the same about the United States and the chosen country and two things that are different.

What to Look For Children's countries of choice should be in the Western Hemisphere; children should indicate an understanding that countries interact with one another in many ways, for example, through tourism, trade, and disaster assistance.

Using the Activity Book Distribute a copy of Activity Book page 74 to each child. Invite children to study the map and answer the questions about the countries of the Western Hemisphere. Suggest that children compare answers with partners.

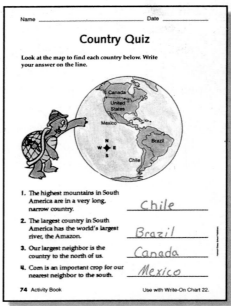

Activity Book page 74

23

CELEBRATIONS AROUND THE WORLD

OBJECTIVES

1. Explore different cultures through their celebrations.

2. Recognize that people all over the world have things in common.

RESOURCES

Write-On Chart 23
Clings
Activity Book, p. 75
The Amazing Writing Machine

1. ACCESS

Ask children to recall some of the customs in their families and the special days celebrated in their community. Invite children to describe some of their favorite special times, identifying holiday foods and customs.

Q. **How are most celebrations alike?** People eat good foods, dance, sing, and honor special people or events.

Focus on the Main Idea

In this lesson children learn about a variety of cultures by exploring their celebrations. They compare elements common to most celebrations, such as decorations, music, dancing, and costumes. Tell children that in this lesson they will celebrate with people from around the world.

ACTIVITY CHOICES

Link to Language Arts

JOURNAL Ask children to name in their journals a celebration from another country. The celebration should be one they would like to know more about. Suggest that they write questions they would like to have answered. For example: What kinds of foods, music, dancing, and decorations are part of the celebration? If children have difficulty thinking of a celebration, you might suggest that they write questions about one held in their family's country of origin.

POETRY Children can work in small groups to write acrostic poems. Distribute to each group a sheet of paper that has the word *HOLIDAYS* written vertically down the page. Instruct children to write a poem about holidays by using one letter of the word to begin each line. Suggest that one group member serve as the recorder while the others illustrate the poem. Invite one group member to serve as the reporter and share the poem with the class. Display children's work in the classroom.

TECHNOLOGY

Use THE AMAZING WRITING MACHINE™ to complete the activities.

Unit 6: Celebrations Around the World (Teacher's Edition pp. W71–W73)
Compare ways that people celebrate around the world.

Write-On Chart 23

WRITE-ON CHART

Children compare and contrast cultural celebrations, identifying elements common to most, such as music, dancing, and costumes.

Geo Flag Clings (optional)

ACTIVITY CHOICES

Background

1. PURIM On the 14th day of the Hebrew month Adar (February or March), the festival of Purim commemorates the rescue of the Jews of Persia from a plot to kill them. This story, called the Megillah, is read aloud in the synagogue. Children enjoy making noise to drown out the name of the villain each time he is mentioned. Purim is a joyous holiday of costumed carnivals and dances.

2. BASTILLE DAY commemorates the creation of France's republic on July 14. It is celebrated with parades, street fairs, and brilliant fireworks.

3. CH'USOK In late summer or early fall, Koreans honor the dead during Autumn's Eve or The Moon Festival. Ch'usok (CHEW•sahk) is a time of thanksgiving and a time for families to reconnect with their past. The oldest male in a family places incense and food on a stone table before the graves of his family's ancestors.

4. DIWALI (DEE•WAH•LEE) is celebrated in India. This Festival of Lights falls in late October or early November. Thousands of tiny clay lamps and colored lights are lit around each house. Children hope the twinkling lights will guide Lakshmi (LAHK•shmee), the goddess of wealth, to their homes.

5. MAY DAY festivals are held in small towns and villages in England on the first day of May. May Day celebrates the coming of spring. Children hold long ribbons as they dance around a decorated Maypole.

2. BUILD

Culture

Shared Humanity and Unique Identity Explain that each segment of the chart shows a celebration from a different culture or country. Use information from Background to identify the pictures in each segment. You may wish to have volunteers place the appropriate Flag Cling to show each culture as you discuss it. Help them to write the names of the holidays in the spaces. Point out that although these celebrations take place in other countries, some Americans from those cultures celebrate them, too. Help children recall that celebrations observe different kinds of events—patriotic, religious, and seasonal. Invite them to use a dry-erase marker to label the category of each holiday pictured.

Thought and Expression Invite children to write sentences on chart paper or on the board to compare the common elements of the celebrations pictured, such as parades, costumes, and dancing.

Q. **How are these celebrations like ones we have in the United States?** Bastille Day is like the Fourth of July because both honor a country's freedom; most celebrations have good food, music, costumes, and people getting together to honor a special person or event.

3. CLOSE

Display Write-On Chart 23. Ask children to summarize the lesson by telling what they have learned about the ways people in each culture celebrate. Invite them to cite U.S. holidays that are similar in some way.

Check Understanding

The child can

—— explore different cultures through their celebrations.

—— recognize that people all over the world have things in common.

Think Critically

Q. **What can you learn about a culture from its celebrations?**
Responses should show that children understand the need for people to honor events and people that are important to them. Celebrations can show what kinds of foods, music, and dancing a culture's people enjoy, as well as what kinds of costumes they wear and decorations they use.

Show What You Know

Performance Assessment Give each child an index card. Ask children to imagine that they have just attended one of the celebrations pictured on Write-On Chart 23. Invite children to create a postcard, on which they describe the event, to send to a friend. Show a real postcard, and suggest that children draw a line down the middle of theirs, too, writing their message on the left side and the name and address of their friend on the right. Ask children to draw on the front of the card things they saw or did at the celebration.

What to Look For Children should name one of the five events pictured and describe some of its elements, such as food, costumes, decorations, music, or dancing. Children's illustrations should accurately reflect the event they describe.

Using the Activity Book Distribute a copy of Activity Book page 75 to each child. Invite children to choose and plan a celebration and to complete the invitation. Ask children to draw a picture about their celebration. After children have cut out their invitations, call on volunteers to share their celebration with the class. Display the invitations on the bulletin board.

Activity Book page 75

Extend and Enrich

CELEBRATE A HOLIDAY Plan a celebration that is observed in the United States as well as in another country—for example, Mexico's Diez y seis de Septiembre (September 16) or Cinco de mayo (May 5). Read poems and stories, sing songs, and play music of the other country. You may wish to have children read or sing for invited family members or for the school. Discuss the selected country's heroes, and display its flags and artifacts. If possible, serve some traditional foods of the country. You may also wish to invite a person from that culture to speak to the class about the holiday.

Reteach the Main Idea

IDENTIFY CELEBRATIONS Bring to class a party hat of the kind worn at birthday parties or New Year's Eve celebrations. Invite children to list common elements of celebrations. As children name *foods, costumes, decorations, music,* and *dancing,* record their responses on slips of paper. Put the slips of paper in the party hat. Invite volunteers to draw a slip of paper, read the element of celebration, and give an example for a particular celebration they know.

HOLIDAY ACTIVITIES

For information and activities related to Christmases Around the World, see the Holiday Activities section at the back of the Teacher's Edition.

24

LEARNING ABOUT OURSELVES AND OTHERS

Multicultural Link

Explain that many cultures express themselves artistically through fabric art. If possible, display some examples of fabric art, such as Mexican embroidery or Japanese paintings on silk, and invite children to compare them.

WRITE-ON CHARTS

Use **WRITE-ON CHART 27** to record ways people tell about themselves.

Link to Art

FOLK ART Invite children to decorate fabric in various ways. They may embroider it with heavy thread, stamp it with potato halves cut into patterns, paste felt cutouts onto it, or draw on it with markers. Display children's fabric art in a class museum.

Link to Reading

READ FOR A PURPOSE Invite children to read *The Whispering Cloth: A Refugee's Story* by Pegi Deitz Shea. It describes brightly colored pa'ndan—embroidered story cloths that portray the Hmong people in Thailand.

OBJECTIVES

1. Draw conclusions about another culture through its art.
2. Explain the importance of knowing about other people.
3. Participate in self-discovery and self-expression through art.

RESOURCES
Write-On Charts 24, 27
Activity Book, p. 77

1. ACCESS

Start a word web with the title *Ways People Tell About Themselves* in the center. List children's ideas about ways people tell about themselves, their families, and their cultures.

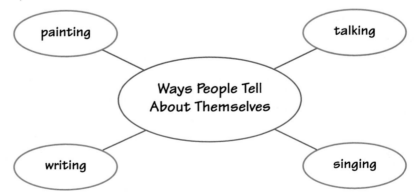

Focus on the Main Idea

In this lesson children explore how people all over the world express themselves and record their histories, using words, pictures, and symbols. Children will create their own symbolic banners to tell others about themselves and their school. Tell them that in this lesson they will describe a mud painting made in West Africa.

Unit 6: Learning About Ourselves and Others (Teacher's Edition pp. W74-W76)
Draw a picture story to communicate something about a group of people.

Write-On Chart 24

WRITE-ON CHART

Children describe the mud painting made on woven cloth and discuss the significance of the symbols used. Then they create their own "story cloth."

2. BUILD

Visual Analysis

Learn from an Artifact   Direct children's attention to the mud painting on Write-On Chart 24. Explain that it is patterned after the mud-on-cloth paintings of the people of West Africa. Then ask children to describe what they see in the painting.

Culture

Thought and Expression   Remind children that a symbol is a simple picture used to stand for an object or an action. Explain that the people of Mali decorated the cloth with symbols that tell about their way of life. Invite children to speculate about the significance of those symbols. Point out the symbols for fish and birds, and help children understand that fishing and raising livestock are probably important to the people of West Africa. Then invite children to plan symbols for a classroom design. Ask volunteers to use dry-erase markers to create school "story cloths" on the chart. Ask children to explain the significance of each symbol they use.

History

People and Events Across Time and Place   Provide children with the information about mud-on-cloth painting from Background. If possible, allow children to examine reference books with photos of the art and artifacts of different countries around the world.

Q. **Why do you think people want to write about or draw pictures about themselves?** They want to be remembered; they like stories; they want to teach others.

Extend and Enrich

COMMUNICATE WITH SYMBOLS

Invite children to explore other methods of communication that employ symbols. Provide examples, such as rebuses, Japanese and Chinese symbols, and Native American pictographs. Ask children to draw the symbols and then use them in telling a story to a friend.

Reteach the Main Idea

REVIEW SYMBOLS   Review Write-On Chart 24 with children. Ask them to describe the symbols on the painting, and guide them to realize what each symbol represents. Point out that each symbol tells us something about the person who made the painting.

Meet Individual Needs

AUDITORY LEARNERS   Children might enjoy making a "sound banner"—a collection of three or four sounds that represent important activities or events. Children can tape-record the sounds or produce them with voices, hands and feet, or noisemakers and invite classmates to guess what the sounds represent.

Link Literature

Invite children to read *Abuela's Weave* by O. S. Castañeda. This book tells the story of a Guatemalan girl and her grandmother who weave beautiful tapestries to sell at a market. Ask children to compare their own ways of life with those of the girl and her grandmother.

3. CLOSE

Ask children to summarize the lesson by inviting them to explain how we can learn about others from story cloths.

Check Understanding

The child can
—— draw conclusions about another culture through its art.
—— explain the importance of knowing about other people.
—— participate in self-discovery and self-expression through art.

Think Critically

Q. **If you could choose only one symbol to represent you on a mud painting, what would it be? Why?** Responses should show that children understand that the symbol they use will help others learn about them.

Why do you think people of West Africa create mud paintings? to express their feelings, to share the things that are important to them

Show What You Know

Performance Assessment   Invite children to create clay sculptures that show something about themselves. Then ask children to exchange their completed sculptures with partners. Have each child describe what he or she can tell about the partner by looking at the sculpture.

What to Look For   Children's symbols should reveal what is important to them.

Using the Activity Book   Distribute Activity Book page 77. Explain that Mandy stitched a picture to tell about herself and her family. Invite pairs of children to examine and discuss the picture. Then have partners work together to write a paragraph telling what they have learned about Mandy by looking at her picture. Invite partners to share their paragraphs with other pairs.

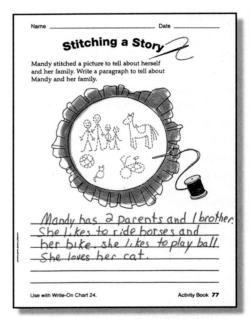

Activity Book page 77

Scope and
Sequence

Scope and Sequence

Harcourt Brace Social Studies builds consistent and cumulative learning from Kindergarten through Grade 6. The program allows students at each level to build on major understandings and skills already acquired and to prepare for learning yet to come. The powerful ideas in *Harcourt Brace Social Studies* provide the principal contexts within which students can integrate major understandings, skills, and their own experiences. These powerful ideas have been selected to help students organize their thinking and develop the competencies they will need as citizens in a diverse, changing, and interdependent world.

THE POWERFUL IDEAS
THEMES AND STRANDS OF SOCIAL STUDIES

Commonality and Diversity

Interaction Within Different Environments

OUR WORLD
Geography
History
Civics and Government
Economics
Culture

Continuity and Change

Individualism and Interdependence

Conflict and Cooperation

Major Understandings

	K	1	2	3	4	5	6
Geography							
understanding location	•	•	•	•	•	•	•
relative and absolute (exact) location		•	•	•	•	•	•
factors influencing location		•	•	•	•	•	•
understanding place	•	•	•	•	•	•	•
physical features (landforms, bodies of water, vegetation)	•	•	•	•	•	•	•
human or cultural features		•	•	•	•	•	•
understanding human-environment interactions	•	•	•	•	•	•	•
seasons and climate	•	•	•	•	•	•	•
land use and natural resources	•	•	•	•	•	•	•
conservation and pollution	•	•	•	•	•	•	•
population density				•	•	•	•
understanding movement	•	•	•	•	•	•	•
people (immigration, colonization, settlement patterns)		•	•	•	•	•	•
products (trade)	•	•	•	•	•	•	•
ideas (cultural borrowing and cultural diffusion)		•	•	•	•	•	•
understanding regions		•	•	•	•	•	•
physical regions		•	•	•	•	•	•
cultural regions		•	•	•	•	•	•
political regions			•	•	•	•	•
economic regions			•	•	•	•	•
functional regions					•	•	•
time zones					•	•	•
History							
understanding time patterns and relationships among events	•	•	•	•	•	•	•
sequence of events (indefinite time order)	•	•	•	•	•	•	•
chronology (definite time order)		•	•	•	•	•	•
cause and effect		•	•	•	•	•	•
identifying and using historical evidence	•	•	•	•	•	•	•
types of evidence		•	•	•	•	•	•
quality of evidence		•	•	•	•	•	•
understanding the importance of individuals and groups across time and place	•	•	•	•	•	•	•
leaders and achievers	•	•	•	•	•	•	•
all people make a difference	•	•	•	•	•	•	•
founders and first persons		•	•	•	•	•	•
contributors to change	•	•	•	•	•	•	•
understanding the importance of events across time and place	•	•	•	•	•	•	•
innovations and inventions		•	•	•	•	•	•
impacts and turning points				•	•	•	•
revolutions and transformations				•	•	•	•
debates and controversies				•	•	•	•
understanding the times in which people lived	•	•	•	•	•	•	•
historical empathy		•	•	•	•	•	•
understanding origins, spread, and influence	•	•	•	•	•	•	•
growth and expansion			•	•	•	•	•

• A bullet indicates levels at which understandings are introduced, taught, applied, reinforced, or extended.
For more detailed information, refer to the index for each level.

	K	1	2	3	4	5	6
development of ideas					•	•	•
connecting past with present	•	•	•	•	•	•	•
comparing past with present	•	•	•	•	•	•	•

Civics and Government

	K	1	2	3	4	5	6
understanding patriotic identity	•	•	•	•	•	•	•
flags, symbols, anthems, mottoes, and pledges	•	•	•	•	•	•	•
patriotic customs, celebrations, and traditions	•	•	•	•	•	•	•
understanding civic values	•	•	•	•	•	•	•
recognizing and respecting authority figures	•	•	•	•	•	•	•
accepting and respecting others	•	•	•	•	•	•	•
working for the common good	•	•	•	•	•	•	•
understanding democratic principles	•	•	•	•	•	•	•
citizens as the source of government's authority			•	•	•	•	•
due process and equal protection under the law				•	•	•	•
majority rule and minority rights				•	•	•	•
government by law		•	•	•	•	•	•
understanding rights and freedoms of citizens	•	•	•	•	•	•	•
voting rights, property rights, civil rights, human rights		•	•	•	•	•	•
freedom of expression, worship, assembly, movement		•	•	•	•	•	•
understanding the responsibilities of citizens		•	•	•	•	•	•
voluntary responsibilities (voting, keeping informed)		•	•	•	•	•	•
responsibilities under the law (obeying laws, paying taxes)		•	•	•	•	•	•
understanding purposes of government	•	•	•	•	•	•	•
promoting order and security	•	•	•	•	•	•	•
promoting well-being and common good	•	•	•	•	•	•	•
providing for distribution of benefits and burdens of society	•	•	•	•	•	•	•
providing means of peaceful conflict resolution		•	•	•	•	•	•
protecting rights and freedoms of individuals			•	•	•	•	•
understanding types of government (democracy, monarchy, dictatorship)					•	•	•
understanding democratic institutions	•	•	•	•	•	•	•
levels of government (local, state, national)		•	•	•	•	•	•
branches of government (executive, legislative, judicial)			•	•	•	•	•
government bodies (councils, boards, legislatures)			•	•	•	•	•
government services and activities			•	•	•	•	•
government documents (Constitution, Bill of Rights, etc.)			•	•	•	•	•
political parties						•	•
understanding democratic processes		•	•	•	•	•	•
making, amending, and removing rules and laws		•	•	•	•	•	•
enforcing laws		•	•	•	•	•	•
voting and elections		•	•	•	•	•	•
becoming a citizen					•	•	•

Economics

	K	1	2	3	4	5	6
understanding scarcity and economic choice	•	•	•	•	•	•	•
wants and basic needs	•	•	•	•	•	•	•
goods and services		•	•	•	•	•	•
production and consumption		•	•	•	•	•	•
trade-offs and opportunity cost		•	•	•	•	•	•

• A bullet indicates levels at which understandings are introduced, taught, applied, reinforced, or extended.
For more detailed information, refer to the index for each level.

	K	1	2	3	4	5	6
economic resources		•	•	•	•	•	•
spending and saving		•	•	•	•	•	•
conservation	•	•	•	•	•	•	•
understanding interdependence and income	•	•	•	•	•	•	•
transportation and communication links	•	•	•	•	•	•	•
mediums of exchange (barter and use of money)		•	•	•	•	•	•
trade		•	•	•	•	•	•
imports and exports (international trade)		•	•	•	•	•	•
understanding markets and prices		•	•	•	•	•	•
supply and demand			•	•	•	•	•
competition			•	•	•	•	•
understanding productivity and economic growth	•	•	•	•	•	•	•
kinds of work (jobs)	•	•	•	•	•	•	•
division of labor and specialization		•	•	•	•	•	•
production process		•	•	•	•	•	•
factors of production				•	•	•	•
effects of technology		•	•	•	•	•	•
understanding economic systems and institutions	•	•	•	•	•	•	•
public and private property	•	•	•	•	•	•	•
taxes			•	•	•	•	•
free enterprise and entrepreneurship		•	•	•	•	•	•
command, traditional, and market systems							•

Culture

	K	1	2	3	4	5	6
understanding ideas of shared humanity and unique identity	•	•	•	•	•	•	•
culture and cultural identity	•	•	•	•	•	•	•
customs and traditions (one's own and others)		•	•	•	•	•	•
cultural diversity and pluralism		•	•	•	•	•	•
multicultural societies		•	•	•	•	•	•
understanding social organizations and institutions	•	•	•	•	•	•	•
belonging to groups	•	•	•	•	•	•	•
family and community	•	•	•	•	•	•	•
social class structures	•	•	•	•	•	•	•
roles (gender, age, occupation)	•	•	•	•	•	•	•
religion and beliefs		•	•	•	•	•	•
education		•	•	•	•	•	•
understanding means of thought and expression	•	•	•	•	•	•	•
art, literature, music, dance, and architecture	•	•	•	•	•	•	•
language and communication	•	•	•	•	•	•	•
recreation	•	•	•	•	•	•	
food preparation				•	•	•	•
understanding human relationships	•	•	•	•	•	•	•
between and among individuals	•	•	•	•	•	•	•
within a culture or society		•	•	•	•	•	•
between and among cultures or societies		•	•	•	•	•	•
philosophy and ethics	•	•	•	•	•	•	•
ideas and standards of behavior	•	•	•	•	•	•	•
resolving ethical issues	•	•	•	•	•	•	•
effects of belief on behavior				•	•	•	•

• A bullet indicates levels at which understandings are introduced, taught, applied, reinforced, or extended.
For more detailed information, refer to the index for each level.

Skills

BASIC STUDY SKILLS	K	1	2	3	4	5	6
Map and Globe Skills							
understanding globes	•	•	•	•	•	•	•
North and South Poles		•	•	•	•	•	•
equator			•	•	•	•	•
hemispheres			•	•	•	•	•
prime meridian					•	•	•
Tropics of Cancer and Capricorn					•	•	•
Arctic and Antarctic Circles					•	•	•
understanding the purpose and use of maps	•	•	•	•	•	•	•
map title		•	•	•	•	•	•
map key (legend)		•	•	•	•	•	•
compass rose (direction indicator)		•	•	•	•	•	•
map scale				•	•	•	•
grid system			•	•	•	•	•
comparing maps with globes	•	•	•	•	•	•	•
comparing maps with photographs		•	•	•	•	•	•
understanding map symbols	•	•	•	•	•	•	•
land and water	•	•	•	•	•	•	•
colors, tints, and patterns		•	•	•	•	•	•
object and picture symbols		•	•	•	•	•	•
lines and borders				•	•	•	•
roads, routes, and arrows		•	•	•	•	•	•
location symbols			•	•	•	•	•
relief and elevation					•	•	•
understanding directional terms and finding direction	•	•	•	•	•	•	•
cardinal directions		•	•	•	•	•	•
intermediate directions				•	•	•	•
understanding and measuring distance				•	•	•	•
miles and kilometers				•	•	•	•
insets				•	•	•	•
understanding and finding location		•	•	•	•	•	•
number and letter grids			•	•	•	•	•
lines of latitude and longitude (parallels and meridians)					•	•	•
measurements in degrees					•	•	•
understanding map projections and distortions						•	•
understanding cartograms							•
Chart and Graph Skills							
understanding and using pictographs	•	•	•	•	•	•	•
understanding and using charts and diagrams	•	•	•	•	•	•	•

• A bullet indicates levels at which skills are introduced, taught, applied, reinforced, or extended.
For more detailed information, refer to the index for each level.

	K	1	2	3	4	5	6
understanding and using bar graphs	•	•	•	•	•	•	•
understanding and using calendars and time lines	•	•	•	•	•	•	•
understanding and using tables and schedules			•	•	•	•	•
understanding and using line graphs					•	•	•
understanding and using circle (pie) graphs						•	•
understanding and using climographs							

Reading and Research Skills

	K	1	2	3	4	5	6
understanding photographs and other picture illustrations	•	•	•	•	•	•	•
understanding artifacts and documents	•	•	•	•	•	•	•
understanding fine art		•	•	•	•	•	•
understanding safety and information symbols	•	•	•	•	•	•	•
understanding political cartoons						•	•
using context clues to understand vocabulary	•	•	•	•	•	•	•
using illustrations or objects to understand vocabulary	•	•	•	•	•	•	•
grouping and categorizing words (semantic maps)	•	•	•	•	•	•	•
understanding multiple meanings of words		•	•	•	•	•	•
understanding literal and implied meanings of words				•	•	•	•
understanding root words, prefixes, and suffixes				•	•	•	•
identifying abbreviations and acronyms				•	•	•	•
understanding facts and main ideas	•	•	•	•	•	•	•
identifying stated main ideas		•	•	•	•	•	•
generating unstated main ideas		•	•	•	•	•	•
recalling facts and details that support a generalization		•	•	•	•	•	•
using headings and prereading strategies to identify main ideas	•	•	•	•	•	•	•
identifying and understanding various types of text	•	•	•	•	•	•	•
informational and expository	•	•	•	•	•	•	•
narrative	•	•	•	•	•	•	•
fiction and historical fiction	•	•	•	•	•	•	•
biography and autobiography		•	•	•	•	•	•
journal, diary, and log		•	•	•	•	•	•
essay		•	•	•	•	•	•
letter		•	•	•	•	•	•
speech		•	•	•	•	•	•
legend, myth, and folklore		•	•	•	•	•	•
locating and gathering information		•	•	•	•	•	•
almanac			•	•	•	•	•
atlas and gazetteer		•	•	•	•	•	•
dictionary and glossary		•	•	•	•	•	•
encyclopedia		•	•	•	•	•	•
current news sources (television, radio, newspapers)		•	•	•	•	•	•
library and community		•	•	•	•	•	•
electronic resources (databases, CD-ROMs, Internet)		•	•	•	•	•	•
writing and dictating	•	•	•	•	•	•	•
expressing ideas in various ways (to inform, explain, persuade, describe)	•	•	•	•	•	•	•

• A bullet indicates levels at which skills are introduced, taught, applied, reinforced, or extended.
For more detailed information, refer to the index for each level.

	K	1	2	3	4	5	6
speaking and listening	•	•	•	•	•	•	••
expressing a point of view or opinion	•	•	•	•	•	•	•
dramatizing and role-playing simulations	•	•	•	•	•	•	•
making observations	•	•	•	•	•	•	•
asking questions	•	•	•	•	•	•	•
listing and ordering	•	•	•	•	•	•	•
constructing and creating	•	•	•	•	•	•	•
displaying, charting, and drawing	•	•	•	•	•	•	•
distinguishing primary from secondary sources					•	•	•
distinguishing fact from nonfact (fantasy, fiction, or opinion)			•	•	•	•	•

BUILDING CITIZENSHIP

Critical Thinking Skills

	K	1	2	3	4	5	6
identifying cause-and-effect relationships	•	•	•	•	•	•	•
following sequence and chronology	•	•	•	•	•	•	•
classifying and grouping information	•	•	•	•	•	•	•
summarizing		•	•	•	•	•	•
synthesizing				•	•	•	•
making inferences and generalizations				•	•	•	•
forming logical conclusions	•	•	•	•	•	•	•
understanding and evaluating point of view and perspective		•	•	•	•	•	•
evaluating and making judgments	•	•	•	•	•	•	•
detecting bias or stereotypes						•	•
predicting likely outcomes		•	•	•	•	•	•
making thoughtful choices and decisions	•	•	•	•	•	•	•
solving problems	•	•	•	•	•	•	•

Participation Skills

	K	1	2	3	4	5	6
working with others	•	•	•	•	•	•	•
resolving conflict	•	•	•	•	•	•	•
acting responsibly	•	•	•	•	•	•	•
identifying the consequences of a person's behavior	•	•	•	•	•	•	•
keeping informed	•	•	•	•	•	•	•
respecting rules and laws	•	•	•	•	•	•	•
participating in a group or community	•	•	•	•	•	•	•
respecting people with differing points of view	•	•	•	•	•	•	•
assuming leadership and being willing to follow		•	•	•	•	•	•
identifying traits of a leader and a follower			•	•	•	•	•
making decisions and solving problems in a group setting		•	•	•	•	•	•
understanding patriotic and cultural symbols		•	•	•	•	•	•

• A bullet indicates levels at which skills are introduced, taught, applied, reinforced, or extended.
For more detailed information, refer to the index for each level.

Test Preparation

Contents

The lessons in this section have been designed to provide

- additional, motivating reading experiences for your children.
- content related to units in *Making a Difference.*
- opportunities to build background and reinforce reading skills.
- practice opportunities for standardized tests.
- reading strategy activities to help children organize information.

Conversion Chart for Scoring

After children have read the article and answered the questions,
you can use the following chart to determine a grade.

Correct Number of Responses	Percentage Score
6	100%
5	83%
4	67%
3	50%
2	33%
1	17%

A·B·C LESSON PLANNER

1. Access

- **READING STRATEGY:** Use the Word Splash on page TP4 to help children make predictions about the article. Write the words on the board, or use the sheet as a copying master. Invite children to predict how each word or phrase relates to Scouting activities. Children can write their predictions in their journals or learning logs. Do not expect children to know the answers. This activity is designed to help build interest, activate prior knowledge, and set purposes for reading.

2. Build

- Have children read the article, or read it aloud to them.
- As children read or after they have finished reading the article, they may change their Word Splash predictions. Have them identify the predictions that were correct, and have them state what they have learned from reading the article.

3. Close

- Have children complete the copying master *A Special Badge*. Invite children to design a badge for something they would like to learn to do.
- **LANGUAGE ARTS ACTIVITY:** Have children write a letter to a local Scouting organization to invite a leader or spokesperson to come talk to the class.

Harcourt Brace School Publishers

Scouting Experiences
Word Splash

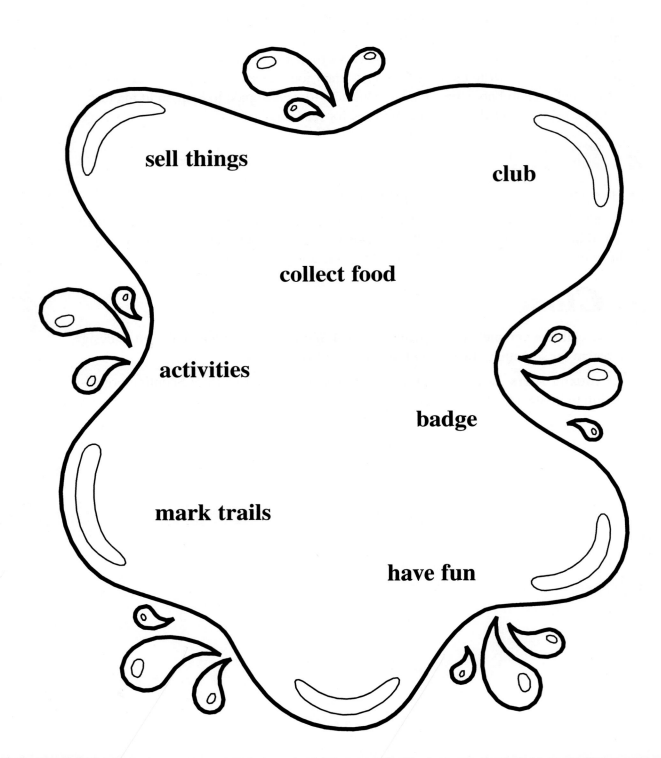

sell things

club

collect food

activities

badge

mark trails

have fun

Name_____

Scouting Experiences

Many boys and girls enjoy Scouting. The Scouts are clubs for boys and girls. Girls six to eight years old can join Brownies. Boys six to ten years old can join Cub Scouts.

In Brownies and Cub Scouts, boys and girls learn to do many things. Some Scouting activities are outdoors, such as learning to mark a trail. Other activities include sewing and cooking. For each activity that a Scout completes, he or she gets a badge. The badge shows that the Scout knows how to do something special. Scouts wear uniforms and attend regular meetings.

Some Scouts sell things to earn money for their clubs. They may sell cookies or candy. With the money they collect, they support their clubs. Scouts also collect food for people who live in shelters.

There are Scouting clubs for older boys and girls, too. Older boys join the Boy Scouts. Older girls join the Girl Scouts. These clubs teach boys and girls how to do many things and give them a chance to have fun together.

A Special Badge

What to do: Draw a design for a badge for something you want to learn to do.

A·B·C *Lesson Planner*

1. *Access*

• **Reading Strategy:** Use the Word Splash on page TP8 to help children make predictions about the article. Write the words on the board, or use the sheet as a copying master. Invite children to predict how each word or phrase relates to Native American homes. Children can write or draw their predictions in their journals or learning logs. Do not expect children to know the answers. This activity is designed to help build interest, activate prior knowledge, and set purposes for reading.

2. *Build*

• Have children read the article, or read it aloud to them.

• As children read or after they finish reading the article, they may change their Word Splash predictions. Have them identify the predictions that were correct, and have them state what they have learned from reading the article.

3. *Close*

• Have children complete the copying master *A Native American Home.* Invite children to draw a kiva with wall paintings.

• **Science Activity:** Have children research the mesas of the Southwest. Invite children to write three facts that they find.

Harcourt Brace School Publishers

Name _____

Native American Homes

Word Splash

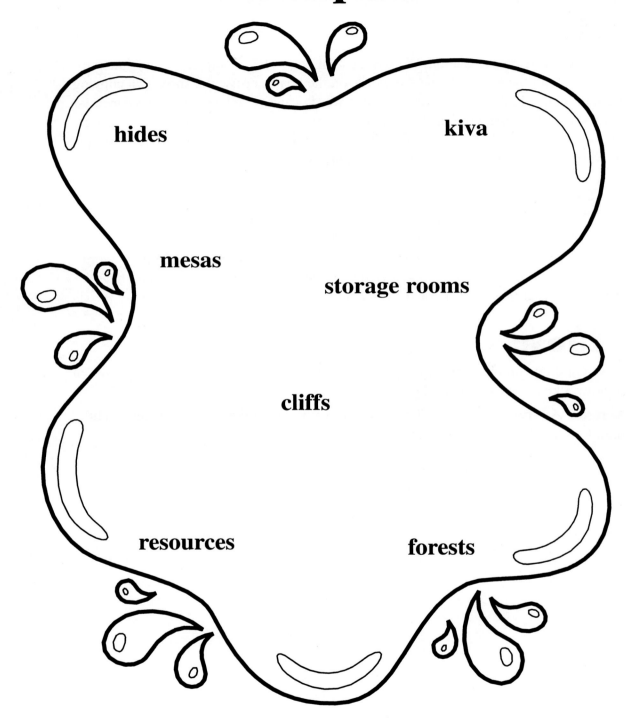

hides

kiva

mesas

storage rooms

cliffs

resources

forests

Harcourt Brace School Publishers

Name_____

Native American Homes

Native Americans used resources from the land around them to make their homes. The Cheyenne lived in an area where there were many buffalo. They used buffalo hides to make their houses. The Iroquois lived near forests. They used wood to make their homes.

Some Native Americans living in what is now Arizona used the cliffs and mesas of their area for their homes. They built houses with many rooms in the sides of cliffs. These houses had storage rooms for grain. They also had rooms for eating and sleeping.

A special room was called a kiva. Some Native Americans used this room for religious ceremonies. This room was mainly underground. It was entered through a hole dug in the ground. The men of the village climbed down a ladder to enter the kiva. The walls of the kiva had many paintings on them. There might be a fire in the middle of the kiva for warmth.

Where Native Americans lived was important to them. They depended on the land for many things. They used what they found on the land to build the kinds of homes they needed.

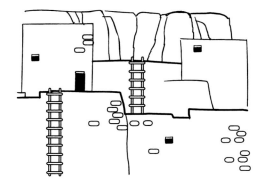

Name_____

A Native American Home

What to do: Draw a kiva with wall paintings.

Harcourt Brace School Publishers

A·B·C *Lesson* *Planner*

1. *Access*

- **READING STRATEGY:** Use the Anticipation Guide on page TP12 before having small groups of children read the article. Write the statements on the board, or use the sheet as a copying master. Invite children to tell whether they agree or disagree with each statement. They can write or draw their responses in their journals or learning logs. Do not expect children to know the answers. This activity is designed to help build interest, activate prior knowledge, and set purposes for reading.

2. *Build*

- Have children read the article, or read it aloud to them.

- As children read or after they finish reading the article, they may change their opinions about the statements. If they do, have them discuss why they revised their opinions, and have them state what they learned from their reading that allowed them to confirm or revise their opinions.

3. *Close*

- Have children complete the standardized-test-format questions after they read the article. (An item analysis that identifies the test objectives covered by each question, as well as an answer key, can be found on page TP27.)
- **MATHEMATICS ACTIVITY:** Have groups of children discuss some of the trade items in the article. Invite children to assign prices to the items. Then encourage children to use the prices to write number problems for members of the group to solve.

Harcourt Brace School Publishers

Name _____

Let's Trade
Anticipation Guide

	Check One	
	Agree	**Disagree**
1. People used to trade things they had for things they needed.		
2. Some people thought feathers were worth a lot.		
3. People who had nothing to trade went hungry.		
4. People still trade today.		
5. Things that are traded for each other are usually worth different amounts.		

Name_____

Let's Trade

Step back in time and picture a world without money. There are no dollar bills. There are no coins. How can a person get food or clothing?

In the past, people traded things they had for things they needed or wanted. Items that were traded were thought to be worth about the same amount. People might trade ten chickens for a pig. They might trade some sugar for a bowl or a cup.

Some groups of people thought certain items were **valuable,** or worth a lot. In the Santa Cruz Islands, people thought that feathers were valuable. They glued together tiny red feathers and traded with them. Some North American Indians made belts out of beads. They called the belts wampum. They traded them for things they wanted. In Ethiopia people traded rock salt for the things they wanted.

How did people who did not have much to trade get the things they wanted? Sometimes people would trade their skill. They might fix someone's roof to get a place to sleep. They might help care for someone's animals to get food for their families.

Today, people still trade for things other than money. A sister might help her younger brother with his homework if he agrees to make her bed. There is no limit to what can be traded.

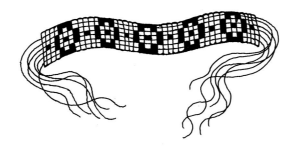

Name _____

Let's Trade

Choose the best answer and mark the oval of your choice.

1. Which of these is the best summary for this article?
   - ⬭ People today use money.
   - ⬭ People trade things to get what they want or need.
   - ⬭ Ten chickens are worth one pig.
   - ⬭ Beads and feathers can be worth a lot.

2. Why do people trade things?
   - ⬭ They have a lot of one thing.
   - ⬭ They want to be friendly.
   - ⬭ It is the law.
   - ⬭ They want to get the things they need.

3. In this article, the word **valuable** means
   - ⬭ worth a lot.
   - ⬭ having a lot.
   - ⬭ given to someone else.
   - ⬭ making yourself.

4. What did the people in Ethiopia trade?
   - ⬭ They traded rock salt.
   - ⬭ They traded beads.
   - ⬭ They traded feathers.
   - ⬭ They traded shells.

5. What is the main idea of the fourth paragraph?
   - ⬭ People have many skills.
   - ⬭ People can trade their skills for what they need.
   - ⬭ People who can fix a roof can become rich.
   - ⬭ Trading is hard work.

6. Which of these is a fact presented in the article?
   - ⬭ Everyone trades every day.
   - ⬭ People who have a lot of money never trade.
   - ⬭ People still trade goods or skills for things they want.
   - ⬭ Friends always trade with each other.

Harcourt Brace School Publishers

A·B·C LESSON PLANNER

1. Access

- **READING STRATEGY:** Use the Word Splash on page TP16 to help children make predictions about the article. Write the words on the board, or use the sheet as a copying master. Invite children to predict how each word or phrase relates to the *Mayflower*. Children can write or draw their predictions in their journals or learning logs. Do not expect children to know the answers. This activity is designed to help build interest, activate prior knowledge, and set purposes for reading.

2. Build

- Have children read the article, or read it aloud to them.

- As children read or after they finish reading the article, they may change their Word Splash predictions. Have them identify the predictions that were correct, and have them state what they have learned from reading the article.

3. Close

- Have children complete the copying master *The Mayflower Log.* Invite children to draw or write what the voyage might have been like.

- **LANGUAGE ARTS ACTIVITY:** Have children imagine that they are passengers on the *Mayflower.* Have each child write or draw a journal entry for the day that they first see land. Children can share their entries.

Harcourt Brace School Publishers

Name _____

The <u>Mayflower</u>

Word Splash

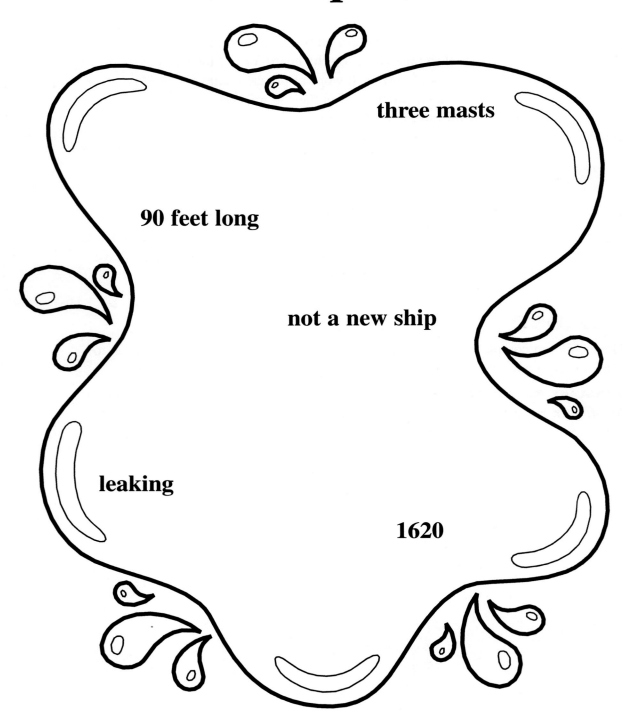

three masts

90 feet long

not a new ship

leaking

1620

Name _____

The <u>Mayflower</u>

In 1620, about 100 passengers sailed to America to find a new life. They sailed on a ship called the <u>Mayflower</u>. The <u>Mayflower</u> was not a new ship. It had been used by the English in many trading voyages before it set sail for America. Some historians think that the <u>Mayflower</u> had been used to fight sea battles with Spain.

The <u>Mayflower</u> was 90 feet long from stem to sternpost. It had three masts for sails. It was armed with several cannons. On each side of the ship were openings for the cannons to shoot from.

One of the sailors on the <u>Mayflower</u> called the ship a "leaking, unwholesome ship." The voyage on the <u>Mayflower</u> was not an easy one. The people who made the voyage wanted a new life badly. That was why the long voyage was worth it to them. Today, we know how brave the Pilgrims were to make the trip.

Harcourt Brace School Publishers

Name_____

The <u>Mayflower</u> Log

What to do: Draw or write what the voyage on the <u>Mayflower</u> might have been like.

A·B·C *Lesson Planner*

1. *Access*

- **READING STRATEGY:** Use the Anticipation Guide on page TP20 before having small groups of children read the article. Write the statements on the board, or use the sheet as a copying master. Invite children to tell whether they agree or disagree with each statement. They can write or draw their responses in their journals or learning logs. Do not expect children to know the answers. This activity is designed to help build interest, activate prior knowledge, and set purposes for reading.

2. *Build*

- Have children read the article, or read it aloud to them.

- As children read or after they finish reading the article, they may change their opinions about the statements. If they do, have them discuss why they revised their opinions, and have them state what they learned from their reading that allowed them to confirm or revise their opinions.

3. *Close*

- Have children complete the standardized-test-format questions after they read the article. (An item analysis that identifies the test objectives covered by each question, as well as an answer key, can be found on page TP27.)

- **MATHEMATICS ACTIVITY:** Have children count the number of students in the class. Then invite children to have an election of class officers. Encourage children to count the ballots for each candidate and tally the results.

Harcourt Brace School Publishers

Name _____

It's a Secret
Anticipation Guide

Check One

	Agree	Disagree
1. Every citizen has the right to vote in secret.		
2. Most adults vote by raising their hands.		
3. Everyone votes in a voting booth.		
4. When people fill out ballots, no one else can see what they are doing.		
5. Even the ancient Greeks voted in secret.		

Harcourt Brace School Publishers

Name _____

It's a Secret

It's time to pick a class president. Will you cast your vote by raising your hand? Or will you write your choice on paper?

When adults in the United States cast their votes in an election, they do it in secret. This is so no one will know who another person votes for. It is a way of protecting people.

Some people vote in a voting booth. The voter closes a curtain so that he or she can vote in secret. On the back wall of the booth is a list of all the people the voter can vote for. The voter picks the candidate. When the voter is finished voting, he or she pulls a handle and moves it to one side. This tells the machine to count the vote. The first voting machines were used in 1892 in New York State.

Some people fill out a **ballot,** or sheet of paper. The voter stands in a small desk-like space that has a border on each side. No one can see how the voter is filling in his or her ballot. When the voter is finished voting, he or she puts the ballot through a machine and the vote is counted in secret. Paper ballots have been used in the United States since the late 1700s.

No matter how or where people vote in the United States, their votes are secret. That is an important right for every citizen of the United States.

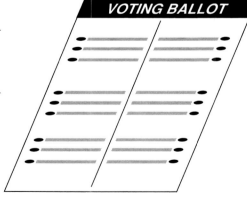

Name _____

It's a Secret

Choose the best answer and mark the oval of your choice.

1. Which of these is the best summary for this article?
   - ⬭ Voting in secret is a right of every citizen of the United States.
   - ⬭ Some people vote in a voting booth.
   - ⬭ Some people vote by filling in a secret paper ballot.
   - ⬭ Colored balls were used for voting.

2. The first voting machines were used in
   - ⬭ New York City.
   - ⬭ Austin, Texas.
   - ⬭ the Republic of Texas.
   - ⬭ New York State.

3. In this article, the word **ballot** means
   - ⬭ a sheet of paper.
   - ⬭ a machine.
   - ⬭ a voting booth.
   - ⬭ a vote.

4. What is the main idea of the third paragraph?
   - ⬭ Some voters vote in a voting booth.
   - ⬭ Ballots are put through a machine.
   - ⬭ No one can see how a voter fills out a ballot.
   - ⬭ Some voters use a ballot to cast their votes.

5. Which of these is a fact presented in the article?
   - ⬭ People would rather vote in a voting booth.
   - ⬭ Black and white balls make good ballots.
   - ⬭ Paper ballots have been used in the United States since the late 1700s.
   - ⬭ Children vote by raising their hands.

6. How is voting in secret a way of protecting people?
   - ⬭ Voting booths make sure a person's vote is a secret.
   - ⬭ No one else can know how a person is voting.
   - ⬭ No one wants to know how another person votes.
   - ⬭ Secret ballot is the best way to vote.

A·B·C LESSON PLANNER

1. Access

• **READING STRATEGY:** Use the Word Splash on page TP24 to help children make predictions about the article. Write the words on the board, or use the sheet as a copying master. Invite children to predict how each word or phrase relates to greeting cards. Children can write or draw their predictions in their journals or learning logs. Do not expect children to know the answers. This activity is designed to help build interest, activate prior knowledge, and set purposes for reading.

2. Build

• Have children read the article, or read it aloud to them.

• As children read or after they finish reading the article, they may change their Word Splash predictions. Have them identify the predictions that were correct, and have them state what they have learned from reading the article.

3. Close

• Have children complete the standardized-test-format questions after they read the article. (An item analysis that identifies the test objectives covered by each question, as well as an answer key, can be found on page TP27.)

• **ART ACTIVITY:** Have children work with a partner to design a greeting card for someone they know. Children may wish to create a birthday card or a card for another special occasion.

Harcourt Brace School Publishers

Name _____

Greetings!
Word Splash

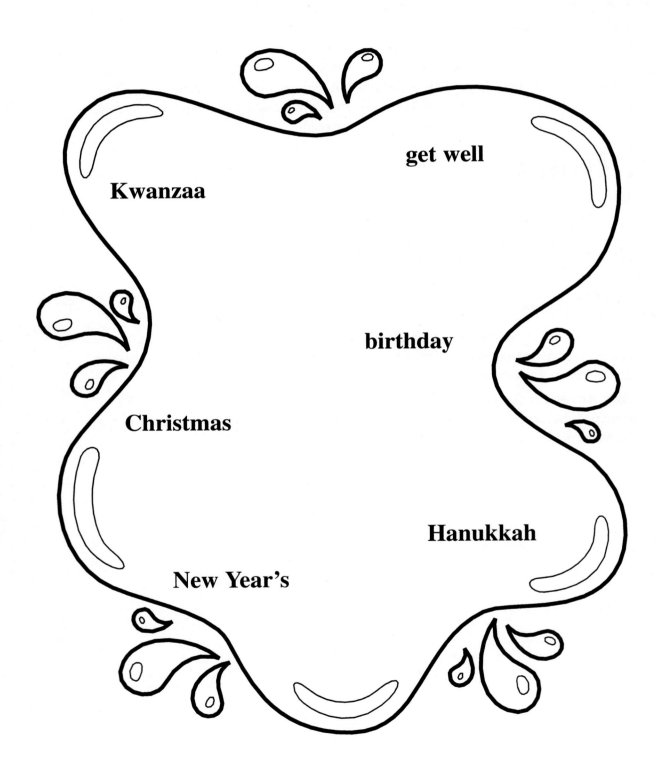

get well

Kwanzaa

birthday

Christmas

Hanukkah

New Year's

Harcourt Brace School Publishers

Harcourt Brace School Publishers

Name _____

Greetings!

"Happy birthday!" "Get well soon!" People send greeting cards to one another each year for holidays and on other special days.

The people in Egypt over 4,000 years ago sent New Year's greetings and gifts to one another. The Romans would also send gifts.

Now, billions of cards are made and sold each year. More than half of them are Christmas cards. Many other holidays, such as Hanukkah and Kwanzaa, have special cards. Most of the other cards that are made are birthday cards. Other cards are made to help people say "Thank you," or "Feel better," or "Congratulations."

The first modern Christmas card was made in London, England. It was designed in 1843 by John C. Horsley, an artist. The card had three parts. In the center was a family having Christmas dinner. On one side the artist drew people feeding the hungry. On the other side was a picture of people giving clothes to poor families.

In the United States the first Christmas card was made in 1875. A printer named Louis Prang had a printing shop in Boston. He designed and sold the first color Christmas card in the country. Soon he was known as the father of the American greeting card.

There are many different kinds of cards today. Some play music. Others hold money or become games and puzzles. One thing hasn't changed, though—cards can still make people happy.

Name _____

Greetings!

Choose the best answer and mark the oval of your choice.

1. Which of these is the best summary for this article?
   - ⬭ Everyone enjoys receiving a birthday card.
   - ⬭ There are many different greeting cards, and they can make people feel happy.
   - ⬭ Many greeting cards are sold all over the United States.
   - ⬭ Some greeting cards play music, hold money, and turn into games and puzzles.

2. Which of these is a fact presented in the article?
   - ⬭ The Egyptians and the Romans were the first people to celebrate New Year's.
   - ⬭ The Romans sent musical Christmas cards to friends.
   - ⬭ The Egyptians sent New Year's gifts to one another.
   - ⬭ All Egyptians received special New Year's gifts.

3. What is the main idea of the third paragraph?
   - ⬭ There are special cards for Kwanzaa.
   - ⬭ There are billions of cards for holidays and other special days.
   - ⬭ Most people send birthday cards to each other every year.
   - ⬭ There are only a few kinds of Christmas cards for people to send.

4. The first Christmas card was made in
   - ⬭ London in 1843.
   - ⬭ Boston in 1843.
   - ⬭ Egypt, over 4,000 years ago.
   - ⬭ the early Roman Empire.

5. Why was Louis Prang called the father of the American greeting card?
   - ⬭ He was the father of many children.
   - ⬭ His family had made greeting cards for many years.
   - ⬭ The American Revolution started in Boston where Louis Prang lived.
   - ⬭ He made the first Christmas card in the United States.

6. The most popular kind of greeting cards are for
   - ⬭ Hanukkah.
   - ⬭ Christmas.
   - ⬭ birthdays.
   - ⬭ Kwanzaa.

Harcourt Brace School Publishers

Item Analyses and Answer Keys

Unit 3

Let's Trade

Item Analysis: 1. Identify the best summary; 2. Identify cause and effect; 3. Identify specialized/technical terms; 4. Recall supporting facts and details; 5. Identify the main idea; 6. Distinguish between fact and nonfact.

Answers: 1. People trade things to get what they want or need. 2. They want to get the things they need. 3. worth a lot. 4. They traded rock salt. 5. People can trade their skills for what they need. 6. People still trade goods or skills for things they want.

Unit 5

It's a Secret

Item Analysis: 1. Identify the best summary; 2. Recall supporting facts and details; 3. Identify specialized/technical terms; 4. Identify the main idea; 5. Distinguish between fact and nonfact; 6. Draw conclusions.

Answers: 1. Voting in secret is a right of every citizen of the United States. 2. New York State. 3. a sheet of paper. 4. Some voters vote in a voting booth. 5. Paper ballots have been used in the United States since the late 1700s. 6. No one else can know how a person is voting.

Unit 6

Greetings!

Item Analysis: 1. Identify the best summary; 2. Distinguish between fact and nonfact; 3. Identify the main idea; 4. Recall supporting facts and details; 5. Make inferences and generalizations; 6. Recall supporting facts and details.

Answers: 1. There are many different greeting cards, and they can make people feel happy. 2. The Egyptians sent New Year's gifts to one another. 3. There are billions of cards for holidays and other special days. 4. London in 1843. 5. He made the first Christmas card in the United States. 6. Christmas.

Index

Index

C